D0998018

99

Natural
Resource and
Environmental
Economics

ROGER PERMAN
YUE MA
JAMES McGILVRAY

WITHDRAWN FROM
THE LIBRARY
UNIVERSITY OF
WINCHESTER

Longman
London and New York

KA 0197413 0

Addison Wesley Longman Limited
Edinburgh Gate, Harlow
Essex CM20 2JE, England
and Associated Companies throughout the world

Published in the United States of America
by Longman Publishing, New York

© Addison Wesley Longman Limited 1996

All rights reserved; no part of this publication may be
reproduced, stored in any retrieval system, or transmitted
in any form or by any means, electronic, mechanical,
photocopying, recording, or otherwise without either the
prior written permission of the Publishers or a licence
permitting restricted copying in the United Kingdom issued
by the Copyright Licensing Agency Ltd,
90 Tottenham Court Road, London W1P 9HE.

First published 1996

ISBN 0-582-257271 PPR

British Library Cataloguing in Publication Data

A catalogue record for this book
is available from the British Library

Library of Congress Cataloging-in-Publication data

Perman, Roger, 1949–
    Natural resource and environmental economics / Roger Perman,
Yue Ma, James McGilvray.
        p.   cm.
    Includes bibliographical references and index.
    ISBN 0-582-25727-1
    1. Environmental economics.   2. Natural resources – Management,
3. Sustainable development.   I. Ma, Yue, 1963–   . II. McGilvray, James.
III. Title.
HC70.E5P446   1996   95-42107
333.7 – dc20   CIP

set by 22 in 9 on 11pt Times

Produced by Longman Singapore Publishers (Pte) Ltd.

Printed in Singapore

KING ALFRED'S COLLEGE
WINCHESTER

333.7 PER | 01974130

Contents

A personal note

Just before the completion of this book, one of its authors – Professor James McGilvray – died suddenly. Our sadness at the loss of a friend and colleague is softened by the memories we shall retain of Jim.

Among these, we recall the pleasure and intellectual stimulus obtained in collaborating with Jim in the process of writing this book. For this reason, the book will always retain a special significance for us.

The preface which follows was written by Jim a few days before his tragic death.

ROGER PERMAN
YUE MA

Preface

Classes in environmental and/or in natural resource economics are commonly offered at graduate level, typically in a Master's course in environmental studies, and delivered to students from a wide range of academic disciplines, or as third or fourth year electives in undergraduate degree courses in economics or business. This diversity of background training and skills amongst the students of environmental economics poses a considerable challenge to those lecturing on the subject, as well as to authors of textbooks in this field – as we have discovered to our cost on both counts! However, it is in response to this challenge that the present text has evolved, based on several years of teaching very distinct cohorts of graduate and undergraduate students. Although there are now a number of contemporary textbooks on environmental and natural resource economics, the range of choice of texts suitable for a full semester class is relatively limited, and in our view leaves many unsatisfied customers. While we do not claim that this text will satisfy all those customers, we believe it is a distinct contribution to the menu of available texts. In particular, we have sought to establish the subject-matter on firm and explicit microeconomic foundations, and thus provide a degree of rigour which we believe to be appropriate to a modern up-to-date text at the present stage of development of the subject. Although in this respect the book is directed principally at graduate or undergraduate economics students, welfare theoretic axioms and results which underpin the text are developed from basic principles, and with careful reading should be accessible to non-economists.

A supporting reason for a more rigorous approach is the rapidly-growing use of environmental criteria in appraising and evaluating investment projects, particularly public sector infrastructure projects (or mixed public–private sector projects) which may have significant environmental effects. Cost–benefit analysis is the established technique of evaluation for projects of this type, and will remain so. However, there is now much greater emphasis on the identification and inclusion of environmental costs and benefits in the overall cost–benefit appraisal. It is desirable that those with an interest in the outcomes of such assessments – and not simply the economists who undertake the calculations – have an understanding of the theoretical foundations and methods of application of the cost–benefit approach. Given the uncertainties and imprecision involved in attempting to value environmental costs and benefits, wider understanding of basic principles on the part of those involved can hopefully inform and enhance the process of environmental assessment and decision-making.

Gratitude as well as prudence prompts a heartfelt thanks to our wives – Val Perman, Hong Lin and Alison McGilvray – who patiently bore many externalities of the type discussed in this book. Various colleagues provided helpful advice and comments on aspects of the book; in particular we would like to thank Darryl Holden (Economics Department, Strathclyde University) and Sue Scott (Economic and Social Research Institute, Dublin). Chris Harrison of Longman provided support and encouragement throughout, and editorial staff at Longmans have been prompt and efficient in executing the various stages of conversion from what used to be called manuscript (diskscript?) to the hard copy in hand.

ROGER PERMAN
YUE MA
JAMES McGILVRAY

November 1995

Acknowledgements

We are grateful to the copyright holders for permission to reproduce copyright material.

Whilst every effort has been made to trace the owners of copyright material, in a few cases this has proved impossible and we take this opportunity to offer our apologies to any copyright holders whose rights we may have unwittingly infringed.

Notation

U	$=$ Utility per period
V	$=$ Value flow per period
W	$=$ Social welfare flow per period
Z	$=$ quantity of pollution abated per period
δ	$=$ Social rate of return on capital
θ	$=$ Pollution stock decay rate
ρ	$=$ Rate of utility time preference
Ψ	$=$ Pollution flow per period

The following symbols are used in a variety of different ways in the text, depending on the context in question:

X
Y

Mathematical notation

Where we are considering a function of a single variable such as

$$Y = Y(X)$$

then we write the first derivative in one of the following three ways:

$$\frac{\mathrm{d}Y}{\mathrm{d}X} = \frac{\mathrm{d}Y(X)}{\mathrm{d}X} = Y'(X)$$

Each of these denotes the first derivative of Y with respect to X. In any particular exposition, we choose the form that seems best to convey meaning.

Where we are considering a function of several variables such as the following function of two variables:

$$Z = Z(P, Q)$$

we write first partial derivatives in one of the following ways:

$$\frac{\partial Z}{\partial P} = \frac{\partial Z(P, Q)}{\partial P} = Z_P$$

each of which is the partial derivative of Z with respect to the variable

Introduction

Who is this book for?

All textbooks are written with certain target audiences in mind, and this one is no exception. It is directed at students of economics, undertaking a specialist course in resource and/or environmental economics. Its primary use is expected to be as a principal textbook in upper level undergraduate (final year) and taught masters' level postgraduate programmes that involve an option in resource and environmental economics. However, it will also serve as a main or supporting text for second-year courses (or third-year courses on four-year degree programmes) that have a substantial environmental economics component.

We assume that the reader has a firm grasp of the economic principles covered in the first year of a typical undergraduate economics programme. In particular, it is expected that the reader has a reasonable grounding in microeconomics; little, if any, knowledge of macroeconomics is necessary for using this textbook. We make extensive use throughout the book of welfare economics. This is often covered in second-year micro courses, and those readers who have previously studied this will find it useful. However, the authors have written the text so that relevant welfare economics theory is developed and explained as the reader goes through the early chapters.

The authors have also assumed that the reader will have a basic knowledge of algebra. Some parts of the book make use of the algebra of calculus, but only to an elementary level. In a few chapters (specifically, Chapters 5 to 7), appendices make use of the techniques of dynamic optimisation to derive results given in the text. However, we do not assume the reader will know these techniques or have experience in their use, and so they are explained carefully at appropriate places. We do not anticipate that any student of economics will find the mathematics used in this book to be particularly daunting, given the care we have devoted to assisting the reader through those parts of the text that do use mathematical analysis.

Some characteristics of this book

Not surprisingly, this is intended to be a completely modern text, dealing with all major areas of natural resource (renewable and non-renewable) and environmental economics. We seek to present the subject in a way that gives a more rigorous grounding in economic analysis than is common in existing texts at this level. It has been structured to achieve a balance of theory, applications and examples, that is appropriate to a text of this level, and which will be, for most readers, their first systematic analysis of environmental economics.

A second distinctive characteristic of the text is its careful presentation of related material in the fields of ecology and the physical and environmental sciences, explaining and illustrating how they have shaped the development of the new environmental economics. Emphasis is given to the laws of thermodynamics, the materials balance principle, and ecological concepts of resilience and stability.

Thirdly, the text provides extensive discussion of the ethical basis of economics, and comparison of the conventional utilitarian ethic with rival frameworks (including those of Rawls, Nozick and other libertarian philosophers, and non-humanist ethics). We demonstrate how results and conclusions of environmental economics analysis depend upon the ethical framework adopted.

Applied welfare economics is used as an organising principle for the book, with relevant theory being explained early in the text. A careful distinction is drawn throughout the text between the concepts of efficiency and optimality, and the reader is shown how efficient outcomes are not necessarily desirable outcomes.

The very long run is given proper attention, particularly in an extensive chapter on sustainability, elucidating and comparing rival concepts, and linking sustainability to developments in ecology and the physical sciences. A second way in which the very long run enters is through the analysis of environmental resource allocation choices presented within the growth theory framework of Dasgupta, Heal and Solow. This allows the text to give due attention to the consequences of population change, resource substitutability, and technological progress.

Other important features of the book are

(a) a presentation of the principles and practice of environmental accounting, based around the proposals contained in the revised UN System of National Accounts, and suggestions for further reform of these accounts;

(b) a chapter devoted to the use of environmental-augmented input–output analysis;

(c) a focus on environmental policy that gives proper recognition to the design of policy in circumstances of uncertainty, irreversibility, and the constraint of a safe minimum standard of conservation;

(d) analysis of pollution and pollution control, emphasising the important case of stock pollutants – pollutants where damage is at least partly related to the concentration or stock level of the pollutant in the air, ground or water.

Contents

Many readers find it useful to have some overview of the contents of a textbook, and to have some feel in advance for the orientation that the book will take towards its subject matter. It is to this that we now turn. If you do not wish to read such a preview, please omit this section and go on to the next.

Natural resource economics and the newer field of environmental economics have tended to be treated as separate sub-disciplines until relatively recently, and

even where textbooks deal with both areas, it is common to find that the two are treated as if they were autonomous fields of study. The authors of this text believe that the two areas should be regarded as a unified discipline, and have structured the book accordingly.

We also maintain that much valuable insight into subject areas within economics can be obtained by examination of the evolution of the discipline from its origins. This task is undertaken in the first chapter. There we examine the treatment of resource and environmental issues in the evolution of economic theory, beginning with the classical economists Malthus, Ricardo, and Mill, then turning to the neoclassical analysis of marginal theory and value, and the full development of welfare economics theory, and the central place it accords to the concepts of efficiency and optimality in economic analysis. The neoclassical concern with efficiency and optimality is given a central place in our text; given limited resources and the wide variety of competing claims on resources, it is of utmost importance to use resources efficiently, and to ensure that environmental policy gives a high (although not exclusive) priority to the pursuit of efficiency.

Environmental economics has not developed, however, in isolation from other disciplines, and we attempt to show the reader how environmental economics incorporates fundamental insights from other disciplines. In particular, developments in the environmental and natural sciences have encouraged economists to take account of the laws of thermodynamics, and to develop materials balance models in which appropriate accounting constraints – determined by physical principles – are satisfied. Ecological science has had a profound influence upon economists' understanding of system stability, and the various relationships between the economic and environmental sub-systems.

Finally in Chapter 1, we outline the fundamental elements of the economic approach to resource and environmental issues, and attempt to identify the distinguishing characteristics of what might be called the New Environmental Economics; these elements form an agenda of issues that are examined at length throughout the book.

Ethics, discounting the future, and the environment

We have already noted that economists hold no monopoly over the concern with environmental issues. Many environmentalists from other disciplines maintain a distrust of the economic approach to the environment. We believe that much of this distrust can be explained by concern about the ethical underpinnings of much economic analysis. Whilst it is common to find economists arguing that their analyses are value-free (or positive as opposed to normative in terms of some notation made famous by Richard Lipsey), it is clear that a substantial part of mainstream environmental economics is based around a particular ethical framework: utilitarianism. Indeed, much of the analysis in this book also adopts a utilitarian foundation. However, utilitarianism is not the only ethical framework in which one can analyse environmental issues, and the conclusions one reaches about environmental issues tend to be very sensitive to the framework one adopts. In the second chapter, we investigate a variety of ethical frameworks – including non-humanistic moral philosophies – and contrast these carefully with the utilitarianism that remains dominant in much economic analysis.

Our text stresses the importance of time and intergenerational choices and trade-offs. Chapter 2 carefully takes the reader through the concept of a social welfare function, and the practices of discounting future monetary values and cost–benefit analysis. In each case, our prime concerns are their ethical and distributional implications, particularly in intertemporal terms. We shall see, in particular, that the concept of discounting is widely misunderstood. Whilst many commentators argue that any positive discount rate is morally indefensible, our analysis makes clear that it is invalid to argue that discounting inevitably benefits those currently living at the expense of those in the future.

Sustainability and sustainable development

It is also incorrect to argue that sustainable economic behaviour requires the adoption of a zero discount rate. This brings us to the central topic of Chapter 3 – sustainability and sustainable development. Despite the vagueness associated with much use of the notion of sustainability, there can be no doubt about the central role and importance it plays in current thinking. We shall review a range of definitions and meanings of this idea, consider the reasons why concern about sustainability has become so prominent, and consider the conditions for economic sustainability. The conservation of resources – or, put differently, the maintenance of natural capital – is

intimately linked with sustainability. Conservation of resources is likely to be particularly important where resource use has irreversible outcomes, or where ecological linkages are poorly understood but suggest that economic activity may interfere with the stability or resilience of ecosystems.

Welfare economics and the conceptual framework of environmental economics

The discerning reader may already have noticed that this text is a blend of the conventional and the modern. One key element of conventional economics that permeates the book is its use of neoclassical welfare economics. It is not possible to understand the economics of pollution policy, for example, without an appreciation of the concepts of efficiency, externalities and market failure. A weakness of many environmental economic texts is the failure to give a clear exposition of the methodology and key results of welfare economics; this is what we endeavour to do in Chapter 4. Our text also differs from many others in the attention it pays to intertemporal efficiency; environmental economics is all about the use of limited resources over long periods of time. We therefore give equal consideration to the static and intertemporal aspects of environmental resource use, giving these a rigorous foundation in terms of key principles of economic theory.

Efficient outcomes are not necessarily desirable outcomes, however, a conclusion which is rarely explained with sufficient clarity. We use the notion of a social welfare function to explain what is meant by an optimal allocation of resources, and contrast this with an efficient allocation of resources. Markets may, in certain circumstances, be relied upon to produce efficient outcomes; there is no way in which one can rely upon markets to produce optimal outcomes. Nevertheless, efficiency can still be justified as a goal worth pursuing, if only because it helps to create the conditions in which desirable outcomes are possible.

However, markets will not even allocate resources efficiently (let alone optimally) in the presence of externalities and public goods. As these phenomena permeate the use of environmental resources, one must be pessimistic about the outcomes of unregulated market economies, a pessimism reinforced by recognition of the pervasiveness of imperfect information, risk and uncertainty, and irreversibilities. We now know that market mechanisms alone will not always bring about efficient outcomes, and this suggests a role for government intervention, discussed at length throughout the book. However, it is by no means certain that government intervention will efficiently rectify market failure, a matter we examine in Chapter 4.

The efficient and optimal use of renewable and non-renewable environmental resources

Chapters 5, 6 and 7 form the heart of that part of the book dealing with the extraction or harvesting of natural resources. The material in these three chapters is the most difficult in the book, largely because of the use made of models of the economy that are investigated by mathematical argument. We have chosen to present this material in a relatively rigorous manner, stressing the intertemporal and intergenerational issues involved. One cannot hope to gain a good understanding of natural resource use without using the techniques of dynamic optimisation. It is this that leads to the material being quite difficult in places. However, the reader is led through the arguments slowly and carefully; every stage of the analysis is explained thoroughly, and where particular mathematical techniques are used, they are explained either as they are being used or in appendices.

In Chapter 5, we present an overview of the theory of the efficient and optimal use of environmental resources, using a simplified model of the economy built around a production function that incorporates natural resources inputs. An important area of debate concerns the best way of using an exhaustible resource over time. The answer depends, among other things, on whether the resource is 'essential', on the substitution possibilities between the exhaustible resource and other productive inputs, on the rate of population growth, and on the presence and pace of technical progress.

In addition to these considerations, an efficient extraction or harvesting programme for a natural resource will be affected by the discount rate that is thought to be appropriate, on the behaviour of extraction and harvesting costs, and upon whether damage arises from the extraction and use of the resource. Each of these matters is carefully examined, and we conclude Chapter 5 by considering whether the exhaustibility of some natural resources poses a problem.

Having dealt with the efficient use of natural resources in a very general way in Chapter 5, the next chapter deals specifically with issues relating to the extraction of non-renewable resources. We centre the chapter around a hypothetical example from which it is possible to obtain precise analytical results. Resource extraction in competitive markets is compared with that in monopolistic markets, and we use comparative dynamic analysis to investigate the consequences of changes in the interest rate, the size of the known resource stock, the level of demand, the price of backstop technology, and extraction costs.

Chapter 7 considers the economics of using or harvesting renewable resources such as fisheries or forests. Particular attention is paid to the consequences of resource use under conditions of open access. The absence of enforceable private property rights leads to a high likelihood of major inefficiencies, and many of the problems in ocean fisheries and tropical deforestation can be explained in this way.

Pollution and pollution control policy

Much of the new environmental economics is concerned with issues of pollution and the design and administration of pollution control programmes. One of the ways in which we integrate resource and environmental economics is by analysing pollution within the framework of resource depletion models, viewing pollution in terms of depletion of the quality or quantity of environmental resources.

Pollution is dealt with in Chapters 8 and 9. Most textbook discussions of pollution and pollution control deal exclusively with flow pollution, where the damages are related to the current rates of emission flows. This seriously limits one's analysis, however, as almost all forms of pollution have a stock dimension too. That is, the damages are related to the stock level of the pollutant in the environmental medium in question. A moment's thought makes it clear that water and atmospheric pollution are predominantly examples of stock pollutants; it is the concentration of the pollutant in the water or the air that matters, rather than the rate at which the pollutant is being emitted currently. We have chosen, therefore, to give stock pollution the emphasis it deserves. By doing so, our analysis of pollution control is far richer than that conventionally found in introductory texts.

Moreover, not all forms of pollution are amenable to control by the same policy instruments. Conventional treatments of pollution focus upon stationary-source flow pollution, where the pollutant mixes rapidly and uniformly. We cover this simple case, but also extend the analysis to deal with mobile pollution sources, the emission of persistent toxins, and pollutants whose mobility and mixing is limited, and which therefore have localised impacts.

We begin our discussion of pollution control policy (in Chapter 9) with a discussion of the theory of bargaining, pioneered by Ronald Coase. Coase's work suggests that governmental intervention to redress efficiency losses arising from externalities may have less scope than is often thought; where efficiency gains are possible, private bargains may well exploit these gains, so obviating the need for outside intervention. However, as our discussion suggests, there are grounds for believing that bargaining solutions to many environmental problems are very unlikely.

In a world where government had complete information, one would hope that government policy is designed to secure, among other things, economically efficient outcomes. But in many circumstances, insufficient information exists to realise such an objective. A weaker criterion that is often advocated by economists as a measure of a good policy instrument is that of cost-effectiveness. An instrument is cost-effective if it can achieve some arbitrarily chosen target at least cost. It turns out to be the case that several instruments including pollution taxes and pollution abatement subsidies, and marketable emissions permits have this property, at least in some circumstances. However, until recently, little use has been made of such pollution control instruments; instead, quantitative controls over output or pollution flow levels, or mandatory technological regulations, have been the instruments actually used. These do not possess the property of cost-effectiveness, which goes some way to explaining why they receive little support from economists.

Once we recognise the existence of uncertainty, however, the case for market-based instruments over command-and-control considerably weakens. We investigate the consequences of uncertainty for the design of pollution control programmes in Chapter 9, and also consider what implications the so-called precautionary principle has for such programmes in the face of uncertainty. It is sometimes suggested that pollution policy should be subject to an overriding constraint: a safe minimum standard of conservation. What exactly is this and how might it be achieved?

The valuation of environmental resources

Where a good or service is subject to regular exchange in markets, its market price serves as an indicator of its value at the margin. In practice, observed prices may not be reliable indicators of value, because of market imperfections, the presence of taxes or subsidies and so on. But at least a first approximation to value can be gained from observation of prices. But in many cases, economic activity has impacts upon the quantity or quality of environmental resources, or the services derived from those resources, and these resources of services are not the subject of market exchanges. In the absence of market prices, other ways of obtaining valuations of such impacts are required.

We begin Chapter 10 with an analysis of the different types of values that environmental resources may possess. It will be seen that economic analysis does *not* entail that only narrowly defined 'use values' enter into appraisals of the costs and benefits of resources. Non-use values, including bequest and existence values, are likely to be of considerable importance, too, for environmental resources, and we demonstrate how these can be estimated and incorporated into economic appraisals. The next part of the chapter examines and appraises several techniques for the evaluation of environmental resources. It is important to recognise the time domain in all of this; environmental resources have value not only for this generation, but for many subsequent ones. We shall examine how intergenerational values can be obtained, giving particular emphasis to the manner in which irreversibility influences resource valuation.

Population growth, economic growth, and the natural environment

Readers of this text will come from countries with widely differing levels and rates of growth of national income and population. What implications do population growth and economic growth have for the future of our natural environment? Are there limits to the growths of population and the economy? Is it possible, as some people argue, that the process of economic development can generate improvements in the quality of the environment, rather than inevitably worsening it as others argue? The examination of these relationships and questions forms the subject matter of Chapter 11.

In addressing these issues, we shall examine the processes of population change in some detail. Economic theory regards population size as a choice variable, not as an exogenous process outside our choice set. We outline the microeconomic theory of fertility a simplified representation of this choice process, but we will also consider the social and cultural contexts in which these choices are made. If the control of population is selected as a policy instrument for environmental policy, this analysis will give us some tools to devise appropriate policy prescriptions.

Much concern has been expressed in recent years about the impacts of demographic and economic change on soil and groundwater quality, and the prospects for future food availability from both land and marine resources. Chapter 11 reviews some of this literature, and we devote one case study to an examination of the extent, causes and control of loss of soil fertility and desertification.

International and global environmental pollution problems

It is common in textbook presentations of environmental pollution and pollution control policy to limit the theoretical presentation to 'within country' problems. Environmental pollution problems that have impacts beyond national boundaries are often not well related to the theory of pollution control in the context of a single economy. We regard international and global environmental problems as sufficiently serious to warrant addressing them in a separate chapter, but do so in a way that grounds the analysis clearly in terms of the basic theory of pollution control.

It will be seen that where environmental problems spill over national boundaries, their regulation and control is particularly difficult, particularly in those cases where the distribution of the costs and benefits of control is very uneven between countries.

In this situation, there no longer a single decision-making authority capable of acting in the collective interest; rather, choices are made by a number – sometimes a large number – of actors, with very different interests. Two items of economic theory are particularly helpful here. First, the economic theory of externalities can be used to analyse behaviour in the case of reciprocal externalities. Secondly, the techniques of game theory analysis are used to illuminate the benefits that can be derived by cooperation, and also to explain why such cooperation may be hard to achieve. Such cooperation is particularly difficult where decision making confronts profound uncertainty about the costs or benefits of pollution control.

Our main focus of attention in the chapter is three international environmental pollution problems widely regarded as actually or potentially the most serious for the world economy: climate change, ozone depletion, and acid rain. These case studies will be examined using the analytical tools developed in this and previous chapters.

Environmental input–output analysis and its applications

Many of the analytical and policy issues related to the environment require us to model the interaction between the economy and the environment. The exercise of modelling forces us to think carefully about the exact nature and extent of the relationships between the behaviour of economic agents and the environment and, if possible, how these might be expressed in quantitative terms. Examples of models used to clarify and analyse economic environmental issues have appeared in earlier chapters, notably in Chapters 5–7. In Chapter 13, we present and discuss the use of input–output models to analyse the impact of economic activity on the environment. This type of model has been extensively used in recent years, notably for studies of pollution control and abatement, and for a wide range of applications in energy studies. Since many readers may be unfamiliar with input–output analysis, we begin the chapter with a simple introductory guide to input–output models, and then show how the basic model can be extended to encompass economy–environment interactions. It is then explained, using published case-studies, how the extended input–output model may be used to predict or simulate the consequences of particular economic changes, including for example policy instruments designed to limit or reduce environmental damage. Policy measures such as carbon taxes also influence economic behaviour through their effects on prices, and we show how the input–output framework may be used to explore the effects of environmental policy measures on relative prices and incomes.

Despite providing considerable detail on inter-sectoral flows within an economy, input–output models are highly tractable and easy to understand. They achieve these advantages at the cost of a number of highly simplified assumptions about technology and the behaviour of economic agents. Efforts to allow for maximising behaviour by economic agents, to permit substitution of inputs as relative prices change, and to account for capacity or supply constraints, lead us from input–output to applied or computable general equilibrium (CGE) models. Although computationally much more complex, the huge growth in computing power has made it easier to solve CGE models, and these have been increasingly used in environmental modelling work in the last few years. The use of CGE models in environmental studies is reviewed in the concluding section of Chapter 13.

Accounting for the environment

Successful development of any field of applied science is dependent on observation, measurement and recording of the phenomena which are the subject of that field's interest – in short, on scientific data. The systematic compilation of what can be termed *environmental statistics* is relatively recent and still evolving. There is now available in many countries (though there are great variations) a considerable volume of data on environmental phenomena measured in physical units, though there is as yet no internationally-agreed system of classification. Environmental data expressed in value terms, which would permit the application of economic calculus to environmental issues, is much less common. It is widely recognised, for example, that the conventional national accounts aggregates, such as gross domestic product and national income, do not adequately reflect the consumption and depletion of environmental assets.

The question of how environmental costs and benefits might be treated within a system of national accounts is the subject-matter of Chapter 14. One solution is to establish a quite separate system of environmental accounts without the conventional national accounts framework. Stocks and flows in these accounts could be expressed in physical units, thus avoiding difficult problems of valuation. This however is also the major disadvantage of this approach; the absence of a standard unit of measurement (such as monetary value) greatly reduces the usefulness of the data. While physical indicators have an important role to play, especially in monitoring and assessing environmental status, the development of environmental accounts in value terms is a necessary condition for progress in many of the areas of environmental economics discussed in this book. This need is widely recognised, and finds expression in the most recent (1993) version of the United Nations System of National Accounts (SNA). The SNA's proposal for a 'satellite' set of environmental accounts is examined in some detail in this chapter, which also discusses the nature of the environmental stocks and flows to be incorporated in the accounts, and alternative methods of valuation.

Chapter 14 concludes with a brief review of environmental accounting at the firm or company level.

Mode of study

Alternative course structures

A: Full course

A full course of study in resources and environmental economics would involve study of the material in each of the 14 chapters of this text, typically over one semester.

B: Environmental Economics course

For those readers undertaking a course in environmental economics, the relatively technical material on exhaustible resources in Chapters 5 and 6 could be omitted without loss of continuity. This might also lead to a structure suitable for study by individuals who strongly dislike the use of mathematics in economics, or who are worried about their quantitative ability. Such a course has less need of input–output techniques, and so Chapter 13 might also be omitted. This leads to the following programme:

1 Introduction to resource and environmental economics
2 Ethics, discounting the future and the environment
3 Sustainability and sustainable development
4 Welfare economics and the conceptual framework of environmental economics
7 The theory of optimal resource extraction renewable resources
8 The economics of pollution
9 Pollution control policy
10 The valuation of environmental resources
11 Population growth, economic growth, and the natural environment
12 Global environmental pollution problems
14 Environmental accounting

C: Environmental Policy course

For the reader interested primarily in a course in the economics of environmental policy, we suggest that a self-contained and internally consistent course programme can be constructed by combining the following chapters. Such a programme would be particularly suitable for a short, half-semester, policy-oriented introduction to environmental economics.

1 Introduction to resource and environmental economics
2 Ethics, discounting the future and the environment
3 Sustainability and sustainable development
8 The economics of pollution
9 Pollution control policy
10 The valuation of environmental resources
12 Global environmental pollution problems
13 Environmental input–output analysis and its applications
14 Environmental accounting

Suggestions for study

Further reading

It is not possible to include in any single text of reasonable length all the material that one might conceivably wish for in an introduction to resource and environmental economics. Furthermore, the reader will inevitably find some topics of particular interest that he or she wishes to study at greater depth. To facilitate the reader in selecting directions for additional study, each chapter concludes with suggestions for further reading. Unless otherwise indicated, each item of recommended further reading is presented at a technical level accessible to readers of this text. We have also indicated, where appropriate, sources of empirical data that the reader may find useful for purposes of further study or research.

Discussion questions and problems

Each chapter of the book contains a small number of discussion questions and problems that you are strongly recommended to work through. Suggested answers are not provided in the text, but are available in the Instructor's Manual that will accompany this text.

The use of appendices in this textbook

Several of the chapters make use of appendices to provide complete derivations or explanations of results discussed in the main part of the relevant chapter. It is, we would conjecture, common practice for readers to take these as signals that the material is of lesser importance, or is excessively complicated, and can easily be ignored. These are not the signals we wish to send out!

Our use of appendices serves a distinct purpose: they are designed to facilitate a relatively quick reading of chapters. By putting technically difficult sections in an appendix, the reader may omit these on first reading, obtain an overview of the main arguments of the chapter, and then return to the material which is slower and more demanding to study in a second reading. You are strongly recommended to read every appendix in this way. If any appendix turns out to be too difficult to understand, ask your instructor for some assistance. If this fails, do not worry! No section of this book *requires* that the material in any appendix be mastered.

A final comment

The authors of this book have one advantage over you: we have studied the subject of resource and environmental economics for a number of years, and know how stimulating and fascinating its study can be. We expect that you will find the same qualities as you master the subject, and hope that this text stimulates you to further study in the future.

CHAPTER 1

An introduction to resource and environmental economics

'Contemplation of the world's disappearing supplies of minerals, forests, and other exhaustible assets has led to demands for regulation of their exploitation. The feeling that these products are now too cheap for the good of future generations, that they are being selfishly exploited at too rapid a rate, and that in consequence of their excessive cheapness they are being produced and consumed wastefully has given rise to the conservation movement.'

Hotelling (1931)

Introduction

We have four objectives in this chapter. Given that the discipline of economic theory is often viewed as the study of the allocation of limited resources to satisfy human wants or desires, our first objective is to identify the meaning or meanings attached to the term *resources*. In so doing, we will consider the related concepts of natural and environmental resources. Our first task, then, is to ascertain exactly which meanings can be given to the concepts of natural and environmental resources, and to understand how these relate to the more general category of economic resources.

Secondly, we review the manner in which issues of resource use in general and environmental resources in particular have been analysed in economic theory, as it has developed from the period of classical political economy. As the opening quotation demonstrates, the existence of a conservation movement has been recognised by economists for at least 60 years. However, we will show that concern with the exhaustion of finite environmental resources has far older antecedents, and was a fundamental component in the development of modern economic analysis.

Our third goal is to describe and explain a set of theoretical developments and principles that originated outside economic theory, but which have made important contributions to modern environmental economics.

Finally, we seek to present a summary of the distinctive features of natural resource and environmental economics as it stands today. It will be shown that the subject is eclectic, based predominantly on conventional neoclassical microeconomic foundations, but drawing significantly from developments in the natural and physical sciences. As in other branches of economic theory, differing normative perspectives and perceptions of the efficiency of market mechanisms in allocating resources have resulted in a discipline which is far from having achieved a consensus in the prescriptions which it advocates.

In addition to the four objectives that have just been described, this chapter serves two other purposes. First it is intended to be an introduction to the central issues confronted by environmental economists. Most of the ideas presented here will be given in a brief, simplified form. Subsequent chapters in this book will analyse the issues more carefully. Secondly, the chapter will give you some insight into the way in which this book is structured, by indicating where those more complete analyses are to be found.

Natural and environmental resources

Resources and production

In many economics texts, the term resources is used synonymously with the factors of production. The latter are defined to be those inputs without which the production of goods and services could not take place. Economic analysis typically adopts the premise that, for any given state of technology, a mathematical relationship exists between quantities of production inputs (factors of production) and the associated maximum output quantities. This relationship can be represented by a production function

$$Q = Q(X_1, X_2, \ldots, X_n) \qquad (1.1)$$

where Q is the maximised quantity of output flow for given values of the arguments of the production function, and $X_1, X_2, \ldots, X_n$ denote (suitably defined) quantities of n productive inputs or factors of production. In theoretical analysis, it is common to identify three distinct classes of productive input, namely L, K, and D, denoting respectively quantities of labour, capital, and land employed in production. Applied empirical analyses sometimes specify a fourth factor, energy (E), as a separate productive input. These productive inputs are measured either as a flow of input services over some specified period of time (L and E are usually measured in this way), or as input stocks employed at some point in time (K and D are usually measured in this way). In this case, we can express the production function as

$$Q = f(L, K, D, E) \qquad (1.2)$$

There is no reason, however, to suppose that this fourfold categorisation of factors is necessarily best. We can classify the factors of production in many ways; the most appropriate way will depend upon the particular questions we address, or the particular characteristics of inputs that we choose to stress. In much of modern economic growth theory, for example, the highly aggregate and long-run nature of the analysis has resulted in presentations in which output is viewed as a function of just two inputs, labour and capital. In contrast, analyses which have the objective of deriving the economic implications of taxes on energy use tend to be more disaggregated in scope, identifying a wider set of distinct inputs, including energy as a whole or different forms of energy as production inputs.

Notice that the specification of the production function in Equation 1.1 does not admit *intermediate inputs* (semi-manufactured goods and services) as separate factors of production, despite the evident fact that spending on such inputs constitutes a large component of the gross costs of many productive units. It will usually be legitimate to abstract from the presence of intermediate inputs in analyses posed at a high level of aggregation, by recognising that these are not primary inputs but are the outputs of prior production processes.

Private and social costs of production

A fundamental principle of economic theory argues that economic resources are scarce. They are scarce in the particular sense that whilst being available in limited or finite quantities, the claims to which these resources are put are, at least to a reasonable approximation, infinite or limitless. Scarcity of resources implies that their use is costly; using a resource incurs an opportunity cost, in the form of an alternative foregone benefit.

In those cases where a resource user directly incurs this opportunity cost, the cost is known as a private cost. However, the costs incurred in the use of resources may not be met by the user, but are borne by another person or persons. These costs are known as external costs. The full cost of the resource use – the social cost – is the sum of all relevant private and external costs associated with that resource use.

Many productive inputs exist in forms that allow appropriability (that is, they can be possessed and owned by one or more individuals) and exclusive use. In these cases, as we shall see in Chapter 3, private (or at least well-defined) ownership and the existence of competitive markets may well ensure that private costs of production accurately reflect the true social costs in question, and so one important condition for their efficient use will be satisfied. However, as we show in a moment, for some types of resource, an important property that they possess is that their use does impart value but is not usually associated with any monetary payment by the user in a pure market economy (at least in the absence of some system of charges established by government). An obvious example here is the set of services provided by the natural environment in transforming toxic wastes into less harmful residues. As we shall demonstrate in Chapter 3, there is, at least, a *prima facie* case for believing that market economies will not efficiently allocate what we shall call environmental resources.

Environmental resources and production

The production function given in Equation (1.2) specified four inputs, labour, capital, land, and energy. Is this sufficiently comprehensive for our purpose? The answer to this question will depend to some extent on how broadly one chooses to define land and energy. In some economic analysis, land is treated in terms of its provision of *space* alone. Broader interpretations also recognise the fertility of land and its biological growth potential. This aspect of land, as we shall see, was of particular interest to the classical economists.

However, even this broader interpretation of land is not sufficient for our purposes, for at least two reasons. Firstly, areas of land and water may contain stocks of natural resources, in the form of both non-renewable resources (such as mineral fuels) and potentially renewable resources (such as timber or fisheries). Such stocks obviously contribute inputs to the production process, and are conceptually distinct from the space in which they happen to be situated.

Secondly, conventional interpretations of land and energy resources ignore a set of productive services offered by environmental resources. These services, for which no financial payment is (usually) made by the user, include

- waste assimilation and processing by ecological systems;
- the direct provision of environmental inputs (such as clean air, water for cleaning and cooling);
- environmental systems maintenance processes, which sustain clean air and water, maintain climatic conditions, regulate soil fertility, support stocks of renewable resources (such as fish and timber stocks), and regulate water flows in river systems and aquifers.

Resources and consumption

Looking at resources as being synonymous with factors of production (even in a wide sense) focuses on their role in the production of goods or services, from which satisfaction (or utility) is obtained in consumption. Equating 'resources' with 'productive inputs' is too restrictive for the purposes of environmental economics analysis as it envisages resources only contributing indirectly to utility, through the intermediary of production. It is clear, however, that resources can also yield utility directly. For example, if land is interpreted broadly, we note that it creates utility directly when areas of beauty are visited or used for recreation. Resources, therefore, generate value both directly (through consumption of environmental amenities) and indirectly (through produced goods or services). Chapters 2 and 10 will investigate the conditions under which these direct consumption amenities will be adequately reflected in decisions affecting the supply of environmental resources. At the moment, the purpose of these preliminary remarks is just to establish the fact that resources possess value through consumption use as well as through production use.

Intrinsic values

A more awkward issue arises when one considers whether resources have intrinsic value; that is, whether resources have value irrespective of any use that humans make of them (in production or consumption) now or in the future, or of any feelings of satisfaction that humans might have from knowing that the resource exists. Conventional economic analysis does not accord intrinsic value (in this sense) any relevance to the evaluation of costs and benefits; not surprisingly, this is a matter of considerable contention. We shall examine this question in some depth in the second chapter.

The main conclusion one should draw from these remarks is that 'resources' provide a broader set of services than is sometimes recognised in economic analysis; environmental resources play a multifunctional role. Whereas some services derived from environmental resources command market prices, others are 'free' in a monetary sense. We argue below that it is reasonable to treat resources or the services derived from them as free goods if they are in unlimited supply, or if the use of the service is non-rivalrous. Whereas this may have been true for some services when the demands made by economic activity were relatively low, this has become less true with the passage of time. Most environmental resources have become increasingly scarce as the scale of economic activity has expanded, and many have been exploited or degraded to very considerable degrees.

Ecologists and environmental scientists have for a long time recognised the tendency of economic activity to degrade and deplete natural environments, and have shown how the stability and resilience of ecosystems can be threatened by excessive rates of economic activity. Ecologists and environmentalists have sometimes taken the view that economics has failed to address these deeper, system-wide implications of economic activity. Indeed, this is the fundamental critique of economic analysis by ecologists, and we examine the extent to which this critique has resulted in new developments within environmental economics later in this chapter.

Classifications of environmental resources

We shall conclude this initial discussion of resources by considering some ways in which environmental resources may be usefully classified. One fundamental property concerns the reproducibility of a resource stock. The criterion of interest in this regard is the extent to which a resource exhibits economically significant rates of regeneration. This suggests one type of classification which is very commonly used. Where the rate of resource regeneration is significant, we describe the resource as being renewable; otherwise, the resource is non-renewable.

This distinction is useful, but is limited in so far as it does not relate in any straightforward way to the potential for exhaustibility of resource stocks. Potential exhaustibility of a resource is related to the manner in which the resource is available and the way it can be used. To understand this, consider energy resources such as those in the forms of wind, tidal, wave, and solar flows. These are often labelled as 'renewable resources' but the most important property which they possess is that they are not exhaustible (at least in economically relevant time horizons). These energy flow resources are not exhaustible in the sense that one person's consumption of the energy flow does not reduce the magnitude of the flow available to others; the reason for this non-exhaustibility derives from the fact that the stock from which the energy flow ultimately derives is extra-terrestrial, and unaffected by human behaviour. For example, solar energy flows derive from stocks of matter in the sun, and tidal energy derives from gravitational forces related to the conjunction of the earth and the moon.

On the other hand, biological stock resources such as forests, fish and animal populations and other biomass stocks are often renewable, but are also potentially exhaustible. If the resource stock size or population level is sufficiently large, and the environmental conditions are benign, reductions in stock through harvesting can be regenerated through biological growth processes. However, for any given environmental system, there may be some population threshold size below which positive rates of biological growth are not possible. If the population or stock size were ever to fall below this threshold, the population would fall to zero. This dual property will be examined at length in Chapter 7.

Finally, mention should also be made of resource systems that we shall describe as renewable physical stock resources. These resource systems are capable of regeneration in relatively short periods of time through physical as well as biological transformation processes. Examples include soil structures and fertility levels, aquifers (water systems), the earth's ozone layer, and various parts of the lower, middle and upper layers of the earth's atmosphere, and the assimilative or waste processing capacities of environmental systems. Just as in the case of biological stock resources, though, these resource systems are also depletable and potentially exhaustible.

Notice that the classification scheme that has just been proposed enables us to view pollution as a form

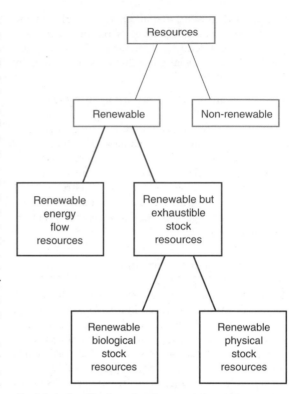

Fig 1.1 A classification of environmental resources.

of environmental resource depletion, in so far as pollutant flows result in reductions in the quantity or quality of one or more of the resource types we have discussed. The analysis of pollution viewed in terms of resource depletion will figure prominently in several places in later chapters. A classification based on these principles is presented in Figure 1.1. This classification will be used throughout the rest of this book.

The emergence of resource and environmental economics

As we noted above, an important characteristic of environmental economics is its eclecticism. This branch of economics draws its techniques largely from the fields of pure and applied economic theory, but it has incorporated elements from the natural sciences, from systems analysis, and from the domain of ethics. The resulting body of knowledge, however, is far from having achieved a synthesis of these components, and no consensus has been reached regarding the way in which such a synthesis could be achieved.

We now turn our attention to a historical review of the development of environmental economics from the time of the industrial revolution. Some important foundations of environmental economics can be found in the writings of the classical economists, and most of the foundations had been laid by the time that neoclassical economics achieved dominance in orthodox economics. From the 1960s, concern with possible environmental degradation or limits to growth encouraged the development of environmental science, drawing on elements from the natural science disciplines. Some of these developments found a reflection in the emerging discipline of 'new environmental economics'.

The treatment of resource and environmental issues in the evolution of economic theory

The emergence of environmental economics as a distinct sub-discipline has been a relatively recent event. However, concern with the substance of natural resource or environmental issues has much earlier antecedents, and can, for example, be identified in the writings of the classical economists. Whilst the subject matter of environmental economics has precursors from the time of Adam Smith onwards, the reasons for interest in this material have differed over time.

A survey of the development of economic theory from the period of classical economics onwards is a useful exercise to the student of environmental economics for several reasons. It contributes to an understanding of the methodological framework and conceptual tools used in modern environmental economics analysis. Our survey will point to a number of important links and relationships that are relatively easy to miss in the analysis of environmental issues, but which will be examined at length in this book. Finally, an excursion into the history of economic theory will reveal a number of interesting continuities between the concerns of economists over a period of 200 years.[1]

Classical economics: the contributions of Smith, Malthus, Ricardo, and Mill to the development of natural resource economics

The label *classical* has been given to a number of economists writing in the eighteenth and nineteenth

centuries, a period during which the Industrial Revolution was taking place (at least in much of Europe and North America) and agricultural productivity was growing rapidly. A recurring theme of political–economic debate concerned the appropriate institutional arrangements for the development of trade and growth.

These issues are central to the work of Adam Smith (1723–1790). Smith was the first writer to systematise the argument for the importance of markets in allocating resources, although his emphasis was placed on what we would now call the dynamic effects of markets. His major work, '*An Inquiry into the Nature and Causes of the Wealth of Nations*' (1776), contains the famous statement of the role of the *invisible hand*:

> But it is only for the sake of profit that any man employs a capital in the support of industry; and he will always, therefore, endeavour to employ it in the support of that industry of which the produce is likely to be of the greatest value, or to exchange for the greatest quantity, either of money or of other goods.
>
> As every individual, therefore, endeavours as much as he can both to employ his capital in the support of domestic industry, and so to direct that industry that its produce may be of the greatest value; every individual necessarily labours to render the annual revenue of the society as great as he can. He generally, indeed, neither intends to promote the public interest, nor knows how much he is promoting it. . . . he is, in this as in many other cases, led by an invisible hand to promote an end which was no part of his intention . . .
>
> . . . By pursuing his own interest he frequently promotes that of society more effectively than when he really intends to promote it.

Smith (1776), Book IV, Chapter 2, page 477

This belief in the efficacy of the market mechanism is a fundamental organising principle of the policy prescriptions of much modern environmental economics. In particular, as we show in Chapter 9, it provides the foundation for much of the policy advice given by economists regarding pollution control.

Of more immediate relevance to our current objective is the interest of classical economists in standards of living and the process of economic growth. Natural resources were seen as determinants of national wealth and growth; moreover, differences in resource endowments were perceived as influencing income differentials between economies. A strand running through classical political economy concerns the prospects in the long term for an economy (and so

---

[1] See Blaug (1985) for a much more extensive survey.

for living standards of the majority of people) subject to constraints on the supply of land.[2] Land (sometimes used in the sense of what we might now call natural resources) was taken to be fixed in some sense. Taken together with the assumptions that land was a necessary input to production, and that it exhibited diminishing returns, the conclusions drawn by early classical economists pointed to the transience of economic progress and the inevitability of an eventual stationary state, in which the prospects for the living standard of the 'mass' were bleak.

This thesis is most strongly associated with Thomas Malthus (1766–1834), and is most forcefully argued in his '*Essay*' of 1798. Given a fixed land quantity and an assumed continual positive population growth, diminishing returns in agriculture imply a tendency for output per capita to fall over time, and so a long-run tendency for the living standards of the mass to be driven down to a subsistence level. At the subsistence wage level, conditions would permit reproducibility of the population at an unchanging level, and the economy would attain a steady state. This notion of a steady state was formalised and extended by David Ricardo (1772–1823), particularly in his *Principles of Political Economy and Taxation* (1817). Malthus's assumption of a fixed stock of land was replaced by a conception in which land was available in parcels of varying quality. Agricultural output could be expanded by increasing the intensive margin (exploiting a given parcel of land more intensively) or by increasing the extensive margin (bringing previously uncultivated land into productive use). However, in either case, returns to the land input were taken to be diminishing. Economic development proceeds in such a way that the 'economic surplus' is appropriated increasingly in the form of rent, the return to land, and development again converges toward a Malthusian stationary state.

---

[2] The classical economists' analysis of the consequences of a limited supply of land was by no means the first time that writers had been concerned with limited resources. Rosenberg (1973, page 112) documents the long-standing concern within England about the supply of timber. Nor did fears about limited resources close with the evolution from classical to neoclassical economics. Apart from more recent analysis of the consequences of finiteness, to be discussed later in this chapter, we can find recurring examples during the nineteenth and twentieth centuries. Jevons (1865), for instance, observed the physical limits to coal supply in industrial Britain, and predicted that these limits would force an end to the Industrial Revolution there.

In the writing of John Stuart Mill (1806–1873) (see in particular Mill (1857)) one finds a full statement of classical economics. Mill's work utilises the idea of diminishing returns, but recognises the countervailing influence of the growth of knowledge and technical progress in agriculture and in production more generally. Writing in Britain when output per person was apparently rising, not falling, he placed less emphasis on diminishing returns, reflecting the relaxation of the constraints of the extensive margin as colonial exploitation opened up new tranches of land, as fossil fuels were increasingly exploited, and as innovation rapidly increased agricultural productivity. The concept of a stationary state was not abandoned, but it was thought to be one in which a relatively high level of material prosperity would be attained.

Perhaps foreshadowing later developments in the economics of conservation, Mill adopted a broader view of the roles played by natural resources than his predecessors. In addition to agricultural and extractive uses of land, land was a source of amenity values (such as the intrinsic beauty of countryside) that would become of increasing relative importance as material conditions improved. These views of Mill are clearly revealed in the following extracts from his major work.

> I cannot . . . regard the stationary state of capital and wealth with the unaffected aversion so generally manifested towards it by political economists of the old school . . . I confess that I am not charmed with the ideal of life held out by those who think that the normal state of human beings is that of struggling to get on; that the trampling, crushing, elbowing and treading on each other's heels which form the existing type of social life, are the most desirable lot of human kind, or anything but the disagreeable symptoms of one of the phases of industrial progress . . . . Those who do not accept the present very early stage of human improvement as its ultimate type may be excused for being comparatively indifferent to the kind of economic progress which excites the congratulations of ordinary politicians: the mere increase of production . . . . It is only in the backward countries of the world that increased production is still an important object; in those most advanced, what is needed is a better distribution . . . . There is room in the world, no doubt, and even in old countries, for a great increase in population, supposing the arts of life to go on improving, and capital to increase. But even if innocuous, I confess I see very little reason for desiring it. The density of population necessary to enable mankind to obtain, in the greatest degree, all of the advantages both of cooperation and of social intercourse, has, in all the most populous countries, been attained. A population may be too crowded, though all be

amply supplied with food and raiment. It is not good for man to be kept perforce at all times in the presence of his species.... Nor is there much satisfaction in contemplating the world with nothing left to the spontaneous activity of nature: with every rood of land brought into cultivation, which is capable of growing food for human beings; every flowery waste or natural pasture ploughed up, all quadrupeds or birds which are not domesticated for man's use exterminated as his rivals for food, every hedgerow or superfluous tree rooted out, and scarcely a place left where a wild shrub or flower could grow without being eradicated as a weed in the name of improved agriculture. If the earth must lose that great portion of its pleasantness which it owes to things that the unlimited increase of wealth and population would extirpate from it, for the mere purpose of enabling it to support a larger, but not a happier or better population, I sincerely hope, for the sake of posterity, that they will be content to be stationary long before necessity compels them to it.

Mill (1857), Book IV

Neo-classical economics: marginal theory and value.

By the late nineteenth century, classical economics was being challenged by what subsequently became labelled *neoclassical economics*, in a series of major works published in the 1870s. One consequence of this was a change in the manner in which value was explained. Classical economics saw value as arising from the labour power embodied (directly and indirectly) in output, a view which had found its fullest embodiment in the work of Karl Marx. Neoclassical economists envisaged value as being determined in exchange, so reflecting preferences and costs of production. The concepts of price and value ceased to be distinct. Moreover, previous notions of absolute scarcity were replaced by a relative concept of scarcity. This change in emphasis paved the way for the development of welfare economics, in which values could be measured in terms of consumer preferences.

At the methodological level, the technique of marginal analysis became adopted, allowing earlier notions of diminishing returns to be given a formal basis in terms of diminishing marginal productivity in the context of an explicit production function. Jevons (1835–1882) and Menger (1840–1921) formalised the theory of consumer preferences in terms of utility and demand theory. The evolution of neoclassical economic analysis led to an emphasis on the structure and degree of efficiency, rather than the level, of economic activity. Concern with economic growth

receded in importance, perhaps reflecting the apparent inevitability of growth in Western Europe at this time. Leon Walras (1834–1910) developed neoclassical General Equilibrium Theory, and in so doing provided a rigorous foundation for the concepts of efficiency and optimality that we employ extensively in this text. Alfred Marshall (1842–1924) (see *Principles of Economics*, 1890) was responsible for elaboration of the partial equilibrium supply and demand-based analysis of price determination so familiar to students of modern microeconomics. A substantial part of modern environmental economics continues to use these techniques as tools of exposition.

We remarked earlier that concern with the level (and the growth) of economic activity had been largely ignored in the period during which neoclassical economics was being developed. Economic depression in the industrialised economies in the inter-war years provides the backcloth against which John Maynard Keynes (1883–1946) developed his theory of income and output determination. The Keynesian agenda switched attention to aggregate supply and demand, and the reasons why market economies may fail to achieve optimal aggregate levels of activity.

This direction of theoretical development, whilst undoubtedly of importance, has little of intrinsic interest to environmental economics *per se*. However, Keynesian macroeconomics was of indirect importance in stimulating a resurgence of interest in growth theory in the middle of the twentieth century (Harrod, Domar, Kaldor), and the development of a neoclassical theory of growth (Solow). What is noticeable in early neoclassical growth models is the absence of land, or any wider category of natural resources, from the production function underlying these growth models. Classical limits to growth arguments, based on a fixed land input, do not have any place in these models.

The introduction of natural resources into neoclassical models of economic growth followed some pathbreaking work completed during the 1960s and 1970s, in which economists systematically investigated the efficient and optimal depletion of resources. The original investigation of optimal depletion of exhaustible resources dates back to Gray (1914) and the classic paper by Hotelling (1931). These provided a foundation upon which a more general and extended structure was built later by Dasgupta, Heal, Solow, and Hartwick. These writers developed models of efficient and optimal growth for economies whose production function included as arguments exhaustible and non-exhaustible natural resources, as well as capital and labour inputs resources. Good examples of these models are found in the 1974 Special Issue of the *Review of Economic Studies*. The models of optimal extraction of resources that we present and discuss in Chapters 5, 6 and 7 are based on the writings of those authors. One important and related issue addressed in this literature, and examined below in Chapter 2, concerns the conditions necessary for sustainable growth, the seminal works of which are Solow (1974a) and Hartwick (1977, 1978).

Welfare economics

The final development in mainstream economic theory that needs to be addressed is the development of a rigorous theory of welfare economics. Welfare economics, as you will see in Chapter 3, attempts to provide a framework in which normative judgements can be made about alternative configurations of economic activity. In particular, it attempts to identify circumstances under which one can claim that one allocation of resources is better (in some sense) than another.

Not surprisingly, it turns out to be the case that such rankings are only possible if one is prepared to accept some ethical criterion. The most commonly used ethical criterion adopted by classical and neo-classical economists derives from the utilitarian moral philosophy, developed by David Hume, Jeremy Bentham and John Stuart Mill. We explore this ethical structure in some depth in the next chapter. Suffice to say now that utilitarianism suggests that social welfare consists of some weighted average of the total utility levels enjoyed by all individuals in the society.

Economists have attempted to find a method of ranking different states of the world which does not require the use of a social welfare function, makes little use of ethical principles, but is nevertheless useful in making prescriptions about resource allocation. A criterion which has been proposed for this purpose is that of economic efficiency, developed by Vilfredo Pareto (1897). Using this criterion, one can explore which sets of institutional arrangements are consistent with outcomes which are economically efficient. Conversely, one can identify circumstances which would make it possible (or likely) that efficient outcomes will not be forthcoming. These ideas are briefly previewed in the next section, and examined at length in Chapter 4.

Important early work in this field is found in the analysis of externalities and market failure in Marshall (1890). The first systematic analysis of pollution as an externality is to be found in Pigou (1920, pages 159–161). The systematisation of welfare economics was finally achieved in the 1960s, following important contributions by Debreu, Arrow and Samuelson. Ronald Coase developed the argument that the existence of well-defined and transferable property rights may be necessary conditions for efficient allocation of resources. Edward Mishan and others developed the technique of cost-benefit analysis as a practical vehicle for evaluating the welfare implications of changes in the pattern of resource allocation. These foundations have led to a burgeoning literature in the area of applied welfare economics, and much of this recent work concerns the relationship between resource use, market failure and environmental issues.

The concepts of efficiency and optimality in economic analysis

With the full development of welfare economics theory, most of the foundations of modern economic analysis were in place. We will move in the following sections to see how resource and environmental economics has adapted this literature to its objects of focus, whilst at the same time drawing on developments that originated outside economics itself. Before we do this, it will be useful to review how this development of economics has led economists to understand and use the terms efficiency and optimality, concepts that we shall apply extensively throughout this book.

Economists use the concept of efficiency in a special way. An outcome (a particular allocation of resources) is Pareto efficient if it is not possible to make anyone better off without making at least one other person worse off. In other words, no transaction possibilities exist that are mutually beneficial to all parties affected by the transaction.[3] In a Pareto efficient situation, there are no 'free lunches' available. Changes in the way that resources are allocated

---

[3] Note, though, that if we introduce the possibility of actual (or potential) compensation by the gainers from any project to the losers from a project, a weaker version of efficiency can be defined. If all persons could be made better off, provided the direct gainers compensate (or could compensate) the direct losers, then an allocation of resources cannot be efficient.

will involve trade-offs, such that gains by one person are only possible if one or more other persons suffer losses. Conversely, this implies that in an inefficient situation, positive gains are possible to some persons without losses to others, so-called 'no regrets' options.[4]

Notice that the ability to say whether a particular allocation of resources is efficient or is not does not require that any interpersonal comparison be made. By definition, an allocation of resources cannot be efficient if one or more persons could gain with no-one else losing. Similarly, an efficiency gain is said to take place if a change occurs which benefits all affected parties. But as no trade-offs between individuals are required in these cases, it is not necessary that any judgement be made about the relative worthiness of different individuals.

Indeed, one reason why the criterion of efficiency has proved so attractive to economists is precisely that the concept carries little (if any) ethical content. But the converse of this, of course, is the fact that there is no reason whatsoever to believe that resource allocations are ethically desirable just because they are efficient. We can show this with a simple example. Suppose a situation exists in which I happen to possess nearly all the world's resources and you possess almost none. This situation would be efficient if no change were possible that did not result in a loss to me (in terms of my scale of preferences), irrespective of how much you would benefit. Clearly there is no reason for attributing any ethical goodness or optimality to this situation, just because it is efficient. When we discuss efficient or inefficient situations, we do so conditionally on a given distribution of income and wealth. This distribution may or may not be a fair one.

On the other hand, claims about the optimality of particular circumstances do require that ethical judgements be made. Following the conventional practice of using the phrase 'social optimality' to mean a situation in which social welfare is at its maximum value, it should be clear that any claim about optimality can only be assessed in terms of social welfare. But the criterion of social welfare is

only meaningful if there are agreed ethical principles that allow one to judge the relative merits of different distributions of stocks of wealth or flows of income.

Unfortunately, not all uses of the concept are made in this sense. Some authors use optimal as another word for efficient. It is important, therefore, to be particularly careful to note the sense in which the word *optimal* is being used in any particular argument. Throughout this text, we use the word optimal to refer to an arrangement which maximises some relevant social welfare function. As you might expect (and as we shall demonstrate in Chapter 3) an optimal arrangement is necessarily efficient. But the converse is not true: an efficient arrangement is not necessarily an optimal one.

The concepts of efficiency and optimality are explored extensively in Chapter 3. Given that much of the literature in the field of environmental economics pays no attention to distribution of income and wealth, or how these might be affected by the changes being considered, we also investigate in that chapter the circumstances in which it might be reasonable to discuss matters of efficiency in isolation from any social welfare function. We will then apply these theoretical tools to general issues relating to environmental resource use in Chapter 4, and to the extraction and harvesting of non-renewable and renewable resources in Chapters 5 to 7.

Associated developments in the environmental and natural sciences

The materials balance principle

Concern with issues relating to resource use and the environment has not been exclusively (or even mainly) the subject of economic analysis, of course. Whilst the developments referred to above were taking place in the field of economics, attention was being given to environmental issues in the natural sciences. In this section, we identify a number of the developments that had significant implications for the subsequent evolution of environmental economics.

We shall begin with the *materials balance principle*. The materials balance principle concerns identities that must hold between physical flows in any closed system, given the laws of thermodynamics (see Box 1.1). An early exposition of the principle as it applies to economic activity is found in Kneese *et al.* (1970). The materials balance principle, and its applications

---

[4] Whether this hypothesis is true or not is an empirical question. However, one question we should always ask when it is suggested that 'no regrets possibilities exist is the following: If it is possible for us to all get better off (with none losing), why have these opportunities not been exploited already? If such possibilities *do* exist, and we can answer this question, then it should provide insights into appropriate policies to achieve these potential gains.

Box 1.1 The laws of thermodynamics

The three laws of thermodynamics and their implications for environment–economy interactions are here described in a non-technical way. We begin by stating the three laws.

The so-called zeroth law

Every body has a property called temperature. When two bodies are found to be in thermal equilibrium, their temperatures are equal.

The first law

The first law of thermodynamics states that total energy and matter remain constant in any closed system. This is otherwise known as the 'law of conservation of energy' and the 'law of conservation of matter'.

The second law

In any thermodynamic process that proceeds from one equilibrium state to another, the entropy of the system *plus* the environment either remains unchanged or increases.

Implications of the laws of thermodynamics

The two laws that are relevant for thinking about the long-term nature of economy–environment interactions are the first and second laws. The first law underpins the materials balance principle. It states that matter/energy cannot be created or destroyed, and so leads to the accounting identities of material balance models. Matter and energy used in human production and consumption activities must eventually end up in environmental systems. When discharged as residuals, although their mass will not have altered, their form will have. These altered forms may result in significant amounts of environmental and economic damage.

The second law is sometimes known as the entropy law. What is entropy? Entropy describes the extent to which material and energy is organised or structured. The less structured it is – that is, the more uniformly and homogeneously it is distributed throughout a system – the higher is the entropy of that system. Conversely, entropy is low when material and energy are highly organised and structured. For matter and energy to be biologically and economically useful, they must be organised in highly structured forms; that is, matter and energy are useful when entropy is low. Consider fossil fuel mineral deposits. These constitute highly ordered and structured forms of organic matter, which can deliver economically useful services. Once combusted, however, whilst the total amount of mass/energy remains unchanged, its form becomes less ordered and less structured: combustion results in an increase in entropy. Recycling and waste management can reconvert high entropy (non-useful) matter into low entropy (useful) forms, but only by using energy. In such a process, energy is converted into high entropic form. The importance of the second law resides in the fact that it tells us that the overall entropy of the system must increase over time; the penalty we pay for recycling residuals into useful forms is a larger loss of usefully organised banks of energy.

So the second law of thermodynamics implies that the total amount of usefully concentrated energy and matter in an isolated system must decline over time. Many authors regard the second law as implying ultimate limits to the sustainability or reproducibility of an ecological system over time, because as continuing economic activity causes entropy to rise relentlessly, so the proportion of usefully available mass and energy decreases toward zero. Georgescu-Roegen (1971), for example, argues that the entropy law condemns civilisation to decline once earthly stocks of concentrated matter and energy have been dissipated. The best humans can do is to manage their behaviour so as to reduce the rate at which society approaches this limit.

However, things are not quite as bleak as this suggests. The earth is not a closed physical system. On the contrary, it does exchange energy with outside systems. Some positive level of continued resource use is therefore possible on a sustained basis, using, for example, solar energy-powered recycling (see Young, 1991).

Whilst physical principles do not imply that some positive level of activity is non-feasible on a perpetual basis, a number of authors (for example Daly, 1987) argue that sustained economic growth is not possible because current rates of material and energy use already exceed solar-powered recycling potential.

Let us end on an optimistic note, though. Economic growth is usually taken to be growth in the value of output. It is quite possible that higher values of output do not require equi-proportional increases in material/energy throughputs. This appears to mean that indefinitely sustainable growth is feasible, provided the materials component of output can be continually reduced.

Source: Halliday and Resnick (1988).

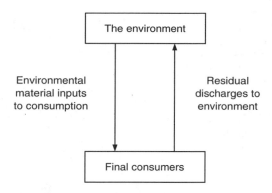

Fig 1.2a The materials balance principle.

to environmental issues, are examined in depth in Chapter 2 (in the section on sustainability). There, we attempt to use the principle to identify the conditions which should be satisfied for economic processes *and* environmental systems to be sustainable over time.

A simple statement of this principle, which will suffice for our present purpose, is that the mass of residuals flows into the environment from all forms of activity in the system equals the mass of resource flows from the environment. In Figure 1.2a, the materials balance principle is portrayed in its most simple form. In this representation, environment–economy interactions are shown as taking place, without any intermediation, between the environment itself and a final consumption sector. In this case, the material balance principle states that, provided no net accumulation of stock of goods takes place in the consumption sector, the mass of inputs from the environment into consumption must equal the mass of residual discharges from the consumption sector to the environment.

The representation given in Figure 1.2a is, of course, grossly oversimplified, and a more complete portrayal is given in Figure 1.2b, which is taken from Herfindahl and Kneese (1974, page 355). This shows, again in a very simplified manner, the physical relationships implied by the materials balance principle, taking into account the presence of intermediate production and recycling processes.

Commencing from the top of the diagram, we see that basic primary inputs (ores, liquids and gases) are taken from the environment and converted into useful products (basic fuel, food and raw materials) by 'environmental' firms. The outputs of these processes become inputs into subsequent production processes (shown as a product flow to non-environmental firms) or to households directly. Households also receive

final products from the non-environmental firms sector.

The essence of the materials balance principle is the identity between the mass materials flow from the environment (the flow A) and the mass of residual material discharge flows to the environment (flows $B + C + D$). So, in terms of mass, we have

$$A = B + C + D$$

Notice that several other sets of identities are suggested by Figure 1.2b. Each of the four sectors shown by rectangular boxes receives an equal mass of inputs to the mass of its outputs. So we have the following four mass identities:

The environment: $A = B + C + D$ as above

Environmental firms: $A = A_1 + A_2 + C$

Non-environmental firms: $B + R + E = R + A_1 + F$

Households: $A_2 + E = D + F$

Several interesting and important insights can be derived from this model. Firstly, in a closed economy (no material flows to or from the outside) in which no net stock accumulation takes place (i.e. the stocks of buildings, plant, other capital and consumer durables do not change in magnitude), the mass of residuals into the environment ($B + C + D$) must be equal to the mass of fuels, foods and raw materials extracted from the environment and oxygen taken from the atmosphere (flow A). This merely restates the fundamental identity stated above, but a corollary of this is that the mass of residual discharges is larger than the mass involved in basic materials production (the difference being accounted for by the oxygen consumed).

Secondly, the materials balance principle shows that 'treatment' of residuals from economic activity does not reduce their mass, it merely alters their form. This is a consequence of the law of conservation of mass: matter cannot be created or destroyed, although its form can be altered. Nevertheless, whilst it is important to be clear that waste treatment does not 'get rid of' waste, it is nevertheless true that the form in which residual discharges enter the environment can have a considerable impact on the damages that discharge flows create. Waste management is useful, therefore, not because it reduces the mass of waste but because it alters residuals from a less to a more benign form.

Thirdly, the extent of recycling is important. To see how, look again at the identity

$$B + R + E = R + A_1 + F$$

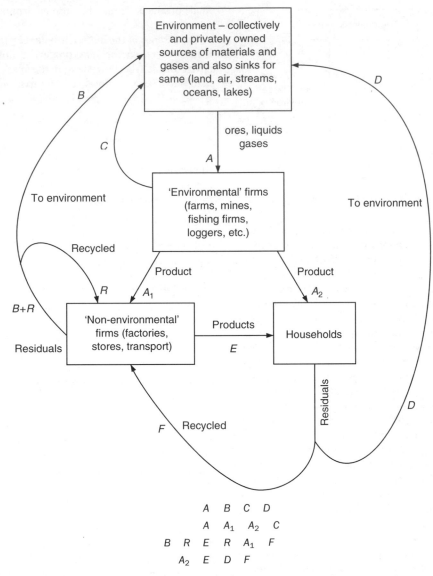

Source: Adapted from Herfindahl and Kneese (1974).

Fig 1.2b A materials balance model of economy–environment interactions.

For any fixed magnitude of final output, E, if the amount of recycling of household residuals F can be increased, then the quantity of inputs into final production A_1 can be decreased. This in turn implies that less primary extraction of environmental resources A need take place. This is of fundamental importance; the total amount of material throughput in the system (the magnitude A) can be decreased for any given level of production and consumption if the efficiency of materials utilisation is increased through recycling processes. As many ecologists argue that the ultimate determinant of environmental damage is the level of materials throughput in the system, a very strong case for recycling is apparent. But note that there are limits to how far recycling should be undertaken. It is not a costless activity. Recycling of materials uses materials too; recycling should not (even from a purely ecological perspective) be pushed beyond the point where the mass of inputs used in recycling exceeds the reduction in material throughputs that it allows.

The importance of the materials balance principle resides in the fact that it provides a coherent framework in which an economic analysis of resource use and its implications for the environment can be placed. It draws one's attention to the long-term implications of economic activity, by focusing on the stock–flow relationships implied by that behaviour, and its importance follows from the discipline it imposes in thinking about stock and flow relationships. Typical analyses of the optimal depletion of an exhaustible resource, for example, pay no attention to the residual flows into the environment as an extracted resource is consumed. In our discussion of the optimal extraction path of non-renewable fossil fuel stocks in Chapters 5 and 6, policy implications are initially derived under the assumption that the associated pollutant emissions are harmless. Subsequently in those chapters, we examine how the conclusions differ when proper account is taken of the damaging nature of residual products. As we analyse the Greenhouse Effect and the problems associated with acid rain in Chapter 12, these issues will adopt a central place in our analyses.

Finally, we note that the materials balance principle has important implications for the economic analysis of pollution in general. If we model pollution *flows* only, and ignore the *stock* considerations implied by the materials balance principle, we show in Chapter 8 that one is likely to overestimate the optimal flow level of pollution for any emission that is persistent over time.

Environmental-augmented input–output models

A means of describing and analysing the interaction between the environment and the economy implied by the materials balance principle, is through the construction of environmental input–output tables, which in turn provide the statistical foundation for the development of environmental input–output models. The key feature of input–output tables and models is the degree of detail they provide on flows of goods and services (inputs and outputs) between different sectors of the economy. In principle, it is easy to extend this system to incorporate environmental sectors (e.g. land, air, water) producing a variety of environmental goods (e.g. timber, oxygen, fish) and bads (e.g. carbon

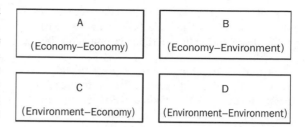

Fig. 1.3 Schematic environmental input–output system.

dioxide, polluted soil, waste water). This is illustrated in Figure 1.3, where submatrix **A** records flows between the different sectors and economic agents, as in the conventional input–output model. Submatrices **B**, **C** and **D** represent extensions of the system, in this instance including not only environment–economy interaction but also interaction between elements of the environment independent of the economy (e.g. coastal erosion). Submatrix **C** records environmental inputs to the economy, i.e. the extraction and use of natural resource products, while submatrix **B** records environmental outputs from the economy such as pollutants.

In practice the construction of complete systems such as that sketched above is extremely difficult, but there are an increasing number of examples of models which incorporate a limited range of environmental inputs and outputs i.e. partial implementation of submatrices **B** and **C**, though none as yet which also attempts to include elements of submatrix **D**.

The development and use of environmental input–output models are discussed in Chapter 13. Like any other model, the construction of an input–output model requires data, and input–output models are particularly data-hungry. In fact, an input–output table is essentially a very detailed form of the national accounts, and this leads us to consider whether and in what ways the system of national accounts might be modified or extended to include environment–economy interaction. For example the national accounts presently include estimates of depreciation or capital consumption of the nation's capital assets, defined as the stock of buildings, plant and equipment. They do not include estimates of the depletion of the nation's stocks of natural resources, such as the national forest (renewable) or coal stocks (non-renewable), and in this respect may be said to underestimate the amount required to maintain the nation's capital stock, and to overestimate net national product or national income. Moreover, while the national accounts may well include the cost of cleaning up environmental damage (e.g. an oil slick), they do not include (as a negative item) any estimate of the value of the environmental damage caused.

Proposals to create more environmentally conscious national accounts are, however, included in the most recent (1993) United Nations System of National Accounts, which is the basis of most countries' systems of national accounting. The concepts and practices of environmental accounting are reviewed in Chapter 14.

Systems analysis

Systems analysis is a methodological technique that was developed in the physical sciences. During the early 1970s, a number of attempts were made to apply this approach to consider the long-term prospects for economic development.

One well-known example of this systems approach is the model developed in Forrester's *World Dynamics* (1971) for very long-term projection of historical trends. The model was applied in *The Limits to Growth* (1972) by Meadows *et al*. Box 1.2 presents the main elements of Meadows' methodology, together with an example of one of the simulation runs presented in *The Limits to Growth*. Meadows' simulations, and others using a similar approach, led to the conclusion that, given finite quantities of natural resource stocks, sustained positive flows of natural resource services were impossible. This conclusion is reminiscent of that suggested by the early classical economists, but was given a foundation in the laws of thermodynamics, rather than being based on the principle of diminishing returns. The notion that the natural environment imposes some form of constraint on economic growth is not particularly controversial in itself. The base run simulation of the Meadows' model, however, implied resource exhaustion and system collapse, and, not surprisingly, attracted much criticism from economists.

The main conclusion reached by Meadows is precisely what the title of the book states: economic growth is subject to fundamental limits, and will ultimately have to cease if the economy is to continue in perpetuity. But an interesting side argument is developed in the report. The conventional wisdom held that the key to alleviation of poverty in the global economy was economic growth. In *The Limits to Growth*, Meadows *et al*. argue that growth is not an appropriate vehicle for achieving that objective; rather, redistribution of income and wealth was a more appropriate instrument. Very little attention was given at the time of publication of '*Limits*' to this proposition, but it is now by no means uncommon to find this view being advocated. Indeed, the need for a redistribution of resources now finds wide support, and was one of the central themes of the Brundtland Commission's report *Our Common Future* (WCED, 1987).

Returning to the theme of the limits to growth, the response by economists to '*Limits*' was almost entirely hostile. Prominent among these responses were those by Page (1973), Nordhaus (1972), Beckerman (1972, 1974), Cole *et al*. (1973) and Lecomber (1975). Various criticisms were made of the research. Firstly, it was argued that the model's predictions were dominated by unrealistic growth projections. Secondly, Nordhaus and other critics claimed that the empirical underpinnings of the model were flawed so that, contrary to what the authors claimed, the simulations failed to track twentieth-century historical data to acceptable levels of statistical significance. The most serious attack was reserved for the claim that the '*Limits*' model contained poorly specified feedback loops, as it failed to take account of behavioural adjustments operating through the price mechanism. In particular, changing patterns of relative scarcity would alter the structure of prices, inducing behavioural changes in resource use patterns. In a well-functioning market mechanism, the criticism went, limits to growth would not operate in the way stated by Meadows *et al*. The following extract from Page (1973, pages 41–42) is typical of the criticism that *The Limits to Growth* attracted from economists.

One of its main modes of 'collapse' is resource depletion. The main reason for this is the assumption of fixed economically-available resources, and of diminishing returns in resource technology. Neither of those assumptions is historically valid. The relative cost of minerals has remained roughly constant, and has not increased over the past eighty years as a consequence of diminishing returns. And new economically exploitable reserves are being discovered all the time.... If one also includes the possibilities of improvements in recycling, and of further economy in the use of resources in industry, then we can conclude the following: If the sum of the annual rates of increase of resource discovery, of recycling, and of economy of use in industry add up to more than around 2%, then the resource mode of collapse in the model will be avoided and there will not be any net drain on 'available' reserves.

However, this rebuttal of Meadows *et al.* relies upon the presence of a well-functioning market mechanism. In the absence of a complete set of markets, the appropriate substitution effects that economists have in mind may not take place. As we shall see in the following chapters, the possibility (and indeed likelihood) of market failure is recognised in, and forms an important component of, modern environmental economics.

Even if one were to find fault with the particular assertions made in the limits to growth literature, there may nevertheless be limits to growth for other reasons. Daly (1987), for example, argues that whilst growth processes do not face limits in all circumstances, the level of material throughput has now reached sufficiently high rates for some limits to start biting. Daly identifies two classes of limits to growth. The first consists of biophysical limits; these arise from three related matters – the finiteness of the material and energy base, the second law of thermodynamics (the entropy law) and the existence of complex ecological interdependencies. The consequence of these three facts is that economic activity leads to an increasing disordering of the overall system of which the economy is one part. This disordering interferes with the complex life-support systems of the biosphere and disrupts the nature of what Daly calls biogeochemical cycles.

Despite these being serious problems, Daly contends that the more serious limits may be of what he calls the ethicosocial type. We shall defer a detailed examination of these until discussing economic growth in Chapter 11. Suffice it to say here is that what Daly has in mind is that the pursuit of growth tends to be self-defeating or seriously objectionable on social, welfare and moral grounds; presumably, he believes that the growth goal will be abandoned as these limits become sufficiently evident, although one may regard this as being a rather optimistic position to take.

Ecological science developments

A central interest of ecological science is the study of the developmental processes occurring over time in interrelated biological and physical systems – what we shall call ecosystems. Ecosystems can be analysed at many different levels, but in all cases an ecosystem is a complex set of interdependencies between the system's components, and is continually in a dynamic process of development and change.

The structure of a system can be expressed in terms of mathematical relationships. When any particular ecosystem is subjected to disturbances, an important property of the system is whether the disturbance merely changes the levels of variables in the system, or whether the parameters of the relationships themselves change. The resilience of an ecosystem is a measure of the extent to which it can be subjected to disturbances without the system's parameters being changed. A system's resilience is not constant, however. Ecologists suggest that resilience tends to be greater the higher is the degree of complexity, diversity and 'interlockedness' of the ecosystem.

Economic behaviour tends to reduce ecosystem complexity, diversity and interlockedness, sometimes at very dramatic rates. As resilience is reduced, so the level of disturbance to which the ecosystem can be subjected without parametric change taking place is reduced. Expressed another way, the threshold levels of some system variable, beyond which major changes in a wider system take place, can be reduced as a consequence of economic behaviour. Safety margins become tightened, and the integrity and stability of the ecosystem is put into greater jeopardy.

When change takes place, the dose–response relationship may also exhibit very significant non-linearities and discontinuities. Pollution of a water system, for example, may have relatively small and proportional effects at low pollution levels, but at higher pollutant concentrations, responses may increase sharply and possibly jump discontinuously to much greater magnitudes. Such a dose–response relationship is illustrated in Figure 1.5.

These insights from ecology have important implications for human behaviour, and in particular for the rates of depletion and harvesting of non-renewable and exhaustible resources, and the processes of residual disposal into the environment. Ecologists often suggest three behavioural rules that should be followed to minimise the likelihood of ecosystem disruption:

1 Harvesting of renewed resources should take place within natural and managed rates of regeneration.

2 Extraction of exhaustible resources should be limited to the rate at which renewable resources can be substituted for them. There should, in other words, be a zero rate of extraction of the composite environmental resource stock.

Box 1.2 The limits to growth

One example of a systems approach is Forrester's *World Dynamics* (1971), applied in *The Limits to Growth* (1972). In *The Limits to Growth*, Meadows *et al.* state that

> [The *Limits to Growth* model] was built to investigate five major trends of global concern-accelerating industrialisation, rapid population growth, widespread malnutrition, depletion of non-renewable resources, and a deteriorating environment. These trends are all interconnected in many ways, and their development is measured in decades or centuries, rather than in months or years. With the model we are seeking to understand the causes of these trends, their interrelationships, and their implications as much as one hundred years in the future.
>
> Meadows *et al.* (1972), page 21.

The projection of trends is not one of simple extrapolation *per se*, but is rather one which takes account of the existence of *feedback loops*. Changing levels of the variables being forecast feed back to alter the levels or explanatory variables. Moreover, feedback loops in particular parts of the overall model interact with those in other parts. The world economy is viewed as a complex organism, in which all parts are interrelated, but each part nevertheless possesses considerable autonomy. In the Meadows model, these feedback mechanisms are modelled for population, capital, agriculture and pollution. The evolution of the system as a whole over time is studied through computer simulation analysis. In order to do this simulation, the interrelationships between variables in each part of the system, the

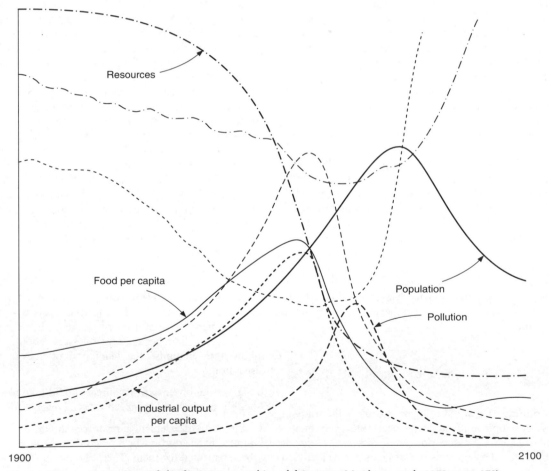

Fig 1.4 Base run projections of the 'limits to growth' model (*source:* Meadows *et al.*, 1972, page 176).

Box 1.2 Continued

associated feedback loops within each component, and the linkages between different components of the system must be numerically specified. Also, initial values must be selected for each system variable. The next step involves adjustment to the model specification and parameter values so that the model simulations can replicate or track historical data fairly accurately. Meadows *et al.* claim to have tuned the model well enough for it to track historical data on key variables over the period 1900 to 1970 reasonably well. Once this point is reached, the model can be allowed to simulate over future periods. The predictions that emerge from such simulations in the absence of any explicit governmental intervention are known as the *base run* or standard run projections. Meadows base or 'standard' run projections are reproduced in Figure 1.4.

The authors comment that the standard world model simulation assumes no major changes in the social, economic or physical relationships that have historically characterised the world system. The variables shown in the figure all follow actual historical values until the year 1970. Food, industrial output and population grow exponentially until the rapidly diminishing resource base causes a slow-down in industrial growth. System lags result in pollution and population continuing to grow for some time after industrial output has peaked. Population growth is finally halted by a rise in the mortality rate, as a result of reduced flows of food and medical services.

The base run projections are clearly very dismal ones, being dominated by rapid population growth during the first part of the simulation time period, which forces downwards all measures expressed in *per capita* terms. It is clear from Figure 1.4 that food *per capita* and industrial output *per capita*, for example, fall back after 2000 to levels below the minimum ones attained during the twentieth-century. The standard run simulations were extremely depressing, and the modellers devoted much effort to reparametrising and respecifying the model in an effort to generate more optimistic simulated outcomes. These changed simulations formed the basis of the policy advice presented by Meadows *et al.*

3 Emission of wastes should take place within the assimilative capacity of the environment.

Some important contributions to this debate are to be found in, or are surveyed in, Common and Perrings (1992), Commoner (1963, 1972), Darnell (1973), Barbier (1989a), and Barbier and Markandya (1990). Barbier provides analyses of some ecosystems that have been subjected to extensive ecosystem disturbance, including extensive deforestation of tropical rainforests, such as Amazonia, upper watershed degradation through inappropriate upland farming, and the phenomenon of global warming, which we discuss at length in Chapter 12.

Fundamental elements of the economic approach to resource and environmental issues

Resource allocation, property rights and efficiency

A central question in the new environmental economics concerns the efficient allocation of environmental resources at a given point in time. We explore this

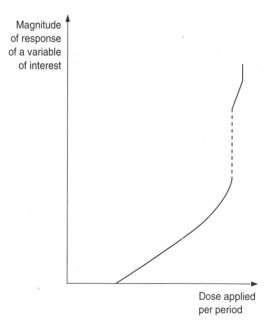

Fig 1.5 Non-linearities and discontinuities in dose–response relationship.

question at length in Chapter 3. The role of prices in allocating resources turns out to be crucial in this analysis. Because property rights do not exist, or are not clearly defined, for many environmental resources, markets do not exist for such resources or they fail to allocate resources efficiently (see Chapters 5, 7 and 8). In such circumstances, where price signals fail to reflect true relative costs, a *prima facie* case exists for government intervention in the allocation of resources to seek efficiency gains (Chapter 9).

The time dimension of economic decisions

It is important to regard environmental resources as forms of capital, yielding flows of environmental services over time. Two sets of considerations are implied by this perspective: one relates to the efficient use of environmental capital over time, the other relates to the optimal use of environmental capital over time (in the sense of maximising the value of some social welfare function).

Most forms of capital possess the property of productiveness. If an individual defers consumption to a later period through directing current resources into capital accumulation, the increment to future consumption that follows from such investment will exceed the initial consumption quantity deferred. In addition, if technical progress is taking place through time, this may augment the magnitude of the return to capital. Environmental capital stocks (or at least some components of them) also possess such an intrinsic productive capacity. This raises the question of the economically efficient path of capital accumulation (or depletion) over time. One important set of issues concerning natural resources, therefore, concerns the choices that are made as to how these stocks are managed, harvested and extracted. Different choices will yield different time profiles of the environmental services which are yielded. We explore the theory of efficient harvesting or depletion rates in Chapters 4 to 8.

Under some circumstances (roughly speaking, where all goods and services are traded in competitive markets, resources are privately owned and no external effects arise in extraction, production or consumption), market mechanisms will result in efficient rates of resource depletion or harvesting over time. However, many environmental resources are not subject to private property ownership. In addition, where resources are collectively owned, it is often the case that access to or use of the resources is not carefully regulated, either by the state or by the

users themselves as a group. Resources that are neither privately owned nor collectively managed in the common interest are known as open access resources.

Intuition suggests that such resources may not be used in an efficient manner, as the incentives on individual users will tend to lead to high rates of harvesting, given that the benefits to an individual from deferring consumption until the future can only be reaped by him or her to a small extent in a situation of open access. In other words, individually rational behaviour often results in collectively irrational behaviour in conditions of open access. We shall demonstrate that this intuition is substantially correct, and carefully analyse resource depletion and harvesting under conditions of open access, in Chapters 3 and 7. But our provisional conclusion at this point must be that it is unlikely that environmental resources will be efficiently allocated in unregulated market economies.

However, the time horizons with which environmental economists deal are usually sufficiently long to permit generational change. When we consider the appropriate way in which resources should be allocated over time, it will not be reasonable to maintain the 'fiction' of a cohort of given individuals choosing the time-paths of their own consumption. Instead, decisions made about resource use will affect the welfare of different individuals, in different generations, over time. If we wish to discuss how resources should be allocated over time, answers can only be given when particular ethical principles have been agreed as being relevant. This ethical dimension pervades all economic analysis, of course. In conventional static economic analysis, the distribution of output between individuals can only be regarded as good or bad in terms of some ethical principle. In practice, this dimension is abstracted from by making some assumption which allows one to discuss issues of efficiency in isolation from issues of justice or fairness.

It is much less easy to do this in dealing with long-term allocation of environmental resources. In these circumstances, intertemporal choices correspond to intergenerational choices. One way in which economists have tried to incorporate considerations of distributional justice into their analyses has been through the use of discounting. Different choices of the discount rate are argued to accommodate different views regarding distributional fairness. We shall discuss these questions at some length in Chapter 2. It will be shown, however, that it is not possible to reduce all (or even most) important matters of distributional justice to a choice of discount rate.

Environmental resources: exhaustibility, substitutability irreversibility and sustainability

It is conventional (if somewhat simplistic) to classify resources in terms of whether they are non-renewable or renewable. The former category, by virtue of existing in a finite quantity, is certainly exhaustible. Renewable resources are potentially 'exhaustible' if harvested for too long at a rate exceeding their regeneration capacities.

A property of production functions that is of interest is the extent to which inputs are substitutable for one another. Some production functions admit possibilities of substitution, others do not. Of central importance to us is the degree to which environmental resources can be substituted by other resources (labour, capital). This is of particular significance when we address questions concerning long-run economy–environment interactions.

The substitutability of environmental resources is investigated in Chapter 5 and in many places throughout the text. Unfortunately, we shall see that this is a largely unresolved question. Not surprisingly, policy recommendations are highly sensitive to the assumptions one makes about resource substitutability, and differences in conclusions between writers can often be attributed to differences in the assessment of these substitution possibilities.

A distinguishing characteristic of many environmental resources is that they are non-producible. Unlike man-made capital, if a natural resource is depleted, degraded or exhausted, it is not possible to reproduce the resource in its original form (i.e. with its original bundle of characteristics), at least in any time frame relevant to humans. To establish the relevance of this point, let us simplify matters by assuming that a resource stock (such as a wilderness area, or a tropical rainforest) can either be 'developed' (which will result in the loss of some or all of the bundle of resource services it offered) or not developed (i.e. conserved). Given non-producibility, the development decision would be irreversible, whereas the conservation decision would be reversible. We show in Chapter 10 that under certain (reasonably likely) conditions this asymmetry implies a stronger preference for non-development than would be the case where all decisions are reversible.

Sustainability is, as we will see, a many-faceted concept. However, one dimension of it which may interest us is concerned with whether or not some pattern of resource use can be continued indefinitely. Clearly, whilst a renewable resource can be harvested indefinitely at some positive rate (a sustained yield), any non-zero use of a finite resource cannot be continued indefinitely. For any exhaustible resource, current use implies an opportunity cost, and so choices are required as to how they should be used over time. We demonstrate in Chapters 2 and 5 that the economically optimal use of resources, and the extent to which alternative use patterns are sustainable, depends crucially upon the extent to which the resources in question are necessary, substitutable, and possess the characteristic of irreversibility discussed above.

Economic growth, the environment and the limits to growth

At several points in this chapter, we have been considering the question of whether continuing (positive) economic growth is limited by resource constraints. The process of economic growth has, for most economies and at most times in the past, been associated with higher material throughput. This pattern of increasing materials use inevitably places greater demand on the world's stocks of environmental resources, and it is from this basis that pessimism regarding the long-term prospects for economic performance tends to be based. Even if one were to grant, for the sake of argument, that these premises are valid, the conclusions which can be derived from these premises are far from clear (and are certainly not necessarily catastrophic). At the risk of simplifying matters too much, we consider three alternative lines of reasoning.

Perspective 1

Environmental resources are ultimately finite, as is the residual carrying-capacity of the environment. The growth process depletes and eventually exhausts this finite resource base, and reduces the capacity of ecological systems to transform residuals into harmless forms. Growth, in this view, is not indefinitely sustainable, as the economy will eventually reach a point at which an absolute resource constraint becomes binding, and further economic activity becomes impossible. This perspective actually implies a conclusion even stronger than the impossibility of indefinite economic growth: there is some absolute upper limit on the level of output of the system which is perpetually sustainable. This upper level is determined by the amount of recycling that can be carried out using energy flows in perpetually renewable form, such as solar power. The level of material throughput of the system cannot, in the long run, exceed this quantity of material recycling. We might call this version of the first perspective the strong version of limits to growth.

A variant of this view – the weak version of limits to growth – would stress the relative importance of impairments to the ecosystem's capacity to assimilate and transform pollutants. The growth process leads to a continuous reduction in the flows and qualities of environmental services, which feeds back into an increasing difficulty of the system in providing continued growth. In this view, the absolute limit to growth arising from finiteness of resources is not binding, as it is preceded by a relative limit imposed by ever-increasing environmental degradation. Such a view is strongly reminiscent of the later writings of John Stuart Mill; the limit to growth arises from the perceived human unwillingness to tolerate environmental degradation, as well as from the physical difficulties of sustaining rising levels of material–energy throughput in a 'finite world'.

Perspective 2

A second line of reasoning is associated with what we may call the 'optimistic' economic perspective. Economic growth is associated, at least initially, with rising rates of depletion of non-renewable resources, increased harvesting of renewables, and increasing flows of residuals, some proportion of which will be harmful. However, these consequences of the growth process result in relative price changes, which set in motion behavioural adjustments by producers and consumers. The net effect of these behavioural changes are changes in the input–output–emissions relationships, which permit continuing economic growth. This view corresponds roughly to that taken by those economists who most vehemently attacked the conclusions of *The Limits to Growth*.

First, consider the issue of rising rates of residual production. As residual flows increase, the costs of waste disposal and management rise. Waste producers, minimising their costs, will adopt technologies that produce less residuals, and so the ratio of residual to output flows will tend to fall over time. Resource depletion will induce rising real resource prices. This change in relative prices will promote the extent of materials recycling, and encourage the adoption of production methods which use relatively fewer environmental resources (in proportion to other inputs). The net effect of these responses will be a diminishing residual-to-output and a diminishing resource-to-output ratio. Under certain conditions that we explore later, this should allow growth to proceed unconstrained by absolute resource limits. The essence of this reasoning is the presence of powerful price-induced substitution effects.

Perspective 3

The reasoning we now explore might be said to be the consensus opinion of orthodox environmental economists. The behavioural adjustments described in the second view presume the existence of markets for environmental resources, the technical possibility of large substitutability between environmental resources and other inputs, and speedy and powerful behavioural adjustments to relative price changes.

Unfortunately, these mechanisms work at best imperfectly, and sometimes not at all, due to failures of markets to function efficiently or to non-existence of markets. The reasons for market failure include

- absence of property rights
- missing future markets
- imperfect information

Substitution possibilities may be limited for physical reasons too. We may infer that it is not growth as such which leads to environmental 'problems', but rather the failure of the price mechanism to generate correct signals. The objective of policy should be to adopt instruments (and set their levels) so as to mimic a properly functioning price mechanism, in which 'prices' reflect true opportunity costs. If this were achieved, growth should proceed at a socially desirable rate. Note, however, that it is not always possible for a 'price mechanism solution' to be found for an environmental problem.

The policy instruments that might be required include

- use of taxes or subsidies
- use of direct controls
- creation of property rights
- facilitation of redress for damage through judiciary

Conclusions: what are the distinguishing characteristics of the new environmental economics?

It is difficult to identify a single methodology that could be ascribed to all environmental economists.

Box 1.3 Economics of 'spaceship earth'

In a classic paper written in 1966 – 'The economics of the coming Spaceship Earth' – Kenneth Boulding discusses a change in orientation that is required if mankind is to achieve a perpetually sustainable economy. He begins by describing the prevailing image which man has of himself and his environment. The 'cowboy economy' describes a state of affairs in which the typical perception of the natural environment is that of a virtually limitless plane, on which a frontier exists that can be pushed back indefinitely. This economy is an open system, involved in interchanges with the world outside. It can draw upon inputs from the outside environment, and send outputs (in the form of waste residuals and so on) to the outside. In the cowboy economy perception, no limits exist on the capacity of the outside to supply or receive energy and material flows.

Boulding points out that, in such an economy, the measures of economic success are defined in terms of flows of materials being processed or transformed. Roughly speaking, income measures such as GDP or GNP reflect the magnitudes of these flows – the cowboy perception regards it as desirable that these flows should be as large as possible.

However, Boulding argues, this economy is built around a flawed understanding of what is physically possible in the long run. A change in our perception is therefore required to one in which the earth is recognised as being a closed system or, more precisely, a system closed in all but one respect – energy inputs are received from the outside (such as solar energy flows) and energy can be lost to the outside (through radiative flows, for example). In material terms, though, planet earth is a closed system; matter cannot be created or destroyed, and the residuals from extraction, production and consumption activities will always remain with us, in one form or another.

Boulding refers to this revised perception as that of the 'spaceman economy'. Here, the earth is viewed as a single spaceship, without unlimited reserves of anything. Beyond the frontier of the spaceship itself, there exist no reserves from which the spaceship's inhabitants can draw resources nor sinks into which they can dispose of unwanted residuals. On the contrary, the spaceship is a closed material system, and energy inputs from the outside are limited to those perpetual but limited flows that can be harnessed from the outside, such as solar radiation.

Within this spaceship, if mankind is to survive indefinitely, man must find his place in a perpetually reproduced ecological cycle. Materials usage is limited to that which can be recycled in each time period; that, in turn, is limited by the quantity of solar and other external energy flows received by the spaceship.

What is an appropriate measure of economic performance in spaceship earth? It is certainly not the magnitude of material flows, as measured by GNP or the like. Quite the contrary, it is desirable that the spaceship maintain such flows of material and energy throughput at low levels. Instead, the well-being of the spaceship is best measured by the state – in terms of quality and quantity – of its capital stock, including the state of human minds and bodies.

So for Boulding, a 'good' state to be in is one in which certain stocks are at high levels – the stock of knowledge, the state of human health, and the stock of capital capable of yielding human satisfaction. Ideally we should aim to make material and energy flows as small as possible to achieve any chosen level of the spaceship's capital stock, maintained over indefinite time.

Boulding is, of course, arguing for a change in our perceptions of the nature of economy–environment interactions, and of what it is that constitutes economic success. He states that

> The shadow of the future spaceship, indeed, is already falling over our spendthrift merriment. Oddly enough, it seems to be in pollution rather than exhaustion, that the problem is first becoming salient. Los Angeles has run out of air, Lake Erie has become a cesspool, the oceans are getting full of lead and DDT, and the atmosphere may become man's major problem in another generation, at the rate at which we are filling it up with junk.

Boulding concludes his paper by considering the extent to which the price mechanism, used in a way to put prices on external diseconomies, can deal with the transition to spaceship earth. He accepts the need for market-based incentive schemes to correct such diseconomies, but argues that these instruments can only deal with a small proportion of the matters which he raises. Boulding concludes:

> The problems which I have been raising in this paper are of larger scale and perhaps much harder to solve.... One can hope, therefore, that as a succession of mounting crises, especially in pollution, arouse public opinion and mobilise support for the solution of the immediate problems, a learning process will be set in motion which will eventually lead to an appreciation of and perhaps solutions for the larger ones.

Source: Boulding (1966).

Some practitioners have proposed the need to work towards a more holistic discipline, that would integrate natural scientific and economic paradigms. Whilst movement has been made in this direction by a number of writers, we will show that the subject is still a long way from having achieved such an integration.

At the other end of a spectrum of methodologies, we can observe analysts who propose the application of neoclassical techniques to environmental issues, stress the importance of constructing a more complete set of quasi-market incentives to induce efficient behaviour, and would reject the necessity of a change in methodology for a proper understanding of those issues.

Common ground exists between virtually all environmental economists, however, and it is this that we focus upon in this text. A consensus appears to exist regarding the likelihood of market failure in the allocation of environmental resources, at one time and over time. Similarly, to the extent that economic growth is associated with greater material through-put, pollution problems are likely to become ever more pressing. Pollution imposes pressures upon the assimilative capacities of the environment, capacities which at any point in time are limited in scope.

However, most economists would disagree with a claim that pollution problems must eventually become intolerable if growth is allowed to continue. The natural environment has some reproductive capacity, and provided pollution flows do not reach critical levels, polluted systems can renew and become cleansed through natural processes. Changing relative scarcities will induce substitution effects and other behavioural changes that will mitigate environmental degradation. The extent to which the operation of market forces alone can mitigate these effects is, though, very controversial. The desirability of growth, at least as this term is conventionally understood, has been challenged by some economists, for example by Schumacher (1973) and Mishan (1967), but more so on the grounds of social limits to growth rather than on physical or environmental limits as suggested by Boulding (1966, 1981), Hirsch (1977), Daly (1987) and Meadows *et al.* (1972).

Key characteristics of new environmental economics include the importance attached to the amenity services derived from natural environments. In some respects, this attention may be seen as a continuation of John Stuart Mill's concern with the implications of economic development for mankind's environment and so for the quality of life. However, it is now recognised that many economic activities entail irreversible consequences (see the work of Krutilla, summarised in Chapter 10). Once extracted and used, the services of an exhaustible resource are lost forever. But this is also true for the amenity and other services offered by natural environments; whilst a decision not to develop such an environment is reversible, the decision to develop is irreversible.

During the 1970s and 1980s, a number of factors placed resource and environmental issues more highly on the political agenda in the OECD countries. So-called oil 'crises' drew attention to the finiteness and exhaustibility of fossil fuel reserves. In the affluent developed economies, conflicts were becoming more apparent between the development uses of resources and the demands for environmental services flowing from preserved environments (for wilderness, recreation, and amenity purposes).

Discussion questions

1 Many economists accept that a spaceship earth characterisation of the global economy is valid in the final analysis, but would dispute a claim that we are *currently* close to a point at which it is necessary to manage the economy according to strict principles of physical sustainability. On the contrary, they would argue that urgent problems of malnutrition and poverty dominate our current agenda, and the solution to these is more worthy of being our immediate objective. The objective of physically sustainable management must be attained eventually, but is not an immediate objective that should be pursued to the exclusion of all else. To what extent do you regard this as being a valid argument?

2 Do environmental resources have *intrinsic* values, independent of any use that human beings may have for them now or at any point in the future, and independent of any values that human beings would be willing to pay to preserve them in existence? If your answer is in the affirmative, how could one establish a figure for the magnitude of such an intrinsic value?

Problems

This problem is concerned with the distinction between private and social costs of production (see the section on resources and production) and the implications of external costs for the overall, social level of well-being.

Suppose that a wood pulp mill is situated on a bank of the River Tay. The private marginal cost of producing wood pulp (in £ per ton) is given by the function

$$MC = 10 + 0.5Y$$

where Y is tons of wood pulp produced. In addition to this private marginal cost, an external cost is incurred. Each ton of wood pulp produces pollutant flows into the river which cause damage valued at £10. This is an external cost, as it is borne by the wider community but not by the polluting firm itself.

The marginal benefit to society of each ton of produced pulp, in £, is given by

$$MB = 30 - 0.5Y$$

The following questions can be answered using carefully drawn diagrams or with algebra. Recall that profit maximisation requires selection of an output that equates marginal revenue and marginal cost. Furthermore, maximisation of social net benefits should be taken to imply equating marginal social benefits with marginal social costs.

1 Draw a diagram illustrating the marginal cost (MC), marginal benefit (MB), external marginal cost (EMC) and social marginal cost (SMC) functions.
2 Derive the profit maximising output of wood pulp, assuming the seller can obtain a marginal revenue equal to the marginal benefit derived from wood pulp.
3 Derive the pulp output which maximises social net benefits, defined as

   Social net benefit

   = (gross) social benefit − social cost

4 Explain why the socially efficient output of wood pulp is lower than the private profit maximising output level.

5 How large would external marginal cost have to be in order for it to be socially desirable that no wood pulp is produced?

Further reading

As most of the topics and issues discussed in this chapter will be dealt with more comprehensively in subsequent chapters, we shall make few suggestions for further reading at this stage. No more explicit discussion of the history of economic theory will be given, however; the classic reference for this is Mark Blaug (1985), *Economic Theory in Retrospect* (4th edition), Cambridge University Press.

A useful area for additional reading would be some of the classic works deriving from the materials balance principle, and its applications to environmental economics. Very good, easy and stimulating works include Boulding (1966) and Daly (1987). An interesting preview of many of the major resource-allocation questions to be investigated throughout this text is given in Solow (1986), a contribution by one of the seminal thinkers in this field. If you have a strong grasp of mathematics, D'Arge, R.C. and Kogiku, K.C., 'Economic growth and the environment', found in the *Review of Economic Studies*, 1972, presents an analysis of optimal economic growth in an economy subject to a materials balance constraint, and in which residuals build-up is economically damaging.

The first two chapters of Markandya and Richardson (1992), also add substance to these introductory remarks. See also Cipolla (1962), *The Economic History of World Population*, for a discussion of population history and economic growth, and Leach (1975) *Energy and Food Production*, International Institute for Environment and Development, on the use of energy in agricultural systems.

CHAPTER 2

Ethics, discounting the future and the environment

And God said, Let us make man in our image, after our likeness: and let them have dominion over the fish of the sea, and over the fowl of the air, and over the earth, and over every creeping thing that creepeth upon the earth.

Genesis 1:24–8.

Introduction

Environmental economics is concerned with the allocation, distribution and use of environmental resources. To some extent, these matters can be analysed in a framework that does not require the adoption of any particular ethical viewpoint. We can focus our attention on answering questions of the form 'If X happens in a particular set of circumstances, what are the implications of X for Y?'. Analyses of this form constitute what is sometimes described as *positive economics*.

The best known statement of the desirability of restricting the practice of economic analysis to the domain of positive economics is to be found in Lionel Robbins' work *An Essay on the Nature and Significance of Economic Science*. Robbins argues that

> ... it does not seem logically possible to associate the two studies [economics and ethics] in any form but mere juxtaposition.

Robbins (1935), page 148

Limiting our attention to answering questions of this form may be considered somewhat restrictive. This was certainly the position taken by the early classical economists, perhaps reflecting the historical evolution of economics as an offshoot of ethics. Indeed, Adam Smith's post at the University of Glasgow was as Professor of Moral Philosophy. It remains the case that many economists wish to address questions concerning what *should* be done in a particular set of circumstances, or which is the *best* policy in a given context. To broaden our domain of interest in this way, it is necessary that ethical judgements be made. This does not imply that the economist need bring his or her own moral principles into an analysis. Rather, the economist should be aware of the ethical positions

that underpin particular conclusions, and recognise that different ethical foundations lead to different conclusions. One may, for example, choose to investigate what a utilitarian moral philosophy implies about how incomes should be distributed, and then compare this outcome with the distributional consequences of alternative moral bases. Indeed, this is something we shall do in this chapter.

Most economists have tended to employ some variety of utilitarian ethical position whenever their work has gone beyond matters of positive economics. This reflects the fact that the conventional welfare economics underlying much of modern economics incorporates a utilitarian moral philosophy, the antecedents of which are found in the writings of Jeremy Bentham and John Stuart Mill. Moreover, mainstream resource and environmental economics is similarly infused with a predominantly utilitarian ethic.

The utilitarian ethic is not universally accepted though. Other rival moral philosophies exist, with quite different implications for right or just behaviour. Conservationists and environmentalists often appear to subscribe to a quite different naturalist ethic, according human preferences much less primacy. Indeed, it is not possible to understand the arguments and debates which take place between 'environmentalists' and 'economists' without recognising these fundamental ethical differences.

Some economists, whilst not adopting a naturalist ethic, have become increasingly unwilling to adhere to utilitarian moral principles, particularly when considering the intertemporal and intergenerational allocation of resources. One stimulus to this has come from an increasing unease with the application of cost–benefit analysis to issues involving the allocation of environmental resources. Economics has also been influenced by developments in moral philosophy, and in particular by the work of John Rawls in his book *A Theory of Justice*, to be discussed below. In the first two sections of Part 1, we attempt to classify and explain a variety of moral principles that have been invoked when environmental issues have been discussed by economists, philosophers and environmental scientists. In the third section of Part 1, we devote attention to the utilitarian ethical system, and demonstrate that variants of this underpin much conventional economic analysis.

Part 2 of the chapter looks in detail at the discounting of future costs and benefits, a practice that has been the subject of much controversy. Within the economics profession, views differ widely as to how discounting should be undertaken and what criteria should be used in selecting a discount rate. Many non-economists regard the entire practice of discounting as being ethically indefensible. Finally, in Part 3 of the chapter, we investigate the practice of cost–benefit analysis (CBA), one of the principal weapons in the armoury of the research economist. The application of CBA to the appraisal of projects that are expected to have significant and long-lasting environmental impacts pushes this technique to the limits of its validity or even, some would argue, beyond those limits.

PART 1
Ethical foundations for environmental economics[1]

Naturalist moral philosophies

A fundamental distinction can be drawn between two broad families of ethical systems, humanist and naturalist moral philosophies. In humanist philosophies, rights and duties are accorded exclusively to human beings, either as individuals or as communities. Whilst humans may be willing to treat other species tenderly or with respect, non-human things have no rights or responsibilities in themselves. A naturalist ethic denies this primacy or exclusivity to human beings. In this ethical framework, values do not derive from human beings, have no human psychological basis, nor reside in humans exclusively.

Rather, rights can be defined only with respect to some natural system, including living and non-living components. A classic exposition of this ethic is to be found in Aldo Leopold's *A Sand County Almanac* (1949), page 262:

> A thing is right when it tends to preserve the integrity, stability and beauty of the biotic community. It is wrong when it tends otherwise.

It is probably fair to say that this position is taken by a large number of environmentalist writers. Peter Singer (1993) describes it as a 'deep ecology' ethic. For example, when industrial developments are being proposed that would entail large environmental impacts, a deep ecologist might argue that the project would not be right if significant disturbances to affected ecosystems are likely to occur. What is of particular interest is the inference for policy from this ethical perspective. Presumably, if an action is deemed not to be right, it should not be done. Given that a large part of human behaviour does have 'significant' ecological implications, it seems likely that much current economic activity would be regarded as morally wrong by a naturalist philosopher, and the requirement of preserving the integrity of the biotic community, if interpreted strictly, could prohibit a large proportion of all conceivable human behaviour.

The implications of a thorough-going adherence to such a moral philosophy seem to be quite profound, although much presumably depends upon how strictly the word *significant* is to be interpreted. It appears to be the case in practice that arguments based on a naturalistic ethic tend to draw a distinction between projects having any ecological impact and those having significant impacts on parts of the biosphere considered to be particularly deserving of safeguard, perhaps because of their unusualness or scarcity. In the UK, the designation of Sites of Special Scientific Interest and the consequent special provisions for management of these sites are based on this latter criterion. A similar comment applies to the system of National Parks in the USA, and the designation of Internationally Important Sites by the World Wide Fund for Nature (formerly the World Wildlife Fund).

In the period since 1970, a large number of important works have emerged from a background that is largely but not exclusively naturalistic. The majority of these can be interpreted as attempting to establish the nature of man's obligation to non-human beings. It is our intention to give you an

---

[1] This section relies heavily upon the discussion in Kneese and Schulze (1985).

awareness of the kinds of argument being deployed and the conclusions being obtained; if you wish to examine them more carefully, we recommend some additional reading at the end of this chapter. Alternatively, you may choose to go directly to the original sources. Many of these recent writings have made use of Immanuel Kant's *categorical imperative* as the basis for ethical behaviour. In Kant's philosophy, the basis of moral behaviour is to be found in duty and the adherence to rules. For Kant, an action is morally just only if it is performed out of a sense of duty, and is based upon a valid ethical rule. Rightness or justice is not to be assessed, Kant argues, in terms of the consequence or outcomes of an action, but only in terms of whether the action is undertaken in response to a valid ethical rule.

But what is a valid rule? According to Kant, rules that are just or valid are universal rules; they are made valid by their universality, the property that they can be applied consistently to every individual. He writes

> I ought never to act except in such a way that I can also will that my maxim *[rule]* should become a universal law.

This principle is Kant's categorical imperative. It is categorical as it admits of no exceptions, and imperative as it gives instructions on just behaviour. So, for Kant, the basis of ethical behaviour is found in the creation of rules of conduct which each person believes should be universalised. For example, I might argue that the rule 'No person should steal another's property' is an ethical rule if I believe that everyone should be bound by that rule.

One categorical imperative, Kant suggests, is the principle of respect for persons. This states that no person should treat another exclusively as a means to his or her end. It is important to stress the qualifying adverb *exclusively*. In many circumstances we do treat people as means to an end; an employer, for example, regards members of his or her workforce as means of producing goods, to serve the end of achieving profits for the owner of the firm. This is not wrong in itself. What is imperative, and is wrong if it is not followed, is that all persons should be treated with the respect and moral dignity to which any person is entitled.

Kant was a philosopher in the humanist tradition. His categorical imperatives belong only to the domain of human creatures, and respect for persons is similarly restricted. Writers in the naturalistic tradition deny that such respect should be accorded only to humans. Richard Watson (1979) begins from this Kantian imperative of respect for persons, but amends it to the principle of respect for others. He then discusses who is to count as 'others'. In order to answer this question, Watson makes use of what is known in philosophy as the principle of reciprocity. Reciprocity refers to the capacity of beings to *knowingly* act with regard to the welfare of others. Many writers argue that what makes humans moral agents whereas other beings are not is that only humans have this capacity for reciprocity: that is, they can act in ways that consciously take into account the welfare of others. Whilst accepting much of this, Watson denies that only humans have the capacity for reciprocal behaviour. In his opinion, reciprocal behaviour is also evident in some other species of higher animal, including chimpanzees, gorillas, dolphins and dogs. Such animals, Watson argues, should be attributed moral rights and obligations: at a minimum, these should include intrinsic rights to life and to relief from unnecessary suffering. The validity of Watson's argument depends upon these higher forms of non-human animals actually possessing this capacity for reciprocity, and so being able to act as moral agents, rather a moot point. But note that even if one were to accept the validity of Watson's position, it still leaves considerable scope for deciding the relative weights that should be accorded to human and non-human interests when choices are being made.

What bearing do these matters have on the economic analysis of environmental issues? Human behaviour has many impacts on the world around us – on the natural environment, in other words. The environmental impacts of our behaviour are pervasive, affecting the conditions of existence of almost all plants and animals, and influencing the relationships and evolution of the component parts of the biosphere. When humans take economic decisions, to whom or to what do we owe obligations? Is it only human interests that 'matter' or have we a moral duty to take account of the interests or rights of things other than humans?

You have just seen that Richard Watson believes that humans do have an obligation to others – specifically to some higher-order animals that he claims can act consciously with regard to others. Many people regard this position as being too restrictive, and believe that human obligations extend to broader classes of 'others'. The philosopher G. J. Warnock grappled with the concept of 'consideration', the circumstances which imply that something has a right to be considered (its interests be taken into account) in the conscious choices of others. Warnock concluded that all sentient beings – that is, beings which have the capacity to experience pleasure or pain – deserve to be considered by any moral agent. So for Warnock, when you and I make economic decisions, we have a moral obligation to give some weight to the effects that our actions might have on any sentient being. Peter Singer (1993) also arrives at this conclusion, but from a utilitarian standpoint. In his view, all sentient beings have utility functions. Utility maximisation should take place over all utility functions, not just those of humans. We shall explain and discuss utilitarian ethics in the next section of this chapter.

Many naturalist philosophers, whilst agreeing with the general premise that not only human interests matter, argue that the condition of sentience is itself too narrow. Our obligations to others extend far beyond the class of other animals that can experience pain and pleasure. Kenneth Goodpaster (1978) concludes that all living beings have rights to be considered by any moral agent. The philosopher W. Murray Hunt adopts an even stronger position. He concludes that 'being in existence', rather than being alive, confers a right to be considered by others. For Hunt, all things which exist, living or dead, animate or inanimate, have intrinsic rights. This is, in effect, the deep ecology position of Leopold that we mentioned earlier.

This summary of naturalistic philosophies has, necessarily in a book of this kind, been exceedingly brief. There is, and probably never can be, any universally agreed principle which can be used to provide a single ethical criterion for human behaviour. Our review demonstrates that the typical humanist philosophy adopted by most economists has not gone unchallenged. Furthermore, as we shall show in the following sections, the utilitarian ethical basis of conventional economic analysis implies a particular, and arguably very narrow, form of humanism. Although we have not tried to make the link explicit, it seems to be the case that the philosophic positions which underpin the arguments of many ecologists and environmentalists owe much to naturalistic ethics. This difference in the ethical foundations of the two disciplines may account for why economists and ecologists find it so difficult to agree on many environmental issues.

Humanist moral philosophies

It is useful to consider two broad strands within the humanist moral philosophy tradition, the utilitarian and libertarian schools. Whilst both see rights as residing exclusively within humans, they differ in how outcomes are to be assessed. Utilitarian philosophers judge outcomes in terms of the degree of utility which is achieved by society as a whole. We shall attempt to ascertain what utility consists of in the following section; for the moment, we interpret it to mean happiness or pleasure. A situation is a good one, from a utilitarian point of view, if the total level of happiness or pleasure in society is high. Not surprisingly, we shall see that if utilitarianism is to be useful as a practical principle, it will be necessary to specify what it means when one refers to 'the total level of happiness or pleasure in society'.

Libertarianism asserts and is built upon the fundamental inviolability of individual rights. There are no rights other than the rights of individuals, and economic and social behaviour is assessed in terms of whether or not it respects the rights of individuals. Actions that infringe individual rights cannot be justified by appealing to some supposed improvement in the level of social well-being. Indeed, to a libertarian philosopher, a phrase such as 'the social good' or 'social well-being' has no meaning except that of a situation in which individual rights are respected. Nor is it meaningful, in a libertarian framework, to define community or group rights. Clearly, this perspective carries profound implications for political and economic behaviour, and for human activity with environmental impacts. We will examine the implications of a libertarian ethic shortly, but first we examine utilitarianism and the way in which it has been used in economic analysis.

Utilitarianism

Utilitarianism originated in the writings of David Hume (1711–1776) and Jeremy Bentham (1748–1832), and found its most complete expression in the work of John Stuart Mill (1806–1873), particularly in his *Utilitarianism* (1863). Unlike rules-based moral philosophies, such as that of Kant, utilitarianism is a consequentialist philosophy; the moral worth of an action is determined solely by the consequences or outcomes of the action.

What kind of outcome is ethically praiseworthy according to utilitarians? Classical utilitarianism, as developed by Jeremy Bentham and John Stuart Mill, judges actions solely in terms of their effect on the 'good' of a whole society. More specifically, Mill proposes the principle of utility or the 'greatest happiness principle' as the foundation of an ethical theory. Actions are right or just in proportion to the extent to which they tend to promote happiness, pleasure or the absence of pain. Pleasure and the absence of pain are the sole desirable ends of human activity.

Classical utilitarianism possesses three main components:

1 An assertion that outcomes can be assessed only in terms of the extent to which they contribute to the social good.
2 A criterion as to what constitutes the social good.
3 The principle that individual good or well-being is cardinally measurable and comparable over persons and time.

The first component states that behaviour should be directed to producing the greatest possible amount of good for all persons, considered as a single group. The second is concerned with a criterion for good. Early utilitarian writers tended to interpret this rather narrowly: the good of an individual (his or her utility) was equated with the individual's pleasure or happiness. The social good is some aggregate of individual utilities. Subsequent utilitarian writers have often adopted a broader view, arguing that other values, such as friendship, knowledge, courage and beauty, have intrinsic worth, and so affect individual utilities and the social good. One of the principal goals set by the early utilitarian thinkers was to establish precisely what utility consisted of, and what things conferred utility. Most of these attempts were unsuccessful; later writers, particularly economists writing after the times of the so-called 'neoclassical revolution' in the late nineteenth century, have regarded this as a futile exercise. Instead, they argued that individuals obtain utility from the satisfactions of their wishes or preferences. But as individuals have different preferences, and these preferences are satisfied in different ways, it is not possible to develop a general description of what utility is, nor what things lead to it. All that can be said in general is that utility is the pleasure or happiness which individuals experience from the satisfaction of their preferences. This still leaves the question of how the social good is defined. One thing which is agreed by all utilitarians is that the social good is some form of aggregation of the utilities of all relevant persons. We shall examine shortly how such an aggregate might be obtained. But whatever the answer to this, we can only obtain such an aggregate if individual utilities are comparable over

persons and time. This explains the need for the third component of utilitarianism that we identified earlier.

For the majority of economists, whilst there may be disagreement as to what utility is and from what it derives, there is a consensus that the only relevant utilities are human utilities. But this is not, of course, the only position that one could take. We mentioned earlier a conclusion reached by the philosopher Peter Singer. In his book *Practical Ethics*, Singer adopts what he regards as being a utilitarian position, but he applies the concept in a rather different way. All sentient beings, by definition, can experience pleasure or pain. Utility is derived from gaining pleasure and avoiding pain. But since all sentient beings can experience pleasure or pain, all can be regarded as capable of enjoying utility. Utility is a characteristic of sentience, not only of humanity. Singer concludes that the utilitarian principle of judging actions on the basis of maximisation of utility is morally valid, but asserts that weight should be given to human and non-human utilities in this process.

Such an approach is certainly an interesting one, and has much to commend it, but the approach we take in this text is a more conventional one. We regard human utilities only as components of the social good. There are two reasons, though, why this need not imply purely human-centred behaviour. The first explanation derives from the point that human utility functions may depend upon the condition of other (animal or plant) lives. Nothing prevents us from incorporating altruism or concern for other beings in human utility functions if these things do affect human utility (which certainly does seem to be the case). Secondly, if society deems it correct that other animals or plants do have intrinsic rights (such as rights to be left undisturbed or rights to be reasonably protected), then we can incorporate such rights by imposing them as constraints on what is legitimate human behaviour. For more on this, see Discussion Question 3 and the last section in this chapter.

The term utilitarianism has evolved in meaning since the time of Mill, and is used today in a variety of ways by different writers. It is, therefore, a concept that is difficult to define in a precise way. According to Robert Solow (1974b), utilitarianism, in its broad sense, values social good or well-being as some function of the utilities of the individuals in a society. How is the good of a society to be measured, at least in principle? Given that the social good is taken to be some function of the utility of the individual members of that society, a particular form of this function is required. One form this function may take (and the one which seems to have been assumed by the majority of classical utilitarian writers) is additive: the social good is a weighted sum of the utilities of the individual members of the society. Such an additive form of social good or social welfare function is contained in what Solow terms narrow sense utilitarianism.

We remarked earlier that the classical economists regarded utility as being cardinally measurable. Ordinally measurable utility merely requires that each person be able to rank different packages or amounts of goods in terms of a preference ordering. Cardinally measurable utility involves a much stronger assumption, namely that the individual be able to express utility in terms of a numeric value, indicating the quantity of utility obtained. For an aggregate or social measure to exist, it must also be meaningful to make interpersonal comparisons of one person's utility with another's. Typically, the weights in an aggregate measure reflect society's judgement of the relative worth of each person's utility. In the simplest case, weights are equal and social welfare is a simple sum of utilities of all individuals.

Classical utilitarianism clearly makes extremely strong assumptions, assumptions that not everyone would be willing to accept. Within orthodox micro-economics, the problems associated with the assertion that utility is cardinally measurable have led economists to search for a theoretical structure that does not require one to make such an assertion. The modern theory of consumer demand is one result of this search. A large part of modern economics does not require that utility be cardinally measurable. Kneese and Schulze use the term neoclassical utilitarianism to describe such a weaker form of utilitarian theory. As we shall see in the following chapter, a fundamental theorem of welfare economics implies the following result. Assume that each person acts in a rational, self-interested manner, and that wealth is distributed in some predetermined manner. Then, under certain conditions that we state and discuss in Chapter 3, individual utility-maximising behaviour results in a welfare maximum for society as a whole, for that particular distribution of wealth.

It is important to be careful here. This welfare maximum is a constrained one, the highest welfare attainable given a particular distribution of wealth. However, to every other initial allocation of wealth there will correspond another (constrained) welfare maximum. The unconstrained welfare maximum would be the highest one of all these constrained maxima. It should be clear that for any arbitrary

choice of initial allocation of wealth, the likelihood is very low that this would be consistent with welfare being at such a maximum of all maxima. We discuss this matter in some depth in Chapter 3.

Modern neoclassical utilitarianism does not make use of the assumption that utility is cardinally measurable. By not invoking such strong assumptions as classical utilitarianism, its results are more general, and are more likely to be ones to which we can give credence. But a price is paid for this advantage. Neoclassical utilitarianism is unable in itself to compare and rank the welfare outcomes corresponding to different initial allocations of wealth. In order to do that, it would need to adopt a social welfare function – a criterion that allows such a ranking to be done. But if this adoption is made, we are essentially back to the classical form of utilitarianism!

There is a trade-off here. The price paid for not assuming that utility is cardinal and comparable between individuals is the inability to decide whether one distribution of wealth is better than any other, because in this situation one is unable to make interpersonal comparisons of utility in order to assess the goodness of different possible distributional outcomes.

As we shall see later in this and subsequent chapters, a common assumption made in some applied analysis (particularly in cost–benefit analysis) is that the marginal utility of consumption is equal for all individuals. If this is so, then actions which lead to net consumption gains (i.e. consumption gains are greater than consumption losses) unambiguously increase social welfare irrespective of who gains and loses, provided the changes are small. But it is extremely difficult to believe that all individuals do have an equal marginal utility of consumption, If marginal utilities are not equal, then we can no longer validly claim that 'distribution does not matter'.

In general throughout this text, we shall be working in a utilitarian framework, and assuming that a social welfare function does exist. When comparing utility levels between different generations, we shall often be adopting a classical utilitarian position, taking utility to be cardinally measurable. This will allow us to confront ethical questions relating to the distribution of income and wealth over time in an open and explicit manner.

Some distributional implications of utilitarianism

Let us continue our examination of utilitarian philosophy by considering a hypothetical society, consisting of two individuals, A and B, living at some particular point in time. One aggregate good (X) exists, the consumption of which is the only source of utility. Let U^A denote the total utility enjoyed by A, and U^B the total utility enjoyed by B, so we have

$$U^A = U^A(X^A)$$
$$U^B = U^B(X^B)$$
$$(2.1)$$

where X^A and X^B denote the quantities of the good consumed by A and B respectively. For simplicity, we also assume that there is a fixed quantity of the good X, denoted $\bar{X}$.

The social welfare function

Let W denote social welfare. Broad sense utilitarianism asserts that social welfare is determined by a function of the form

$$W = W(U^A, U^B) \qquad (2.2)$$

Social welfare depends in some particular (but unspecified) way on the levels of total utility enjoyed by each person in the relevant community. Utilitarianism ranks states in terms of the value attained by social welfare, W. In particular, the best state is the one at which W is maximised, and ethical considerations imply that such a state should be the objective of a social decision maker (if one were to exist), or that the 'worth' of market outcomes should be assessed in terms of the extent to which W approaches its maximum value.

In this broad sense, utilitarianism does not carry any particular implication for the way the good should be distributed between the two individuals, as the function does not specify in which way social welfare is related to individual utilities. However, if one is prepared to specify a particular form for the social welfare function and to specify the particular form of utility function for each individual, then matters change. Recall from earlier in this chapter that we use the term narrow sense utilitarianism to refer to the case in which social welfare is an additive function of individual utilities, so that

$$W = \beta_1 U^A + \beta_2 U^B \qquad (2.3)$$

where β_1 and β_2 denote the weights used in summing individual utilities to an aggregate measure of welfare.

Figure 2.1a illustrates one indifference curve, drawn in utility space, for such a welfare function. The social welfare indifference curve is a locus of combinations of individual utilities that yield a constant amount of social welfare, $\bar{W}$. Note that

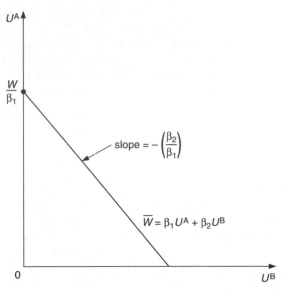

Fig 2.1a Narrow form utilitarian social welfare function indifference curve.

because of our assumption that the welfare function is additive, the indifference curve, when drawn in utility space, is linear. The weights in the welfare function determine the relative importance attached to individual utilities in determining social welfare. Thus if one believed that some level of utility enjoyed by a female contributes twice as much to social welfare as the same quantity of male utility, and if A is male and B female, then one could incorporate this belief in the welfare function by choosing $\beta_1 = 1$ and $\beta_2 = 2$. Alternatively, an egalitarian ethic might imply that individual weights should be equal so that, with a suitable choice of units in terms of which W is measured, we obtain

$$W = U^A + U^B \qquad (2.4)$$

To keep our presentation simple, we focus below on the special case in which the weights on individual utilities are equal. The analysis of the more general case in which the weights are not constrained to be equal is given in Appendix 1. To maximise welfare, we choose X^A and X^B so as to maximise[2]

$$W = U^A + U^B \qquad (2.5)$$

subject to the constraint that

$$X^A + X^B \leq \bar{X}$$

---

[2] Remember that we assume utilities to be functions of consumption levels, denoted X^A and X^B.

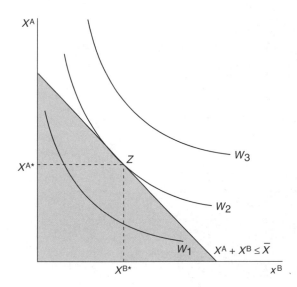

Fig 2.1b Maximisation of social welfare subject to a constraint on the total quantity of goods available.

It is shown in Appendix 1 that the solution to this problem requires that

$$\frac{dU^A}{dX^A} = \frac{dU^B}{dX^B} \tag{2.6}$$

What interpretation do we give to this equality? The terms dU^A/dX^A and dU^B/dX^B are the marginal utilities of consumption for each person respectively. So the condition states that marginal utilities must be equal for each person.

However, this still does not tell us how goods should be distributed. To find this, we need some information about the utility function of each individual. Consider first the case where every person has the same utility function. That is

$$U^A = U^A(X^A) = U(X^A)$$
$$U^B = U^B(X^B) = U(X^A) \tag{2.7}$$

It is then easy to see that in order for marginal utility to be equal for each person, the consumption level must be equal for each person. An additive welfare function, with equal weights on each person's utility, and identical utility functions for each person, implies that, at a social welfare maximum, consumption levels are equal over individuals. A proof of this can also be found in Appendix 1.

The solution to this problem is illustrated in Figure 2.1b. Notice carefully that the diagram is now drawn in commodity space, not utility space. Under

the common assumption of diminishing marginal utility, the linear indifference curves in utility space in Figure 2.1a map into indifference curves which are convex from below in commodity space. A proof of this is given in the answer to Problem 2. The curves labelled W_1, W_2 and W_3 are social welfare indifference curves, corresponding to different levels of welfare. Remember that in this example we are assuming that there is a fixed quantity of the good $\bar{X}$ available to be distributed between the two individuals. Maximum social welfare, W_2, is attained at the point z where the consumption levels enjoyed by each person are X^{A*} and X^{B*} respectively. Under the assumptions we have made, the two individual consumption levels are equal. The maximised level of social welfare will, of course, depend on the magnitude of $\bar{X}$. But irrespective of the level of maximised welfare, the two consumption levels will be equal.

In the example we have just looked at, the result that consumption levels will be the same for both individuals was a consequence of the particular assumptions that were made. But utilitarianism does not in general imply equal distributions of consumption goods. An unequal distribution of goods at a welfare maximum may occur under either of the following conditions:

1 The weights attached to individual utilities are not equal (a proof of this can be found in Problem 2).
2 Utility functions differ between individuals.

To illustrate the second condition, suppose that the utility functions of two persons, A and B, are as shown in Figure 2.2. The diagram makes it clear that individual A enjoys a higher level of utility than individual B for any given level of consumption. It is evident that, in this example, A and B have different utility functions. Now because of that difference in the utility functions, the marginal utilities of consumption of the two individuals can only be equal at different levels of consumption by A and B. It may help in interpreting the diagram to recall that the value of marginal utility at a particular level of consumption is indicated by the slope of the (total) utility function at that point. Problem 2 takes you through this argument algebraically.

The conclusions we can derive from this are as follows. In circumstances where individuals do not have the same utility functions, social welfare maximisation implies that individuals will consume different quantities, and will enjoy different levels of

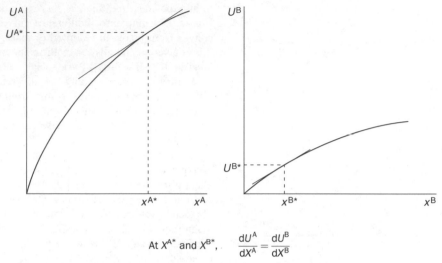

At X^{A*} and X^{B*}, $\dfrac{dU^A}{dX^A} = \dfrac{dU^B}{dX^B}$

Fig 2.2 Maximisation of social welfare for two individuals with different utility functions.

total utility. Secondly, if the social welfare function attributes different weights to the utilities of different individuals, it will also be true that social welfare maximisation implies that individuals will consume different quantities, and will enjoy different levels of total utility. The only circumstance where one would expect to find equal consumption and equal utility levels between individuals is the case in which each individual utility is weighted equally in the social welfare function and all utility functions are identical.

Other forms of utilitarian welfare function

So far we have investigated the general nature of utilitarianism, and considered one particular form the social welfare function might take: what we have termed narrow sense utilitarianism. However, many other special forms of the social welfare function are consistent with utilitarianism defined in a broad sense. A second variant is what we might label an élitist function of the form

$$W = \max\{U^A, U^B\} \tag{2.8}$$

In this case, social welfare is determined by the maximum of the utilities enjoyed by A and B. Notice that if $U^A > U^B$, then $W = U^A$, irrespective of the size of U^B. Not surprisingly, maximisation of welfare given this welfare function will tend to favour an unequal distribution of consumption. But

contrary to what one might first think, it is not likely that this function would imply transferring all consumption to one person. The utility of any person is likely to depend in some way on the utility of others. One would expect to reach a point at which further transfers of consumption from B to A would not only reduce B's utility, but would also reduce A's. In the section below on Rawls, we investigate the properties of another particular form of utilitarian social welfare function that implies egalitarian distributions, and which has gained considerable support among economists and moral philosophers.

Utilitarianism: individuals and generations: the (intertemporal) social welfare function

Many of the issues with which we shall deal in this text involve choices which affect different generations of people over time, so it would be useful if we were able to understand utilitarianism in an intertemporal framework. It is easy to do this by a simple reinterpretation of 'individuals' and 'society'. We could think of an individual as one particular generation of people. Another individual might consist of the following generation of people. Society is then a sequence of individual generations living through some specified interval of time. With this change in interpretation, utilitarianism can address the relationship between the social welfare of a set of

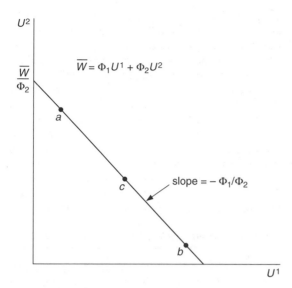

$$\overline{W} = \Phi_1 U^1 + \Phi_2 U^2$$

slope $= -\Phi_1/\Phi_2$

Fig 2.3a Intertemporal utilitarian social welfare function indifference curve.

consecutive generations and the utility of the individual generations existing over that interval of time.

Let us now investigate a graphical representation of the indifference curves corresponding to a utilitarian intertemporal social welfare function. We collapse all generations into two; generation 1 is the present generation; 2 represents all future generations. U^1 and U^2 denote the total utility enjoyed by members of generations 1 and 2, respectively. W denotes *intertemporal* social welfare. A broad sense intertemporal social welfare function can be written as[3]

$$W = (U^1, U^2) \tag{2.9}$$

Narrow sense utilitarianism, as illustrated in Figure 2.3a, implies an additive form of welfare function

$$W = \Phi_1 U^1 + \Phi_2 U^2 \tag{2.10}$$

so that W is a weighted average of the utilities of each generation, where Φ_1 and Φ_2 are the weights used in summing utility over generations to obtain a measure of social welfare. But from where might such weights come? One answer is obtained from the common practice of 'time discounting' in which the weights can

[3] Note, before we continue, that this form of social welfare function is already quite restrictive. It assumes that we can meaningfully refer to an aggregate level of total utility for each generation, and that social welfare is a function of these aggregate quantities, but not of the distributions of well-being within generations (except in so far as this affects the relevant aggregate). We do not pursue this any further, but see Broome (1992) for further analysis.

be interpreted as time discount factors. For example, setting $\Phi_1 = 1$ and $\Phi_2 = 1/(1 + \rho)$, where ρ is a social discount rate, we obtain a utilitarian social welfare function in which (one period ahead) future utility is discounted at the proportionate rate ρ. That is

$$W = U^1 + \frac{U^2}{1 + \rho} \tag{2.11}$$

Time discounting, as we shall see in more detail in Part 2 of this chapter, implies (if $\rho > 0$) that future utility 'counts for less' than the same quantity of present utility in obtaining a measure of intertemporal welfare.

Criticisms of utilitarianism

Utilitarianism is open to many criticisms. One set of criticisms is fundamental in the sense that it arises from those who challenge the philosophical basis of utilitarianism. We earlier examined the nature of naturalistic ethics. It is clear that an adherent to a naturalistic moral philosophy will be unable to accept the validity of any ethic which views rights and values as being inherent only in human beings. However, it is possible to broaden the scope of utilitarianism so that the pleasure or happiness of non-human beings is accorded weight in a social welfare function. A second alternative ethical stance – libertarian moral philosophy – also poses a fundamental challenge to utilitarianism. However, we shall defer consideration of this critique until the last section of Part 1 where libertarian views are explored more fully. In this section, we limit our attention to criticisms of the kind of utilitarianism that is commonly used by economists, but where the criticism does not represent a fundamental challenge to utilitarianism *per se*.

One such criticism is the claim that utility, in the usual sense in which that term is used, is defined too narrowly to be an adequate description of human economic behaviour. Utilitarians regard the objective of economic behaviour as being the maximisation of utility; this is equated with pleasure or happiness. It is common to regard the amount of utility that a person enjoys as being dependent on the quantity of goods and services that he or she enjoys in a given period of time. Now one aspect of this criticism is the assertion that individuals are, as a matter of fact, motivated by something rather broader than utility in the sense we have just used. For want of a better term, let us call this well-being. It is clear that whether this argument has any real substance depends upon the extent to which the distinction between utility and well-being is a significant one.

Sen (1987) certainly believes that this distinction exists and is significant, and he develops the critique forcefully. Sen regards well-being as a multi-dimensional quantity, depending not only on what individuals have achieved or attained in the way of goods and services, but also on various attributes they enjoy as citizens. Of particular importance is the nature and extent of the freedoms they possess. The possibility of being able to do something is, according to Sen, intrinsically valuable, irrespective of what use a person makes of that freedom. So for Sen, social welfare is a function of something much broader than the utility enjoyed through consumption. In this, Sen shares similar beliefs to libertarianism philosophers who accord liberties, rights and freedoms inherent values (and who is some cases see these things as the only source of value). So the existence of such things as democracy, free speech and tolerance may well be intrinsically valuable, whereas narrow utilitarian positions might only see these as being instrumentally valuable; that is, the value they generate arises from the pleasures and satisfaction that people can achieve though them.

But this is not the end of Sen's critique. Well-being itself, even in this broad sense, is not the only thing which is valuable. All persons have a fundamental dualism, being concerned with their well-being but also being agents with objectives which they would like to see obtained. These objectives will rarely be exclusively self-interested. Individuals may seek to eliminate nuclear defence, may promote the conservation of whales, may wish poverty to be eliminated in parts of the world. For some people, much of their activity may be directed to pursuing such goals, even though their well-being, in some narrowly defined sense, is not likely to be affected by the success the person has in this goal pursuit.

Once the scope of things which are regarded as being inherently valuable is extended in the two directions we have just been discussing, the problems of quantification and comparability mentioned earlier become massively more complex. This does not in itself imply that utilitarianism should be abandoned, but rather that its practice is far more problematic than many would usually admit.

The final criticism of utilitarianism that we consider is the problem of unjust consequences. In simple or classical versions of utilitarianism, the good of actions is judged by their effect on overall, aggregate welfare. But this poses great difficulties in cases where sacrifices by a few are demanded to improve the overall lot. The logic of utilitarianism might lead someone to advocate the killing of all persons over the age of 65 on the grounds that this would improve social welfare. To some extent, such 'problems' arise from the fact that classical utilitarianism is essentially a consequentialist philosophy, in which good is measured only by the outcome attained, and not by the means of achieving that outcome. If the nature of social welfare is defined in a broad way, taking adequate account of well-being and agency, the problems inherent in a philosophy in which unbridled self-interest is the only source of value can be avoided. The philosopher John Rawls would dispute the claim that utilitarianism can be rescued in this way, however, and it is to his views that we now turn.

Rawls: a theory of justice

The work of John Rawls in *A Theory of Justice* (1971) has had a remarkable influence upon the consideration given by economists to ethical issues. In many respects, Rawls's work is an explicit challenge to utilitarianism, or more precisely to classical utilitarianism. His objection to that ethic is grounded in the assertion that by being indifferent to the distribution of satisfaction between individuals (and only being concerned with the magnitude of the sum of utilities), a distribution of resources produced by maximising utility could violate fundamental freedoms and rights which are inherently worthy of protection.

In common with many moral philosophers, Rawls seeks to establish the principles of a just society. Rawls adopts an approach which owes much to the ideas of Immanuel Kant. Valid principles of justice are those which would be agreed by everyone if we could freely, rationally and impartially consider just arrangements. In order to ascertain the nature of these principles of justice, Rawls employs the device of imagining a hypothetical state of affairs (the 'original position') prior to any agreement about principles of justice, the organisation of social institutions, and the distribution of material rewards and endowments. In this original position, individuals exist behind a 'veil of ignorance'; behind this veil, each person has no knowledge of his or her inherited characteristics (such as intelligence, race, gender), nor of the position he or she would take in any agreed social structure. Additionally, individuals are assumed to be free of any attitudes that they would have acquired through having lived in particular sets of circumstances. The veil of ignorance device would, according to Rawls, guarantee impartiality and fairness in the discussions leading to the establishment of the social contract. Rawls then seeks to establish the nature of the social contract that would be created by freely consenting individuals in the original position.

He reasons that, under these circumstances, people would unanimously agree on two fundamental principles of justice. These are

> First: each person is to have an equal right to the most extensive basic liberty compatible with a similar liberty for others.

> Second: social and economic inequalities are to be arranged so that they are both (a) reasonably expected to be to everyone's advantage, and (b) attached to positions and offices and open to all.... [The Difference Principle]

The first of these principles is asserted to have primacy over the second, and is similar to a principle of justice derived by many philosophers. It is the second principle which is of principal interest in our study of environmental economics. The Difference Principle asserts that inequalities are only justified if they enhance the position of everyone in society (if they lead to Pareto improvements). In other places, Rawls seems to advocate a rather different position, however, arguing that inequalities are justified in particular when they maximally enhance the position of a representative, least advantaged person in society.

Many commentators have interpreted the Difference Principle as a presumption in favour of equality of position; deviations from an equal position are unjust except in the special cases where all persons would benefit (or perhaps where the least advantaged benefit). When economists have commented upon or interpreted Rawls's conclusions, it has been common to try to infer what a Rawlsian position would imply for the nature of a social welfare function (SWF).[4] Robert Solow, for example, argues that a Rawlsian SWF for a society of individuals at one point in time is of the so-called *max–min* form, which for two individuals would be

$$W = \min\{U^A, U^B\} \qquad (2.12)$$

Two SWF indifference curves from such a function are illustrated in Figure 2.3b. Does such a SWF convey any implications for the distribution of utility between persons? Such a SWF seems to imply that welfare can be increased by raising the utility level of the person with the lowest utility level. This point is

---

[4] However, notice that one could argue that such an attempt forces Rawls's theory into a utilitarian framework, something of which he would probably strongly disapprove.

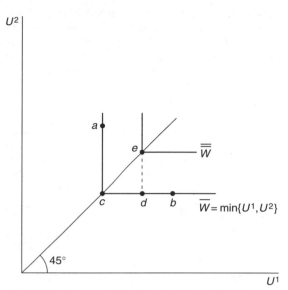

Fig 2.3b Intertemporal Rawlsian social welfare function indifference curve.

illustrated in Figure 2.3b. Compare the two points labelled **b** and **c**, which by definition generate identical levels of social welfare. Now, starting from point **b**, reallocate utility between persons, by subtracting (**b** − **d**) utility from person 1 and adding this to person 2. The point labelled **e** will have been attained on another indifference curve with a higher level of social welfare. It is clear that the only combinations of utility for which higher welfare levels are not possible through interpersonal transfers of utility are combinations along the 45° ray from the origin; along this locus, utility is allocated equally between individuals. So for any given total of utility, a Rawlsian social welfare function implies that, where utility levels differ between individuals, it is possible to increase social welfare by redistributing utility from individuals with higher utility to those with lower utility. If the total level of utility were independent of how it was distributed, an egalitarian distribution is implied by this logic.

But there is no reason to believe that the total level of utility will necessarily be independent of its distribution. Indeed, there are some grounds for believing that total utility could be higher in an unequal position if incentive effects enhance productive efficiency. But note carefully that Rawls is not a utilitarian, and the fact that total utility might be higher in a situation in which utility is unequally distributed than one in which it is equally distributed does not of itself make the former a just distribution.

Rawls's Difference Principle asserts that it is only just to have an unequal distribution if all persons benefit from that allocation. Clearly, such results have important implications for the distribution of resources both within and between countries. Discussion Question 1 investigates these implications.

But let us now turn our attention to the distribution of resources between generations; that is, intertemporal distributions. Rawls writes very little about this, and it is fair to say that he does not reach any firm conclusion. Robert Solow suggests that a consistent extension of Rawls's logic implies that a two-period SWF would be of the form

$$W = \min\{U^1, U^2\} \qquad (2.13)$$

Such a SWF implies that welfare can be increased by raising the utility level of the generation with the lower utility level, for the same reasons as we indicated above in the interpersonal case. The only combinations of utility for which higher welfare levels are not possible through intergenerational transfers of utility are combinations along the 45° ray originating from the origin; along this locus, utility is allocated equally between generations. If utility functions were time invariant, this would imply equality of consumption levels over time as well. Of course, the Difference Principle will still apply in this context, and so unequal distributions between generations will be justified if they enhance the utility levels of all generations.

Libertarian moral philosophy

A libertarian ethic asserts the primacy of processes, procedures and mechanisms for ensuring that fundamental liberties and rights of individual human beings are respected and sustained. For a libertarian, rights are inherent in persons as individuals, and concepts such as community or social rights are not meaningful. In this school of thought, actions cannot be assessed as right in terms of their consequences or outcomes, but only in terms of whether they conform to certain rules or procedures which encapsulate individual rights.

In this brief review, we will discuss the work of one recent libertarian philosopher, Robert Nozick (1974). Nozick's intellectual foundations are found in the work of Adam Smith, and in the writings of the philosopher John Locke. A key principle in Locke's philosophy is that of just acquisition. Locke attempted to specify a principle of justice in the acquisition of previously unowned property. Locke's answer is that legitimate or just acquisition arises when an individual mixes his labour power with it. Provided the item(s) with which the labour was mixed were no-one's property previously, Locke regards this as the source of original and just property rights.

Nozick extends this argument. He asks when is a holding a just holding, i.e. when is someone entitled to hold something? His answer is a simple one:

> Whoever makes something, having bought or contracted for all other held resources used in the process (transferring some of his holdings for these cooperating factors), is entitled to it . . .

So any holding I have is a just holding (and I am entitled to it) if it was obtained via a contract between freely consenting individuals. Nozick introduces one qualification, however. The thing transferred in a contract must have been the entitlement of the seller for the buyer's holding to be just. Because, in practice, not all people will be entitled to their holdings (because they were obtained by theft, deception, etc.), some processes and principles of rectification of past injustices are discussed by Nozick. The key point in all of this is free action. Distributions are just if they are entirely the consequence of free choices, but not otherwise.

Libertarians, such as Nozick, are entirely opposed to all concepts of justice based on the results, consequences or outcomes of behaviour. No particular pattern of outcome can be regarded as morally good, according to a libertarian. Moral philosophies such as utilitarianism or egalitarianism imply something about an outcome which should be sought after. But to achieve such an outcome, Nozick argues, coercion would be required (such as progressive taxation) which would inevitably violate individual freedoms and interfere with just acquisitions. This is not to say that egalitarian outcomes are not just or valid, but that they are just only if they have been freely chosen by all persons concerned or affected. A libertarian moral philosophy is likely to drastically limit the scope of what government may legitimately do. No redistributive policy, whether between people, between countries or between generations, would seem to be just. Government action would be limited to maintaining the institutions required to support free contract and exchange. It is interesting to ponder over the range of actions that a strict adherence to such an ethic would close off.

In practice, libertarian ethics have been adopted most enthusiastically by those people who believe in a limited role for government. However, it by no means clear that a laisser-faire approach is necessarily implied. Three issues arise from the notion of just acquisition:

1 What should government do about unjust holdings?
2 How are open access or common property resources to be dealt with?
3 How do external effects and public goods relate to the concept of just acquisition?

We invite you to consider these issues in Discussion Question 2.

PART 2
Utilitarianism and discounting

Utility discount rate and consumption discount rate

We have seen that the ethical framework which underpins conventional environmental economics is utilitarianism. Broad sense utilitarianism asserts that the welfare of a society at some point in time is a function of the levels of utility of the members of that society. The general form of welfare function was written as

$$W = W(U_0, U_1, \ldots, U_T) \qquad (2.14)$$

where U_0 through to U_T denote the utility levels of $T + 1$ individuals. Classical utilitarianism restricts this function to be additive in the form

$$W = \alpha_0 U_0 + \alpha_1 U_1 + \ldots + \alpha_T U_T \qquad (2.15)$$

in which the parameters α_0 to α_T are the weights being attached to individual utilities in the aggregation to social welfare.

When our attention turned to *intertemporal* social welfare, we interpreted 'individuals' 0 to T as a sequence of successive generations. In this case, the classical utilitarian form of intertemporal welfare function is usually written as

$$W = \frac{1}{(1+\rho)^0} U_0 + \frac{1}{(1+\rho)^1} U_1 + \ldots + \frac{1}{(1+\rho)^T} U_T$$
$$= \sum_{t=0}^{t=T} \frac{1}{(1+\rho)^t} U_t \qquad (2.16)$$

In this formulation, ρ is known as the *utility discount rate*. The utility discount rate is the rate at which the

value of a small increment of utility changes as its date is delayed. It is conventional to multiply this rate of change by minus one. Then a negative rate of change of the value of utility will result in a positive utility discount rate. Thus if one unit of utility received next period were regarded as less valuable by a proportion of 0.1 (or 10%) than one unit of utility received this period, then $\rho = 0.1$.

Later in this chapter, and at many points in the book, we shall wish to use the continuous time counterpart of Equation 2.16:

$$W = \int_{t=0}^{t=T} e^{-\rho t} U_t \, dt \qquad (2.17)$$

The discrete and continuous time versions of the utilitarian social welfare function (2.16 and 2.17) contain utility levels as arguments. Suppose that utility is a function of consumption. Then, in discrete time, the welfare function can be written more explicitly as

$$W = \frac{1}{(1+\rho)^0} U(C_0) + \frac{1}{(1+\rho)^1} U(C_1) + \ldots$$
$$+ \frac{1}{(1+\rho)^T} U(C_T)$$
$$= \sum_{t=0}^{t=T} \frac{1}{(1+\rho)^t} U(C_t) \qquad (2.18)$$

As W is indirectly a function of C, it is possible to rewrite the welfare function directly in terms of consumption (as opposed to utility). The precise form taken by this function will depend upon $U(C)$, the relationship between consumption and utility. In some special cases of utility function, the welfare function will be of the form

$$W = \frac{1}{(1+r)^0} C_0 + \frac{1}{(1+r)^1} C_1 + \ldots$$
$$+ \frac{1}{(1+r)^T} C_T \qquad (2.19)$$

In this case, r is a constant parameter that we shall call the *consumption discount rate*. The consumption discount rate is the rate at which the value of a small increment of consumption changes as its date is delayed. However, in general it will not be the case that there is a single consumption discount rate as in Equation 2.19; instead that rate will change over time, as we show later in this section.

We have now seen that there is not one discount rate, but two – a utility rate and a consumption rate. It is important to be careful about which rate we are referring to when discussing the process of discounting. Much confusion arises in the literature as a result of a failure to make this distinction when discussing 'the discount rate'.

The consequences of discounting

Let us examine the consequences of discounting. We restrict our attention to the consequences of discounting utility, but similar arguments can be made about the consequences of consumption discounting. This is left to the reader as an exercise. Consider the relative contributions of utility at different points in time to the level of welfare, using the welfare function (Equation 2.16). Suppose that the level of utility in each generation is 100 units, and that the utility discount rate is 0.1 (or 10%) per period. Let T be 50. Now compare the contributions to total welfare of these 100 units of utility today (period 0) and 50 periods later. The welfare contribution of 100 units of utility in period 0 is 100; that is, $100/(1.1)^0 = 100$. The welfare contribution of 100 units of utility in period 50 is approximately 0.852 (i.e. $100/(1.1)^{50} = 0.852$). The effect of discounting utility at the rate $\rho = 0.1$ over 50 periods is to make the contribution of some given amount of utility about 117 times smaller than the same level of utility gained currently.

If policy is dictated by trying to maximise the value of W, a utility-discounted welfare function might well be loosely described as discriminating against future generations, by giving their utility levels much less weight in the maximisation exercise. It is this feature of discounting which leads many persons to regard any positive discount rate as ethically indefensible.

In subsequent chapters of this book (especially Chapters 5, 6 and 7) we shall be analysing the optimal use of resources over time, assuming that society's welfare function is of the discounted utilitarian form. It will be shown that the optimal path over time of consumption and resource use does depend critically upon the particular utility discount rate selected. Intuition suggests that higher utility discount rates will lead to patterns of resource use that are more rapacious, implying greater depletion in earlier years. This intuition is shown to be more or less correct. However, it is not valid to argue that consumption (or real income) will fall over time if high discount rates are used. We will demonstrate that rising consumption over time is quite consistent with a high positive utility discount rate.

Relationship between the utility and consumption discount rates

To deduce the relationship between the utility and consumption discount rates, we need to specify a particular welfare function. Let us continue to assume that this is of the discounted utilitarian form. In continuous time, this was given as Equation (2.17), that is

$$W = \int_{t=0}^{t=T} e^{-\rho t} U_t \, dt$$

Suppose that the utility function

$$U = U(C)$$

is such that utility is an increasing function of consumption, but that it increases at a decreasing rate. In mathematical terms, the first derivative of utility with respect to consumption is positive, but its second derivative is negative:

$$\frac{\partial U}{\partial C} = U'(C) > 0$$

$$\frac{\partial^2 U}{\partial C^2} = U''(C) > 0$$

A utility function which satisfies these assumptions is illustrated in Figure 2.4.

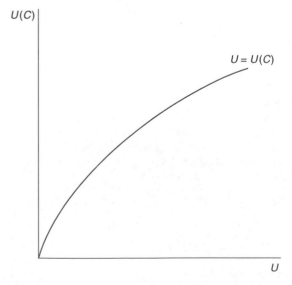

Fig 2.4 Conventional form of an individual's utility function.

Now define the elasticity of marginal utility with respect to consumption, η, to be

$$\eta(C) = -\frac{C \cdot U''(C)}{U'(C)} > 0$$

We have defined the consumption rate of discount, r, to be the rate at which the value of a small increment of consumption changes as its date is delayed. It is shown in Appendix 2 that the consumption discount rate, r, is given by

$$r = \rho + \eta \frac{\dot{C}}{C} \qquad (2.20)$$

It is clear from this expression that the consumption rate of discount depends upon three things:

- the utility discount rate ρ
- the elasticity of marginal utility with respect to consumption η
- the proportionate rate of growth of consumption, $\dot{C}/C$.

The consumption and utility discount rates will only be equal when $\eta \dot{C}/C$ is zero. This would occur if (a) $\dot{C}/C = 0$, implying that $\dot{C} = 0$, and so that consumption remains at a constant level over time, or (b) $\eta = 0$. Now it can be shown that $\eta = 0$ only if the utility is a linear function of consumption, a most implausible relationship.[5]

Notice also, from Equation 2.20, that even if the utility discount rate ρ is greater than zero, it is possible that the consumption discount rate r will be negative. This would occur if the level of consumption is falling at a sufficiently high rate.[6]

What numerical values should be selected for the utility and consumption discount rates?

Our purpose in this section is to discuss how one might arrive at figures for the utility and consumption

---

[5] By definition, $\eta = -CU''(C)/U'(C)$. So for $\eta = 0$, we require that $-CU''(C)/U'(C) = 0$. As in any economy $C > 0$ and $U'(C) > 0$, this equality will only be satisfied if $U''(C) = 0$. The second derivative of the utility function will only be zero everywhere if the utility function is linear.

[6] Let us show this result more formally:

$$r = 0 \quad \text{if} \quad \rho + \eta \dot{C}/C = 0$$

$$r < 0 \quad \text{if} \quad \rho + \eta \dot{C}/C < 0$$

So if consumption is falling at a rate sufficient that $\eta \dot{C}/C$ is larger in absolute value than ρ, then the consumption discount rate r will be negative.

---

discount rates that are justifiable in both ethical and economic terms.

Utility discount rate

The utility discount rate, ρ, is sometimes described as the pure rate of time preference. If the time preference rate is positive, this implies some form of impatience; utility is preferred sooner rather than later. Whilst it may be true that individuals exhibit such impatience, it is not necessarily the case that society as a whole either does or should exhibit such impatience. Indeed, many people argue that in comparing utilities over successive generations, the only ethically defensible position is that utilities attaching to each generation should be treated equally, implying a zero rate of utility discounting.

One argument used to justify a positive utility discount rate is that there is, for every point in time in the future, a positive probability that the human species will become extinct. Presumably this probability is very small, but one would expect it to increase as the length of time into the future exists. One may take the view that future generations should be given less weight than the present, given that we cannot be certain of the existence of any future generation.

The consumption discount rate

Even if one were to accept that ρ should be (or actually is) zero, then this does not imply that the consumption discount rate will necessarily be zero, as the term $\eta \dot{C}/C$ may be non-zero. Under the quite plausible assumptions we have made about the form of the utility function, η will be a positive number. The value of $\eta \dot{C}/C$ will then depend on the sign of the consumption growth rate, $\dot{C}/C$. If consumption is growing over time, $\dot{C}/C > 0$, and so the consumption discount rate would exceed the utility discount rate. To many people, this is an intuitively reasonable conclusion. If an economy is experiencing a growth in income and consumption through time, then an additional unit of consumption will be worth less to a typical person in the future than to such a person now, as the former will be more affluent. Suppose that an individual receives less additional (marginal) utility from further units of the good as his or her total consumption level increases, then additional units of consumption are worth less to an individual the higher the initial level of consumption. Arguments that the expectation of continuing technical progress justifies discounting can be regarded as a variation on

---

Box 2.1 Discount rate choices in practice

As our analysis has shown, there is no unequivocally correct single rate of discount. Indeed, Heal (1981) argues that

> The discount rate is not something we measure; it is something we choose.

and Page (1977) writes

> After a lot of time trying to discover an unassailable definition of the social rate of discount, economists are beginning to decide that a totally satisfactory definition does not exist.

When pressed for a particular number, economists have conventionally advocated setting the social discount rate at the level of long-term interest rates on government bonds, plus a risk premium where appropriate. Here we briefly survey the values that have been used for social discount rates in the USA and the UK.

In 1969, a United States Congressional hearing found that agencies were using discount rates from zero to 20%, with no clear logic dictating the level in any particular instance. Very often, rates are set reflecting political pressures and goals. For example, in the years of the Nixon administration, the federal government chose to use rates near the top of the then prevailing 3–12% band in order to reduce the level of public expenditure. From time to time, single target rates have been set by the federal authorities. In 1970, the Office of Management and Budget required all federal agencies to use a 10% discount rate, although some project areas were treated differently.

In particular, water resource projects were set annually by the US Treasury Department, and have typically been around 2.5%. In 1986, the US Congressional Budget Office has required the general use of a 2% discount rate, roughly equal to the real cost of borrowing on world markets. A detailed analysis of recent US discounting practices can be found in the March 1990 Special Issue of the *Journal of Environmental Economics and Management* (**18**, No. 2, Part 2).

Little more consistency seems to characterise choices of social discount rates in the UK. Some recent choices have been:

- 1988: UK Treasury 'Test' Discount Rate of 5%
- 1990: UK Treasury: 6% rate on most public sector investments, but 8% for public transport
- 1994: UK Treasury 'Target' Discount Rate for public sector investment, 8%. Forestry projects to be discounted at 6% if non-market benefits included

One particularly awkward matter has been the use of different discount rates where project areas are deemed to carry positive external benefits. In the USA, this has been true for water resource project appraisal, whilst in the UK, forestry projects have often been discounted at unusually low rates. This practice is not desirable; the appropriate way of proceeding is to measure externalities in a project appraisal, rather than to assume they exist and set *ex ante* an adjusted discount rate to reflect this assumption.

---

this theme. Technical progress leads, other things being equal, to consumption possibilities being increased over time. Note that the arguments based on consumption growth and technical progress are related to the consumption (but not the utility) discount rate.

Market interest rates and the consumption rate of interest

We demonstrate in the next chapter that, *under certain conditions*, the market rate of interest will be equal to the consumption discount rate. The result we shall demonstrate there is that

$$i = r = \delta \qquad (2.21)$$

where i denotes the market interest rate on risk-free lending and borrowing, δ denotes the rate of return on capital, and r is the consumption discount rate (or

consumption rate of interest). The importance of these equalities should be clear. As i (and possibly δ) are observable quantities, Equation 2.21 provides us with a criterion for selecting r, should we need it.

Notice that Equation 2.21 implies that $r = \delta$. This provides the rationale for another argument which is often made: the discount rate should be equal to the marginal product of capital. If one unit of output is not consumed today, but is invested in new capital, the extra consumption available tomorrow will (on average) be greater than one unit. In other words, capital is productive.

Divergences between the social and private rates of time preference

The argument that the market rate of interest serves as an observable benchmark in terms of which one might choose a consumption discount rate is an attractive one. But its validity does depend, as we shall see, on the existence of a set of conditions that are unlikely to be met in practice. These amount, more or less, to the requirement that the economy is a perfectly competitive market economy in which no forms of market failure exist.[7] The rates of time preference or rates of return on capital observed in actual markets may, however, be inappropriate guides to their unobservable 'social' counterparts.

Marglin (1963) compares individual and social time preference. He argues that society as a whole would choose to save more collectively than the sum of individuals' private savings decisions. This follows from the fact that the investment of saved funds provides external consumption benefits in the future. No individual expects to be able to appropriate more than a tiny proportion of these external benefits, and so private savings decisions will tend to ignore these external returns. An example of this might be investment in water resource projects: if such investments improve public health, the project will certainly have positive external effects in the future. The government, acting as a collective agent, can compare total returns with total sacrifices of present consumption. In evaluating projects with substantial external future consumption benefits, therefore, a lower discount rate should be adopted than that used in private markets. The essence of this argument is that the social rate of time preference is the relevant magnitude to use when trying to determine a social discount rate. Market failure makes it unlikely that social and market (private) rates of time preference will coincide.

Another very similar argument revolves around the distinction that Sen draws (see Part 1) between the roles of individuals as citizens and as consumers. As citizens, individuals may prefer to discount future costs and benefits at a lower rate than they do as consumers. However, even if this were true, the question arises of whether it would be legitimate for government or some other environmental planner to impose what it regards as people's 'true' citizen-preferences on their behalf. A democracy requires that government action reflects the expressed opinions of its citizens. It is very unclear to what extent democracy is consistent with government doing what it claims is in 'our best interests as citizens' in cases where these are not the ones we actually express.

[7] The concept of market failure is explained at length in Chapter 4.

Pigou (1920) argued that individuals may underestimate the pleasure that future consumption would in fact give them. Individuals who are myopic in this way, underestimating the utility of future consumption, are suffering from 'defective telescopic faculty'. One might then argue that the discount rates which should be used in intertemporal comparisons are lower than those that myopic individual behaviour implies. Once again, this raises the very difficult question of the extent to which government should act against the expressed opinions of individuals, even where those opinions might not in fact be in their best interests.

The principles and practice of discounting are very controversial, with many fundamental and largely unresolved theoretical controversies. In addition, a whole set of 'practical' problems exist that are very difficult to resolve satisfactorily. For example, taxes and transaction costs drive a wedge between market rates of return and time preference rates; in practice, the market rate of return exceeds the time preference rate, destroying the equality given in Equation 2.21. This has led some authors to suggest the use of a weighted discount rate. See the Further reading section at the end of this chapter for some suggestions on where to read about this and other matters relating to the choice of discount rate in practice.

Discounting over very long periods

It seems to be especially difficult to find convincing criteria for making choices about discount rates when long-term *intergenerational* comparisons are being made. It is the usual practice in conventional environmental economics analysis to use positive utility discount rates, even when very long time periods are being considered. However, the derivations presented in this chapter should have made it clear that this may or may not imply that consumption discounting is being undertaken.

A number of writers argue that a market determined interest rate is inappropriate as a long-term social consumption discount rate as the market only takes account of the preferences of currently living people. Whilst currently living people might give proper attention to the needs of future persons, this is rather unlikely. Individuals with finite life expectancies are likely to behave differently from a planner presiding over a society that is expected to remain in existence for perpetuity. It is this distinction that lies at the heart of two of the most famous statements regarding discounting. Frank Ramsey (1928) pronounced discounting to be 'ethically indefensible and arises merely from the weakness of the imagination'. Roy Harrod (1948) remarked that discounting is 'a polite expression for rapacity and the conquest of reason by passion'.

Many writers seem to argue that the only ethically defensible discount rate for projects having effects spread over several generations is zero. Without wishing to deny that zero may be a valid rate for some purposes, our arguments should have made it clear that non-zero rates may also be ethically defensible. If consumption is growing rapidly over time, there are good ethical grounds for the use of a positive consumption discount rate. On the other hand, if consumption is falling over time, there are good ethical grounds for the use of a negative consumption discount rate. It is also important to ask which rate – the utility or consumption rate of discount – is being referred to whenever a writer is proposing a zero rate of discount.

PART 3
Cost–benefit analysis

Principles of cost–benefit analysis

Cost–benefit analysis (CBA) is a widely practised technique of project appraisal. It is used in circumstances where it is felt that important components of either the real costs or the real benefits of a project would not be adequately represented by market prices, or would not be traded through markets at all (and so do not have market prices). In these circumstances, markets are failing to value all relevant flows correctly, and so some non-market evaluation procedure is required to assess the net worth of the project. Suppose that a project has been put forward, and that the government wishes to estimate the impact that this project would have on social welfare if it were to be undertaken. We begin by noting that any non-trivial project would tend to affect many individuals, and have impacts over many periods of time.

The key principle which underpins CBA is very simple. The impact of the project on each affected person at each point in time is identified. The value to

each person of any gain or loss is then estimated. In principle, these valuations should be based on the preferences of the affected individuals, and ideally should reflect each person's willingness to pay for an improvement or compensation willingly accepted for a loss. The methods by which such valuations might be made are not described here, but are presented and discussed in Chapter 10. Having arrived at the values of the impacts of the project to each affected person, some procedure is then used to obtain an aggregate or social measure of the impacts of the project. The project is approved if its aggregate net value is positive.

For simplicity, imagine that three individuals (A, B and C) are affected in each of four consecutive intervals of time, labelled 0, 1, 2 and 3, where we take period 0 to be the present period. Table 2.1 presents the impacts on each person's utility at each time. Thus $\Delta U_{B,2}$ denotes the change in utility (post-project utility minus pre-project utility) experienced by individual B during time period 2.

However, utilities are unobservable, and not all economists believe that utilities are comparable across people. As a result, the usual practice in CBA is to assess changes in terms of observable consumption (or output) gains and losses. Then defining net benefit (NB) as the gross benefit from the project less the costs associated with the project, both being measured in units of consumption, we can re-express the impacts of the project as in Table 2.2.

The net value of the project is defined as

$$NV = NB_0 + NB_1 + NB_2 + NB_3$$

which is the sum of what are labelled in Table 2.2 the 'social' net benefits in each of the four time periods. Note that in this measure of net value, the gains or losses of each individual are weighted equally in arriving at the social net benefit for each time period, irrespective of characteristics or circumstances of the

Table 2.1 Notation for change in utility ΔU (impact) for individuals A, B, C over consecutive time periods

Individual	Time period				
	0	1	2	3	Overall
A	$\Delta U_{A,0}$	$\Delta U_{A,1}$	$\Delta U_{A,2}$	$\Delta U_{A,3}$	ΔU_A
B	$\Delta U_{B,0}$	$\Delta U_{B,1}$	$\Delta U_{B,2}$	$\Delta U_{B,3}$	ΔU_B
C	$\Delta U_{C,0}$	$\Delta U_{C,1}$	$\Delta U_{C,2}$	$\Delta U_{C,3}$	ΔU_C
Society	ΔU_0	ΔU_1	ΔU_2	ΔU_3	

Table 2.2 Notation for net benefit NB for individuals A, B, C over consecutive time periods

Individual	Time period				
	0	1	2	3	Overall
A	$NB_{A,0}$	$NB_{A,1}$	$NB_{A,2}$	$NB_{A,3}$	NB_A
B	$NB_{B,0}$	$NB_{B,1}$	$NB_{B,2}$	$NB_{B,3}$	NB_B
C	$NB_{C,0}$	$NB_{C,1}$	$NB_{C,2}$	$NB_{C,3}$	NB_C
Society	NB_0	NB_1	NB_2	NB_3	

individuals concerned. More generally, for T time periods ($T > 0$), the net value of a project is given by

$$NV = NB_0 + NB_1 + NB_2 + \ldots + NB_T$$

The net present value (NPV) of a project is then defined as

$$NPV = NB_0 + \frac{NB_1}{(1 + r_1)} + \frac{NB_2}{(1 + r_1)(1 + r_2)} + \ldots$$
$$+ \frac{NB_T}{(1 + r_1)(1 + r_2) \ldots (1 + r_T)}$$

Because we are here summing consumption (or consumption equivalents) over a sequence of periods, if a discount rate is deemed to be relevant the appropriate rate should be the consumption rate of discount. There is no reason why the consumption discount rate need be equal between periods, and so we have written the expression for NPV in a way that allows for varying consumption discount rates. However, if that rate were constant, so that $r_i = r$, for $t = 1, \ldots, T$, as it is commonly assumed to be when CBA is undertaken in practice, then we can express the NPV of a project as

$$NPV = \sum_{t=0}^{t=T} \frac{NB_t}{(1 + r)^t}$$

As we mentioned earlier, the CBA decision rule is of the form:

Do the project if $NPV > 0$, otherwise do not do the project.

Why is this a sensible rule? Suppose for the moment that r denotes the marginal rate of return (in units of consumption) on the best available alternative project in the economy. If scarce resources were not to be used in the project being considered, they could be invested elsewhere at a rate of return r. The NPV of a project will only exceed zero if its marginal rate of return exceeds r. Hence, scarce funds will

only be allocated to the project if its rate of return is at least as good as the best alternative returns available. But this is precisely what efficient investment appraisal requires – allocating scarce funds to their highest valued use. It is clear from this that CBA is a technique whose object is to ensure the attainment of economic efficiency in the allocation of resources.

Could this decision rule have any ethical justification as well? It turns out to be the case that we are able to claim that a positive net present value is equivalent to an increase in social welfare if some additional assumptions are satisfied. One condition required is that the marginal utility of consumption is equal for each individual. This ensures that if the sum of individual consumption (or consumption equivalent) changes is positive in any period, the sum of utility changes must also be positive in that period. Then, provided we are willing to accept the ethic underlying utilitarianism, it is valid to argue that the social welfare in that period has risen.

This is not enough by itself, though. The NPV criterion asserts that if the sum of the discounted welfare changes for each period is positive, then intertemporal social welfare has increased. This requires that we also accept that the intertemporal SWF has a utilitarian form, and that the discount rate chosen is a fair one. There are clearly a large number of assumptions here that underpin any attempt to give the cost–benefit analysis technique of appraisal ethical support.

As we shall see in the following chapter, another way of thinking about these assumptions is that they amount to a claiming that the existing distribution of wealth, at each point in time, is an optimal one. In this situation, the distribution of the gains and losses between individuals does not affect the magnitude of the welfare gains arising from a project, provided the gains and losses are relatively small.

Do any additional complications arise when we undertake CBA for projects whose impacts are spread over several generations? Many writers would certainly answer in the affirmative. The technique was developed to deal with project evaluation in which costs and benefits, while being spread out over time, were not thought to be distributed over very long periods of time into the future, having significant effects (adverse or beneficial) on future generations. It is by no means clear whether the technique can be applied in the simple manner we have just indicated, where significant intergenerational impacts take place. However, as we have already discussed a variety

Box 2.2 A CBA of temperate zone forestry

What are the benefits and costs of afforestation programmes in temperate zones such as the UK? David Pearce argues that afforestation programmes are multiple-output activities. The outputs he identifies are listed below.

T   Timber values
R   Recreational amenities
D   Biological diversity
L   Landscape values
W   Water-related effects: watershed protection, affecting soil erosion and water run-off, fixation of airborne pollutants, typically increasing pollutant concentrations locally but reducing them elsewhere
M   Microclimate effects
G   Carbon stores
S   Economic security
I   Community integration

Each of these outputs can be beneficial, relative to alternative uses of the land. However, in some cases the benefits may be negative. For example, if single-species spruce afforestation displaces the provision of wilderness areas, biological diversity is likely to diminish. On the other hand, the creation of urban forests in areas of industrial dereliction would, in most cases, increase diversity.

What are the costs of afforestation? These costs comprise land acquisition, planting, maintenance, thinning and felling. Denoting the total benefits by B and the total costs by C, and using subscripts f and a to denote afforestation and the best alternative use respectively, then ignoring time for a moment, Pearce argues that afforestation is economically justified if

$$B_f - C_f > B_a - C_a$$

although there are grounds for disagreeing with this particular formulation.[8]

Pearce then notes that only one of the joint products – the produced timber – is actually traded through market exchanges. All other products are beneficial (or sometimes adverse) external effects, not captured in market valuations. On the other hand, the

costs of afforestation are internalised in market transactions. The consequence of this is that afforestation programmes in temperate regions such as the UK are rarely commercially profitable. By way of example, Pearce quotes results from an earlier study. He introduces time into his analysis, discounts consumption-equivalent benefits and costs at a discount rate of 6%, and then estimates the net present value (NPV) of various types of forestry plantations (on various types of land) under a variety of assumptions about the costs of land.

Pearce investigates eight types of forestry scheme. For each scheme, the commercial[9] NPV is calculated under high and low (and sometimes zero) assumed costs of land. Of the 17 cases this generates, all but one result in negative NPV's. The sole exception is mixed fir/spruce and broadleaf plantations in low-lands, assuming the true value of land is zero (that is, the land has no alternative use)!

Having evaluated the commercial returns to afforestation, Pearce then investigates each of the non-marketed benefits, and gives estimates of the net benefits for each of the outputs R, D, L, W, G, S and I. For two of these (R and G) the benefits are quantified in money terms; for others (D, W, S and I) Pearce identifies and describes the benefits but does not attempt any monetary quantification. Unquantified benefits will have to be judgementally taken into account when project decisions are made.

Recreational benefits for various forms of afforestation are taken from Benson and Willis (1991). The gross values for recreational benefits in the UK range from £3 per hectare on low amenity woodlands in the uplands to £424 per hectare on very high amenity lowland woodlands (in 1989 prices). Pearce suggests these values are likely to grow in real terms by at least 1% per annum. Wildlife conservation and biodiversity benefits (W) and landscape amenity values (L) are two outputs which Pearce does not quantify and monetise. He argues that these benefits will vary widely depending upon woodland form and location, but that they are likely to be positive in the UK, where land for afforestation tends to be drawn from low wildlife-value agricultural land. However, if afforestation takes the form of non-native conifer species, and is at the expense of previously semi-natural land use, these effects on both landscape amenities and biological diversity could be strongly

---

[8] The problem with this expression is actually twofold. In a CBA, the benefits and costs of a project should be valued in opportunity cost terms – that is, they are valued in terms of the best alternative. This suggests that, if B and C are measured correctly, there is no need to make any comparison of the type Pearce does. Using a CBA criterion, afforestation should be done if $B_f > C_f$. Indeed, the logic of this approach suggests that if $B_f > C_f$ (and so afforestation is actually best), then $B_{+a} < C_a$, as the cost of the alternative is the lost net benefits of afforestation.

[9] This is not a true calculation of the commercial NPV: in that case, the actual market price would enter the cost calculations. Pearce assumes the true (economic) cost of land is at most 80% of its marker value, and at worst is of zero economic cost.

Box 2.2 Continued

negative. The picture is thus a very mixed one, with the magnitude (and direction) of the effects varying greatly from one case to another.

Water-related ecological outputs (W) discussed by Pearce include the effects of afforestation on water supply, water quality, the deposition of air pollution, soil erosion, and the impacts of fertiliser and pesticide use and harvesting practices. Qualitative estimates only are presented for these impacts.

Greenhouse warming related effects (discussed at length in Chapter 12 of this book) are quantified in monetary terms by Pearce. His estimates of the present value of benefits from carbon-fixing, in £ per hectare at a 6% discount rate, range from £142 on upland semi-natural pinelands to £254 on lowland mixed woodlands.

Pearce's conclusions

In terms of the commercial costs and benefits, together with the two benefit categories that he was able to quantify (recreation and carbon-fixing), Pearce concludes that only four of the eight general classes of woodlands he investigates have a clear justification for increased afforestation at a discount

Forest type	Assumptions giving positive NPV at $r = 6\%$
FT5 Community forests	Very high recreational values
FT4 Spruce in uplands	Moderate recreational values and land values at $0.5 \times$ market price
FT8 Fir, spruce, broadleaves in lowlands	High recreational values and land values at $0.8 \times$ market price
FT7 Pine in lowlands	Moderate recreational values and land values at $0.5 \times$ market price

rate of 6%. His summary conclusions are presented in the table above.

As explained above, these conclusions are drawn without looking at non-monetised benefits (or costs). In those cases where the NPV of an afforestation project is negative, however, the decision maker may regard the project as socially desirable if he or she forms a judgement that the non-monetised benefits are sufficiently large to offset the negative (monetised) NPV.

Source: Pearce (1994).

of ethical arguments relating to intergenerational distributions, we shall not pursue this debate any further here.

Cost–benefit analysis in practice

The history of CBA is an interesting case study of the way in which a technique has been developed and refined gradually in response to the need to address practical problems. The original theoretical basis for CBA arose from the need in the USA to evaluate flood control and irrigation projects. The original applications made little or no attempt to analyse the welfare implications of the projects, requiring only that the aggregate total of benefits exceeded the aggregate costs, irrespective of distribution (see Maass *et al.*, 1962; Ecstein, 1958). After 1960, the types of project to which CBA was directed and the number of applications grew enormously. CBA has become a commonly used appraisal tool in developed countries, and is used routinely for some classes of project appraisal in developing countries where official assistance is sought from the World Bank,

the United Nations, or other international agencies.

Most applications have tended to ignore certain problems associated with the technique. One of these – arriving at simple aggregate totals, without any clear theoretical justification for so doing – has already been mentioned. We have seen that distributional questions can be ignored if a set of conditions are satisfied. But it seems most unlikely that these would be satisfied in practice. A second set of difficulties concerns measurement issues, which we shall ignore in the present discussion but will cover in depth in Chapter 10. Finally, as many projects imply costs and benefits which are spread out through very long periods of time, often affecting generations long into the future, the question of the appropriate way in which to discount future net values has been an issue of continuing interest.

In the last 20 years, CBA has routinely been applied to the evaluation of schemes having significant environmental implications. There are a number of additional difficulties posed by this. First, there are several issues related to scale. In some cases, the projects have impacts which are considerably greater than 'marginal' impacts. Given that most applications of CBA either ignore the conditions required for valid aggregation, or simply assume that these are satisfied, this is particularly problematic. Consider, for example, the assumption of constancy of the marginal utility of income; this seems to be an untenable assumption when significant impacts change the real income of individuals by greater than marginal magnitudes.

Secondly, many projects affecting the environment in non-trivial ways imply actual physical harm or threats to life, rather than just small changes in the risk of certain types of ill-health. There are profound problems in evaluating impacts of this form. Thirdly, projects may have very small impacts, but on very many individuals, over very long periods. In these cases, individuals may be unaware of the relevant impacts, or have great difficulty in identifying their magnitudes. Attempting to infer values through human behaviour which is assumed to reveal preferences may be a very poor basis for valuation in these cases. In circumstances where future impacts are likely to be significant, the analyst also faces the difficult task of deciding how the preferences of people not yet born are to be measured and incorporated. Finally, many of the costs and benefits of projects with environmental impacts possess the characteristics of public goods. There are additional valuation difficulties here that we shall discuss in Chapters 3 and 10.

Discounting as questions of efficiency and of intergenerational distribution and equity

We have been attempting, in the last few paragraphs, to deduce a relationship between ethics and the practice of discounting. Some authors, for example Hanley and Spash (1993), argue that such an exercise is ill-conceived and incapable of yielding unambiguous answers. In this view, questions relating to the equitable distribution of wealth between generations are not amenable to being translated into questions regarding what is the appropriate discount rate; the whole exercise of asking which discount rate will ensure an ethically just distribution of resources between generations is futile.

If one accepted this view, how would ethics be incorporated into discussions about the distribution of resources over generations? The answer has to be by incorporating ethical positions that we believe are right as constraints over acceptable behaviour. If, for example, you believe that future generations have

certain intrinsic rights, there is almost certainly no way in which those rights could be safeguarded merely by the choice of some particular discount rate. Exactly the same comments apply about views regarding what kind of distribution of resources or wealth are just. If one believes that each generation should have the same level of well-being as every other one, we could not ensure the attainment of this merely by the choice of a discount rate. On the other hand, it might be possible to realise such an objective through the incorporation of certain constraints on our behaviour.

Let us conclude our discussion of discounting by considering the merits of the view that the rate of discount that should be used in appraising projects that have significant environmental impacts should be zero. Many people regard a zero discount rate as being the only one that is ethically defensible. Another view is that a discount rate of zero (as opposed to a positive number) will be more likely to result in environmentally-friendly economic behaviour. Do these arguments have any merit?

The first point to note is one we have already discussed; which discount rate is it that should be set to zero – the consumption or the utility discount rate? Asking this question should warn you that the view that discount rates should be zero may be at odds with many sensible ethical stances. If real income were expected to fall, it may be appropriate to have a negative consumption rate of discount, as consumption in the future will be worth more than consumption today. What if consumption were expected to rise over time – should one really argue that one unit of future consumption is of the same value as one unit of present consumption? It does not seem that any single discount rate can ever be right for all circumstances.

The second argument probably carries more weight. Page (1977), for example, argues convincingly that a zero discount rate would tend to prevent environmental damage from implicitly being ignored. However, it can easily be demonstrated that the selection of a low or zero discount rate does not necessarily make development projects of a 'sustainable' form more likely.

Discussion questions

1 We argued in the text that Rawls's Difference Principle asserts that it is only just to have an

unequal distribution of wealth if all persons benefit from that allocation, relative to the situation of an equal distribution. But we also argued that the total level of utility attainable may depend on the distribution of wealth, as utility could be higher in an unequal position if incentive effects enhance productive efficiency.

Discuss the implications of these comments for a morally just distribution of resources within counties and between countries.

2 In discussing the work of Robert Nozick, it was argued that libertarian ethics have been adopted most enthusiastically by those who believe in a limited role for government. But we also noted that it is by no means clear that a *laissez-faire* approach is necessarily implied. Three difficult issues arise in connection with the principle of just acquisition:

(a) What should government do about unjust holdings?
(b) How are open access or common property resources to be dealt with? (See Locke's proviso).
(c) How do external effects and public goods relate to the concept of just acquisition?

Sketch out reasoned answers to these three questions.

3 In the main text, we wrote that if society deemed it to be correct that some animals or plants have intrinsic rights (such as rights to be left undisturbed or rights to be reasonably protected), then such rights can be protected by imposing them as constraints on what is legitimate human behaviour. Do humans appear to regard whales as having intrinsic rights, and if so, what rights are these? In what ways, if at all, do humans defend these rights by imposing constraints on human behaviour?

4 A river tumbles through forested ravines and rocky gorges towards the sea. The state hydro-electricity commission sees the falling water as untapped energy. Building a dam across one of the gorges would provide three years of employment for a thousand people, and provide longer-term employment for twenty or thirty. The dam would store enough water to ensure that the state could economically meet its energy needs for the next decade. This would encourage the establishment of energy-intensive industry thus further contributing to employment and economic growth.

The rough terrain of the river valley makes it accessible only to the reasonably fit, but it is nevertheless a favoured spot for bush-walking. The river itself attracts the more daring whitewater rafters. Deep in the sheltered valleys are stands of rare Huon Pine, many of the trees being over a thousand years old. The valleys and gorges are home to many birds and animals, including an endangered species of marsupial mouse that has seldom been found outside the valley. There may be other rare plants and animals as well, but no one knows, for scientists are yet to investigate the region fully.

Peter Singer, *Practical Ethics*, page 264

Peter Singer's discussion of ethics and the environment begins with this scenario. His description is loosely based on a proposed dam on the Franklin River in southwest Australia. Singer notes that this is an example of a situation in which we must choose between very different sets of values. Please answer the following question, as put by Singer:

Should the dam be built?

Problems

1 Suppose that one believed that each generation should have the same level of well-being as every other one. Demonstrate that we could not ensure the attainment of this merely by the choice of a particular discount rate, zero or otherwise.

2 Prove that, under the assumption of diminishing marginal utility, the linear indifference curves in utility space in Figure 2.1a map into indifference curves which are convex from below in commodity space, as illustrated in Figure 2.1b.

3 Demonstrate that an unequal distribution of goods at a welfare maximum may occur when the weights attached to individual utilities are not equal, and/or when individuals have different utility functions.

4 Consider the two social welfare functions

$$W_U = U_1 + U_2 \qquad \text{(Utilitarian)}$$
$$W_R = \min(U_1, U_2) \qquad \text{(Rawlsian)}$$

where $U_i = \log(X_i)$ is the utility enjoyed by the ith generation from the consumption $X_i, i = 1, 2$. Consider two projects:

Project A: Generation 1 reduces consumption by 10 units. The investment yields 20 additional units of consumption for Generation 2.

Project B: Generation 1 reduces consumption by 15 units. The investment yields 15 additional units of consumption for Generation 2.

Let the pre-project level of consumption in Generation 1 be 100 units. Now consider three scenarios:

Scenario	Pre-project level of X_2
(i) No technology change	100
(ii) Technology improvement	120
(iii) Technology worsening (or loss of inputs)	80

Use a tick ($\checkmark$) to denote *Do project* or a cross ($\times$) to denote *Do not do project* in each cell of the following table to denote whether the project (A or B) should be undertaken under each of the three scenarios, for the two cases of a utilitarian SWF (U) and a Rawlsian SWF (R).

		Scenario					
		(i)		(ii)		(iii)	
		U	R	U	R	U	R
Project	A						
	B						

5 The Safe Water Drinking Act required the United States Environmental Protection Agency to establish action standards for lead in drinking water. The EPA evaluated three options (labelled A, B and C below) using cost–benefit techniques. A selection of the results of this analysis is presented in the following table.

	Option		
	A	B	C
Total benefits	$68 957	$63 757	$24 325
Total costs	$6 272	$4 156	$3 655
Benefit to cost ratio	11.0	15.3	6.7
Marginal benefit (MB)	$5 192	$39 440	$24 325
Marginal cost (MC)	$2 117	$500	$3 655
MB to MC ratio	2.5	78.8	6.67

Monetary values in the table are 1988 $ million, based on a 20-year life, discounted to present value at 3%. Option A involves the strictest standard, Option C the least strict, with B intermediate. The marginal cost and benefit figures refer to incremental costs/benefits incurred in moving from no control to Option C, from Option C to Option B, and from Option B to A respectively.

Source: EPA (1991). The EPA decision is discussed at length in Goodstein (1995), pages 133–140.

The US Environmental Protection Agency selected Option B. Is Option B the economically efficient choice?

Further reading

Ethics

A superb introduction to ethics, including environmental applications, may be found in Singer (1993). Beauchamp and Bowie (1988) give a good presentation, especially in Chapters 1 and 9; the book contains an interesting analysis of the business implications of ethical principles. Other useful sources include Sen (1987) and Kneese and Schulze (1985). Interesting applications and discussions of ethical issues are to be found in the journal *Environmental Values*.

Discounting

Excellent extensive presentations are found in Hanley and Spash (1993, Chapter 8) and in Layard and Glaister (1994), particularly in the Introduction, Chapter 3 (by Stiglitz), Chapter 4 (by Arrow and Lind), and Chapter 11 (by Dasgupta on discounting and the environment). Lind (1982) investigates discounting and risk in energy policy, and Harberger (1971), Common (1995), Heal (1981), Marglin (1963) and Broome (1992) provide stimulating analyses of discounting. Mikesell (1977) looks in detail at the practical choice of discount rates, and the implications of that choice.

CBA

The texts by Hanley and Spash (1993) and by Layard and Glaister (1994) are excellent surveys of the theory and practice of cost–benefit analysis. Good accounts are also to be found in the general microeconomic texts by Layard and Walters (1978) and Varian (1987).

Appendix 1

Suppose that there are two persons, A and B, consuming a single type of good, X. In order to maximise the combined welfare of these two persons, it is necessary to obtain the solution to the following constrained optimisation problem. Choose X^A and X^B so as to maximise

$$W = \beta_1 U^A + \beta_2 U^B$$

subject to the constraint that

$$X^A + X^B \leq \bar{X}$$

where $U^A = U^A(X^A)$ and $U^B = U^B(X^B)$. Assume that U^A and U^B are increasing in X^A and X^B, but at a decreasing rate. The Lagrangian for this problem is

$$L = \beta_1 U^A + \beta_2 U^B + \lambda(\bar{X} - X^A - X^B)$$

The first-order conditions include

$$\frac{\partial L}{\partial X^A} = \beta_1 \frac{dU^A}{dX^A} - \lambda = 0$$

$$\frac{\partial L}{\partial X^B} = \beta_2 \frac{dU^B}{dX^B} - \lambda = 0$$

which together imply that

$$\beta_1 \frac{dU^A}{dX^A} = \beta_2 \frac{dU^B}{dX^B}$$

If $\beta_1 = \beta_2$, then this reduces to

$$\frac{dU^A}{dX^A} = \frac{dU^B}{dX^B}$$

as given in the main text. As dU^A/dX^A and dU^B/dX^B are the marginal utility functions for each person, we obtain the requirement that maximisation of welfare requires that the good be distributed so that marginal utilities are equal for everyone.

Note also that if $U^A = U^A(X^A)$ and $U^B = U^B(X^B) = U(X)$ (i.e. both individuals have an identical utility function), then this maximisation condition gives

$$\frac{dU}{dX^A} = \frac{dU}{dX^B}$$

This equality can only hold when $X^A = X^B$.

Appendix 2

This appendix analyses the relationship between the utility and consumption discount rates. The welfare function is

$$W = \int_{t=0}^{t=T} e^{-\rho t} U(C_t) \, dt$$

and the utility function

$$U = U(C)$$

satisfies the restrictions that

$$\frac{\partial U}{\partial C} = U'(C) > 0$$

$$\frac{\partial^2 U}{\partial C^2} = U''(C) < 0$$

We have defined the elasticity of marginal utility with respect to consumption, η, to be

$$\eta(C) = -\frac{C \cdot U''(C)}{U'(C)} > 0$$

We have defined the consumption rate of discount, r, to be the rate at which the value of a small increment of consumption changes as its date is delayed. The value of an incremental unit of consumption at date t is given by the marginal utility of consumption at that date, which is

$$\frac{d}{dC_t} [e^{-\rho t} U(C_t)] = U'(C_t) e^{-\rho t}$$

The proportionate rate of change of this value with respect to time is

$$\frac{\frac{d}{dt}[U'(C_t) e^{-\rho t}]}{U'(C_t) e^{-\rho t}}$$

Differentiating the numerator with respect to time, we obtain

$$\frac{U''(C_t) \frac{dC}{dt} e^{-\rho t} - \rho U'(C_t) e^{-\rho t}}{U'(C_t) e^{-\rho t}}$$

Letting $\dot{C} = dC/dt$, this simplifies to

$$\frac{U''(C_t)}{U'(C_t)} \dot{C} - \rho$$

Now, remembering that we have defined the consumption rate of discount, r, as the negative of this magnitude, we obtain

$$r = \rho - \frac{U''(C_t)}{U'(C_t)}\dot{C}$$

Finally, to obtain an expression for r in its most useful form, note that using the definition of η we obtain

$$r = \rho + \eta\frac{\dot{C}}{C}$$

CHAPTER 3

Sustainability and sustainable development

> But we can be fairly certain that no new technology will abolish absolute scarcity because the laws of thermodynamics apply to all possible technologies. No one can be absolutely certain that we will not some day discover perpetual motion and how to create and destroy matter and energy. But the reasonable assumption for economists is that this is an unlikely prospect and that while technology will continue to pull rabbits out of hats, it will not pull an elephant out of a hat – much less an infinite series of ever-larger elephants!

Daly (1974), page 19

Introduction

This chapter addresses the issue of *sustainability*. Interest in this concept has arisen because of a reawakening of concerns about the possibility of continuing economic growth that we looked at in Chapter 1. There are two central issues here. One is an issue of positive economics: is it possible for the economy to attain a state in which production and consumption track along non-declining paths (or grow at positive rates) over indefinite periods of time, in the presence of finite stocks of exhaustible resources and constraints imposed by natural environmental processes? The second issue is a normative one: what form *should* the path of resource allocation over time take?

The concept of sustainability carries a variety of meanings, exemplified by the very different interpretations given to it by economists and ecologists. We shall begin by presenting, and then discussing, several interpretations of the concept and the implications which follow from them. Assuming that sustainability (in some sense) is regarded as an important objective, its attainment presumably implies some constraints on economic behaviour. What would be the characteristics of such constraints, and what other consequences might follow from imposing sustainability constraints on economic activity? We provide some tentative answers to these questions in this chapter.

In the previous chapter, a number of alternative ethical frameworks were examined, and we showed how these can affect our attitudes towards issues concerning economy–environment interactions. Within the general field of environmental economics, ethics currently figure most prominently in the analysis of sustainability and sustainable development.[1] One explanation for the force which the concept of sustainability exerts in current debate derives from the fact that the concept has a powerful ethical content. But this is only one of its components. A second element in the mixture of meanings it carries relates to the ability of a system to reproduce itself over long periods of time. As our examination of the development of environmental economics in Chapter 1 suggested, this facet of sustainability has had a long history in economic analysis. A major concern of the classical economists was the prospect for continuing economic development. The conjunction of fixedness of land resources, population growth, and diminishing returns in production, led early classical economists such as Malthus and Ricardo to argue that the economy had a tendency to converge in the long run to a stationary state. In this state, the majority of people would live at a subsistence level, closing off any tendency for population to rise. The long-run tendency towards the stationary state would be punctuated intermittently by periods of rising living standards and increasing population: these periods of material progress would be brought to an end by the diminishing returns that would inevitably follow as a consequence of the population increase.

So the early classical writers, stressing the constraints imposed by finite resources and the principle of diminishing returns, regarded the economy as sustainable in the sense that it could be reproduced over indefinite periods of time. The prognosis for the level of well-being of an average person was, however, very bleak. Later classical writers, without departing from the basic premises of this argument, took a more optimistic view of the prospects for economic development, pointing out the ways in which new

---

[1] The terms *sustainability* and *sustainable development* shall be treated as synonyms throughout this book.

resource discoveries and technical progress could offset diminishing returns, and stressing the benefits to be obtained from decisions to limit population growth. Neoclassical growth theory, developed in the twentieth century, almost entirely rejected the classical hypothesis of a long-run tendency towards a stationary state. The increasing share of output generated by manufacturing industry led economists to downgrade the importance they attached to land as a productive input. Indeed, neoclassical growth theory no longer posited the existence of any fixed factor; productive inputs were visualised as either growing naturally over time (labour inputs) or capable of being accumulated indefinitely (capital). An assumption of continuing technical progress was sufficient, in this framework, to generate the conclusion that economic growth (rather than merely some level of output) could be sustained perpetually.

But economists, of course, have not been alone in their concern with growth and development. In the years after 1950, fundamental principles of physics and biology were reflected in developments in ecological science, and the new discipline of environmental science emerged. Threats to the sustainability of ecosystems became the objects of attention, and these developments, in conjunction with the implications of the materials balance principle, began to be incorporated into environmental economics. Initial applications of these principles in economics were to the analysis of environmental pollution and residuals disposal, important early contributions being made by Daly (1974), Boulding (1966) and Ayres and Kneese (1969). These new insights collectively pointed to the existence of limits to growth, and so for the first time raised the possibility that the economic process may not be sustainable.

During the 1970s, concern with sustainability began to appear on the national and international political agenda, most visibly in the proceedings of a series of international conferences. In 1972, the meeting in Stockholm of the United Nations Conference on the Human Environment led to the formation of the United Nations Environmental Programme (UNEP), and the creation of a set of national environmental protection agencies in a number of countries. The first explicit attempt to develop a programme of action centred on sustainability was the 1980 World Conservation Strategy of the International Union for the Conservation of Nature.

Early variants of the limits to growth literature, such as the contributions by Meadows et al. (1972)

and Barney (1980), were widely (and often unfairly) criticised by economists. However, the limits to growth literature and the critiques made of it stimulated interest in the role of poverty in natural resource degradation in developing economies, and the potential value of market forces as efficient instruments for environmental regulation and control. It became evident that the linkages between growth, resource depletion and environmental degradation could be radically altered through an appropriate use of policy instruments. Useful accounts of these debates are to be found in *The Resourceful Earth* (Simon and Kahn, 1984) and *The Global Possible* (Repetto, 1985).

Perhaps the best known statement of the concept of sustainability (see Box 3.1 below) derives from the 1987 report of the World Commission on Environment and Development (WCED), established by the United Nations in 1983. The report – *Our Common Future* (WCED, 1987) – of what is commonly known as the Brundtland Commission, after the name of its Norwegian chairman, contained a set of recommendations that are rather different from what they are popularly perceived to be, however. Firstly, sustainable development was interpreted in terms of the extent to which economic activities can meet human needs, rather than in terms of protection of the biosphere or specific natural systems. Secondly, no presumption was made against the desirability and feasibility of economic growth itself. On the contrary, further growth and development was welcomed:

> Far from requiring the cessation of economic growth, [sustainable development] recognises that the problems of poverty and underdevelopment cannot be solved unless we have a new era of growth in which developing countries play a large role and reap large benefits.

> WCED (1987), page 40

Moreover,

> Growth must be revived in developing countries because that is where the links between economic growth, the alleviation of poverty, and environmental conditions operate most directly. Yet developing countries are part of an interdependent world economy; their prospects also depend on the levels and patterns of growth in industrialised nations. The medium term prospects for industrial countries are for growth of 3–4 per cent, the minimum that international financial institutions consider necessary if these countries are going to play a part in expanding the world economy. Such growth rates could be environmentally sustainable if industrialised nations

can continue the recent shifts in the content of their growth towards less material- and energy-intensive activities and the improvement of their efficiency in using materials and energy.

WCED (1987), page 51

The emphasis in the Brundtland Report is placed on growth alleviating poverty, rather than on poverty being eliminated through redistribution. What makes this option environmentally sustainable is the scope for economising in the use of resources as the value of output increases, and the existence of possibilities for substitution. A host of international conferences have taken place in the last decade, and we present a summary of the agenda and recommendations of one of these in Box 3.1.

One question – the appropriate treatment of population in sustainability analysis – has remained particularly difficult to address in all these discussions. The largest single threat to sustainability appears to come from human population increase. Should a researcher assume that population growth is an exogenous process, and analyse the conditions for sustainability given the expected future path of population over time? Or should he or she regard population as an endogenous variable, so that choices are to be made about future population levels as well as about future patterns of resource use? We deliberately avoid these difficult issues in this chapter, and leave analysis of population and the environment until Chapter 11.

The discussion of sustainability that follows in the rest of this chapter contains three main parts. First, we attempt to establish why one should be concerned about sustainability. One of the outcomes of this exercise will be to show that the concept of sustainability carries a variety of meanings, not all of which are necessarily consistent with one another. The second part elucidates the various meanings which the concept carries. Thirdly, assuming one were to accept that economic behaviour should be subject to some form of sustainability constraint, we consider some of the forms that such a constraint might take.

Reasons for concern about sustainability

There are at least three classes of argument one could make to justify a claim that economic activity should be sustainable. The first argument is a moral one: we, the present generation, have moral obligations to those generations which will come after us. Such an obligation might imply that we do not act in such ways as to jeopardise the chances of future generations having equal opportunities to those that are currently enjoyed. This is not the only way of presenting a moral argument for sustainable behaviour, nor is it even the best way. We merely use it to illustrate the point that moral arguments can be used to justify sustainability as a constraint on behaviour.

The second type of argument is an ecological one. Suppose that you believe that ecological diversity is an important objective in its own right. Then economic activity that threatens to reduce such diversity is intrinsically undesirable. We should organise our behaviour so as to avoid serious ecological disruption – or in other words, economic activity should be organised so as to sustain ecological diversity. Once again, there are different ways in which one could argue an ecological case for sustainability: diversity may be replaced by a related concept such as ecological stability, integrity, or resilience, for example. One might also claim that such an argument is, in the final analysis, a moral one, and so could be included in the first class we looked at.

The third approach to justifying a sustainability goal is an economic one. To develop an economic case, one would need to argue either that sustainable economic behaviour is more efficient than non-sustainable behaviour, or that sustainable behaviour is that which maximises intertemporal social welfare. Perhaps such an argument could be made in a convincing way, but it is not clear to the authors of this text that sustainable economic behaviour is necessarily efficient nor that it necessarily maximises social welfare. Our view is that the only convincing way of arguing for sustainability is by invoking ethical principles of justice or fairness. If the sustainable development is ethically correct, we should seek to attain it. If not, then it is irrelevant to economic analysis.

The whole question about whether or not economic behaviour *should* be required to satisfy sustainability constraints would be of no more than philosophical interest if economic activity were sustainable anyway, and could be shown to be sustainable for all foreseeable times in the future. Presumably, the reason why this area has become such an important part of current debate is that there are good reasons to believe that current economic activity is *not* sustainable. What are the grounds for this belief?

Box 3.1 International institutions and sustainable development

An important and growing role in environmental policy-making is being played by international policy institutions, particularly agencies of the United Nations (UN). The World Resources Institute points out, in the 1994–95 edition of its biennial publication *World Resources*, that of the more than 170 international environmental treaties which have been adopted to date, two-thirds have been signed since the 1972 UN Conference on the Human Environment in Stockholm. It argues that

> The opportunity for international and regional institutions to encourage actions by national governments that promote sustainable development has never been greater. Public awareness of the urgent need for concerted action has been growing in many countries.
>
> *World Resources 1994–95*, page 223

It is also clear that the last ten years in particular have been marked by increasing attention being paid to environmental issues in the conduct of international relations. This reflects an awareness that the issues of environmental protection, liberalisation of world trade, poverty and economic development and North–South relationships are inextricably linked, a theme forcibly argued in the 1987 Report of the Brundtland Commission.

The importance, or even necessity, of the contribution played by international agencies stems from the absence of incentives at national levels to commit resources unilaterally to deal with regional or global environmental problems, such as transboundary airborne and water pollution, loss of biological diversity, ozone depletion and global climate change. Only concerted international behaviour can hope to make much headway in dealing with these processes. In this survey, we focus on the contribution of the UN system of international institutions; the proactive role played by the UN has been one of the major successes of international diplomacy in the post Cold War period.

The 1992 United Nations Conference on Environment and Development (UNCED), held in Rio de Janeiro and commonly known as the Earth Summit, was the largest international conference ever assembled. Its size is partly explained by the large representation and active involvement of interested and expert non-governmental organisations (NGOs) from many countries. The Earth Summit approved three documents:

1 The Rio Declaration on Environment and Development, consisting of 27 principles stating the rights and responsibilities of individual nations with respect to the environment, aiming to ensure the integrated pursuit of economic development and environmental protection. These principles are not binding on signatory countries.

2 A non-binding declaration, containing general principles for sustainable forest management. Wide conflicts of opinion between industrialised and developing countries prevented the adoption of any specific plans of action on forest management.

3 A comprehensive programme for national and international action towards sustainable economic development, known as Agenda 21.

Also noteworthy at the Rio summit was the adoption of two other treaties that were not on the original agenda of the conference: the UN Framework Convention on Climate Change (requiring signatories to conduct periodic inventories of greenhouse gas emissions and to submit (non-binding) action plans for emissions control), and the UN Convention on Biological Diversity.

Two matters warrant attention at this point. Firstly, the adoption of a treaty (particularly one that is non-binding) does not of itself imply that objectives and targets will be met. However, the moral, financial and political pressures that such treaties can bring to bear are very large. Secondly, the UN environmental strategy makes no attempt to treat issues of environmental protection and environmental sustainability in isolation from issues of economic development, particularly in the poorer nations. On the contrary, the whole thrust of the institutional structure established over recent years is towards a joint approach to the two objectives.

What arrangements have been made to monitor and enforce these treaties? Monitoring is the principal responsibility of a newly created (1993) institution, the UN Commission on Sustainable Development (CSD), which is to work in close collaboration with interested NGOs. In terms of enforcement, CSD has little direct power, having no budgetary or legal authority over national governments. Its major influence is expected to derive from the role it plays in organising information, and harnessing the influence of NGOs in the political processes of individual countries and regional organisations such as the European Community.

Coordination and integration of policy between the work of the various UN agencies is promoted with the assistance of two other institutional mechanisms, the UN Administrative Committee on Coordination, and the Inter-Agency Committee on Sustainable Development. Agenda 21 of the Rio summit also

Box 3.1 Continued

recommended the strengthening of the other UN organs dealing with environmental and development issues, particularly the UN Environment Programme (UNEP) and the UN Development Programme (UNDP). A full account of the complex environmental/development structure of the UN, and an appraisal of its performance, is found in World Resources: 1994–95, Chapter 13.

Our focus on the United Nations Organisation in this section should not, of course, be taken to imply that it is the sole international body concerned with environmental issues. As we shall see in Chapter 12, a substantial number of organisations also have interests in this area, and play important roles in environmental policy. These organisations include the Committee on International Development Institutions on the Environment (CIDIE), the Organisation for Economic Cooperation and Development (OECD), the World Bank, NGOs, research institutions such as the World Resources Institute, and multilateral development banks. The Global Environmental Facility (GEF), a three-year programme running until 1994 intended to help developing countries deal with global environmental concerns, is examined in Chapter 12.

Physical stocks and flows and the laws of thermodynamics

We have already considered the laws of thermodynamics. The first law – matter/energy can be neither created nor destroyed is the basis of materials balance models of economic activity. Matter and energy used in human production and consumption activities must eventually end up as residual flows into environmental systems. Some proportion of these flows will have damaging consequences. Externalities such as environmental pollution are not, therefore, unusual consequences of thoughtless or selfish behaviour (which could be eliminated by 'better' behaviour) but are pervasive and inescapable. The second law states that the total amount of usefully concentrated energy and matter in an isolated system must decline over time – the degree of entropy of the system inevitably increases.

Some writers suggest that these laws necessarily imply very grave long-term consequences. Georgescu-Roegen (1971), for example, sees the second law as condemning civilisation to decline once the global stocks of usefully concentrated matter and energy have been dissipated. However, even if such an inference were correct, it would not be of much interest to the economist: if the decline of human civilisation is an inevitable outcome of physical laws, then there is nothing we can do about it. That would seem to be the end of the matter!

Luckily, there are good grounds for not wringing our hands in despair. First of all, one may argue that the inevitability of collapse refers to times completely beyond anything that is of relevance to humans. But more importantly, the inference is not warranted as it stands. The earth is not an isolated (closed) physical system, as it exchanges energy with outside systems. As Boulding (see Box 1.3 in Chapter 1), Daly (see Box 3.2) and Young (1991) argue, some level of perpetually reproduced resource use is possible with the employment of solar-powered material recycling. Now the thermodynamic arguments become interesting and important to economists. Are present and predicted future levels of economic activity physically sustainable? Daly (1987) argues that sustained economic growth at any positive rate is not possible, as current rates of material and energy use already exceed solar-powered recycling potentials.

A second (and probably more important) reason why Georgescu-Roegen's conclusion is unwarranted arises from the neglect of substitution possibilities. Economic growth is a growth in the value (rather than the physical quantity) of output. It is quite conceivable that the level of output value can be sustained (or even raised) over time using flows of material/energy throughputs at continually declining levels, through substitution and innovation on both the input and output sides of the economy. We return to this theme later in this chapter, and at many places throughout the book.

Ecological and economic steady state

Ecological considerations also suggest that current levels and patterns of economic activity may be unsustainable. As we showed in Chapter 1, ecological science points to three main features of biological systems that are relevant to sustainability. First, human life depends upon a highly complex web of food chains. These food chains can be disturbed or disrupted in many ways. Secondly, ecological systems are processes in which development and change occur. Component parts of these systems may be induced into processes of decline, and such declines are typically characterised by thresholds, at which catastrophic and irreversible change sets in. Thirdly, there appears to be evidence pointing to the fact that simple and novel ecosystems tend to be more unstable than complex ones – see Krebs (1985, page 581) and Lovelock (1989, page 50). Human activity tends to simplify ecosystems and reduce biological diversity, and so leads to less stability in the relevant ecosystem. Continued economic growth may, therefore, result in catastrophic ecosystem collapse, rendering economic activity unsustainable at levels that would be considered reasonable.

Clearly, much of this is based on possibilities rather than expected outcomes. However, at the very least, these kinds of arguments suggest the desirability of cautious behaviour, minimising ecological disruption whenever we can reasonably do so. For many ecologists, this is the essence of what constitutes sustainable behaviour. But note that there are still some very awkward choices that have to be made: how cautious should behaviour be? When is it reasonable to do something that entails ecological disturbance and when is it not? Does any disturbance matter, or just large disturbances?

Definitions and meanings of sustainability

In terms of usage, the concept of sustainability does not possess any single meaning or definition. In order to structure our thoughts and discussions on sustainability, it will be useful to classify in as simple a way as possible the alternative manners in which writers have treated the concept. At least five alternative conceptualisations can be identified:

(1a) A sustainable state is one in which utility is non-declining through time.

(1b) A sustainable state is one in which consumption is non-declining through time.

(2) A sustainable state is one in which resources are managed so as to maintain production opportunities for the future.

(3) A sustainable state is one in which the natural capital stock is non-declining through time.

(4) A sustainable state is one in which resources are managed so as to maintain a sustainable yield of resource services.

(5) A sustainable state is one which satisfies minimum conditions of ecosystem stability and resilience through time.

There are two points to note about this set of concepts from the outset. First, the concepts are not necessarily mutually exclusive. One may argue, for example, that (2) implies (3). Secondly, what is the relevant time scale for discussions of sustainability? At the very least, one must be thinking in terms of very long time horizons. However, this statement just begs the question of what is meant by a very long period of time. Some writers choose to think of indefinitely long (infinite) time horizons. Put another way, a state is sustainable if the criterion being used for sustainability is capable of being satisfied in perpetuity. Other writers choose time periods defined in terms of millennia or the like; what they appear to have in mind is periods of time in which human populations are, on average, genetically constant. However, it is probably neither necessary nor even fruitful to decide upon some particular time horizon, as sustainability questions can be addressed in a two-period framework. Thus, we may choose to define a sustainable state as one in which some relevant magnitude is bequeathed to the following period in at least as good a state as it is in the present period. Sustainable development implies that this is true whichever pair of successive periods is chosen (which then suggests that we are thinking about unlimited horizons in time). This is the way that we shall use the concept of sustainability in this text.

Table 3.1 presents a number of definitions presented by leading authors in this field; in each case, we make some preliminary observations about the definition that will be taken up more thoroughly in what follows. Our main task in this section is to analyse and discuss each of the five conceptualisations of sustainability.

Concepts (1a) and (1b)

Concept (1a) is that a sustainable state is one in which utility is non-declining through time. Concept (1b) is that a sustainable state is one in which consumption is non-declining through time.

We have grouped these two criteria as they will be equivalent in some (but not all) circumstances, and because it is convenient to treat them together for expositional purposes. One or other of these concepts has been the conventional way in which

Table 3.1 Some definitions of sustainability

Definition 1: *Every generation should leave water, air and soil resources as pure and unpolluted as when it came on earth. Each generation should leave undiminished all the species of animals it found on earth.*

Source: UNESCO Document.

Comment: Robert Solow's (1991) comment on this definition succinctly sums up the problem with this and other similar interpretations of sustainability. He writes: 'If you define sustainability as an obligation to leave the world as we found it in detail, I think that's glib but essentially unfeasible. It is, when you think about it, not even desirable.'

Definition 2: *Sustainability is defined as ... non-declining utility of a representative member of society for millennia into the future.*

Source: Pezzey (1992), page 323.

Comment: Pezzey notes that his criterion is actually one of 'sustainedness', as it refers to actual achievement rather than just a potential for this. His definition is built around an explicit goal in terms of human well-being. This definition relates to final outcomes, and if one were confident about the likelihood of continuing technological progress, this would imply a reduced need to bequeath some forms of capital inputs to future generations.

Definition 3: *Sustainable activity is ... that level of economic activity which leaves the environmental quality level intact, with the policy objective corresponding to this notion being the maximisation of net benefits of economic development, subject to maintaining the services and quality of natural resources over time.*

Source: Barbier and Markandya (1990), page 659.

Comment: A standard economic objective: but what exactly does it mean to require that the services and quality of natural resources be maintained?

Definition 4: *Sustainable development is development that meets the needs of the present without compromising the ability of future generations to meet their own needs.*

Source: WCED (1987) page 43.

Comment: The definition requires that we can satisfactorily define a reasonable standard for human needs. Can this be done?

Definition 5: *Preserving opportunities for future generations as a common sense minimal notion of intergenerational justice.*

Source: Page (1977, 1982), pages 202 and 205, survey.

Comment: Page appeals to John Locke's concept of just acquisition: the present generation does not have the right to deplete the opportunities afforded by the resource base since it does not 'own' it. Page's ethical position owes much to the writings of the philosopher John Rawls.

Definition 6: *A safe minimum standard of conservation as a matter of resources and economic policy. To be achieved by avoiding the 'critical zone' – that is, the physical conditions, brought about by human action, which would make it uneconomical to halt and reverse depletion'.*

Source: Ciriacy-Wantrup (1952), page 253.

Comment: A definitive statement of the views of an ecological economist about sustainability.

Definition 7: *The alternative approach [to sustainable development] is to focus on natural capital assets and suggest that they should not decline through time.*

Source: Pearce *et al.* (1989), page 37.

Comment: A necessary condition; based on the assumption that there are limits beyond which the substitution of man-made for natural capital is not possible. This approach does not identify goals as such, but focuses on physical and ecological constraints.

---

economists have interpreted and used the concept of sustainability in recent years. In a seminal paper written in 1974, Solow began from the premise that a sustainable state is one which satisfies some relevant criterion of intergenerational equity. He proceeded to argue that a Rawlsian ethical framework was an appropriate one in which to develop principles of intertemporal distributive justice. Suppose that society were to make a decision as to how utility should be allocated over time. A Rawlsian ethic would suggest that the allocation would confer equal utility on each generation of people through time. More precisely, Solow's assertion is that a consistent application of this framework leads one to the conclusion that the undiscounted utility of per capita consumption should be constant over infinite time. One might then choose to interpret the term sustainability as meaning the attainment of

such a target, as does Pezzey in Definition 2 in Table 3.1.

Unfortunately, it is very difficult to deduce the conditions that would be necessary or sufficient for an economy to reach and sustain a constant level of undiscounted utility of per capita consumption. Analysis becomes much easier if the problem is converted to one in terms of consumption rather than utility. Under some circumstances, the criterion of constant consumption would be equivalent to that of constant utility. The two would be identical, for example, in an economy producing a single aggregate output, in which no growth occurred, and in which the function relating utility to consumption is constant over time. Clearly these are very restrictive conditions.

John Hartwick (1977, 1978) chooses to interpret sustainability in terms of non-declining consumption.

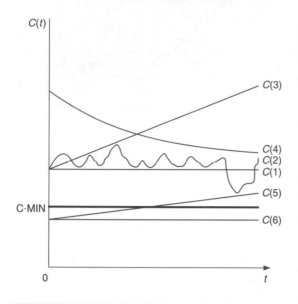

Consumption path	Criterion	
	Solow–Hartwick	Minimum Condition
C(1)	S	S
C(2)	NS	S
C(3)	S	S
C(4)	NS	S
C(5)	S	NS
C(6)	S	NS

Key: S = sustainable, NS = not sustainable.

Fig 3.1 Consumption paths over time, illustrating the Solow–Hartwick sustainability criterion.

He seeks to identify conditions under which such a target would be achievable. The conditions derived centre around a particular savings rule, commonly known as Hartwick's Rule. This rule states that if the rents (the surplus of revenues over production costs) derived from exhaustible resource extraction are saved and then invested entirely in reproducible (physical) capital, then under certain conditions the levels of output and consumption will remain constant over time. We shall discuss and interpret this result later in this chapter.

Hartwick and Solow were particularly interested in the conditions under which consumption can be indefinitely maintained at non-declining levels. One might argue that a more important case to consider is one in which consumption is not allowed to fall below some minimum level over time, where the relevant

minimum is determined by what is judged to be a decent living standard that any human being could reasonably expect. We shall not discuss how such a level might be identified, but merely assume that it is possible to do so. In Figure 3.1, we illustrate a number of hypothetical consumption paths over some period of time. The vertical axis measures the level of consumption, at points of time from the present ($t = 0$) indicated on the horizontal axis. We represent the minimum acceptable level of consumption by the heavy line denoted C·MIN. It is interesting and informative to see which of the paths shown constitutes a sustainable path according to the Solow–Hartwick criterion (non-declining consumption) and according to the minimum condition criterion that we have just outlined. The results of this test are displayed below Figure 3.1.

The time paths which are sustainable using the Solow–Hartwick criterion are C(1), C(3), C(5) and C(6), as each exhibits a strictly non-declining level of consumption. But notice that this criterion does not distinguish between paths for which consumption is always higher than the minimum level (C(1) and C(3)) and those for which it is not (C(5) and C(6)). This illustrates one of the weaknesses of that criterion: it does not impose any requirements on how large the non-declining level of consumption should initially be; an economy can be sustainable if living standards are abysmally low, provided they do not get any lower! Many people would find it difficult to describe such a state of affairs as sustainable. What can be said about path C(2)? It is clearly not Solow-sustainable, as consumption falls at the end of the period below its initial level. Whether it would be an unsustainable case if the final drop below the initial level did not occur is a moot point, and depends upon how strictly one interprets the non-declining requirement. If 'averaging' is allowed, one might be tempted to regard C(2) as sustainable because there is not a downward trend, even though there are many times at which it is actually falling.

Paths C(1), C(2), C(3) and C(4) are all sustainable, but C(5) and C(6) are unsustainable, in terms of the minimum condition. Clearly, whether or not a path of consumption over time is sustainable or not can vary according to the criterion we tend to use. One other point is worthy of special mention here: path C(4) is not sustainable on the Solow–Hartwick criterion, whereas C(1), C(5) and C(6) are all sustainable. But it would be easy to make a strong case that C(4) is superior to each of C(1), C(5) and C(6) as consumption is higher for all time in the former case. Sustainable outcomes may not be best outcomes, therefore. Finally, we note that in Table 3.1, the Brundtland Report definition of sustainability (Definition 4) appears to be close to the minimum condition criterion we have just presented.

Concept (2)

In this concept, a sustainable state is one in which resources are managed so as to maintain production opportunities for the future.

In some important later works, Solow proposes a second criterion of sustainability based on a weaker criterion of maintaining production opportunities for the future (Solow, 1986, 1991). He observes that one very common way of discussing ethical matters in the context of the sustainability issue is in terms of a parable: the so-called cake-eating problem. This is concerned with the situation in which some fixed quantity of a non-renewable resource is available; the question for which an answer is sought concerns how the resources should be distributed over time. Put another way, what is the appropriate way of dividing the cake intertemporally?

Solow regards as erroneous and unhelpful attempts to define sustainability (or to identify conditions that should be satisfied for sustainability to be achieved) in terms of the way in which non-renewable resources should be distributed. Solow (1986) argues that:

At the level of popular discussion, the usual form of intergenerational equity argument is

How much of the world's resources (non-renewable) is it fair for the current generation to use up, and how much should be left for later generations who have no active voice in contemporary decisions?

This is a damagingly narrow way to pose the question. We have no obligation to our successors to bequeath a share of this or that resource. Our obligation refers to generalised productive capacity or, even wider, to certain standards of consumption/living *possibilities* over time.

Solow regards the cake-division parable as inappropriate because the present generation can have no firm knowledge of what future people's preferences will be, what technologies will be available, or even how long the human species will survive. Unless one knew these things, it would not be possible to arrive at any sensible decision about how the cake of non-renewable environmental resources should be distributed through time. The final sentence of our extract from Solow's paper seems to suggest a criterion very similar

to the first one we investigated, but that equivalence largely disappears when one looks at matters closely. Ultimately, claims Solow, what we owe our successors is the potential to do as well as we have done. Providing we bequeath them sufficient to do that, we will have done all that can be reasonably expected. It might make very good sense to bequeath a smaller non-renewable resource stock to future generations if that is compensated for by a more developed stock of scientific knowledge. Looking at Table 3.1 again, it is clear that this is also the concept of sustainability that Talbot Page has in mind.

The point of this argument, therefore, is that one might choose to define sustainability in terms of the maintenance of productive or consumption potential over time. Let us now develop this argument more fully. Production potential at any point in time depends predominantly on the stock of productive assets available for use. First, divide this stock of productive resources into human labour power and all other productive resources. Let us define the term capital in a very broad sense, to include any economically useful stock, other than raw labour power. In this broad sense, capital consists of:

1 Natural-capital: any naturally provided stock, such as aquifers and water systems, fertile land, crude oil and gas, forests, fisheries and other stocks of biomass, and the earth's atmosphere itself. The category is thus broadly equivalent to what are often termed natural resources.
Natural capital thus comprises exhaustible resources, if we use that term to mean renewable stock and non-renewable stock resources. We do not include the human population stock in this category.
2 Physical capital: plant, equipment, buildings and infrastructure, accumulated by devoting part of current production to investment purposes.
3 Human capital: stocks of learned skills, embodied in particular individuals. In some loose sense, therefore, this enhances the productive potential of the person above that of his or her pure labour power alone.
4 Intellectual capital: disembodied skills. This comprises the stock of useful knowledge, which we might otherwise term as the state of technology. These skills are disembodied in that they do not reside in particular individuals, but are part of the culture of a society.

If human-made capital is defined to be the sum of physical, human and intellectual capital, then the capital stock consists of two parts: natural and human-made capital. In terms of the production function notation that we introduced in Chapter 1, this way of classifying production inputs suggests that output Q is a function of labour, L, and capital, K. Capital consists of natural capital, K_N and human-made capital K_H, so we could write the economy's production function as

$$Q = Q(L, K_N, K_H)$$

Maintenance of the productive potential of the economy will be achieved if the composite capital stock is non-declining over time. If the individual elements of this stock were unable to substitute for one another to any degree and each element were necessary for production, then maintenance of productive potential would imply that each element should be non-declining over time.[2] Most economists would argue that the different elements are substitutable to some degree. If so, then whilst it is necessary to bequeath some aggregate value of capital assets to ensure the maintenance of productive opportunities, there is no necessary reason why any particular element of the capital stock has to remain at a non-decreasing level. In particular, two kinds of substitution effect are particularly important. First, as Dasgupta and Heal (1974) show, productive potential can in some circumstances be maintained in the face of falling availability of exhaustible resources if these can be substituted for by rising quantities of physical capital. Secondly, as Solow (1986) and Dasgupta and Heal (1979, page 207) argue, knowledge appears to be a good substitute for exhaustible resources, and so it may well be the case that falling quantities of exhaustible resources could be more than compensated for by increasing human and intellectual capital.

Concept (3)

In this concept, a sustainable state is one in which the natural capital stock is non-declining through time.

[2] If resources cannot be substituted for one another, this means that more of one type cannot be used in place of less of another type. So, if we wished to at least maintain the existing level and pattern of output, each different element of the resource mix would need to be maintained at non-declining levels. However, if we were prepared to accept changes in the output mix, it may then be possible to maintain overall output by producing more of those goods using large shares of the growing resource and less of those goods using large shares of the depleting resource.

The argument that policy should be directed towards maintaining a non-declining natural capital stock has found much support among economists (see Box 3.3 later in this chapter). This would be a necessary condition for sustaining the economy's productive potential if natural capital is *essential* to production, and is not substitutable by other productive resources. In the final analysis, the extent to which natural capital is substitutable by other forms of productive input is an empirical matter, not one that can be decided by theoretical considerations alone. But theory is suggestive on this matter. A number of writers argue that substitutability is much lower than we have previously thought. Moreover, as the natural capital stock depletes, it may well be the case that substitutability falls too. Therefore, even if we found evidence confirming substitutability, this may not constitute grounds for believing that this will remain true in the future. When we look at the different functions of the natural environment, it seems clear that some of these functions can be performed only by natural capital stocks, and so these functions are ones for which no substitutability is possible. Finally, as we show in Chapter 10, economic progress and development may well lead societies to place increasing emphasis and value on the consumption amenities yielded by natural capital.

How do the various definitions of sustainability given in Table 3.1 relate to the concept we have just discussed? Clearly, Definition 7 is an exact statement of it. The third definition, due to Barbier and Markandya, also emphasises maintenance of environmental quality and of services and quality of natural resources. A very strong version of the non-declining natural capital stock criterion is given in the UNESCO version, Definition 1. In this case, there appears to be a requirement that each element of the natural capital stock should be maintained, a stronger condition than one which merely constrains the total stock of natural capital to not fall.

Concept (4)

In Concept (4), a sustainable state is one in which resources are managed so as to maintain a sustainable yield of resource services.

The concept of a sustainable yield is often used in biological models of renewable resource stocks, such as forests and fisheries. These models will be investigated in Chapter 5, and so we restrict attention here to a few general remarks. A *sustained yield* describes a steady state in which some stock is held at a constant level and delivers a constant flow of resource services over time. For example, a forest stand is a resource stock which, when subjected to a suitable thinning and replanting regime, can deliver a constant flow of services in the form of felled timber.

The maximum sustainable yield of a resource is the highest feasible flow of services that can be maintained over time from some environmental system. Some writers advocate that stocks should be regulated so as to deliver maximum sustained yields, equating a maximum sustained yield with optimal practice. We show in Chapter 5 that it is not necessarily sensible to advocate a maximum sustainable yield management programme, and in some circumstances, it is not even desirable to have any sustainable yield from a resource!

What is of interest to us at the moment is to note that one interpretation of 'sustainable development' is in terms of sustainable yields from resource stocks looked at in some aggregate sense, although not necessarily maximum sustainable yields. But choosing to think in terms of aggregates poses some difficulties. When one refers to maintaining a stock of resources constant, or a flow of resource services constant, what does this mean when the stock and flow are made up of heterogeneous elements? Does it mean that each different element must be kept constant, or rather that some weighted sum should be maintained? If the latter interpretation is chosen, how are the weights to be selected and will they be constant?

An alternative interpretation of this concept follows from the steady state models of Daly (see Box 3.2) and Boulding (Box 1.3) that we examined in Chapter 1, and which follow from a strict application of the laws of thermodynamics. In a spaceship earth economy, perpetual reproducibility of the economic/physical system (the spaceship) requires that a steady state be achieved in which the waste flows from production and consumption are equated with the system's recycling capacity. Reproducibility of the spaceship over time implies that waste flows cannot be ejected into outer space through the air lock, as that would lead to a gradual depletion of the material resource base upon which the spaceship is reliant. As the maximum recycling capacity of the system is determined by the (constant) flow of incoming energy that can be harnessed from extra-terrestrial sources, so there must be in this steady state a maximum rate of sustainable materials usage in the economy.

Concept (5)

In this concept, a sustainable state is one which satisfies minimum conditions of ecosystem stability and resilience through time.

Ecological science is founded upon looking at its subject matter within a systems perspective: indeed the term for this subject matter – the ecosystem – indicates immediately that this is to be the perspective that is adopted. The whole system – the biosphere – consists of an interlocking set of ecological subsystems or ecosystems. Systems analysts are concerned with organisational characteristics and structure, and with the systems dynamics; the processes of evolution and change.

Ecologists look at sustainability from the point of view of the ecological system of which humans are just one part. Sustainability is assessed, loosely speaking, in terms of the extent to which the structure and properties of the prevailing ecosystem can be maintained. Human interests are not regarded as paramount; rather, they are seen as being identified with the continuing existence and functioning of the biosphere in a form more or less similar to that which exists at present. Ecological views are more human-centred than is often admitted, as there is a presumption that the present system structure, including the important place in it occupied by humans, is preferred to any other. To confirm that this is so, consider the attitude an ecologist might take to the threat of global warming. If large-scale global warming were to occur, there is a reasonably high chance that major ecosystem change would occur. The biosphere would not cease to operate, of course – it would just operate in a different way. We guess that nearly all ecological scientists would take a stand against global warming, and most would do so on the grounds that human life is more threatened in a changed ecosystem than in the present one.

The biosphere and its component ecosystems are in continuous process of change, some of which is gradual and continuous, and some of which is disruptive and discontinuous. Two concepts which are of fundamental importance in ecological science are *stability* and *resilience*. The ecologist C.S. Holling (1973, 1986) interprets stability as a property of individual species or populations within an ecosystem. Stability is the propensity of a population to return to an equilibrium condition following some disturbance. The stability of a population refers to the strength of the tendency to return to an original equilibrium level after being subjected to some

Box 3.2 Herman Daly: the steady state economy

In his article 'The economics of the steady state' (1974), Daly begins by defining his concept of a steady-state economy:

> A steady-state economy is defined by constant stocks of physical wealth (artifacts) and a constant population, each maintained at some chosen, desirable level by a low rate of throughput − i.e., by low birth rates equal to low death rates and by low physical production rates equal to low physical depreciation rates, so that longevity of people and durability of physical stocks are high. The throughput flow, viewed as the cost of maintaining the stocks, begins with the extraction (depletion) of low entropy resources at the input end, and terminates with an equal quantity of high entropy waste (pollution) at the output end. The throughput is the inevitable cost of maintaining the stocks of people and artifacts and should be minimised subject to the maintenance of a chosen level of stocks.

>   Daly (1974) page 15

According to Daly, the ultimate benefit of economic activity is the services (want satisfaction) yielded by the stocks of artifacts and people. He notes that conventional indicators of economic performance measure the wrong thing: instead of measuring service flows, GDP and the like measure throughputs. But there is no longer any reason to believe that these two will be closely correlated, or have a stable relationship over time. It is possible to make progress in the steady state through two types of efficiency improvement: either by maintaining a given stock level with less throughput, or by obtaining more services per unit of time from the same stock. Unfortunately, the fundamental laws of thermodynamics imply that these two forms of efficiency gain are likely to be unobtainable in the long-term; we are condemned to efficiency losses, not gains. The main reason for this arises from the fact that

> . . . as better grade (lower entropy) sources of raw materials are used up, it will be necessary to process ever larger amounts of materials using ever more energy and capital equipment to get the same quantity of needed mineral.

Daly notes that a choice must be made about the *level* of stocks in the steady state. He observes that there is a large number of stock levels to choose from, and that the choice is a difficult problem of ecology and ethics. Daly suggest that we will never be able to identify an optimal stock level and so, as a matter of practice, we should learn to be stable at or near to existing stock levels.

For Daly, we ultimately have no real choice over whether to seek a steady state. If the economic subsystem is not to eventually disrupt the functioning of the larger system of which it is a part, then at some point the economy will have to be run in a steady state. Note, though, that Daly does not claim that the steady state is infinitely sustainable. Indeed, his view is quite the opposite:

> Thus a steady state is simply a strategy for good stewardship, for maintaining our spaceship and permitting it to die of old age rather than from the cancer of growthmania.

According to Daly, the necessary ultimate demise of the system arises from the irresistible force of increasing entropy. He pours particular scorn upon those economists who see substitution as the salvation of perpetual growth. Conventional economists envisage a sequence of substitution effects; as one input becomes relatively scarce, it will be replaced by another that is less relatively scarce. The possibility of absolute scarcity is assumed away in this approach. But for Daly

> Substitution is always of one form of low entropy matter-energy for another. There is no substitute for low entropy itself, and low entropy is scarce, both in its terrestrial source (finite stocks of concentrated fossil fuels and minerals) and in its solar source (a fixed rate of inflow of solar energy).

Finally, technology does not offer the solution to perpetual economic growth that is often claimed. All technologies obey the logic of thermodynamics, and so we cannot appeal to any technology to wrench us from the grasp of the entropy principle (see the quotation at the start of this chapter).

---

disturbance. Resilience is a property of ecosystems rather than individual populations. It is the propensity of a system to retain its organisational structure and function in essentially the same way following a significant disturbance. A resilient ecosystem need not imply that all populations within the system are stable; it is quite possible that a disturbance can result in a species disappearing even though the ecosystem

as a whole continues to function in broadly the same way (and so is resilient). On the other hand, individual populations can only be stable if the ecosystem is resilient. Common and Perrings (1992) provide an alternative way of describing the difference between these two concepts: stability is a property that relates to the levels of individual variables within a system (so for example, cod populations in North Atlantic waters would be stable if their numbers returned to prior levels after a brief period of very heavy fishing was brought to an end). Resilience, on the other hand relates to magnitudes of the parameters of an ecosystem: a ecosystem is resilient if parameter values governing the relationships between components of the system tend to remain unchanged following disturbances.

Many ecologists believe that ecosystems possess the property of self-organisation, and will be in a state of equilibrium (at what is called an optimum operating point) if the self-organising forces balance with other environmental forces which are disruptive or disorganising. Such an equilibrium will not usually be unique, as systems will tend to have multiple equilibria. The resilience of a system is measured by its ability to maintain its organisation in the face of disruptive perturbations, without undergoing catastrophic, discontinuous change. Some research points to the claim that resilience tends to be higher the greater is the extent of interconnectedness or complexity of the ecosystem, but there also appear to be many circumstances in which this is not correct.

Let us now relate these ideas to the concept of sustainability. Common and Perrings (1992) define a system as being ecologically sustainable if it is resilient. By implication, therefore, any behaviour which reduces the system's resilience is potentially unsustainable behaviour. Unfortunately, we can not know whether any ecosystem is resilient or not; by the nature of the property, it can only be determined *ex post*. We may be able to observe whether a system was resilient after a disturbance took place, but the best one can do *ex ante* is to make informed guesses whether existing systems would be resilient in the face of future shocks. Uncertainty pervades the behaviour of ecological systems, ensuring that we cannot 'know' *ex ante* whether some system is or is not resilient.

Suppose that one were to accept that ecological sustainability is a good objective to pursue (or that it should be imposed as a constraint on economic behaviour). Then economic affairs should be organised so as to keep to a reasonably low level the likelihood that disturbances alter the system's parameters to a point where resilience of the whole ecosystem is threatened. One task of ecological economics is to identify what kinds of economic activity seem to be consistent with ecological sustainability, and what kinds do not.

For the reasons suggested above, it will never be possible to answer such questions with certainty.

Prudent behaviour, based on informed judgement, may be the best we can do. Some authors have suggested that some indicators are useful as monitoring devices: they can be used to make inferences about potential changes in the degree of resilience of ecosystems in which we are interested. Schaeffer *et al.* (1988) propose a set of indicators including the following ones:

- changes in the number of native species
- changes in standing crop biomass
- changes in mineral micronutrient stocks
- changes in the mechanisms of and capacity for damping oscillations

Suggestive as these and other indicators might be, none can ever be a completely reliable instrument in the sense that a satisfactory rating can be taken as guarantee of resilience. They may, nonetheless, help us to avoid entering the 'critical zone' about which Ciriacy-Wantrup warns (Definition 6, Table 3.1).

Attaining sustainable economic behaviour

Consider the following types of question:

- Is UK economic behaviour sustainable?
- What growth rate of the USA economy is sustainable?
- What policy programme should the EC adopt to ensure that future economic activity is sustainable?

Many people would like to be able to answer questions of this form, which for want of a better term I shall call concrete questions. Can these questions be answered?

Clearly they cannot be answered without knowing what sustainability means. Suppose that we do have a criterion that is unanimously accepted, whether it be one of the five we looked at earlier or any other. Can we answer concrete questions about economic behaviour and sustainability? The answer is that we probably cannot, if for no other reason than the fact that economic/environmental systems are complex entities, subject to random forces, in which prediction is inherently uncertain.

Orthodox economic theory and analysis does not attempt to provide answers to concrete questions; it attempts to provide frameworks in which useful understanding can be gained and applied. This is also true of much environmental economic analysis. Where it is concerned with the issue of sustainability,

Box 3.3 Measuring sustainable development

If sustainable development is to be pursued, it is important that we have the ability to monitor the extent to which such a goal is being attained. This requires, in turn, that a measure of sustainable development (SD) is available. How can such a measure be constructed?

Giles Atkinson and David Pearce have been attempting to develop indicators and measures of SD. The most widely accepted definition of SD, they claim, is economic and social development that increases in *per capita* terms over time. There is, of course, a major problem one confronts at this point: is development to be measured in narrow terms (such as GDP *per capita*) or in broad terms (such as measures of economic or social welfare, possibly

including indices of educational attainment and health status)? Most writers would choose the broader criterion as the relevant measure.

But for Atkinson and Pearce, a more interesting and important question concerns the *conditions* required for achieving SD. They describe two approaches to the identification of these conditions: an economic approach and an ecological approach.

The economic approach

As we explain in the text of this chapter, Pearce has proposed a constant capital stock rule as a criterion for sustainability. An essential condition for sustainability is that a nation's capital stock should not

Table 3.2 Testing for sustainable development

National economy	Test calculation[a]			
	S/Y	$-\delta M/Y$	$-\delta N/Y$	$= Z$
Sustainable economies				
Brazil	20	7	10	+3
Costa Rica	26	3	8	+15
Czechoslovakia	30	10	7	+13
Finland	28	15	2	+11
Germany (pre-unification)	26	12	4	+10
Hungary	26	10	5	+11
Japan	33	14	2	+17
Netherlands	25	10	1	+14
Poland	30	11	3	+10
USA	18	12	3	+3
Zimbabwe	24	10	5	+9
Marginally sustainable				
Mexico	24	12	12	0
Philippines	15	11	4	0
United Kingdom	18	12	6	0
Unsustainable				
Burkina Faso	2	1	10	−9
Ethiopia	3	1	9	−7
Indonesia	20	5	17	−2
Madagascar	8	1	16	−9
Malawi	8	7	4	−3
Mali	−4	4	6	−14
Nigeria	15	3	17	−5
Papua New Guinea	15	9	7	−1

[a] An economy is sustainable if it saves more than the depreciation on its man-made and natural capital, i.e. $Z \geq 0$

    S = Gross Domestic Savings
    Y = Gross Domestic Product
    δM = Value of depreciation of man-made capital
    δN = Value of depreciation of natural capital
    Z = Sustainability Index

Source: Atkinson and Pearce (1993), page 3.

Box 3.3 Continued

decline over time. The concept of capital Pearce has in mind is a very broad one, including physical, human and natural capital. In a world in which the population level is changing, we might wish to amend the rule to one in which the nation's stock of capital *in per capita terms* is non-declining.

The constant capital stock rule has two variants. *Weak sustainability* is achieved when the total capital stock — physical, human and natural — is non-declining through time. In this variant, development is sustainable even if some component (such as natural capital) is declining, provided the total capital stock is not falling. For this to be a meaningful criterion (on its own terms), it is necessary that different elements of the capital stock are substitutes for one another. An example of substitutability of this sort would be if the loss of a particular ecosystem is compensated for by an increase in the stock of human knowledge. By 'compensated for', one presumably means that the environmental and economic losses due to the former are more than outweighed by environmental and economic benefits from the latter, and that the overall system stability and resilience does not suffer in the process.

The second variant — strong sustainability — affords environmental (or natural) capital a special place. SD is attained, in a strong sense, if the nation's stock of environmental capital is non-decreasing. Atkinson and Pearce point out that one may wish to modify this; some part of the capital stock is likely to be of particular importance, providing valuable and non-substitutable environmental services to the economic process. If we call this critical natural capital, then the modified version of strong SD requires that

development does not lead to a decline through time of a nation's stock of critical natural capital.

Table 3.2, reproduced from Atkinson and Pearce (1993), shows the results of a simple test for weak sustainability. The test statistic measures the nation's savings less the depreciation of man-made and natural capital, each expressed as a proportion of Gross Domestic Product (Y). The resulting number, Z, constitutes a measure of SD. If Z is positive, development is sustainable; if Z is negative, development is not sustainable.

The authors are able to obtain this index for 22 economies, but urge caution in the degree of reliance that should be placed on the index. They argue that

... even on a weak rule many countries are unlikely to pass a sustainability test.

Ecological approaches

A second approach to defining a criterion of SD is to use ecological indicators. One might define an economy–environment system as being sustainable if it is resilient to a wide variety of shocks and stresses. Given this, a SD measure should take the form of some indicator of resilience. This is likely, however, to be difficult to construct in practice. Alternatively, if resilience is a function of the degrees of complexity and diversity of an ecosystem, one might develop indirect measures of resilience (and hence of sustainability) using indicators of a system's complexity and/or diversity. Conway (1992) has developed and applied a variety of such indicators, with promising results.

Source: Atkinson and Pearce (1993).

it proceeds by adopting some criterion of sustainability, and then trying to deduce the conditions under which that criterion could be satisfied. Exercises in analysis of this form are difficult to do unless one works with quite simple, aggregate models, in which a set of simplifying assumptions are made. It should be evident that the methodology of this form of economic analysis means that it cannot give answers to what we have called concrete questions. However, it does provide us with frameworks in which we can gain useful insight about matters that are of interest to us.

The Hartwick rule

The Sollow–Hartwick analysis of the conditions required for economic behaviour to be sustainable

is one example of an abstract economic analysis firmly within this tradition. Hartwick's sustainability criterion, as we have seen, is that of non-declining consumption. He proceeds by characterising the economy and the technological relationships governing production in a very simple way. The emphasis throughout his analysis is on the substitution possibilities between different productive inputs. Hartwick is able to use his model to deduce a particular condition – the Hartwick rule – which, if satisfied, would in the simple economy he has characterised be a sufficient condition for sustainability to be attainable. Appendix 1 proves that constant consumption through time is possible in an economy extracting and using a non-renewable resource if the Hartwick saving rule is followed.

Before we discuss the rule itself, let us follow through Hartwick's thinking. Suppose that an economy has a fixed quantity of some non-renewable resource, and that recycling is impossible. Consuming this resource directly is the only source of human utility. What is the largest constant rate of consumption of this stock that is feasible over indefinite time? The answer must be zero, because of finiteness of the stock. But next suppose that the resource stock is not consumed directly for consumption, but is an input, together with physical capital, into the production process: the output of this production process can be either consumed or accumulated as capital. Let us now repose the question, but in a slightly different form: What is the largest constant rate of consumption in this economy that is feasible over indefinite time? Hartwick shows that under certain conditions, the answer is no longer zero; some positive amount of consumption can be maintained in perpetuity. What conditions are required to obtain this result?

The first condition concerns substitutability between the exhaustible resource and physical capital: these two inputs must be substitutable for one another in a particular way (to be defined precisely in Chapter 5). Intuitively, the condition requires that as the exhaustible resource is depleted, the physical capital stock is accumulated, and that the latter substitutes for the former in the production process in such a way that output does not diminish.

The second condition is known as the Hartwick rule. This rule states that the rents (the surplus of revenues over production costs) derived from exhaustible resource extraction should be saved and then accumulated entirely in physical capital. Finally, a third condition is required too. One particular extraction programme (that is, the amounts to be extracted at each point in time) must be adopted for the exhaustible resource: it should be extracted according to an *efficient* programme. We shall define and explain exactly what is meant by an efficient programme in Chapters 4 and 5; suffice it to say at the moment that the resource should not be extracted in a wasteful way.

What lies behind Hartwick's result is a very simple idea: whilst exhaustible resources are being depleted, the savings rule implies that a compensating increase in the stock of reproducible resources is taking place. In some sense, therefore, the Hartwick rule ensures that an aggregate measure of capital is being maintained at a constant level.

Unfortunately, very strong assumptions are required for the validity of this rule, including as we

have seen the requirement that the resource is extracted efficiently over time and that sufficient substitutability exists between exhaustible resources and capital. Since not all of these conditions will be met in practice, one might argue that the practical usefulness of this rule is close to zero. However, for the reasons we discussed earlier, this is not a fair way in which to appraise the value of this model. On the contrary, its value lies in disciplining us to think in terms of the important roles that substitutability and technology play. We discuss some of the extensions that can be made to the Sollow–Hartwick model in Chapter 5, in which the model is examined more formally.

What implications for actual practice, if any, follow from the Sollow–Hartwick model? The first thing to note is that there is no guarantee that following the Hartwick rule will ensure that consumption will not decline over time, because the actual economy is not identical to the economy in Hartwick's model. However, there are very good grounds for believing that if the rule were adopted, sustainable outcomes would be more likely than if the rule were not adopted. It does make sense to argue that as the exhaustible resource is depleted, the physical capital stock should be accumulated to compensate for the diminishing exhaustible resource base. If we do not do this, then future consumption is more likely to fall as the stock of productive assets declines.

How could the Hartwick rule be implemented? Hartwick shows that the required level of accumulation of physical capital would only be forthcoming in a market economy if all decision makers used a particular socially-optimal discount rate. As this will almost certainly not happen in any market economy, another mechanism would be required. To bring forth the optimal amount of savings over time, Hartwick argues that government could tax resource rents, and invest the proceeds in physical capital.

Sustainability at the level of firms and consumers

What roles can be played by individual firms and consumers in a programme seeking economic and ecological sustainability? One might begin answering this question by identifying forms of behaviour that a sustainability criterion would imply or prohibit. If it were possible to obtain an answer, the next step would entail deciding how business and consumer behaviour could be brought into consistency with this. It is fairly easy to make some headway by listing certain standards of *environmentally responsible* behaviour. Presumably, at the very least, the release of non-degradable and highly toxic wastes into the environment would be prohibited if a sustainability objective were to be adopted. But in more general cases, where pollutants are neither permanently lived nor catastrophically damaging, there remains the very awkward matter of deciding upon the degree to which behavioural adjustments should take place. Consideration of possible ways in which one might try to answer this is the main objective of Chapter 8.

At the present level of knowledge, we simply do not know how much change is required in order for economic activity to be sustainable. There is general agreement among environmental scientists that some change is required if major ecosystem disruptions are not to take place – and many are convinced that the required changes are large. On the other hand, as we show in Chapter 8, it is almost certainly wrong to argue that any pollution abatement programme should be undertaken to the maximum extent that is technically feasible. It may well be sensible to move gradually in a direction towards sustainability, rather than attempting to attain such a goal directly.

Towards sustainability

The prospects for sustainable development will be enhanced if pollution flows are reduced, recycling is encouraged, and more attention is given to the regulation, management and disposal of waste. Indeed, any action of this kind represents a move towards sustainability. How can this be achieved? One school of thought argues that information is of central importance. Businesses sometimes seem able to increase profitability by behaving in environmentally friendly ways, and consumers sometimes appear to give preference to sellers with good environmental credentials. It is easy to find examples to support such claims. Consider the Dow Chemical Corporation: this organisation, by refining its method of synthesising agricultural chemicals at its Pittsburg (California) plant, reduced its demand for a key reactant by 80%, eliminated 1000 tons of waste annually, and reduced costs by $8 million per year (Schmidheiny, 1992, page 268). Much has also been made of the power that the green consumer can have in altering producer behaviour (see Smart, 1992, for one examination).

Proponents of the view that self-interest will stimulate environmentally friendly behaviour sometimes argue that the potential of this is limited only by the amount of relevant information that consumers and producers possess. Environmental problems reflect ignorance; if that ignorance were to be overcome by improving the quality of information flows, much progress could be made towards sustainable economic behaviour.

An interesting example of the role that can be played by information is given by the US Toxics Release Inventory (TRI). In 1986, the US government enacted legislation which required businesses to quantify their emissions of any of the 313 toxic substances covered by the Toxics Release Inventory. The public exhibition of this information, no doubt linked with fears of possible future control, has served as a powerful incentive on firms to revise their production processes, and many large firms have voluntarily committed themselves to very demanding clean-up targets. Similar disclosure schemes are planned or are in operation in the European Community, Canada, Australia and India (Sarokin, 1992; WWF, 1993; *Business Week*, 1991).

There is clearly merit in these arguments, but it is difficult to believe that purely self-interested voluntary behaviour will succeed in moving economies very far towards sustainability targets, unless additional incentives are provided or threatened to steer that behaviour in an appropriate direction. Attempts to show that 'green' behaviour can be privately profitable tend to rely on evidence that is both anecdotal and selective. As we show repeatedly in later chapters, there are strong grounds for believing that, in the absence of policy interventions, financial incentives typically work in the opposite direction: environmentally responsible behaviour is costly, individuals have incentives to pass costs onto others and it is often in the interests of individual resource harvesters to maximise current rates of harvest rather than to manage the resource on a sustainable basis. The fishing industry throughout the world provides one clear example of the last-mentioned point.

Financial incentives can have dramatic effects on corporate behaviour, but there may be a need for government to manipulate these incentives to achieve desired targets. Sometimes the perceived threat of penalties if action is not privately forthcoming can be sufficient to modify business behaviour. An important tool that government has is the announcement of targets to be achieved and timetables for the

Box 3.4 The European Commission Fifth Environmental Action Programme, 1992

In March 1992, the European Commission adopted its fifth environmental action programme entitled 'Towards Sustainability'. The four previous environmental programmes were predominantly reactive, responding to problems after they had occurred. Towards Sustainability differs in being proactive rather than reactive. The programme, intended to run until the year 2000, is firmly centred around the twin concepts of sustainable development, as proposed by the 1987 Brundtland Report, and precautionary action. The Commission argues that the full benefits of growth in the European Community's (EC) internal market may not be attainable if acceptable environmental standards are breached.

The programme is contained in three documents:

Volume I: Proposal for a Community Programme of policy and action in relation to the environment and sustainable development.

Volume II: 'Towards Sustainability' – the Programme's suggestions for action.

Volume III: An overview of the state of the environment in the EC. Volume III is itself in three parts. The first deals with the state of air, water, soil, waste, quality of life, high risk activities and biological diversity in Europe. Part 2 looks at the causes of environmental degradation in five targeted areas. The final part is an economic appraisal of environmental damage and control. We shall focus on the second volume of the programme, containing the actions that the European Commission recommends for adoption by the Council of Ministers.

The programme strategy

The main goals of the programme are to raise public awareness of environmental issues, and to change attitudes and behaviour to become more environmentally friendly. Three main sets of actors are identified: public authorities (at both national and local government levels) which bear the main responsibility for creating appropriate legislative and administrative control frameworks, public and private enterprises in their roles as consumers of materials and producers of waste, and the general public in its role as consumer of goods and producer of waste.

The programme has selected a number of economic sectors as targets for the focus of the programme's action. These target sectors are

- Industry
- Energy
- Transport
- Agriculture
- Tourism

It is interesting to note that the target sectors identified for EC action are virtually identical to those identified for special attention by the Dutch government in its National Environmental Policy Programme (see Case Study 1).

Industry: The main thrust of the programme with respect to industry is the establishment of *standards* for production processes and products. As we shall see in Chapter 9, economists have typically argued that standards (or other forms of direct regulation) are not cost-efficient instruments for pollution control. However, the European Community is not yet in a position to adopt fiscal control measures at the European level, and the Commission believes that if standards enforce the adoption of state-of-the-art technology, European business will gain a competitive edge in world markets. This presumption may well be too optimistic, however, and it is by no means certain that required standards will result in the adoption of least cost technology. Case Study 1 suggests that many in the Netherlands fear the opposite – strict environmental control measures are often extremely expensive, and if adopted unilaterally could harm the Netherlands' competitive position in international trade.

Energy: The main objective is to reduce energy demand, and so to lower emissions of gases which contribute to the greenhouse effect and acid rain. The Commission hopes to tackle this by means of taxes on the carbon used in energy production; however, proposals for a carbon tax have not been accepted by the European Council of Ministers.

Transport: Forecasts of rapidly rising traffic volume in the medium-term future suggest that the Commission's goal of reducing transport demand will be very difficult to achieve. The Commission can do little more at the moment than to suggest a coherent programme of measures, based around road pricing, higher fuel prices, investment in public transport and the promotion of research that seeks to raise fuel efficiency and produce cleaner fuels. These are, indeed, the main elements of its transport strategy.

Agriculture: Ironically, the success of the EC's Common Agricultural Programme (in terms of increasing food output) has come at the expense of severe negative environmental damage, as we explain in Case Study 1. Agriculture contributes to a disproportionately large and growing proportion of

Box 3.4 Continued

total harmful pollution within the EC countries. The Commissions's goals include strict controls over the use of fertilisers, pesticides and herbicides, and improved management of manure. Financial incentives to encourage environmentally-friendly farming practices are the principal instrument sought by the Commission.

Tourism: The environmental degradation associated with tourism activities is very acute in some European regions, in particular the Mediterranean coast and the Alpine zones. Proposals for minimising this impact include the use of stricter planning standards, influencing tourist behaviour and promoting forms of tourism that have little environmental impact.

In addition to the particular target areas selected by the Commission, the programme identifies a wide variety of other environmental objectives, and proposes appropriate policy measures for each of these. The objectives include:

- reduction of greenhouse gas emissions
- reduction of pollutant flows contributing to acidification and air quality deterioration
- preservation of nature and biodiversity
- management of water resources

- improving the quality of the urban environment
- coastal zone protection
- improved waste management
- prevention of environmental risks

Instruments of Environmental Policy

The Commission recognises that legislative measures will continue to be the principal form of environmental control at the EC level. However, an important part of the fifth Environmental Action Programme is the advocacy of a broader set of instruments. Six instruments are specifically advocated in the report:

1 Higher quality environmental data.
2 Scientific research and technological development.
3 Integrated sectoral and spatial planning.
4 Integrating true environmental costs and risks into all economic activity.
5 Informing, and involving in the processes of environmental protection, the general public.
6 Informing, and involving in corporate decision making, the workforces in the private and public sectors.

Source: EC (1992).

---

implementation of various stages of the programme. If government timetables are seen as credible, businesses will often act proactively rather than reactively, as the costs of planned, gradual adjustments are lower than those of enforced, rapid change. One important case in point concerns the distinction between the reduction of waste or pollution at source, as compared with the more conventional 'end-of-pipe' treatment.

Because of lower adjustment costs, there are important economic gains to be got from such announced programmes, particularly when firms are engaged in partnerships with government in the details of programme design. The Case Study at the end of this chapter shows how the Dutch environmental policy planners hope to secure these gains from preannounced programmes.

Let us now turn our attention to the relationship between firms' internal accounting procedures and the structure of incentives facing firms. Many firms appear to have very poor procedures for recording quantities of waste flows, where they originate, how much cost is associated with waste controls and where these costs can be attributed. More generally,

environmental impacts and the costs of environmental management within firms are not usually adequately represented in a cost-accounting framework. Similarly, when legislative or administrative controls impose costs of environmental control on firms, these costs are not usually attributed to particular production processes, and are treated as general environmental management expenses. This tends to hide the true costs of particular products and processes from managers, and undervalues the benefits to the firm of pollution control programmes. The implication of this is that firms should be encouraged to develop cost-accounting procedures so that pollution control costs and benefits can be evaluated at the level of individual products and processes within the firm. Not only will this create correct signals for resource allocation decisions within the firm, but it will create a recording framework that will enable the government to more easily and accurately compile national accounts that pay due attention to environmental impacts of economic activity. The final chapter of this book will examine such national accounting procedures.

The pursuit of sustainability can also be helped by encouraging firms to adopt what are sometimes called green design principles. The objective of green design is to minimise the environmental impact of a product though its life cycle without compromising the product's performance or quality. Green design can be assisted by life cycle assessment, a process which attempts to measure the total environmental impact of a product from its conception through to any effects that result from its final disposal (in whole or in parts) to the environment. Government can encourage firms to adopt green design by extending the legal liability of firms to all damages over the life cycle of the products which they sell (see Chapter 9 for a discussion of this policy instrument).

Sustainability at regional, national, local and individual levels

What role can be played in the development and implementation of sustainability strategies by regional or local governments? One would expect that these organisations would have an important contribution to make for the following reason. Modern economies are complex, interrelated systems; the component parts are highly interconnected. Whilst individual units can do much to reduce their environmental impacts, the existence of interconnectedness suggests there are substantial additional gains to be achieved by environmental planning at higher levels. A well-known example which illustrates this point is integrated systems of waste disposal, power generation and district heating. Establishing and implementing such schemes cannot easily be done at the level of individual units, as the decisions cut across institutional boundaries. A substantial literature on this approach – known as industrial ecology – has developed in recent years. It examines systems in terms of the extent to which flows of materials and energy are efficient and sustainable, and tries to identify 'closed loops' in which no net residual flows occur between the system and its environment. The second law of thermodynamics implies that no integrated process can ever be a perfect closed loop, but with careful design it may be possible to approach such a target.

We conclude our brief examination of techniques for moving towards sustainability by mentioning the role of project appraisal. In Chapter 2, it was shown that a conventional criterion for appraising projects is that of social net present value. If a project has a positive social net present value, then it should be implemented. Some writers argue that project appraisal should involve an additional criterion: if a project is to be adopted, not only should it have a positive social net present value, but also it should have no negative net effects on the environment.

This is a very strong pair of conditions indeed, and a strict adherence to the criteria would probably close off most development proposals. Projects might satisfy the criterion if they involve matching benefits, though, and this seems to be one of the features which makes this an attractive idea. Matching benefits refer to proposals whereby a package is proposed in which environmental losses arising from one activity are at least compensated for by environmental benefits from other elements of the package. This concept is related to the notion of sustainability as a non-declining natural capital stock which was examined in the previous section.

Market economies, economic efficiency and sustainability: the limits of economic incentives

As we shall demonstrate in the following two chapters, economists often argue that, given a 'correct' set of prices, economic incentives will bring about outcomes in which pollution flows and environmental damage levels are socially efficient. Strong versions of this argument suggest that the correct set of prices would also bring about outcomes that are sustainable. Advocates of this view do not claim that actual market prices are the correct ones, but suggest that they could be made correct by an appropriate use of tax or subsidy instruments (or by other methods that we shall explore in Chapter 9). At this early stage in the book, insufficient analysis has been undertaken for us to discuss this view in a rigorous way. However, two intuitive arguments lead one to be sceptical about the claim that sustainable outcomes can be attained through markets in which agents respond to correct sets of prices.

The first issue concerns the part played in market processes by future generations. It seems reasonable to argue that if some mechanism were available that enabled all future generations to express preferences and enter into contracts in market, resource allocation decisions would at least have the potential to be sustainable. Unfortunately, no such mechanisms do exist or could ever exist. As yet unborn individuals will participate in markets when they are born, but they do not participate in current markets. However, it is decisions taken currently, whether through markets or otherwise, that will determine whether patterns of activity can be sustained over time. The fact that future generations cannot affect current resource allocation decisions should urge one to be cautious about the claim that a set of prices could be found that would be consistent with sustainable behaviour.

The second caution follows from the way in which market mechanisms take cognisance of ecological considerations. We suggested earlier that sustainability may require that human activity does not impair too strongly the resilience of the biosphere in its present form. Can prices be found that could ever guarantee that resilience is not lost? Our earlier arguments suggest not. It is not possible to know a priori what kinds of behaviour will and will not threaten ecosystem resilience. But if that is not knowable, then there is no set of prices that can guarantee sustainable outcomes either. If we are risk averse, some form of precautionary principle is probably warranted; we should make a presumption that interference with ecosystems is potentially damaging, and hence behave in a more cautious, conservationist way than would be the case otherwise. But this brings one back to the issue of which people constitute 'we'. Given that currently living individuals are those taking decisions, it is at least possible that current generations will behave less cautiously than our descendants would wish.

None of this implies that human society cannot and will not behave in a sustainable way. It does suggest, though, that there are limits to the extent to which the price mechanism alone, adjusted or otherwise, can bring about such an outcome.

Irreversibility and sustainability

In much of economic analysis, it is assumed that resource-use decisions are reversible. If this were true for all resource use decisions, then much of the force behind sustainability arguments would be lost. If we were to discover that present behaviour was unsustainable in some sense, then our decisions could be changed in whatever way and at whatever time was deemed appropriate. Reversibility implies that nothing would have been irretrievably lost.

But reversibility does not apply in all matters of environmental resource use. The most obvious example concerns exhaustible resources. The use of

these is irreversible in the sense that once extracted, that quantity is lost for ever. We might regret initial choices, but some parts of those choices cannot be reversed. Irreversibility is also important in relation to renewable resources. Suppose that a current harvesting rate leads to some stock level falling below a minimum threshold size for species reproduction over time. The species will then become irreversibly extinct.

Finally, another class of irreversibilities concerns decisions to develop wilderness areas or to change the use of some environmental resource system in some significant way. Once 'developed', a wilderness area cannot be returned to its original state, or at least it cannot return to that state in a time scale relevant to human existence. There is a fundamental asymmetry here: a decision not to develop can be reversed, but a decision to develop cannot be reversed. In the latter case, taking the 'develop' option closes off the 'not develop' option for all future periods. These insights were first systematically analysed by Krutilla (1967) and Krutilla and Fisher (1975). They will be explored systematically in Chapter 10 of this volume.

Of course the principle that extractive uses of resources tend to lead to irreversible changes to natural environments, permanently reducing the flow of amenities available from alternative uses of the site, has been known for a long time. As we saw in the first chapter, John Stuart Mill was aware of this in the nineteenth century. In the late nineteenth and early twentieth centuries, the recognition that natural assets are non-producible in human-relevant timescales was one of the principal arguments used by the emerging American conservation movement, and the creation of the system of National Parks in the USA.

Irreversibility itself may not imply the desirability of caution, or a presumption against development. If we are sure of what assets will be available in the future and of the strength of people's preferences in the future, we can judge whether any particular irreversible choice is a good one. But if we do not know these things with certainty, then there are good grounds for keeping options open, behaving in a cautious manner (with a presumption against development built into each choice) and restricting behaviour to that which is sustainable. The logic behind these assertions will be given in Chapter 10. At this point, we ask you to take these fairly general conclusions on trust from us.

CASE STUDY   Sustainable development: the case of the Netherlands

The Netherlands has been one of the first countries to unilaterally adopt a programme of environmental policies that seek to attain sustainable development. During the 40 years until 1985, the Dutch economy experienced a rapid rate of industrial development, transforming the Netherlands into one of the richest nations in the world in terms of *per capita* income. However, this growth success came at the expense of a gravely deteriorating state of the country's environ- ment. By the mid-1980s, the Netherlands had become one of the most heavily polluted of all industrial economies. This was partly a self-inflicted conse- quence of industrial development, with chemical manufacturing, oil refining and intensive agriculture in particular generating very large quantities of hazardous residuals.

But the environmental pollution is also a con- sequence of geographical location, as can be seen from Figure 3.2.

First, the Netherlands is located in the centre of the heavily industrialised areas of northern Europe, being territories subject to transboundary airborne pollution from Britain, Germany, and other European states. The most serious transboundary pollution problems are waterborne. The Netherlands includes the huge delta formed by three major river systems: the Rhine, Meuse and Scheldt. The Rhine basin acts as a receptacle for vast quantities of waste over an area of more than 185,000 square kilometres in five countries. As more than one-third of Dutch drinking water is drawn from the Rhine and Meuse rivers, their heavy pollution poses serious health risks to Netherlanders. The Dutch economy borders the North Sea, one of the most polluted marine areas in the world, acting as it does as a final receptacle for river-borne pollutants from a variety of north European nations, and as a direct waste disposal facility from many sources.

The economic success of the Netherlands has, to a large extent, been dependent on the land reclamation and coastal defence systems that have been imple- mented since medieval times. More than 30% of the country's land area lies below sea level, with over 60% of the population living on reclaimed land. Land reclamation has enabled an intensive agricultural sector to flourish, but this activity is becoming increasingly vulnerable to periodic flood damage. The scale of the damage that can be caused in this way was vividly illustrated in the floods of January 1995.

continued

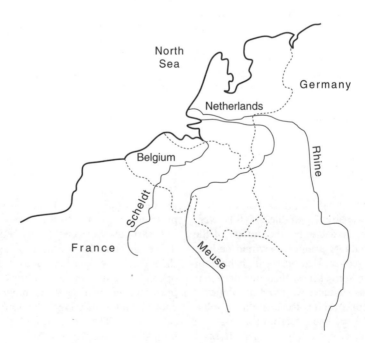

Fig 3.2 The Netherlands: the role of size and location.

CASE STUDY Continued

The impetus for change

In the ten years since 1985, the Netherlands has made remarkable and unprecedented progress towards environmentally and economically sustainable behaviour. The main explanation for this was given in the preceding paragraphs: the Dutch economy had become intolerably dirty. The fact of severe environmental degradation is not, in itself, sufficient to create a political force for drastic environmental policy initiatives; that required the existence of an environmentally conscious electorate in conjunction with a government composed of individuals willing to take the risks inherent in introducing costly control packages. The catalyst to change appears to have been the 1987 Brundtland Report, the framework of which is argued to underpin the Dutch approach to policy. Whatever the particular circumstances were, 1987/88 saw a number of official and academic surveys of the state of the Dutch environment, prognoses for the future, and statements of the appropriate way forward. Queen Beatrix of the Netherlands expressed the Dutch mood in her 1988 Christmas message:

> The Earth is dying slowly, and the inconceivable – the end of life itself – is actually becoming conceivable.

By 1990, the Dutch government had adopted a major environmental programme: the National Environmental Policy Plan (NEPP). It is a mark of the political success of the environmental control lobby in the Netherlands that environmental protection is now ranked equally with full employment and a balanced budget as pre-eminent policy targets.

NEPP – The main themes

Six principles form the basis of NEPP:

1 Environmental problems are interconnected and cannot be tackled effectively on a piecemeal basis.
2 Users of environmental resources should pay for any consequent environmental degradation, and cannot pass on costs to others (now, or in the future, in the Netherlands or elsewhere). The polluters-pay principle is to be interpreted strictly:

continued

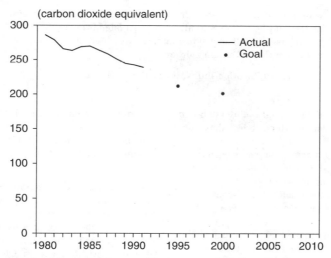

Source: Albert Adriaanse, *Environmental Policy Performance Indicators* (Sdu Uitgeverij Koninginnegracht, The Hague, 1993), pp. 20 and 24.

Note: The Greenhouse Gas Emissions Index was calculated by estimating the emissions of carbon dioxide from fossil fuels, methane – mostly from agricultural activities – nitrogen oxides from combustion processes, and chlorofluorocarbons and halons. These were each weighted by their warming potential compared to carbon dioxide to estimate their carbon dioxide equivalent warming.

Fig 3.3 Greenhouse Gas Emission Index, the Netherlands, 1980–91.

CASE STUDY Continued

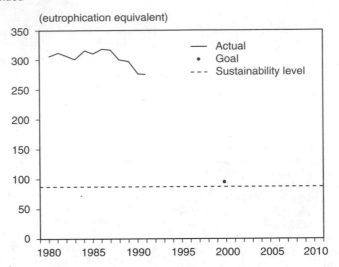

Source: Albert Adriaanse, *Environmental Policy Performance Indicators* (Sdu Uitgeverij Koninginnegracht, The Hague, 1993), pp. 39 and 44.

Note: The Eutrophication Index uses emissions of phosphorus (in the form of phosphate) and nitrogen (calculated from fertiliser and manure use as well as waste dumping), weighted by their natural proportion in the Dutch environment.

Fig 3.4 Eutrophication Index, the Netherlands, 1980–81.

wherever identifiable, individual polluters should pay any clean-up costs to which their behaviour contributes.
3   The basis for environmental control is economic instruments, centred around the use of tax and subsidy to provide appropriate signals and incentives. Traditional 'command-and-control' instruments should be replaced by these fiscal control measures.
4   Environmental policy should be, as far as possible, based on self-regulation and social institutions, rather than being handed down from above. Negotiated covenants between government and business are to play a central role in attaining interim objectives.
5   The principal long-run objective of the environmental control programme is the attainment of sustainable development. SD is defined in terms of three particular targets: consumption of no more energy than can be harnessed from the sun, the treatment of all waste as raw material, and the promotion of high-quality products – products that last, can be repaired, and are recyclable.

6   Medium-term goals, consistent with the long-run objective of SD, and the means of achieving these goals, are to be provided in a four-year environmental plan. The rolling plan is to be revised annually.

Some elements of the programme
NEPP institutes some demanding targets for emissions control. Very large proportionate reductions are called for in the use of energy, water and materials; most emissions are to be reduced to 10–20% of their 1990 levels within 20 years. CFCs are to be phased out entirely by 1998, and greenhouse gas emissions should be below their 1989 levels by the year 2000. Lower materials usage is to be achieved through recycling and integrated life cycle management (see Chapter 9 for more discussion).

The programme is expected to cost the Netherlands government authorities 46 billion dollars over the period 1990–94; to put this in a context which is readily interpretable, this is equivalent to a lump sum tax on each household of $20 per month over the

continued

CASE STUDY Continued

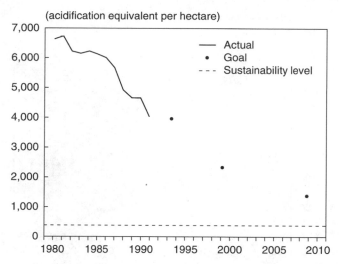

(acidification equivalent per hectare)

— Actual
• Goal
--- Sustainability level

Source: Albert Adriaanse, *Environmental Policy Performance Indicators* (Sdu Uitgeverij Koninginnegracht, The Hague, 1993), pp. 33 and 36.

Note: The Acidification Index was calculated using the three main substances responsible for acid deposition in the Netherlands, sulphur dioxide, nitrogen oxides, and ammonia. The index is the number of acid equivalents deposited per hectare per year (from both domestic and foreign sources) and converts these substances to an acidification equivalent corresponding to 32 grams (g) of sulphur dioxide, 46 g of nitrogen dioxide, and 17 g of ammonia.

Fig 3.5 Acidification Index, the Netherlands, 1980–91.

same period. The major costs of the programme, however – in accord with the polluter pays principle – are to be met by industry. Substantial progress has already been made in controlling a variety of pollutants, as is evident from Figures 3.3–3.6. Nevertheless, the figures also show that longer-term targets are much tighter than the levels of control achieved so far.

Target groups

Agriculture The Netherlands economy contains a highly efficient agricultural sector, with extremely high crop yields supported by inorganic fertiliser, herbicide and pesticide use. Agriculture contributes about 5% to the nation's GDP, but is very important to the Dutch balance of payments, representing about one quarter of her export value. Despite the low share of output for which it accounts, the agricultural sector's share of total pollution rose to 35% in 1992 (from 20% just ten years earlier). Agricultural pollution is a consequence of intensive use of fertilisers, herbicides and pesticides, and the failure of the economy to be able to process animal manures into

benign forms in sufficient quantity. Contamination of water systems by residuals in untreated manure causes eutrophication (the harmful loading of soil and water media with dissolved nutrient matter). This process is harming animal and plant life, reducing the quality of water supplies, and generates feedback effects that reduce crop yields and, ultimately, cattle growth rates. NEPP contains provision for a substantial increase in manure processing capacity. With regard to pesticide use, the Dutch government estimates that of the 21 million kg of active pesticide ingredient applied annually, between 4 and 5 million kg enters air, groundwater and soil media as waste residuals. The Environment Plan provides for a 50% reduction in pesticide use by 2000.

Industry Industrial emissions are the principal form of pollution in the Netherlands, but the early stages of the environmental programme have already achieved much success in reducing industrial

continued

CASE STUDY   Continued

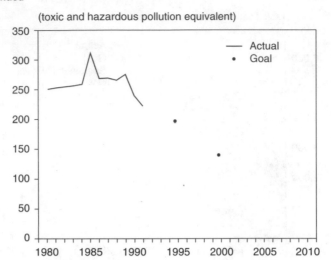

(toxic and hazardous pollution equivalent)

Source: Albert Adriaanse, *Environmental Policy Performance Indicators* (Sdu Uitgeverij Koninginnegracht, The Hague, 1993), pp. 47 and 53.

Note: The Toxic and Hazardous Pollution Index was calculated by using the emissions of the most hazardous substances in three main categories (pesticides, other wastes of high priority, and radioactive substances) weighted according of their toxicity and residence time in the environment.

Fig 3.6 Toxic and Hazardous Pollution Index, the Netherlands, 1980–91.

pollution flows (see Figure 3.4). However, cost-minimising behaviour implies that initial abatement efforts will be focused on the least expensive forms and areas of control; as the overall scale of abatement increases, the marginal cost of pollution reduction will rise, making further control more expensive to the economy than has been the case hitherto.

Transportation Attempts to reduce pollution associated with transport are based upon a threefold approach. Fiscal measures are being implemented to provide economic incentives to reduce fuel demand; regulations will be used to control vehicle use in urban areas; and supply side improvements, together with price incentives, are intended to increase the use of public rather than private transport.

Other elements of NEPP The NEPP places a strong emphasis on attempts to reduce acidification effects associated with energy production, and envisages that the incineration of waste products will play an important role in the provision of energy in the future. The construction sector is expected to modify its choice of methods and materials; more recycled

materials are to be used, and design should incorporate the potential for recyclability. Less use is to be made of non-renewable and tropical region materials. Very demanding targets have been set to reduce the sectors environmental impact. In the consumption sector, separated waste collection systems are gradually being introduced, the composting of biological waste is to be increased, and pricing policy is designed to increase end-use energy efficiency. The retail trade sector is expected to provide sufficient information to enable consumers to make choices which are well informed in terms of their environmental consequences.

Economic costs and political support
To date, NEPP appears to have won widespread support throughout the Netherlands. Business participation and involvement in designing programmes has been important not only in creating corporate support for NEPP, but also on minimising the costs of attaining the standards that have been achieved so far.

But the costs of abatement are large, and are expected to become substantially larger as the target

continued

CASE STUDY   Continued

constraints bite more strongly. Many of the elements in NEPP are being pursued unilaterally by the Nether-lands, or are being taken to higher degrees of control than in other countries. Environmental control does impose real costs, although it also yields real benefits. However, these benefits will not typically be incorpo-rated in the traded output of Dutch business. To the extent that control has this effect, the competitive position of Dutch goods and services in world markets will deteriorate. This is of course a problem that could be

experienced by any single country or group of countries imposing unilateral or regional pollution control pro-grammes. The Netherlands is a small open economy, very dependent on international trade, and with an export portfolio that includes large shares of goods that have adverse environmental impacts (such as agricul-ture and chemicals). The magnitude of this competitive disadvantage could, therefore, be quite large.

Source: World Resources 1994–95, Chapter 14.

Discussion questions

1 Strong sustainability was defined as a process of development through time in which the nation's stock of environmental capital is non-decreasing. Is activity sustainable, however, even if the stocks of other forms of capital are falling through time?
2 To what extent are the ecologist's and the economist's concepts of sustainable behaviour mutually consistent?
3 Discuss the implications for accounting practices at the level of the firm if government seeks to pursue a programme of sustainable economic development.

Problems

1 Suppose Mr Field owns a plot of land which contains an oil well containing 1 million barrels of oil. A local extraction company has offered to extract this oil for Mr Field at $1 per barrel, the best deal he can obtain. The current market price of extracted oil is $3 a barrel, and is expected to stay at that level indefinitely.

   Now suppose that Mr Field decides to extract immediately and sell all the oil on his plot of land.

   (a) How much economic profit (or rent) does Mr Field obtain?
   (b) What is the effect on the GDP of the country in which Mr Fields plot is located?
   (c) What will be the effect of the extraction decision on Mr Field's descendants?
   (d) If Mr Field wished to arrange his affairs so that his descendants were at least as well off as he is, what actions might Mr Field take?
2 With computer economic modelling, Dow Chemical Corporation has been able to cut the

need for a key reactant by 80%, eliminating 1000 metric tonnes of waste per year, and saving $8 million annually (*source: World Resources 1994–95*, page 218).

(a) Has this change been economically efficient?
(b) Has this change contributed to more sustainable economic behaviour?

Further reading

Sustainability and sustainable development

There are many different interpretations of what sustainable development actually involves, and many different views on whether it can be achieved. Redclift (1992) examines a number of the dimensions within which the idea can be explored, as do Pezzey (1992), Barbier and Markandya (1990), Common and Perrings (1992), Common (1995) and Lele (1991). The particular contributions of environmental economists to the debates are well represented by Pearce *et al.* (1989), Pearce (1991a), Common and Perrings (1992), Common (1995), Pezzey (1992) and Toman, *et al.* (1993). More conventional economic contributions to the discussions, in the framework of a neoclassical growth model, are to be found in Solow (1974b, 1986) and Hartwick (1977, 1978). The long-term system implications of economic development and growth are discussed in Boulding (1966) and Daly (1974, 1977, 1987). An interesting assessment of the con-tribution of scientific understanding to the debate is to be found in Ludwig *et al.* (1993). Other good surveys are presented in Barbier (1989a), Klassen and Opschoor (1991) and Markandya and Richardson (1992). The argument that policy should be directed towards maintaining a non-declining natural capital stock is developed in Pearce and Kerry Turner (1990).

Ecological economics

Further discussion of ecological sustainability can be found in Common and Perrings (1992), on which our presentation relies heavily, Common (1995), and various articles in Costanza (1991). Conway (1985) discusses agriculture and ecology. A proposed system of environmental indicators for the UK is presented and discussed in RSPB (1994).

Environmental assessments and profiles

The basic references here are the biennial editions of *World Resources*, and the United Nations Development Report. All of the recent issues of these two periodic publications contain a wealth of environmental data and case study analysis.

Accounting and pollution control at the firm level

Useful additional sources are *World Resources 1994–95*, especially Chapter 12, Hirschborn (1991), EPA (1993), Schmidheiny (1992), Sarokin (1992), WWF (1993) and a *Business Week* special supplement entitled 'Saving the Planet: Environmentally Advantaged Technologies for Economic Growth', 30 December 1991. The role of the green consumer is examined in Smart (1992).

Appendix 1

The Hartwick rule

If all output is either consumed or invested, then from the national income accounting identity we have

$$C_t = f(K_t, R_t) - \dot{K}_1 \tag{3.1}$$

where C is consumption, $f(.)$ is the production function, K is the man-made capital stock, $\dot{K} = dK/dt$ is the rate of change of the capital stock, and R is the rate of extraction and use of the exhaustible environmental resource.

Next, assume that the following two relationships are satisfied:

$$\frac{\dot{f}_R}{f_R} = f_K \tag{3.2}$$

$$\dot{K} = R \cdot f_R \tag{3.3}$$

where $f_R = \partial f/\partial R$ and $f_K = \partial f/\partial K$ are the marginal products of the exhaustible resource and of man-made capital, respectively. Equation 3.2 is Hotelling's efficiency condition for resource extraction, and its interpretation is explained in Chapter 5. For the moment, just take Equation 3.2 to mean that the resource extraction programme is economically efficient. Equation 3.3 is known as the Hartwick rule: it states that the value of resource rents (R, the amount of the resource, times f_R, the net extraction cost return to the resource) should equal the value of new investment in physical (man-made) capital stock. If an economy adheres to the Hartwick rule, it must find some mechanism so that the rents from exhaustible resources are entirely invested in new physical capital.

John Hartwick (1977, 1978) demonstrated that if the Hartwick rule is followed and resources are being extracted efficiently (so that Equation 3.2 is satisfied), then it is possible for the economy to have positive and constant consumption through time. In certain circumstances (that we do not discuss here) this constant consumption can be continued indefinitely, even though an exhaustible resource is being depleted ever more closely to exhaustion. A simple proof is given below.

By differentiating Equations 3.1 and 3.3 with respect to time, one obtains

$$\dot{C}_t = f_K \dot{K} + f_R \dot{R} - \frac{d^2 K}{dt^2} \tag{3.4}$$

$$\frac{d^2 K}{dt^2} = f_R \dot{R} + R \dot{f}_R \tag{3.5}$$

Substituting Equations 3.5 in 3.4 gives

$$\dot{C}_t = f_K \dot{K} + f_R \dot{R} - f_R \dot{R} - R \dot{f}_R \tag{3.6}$$

or

$$\dot{C}_t = f_K \dot{K} - R \dot{f}_R \tag{3.7}$$

Using Equation 3.3 in 3.7 we have

$$\dot{C}_t = f_K R f_R - R \dot{f}_R \tag{3.8}$$

Finally, rearranging Equation 3.2 and substituting in Equation 3.8 we obtain

$$\dot{C}_t = f_K R f_R - f_K f_R R \tag{3.9}$$

and so

$$\dot{C}_t = 0$$

Hence adhering to the Hartwick savings rule allows the economy to have constant consumption over time, provided the exhaustible resource is efficiently extracted (in the particular sense to be explained in Chapter 5).

CHAPTER 4

Welfare economics and the environment

PART 1
Welfare economics: efficiency, optimality and market failure

Introduction

In this chapter, we present, explain, and apply to environmental questions some of the body of economic theory known as welfare economics. This chapter has four main objectives:

1 To define and explain the concept of economic efficiency, and to identify the conditions that must be satisfied if resources are to be used efficiently.
2 To define and explain the concept of an optimal use of resources, and to identify the conditions that must be satisfied if resources are to be used optimally.
3 To analyse the circumstances, if any, under which free market economies will, in the absence of government intervention, allocate resources (a) efficiently and (b) optimally.
4 To identify and explain the circumstances in which markets are likely to fail to allocate resources efficiently.

The approach taken in this chapter involves the use of simple, abstract economic models. In the first part of the chapter, these are analysed to obtain important general results about the efficient and optimal use of resources. The second part of the chapter pays close attention to the special implications that *environmental* resources have for resource use efficiency and optimality.

A few words of warning are required. We shall use algebraic arguments and presentations quite extensively in this chapter. None of the mathematics used is difficult, but it may deter readers who have little confidence in their maths. Please do not be deterred! The material is easily understood, particularly if you adopt the study method of reading the chapter quickly once, followed by a more careful, detailed reading. We advise you to read the Appendices, but none is required for understanding of the main text.

Environmental resources: scarcity and choice

One of the central conclusions reached in Chapter 1 is that the natural environment is a complex system of resource stocks, providing a variety of valuable service flows. For example, stocks of fossil fuels and minerals provide valuable flows of material inputs into the production process; forests and fisheries can be managed to yield sustainable flows of timber and food; wilderness areas yield a large variety of services, including the pleasures of observing unspoilt natural landscapes and the enjoyment of peace and solitude. Environmental resource stocks and flows, therefore, provide benefits to humans in a variety of ways, and so render valuable services. In addition to any value that these resources have to humans, directly or indirectly, one might argue that environmental resources possess intrinsic values. However, in this chapter, we are not concerned with any intrinsic values that they might possess; our only concern here is with the implications that they have for human welfare. The intrinsic values of resources are examined in Chapter 10.

Our second important observation is that environmental resources are available in limited quantities. This is self-evidently true for non-renewable stock resources, such as mineral deposits and fossil fuels. At any point in time, there exists some finite quantity of such resources. Of course, we may not know what this quantity is, and we may not know where these stocks are located. As time goes by, research can, and does, improve our knowledge of these matters. But these considerations do not affect the fact that the resources exist in finite quantities. In the final analysis, therefore, the decision to extract and consume such a resource is irreversible: once extracted, that part of the resource stock is lost forever.

Although the situation is not identical for renewable resources, it remains true that there are finite limits on the quantities that can be harvested in any period of time. Furthermore, if harvesting is persistently above the levels that can be sustained over time, the possibility of the stock irreversibly collapsing to zero arises. These characteristics of renewable resources are explained in Chapter 7. Intuition might suggest that energy flow resources, such as solar radiation or wind energy, are unlimited, but this is misleading. Whilst it may be the case that the energy flow itself is infinite (or is so large that it can be regarded as such), the flow is only useful to the extent that it can be harnessed. A moment's reflection is sufficient to see that this harnessing will require the use, directly or indirectly, of other scarce resources.

Let us pull together the threads of our argument. Environmental resources provide a set of useful, valuable services. However, they are available to us in finite quantities only. Even where the flow is unlimited, it can only be usefully appropriated at the cost of using other scarce resources. Whenever a resource is valuable but is limited in availability, economists refer to the resource as being scarce. To say that a resource is scarce is not to say that there is a shortage of it – although there might well be shortages of resources in some circumstances. The existence of scarcity is important because it implies the inevitability of trade-offs: at the margin, the use of scarce resources in one way precludes the use of those resources in another way.

One of the central tenets of modern environmental economics is the assertion that environmental resources are scarce. In contrast, much behaviour in the past and in the present – by individuals, firms, and governments – appears to be based upon a belief that environmental resources are not limited, that they are inexhaustible 'free gifts of nature'. As we shall see in subsequent chapters, this may well be a perfectly rational position for individual consumers and firms to take. In some cases, the use of these resources is free in a financial sense; there is no economic incentive to

persuade agents to behave in any way other than treating the resources as unlimited or free goods.

Resource scarcity implies the necessity of making choices about how the resources should be allocated among competing uses. At any point in time, there are many uses to which resources could be put, and many different ways in which they could be distributed over individuals and between nations. In addition, choices also relate to the patterns of use over time – the intertemporal allocation of resources. Given that environmental resources are scarce, what requirements could one reasonably expect of any 'sensible' pattern of resource use? We shall discuss two possible requirements:

1 The resource should be used efficiently.
2 The resource should be used optimally.

Our next objective in this chapter is to define and establish the meanings of the concepts of efficiency and optimality. Having done that, we then seek to ascertain what conditions must be satisfied for resource use to be (1) efficient and (2) optimal. The body of analysis known as welfare economics is concerned, among other things, with the conditions which should be satisfied for an allocation of economic resources to be efficient and optimal. In the next two sections of this chapter, we review the main principles and conclusions of welfare economics theory, and indicate how we can apply these to the particular concerns of environmental economics.

Economic efficiency: the efficient allocation of resources

Although we are concerned with environmental resources in this book, it will be convenient to define and discuss the concept of efficiency by thinking about the allocation of resources in general. Let us begin by establishing the meaning of the term 'allocation of resources'. Choose some particular point in time. At this time, there will be available to the economy some particular quantities of a set of environmental and other productive resources. The individuals who make up the economy will have particular preferences for the various goods and services that it is feasible to produce. The productive resources can be used or allocated in many ways, each corresponding to a different configuration of outputs. An allocation of resources can be described by the techniques which are used in production, and the set of outputs that are produced. So much for the production dimensions of the economy. However, there is a second dimension of allocation to consider as well. For any configuration of outputs, there are many ways in which that set of goods and services can be distributed amongst different individuals. The allocation of resources also refers to the particular choice of distribution that is made.

So an allocation of resources will define which goods are produced, which combinations of inputs are used in producing those goods, and how the outputs are distributed between persons. Let us use the term 'static allocation of resources' to refer to the allocation at some single point in time. But this is a rather restrictive interpretation of the concept, as it abstracts from the passage of time. Thus, it is also useful to consider another dimension of resource allocation – allocation over time, otherwise known as the intertemporal allocation of resources. We will investigate both of these dimensions of resource allocation – static and intertemporal – in this text.

Static economic efficiency

Resource allocation choices in practice are intimately tied up with issues relating to time. Time is particularly important, as you will see, when it comes to considering the allocation of environmental resources. However, it is useful to begin by abstracting from time, analysing the allocation of resources between individuals at a given point in time. Therefore, we investigate first the conditions required for an efficient static allocation of resources.

We shall use a simplified and highly abstract model to investigate this matter. The reason why we do this is explained in Box 4.1. Suppose we have an economy in which there is a particular pattern of ownership to *all* resources: what we shall call the initial distribution of property rights, or initial distribution for short. We are not concerned at the moment with whether this initial distribution is just or fair, although we shall return to this matter later.

For this particular initial distribution, an allocation of resources is said to be *efficient* if it is not possible to make one or more persons better off without making at least one other person worse off. Conversely, an allocation is inefficient if it *is* possible to improve someone's position without worsening the position of any other individual. A gain by one or more persons without anyone else suffering is known as a Pareto

improvement (named after the nineteenth century economist Vilfredo Pareto). So the criterion we shall be using is that an efficient allocation is one in which no Pareto improvement is possible. How do we measure whether an individual's position has changed for the better or for the worse? The answer is that this is entirely a matter of the preferences of the individual concerned. I can judge whether a change improves or worsens my utility; you can judge whether a change improves or worsens your utility. However, I cannot judge whether some change improves or worsens your utility, and similarly you cannot know whether a particular change improves or worsens my utility.

What conditions would have to be satisfied in order that an allocation of resources is efficient? To answer this question, we strip the problem down to its barest essentials. Consider an economy in which there are two persons (denoted A and B); two goods (denoted X and Y) are produced; and production of each good uses two inputs (denoted K and L). These productive inputs are available in fixed quantities. We also make a number of other assumptions (which will be explained and illustrated later in this chapter). Firstly, no externalities exist in either consumption or production; roughly speaking, this means that consumption or production activities by any agent do not have uncompensated effects upon any other person's utility. Secondly, both goods are private goods; no public goods exist, and nor do the individuals wish that any be provided.

Let us stress that these assumptions are not intended to be realistic, which they certainly are not. We adopt them simply as a device to enable us to derive some results which are useful, and which can be applied in more realistic and relevant cases subsequently.

Let U denote an individual's total utility or satisfaction. Assume that each person's utility depends only on the quantity that he or she consumes in a particular period of time. Given this, we can write the utility functions for A and B in the form shown in Equation 4.1.

$$U^A = U^A(X^A, Y^A)$$
$$U^B = U^B(X^B, Y^B)$$
(4.1)

The first of these equations states that the total utility enjoyed by individual A (i.e. U^A) depends upon the quantities he or she consumes of good X (X^A) and good Y (Y^A). A comparable statement is being made about individual B's utility.

Box 4.1 Models, abstraction, and their role in economic analysis

In this and subsequent chapters, we shall make extensive use of economic models to develop, explain and illustrate our arguments. The purpose and use of models is sometimes misunderstood, and as a result invalid criticisms are made about their use. What is the nature of an economic model? Why do we use them? What limitations exist on the conclusions drawn from such models?

The essence of an economic model is its abstract quality. In attempting to derive useful conclusions about some matter of economic interest, the modeller proceeds from the premise that useful answers must be general ones; they should not be applicable only to a unique configuration of actual circumstances (including all of the institutional characteristics pertaining to a particular place at a particular time). It is not, then, likely to be useful to address important questions starting from a particular real situation, in which all of the features of that situation are specified.

Instead, the modeller attempts to identify the most fundamental forces and relationships in this and other similar circumstances. Often, this is done by describing these relationships in stylised, simplified forms, which are amenable to qualitative or quantitative forms of mathematical analysis. We then try to deduce conclusions by logical deduction. An economic model is, then, an abstract, stylised representation of what the modeller believes to be the essential relationships operating in some (more or less wide) set of circumstances. Economic conclusions emerge by logical deduction from such a model.

Two features of this process are of fundamental importance:

1 The modeller may fail to identify 'the most fundamental forces and relationships in this and other similar circumstances'.
2 Perhaps more importantly, the questions for which the researcher seeks general answers will determine the nature of the relationships chosen as components of the model, and how these relationships are specified and represented. Models may differ substantially in their nature not just because they are referring to different

situations, but also because they are trying to understand and answer different questions about the same situation. The production functions we employ in this book, for example, include natural resources as an input, but do not attempt to introduce any disaggregation of 'capital' or 'labour'. This arises because we are particularly interested in the long-term consequences of economic growth in the presence of exhaustible natural resources. On the other hand, the time frame within which macro-modellers work, and their particular interests, might lead them to ignore exhaustible resources as an input in the production function, but to model capital in a far more rich and complex way than we do.

It would be inappropriate to claim that either of these two schemas is 'wrong' because it is simplified. Each may be a perfectly satisfactory starting point for addressing different questions of interest. Similarly, in this chapter, we shall consider an economy consisting of just two consumers. Clearly, our model economy is 'unrealistic' in a variety of ways. For example, the UK economy contains around 60 million consumers, and it seems unlikely that any actual economy consists of just two people. But this is to miss the point of abstraction; a model that assumes the existence of two consumers is useful if the conclusions can be easily generalised to any positive finite number (say n), and if the conclusions reached in the two-person case are not different in kind from those in the n-person case.

There are limitations in all this, however. The conclusions we draw will be valid for a given set of assumptions. They may or may not be valid if these assumptions do not hold. It is wrong to argue that conclusions drawn from a model will be true in specific real situations. In the final analysis, it is impossible to obtain results which have such power. Theorising and model building may, perhaps, be useful to us primarily through the discipline it imposes on us when we seek to understand issues. It may help to focus our attention on what information would be required to answer a question. It probably cannot provide definitive answers to questions themselves.

Next, we suppose that the quantity produced of good X depends only on the quantities of the two inputs K and L used in producing X, and that the quantity produced of good Y depends only on the quantities of the two inputs K and L used in producing Y. Thus, we can write the two production functions in the form shown in

Equation 4.2.

$$X = X(K^X, L^X)$$
$$X = Y(K^X, L^X)$$
(4.2)

Note carefully that Equations 4.1 and 4.2 embody our assumptions that there are no externalities in consumption or production. This is explained in Problem 1. Finally, let us establish some additional notation that shall be used throughout this chapter. The marginal utility that A derives from the consumption of good X is denoted U_X^A ; that is, $U_X^A = \partial U^A / \partial X^A$. The marginal product of the input L in the production of good Y is denoted as MP_L^Y ; that is, $MP_L^Y = \partial Y / \partial L^Y$. Equivalent notation applies for the other three other marginal utilities and the three other marginal products. We are now in a position to state and explain three conditions that must be satisfied if resources are to be allocated efficiently.

Efficiency in consumption

Consumption efficiency requires that the ratios of the marginal utilities of goods X and Y are the same for each consumer. That is

$$\left(\frac{U_X}{U_Y}\right)^A = \left(\frac{U_X}{U_Y}\right)^B \qquad (4.3)$$

If this condition is not met, then the two consumers can exchange commodities at the margin in such a way that both gain (and so neither suffers). For example, suppose that the ratios of marginal utilities were as follows:

$$\left(\frac{6}{3}\right)^A = \left(\frac{2}{4}\right)^B \qquad (4.4)$$

A values X twice as highly as Y at the margin, whereas B values X at only half the value of Y. Clearly, if A exchanged one unit of Y for one unit of X from B, both would gain. Individual A would obtain a net utility gain of 3 by giving up 3 units of utility on the marginal unit of Y but gaining 6 units of utility from the additional unit of X. By similar reasoning, individual B would obtain two units of additional utility. A Pareto improvement is possible, therefore, and so the initial position could not have been efficient. The only situation in which a mutually beneficial gain would not be possible is that in which the ratios of marginal utilities are equal.

Efficiency in production

Now turn your attention to the production side of the economy. Recall that we are considering an economy with two inputs, L and K, which can be combined (via the production functions of Equations 4.2 to produce the two goods X and Y. Efficiency in production

requires that the ratio of the marginal product of each input be identical in the production of both goods. That is

$$\left(\frac{MP_L}{MP_K}\right)^X = \left(\frac{MP_L}{MP_K}\right)^Y \qquad (4.5)$$

If this condition is not satisfied, it would be possible for producers to exchange some K for some L so that the total production of both goods would be increased from the same total volume of inputs. If the output of both goods can be increased, then a Pareto improvement must be possible.

Product-mix efficiency

The final condition which is necessary for economic efficiency is 'product-mix efficiency'. Unfortunately, it is less easy to gain an intuitive understanding of this condition than it is for consumption and production efficiency. Product-mix efficiency requires that

$$\left(\frac{U_X}{U_Y}\right) = \left(\frac{MP_K^Y}{MP_K^X}\right) \qquad (4.6)$$

How can this equality be explained? The term on the left-hand side is the ratio of the marginal utilities of goods X and Y. We have omitted specifying to which person this refers, as from Equation 4.3 the ratio will be the same for both individuals, if an allocation is efficient. The left-hand side term can be interpreted as the relative marginal valuation put on the two goods by all consumers; it gives the terms at which consumers are willing to trade Y for X at the margin. The term on the right-hand side of Equation 4.6 is the ratio of the marginal products of capital in the production of the two goods, Y and X. It indicates the rate at which units of Y are sacrificed for units of X, in using the scarce resource, capital. Hence, the product-mix efficiency condition requires that there be an equality of the rate at which consumers value one good in terms of another with the opportunity costs of one good in terms of the other. If this condition were not satisfied, inputs could be reallocated in such a way that a higher total utility could be achieved by each consumer for any given initial level of inputs, and so a Pareto improvement would be possible (see Problem 2).

Note also that by rearranging Equation 4.5 to yield

$$\left(\frac{MP_K^Y}{MP_K^X}\right) = \left(\frac{MP_L^Y}{MP_L^X}\right) \qquad (4.7)$$

the condition of Equation 4.6 can be written more completely as:

$$\left(\frac{U_X}{U_Y}\right) = \left(\frac{MP_K^Y}{MP_K^X}\right) = \left(\frac{MP_L^Y}{MP_L^X}\right) \qquad (4.8)$$

An economy attains a fully efficient static allocation of resources if conditions 4.3, 4.5 and 4.8 are satisfied simultaneously. Although we have stated these results for the special case of a two-good, two-person, two-input economy, the results generalise to economies with many inputs, goods and individuals. The only difference will be that rather than there being just one equality for each of the three efficiency conditions, these equalities have to hold for each possible pairwise comparison that one could make.

The non-uniqueness of efficient allocations

In general, there will not be a unique efficient static allocation of resources in an economy. On the contrary, there will be many efficient allocations that are feasible. To understand this result intuitively, recall that we have been discussing an economy in which there was one particular initial distribution of property rights. Now, if one knew what this initial distribution actually was, and one knew all the relevant utility and production functions, it would be possible to mathematically solve for the efficient allocation of resources in this particular case. The solution would specify what quantities of goods are produced, how the inputs were allocated between different products, and what quantities of goods each individual would receive.

Now consider a case where everything remains the same except for one thing: the initial distribution of property rights is different. It should be clear that if one were to repeat the above exercise, a different efficient allocation would result. Different quantities of goods would be produced, inputs would be allocated in another way, and the quantities of goods that each person receives would vary from the first case. More precisely, it can be shown (although we shall not provide a proof) that if all utility and production functions are 'well-behaved' (that is, they are smooth continuous functions that satisfy standard assumptions regarding their curvatures), there will be a unique efficient allocation corresponding to every possible initial distribution of property rights.

If we restrict attention to the two-person special case, once again, we can represent this idea using the concept of the *Grand Utility Possibility Frontier*, illustrated in Figure 4.1. As the shape of this curve will depend upon the particular forms of the utility and production functions which underlie it, the way in which the grand utility possibility frontier is represented in Figure 4.1 is merely indicative of one possibility. However, in conventional circumstances, one would expect the frontier to be generally bowed outwards in the manner shown. Each point on this frontier is an efficient allocation of resources, satisfying the three necessary conditions. If an economy were to allocate resources efficiently, the position an economy takes on this frontier (and so the distribution of total utility between consumers) depends upon the initial distribution of property rights to the productive resources. There are clearly an infinite number of efficient allocations. Moreover, each point describes a particular pair of utility levels enjoyed by the two individuals. Note also one other implication of this line of reasoning; if one were able, somehow or other, to decide which position *should* be chosen on this frontier, this decision would then imply how property rights should be distributed.

Is it possible though, using the information shown in Figure 4.1, to say which of the points on this frontier is best from the point of view of society? The answer is that it is not possible, for the very simple reason that the criterion of economic efficiency does not give one any basis for making interpersonal

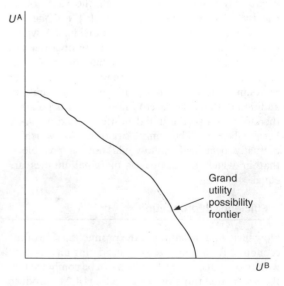

Fig 4.1 The Grand Utility Possibility Frontier.

Box 4.2 Productive inefficiency in ocean fisheries

The total world marine fish catch has increased steadily since the 1950s, rising by 32% between the periods 1976–78 and 1986–88 (UNEP, 1991). However, the early 1990s have witnessed downturns in global harvests, although it is not yet clear whether this is indicative of longer-term trends. The steady increase in total catch until 1989, however, masked significant changes in the composition of that catch; as larger, higher-valued stocks became depleted, effort was redirected to smaller-sized and lower-valued species. This does sometimes allow depleted stocks to recover, as happened with North Atlantic herring which recovered in the mid-1980s after being overfished in the late 1970s. However, many fishery scientists believe that these cycles of recovery have been modified, and that species dominance has shifted permanently towards smaller species.

So rising catch levels have put great pressure on some fisheries, particularly those in coastal areas, but also including some pelagic fisheries. Among the species whose catch has declined over the period 1976 to 1988 are Atlantic cod, haddock, Atlantic herring, South African pilchard and Peruvian anchovy. Falls in catches of these species have been compensated for by much increased harvests of other species, including Japanese pilchard in the north-west Pacific, but it is widely agreed that the prospects of the total catch rising in the future are now very remote (*World Resources 1992–93*).

Where do inefficiencies enter into this picture? We can answer this question in two ways. Firstly, a strong argument can be made to the effect that the total amount of resources devote to marine fishing is excessive, probably massively so. We shall defer giving evidence to support this claim until Chapter 7 (on renewable resources), but you will see there that a smaller total fishing fleet would be able to catch at least as many fish as the present fleet does; furthermore, if fishing effort were temporarily reduced so that stocks were allowed to recover, a greater steady-state harvest would be possible, even with a far smaller world fleet of fishing vessels. There is clearly an intertemporal inefficiency here.

A second insight into inefficiency in marine fishing can be gained by recognising that two important forms of negative external effect operate in marine fisheries, both largely attributable to the fact that marine fisheries are predominantly open-access resources. One type is a so-called crowding externality, arising from the fact that each boat's harvesting effort increases the fishing costs that others must bear. The second type may be called an intertemporal externality: as fisheries are subject to often very weak (or even zero) access restrictions, no individual fishermen has an incentive to conserve stocks for the future, even if all would benefit if the decision were taken jointly.

As the concepts of externalities and open access will be explained and analysed in the second part of this chapter, and applied to fisheries in Chapter 7, we shall not explain these ideas any further now. Suffice it to say that production in market economies will, in general, be inefficient in the presence of external effects.

---

comparisons. Put another way, efficiency carries no ethical content, and so gives us no criterion to say which allocation is best from a social point of view.[1]

The social welfare function and optimality

Any attempt to discuss the well-being or welfare of a society requires that some ethical criterion be adopted. You saw in Chapter 2 that one way in which we might incorporate such a criterion into economic analysis is through the device of a social welfare function (SWF). We shall not discuss here what form such a function might take, as that was investigated in Chapter 2. The social welfare function will be of the general form

$$W = W(U^A, U^B) \qquad (4.9)$$

where W denotes social welfare. This states that social

---

[1] There is, perhaps, a weak ethical principle underpinning the concept of Pareto efficiency. Since a Pareto improvement corresponds to some gaining with none losing, a judgement is being made that more is better than less. Many economists regard this principle as being self-evidently correct. However, not everyone accepts this premise. Consider, for example, the claim that State A is superior to State B if no person is worse off (in terms of his or her own preferences) in State A, but at least one person is better off in State A. But one might argue instead that equality is an ethically desirable principle. Suppose that State B is one in which equality exists, but State A is not. On the ethical grounds of equality, one might challenge the claim that State A is superior. Other arguments that challenge the validity of the efficiency criterion for comparing outcomes are to be found in the writings of Daly and Boulding, discussed in previous chapters. Furthermore, many ecologists would, in some sense, regard 'less' as being better than 'more' when it comes to economic activity.

welfare depends in some deterministic (but as yet unspecified) way on the levels of total utility enjoyed by each person in the relevant community. The only assumptions we make at this point regarding the social welfare function are that one exists, and that it is non-declining in U^A and U^B. In other words, for any given level of U^A, welfare cannot decrease if U^B were to rise.

Once we are armed with the tool of a social welfare function, we are in a position to identify a socially optimal outcome, or just an optimal outcome for short. The social welfare function gives one a criterion that enables interpersonal comparisons to be made. Put another way, it will permit one to rank particular distributions of utility along the utility possibility frontier in (UPF) terms of the level of social welfare that would be attained.

It seems natural to argue that the optimal allocation of resources is the one at which social welfare, W, is at its highest level. The problem we are considering is a familiar one of constrained optimisation, and is illustrated in Figure 4.2. The curves labelled W_1, W_2 and W_3 are social welfare indifference curves. Each one is constructed to represent combinations of individual utilities that yield a constant level of social welfare. The social welfare maximum is attained at point z, where social welfare is W_2 and the utility levels enjoyed by each person are U^{*A} and U^{*B} respectively.

Not surprisingly, it is a necessary condition for a welfare maximum that resources are allocated efficiently. Given our assumption that 'more is better', society cannot be in the best position possible if resources are not efficiently used. As a result, conditions 4.3, 4.5 and 4.8 will be satisfied simultaneously at the welfare optimum. However, maximised welfare implies an additional necessary condition:

$$\left(\frac{U_X^B}{U_Y^A}\right) = \left(\frac{W_{U^A}}{W_{U^B}}\right) \qquad (4.10)$$

This implies that it is not possible to increase social welfare by transferring consumption goods between persons. To see that this is so, note that the left-hand side of this equality is the slope of the utility possibility frontier; the right-hand side term is the slope of the social welfare indifference curve. At a social welfare maximum, these slopes must be equal.

An example may help in understanding this conclusion. Consider the point labelled Ω in Figure 4.2. Imagine that goods were exchanged between the two individuals in such a way that B's utility falls

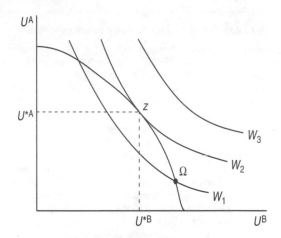

z = Maximised social welfare ('Constrained bliss')

Fig 4.2 Maximised social welfare.

and A's utility rises. The economy would move upwards and to the left along the utility possibility frontier. But in so doing, the economy can move onto a higher social welfare indifference, and so social welfare would rise. The only circumstance where this is not possible is where the slope of the SWF is identical to that of the UPF. Then, small movements along the UPF would be equivalent to movements along a SWF indifference curve, and not movements between indifference curves. We can also think about this numerically. At the point Ω, the slope of the social welfare function (SWF) is lower than the slope of the utility possibility frontier (UPF) in absolute terms. Suppose that the slope of SWF is $-1/1$, and the slope of the UPF is $-2/1$. The latter ratio implies that if B gave up sufficient goods for his or her utility to fall by 1, A's utility would rise by 2. However, the slope of the SWF tells us that if A's utility fell by 1, it would only be necessary for B's utility to rise by 1 if social welfare is to remain constant. As B's utility would in fact rise by 2, this would imply an increase in welfare.

Intertemporal economic efficiency

As much of the content of environmental economics concerns decision-making over time, we must now generalise our analysis to take account of this dimension of economic behaviour. Decisions taken today have implications for the consumption and production possibilities available in the future. When making decisions about the use of resources, provided that we think the future 'matters', it will not be desirable to do so without reference to the subsequent consequences of our actions. Therefore, subsequent chapters of this book will pay careful attention to intertemporal choices, in which we compare the desirability of alternative feasible time paths of variables in which we are interested.

It was argued earlier, in considering the static allocation of resources, that a minimum condition one might require of an allocation of resources is that it be efficient. It seems sensible to apply this idea to intertemporal choices as well. To derive a criterion for intertemporal efficiency, a natural way of progressing is to reinterpret and generalise the static conditions to an intertemporal context. Thus, instead of thinking of different commodities at one point in time, we might alternatively consider one commodity at different points in time. A commodity delivered at a particular point in time can be called a *dated commodity*. Doing this, we can now think of the economy as having a set of commodities, each element of which is a particular good made available at a particular point in time. So, if there were two types of commodity available at each of three points in time, there exist six dated commodities. More generally, if there are n physically distinct commodities available at each of T different points in time, we have nT dated commodities.

We have previously defined an allocation of resources at one point in time (a static allocation) to be efficient if no person can benefit from a change without at least one other person losing utility. A strong version of intertemporal efficiency would require an allocation to have the property that any person at any point in time cannot benefit from a change without one or more other persons losing at that or any other point in time.

It is very difficult to proceed at such a general level, however. Throughout this text, in order to avoid unnecessary complications and to keep our arguments as simple as possible, we shall employ a weaker criterion of intertemporal efficiency. To do this, we shall consider the aggregate of all persons at one point in time. We also suppose that it is possible to define the aggregate utility of this set of persons at the relevant point in time.[2] Given this, an allocation of resources over time is *intertemporally efficient* if, for

some given level of utility at the present time, utility at all future points in time is as high as is economically feasible. In other words, future utility can only be increased at the expense of current utility.

Now before we try to work out some of the implications of this general criterion of intertemporal efficiency, some clarification is needed about our use of the words 'current' and 'future' in this statement. At least two meanings can be attached to them. One interpretation, the most natural one perhaps, relates to the passage of time. Current utility is the rate at which individuals at the present instant are gaining satisfaction; future utility refers to the rate at which individuals at some future instant of time gain satisfaction. Presumably, if the future is not too far away from the present, some of the future individuals will be the same persons as the current individuals, but will, of course, be older. But because of the events of birth and death, the two sets of individuals will not be identical.

But a different interpretation is also possible, and it will turn out to be useful for developing our argument. Suppose we view humans as being members of particular generations. Define Generation 0 to be the set of people living today; at some point of time in the future, this generation of people is replaced by another, Generation 1, and so on. So, with the passage of time, we envisage a sequence of generations of individual people, each new one replacing the previous one. We could then think about 'current utility' as referring to the utility enjoyed through the span of Generation 0 and 'future utility' as referring to utilities enjoyed by members of later generations.

This is, of course, not the way things actually happen in practice; the unfolding of human lives is a continuous process, and it is not the case that all members of one generation are replaced at one point in time by another set of individuals. Nevertheless, this way of looking at things is a useful heuristic device.[3]

Let us now derive some specific conditions that must be satisfied if resources are to be allocated efficiently over time. We focus on two such conditions, which arise from the fact that assets may be productive over time. This is certainly true for some

---

[2] This presumption is far from being a trivial one, and we shall return to this issue throughout this book. Just for the moment, though, we take it to be the case that such an aggregate index of utility can be found.

[3] It is also a device that is widely used. For example, in the USA election campaign of 1992, a group of individuals about whom much discussion took place was the 'baby boomers' generation, of which Bill Clinton was said to be a member. The idea of a generation was being used there in very much the same way as in our text.

biological resources (such as forests and fisheries) which have the property that they grow through natural processes. It is also considered to be an inherent property of capital in general. Thus, if I defer some consumption today, and allow capital to be accumulated instead, my consumption tomorrow may well have increased by a larger quantity than the magnitude of the initial sacrifice. Let δ denote a real rate of return on a single homogeneous asset, and suppose there are M different sectors of the economy in which the asset can be used as a productive input, the ith one of which obtains a return denoted by δ_i.

First intertemporal efficiency condition

The real rate of return on productive inputs and other assets is equalised across all sectors and between all assets at any point in time. That is, $\delta_i = \delta$ for all i, $i = 1, \ldots, M$.

Why is this condition required for intertemporal efficiency? If these rates of return differed, it would then be possible to reallocate a fixed quantity of resources, from low productivity into higher productivity sectors, in such a way that total returns would be increased. But if total returns could be increased in this way, current utility could be higher without there being any reduction in future utility, and so the condition for intertemporal efficiency fails. The only circumstance where such a Pareto improvement would not be possible is that in which the rate of return on assets is equalised throughout the economy. Whichever of the two ways in which we interpret the phrases current and future utility, it should be clear that this condition must be satisfied if intertemporal efficiency is to be satisfied, and so for some given level of utility at the present time, utility at all future points in time is as high as is economically feasible.

Now let us turn our attention to the second intertemporal efficiency condition. Suppose that the marginal worth of present consumption relative to that of consumption in the next period is in the ratio $(1 + r)/1$. That is, one unit of the consumption good in the current period is perceived as having the same effect on utility as $(1 + r)$ units of the good in the next period; an additional unit of consumption in the present period is valued $(1 + r)$ times more highly than the same quantity of consumption in the next period. Clearly, r is the consumption discount rate (see the discussion on discounting in Chapter 2). As before, suppose that the real rate of return that is attained by deferring a marginal unit of consumption

by one period and investing those resources is given by δ. In other words, if one unit of consumption is foregone today, this can be transformed into $(1 + \delta)$ units of consumption in the following period.

Second intertemporal efficiency condition

A necessary condition for the efficient intertemporal allocation of resources is that the real rate of return on investment (δ) is equal to the consumption discount rate (r).

This condition is illustrated in Figure 4.3. The consumption indifference curve is a locus of all combinations of consumption in the current period (C_0) and consumption in the next period (C_1) which confer a constant amount of utility. At any point, the slope of this indifference curve is given by $-(1 + r)$. Note that r is not a constant number; as one moves along any given indifference curve, its slope changes and so r changes. The production possibility frontier shows the combinations of consumption goods that can be produced in each period; its slope at any point is given by $-(1 + \delta)$. Like r, δ is not a constant number; as one moves along any given production possibility frontier, its slope changes and so δ changes. An explanation of these expressions for the slopes of the curves is given in Appendix 2.

An efficient intertemporal consumption allocation

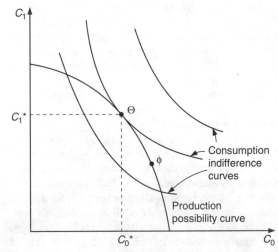

Slope of consumption indifference curve at any point given by $-(1 + r)$, with r varying along the curve. Slope of production possibility curve at any point given by $-(1 + \delta)$, with δ varying along the curve. At the efficient consumption choice (C_0^*, C_1^*), $(1 + r) = (1 + \delta)$ and so $r = \delta$.

Fig 4.3 An intertemporally efficient allocation of resources.

is shown by the point Θ at which the slopes of the intertemporal production possibility frontier and the consumption indifference curve are equalised, and the highest possible consumption indifference curve is attained. At any such point, $r = \delta$.

If this condition were not satisfied, then it would be possible to attain a higher level of two-period utility by moving along the production possibility curve. For example, suppose the economy were currently at the point labelled ϕ in Figure 4.3. An indifference curve going through that point would yield lower two-period utility than the one illustrated in the diagram. By reducing present consumption to C_0^*, consumption could be increased in the next period to C_1^*. At the combination $\{C_0^*, C_1^*\}$ utility is as high as it can be, given the available intertemporal production opportunities.

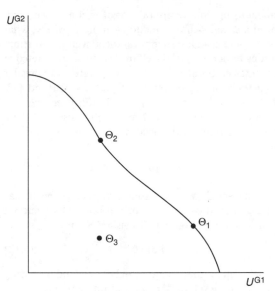

Fig 4.4 The Intertemporal Utility Possibility Frontier.

The intertemporal social welfare function and an intertemporally optimal resource allocation

In the last section we discussed and explained the concept of intertemporal efficiency. An allocation of resources over time is efficient if, for any given level of utility today, future utilities are at their maximum feasible levels. However, just as in the static case, there is no unique intertemporally efficient allocation. On the contrary, there will be an infinite quantity of them. This is illustrated in Figure 4.4.

For simplicity, Figure 4.4 collapses all generations into two; generation 1 is the present generation; 2 represents all future generations. U^{G1} and U^{G2} denote the total utility enjoyed by members of generations 1 and 2, respectively. The intertemporal utility possibility frontier shows the locus of all combinations of total utilities that are feasible. Each point on the frontier corresponds to a particular allocation of rights to use resources between generations. Since there are many different possible ways in which these rights of resource use could be distributed, there are many possible efficient paths of resource usage over time. An example might help you to understand this statement. Suppose that there are no constraints on how much or in what way resources are used by the present generation. The point Θ_1 might denote the combinations of current and future utilities that would be feasible in this case. Now suppose that, somehow or other, restrictions are imposed on the quantities of resources that the current generation is

allowed to use. Maximum attainable utility for G1 may now fall to the level shown at the point Θ_2; the increased resource stock bequeathed to the next generation allows it to obtain greater utility than in the first case. Both Θ_1 and Θ_2 are intertemporally efficient: present utility cannot be increased without future utility falling. However, a point such as Θ_3 is inefficient, as no such trade-off is necessary.

It is important to be clear about the interpretation of the rights of resource use, as this is not a common way of thinking about resource use. In some sense, our generation has at its disposal all the resources known to exist, and could no doubt use them as it sees fit. But that is not the same thing as saying that it has the right to use these resources in any way it chooses. Some people would claim that it does have such a right, but others argue that rights to use resources should be allocated in other ways, presumably implying constraints on how much of the cake of resources we are entitled to use. We do not wish to enter into the debate about how these rights should be distributed; our intention is only to make it clear that there are different ways in which rights could be distributed, and so different possible efficient allocations of resources. Of course, even if agreement could be reached on how rights of this kind should be distributed, it is not clear how such an agreement could be implemented. But this is not something we wish to discuss at the moment.

Once again, if we are to make any claim about which of these efficient paths is best, in the sense of maximising intertemporal social welfare, we shall need a social welfare function – more precisely, what we require is an intertemporal social welfare function.

Let W denote social welfare, this time interpreted in an intertemporal sense. For simplicity, we consider two successive generations of persons, G1 and G2. U^{G1} and U^{G2} denote the total utility enjoyed by members of generations 1 and 2. Suppose that there is an intertemporal social welfare function of the form[4]

$$W = W(U^{G1}, U^{G2}) \qquad (4.11)$$

In Chapter 2, we discussed a variety of particular forms that this function might take. One that we considered was Solow's 'Rawlsian' SWF:

$$W = \min(U^{G1}, U^{G2}) \qquad (4.12)$$

which implies that welfare can be increased by raising the utility level of the generation with the lowest utility level. If it is possible to change the pattern of resource use so as to redistribute utility from generations with higher utility to generations with lower utility, social welfare will be increased. This is true even if the sum of total utility over time is lower after the redistribution. We showed that maximisation of this SWF implies that utility levels should be equalised over generations. Under certain circumstances, this will imply equality of consumption levels over time as well (see the discussion of discounting in Chapter 2).

Previous discussions have also shown that a second, widely used, welfare function is the utilitarian form

$$W = \Phi_1 U^{G1} + \Phi_2 U^{G2} \qquad (4.13)$$

so that W is a weighted average of the utilities of each generation, where Φ_1 and Φ_2 are the weights used in summing utility over generations to obtain a measure of social welfare. Typically, Φ_1 is set equal to unity and Φ_2 to $1/(1 + \rho)$, in which case we have the standard discounted utilitarian SWF in which future utility is discounted at the utility discount rate ρ. Not surprisingly, if we employ a discounted

utilitarian social welfare function, the optimal rates of use of resources over time will depend upon the particular discount rate selected. This will be verified as you read our discussions of the extraction and harvesting of environmental resources in Chapters 5 through to 8.

Achieving an efficient allocation in a market economy

Static and intertemporal allocations and market economies

A variety of institutional arrangements might be employed to allocate resources, such as dictatorship, central planning, and free markets. A well-known result in economic theory is that any of these can, but will not necessarily, achieve an efficient allocation of resources. We are particularly interested in the consequences of free market resource allocation decisions for efficiency. Welfare economics theory can be of use to us here. It points to a set of circumstances which, if they prevailed, would sustain an efficient allocation of resources. For an efficient static allocation, these *institutional arrangements*, as shall call them from now on, include the following:

1 Markets exist for all goods and services exchanged.
2 All markets are perfectly competitive.
3 All transactors have perfect information.
4 Property rights are fully assigned.
5 No externalities exist.
6 All goods and services are private goods. That is, no public goods exist, nor are any resources common property resources.
7 Long-run average costs are non-decreasing.[5]

An efficient static and intertemporal allocation would be sustained if these seven institutional circumstances, generalised to refer to all points in time now and in the future, were satisfied. Thus, for example, we would need to interpret condition (1) as referring to markets for all goods and services being exchanged currently (i.e. spot markets) and at all points of future time (forward markets).

---

[4] Note that this form of social welfare function is already quite restrictive, as it assumes that we can meaningfully refer to an aggregate level of total utility for each generation. Social welfare is a function of these aggregate quantities, but not of the distributions of well-being within generations (except in so far as this affects the relevant aggregate). Despite these limitations, we shall work with this form in most of this text.

[5] This is required for the existence of a competitive equilibrium. If production were characterised by economies of scale, then natural monopolies would exist, and a competitive could not be sustained.

Static allocation and efficiency in a market economy

This section provides an explanation of why a market allocation of resources will be an efficient allocation, if the institutional arrangements we have listed were to exist. Assume that all firms are profit maximisers and all individuals maximise utility. A well-known result from microeconomic theory (a mathematical proof of which is given in Appendix 1) is that utility maximisation subject to a budget constraint requires that the ratio of marginal utilities is equal to the ratio of prices. That is, for any two goods X and Y, and for an individual indexed by i:

$$\left(\frac{U_X}{U_Y}\right)^i = \left(\frac{P_X}{P_Y}\right)^i \quad (4.14)$$

In competitive markets, all consumers face identical prices for each good, so the right-hand side of Equation 4.14 is identical for all consumers. Given this, Equation 4.14 implies that the left-hand side will be identical across persons. This ensures satisfaction of the consumption efficiency condition of Equation 4.3.

Profit maximisation requires that the ratio of marginal products of the productive inputs is equal to the ratio of the input prices. That is, for any firm producing the good j, and using the inputs L and K we have

$$\left(\frac{MP_L}{MP_K}\right)^j = \left(\frac{P_L}{P_K}\right)^j \quad (4.15)$$

where P_L and P_K are the unit input prices of L and K. Because all producers face identical input prices in competitive markets, this ensures satisfaction of the production efficiency condition of Equation 4.5, as the left-side of Equation 4.15 must then be equalised over products, and by implication over all firms.

Furthermore, profit maximisation in the production of any good j implies that

$$P_j = MC_j = \frac{P_K}{MP_K} = \frac{P_L}{MP_L} \quad (4.16)$$

where P_j denotes the output price of good j. This ensures the satisfaction of the product-mix efficiency condition of Equation 4.8. You should try to convince yourself of why it is that Equation 4.16 does satisfy the product-mix efficiency condition; a proof is given in Appendix 1 if you need some help. The intuition behind Equation 4.16 is not easy to obtain. But note that the first equality in that equation states that (in

profit maximising competitive equilibrium) price is equal to marginal cost. This result will probably be one with which you are familiar. It is quite difficult, though, to understand the two other equalities in Equation 4.16 at an intuitive level, except by noting that the last two terms on the right-hand side of the equation are both interpretable as long-run marginal cost. As it is not very satisfactory to take results on trust, the authors strongly recommend that you read through the derivations given in Appendix 1.

Intertemporal allocation and efficiency in a market economy

The circumstances we have just described thus sustain an efficient static allocation of resources. What will ensure an intertemporally efficient allocation? Before we explore this question, recall that an intertemporally efficient allocation requires that:

1 $\delta_i = \delta$ for all $i = 1, \dots, M$

so the return on each asset in each sector of the economy is equalised, and

2 $\delta = r$

so the rate of return on investment is equal to the consumption discount rate.

In looking at behaviour in market economies, we have assumed that the goal of firms is to maximise profits, and the goal of consumers is to maximise utility. The intertemporal generalisations of these assumptions are that firms maximise the present value of profit flows over time, and that consumers maximise the present value of utility flows over time.

It is easy to understand how the first of these conditions will be satisfied in a multi-sector, competitive market economy. Perfectly mobile capital will be invested in the sector yielding the highest rate of return; this will have the effect of equalising the equilibrium real rates of return across all sectors in the economy. Another explanation goes as follows: maximisation of present value by competitive firms implies that they invest to the point where the rate of return on a marginal project equals the market rate of interest, i. But in an economy in which all markets are perfect, firms face a single, exogenously given, interest rate. Thus, since i is at each point in time a constant number, marginal rates of return across sectors will be equalised.

The second condition is satisfied through the mechanism of the market for loanable funds. Those individuals deferring consumption supply loanable funds to the market; individuals or firms undertaking investment projects demand loanable funds from the market. The rate of interest, i, serves as a price which adjusts until equilibrium is achieved in the market, at which demand and supply of loanable funds are equal. This interest rate will be equal to the consumption discount rate, as individual lenders will adjust the quantities of funds lent until the return they receive on the market (i) is equal to their marginal consumption discount rate (r). A similar mechanism operates on the demand side of the market. In equilibrium, the market interest rate will be equal to the real rate of return on capital, as individual borrowers will adjust the quantities of funds invested until the interest rate paid on borrowed funds (i) is equal to their marginal rate of return on investment projects (δ).

Thus we obtain the result that in equilibrium

$$\delta = i = r \qquad (4.17)$$

and so the efficiency condition $\delta = r$ is satisfied. A more complete account of the mechanisms by which Equation 4.17 is obtained is given in Appendix 2. Of course, as is well known, the equalities in (4.17) are only obtained under special conditions, amounting to all the standard assumptions of perfectly competitive markets. However, since at this stage in our discussions we are assuming that all markets are competitive, there is no difficulty here.

The welfare-optimal allocation and a market economy

Our earlier analysis has identified the nature of a welfare maximising allocation of resources. Unfortunately, no 'automatic' (i.e. market based) tendency exists in a market economy for such a welfare maximum to be reached. Perfect competition plus the other circumstances listed above would lead to an efficient allocation, but does *not* lead to the attainment of a welfare maximisation. The only exception to this would be where some chance outcome happened to allocate property rights in the unique configuration that would correspond to optimal welfare. Of course, government can pursue redistributive policy, which might move the economy to such a position. But that is not a process which is in any way intrinsic to the notion of a market economy itself.

In later chapters of this text, we shall often investigate the use by government of a variety of policy instruments. Our discussion of efficiency and welfare should alert us to some problems we might encounter in assessing policy measures. Ideally, all statements about the desirability of changes in resource allocation should be made in terms of their effects upon social welfare. For a variety of reasons, however, it is often not possible to obtain good estimates of the welfare implications of some projects. In these circumstances, the projects are sometimes advocated on the grounds of efficiency gains. But it is easy to see that efficiency improvements are not unambiguously desirable. It is possible that an efficiency improvement might result in a lower value of social welfare. This possibility is illustrated in Figure 4.5 by the efficiency improvement attained by moving from point B to point D. Such a move would result in a welfare loss (as $W_1 < W_2$), even though there is an efficiency gain. Having made this point, it should also be said that whenever there is an inefficient allocation, there is always some other allocation which is both efficient and superior in welfare terms. For example, the move from B to A is both an efficiency gain and a welfare improvement. The reason why the move from B to A is certainly welfare beneficial is that it is a Pareto improvement. On the other hand, going from B to D was an efficiency gain in the sense that an inefficient allocation is replaced by an efficient one; but the change is not a Pareto improvement, unlike the move from B to A.

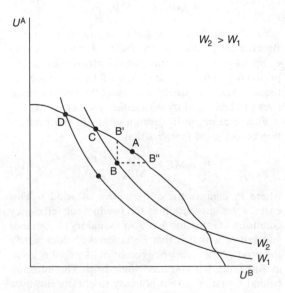

Fig 4.5 Efficient and inefficient static allocations.

The very simple observation that efficiency gains are not necessarily welfare gains, or in other words are not necessarily socially beneficial, is often ignored. Sometimes, claims are made (explicitly or implicitly) that the eradication of a market failure is intrinsically desirable. It is clear that if desirability is defined in terms of effects upon social welfare, an efficiency gain may or may not be beneficial. While it is perfectly reasonable to discuss the means by which efficiency gains may be attained, it is not certain that an efficiency gain would improve social welfare.[6]

PART 2
Market failure and public policy: externalities and public goods

Introduction: efficiency, welfare and the environment

It is worth starting Part 2 by restating the main conclusions of our analysis. We began by laying out the conditions that are required if the allocation of resources within an economy is to be efficient, in both static and intertemporal senses. As we shall make use of these conditions on a number of occasions in the rest of this chapter, it will be convenient to group and present them in a concise form. This is done in Box 4.3.

Our next objective was to identify a set of circumstances which, if they prevailed, would be sufficient to ensure that resource allocation through market processes is efficient. These were labelled the institutional arrangements[7] necessary for efficient

---

[6] In this discussion, we have ignored the possibility of compensation. Thus, imagine some resource reallocation benefited one person but was damaging to another. If, in absolute terms, the size of the gain is greater than the size of the loss, the two parties may be able to negotiate a compensating transfer so that, after compensation is paid, both parties benefit. If the resource reallocation takes place, we can say that there is a *potential* Pareto improvement (also known as a Kaldor improvement). If the resource reallocation *and* compensation take place, an *actual* Pareto improvement will have occurred.

[7] One might argue that not all of the items in Box 4.4 are actually *institutional arrangements*. Nevertheless, this is the term we shall use in referring to this set of conditions or circumstances.

> **Box 4.3 Efficiency conditions in a competitive market**
>
> **Static conditions**
>
> Efficiency in consumption:
> $$\left(\frac{U_X}{U_Y}\right)^A = \left(\frac{U_X}{U_Y}\right)^B = \left(\frac{P_X}{P_Y}\right)$$
>
> Efficiency in production:
> $$\left(\frac{MP_L}{MP_K}\right)^X = \left(\frac{MP_L}{MP_K}\right)^Y = \left(\frac{P_L}{P_K}\right)$$
>
> Product-mix efficiency:
> $$\left(\frac{U_X}{U_Y}\right) = \left(\frac{MP_K^Y}{MP_K^X}\right) = \left(\frac{MP_L^Y}{MP_L^X}\right) \leftrightarrow$$
> $$P_X = MC_X = \left(\frac{P_K}{MP_L}\right)^X = \left(\frac{P_L}{MP_L}\right)^X$$
>
> Intertemporal conditions
> $$r_i = r, \quad i = 1, \ldots, M$$
> $$\delta = r$$

resource allocation; they are restated for convenience in Box 4.4.

Finally, we defined and discussed the concept of an optimal allocation of resources. Our analysis suggested that no market mechanism exists which will ensure that resources are allocated in an optimal way. An optimal outcome requires that endowments (or rights to use property) be distributed in a particular way; markets operate under whatever

> **Box 4.4 The institutional arrangements required for an efficient allocation of resources**
>
> 1 Markets exist for all goods and services exchanged.
> 2 All markets are perfectly competitive.
> 3 No externalities exist.
> 4 All goods and services are private goods. There are no public goods.
> 5 Property rights are fully assigned.
> 6 All transactions have perfect information.
> 7 All firms are profit maximisers and all individuals utility maximisers.
> 8 Long-run average costs are non-decreasing.
> 9 Transactions costs are zero.
> 10 All relevant functions satisfy convexity conditions.

distribution of endowments happens to exist. However, government redistributive policy could alter patterns of endowments in appropriate ways.

The main arguments of the second part of this chapter are as follows.

1 Unregulated private market behaviour can, in principle, lead to efficient outcomes. However, in practice, some of the institutional arrangements required for market economies to allocate resources efficiently are not satisfied.

2 It seems to be very unlikely that any conceivable economy could ever exist in which all these institutional arrangements are satisfied.

3 The special characteristics of environmental resources play an important part in preventing the necessary institutional arrangements from existing or being likely to exist in any economy.

4 If these three assertions are correct, market economies will not allocate resources efficiently; that is, the economy will be characterised by market failure.

5 Even though markets by themselves may fail to allocate resources efficiently, public sector intervention offers the prospect of establishing alternative institutional arrangements that will, by altering behaviour, lead to efficient patterns of resource allocation. It may also be possible for government intervention to generate optimal allocations of resources.

Our objectives in this second part of Chapter 4 are to explain and justify each of these assertions. It has not been our intention to derive the conditions required for an efficient allocation of resources as an end in itself. The purpose in doing this has been to provide a conceptual framework in which questions relating to the efficient and optimal use of environmental resources can be addressed. We shall pay particular attention to points (3) and (5). Identification of the reasons why markets fail is an important step in designing appropriate environmental policy programmes.

resources are not transacted at all through market processes, or the market processes in which they are exchanged are incomplete in some way or another. Examples of environmental resources that are not in general traded at all through markets include the earth's atmosphere, a large proportion of its water resources, and many wilderness areas. In addition, pollution, a negative good, is not transacted through market systems. Unlike many items of man-made capital, natural or environmental resources stocks often cannot be purchased or hired through markets.

Many environmental resources are traded through markets, of course. Most mineral deposits are privately owned and are marketed commodities. However, whereas current (or spot) markets do exist and are highly developed for such resources, it is unusual for futures markets to exist for most commodities. Where they do exist, futures markets are at best incomplete. To the authors' knowledge, there is probably no resource, good or service for which a complete set of future markets exists.

It is possible to envisage alternative forms of organisation to that of the market which can bring about resource allocation efficiency. However, it seems most unlikely that any such substitute does or could exist in practice. The pervasive presence of public goods and externalities implies failure of the static efficiency conditions, and the risks and uncertainties introduced whenever markets are incomplete suggest that it is very unlikely that resource allocation over time will be efficient.

The failure of markets to exist for many environmental resources is often a reflection of the fact that the resources in question are public goods. We shall examine the implications for resource use of public goods and the related issue of common property resources in the present chapter. Implications for the environment and environmental policy of public goods, common property resources and externalities will also be examined in several of the chapters which follow.

Environmental resources and the existence of markets

Where markets do not exist, it is evident that markets cannot allocate resources, efficiently or otherwise. As we shall see on many occasions throughout this book, either many environmental

Environmental resources and market structures

Casual knowledge of markets which do exist for environmental resources suggests that these markets are not always competitive. As is well known from introductory microeconomics courses, monopolistic

Box 4.5 Atmospheric ozone and market failure

We argued in the Introduction to Part 2 that unregulated market economies are likely to be characterised by market failure because some of the institutional arrangements required for efficiency cannot be attained because of the special characteristics of environmental resources. Let us look at a simple example of market failure.

Evidence now suggests that the accumulation of tropospheric ozone in urban areas poses serious threats to human health, and also leads to agricultural crop damage in surrounding areas.[8] A major source of tropospheric ozone is road vehicle exhaust emissions. Because vehicle emissions have real effects on wellbeing through our utility and production functions, these emissions can be termed 'goods' (although it may be preferable to label them as 'bads' as the effects on utility are adverse). However, unlike goods which are exchanged through markets, no charge is made for such emissions in the absence of government intervention. In this example, conditions (1) and (5) of Box 4.4 are not being met, and the analysis below will demonstrate that resources are not being allocated efficiently. An efficient allocation would require lower exhaust emissions, implying lower traffic volumes, change in fuel type used, increased engine efficiency or enhanced exhaust control. We show in Chapter 9 how such objectives might be achieved, but it should be clear at this stage that one method would be through the use of taxes on emissions that cause ozone accumulation. An efficient emissions tax would impose a tax rate on each unit of emission equal to the value of the damages caused by that unit of emission.

In arriving at this conclusion, we did not explicitly consider the time dimension of pollution. But note that if ozone accumulates over time, and damage is dependent on the *stock* of ozone rather than the *flow* of emissions in any particular period, then we need to consider the accumulation of the pollutant over time. As Chapter 9 shows, where emission flows lead to accumulating stocks of pollutants, it may be efficient to impose a tax rate that rises over time.

---

[8] Note that the accumulation of ozone in lower layers of the atmosphere, causing lung-related health problems among other things, is completely distinct from the destruction of the ozone layer in the earth's upper atmosphere (the stratosphere). The latter phenomenon − often known as 'holes in the ozone layer' − causes different problems, and is explained in Chapter 12.

and imperfectly competitive market structures can result in efficiency losses. We investigate these losses in the context of the extraction of exhaustible resources in Chapters 5 and 6, and so do not discuss the matter any further at this point.

Externalities

An external effect, or externality for short, is said to occur when the production or consumption decisions of one agent affect the utility of another agent in an unintended way, and when no compensation is made by the producer of the external effect to the affected party. In our analysis of efficient resource allocation in the first part of this chapter, we excluded the existence of externalities by the assumptions that were made about the utility and production functions. To confirm this, look again at the way we formulated these functions in Equations 4.1 and 4.2. An individual's utility depends only on the quantity of each good chosen and consumed by him or her. Similarly, the quantity of each good produced in a particular interval of time depends only on the quantities of the two inputs that the producer in question chooses to use.

But in practice consumption and production behaviour by some agents does affect, in unchosen and uncompensated ways, the utility gained by other consumers and the output produced by other producers. Economic behaviour does involve external effects. In Chapter 1, we discussed the materials balance approach to economic analysis. The seminal work in this field by Ayres and Kneese (1969) demonstrates that external effects, far from being rare in occurrence and limited in importance, are endemic in modern economies. Negative externalities are inevitable and pervasive in industrial economies, and are intrinsically associated with the use of environmental resources. Ayres and Kneese argued that is not possible for these externalities to be 'internalised' through unregulated market behaviour, and so in the absence of government intervention, inefficient outcomes are inevitable. Our objective here is to explain the basis of these claims, and to show how externalities result in resource misallocation.

Classification of externalities

Let us begin by classifying the forms that external effects may take. A simple classification is given in

Table 4.1 Example of a simple classification of externalities

Effect on others	Consumption	Production
Beneficial	Vaccination against an infectious disease	Pollination of blossom arising from proximity to apiary
Adverse	Noise pollution from radio playing in park	Chemical factory spillages of contaminated water into water systems

Table 4.1. External effects may be the consequence of either consumption or production behaviour, and the unintended effect on other parties may be beneficial or adverse. This twofold classification leads to four types of externality. Vaccination against an infectious disease exemplifies the case of a beneficial consumption externality. Suppose a woman chooses to vaccinate herself against the risk of contracting measles. This is a consumption decision taken presuming that the net benefits she derives will be positive. But her action has effects upon others; her reduced probability of contracting measles will reduce the probability of others contracting the disease. The effect is external in the sense that the effect on others did not influence her choice, and nor will she receive any compensation from others (through a market or otherwise). Put another way, the total benefits of a vaccination decision are greater than the effects derived directly by the individual who is vaccinated. We shall demonstrate later in this section that, relative to economically efficient levels, a market economy will tend to consume too small a quantity of goods that have beneficial external effects. Conversely, a market economy will tend to consume excessive quantities of goods that have adverse external effects.

The example we have just illustrated constitutes one in which the externality is a 'public good'. Public goods externalities include most types of air and water pollution. It is also possible for externalities to take the form of private goods. This suggests a third dimension in terms of which externalities may be classified: they can be public or private, depending upon whether the external effect is a public good or bad, or a private good or bad. As the concepts of public and private goods will be defined in the next section, we shall not explain this distinction at this point. However, it is worth noting that most

externalities associated with the use of environmental resources, or having environmental impacts, are public in nature. As we shall see, the public goods nature of many environmentally relevant externalities poses particular difficulties in designing and administering measures that seek to reduce the problems associated with market failure.

Externalities and economic efficiency

Do the efficiency conditions that are stated in Box 4.3 remain true in an economy in which externalities do exist? Not surprisingly, they do not, or more precisely, they are only valid if we interpret them in a particular way.[9] So how does the presence of externalities change the required efficiency conditions? Let us consider first the production efficiency condition of Equation 4.5 which we wrote as

$$\left(\frac{MP_L}{MP_K}\right)^X = \left(\frac{MP_L}{MP_K}\right)^Y$$

In order for this to remain valid as a condition of productive efficiency, it is necessary to interpret the four marginal products in net terms, or if you prefer, as social marginal products. Let us define some new notation: PMP_L is the private marginal product of labour, EMP_L is the external marginal product of labour and SMP_L is the social marginal product of labour. An equivalent notation applies to capital, and any other input. These three measures of marginal product are related by the identity

$$PMP_L + EMP_L = SMP_L$$

The idea here is a simple one: when a firm chooses to employ an additional unit of labour, the marginal product of labour to that firm is PMP_L. If this employment of labour has an external effect on others, we denote that external effect as EMP_L. The total, net, or social marginal product is the sum of these two. If we interpret all measures in net or social terms, the productive efficiency condition is valid in an economy in which external effects occur, and can then be written as either

$$\left(\frac{SMP_L}{SMP_K}\right)^X = \left(\frac{SMP_L}{SMP_K}\right)^Y$$

---

[9] There is a general point here. None of the efficiency conditions we listed in Box 4.3 remain true (without a suitable reinterpretation) whenever one or more of the institutional arrangements we listed in Box 4.4 fails to hold.

or

$$\left(\frac{\text{PMP}_L + \text{EMP}_L}{\text{PMP}_K + \text{EMP}_K} \right)^X = \left(\frac{\text{PMP}_L + \text{EMP}_L}{\text{PMP}_K + \text{EMP}_K} \right)^Y$$

We have now seen how the efficiency conditions need to be interpreted in situations where economic activity generates external effects. Let us now see why private profit maximising behaviour will fail to allocate resources efficiently in the presence of externalities. The key point here is that, left to act in their individual self-interests, firms will only take account of what we have called private marginal products. So profit maximisation will result in the ratio of private marginal products being equalised between goods. The analysis in Part 1 in the section on achieving an efficient allocations in a market economy, demonstrated, moreover, that these will be equal to the ratio of input prices (see Equation 4.15). That is

$$\left(\frac{\text{PMP}_L}{\text{PMP}_K} \right)^X = \left(\frac{\text{PMP}_L}{\text{PMP}_K} \right)^Y = \frac{P_L}{P_K}$$

Clearly, except for the unlikely event that external effects are exactly offsetting in arithmetic terms, the equalisation of private marginal product ratios will yield a different allocation of resources from that which derives from the equalisation of social marginal product ratios. As the latter is required for efficiency, private market behaviour will be inefficient in the presence of externalities.

We can examine this reasoning a little more deeply by means of a hypothetical example. This example will bring out another way of thinking about efficiency; we show that if firms act uncooperatively (that is, independently of one another) in pursuit of maximising their individual profits, the outcome is less good (and so is inefficient) compared with that where they act cooperatively, maximising their combined profits. The example we investigate is that in which there is a single negative externality in production.

Suppose that good X is produced by one firm, and good Y is produced by another. For simplicity, imagine that X is produced using one purchased input K, whilst Y is produced using another purchased input L. Each producer also makes use of the atmosphere, an environmental resource, as a productive input, but no charge is made for the use of this input. In addition, we assume that the production of Y generates atmospheric pollution. This pollution generates a negative externality, adversely affecting the production of X, but not affecting the production of Y. We denote the quantity of this pollutant emission by Ψ, and assume that its magnitude is an increasing function of the amount of labour used in producing Y. Thus we can write the two production functions as[10]

$$X = X(K, \Psi)$$
$$Y = Y(L)$$

where

$$\Psi = \Psi(L)$$

Assume that $\partial X / \partial K > 0$, $\partial X / \partial \Psi < 0$, and $dY/dL > 0$. Note that the production of Y only involves inputs chosen by its own producer. However, the production of X is only partly determined by inputs chosen by its own producer. Although K is chosen by the firm producing X, Ψ is chosen by the other producer, through its choice of input level L.

In a competitive market economy, each firm maximises profits independently. What is the outcome of this process? Remembering that profit is defined as total revenue less total costs, the profit functions for the two firms can be written as

$$\Pi_X = P_X X - P_K K = P_X X(K, \Psi) - P_K K$$
$$\Pi_Y = P_Y Y - P_L L = P_Y Y(L) - P_L L \tag{4.18}$$

Profit maximisation by each firm separately implies that K is chosen to maximise the profits in producing X, whilst, independently, L is chosen to maximise the profits in producing Y. It is necessary for profit maximisation that the input choices of the two firms satisfy the first-order conditions:

$$\frac{\partial \Pi_X}{\partial K} = P_X X_K - P_K = 0$$
$$\frac{\partial \Pi_Y}{\partial K} = P_Y Y_L - P_L = 0 \tag{4.19}$$

where $X_K = \partial X / \partial K$ and $Y_L = \partial Y / \partial L$. Rearranging Equation 4.19 we obtain the profit maximising

---

[10] Strictly speaking, we should write the production functions as

$$X = X(K, R, \Psi)$$
$$Y = Y(L, R)$$

where

$$\Psi = \Psi(L)$$

to make explicit the fact the environmental resource is actually being used as an input by each firm. However, as this complicates the maths, and is not necessary for our argument, we do not do so here.

conditions

$$P_X X_K = P_K$$
$$P_Y Y_L = P_L$$
(4.20)

The left-hand side of each of these equations is the value (in terms of units of output) of the marginal product of the input. The right-hand side is a marginal cost. Equations 4.20 therefore, state that the quantity employed of each factor input is chosen so that the value of its marginal product is equal to its marginal cost.

Note also that we can derive an alternative interpretation of these profit maximising conditions. Rearranging Equations 4.20 we can obtain

$$P_X = \frac{P_K}{X_K}$$
$$P_Y = \frac{P_L}{Y_L}$$
(4.21)

Equations 4.21 state that in profit maximising equilibrium, the output price for each good equals its private marginal cost of production. We make use of this alternative interpretation later.

Return now to Equations 4.20. These describe the input demands that will exist in a competitive market economy where no price is charged for the pollution externality associated with the output of firm Y. However, this outcome cannot be one in which resources are allocated efficiently. Recall that an efficient allocation implies that no unexploited net benefits exist. But there are unexploited net benefits in this case, because individual competitive behaviour does not maximise overall or combined profits. To see this, consider how profits would change if there were to be a small increase in the use of the input L. The second of Equations 4.20 shows that there would be no change in profits in producing good Y, because the incremental cost of labour (P_L) would be just balanced by the value of the marginal product of the additional unit of labour ($P_Y Y_L$). But the profits of firm X are reduced; the increased use of L raises the quantity of harmful emissions Ψ. Given that $\partial X/\partial \Psi < 0$, this reduces the output of X, and lowers the profits of its producer. A corollary of this is that joint profits would be increased if a smaller quantity of labour were to be employed. Clearly, therefore, the competitive equilibrium is not efficient; it leads to an excessive use of L, reducing combined profits below their maximum level, and leaving unexploited Pareto improvements.

Maximisation of joint profits

Let us now look more closely at the efficient solution, which maximises joint or combined profits. Combined profits, Π_{X+Y}, are given by

$$\Pi_{X+Y} = P_X X(K, \Psi) + P_Y Y(L) - P_K K - P_L L \quad (4.22)$$

The necessary conditions for a maximum of this combined profit function are obtained by differentiation of the joint profit function with respect to K and L:

$$\frac{\partial \Pi_{X+Y}}{\partial K} = P_X X_K - P_K = 0 \qquad (4.23a)$$

$$\frac{\partial \Pi_{X+Y}}{\partial L} = P_X \cdot \frac{\partial X}{\partial \Psi} \cdot \frac{d\Psi}{dL} + P_Y Y_L - P_L = 0 \quad (4.23b)$$

Rearranging Equation 4.23b we obtain

$$P_X \cdot \frac{\partial X}{\partial \Psi} \cdot \frac{d\Psi}{dL} + P_Y Y_L = P_L \qquad (4.24)$$

The first term on the left-hand side of Equation 4.24 is the value of the marginal damage done to X by the pollution produced by Y. The marginal damage in physical units is given by $(\partial X/\partial \Psi) \cdot (\partial \Psi/\partial L)$, what we called earlier the external marginal product of labour. This will be a negative quantity, as $\partial X/\partial \Psi$ is negative whilst the other two components are positive. In value terms, marginal damage is found by multiplying this expression by P_X. The second term on the left-hand side is the value of the marginal product of L in the production of good Y. Combining the two components on the left-hand side gives the value of the marginal product of L, net of the value of the marginal damage done by L in the production of X. Equation 4.24 states that maximisation of combined profits (and so economic efficiency) requires that this should be equal to the marginal cost of L, P_L. So what we have here is another interpretation of the productive efficiency condition in the presence of externalities. The input L should be used to the point where the net value of its marginal contribution in the production of good Y ($P_Y Y_L - P_L$) is just equal to the value of the marginal damage in the production of X, as shown in Figure 4.6a.

Let us recap the argument. Profit-maximising behaviour in a market economy would result in the satisfaction of the second of Equations 4.19, in which $P_Y Y_L = P_L$. However, in the presence of an external effect, this is not economically efficient, as an unexploited Pareto gain exists. The efficient solution is given by Equation 4.24. Efficiency requires that the sum of $P_Y Y_L$ (the value of the output of Y obtained

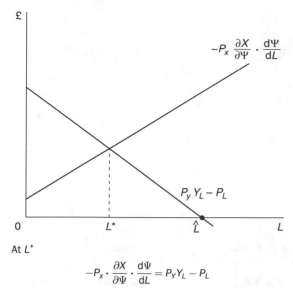

At L^*

$$-P_x \cdot \frac{\partial X}{\partial \Psi} \cdot \frac{d\Psi}{dL} = P_Y Y_L - P_L$$

This is exactly the same as Equation 4.23b in the text. Note that in a private market economy, L will be chosen so that $P_Y Y_L = P_L$, leading to the choice $\hat{L}$ is the diagram.

Fig 4.6a The efficient choice of an input in the presence of a production external effect.

by using an additional unit of labour) and the value of the associated external damage to the production of X is equal to the incremental cost of a unit of labour, P_L. Notice that the first term on the left-hand side of Equation 4.24 represents this adverse external effect, that we earlier called EMP_L. As P_L is a given constant to every firm, it must be equal in the two equations. Also, the first term in Equation 4.24 is negative. Therefore the product $P_Y Y_L$ must be higher in Equation 4.24 than in the second of Equations 4.19.

This in turn implies that Y_L must be higher, implying a lower use of the input L. An illustration of this result is given in Figure 4.6a. The efficient labour choice, L^*, is lower than that implied by private profit maximisation, $\hat{L}$.

Comprehension of this argument can be helped by representing in a slightly different way the information contained in Figure 4.6a. This is done in Figure 4.6b. The diagram on the left portrays the competitive (inefficient) solution, in which the quantity $\hat{L}$ is chosen so that $P_Y Y_L = P_L$. Put differently, if we denote marginal private net benefit by MB, and define this to be $MB = P_Y Y_L - P_L$, then private producers operate so as to employ an input up to the point where MB equals zero. The right-hand side of Figure 4.6b illustrates the combined efficient solution. Defining the marginal net social benefit (MSB) as

$$P_X \cdot \frac{\partial X}{\partial \Psi} \cdot \frac{d\Psi}{dL} + P_Y Y_L - P_L \qquad (4.25)$$

we see that efficiency requires that L^* be chosen so that $MSB = 0$. Finally, Figure 4.7 combines the two sets of information from Figure 4.6b, and allows us to compare L^* with $\hat{L}$. However, one other item of information can be obtained from Figure 4.7. The distance ab represents the magnitude of the value of the adverse external effect *at the socially optimal labour input level*, L^*. This magnitude is a shadow price, and we show in Chapter 8 that this shadow price determines the magnitude of an optimal emission tax.

An alternative interpretation of production externalities

Previously, in Equations 4.21, we derived an alternative formulation of the profit-maximising condition

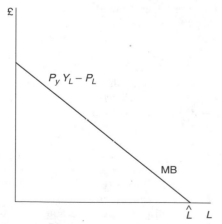

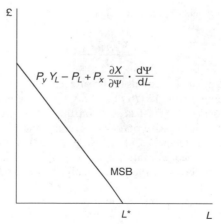

Fig 4.6b The marginal private benefit and the marginal social benefit from the use of labour in the presence of an adverse external effect.

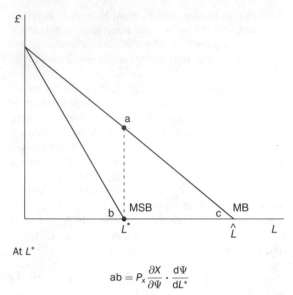

At L^*

$$ab = P_x \frac{\partial X}{\partial \Psi} \cdot \frac{d\Psi}{dL^*}$$

$ab =$ An optimal tax on labour when the employment of labour creates an adverse external effect.

Fig 4.7 An adverse externality, driving a wedge between private and social costs.

in competitive equilibrium, namely

$$P_Y = \frac{P_L}{Y_L}$$

so that the output price of Y equals the private marginal cost of production of good Y. However, we saw above that the efficient allocation requires that

$$P_X \cdot \frac{\partial X}{\partial \Psi} \cdot \frac{d\Psi}{dL} + P_Y Y_L = P_L$$

Rearranging this expression yields

$$P_Y = \frac{P_Y}{Y_L} - \frac{P_X \cdot \frac{\partial X}{\partial \Psi} \cdot \frac{d\Psi}{dL}}{Y_L} \qquad (4.26)$$

so that the price of Y equals the private marginal cost of producing good Y (P_L/Y_L) plus the marginal external cost of Y (the last term on the right-hand side, which is a negative quantity). A comparison of the private but inefficient allocation of good Y with the socially efficient allocation is shown graphically in Figure 4.8, in terms of a familiar supply and demand curve representation.

Private profit maximisation in competitive markets leads to an output level $\hat{Y}$, at which private marginal cost is equal to private marginal revenue. The competitive market price of Y is P_Y, which takes

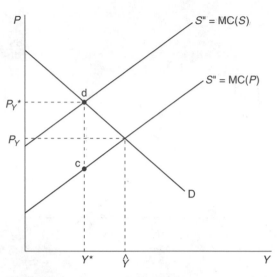

Fig 4.8 The private profit-maximising output and the socially efficient output of a good that creates an adverse external effect.

no account of the external effect that Y has on X. The socially efficient output level is Y^*, which equates the marginal benefit derived from good Y with the social marginal cost of Y – this social cost exceeds the private cost by its inclusion of the external effect.

The distance cd represents a shadow price, which can be interpreted as an efficient externality tax on units of output of Y. The socially efficient price, P_Y^*, is greater than the competitive market price, P_Y, because of the presence of the adverse external effect. We discuss the concept of pollution taxes, designed to 'internalise' externalities, at length in Chapter 9. Just note at this stage in our discussions the pervasiveness of negative external effects in matters relating to the natural environment. Earlier in the chapter, in Box 4.2, we mentioned externalities associated with fishing of marine resources, to be discussed fully in Chapter 7. Perhaps the single most important example relates to negative external effects from the consumption of fossil fuels, discussed extensively throughout the text. The overuse of wilderness areas and other public goods, the loss of biodiversity as economic activity interferes with habitats, the build-up of inorganic pollutants associated with intensive agricultural practices, road congestion, and the increasing real economic costs of waste disposal are all examples of the external effects of economic activities, which we shall investigate in subsequent chapters.

In this discussion of externalities, we have concentrated upon the particular case of negative externalities in production. Clearly, our analysis carries over straightforwardly to beneficial externalities in production, with appropriate changes in sign on the external effects in the appropriate expressions. When it comes to externalities in consumption, whether they be adverse or beneficial, the method of analysis and the results obtained are similar in form. The consumption efficiency condition must be reinterpreted to require an equality between the ratios of *social* marginal utilities. This will not obtain, however, in an unregulated market economy; individual consumers will equate the ratios of their private marginal utilities to the ratios of goods prices. Whenever consumption externalities are present, this will lead to inefficient outcomes. Consumption externalities are investigated in Problem 3. Mention should also be made of 'mixed cases', where production externalities damage individuals as consumers, and vice versa. We will not go through the analyses for these cases, but you should be able to appreciate that these cases will also, in general, lead to market failure.

How can inefficiencies associated with externalities be eliminated? We will not attempt to answer this important question at this point, as it is the major theme of Chapter 9. It will be shown there that, under certain special circumstances, bargaining between producers and consumers of externalities can lead to efficient outcomes. Bargaining solutions are, however, very unlikely in the case of most types of externality rising in the use of environmental resources. The analysis we have done in this section has pointed to one measure that could bring about efficient outcomes: the use of pollution taxes. This policy instrument is examined in Chapter 9.

Public goods

Many environmental resources have the characteristics of *public goods*. The probability of markets existing to provide or conserve public goods is extremely low, even where their existence would yield positive net benefits. As a result, those goods which we shall shortly define as being public goods will tend, in a pure market economy, to be provided in quantities that are too low from the point of view of social efficiency. This assertion will be substantiated shortly. Furthermore, even in the unlikely event that a private market were to develop, we shall show that the outcome would not be efficient. Once again, one is pushed towards the conclusion that efficiency gains may be possible from government intervention.

Consider a good, service or resource which possesses the following two properties. Firstly, when one person consumes a unit of the good, that unit is not available for another person to consume. To give a trivial example, if an ice cream seller in a cinema has just one ice left for sale, when that last unit is consumed no one else can eat it. This property of goods is variously called divisibility, rivalness, or depletability. We will henceforth use the first of these terms, and describe such a good as being a *divisible* good. Notice that divisibility carries an implication about the marginal cost of providing the good: if an additional good can only be produced by using some scarce resources, the marginal cost of a divisible good will be greater than zero.

Secondly, a good may have the property that its owner could prevent access to (and so consumption of) the good by other people, if he or she wished to do so. Returning to the ice cream example, the owner of an ice could refuse to enter into a sale contract with another person, thus preventing its consumption by others. A good possessing this property is said to be an *excludable* good.

A *private good* is defined as a good which is divisible and excludable. However, not all goods and resources are both divisible and excludable. In particular, many environmental resources do not exhibit one or both of these characteristics. Consider an example. Wilderness areas have the property that, as long as use rates are not excessive, they are not divisible. If one person consumes the services provided by a visit to a wilderness area – yielding recreation, wildlife experiences and solitude, for example – that does not prevent others consuming those services as well. There is no rivalry between the consumption of different individuals, provided that the overall rate of usage is not close to some threshold at which congestion occurs and one person's visit does not detract from others' enjoyment. In this sense, we could describe the services provided by wilderness areas as indivisible. What does this imply about the marginal cost of provision of such a resource service, or, more precisely, what is the cost of providing an extra unit of the service to another user? The answer is that this cost is zero, because an additional user's consumption of the resource does not require that the resource stock be increased. This insight has

Box 4.6 Examples of public goods

The classic textbook examples of public goods are lighthouses and national defence systems. These both possess the properties of being non-excludable and indivisibile. If you or I choose not to pay for defence or lighthouse services, we cannot be excluded from the benefits of the service, once it is provided to anyone. Moreover, our consumption of the service does not diminish the amount available to others. Bridges also share the property of being indivisible (provided they are not used beyond a point at which congestion effects begin), although they are not typically non-excludable.

Which environmental resources are public goods? The answer is that very many are, as can be seen from the following examples; you should check, in each case, that the key criterion of indivisibility is satisfied. The benefits from biological diversity, the services of wilderness resources, the climate regulation mechanisms of the earth's atmosphere, and the waste disposal and reprocessing services of environmental sinks all constitute public goods, provided the use made of them is not excessive. Indeed, much public policy towards such environmental resources can be interpreted in terms of regulations or incentives designed to prevent use breaking through such threshold levels.

Some naturally renewing resource systems also share public goods properties. Examples include water resource systems and the composition of the earth's atmosphere. Although in these cases consumption by one person does potentially reduce the amount of the resource available to others (so the resource could be 'scarce' in an economic sense), this will not be relevant in practice as long as consumption rates are low relative to the system's regenerative capacity.

Finally, note that many public health measures, including inoculation and vaccination against infectious diseases, have public goods characteristics, by reducing the probability of any person (whether or not he or she is inoculated or vaccinated) contracting the disease. Similarly, educational and research expenditures are, to some extent, public goods.

concerns property rights; if no person or group is endowed with property rights to an asset, there is no legal right for one person to deny access to another (assuming for the moment that government does not intervene to create rules of access or the like). Secondly, and quite independently of what property rights (if any) characterise the asset, physical properties of the asset may render exclusion infeasible. In the case of wilderness areas, for example, private property rights may be firmly established but exclusion of visitors is not practically possible. Exploitation of virgin frontier lands may at times have been an example of a case where excludability was neither physically nor legally possible.[11]

The term public goods is used in two ways in the environmental economics literature. Some authors define a public good to be a good which is indivisible and non-excludable; that is, both characteristics are required. Other authors use the term to refer to any good which is indivisible in consumption, irrespective of whether it is also excludable or not. We use the second of these definitions in this text, and so take a public good to be a good which is indivisible in consumption.

As you will see, it is probably the case that most indivisible (public) goods are also non-excludable. Moreover, it is this latter aspect which is of most relevance to the place of public goods in market economies; if an owner were unable to exclude another person from consuming a good, it is difficult to see how the owner could sell the good at any positive price. But if prices cannot be charged for a good, it is difficult to imagine how a market could exist for that good. We are drawn to the conclusion that public goods which are also non-excludable will not be provided in pure market economies.

Separating the issue of excludability from the defining characteristic of public goods (i.e. indivisibility) also allows us to define another class of goods for which private property rights have not been established. These are the common-property and open access goods and resources, analysed extensively in Chapter 7. Examples of these include some aquifers, fisheries, forests, the earth's atmospheric resources and wilderness areas. Many of these are private goods, but some may be public.

important implications that are explained later in this section.

Secondly, for many goods, it is not possible to exclude persons from consuming the good if they choose. Note there are really two issues here. The first

[11] On the other hand, if the narratives in many Hollywood 'Western' movies are to be believed, legal excludability was often given to settlers in the American West, but excludability was often impossible in practice!

Public goods and economic efficiency

Let us begin by recalling, from Box 4.3, the consumption and production efficiency conditions for an economy in which all of the institutional arrangements of Box 4.4 are satisfied. In this case, as no public goods exist by assumption, X and Y are each private goods. The production, consumption and product-mix efficiency conditions for this economy are restated in the upper part of Table 4.2.

How do we interpret these conditions? Note that $(U_X/U_Y)^A$ is the number of units of good Y that A is willing to pay for an additional unit of X. As the consumption of X is divisible, the social willingness to pay for one unit of X is equal to one consumer's WTP. Given fixed market prices, P_X and P_Y, this measure of WTP will be identical over all consumers. The expressions involving marginal products refer to the reduction in production of Y that would result from transferring resources into the production of an extra unit of X. In other words, it is the social opportunity cost of X in terms of Y. Efficiency requires that the individual WTP for X in units of Y is equal to the opportunity cost of X in units of Y.

However, now consider the case where one of the goods (Y) is private and the other (X) is a public good. In this case, the efficiency condition is now that given in the lower part of Table 4.2. As the consumption of X is, in this case, non-divisible, the social willingness to pay for one unit of X is the *sum* over all consumers of each person's WTP, rather than being equal to one person's WTP. The interpretation of the terms involving marginal products remains exactly as before. Thus efficiency in the allocation of resources requires that the sum of individual WTP is equal to the opportunity cost of X in terms of Y. As the opportunity cost of X in terms of Y is equal, in a market economy, to the ratio of output prices, P_X/P_Y, we can re-express this result as follows. For

Table 4.2 Private and public goods: consumption efficiency

Efficiency conditions for two private goods, X and Y:

$$\left(\frac{U_X}{U_Y}\right)^A = \left(\frac{U_X}{U_Y}\right)^B = \frac{MP_K^Y}{MP_K^X} = \frac{MP_L^Y}{MP_L^X}\left[=\frac{P_X}{P_Y}\right]$$

Efficiency conditions a private good (Y) and a public good (X):

$$\left(\frac{U_X}{U_Y}\right)^A + \left(\frac{U_X}{U_Y}\right)^B = \frac{MP_K^Y}{MP_K^X} = \frac{MP_L^Y}{MP_L^X}\left[=\frac{P_X}{P_Y}\right]$$

one public and one private good, economic efficiency requires that

$$\sum\left(\frac{U_X}{U_Y}\right) = \frac{P_X}{P_Y}$$

Another interpretation of these efficiency conditions is sometimes given. Recall that we obtained, for two private goods

$$\frac{U_X}{U_Y} = \frac{P_X}{P_Y}$$

and for one private good (Y) and one public good (X)

$$\sum\left(\frac{U_X}{U_Y}\right) = \frac{P_X}{P_Y}$$

Now choose units in such a way that $P_Y = 1$. Given this, we can now write the two efficiency conditions as

$$\frac{U_X}{U_Y} = P_X \qquad (4.27)$$

for two private goods, and

$$\sum\left(\frac{U_X}{U_Y}\right) = P_X \qquad (4.28)$$

for one private good (Y) and one public good (X). We may interpret Equation 4.27 as stating that for any two private goods, consumption efficiency requires that purchases be arranged so that the willingness to pay for X (in units of Y) is equal to the price of X (in units of Y). On the other hand, for the case of X being a public good, Equation 4.28 states that purchases should be arranged so that the *sum of the willingness to pay for X (in units of Y) over all consumers of the good X is equal to the price of X (in units of Y)*.

What is the efficient level of provision of a public good?

Two questions are relevant here:

1 Should a particular public good be provided at all if it does not already exist? If it should be, to what extent should it be provided?
2 Once available, how much use should be made of the public good?

The first question is essentially one which should be answered by means of a cost–benefit analysis project appraisal. The project should be undertaken if its social expected net present value exceeds zero. (See

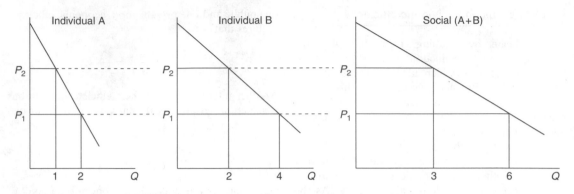

Fig 4.9a The aggregation of individual demands to social demands for a private good

Chapter 2 for an analysis of CBA.) There is one important matter to be careful about here, though. For a private good, the (implicit) demand curve for the resource is the horizontal sum of individual demands. For a public good, the (implicit) demand curve for the resource is the vertical sum of individual demands. This distinction is illustrated in Figures 4.9(a and b).

As far as the second question is concerned, additional use is socially beneficial (and so should be encouraged) whenever a potential user can derive any marginal benefit from the good, no matter how small, provided the marginal cost of that provision is zero. This latter condition will be satisfied, by definition, for a pure public good. However, in circumstances where congestion exists or rivalry between users arises, as for example where the presence of visitors to a wildlife area detracts from other visitors enjoyment, the good in question ceases to be a pure public good. Then limitation on use, possibly through the introduction of user charges, becomes efficient. Wherever a good is private, its use should be such that individual marginal costs and benefits from use are balanced. The efficient use rate of an existing pure public good is illustrated in Figure 4.10.

Property rights, common property resources and environmental resources

The extent to which an economy is able to reach an efficient allocation of resources will depend upon the nature of the property rights which prevail.

Hartwick and Olewiler (1986) define a property right as

> A bundle of characteristics that convey certain powers to the owner of the right.

These characteristics concern conditions of appropriability of returns, the ability to divide or transfer the right, the degree of exclusiveness of the right, and duration and enforceability of the right. Where a right is exclusive to one person or corporation, a private property right is said to exist. In these circumstances, markets will tend to exist and efficient allocations of resources will be possible without government intervention. For several classes of environmental resources, well-defined property rights do not exist. As we show in Chapter 6, outcomes cannot be socially optimal in these circumstances.

Where property rights are non-exclusive, there are common property or open access rights. The title 'common property resources' is used whenever there exist some customary procedures or conventions governing use of the resource in question. This is not implied by the phrase 'open access resources'. In the presence of open access, markets cannot by themselves allocate resources efficiently. It is possible, though unlikely, that resources will be allocated efficiently where common property rights prevail.

Many environmental resources are not privately owned, being characterised by either common property regimes or open access in which ownership is either ill-defined or non-existent. In these circumstances, there are several sources of inefficiency in the use of the resource. Not surprisingly, the major problem arises from the fact that stewardship of the asset is likely to be poor where users cannot expect to receive the fruits of investment in the

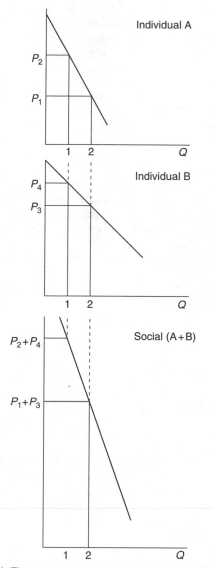

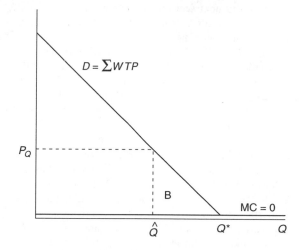

Q^* = Socially efficient level of provision. If a producer were able to extract a price, and that price were P_Q, then the level of demand would be $\hat{Q}$. This would result in an efficiency loss of the area indicated by B.

Fig 4.10 The socially efficient level of provision of a public good.

Fig 4.9b The aggregation of individual demands to social demands for a public good.

environmental assets have the characteristics of public goods, either wholly or partially, and that this can go a long way towards explaining the misuse of these resources.

Imperfect information, risk and uncertainty and irreversibilities

resource. A rapacious attitude often characterises behaviour in the absence of regulatory control. However, since common property resource issues are intimately bound up with the use of resources over time, and because they are characteristic of many renewable resources, these conclusions will not be justified here. They will become evident as you study the economics of renewable resource harvesting in Chapter 7. Indeed, we shall demonstrate at several places in this book that many

The attainment of efficient outcomes through unregulated market behaviour also presupposes perfect information on the part of all transactors of goods and services, of both direct and external effects. To continue our earlier example, those affected by ozone pollution should be fully informed of its origin, and of the damage it causes. This is certainly not true for all persons affected by ozone, and this is likely to be so for many (or even most) forms of pollution externality. In some cases, poor information reflects fundamental scientific uncertainty (for example concerning the Greenhouse Effect). In other cases, poor information about pollution simply reflects the fact that most people are poorly informed about many things in a complex world. Where ignorance is particularly acute, and the potential costs of such ignorance large, government intervention may, again, offer substantial efficiency gains. However, as we show in the next section, there is no guarantee that government intervention will actually achieve these potential net benefits.

Imperfect information and uncertainty become particularly important to our analyses in circumstances where actions have irreversible consequences. It does appear to be the case that many of the consequences of decisions about environmental resource use are irreversible. For example, it is arguable that once developed, a natural wilderness area cannot be returned to its natural state, at least not within time scales that are relevant for human behaviour. We shall demonstrate in Chapter 10 that the conjunction of imperfect information and irreversibility is a potential cause of market failure, as market valuations are not likely to embody so-called option and quasi-option values.

Government policy, government failure and market failure

A central theme throughout this book is that government intervention in the operation of market economies offers the possibility of realising substantial efficiency gains, by eliminating or mitigating situations of market failure, though there are limitations on the ability of government to rectify inefficiencies in the allocation of resources. At this point in the text, all we wish to do is to give a preliminary indication of some of these opportunities.

Firstly, many resources are not traded through competitive market structures in which property rights are clearly established. Efficiency gains may be obtained if government can create and maintain appropriate institutional arrangements for market and property rights. This may well require that the legal and judicial structures of the country in question be developed in such a way that redress for damages arising from external effects can be quickly and cheaply obtained. Similarly, the legal system should ideally allow generators of beneficial public goods and externalities to receive appropriate compensation for the benefits their activities generate but which are not reflected in market transactions.

An alternative direction that government policy might take is to use fiscal instruments – tax and subsidy systems, and marketable permits – to create economically efficient patterns of incentives on private behaviour. We explore this question in depth in Chapter 9. The use of fiscal incentive schemes is likely to be particularly appropriate where markets do already exist, but fail, for one reason or another, to achieve efficient outcomes. However for some goods – public goods – market economies may simply fail to provide them, even though supply at some positive level would be socially desirable. The provision of public goods and services is one area where intervention offers the prospect of very large social benefits.

Governmental intervention may also take the form of providing information, or funding research activity that can reduce uncertainty and increase the stock of knowledge. Given that much research activity has the characteristics of a public good, there is a strong case for its provision or financing by the public sector.

Finally, note that even where markets exist, it might be possible to argue that the allocations that result are ethically undesirable. Many people would argue that the consumption of narcotic drugs, for example, should not be left to market transactions. On the other hand, individuals may choose to consume a lower quantity of some goods than is thought to be desirable. Such goods have been labelled 'merit goods'. A problem with these kinds of arguments, of course, is that they are fundamentally undemocratic and paternalistic. Whilst this does not necessarily mean they are wrong, it does imply that great caution is required in trying to use them as justifications for government intervention.

The arguments we have used so far in this section have all pointed to the possibility of efficiency gains arising from public sector intervention in the economy. But intervention will not necessarily realise such gains. Firstly, the removal of a cause of market failure in one sector of the economy does not necessarily result in a more efficient allocation of resources if other sectors of the economy are characterised by market failure. We cannot pursue this point further, as it takes us into second-best theory which is beyond the scope of this book.

A second important consideration arises from the fact that any government policy can itself induce market failure elsewhere in the economy. Tax and subsidy schemes, for example, may distort the allocation of resources in unintended ways. Any such distortions need to be offset against the intended efficiency gains when the worth of intervention is being assessed.

Intervention in the economy to secure particular policy targets often involves the establishment of

CASE STUDY   Pollution in the Central European ex-planned economies

In this case study, we focus on some of the major industrialised economies of Central Europe, particularly Poland, the previous Czechoslovakia, Hungary, and the former East Germany. Despite historical accuracy, we shall use these names in this study. The heavily industrialised regions of Central Europe are among the most polluted regions in the world, with the most adversely affected region consisting of the coal belt of south-west Poland, north-east Czechoslovakia, and the south-eastern part of East Germany. This part of Europe contains most of the region's heavy industry, particularly the power generation, steel, cement, chemical and petrochemical sectors. The location of this region is shown in Figure 4.11.

Dangerous conditions are thought to prevail in particular 'hot spots' including Katowice in Poland, and Ústí and Most in Czechoslovakia. Very serious environmental conditions prevail in a number of big cities throughout the region; the smogs of Prague, characterised by massive sulphur dioxide

concentrations, are similar to those prevailing in London, the Ruhr valley, Indiana and Pennsylvania in the 1950s and 1960s. The magnitude of the pollution problem can be gauged by noting that in Poland in 1983, areas of 'ecological hazard' covered 11% of the country's land area and 35% of its population. In this total, areas of 'ecological disaster' cover about 4.5% of land. Many parts of Central Europe remain relatively unspoilt, however, including the various mountainous regions, north-east Poland, and border areas that had been largely uninhabited during the Cold War years. The locations of 24 areas thought to be suitable for designation as major conservation areas are shown in Figure 4.12.

What is the environmental legacy that the countries of Central Europe have received? Firstly, and probably of most importance, is atmospheric pollution. In the industrial region referred to above, this is

continued

Source: Compiled by the World Resources Institute, and given in *World Resources 1992–93*, page 58.

Fig 4.11 Central Europe's coal belt.

CASE STUDY continued

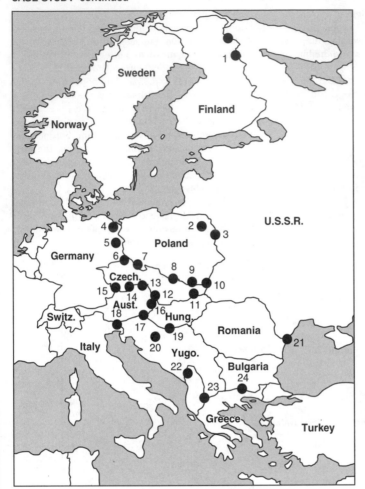

1.   Finish-Russian Woodland Area
2.   Biebrza Marshes
3.   Bialowieza Virgin Forest
4.   Schorfheide/Chorin Area
5.   Spreewald
6.   Sächsische Schweiz
7.   Karkonosze Area
8.   Tatra Area
9.   Pieniny Area
10. Bieszczady Region
11. Slovakian Karst
12. Floodplain Areas of the Danube, Thaya, and March
13. Thaya Valley
14. Trebonsko Pond Region
15. Bavarian Forest, Bohemian Forest Area
16. Lake of Neusiedl
17. Mur Floodplain
18. International Karst Park
19. Lower Reaches of the Drau and Kopacki-Rit
20. Sava Floodplain
21. Danube Delta
22. Lake Scutari
23. Prespa Area
24. Rhodope Mountains, Nestos Delta, and Adjoining Areas

Source: Ecological Bricks for Our Common House of Europe, *Politische Ökologie* (October 1990), pages 16–17, reprinted *World Resources 1992–93*, page 59.

Fig 4.12 Forgotten lands – future preserves?

largely attributable to the use of hard, brown coal, which has both a relatively low energy content and a high pollution propensity. The major atmospheric pollutants are sulphur dioxide (SO_2), soot and other particulate matter and nitrogen dioxide (NO_2), from both heavy industry and smaller-scale production and residential energy use (so-called *low stack emission sources*). Table 4.3 compares the magnitudes of sulphur dioxide emissions between the countries of Central and Western Europe and the USA. Also of importance are carbon monoxide, hydrocarbons and various oxides of nitrogen (NO_x), all of which cause damage to human respiratory systems, and lead, a serious, persistent toxin. In the absence of effective control, this latter class of pollutants is set to rise rapidly with the projected high growth in traffic volume in these countries in the next two decades.

The second category of damage relates to pollution to water systems, as a result of industrial discharges, inorganic fertiliser and pesticide use, and the almost complete absence of sewage treatment in many parts of Central Europe. Forest and soil damage is acute in parts of the region, and can be attributed largely to

continued

CASE STUDY continued

Table 4.3 Sulphur dioxide emissions, 1989

Country	Total emissions (thousand metric tons of SO_2/year)	Per capita emissions (kilograms)	Emissions per dollar GNP (grams)
Central Europe and former USSR			
Albania[a]	50	15.6	13.2
Bulgaria	1 030	114.6	49.4
Czechoslovakia	2 800	178.9	22.7
Eastern Germany (former Dem. Rep.)	5 210	313.3	32.7
Hungary	1 218	115.2	45.0
Poland	3 910	103.3	58.4
Romania	200	8.6	2.5
Yugoslavia	1 650	69.6	27.9
Former USSR[b]	9 318	32.4	3.5
Western Europe and United States			
Austria	124	16.3	1.1
Belgium	414	41.5	2.6
France	1 520	27.1	1.5
Western Germany (Fed. Rep.)	1 500	24.2	1.2
Italy	2 410	41.9	2.8
Sweden	220	25.9	1.2
United Kingdom	3 552	62.1	4.3
United States[c]	20 700	83.2	4.0

[a] Estimated emissions.
[b] Emissions data for European part of former USSR only. Per capita and per dollar emissions calculated using population and GNP for entire country.
[c] 1988 emissions data.

Sources:
1 *World Resources 1992–93*, Chapter 24, *Atmosphere and Climate*, Table 24.5.
2 *World Resources 1992–93*, Chapter 15, *Basic Economic Indicators*, Table 15.1.
3 The World Bank, unpublished data (The World Bank, Washington, DC, June 1991), printed in *World Resources 1992–93*, page 64.

the patterns of activity and emissions that have been mentioned already. The nature of industrial location in Central Europe also leads to massive transboundary pollution problems, of the kind we discuss in detail in Chapter 12. It has been estimated, for example, that only 36% of Czechoslovakia's sulphur emissions are deposited in that country. International externalities of this kind pose immense problems for pollution control.

Finally, the effects on human health remain alarmingly large, with

The health prospects of people living in Central Europe [being] the bleakest in the industrialised world.

World Resources 1992–93

Life expectancy is five years lower in Central than in Western Europe, and morbidity rates for children are very serious.

Pollution control and clean-up to western European standards will be massively expensive. In Poland alone, clean-up costs have been estimated at $260 billion over the next 25 years, and pollution abatement costs have been estimated at $70 billion.

The causes of pollution in Central Europe
Although heavy industrialisation and its associated pollution problems had become established in many parts of this region prior to the Second World War, the magnitudes and pervasiveness of pollution in Central Europe are primarily a consequence of the patterns of economic and political organisation that were imposed in the late 1940s. The Stalinist model of economic organisation placed great stress on the development of heavy industry, centralised control of resource allocation, and limitation of trade between

continued

CASE STUDY continued

the socialist Council for Mutual Economic Assistance (COMECON) countries and the rest of the world. These factors alone did not make it inevitable that the region would be so badly scarred by pollution; however, a number of particular characteristics of the region, together with the way in which planning was implemented, did so.

A fundamental feature of COMECON economic activity has been pervasive productive inefficiency in general, and energy inefficiency in particular. The energy to output ratio was, until recently, between two and three times larger in Central Europe than in Western Europe. Resources have not been allocated in ways that maximised the value of output for any given bundle of resources. Janos Kornai (1986) has attributed this partly to the existence of 'soft budget constraints' under which managers were able to pass on any cost increases and so did not face incentives to minimise production costs. The patterns of incentives facing managers rewarded output increases, irrespective of how they were obtained. Under the material accounting system, output was valued as a weighted sum of the inputs used, creating a situation in which greater rather than lesser resource use was striven for.

A related explanation of production and energy inefficiency is the role of prices. Whereas prices should ideally reflect relative scarcities, they did not do so in the COMECON countries. Administrative or accounting prices often reflected politically set targets, and also reflected quantities of inputs used rather than the 'true' net value of output. Energy prices throughout the region were set at levels well below world prices, creating further incentives to use energy intensively. The region's energy reserves, until oil and gas were imported from the Soviet Union in the late 1970s, are predominantly in the form of brown coal (lignite); as noted previously, this is heavily polluting and low in thermal energy content. The use of brown coal in power generation was promoted by the policy of self-reliance adopted in these countries.

Gabor Hovanyi (in Chandler, 1986) has stressed the important role played by the absence of foreign trade between the COMECON countries and the rest of the world. Trade is an important engine for technology transfer and updating, and the promotion of innovation. Its absence contributed to the continued use of obsolete techniques in Central Europe.

Three others factors have played important roles. First, whilst the damages caused by pollution have long been recognised in Central Europe, and several countries instituted emission charge systems as long ago as the 1970s, little effective account has been taken of the external effects of economic activity in the decision making systems. This partly reflects the second factor, the strongly centralised pattern of decision-making in these countries. When pollution problems became manifest in particular 'hot spots', lines of influence to encourage adaptation of policy were almost non-existent, effectively disenfranchising local communities and preventing bargaining solutions to pollution problems. Finally, maintenance and repair of equipment, being service activities which tended to be regarded as unproductive under the material accounting system, were seriously under-resourced, creating a creeping inefficiency in many areas of activity and encouraging massive waste of capital resources.

The prospects for the countries of Central Europe are far less bleak than these paragraphs indicate. Most now have decentralised political structures and emerging market mechanisms for resource allocation. Prices of energy and other resources are now at world levels, and all have strong pollution control and clean-up programmes. However, the costs of cleaning up hazardous stocks, polluted water systems, and atmospheric and soil media are enormous (for example being estimated at $260 billion for Poland alone) and will place great stress on the public finances of governments already dealing with large public sector budget deficits.

Source: World Resources 1992–93, pages 57–74.

regulatory organisational structures. This opens up the possibility of a third type of 'government failure' that is sometimes described as institutional capture.

In some cases, the chosen policy instruments may just fail to achieve desired outcomes. This is particularly likely in the case of instruments that take the form of quantity controls or direct regulation. One example of this is the attempt by the Greek government to reduce car usage in Athens. Regulations prohibiting entry into the city by cars with

particular letters on their licence plates on particular days has served to promote the purchase of additional cars by households wishing to maintain freedom of mobility in the city. Similarly, the use of quantity controls in fisheries policy (such as determining minimum mesh sizes for nets, maximum number of days of permitted fishing, required days in port for vessels, and so on) have met with very little success, as a result of fishermen making behavioural adjustments to minimise the impact of the regulations. The limited success of quantitative controls in fishing is explored at length in Chapter 7.

Finally, at the risk of excessive repetition, one should always remember that efficiency improvements are not unambiguously desirable, as they may (in the absence of redistributive and reallocative steps) reduce the value of the social welfare function. It is possible in principle to use fiscal adjustments to transfer resources so as to achieve any distributions that might be regarded as fair. Put another way, it is possible to design policy packages that are distributionally neutral. However, this will often not be done in practice.

Discussion questions

1 To what extent do you believe that an economic criterion of efficiency is compatible with
  (a) an economic definition of sustainability?
  (b) an ecological definition of sustainability?
2 What role could taxes on pollutant emissions play in securing economic efficiency?
3 How can the concepts of externalities and public goods be used to shed light on
  (a) losses in biodiversity?
  (b) acid rain pollution?
  (c) research into alternative energy sources?
4 'If the market puts a lower value on trees as preserved resources than as sources of timber for construction, then those trees should be felled for timber.' Discuss.

Problems

1 Demonstrate that Equations 4.1 and 4.2 in the text of this chapter embody an assumption that there are no externalities in either consumption or production. Suppose that B's consumption of Y had a positive effect upon A's utility, and that the use of K by firm X adversely affects the output of firm Y. Show how the utility and production functions would need to be amended to take account of these effects.
2 The product-mix efficiency condition requires that there be an equality of the rate at which consumers value one good in terms of another with the opportunity costs of one good in terms of the other. Demonstrate that if this condition were not

satisfied, inputs could be reallocated in such a way that a higher total utility could be achieved by each consumer for any given initial level of inputs.
3 Show that market economies will, in general, be characterised by inefficient allocations of resources whenever significant consumption externalities are present. What is the necessary condition for consumption efficiency in this case?

Further reading

For a thorough general coverage of welfare economics principles, see Bator (1957), Varian (1987) or Layard and Walters (1978), Chapter 1. Applications of these principles to environmental economics are to be found in Hartwick and Olewiler (1986, especially Chapter 14), Baumol and Oates (1988), and Hanley and Spash (1993). Classic articles on environmental externalities include Ayres and Kneese (1969), and D'Arge and Kogiku (1972). Excellent discussions concerning welfare economics and the environment may be found in Common (1995), Dasgupta (1990), Johannson (1987) and Fisher (1981). An authoritative, but quite difficult, exposition is to be found in Maler (1985). .

Appendix 1

Utility maximisation

Consider an individual consumer, with a fixed money income M and gaining utility from the consumption of two goods, X and Y. The prices of these goods are determined in competitive markets, at the levels P_X and P_Y. Suppose his or her utility function is given by

$$U = U(X, Y)$$

We can express the problem of maximising utility subject to a budget constraint mathematically as

$$\text{Max } U = U(X, Y)$$

subject to

$$M = P_X X + P_Y Y$$

Solving this problem by the method of Lagrange, we obtain

$$L = U(X, Y) + \lambda_1 (P_X X + P_Y Y - M)$$

The first-order conditions for a maximum require that

$$\frac{\partial L}{\partial X} = U_X + \lambda_1 P_X = 0$$

and

$$\frac{\partial L}{\partial Y} = U_Y + \lambda_1 P_Y = 0$$

where $U_X = \partial U/\partial X$ and $U_Y = \partial U/\partial Y$, the marginal utilities of goods X and Y.

From these two equations we can deduce that

$$U_X = -\lambda_1 P_X$$
$$U_Y = -\lambda_1 P_Y$$

and so

$$-\lambda_1 = \frac{U_X}{P_X} = \frac{U_Y}{P_Y}$$

Rearranging this expression, and noting that this is true for each consumer, indexed i, we obtain

$$\left(\frac{U_X}{U_Y}\right)^i = \left(\frac{P_X}{P_Y}\right)^i \qquad (4.29)$$

as given by Equation 4.14 in the main text.

Cost minimisation and profit maximisation

Suppose that a firm wishes to minimise its cost of production subject to satisfying an output constraint. (We will consider where this output constraint might come from shortly.). Let L and K be two inputs with prices P_L and P_K fixed in competitive input markets. Denote the required output level by $\bar{Q}$, and total costs by C. Mathematically we can express the cost minimisation problem as

$$\text{Min } C = P_L L + P_K K$$

subject to

$$\bar{Q} = Q(K, L)$$

Solving this problem by the method of Lagrange, we obtain

$$\Upsilon = P_L L + P_K K + \lambda_2 (Q(K, L) - \bar{Q})$$

The first order conditions for a minimum require that

$$\frac{\partial \Upsilon}{\partial L} = P_L + \lambda_2 Q_L = 0$$

and

$$\frac{\partial \Upsilon}{\partial K} = P_K + \lambda_2 Q_K = 0$$

where $Q_K = \partial Q/\partial K$ and $Q_L = \partial Q/\partial L$, the marginal products of capital and labour.

From these two equations we can deduce that

$$\lambda_2 Q_L = -P_L$$
$$\lambda_2 Q_K = -P_K$$

and so

$$-\lambda_2 = \frac{P_L}{Q_L} = \frac{P_K}{Q_K} \qquad (4.30)$$

Given that we use the notation MP_K for Q_K in the main text, we can rewrite this expression in the form

$$\left(\frac{P_K}{\text{MP}_K}\right) = \left(\frac{P_L}{\text{MP}_L}\right) \qquad (4.31)$$

as given by the last equality in Equation 4.16 in the main text (see Equation 4.36 below).

Next we wish to demonstrate that, for any good, $\text{MC} = P_K/\text{MP}_k = P_L/\text{MP}_L$. Denote L^* and K^* as the cost minimising levels of L and K. By definition

$$C = P_L L^* + P_K K^* \qquad (4.32)$$

Marginal cost is obtained by differentiating this expression for cost with respect to output:

$$\text{MC} = \frac{\partial C}{\partial Q} = \left[P_L \frac{\partial L^*}{\partial Q} + P_K \frac{\partial K^*}{\partial Q} \right] \qquad (4.33)$$

The term in square brackets in Equation 4.33 is equal to the negative of the value of the Lagrange multiplier, $-\lambda_2$. To see that this is so, take the expression for the output constraint at the cost-minimising levels of the inputs:

$$Q(K^*, L^*) = \bar{Q}$$

By differentiation with respect to $\bar{Q}$, we obtain

$$Q_K \cdot \frac{\partial K^*}{\partial \bar{Q}} + Q_L \cdot \frac{\partial L^*}{\partial \bar{Q}} = 1 \qquad (4.34)$$

Substituting from Equation 4.30 into Equation 4.34, we obtain

$$\frac{-P_K}{\lambda_2} \cdot \frac{\partial K^*}{\partial \bar{Q}} - \frac{P_L}{\lambda_2} \cdot \frac{\partial L^*}{\partial \bar{Q}} = 1$$

and then, after multiplication by $-\lambda_2$,

$$\text{MC} = P_K \cdot \frac{\partial K^*}{\partial \bar{Q}} + P_L \cdot \frac{\partial L^*}{\partial \bar{Q}} = -\lambda_2$$

So we have established that $-\lambda_2$ is the marginal cost, MC. But from Equation 4.31 we also know that

$$-\lambda_2 = \frac{P_L}{Q_L} = \frac{P_K}{Q_K} = \frac{P_L}{\text{MP}_L} = \frac{P_K}{\text{MP}_K}$$

This establishes the result we wish to prove, namely that $MC = P_K/MP_K = P_L/MP_L$.

Finally, we also wish to demonstrate that price equals marginal cost in long-run competitive equilibrium. To do this, first note from Equation 4.32, together with the fact that L^* and K^* are functions of P_L, P_K and $\bar{Q}$, that

$$C = C(P_L, P_K, \bar{Q})$$

From the definition of profit we have

$$\Pi(\bar{Q}) = P\bar{Q} - C(P_L, P_K, \bar{Q})$$

The first-order condition for profit maximisation is that

$$\frac{d\Pi(\bar{Q})}{d\bar{Q}} = P - \frac{dC}{d\bar{Q}} = 0$$

which implies that $P = dC/dQ$, and hence at a profit maximum, output price equals marginal cost.

We have now established the result that

$$P = MC = \left(\frac{P_K}{MP_K}\right) = \left(\frac{P_L}{MP_L}\right) \quad (4.35)$$

So for any two goods, X and Y say, we have

$$P_X = MC_X = \left(\frac{P_K}{MP_K}\right)^X = \left(\frac{P_L}{MP_L}\right)^X \quad (4.36)$$

and

$$P_Y = MC_Y = \left(\frac{P_K}{MP_K}\right)^Y = \left(\frac{P_L}{MP_L}\right)^Y \quad (4.37)$$

and dividing Equation 4.36 by Equation 4.37 we obtain

$$\frac{P_X}{P_Y} = \frac{\left(\dfrac{P_K}{MP_K}\right)^X}{\left(\dfrac{P_K}{MP_K}\right)^Y}$$

which implies

$$\frac{P_X}{P_Y} = \frac{\left(\dfrac{P_K}{MP_K}\right)^X}{\left(\dfrac{P_K}{MP_K}\right)^Y}$$

But since all firms face the same price of capital, $P_K^X = P_K^Y$, and so this expression reduces to

$$\frac{P_X}{P_Y} = \frac{MP_K^Y}{MP_K^X}$$

Finally, using the result obtained earlier that in a competitive equilibrium

$$\frac{U_X}{U_Y} = \frac{P_X}{P_Y}$$

we obtain the product-mix efficiency condition

$$\frac{U_X}{U_Y} = \frac{P_X}{P_Y} = \frac{MP_K^Y}{MP_K^X}$$

By replacing K by L in this argument, the proof would be in terms of labour rather than capital, as here.

Appendix 2

The market for loanable funds

Assume that there exists a perfect capital market in which lending and borrowing can take place at a fixed rate of interest, i. Consider two successive periods of time, denoted 0 and 1 respectively. It will be convenient to consider one individual with an initial level of income in each period. This person has two related sets of choices to make: firstly, a consumption choice – the amount to be consumed in each period – and secondly, an investment choice – which of the available investment projects should be taken up. The amounts produced and consumed in the two periods will depend upon the consumption and investment choices that are made.

Maximisation of the present value of utility

Given the interest rate i, an individual can exchange £1 income (and so consumption) today for £1$(1 + i)$ in the next period, as illustrated in Figure 4.13. He or

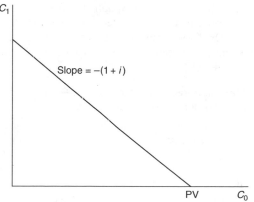

Fig 4.13 The market rate of exchange of present for future income.

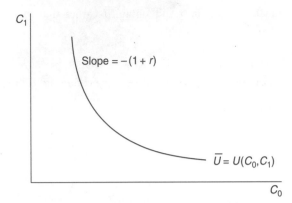

Fig 4.14 The intertemporal indifference curve.

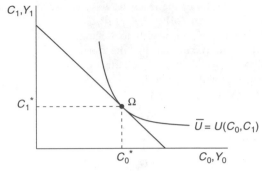

Fig 4.15 Intertemporal consumers' equilibrium.

she can save £1 in period 0, earn interest on the saving at a rate i, and consume an additional quantity of $£1(1 + i)$ in period 1.

The individual's preferences between present and future consumption are reflected in his or her intertemporal utility function

$$U = U(C_0, C_1)$$

Setting utility at some fixed level $\bar{U}$, an indifference curve can be constructed consisting of a locus of combinations of C_0 and C_1 yielding that level of utility. This is shown in Figure 4.14. If we denote by r the person's consumption discount rate, then the absolute value of the slope of an intertemporal indifference curve is given by $(1 + r)$. A necessary condition for the consumer to have achieved an efficient allocation of consumption over time is that the rate at which present consumption can be exchanged for future consumption (i.e. the slope of the intertemporal budget line in Figure 4.13) is equal to the marginal worth of present consumption relative to future consumption (i.e. the slope of an intertemporal utility indifference curve in Figure 4.14). One illustration of an efficient intertemporal consumption allocation is shown by the point Ω in Figure 4.15.

Maximisation of the present value of profits: intertemporal production possibilities

Assume a set of investment projects exists. For each project, an investment reduces present consumption by ΔC_0 and increases the next period's consumption by an amount ΔC_1. Let the rate of return on a project be denoted by δ, defined as

$$\frac{\Delta C_1}{-\Delta C_0} = 1 + \delta \quad \text{or} \quad \frac{\Delta C_1 - \Delta C_0}{-\Delta C_0} = \delta$$

Arranging all available projects in order of rate of return, we can represent available intertemporal production possibilities by means of the intertemporal production frontier shown in Figure 4.16. (In this diagram, we arbitrarily take the coordinates $\{C_0', C_1'\}$ to represent the consumption set if no investments are undertaken.)

As before, assume that unlimited borrowing and lending opportunities are available at the rate i (as shown in Figure 4.13). The rational individual (firm) will undertake all investment projects which have a positive net present value. That is, projects will be selected for which

$$PV = \Delta C_0 + \frac{\Delta C_1}{1 + i} > 0$$

This implies that all projects should be done for which $\delta > i$, and in turn implies that at an efficient allocation $\delta = i$ as indicated in Figure 4.17 at the point ϕ. Maximisation of present value by competitive firms implies that firms invest to the point where the rate of return on a marginal project, δ, equals the market

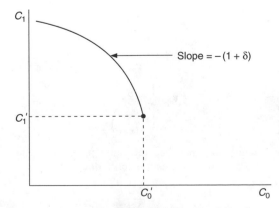

Fig 4.16 The Intertemporal Production Possibility Curve.

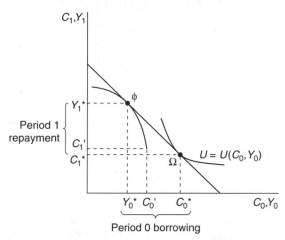

Fig 4.17 Intertemporal consumption–production equilibrium.

rate of interest, i. An efficient production choice, therefore, requires that the rate at which future and present consumption can be exchanged (given by the slope of the intertemporal production frontier) is equal to the rate at which these can be exchanged in the market (determined by the prevailing rate of interest).

Intertemporal production and consumption efficiency

Finally, bringing together the two sides of our argument, we observe that simultaneous satisfaction of the conditions for efficiency in production and consumption requires that $(1 + r) = (1 + \delta)$, as illustrated in Figure 4.17.

We assumed at the outset that all agents face a single given rate of interest. How is such a rate determined? To answer this, we need to look at the borrowing and lending decisions implicit in Figure 4.17. Note first that this individual borrows the amount $C_0^* - Y_0^*$ in period 0, and repays (lends) the amount $Y_1^* - C_1^*$ in period 1. The market rate of interest will be determined by the borrowing and lending decisions of all individuals in the economy. The equilibrium rate of interest (shown in all diagrams) is that for which aggregate lending equals aggregate borrowing at any point in time. Note that the individual we have investigated here is a net borrower initially and a net lender later. In an economy where the interest rate is in equilibrium, this borrowing/lending stance must be offset by an opposite stance by all other persons.

The efficient and optimal use of environmental resources

The Golden Rule is that there are no golden rules.

George Bernard Shaw, *Maxims for Revolutionists*

Introduction

A substantial part of this book is concerned with the use of environmental resources through time. In this chapter, we construct a framework to analyse intertemporal resource use, which provides the basis for the more extensive analyses of non-renewable resource depletion and the harvesting of renewable resources that follow in Chapters 6 and 7.

Our objectives in the present chapter are

1 To develop a simple economic model, built around a production function in which environmental resources are inputs into the production process.
2 To identify the condition or conditions that must be satisfied by any pattern of natural resource use over time that is economically efficient.
3 To establish what is meant by a socially optimal pattern of resource use over time in the special case of a utilitarian social welfare function.
4 To investigate how the characteristics of an efficient and optimal allocation of environmental resources would be affected by
   (a) the presence of external effects (such as pollution) in the extraction or use of these resources;
   (b) the presence of technical progress;
   (c) positive rates of population growth.
5 To identify the parameters which are critical in determining the possibility of sustainable consumption over long periods of time.

Before our attention turns to these matters, some advice on your reading of this chapter may be useful. We shall be constructing a mathematical model of the economy in order to address questions about the use of resources. For the reasons explained in Box 4.1 in Chapter 4, economic models are usually simplified

and highly stylised representations of an economy, and this is certainly true of the model we will develop here. However, although the economics of our model are straightforward, the mathematics required to analyse the model are quite advanced in places.

To keep technical difficulties to a minimum, the main body of text avoids the use of mathematical arguments and proofs wherever possible. It shows the logic behind, and the economic interpretations of, important results. Derivations and proofs of results are presented separately in appendices at the end of the chapter. It is not necessary to read these appendices to follow the arguments in the chapter. But we recommend that you do read them; most of the derivations use quite straightforward maths, and in the few cases where the analysis is more difficult, the techniques are explained thoroughly. Appendix 3 takes the reader through a key mathematical technique used in the book – dynamic optimisation using the Maximum Principle.

PART 1

A simple optimal resource depletion model

The economy and its production function

We aim to develop a model that can help us to understand the use of environmental resources over time, and also is as simple as possible for this task. One way of doing this is to make the model highly aggregated. We investigate an economy producing a single homogeneous output, Q, which can be either consumed or invested. Investing output will increase the capital stock, permitting greater consumption in future periods.

Output is generated through a production function. Environmental resources are inputs to production, and so appear as variables in the production function. We begin by studying the case in which there is a single, 'composite' exhaustible resource, R. Beginning in this way abstracts from any substitution effects that might take place between different kinds of exhaustible resource: in our model there is only one such resource. In Chapter 6, we shall see how our conclusions alter when different kinds of environmental resource enter the production function separately.

Output is produced through a production function with three inputs, capital (K), labour (L) and the exhaustible (non-renewable) resource (R). The economy's production function is represented by

$$Q = Q(K, L, R) \qquad (5.1)$$

This states that output[1] has some functional relationship to the quantities of the three inputs which are used, but it does not tell us anything about the particular form of this relationship. There are many such forms that the production function might actually take. One possible type of production technology is the *Cobb–Douglas* (CD) form; in this case, the economy's input–output relationship comes from the class of functions

$$Q = AK^{\alpha}L^{\beta}R^{\gamma} \qquad (5.2)$$

where A, α, β, and $\gamma > 0$. An alternative form, widely used in empirical analysis, is the *constant elasticity of substitution* (CES) type, which comprises the family of functional forms

$$Q = A(\alpha K^{-\theta} + \beta L^{-\theta} + \gamma R^{-\theta})^{-\epsilon/\theta} \qquad (5.3)$$

where A, ϵ, α, β, $\gamma > 0$, $\alpha + \beta + \gamma = 1$, and $-1 < \theta \neq 0$.[2]

The CD and CES forms of production function do not exhaust all possibilities, of course. Many other

forms exist, and we refer to CD and CES only because they are two of the simplest types, and because they are commonly used in economic analysis. In this chapter we shall not be making any assumption as to which type of production form best represents the production technology of an economy, but rather shall work with a general functional form that might be Cobb–Douglas, might be CES, or might be some other. Ultimately the question of which functional form is the 'correct' one is an empirical question, and cannot be answered by the theoretical argument.

Is the environmental resource essential?

Not surprisingly, it turns out to be the case that the characteristics of an optimal resource depletion path through time will be influenced by whether the environmental resource is 'essential' in some sense. Claiming that a resource is essential could mean several things. Firstly, a resource might be essential as a *waste disposal* and reprocessing agent. Given the ubiquitous nature of waste and the magnitude of the damages that waste can cause, resources do appear to be necessary as waste processing agents. A resource might also be essential for human *psychic satisfaction*. Many humans appear to need peace, quiet, solitude and the aesthetic enjoyment derived from observing or being in natural environments. It may well be that these wishes are so strong that the resource is, in effect, essential. Thirdly, some resource might be *ecologically essential* in the sense that some or all of a relevant ecosystem cannot survive in its absence.

In this chapter, we are only concerned with a fourth meaning: whether a resource is essential for *production*. Some resources are undoubtedly essential for specific products – for example, crude oil is an essential raw material for the production of petrol, kerosene and paraffin. But in this chapter, we wish to look at resources at a high degree of aggregation,

[1] Each output level Q satisfying the production function is the maximum attainable output for given quantities of the inputs, and implies that inputs are used in a *technically efficient* way. Throughout this text, we assume always that technical efficiency is satisfied.

[2] The CD and CES functions given in Equations 5.2 and 5.3 allow returns to scale to be increasing, constant or decreasing. If we restrict attention to the special case in which there are constant returns to scale, then

1 In the CD function, $\alpha + \beta + \gamma = 1$.
2 In the CES function, $\epsilon = 1$.

If $\theta = 0$, the CES production function is not defined; furthermore, it can be shown that the Cobb–Douglas function is a special case of the CES form as θ foes to zero in the limit. In that case, we know that all inputs are essential, in the sense to be defined in the next subsection.

dealing with general classes such as non-renewable and renewable resources. What does it mean to claim that a non-renewable (or exhaustible) resource is an essential productive input? We define a productive input to be essential if output is zero whenever the quantity of that input is zero, irrespective of the amounts of other inputs used. That is, R is essential if

$$Q = Q(K, L, 0) = 0$$

One way of approaching this issue is to investigate some plausible forms for the economy's production function, and see whether the resource is essential in these particular cases. Consider first the Cobb–Douglas production function. For this function, it is always the case that R is essential (as too are K and L). It is easy to verify that this is true. To confirm this for yourself, note that setting any input to zero in Equation 5.2 results in $Q = 0$. Do we obtain the same result if the production function is CES type? Unfortunately, matters are not so straightforward with the CES function. We state (but without giving a proof) that if $\theta < 0$, then none of the inputs is essential, and if $\theta > 0$ then all inputs are essential. This illustrates the fact that, even if one were fortunate enough to know which type of production function is an appropriate one, it can still be the case that whether or not natural resources are essential to production is an empirical question.

What is the relevance of essentialness to our study of resource use over time? If we wish to answer questions about the very long-run properties of economic systems, the essentialness of exhaustible resources will matter. Since, by definition, exhaustible resources exist in finite quantities, it is not possible to use positive amounts of them over infinite horizons. However, if a resource is essential, then we know that production can only be positive if some positive amount of the input is used. This seems to suggest that production and consumption cannot be sustained indefinitely if an exhaustible resource is a necessary input to production.

However, if the rate at which the resource is used were to decline asymptotically to zero, and so never actually become zero in finite time, then production could be sustained indefinitely even if the resource were essential. Whether output could rise, or at least stay constant over time, or whether it would inevitably have to decline gradually towards zero will depend upon the extent to which other resources can be substituted for exhaustible resources, and upon the behaviour of output as this substitution takes place. We now turn to this matter.

What is the elasticity of substitution between *K* and *R*?

In Chapter 1 we examined three different perspectives on the economic growth–natural environment relationship. That discussion demonstrated that the extent of substitution possibilities is likely to have an important bearing on the feasibility of continuing economic growth over the very long-run, given the constraints which are imposed by the natural environment. Let us now look in detail at one particular substitution possibility, that between the exhaustible resource and other productive inputs. It will be convenient for this purpose to consider a production function with an exhaustible resource and just one other input. In this way, we can illustrate the arguments diagrammatically, but without losing anything of importance. So we shall take the economy's production function to be

$$Q = Q(K, R) \qquad (5.4)$$

The elasticity of substitution between capital and resources (σ) can be defined as the proportionate change in the ratio of capital to exhaustible resource used in response to a proportionate change in the ratio of the marginal products of capital and the resource (see Chiang, 1984). That is

$$\sigma = \frac{d(K/R)}{K/R} \bigg/ \frac{d(Q_K/Q_R)}{Q_K/Q_R}$$

where the partial derivative Q_R denotes the marginal product of the exhaustible resource and Q_K denotes the marginal product of capital.[3] The elasticity of substitution, σ, must lie between zero and infinity. We can also represent substitution possibilities between production inputs diagrammatically. Figure 5.1 shows what are known as production function isoquants. For a given production function, an isoquant is the locus of all combinations of inputs

---

[3] It can also be shown (see Chiang, 1984, for example) that if resources are allocated efficiently in a competitive marker economy, the elasticity of substitution between capital and an exhaustible resource is equal to

$$\sigma = \frac{d(K/R)}{K/R} \bigg/ \frac{d(P_R/P_K)}{P_R/P_K}$$

where P_R and P_K denote the unit prices of the exhaustible resource and capital respectively. That is, the elasticity of substitution measures the proportionate change in the ratio of capital to exhaustible resource used in response to a given proportionate change in the relative price of the resource to capital.

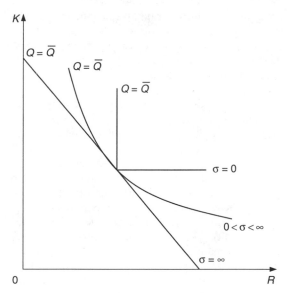

Fig 5.1 Substitution possibilities and the shapes of production function isoquants.

which when combined efficiently yield a constant level of output. The three isoquants shown in Figure 5.1 each correspond to the level of output, $\bar{Q}$, but derive from different production functions. The differing substitution possibilities are reflected in the curvatures of the isoquants.

In the case where no input substitution is possible (that is, $\sigma = 0$), inputs must be combined in fixed proportions and the isoquants will be L-shaped. Production functions of this type, admitting no substitution possibilities, are sometimes known as Leontief functions. As you will see in Chapter 13, they are commonly used in input–output models of the economy. At the other extreme, if substitution is perfect ($\sigma = \infty$), isoquants will be straight lines. In general, one would expect production functions to exhibit an elasticity of substitution somewhere between those two extremes (although not all production functions will have a constant σ for all input combinations). In these cases, isoquants will often be convex to the origin, exhibiting a greater degree of curvature the lower the elasticity of substitution, σ. Some evidence on empirically-observed values of the elasticity of substitution between different production inputs is presented later in Box 5.1.

For a CES production function, we can also relate the elasticity of substitution to the concept of essentialness, discussed in the previous section. It can be shown (see, for example, Chiang (1984) page

428) that

$$\sigma = \frac{1}{1 + \theta}$$

We argued in the previous section that no input is essential where $\theta < 0$, and all inputs are essential where $\theta > 0$. Given the relationship between σ and θ, it can be seen that no input is essential where $\sigma > 1$, and all inputs are essential where $\sigma < 1$. Where $\sigma = 1$ (or $\theta = 0$), the CES production function collapses to the special form of Cobb–Douglas, in which case, as we have already seen, all inputs are essential.

The implications of resource substitutability

The consequences of increasing resource scarcity

As production continues (and perhaps grows) throughout time, stocks of exhaustible resources must decline. One would expect that continuing depletion of the resource stock will be associated with a tendency for the exhaustible resource price to rise relative to the price of capital. We will show later in this chapter and in Chapter 6 that this intuition is correct.

Now productive efficiency implies, as we showed in the previous chapter, that as the relative price of the exhaustible resource rises, the ratio of exhaustible resources to capital employed will fall, thereby raising the marginal product of the resource and reducing the marginal product of capital. However, the magnitude of this substitution effect will depend upon the value of the elasticity of substitution, σ. Where the elasticity of substitution is high, only small changes in relative input prices will be necessary to induce a large proportionate change in the quantities of inputs used. 'Resource scarcity' will be of little consequence as the economy is able to replace the scarce resource by the reproducible substitute. Put another way, the constraints imposed by the finiteness of the exhaustible resource stock will bite rather weakly in such a case.

On the other hand, very low substitution possibilities mean that as resource depletion pushes up the relative price of the exhaustible resource, the magnitude of the induced substitution effect will be very small. 'Resource scarcity' will have much more serious adverse effects as the scope for replacement of the scarce resource by the reproducible substitute is much more limited. Where the elasticity of substitution is zero, then no scope exists for such replacement.

The elasticity of substitution and sustainability

In our discussion of sustainability in Chapter 3, you will recall that mention was made of the so-called Hartwick savings rule. Interpreting sustainability in terms of non-declining consumption through time, John Hartwick (1977, 1978) sought to identify conditions under which such a target would be achievable. The conditions centre around a particular savings rule, commonly known as Hartwick's Rule, which states that if the rents derived from exhaustible resource extraction are invested entirely in reproducible (that is, physical and human) capital, then under certain conditions, the levels of output and consumption will remain constant over time.

We can now be a little more precise about this. If the elasticity of substitution, σ, is greater than or equal to one, then in the absence of technical progress and with no population growth, it is possible to sustain a positive level of consumption indefinitely if the Hartwick rule is followed. If $\sigma < 1$, however, then constant positive consumption may not be possible unless technical progress is sufficiently rapid. A proof of these assertions and a complete analysis of the Hartwick rule and its applications can be found in Hartwick's original articles (Hartwick, 1977, 1978).

Clearly, the magnitude of the elasticity of substitution between exhaustible resources and other inputs is a matter of considerable importance. It would be very useful if policy-makers were to know their values. Unfortunately, as in the case of essentialness, these magnitudes cannot be deduced from theoretical considerations alone, but have to be inferred empirically. Whereas many economists believe that evidence points to reasonably high substitution possibilities (although there is by no means a consensus on this), environmental scientists and ecologists stress the limited substitution possibilities between resources and reproducible capital. Indeed in some cases, ecologists have argued that, in the long-term, these substitution possibilities are zero. These differences probably reflect, in large part, differences in the breadth of functions of the environmental resources being considered. For example, whereas it has appeared to be relatively easy to economise on the use of fossil energy inputs in many production processes, it is difficult to conceive of reproducible capital substituting for environmental capital in the provision of the amenities offered by wilderness areas, or in the regulation of the earth's climate. The reprocessing of harmful wastes is less clear cut; certainly reproducible capital and labour can substitute for the waste disposal functions of the environment to some extent (perhaps through increased use of recycling processes) but there appear to be limits to how far this substitution can proceed.

Finally, it is clear that even if we were to establish that substitutability had been high in the past, this does not of itself imply that it will continue to be so in the future. It may well be that as development pushes the economy to points where environmental constraints begin to bite, substitution possibilities reduce significantly. Recent literature from environmental science seems to suggest this possibility. On the other hand, a more optimistic view is suggested by the effect of technological progress, which appears in many cases to have contributed towards enhanced opportunities for substitution. If you have not already done so, you should now read the material on resource substitutability presented in Box 5.1.

Other resource substitution processes

Up to this point in our theoretical presentation, environmental resources have been treated in a very special way. Let us concentrate on non-renewable resources for a moment. We have assumed that there is a single resource, R, of fixed, known size, and (implicitly) of uniform quality. Substitution possibilities have been limited to those between this resource and other, non-environmental resources. In practice, there is a large number of different natural resources, with substitution possibilities among members of this set. Of equal importance is the non-uniform quality of resource stocks. A particular resource stock does not exist in some fixed amount of uniform quality, but rather in deposits of varying grade and quality. As high-grade reserved become exhausted, extraction will turn to lower-grade deposits, provided the resource price is sufficiently high to cover the higher extraction costs of the lower-grade mineral. Furthermore, whilst there will be some upper limit to the physical occurrence of the resource in the earth's crust, the location and extent of these deposits will not be known with certainty. As known reserves become depleted, exploration can, therefore, increase the size of available reserves. Finally, renewable resources can act as backstops for exhaustible, non-renewables; wind or wave power are substitutes for fossil fuels, and wood products are substitutes for metals for some construction purposes, for example.

Box 5.1 Resource substitutability: one item of evidence

A huge amount of empirical research has been devoted to attempts to measure the elasticity of substitution between particular pairs of inputs. Results of these exercises are often difficult to apply to general models of the type we use in this chapter, because the estimates tend to be specific to the particular contexts being studied, and because many studies work at a much more disaggregated level than is done here. We restrict comments to just one estimate which has been used in a much-respected model of energy–environment interactions in the United States economy.

Alan Manne, in developing the *ETA Macro* model (reported in Pindyck 1979) considers an economy-wide production function in which gross output (Q) depends upon four inputs: K, L, E and N (respectively capital, labour, electric and non-electric energy). Manne's production function incorporates the following assumptions:

1 There are constant returns to scale in terms of all four inputs.
2 There is a *unit* elasticity of substitution between capital and labour.
3 There is a *unit* elasticity of substitution between electric and non-electric energy.
4 There is a *constant* elasticity of substitution between the two pairs of inputs, capital and labour on the one hand and electric and non-electric energy on the other. Denoting this constant elasticity of substitution by the symbol σ, the production function used in the ETA Macro model that embodies these assumptions is

$$Q = [a(K^\alpha L^{1-\alpha})^{-\theta} + b(E^\beta N^{1-\beta})^{-\theta}]^{-1/\theta}$$

where, as noted in the text,

$$\sigma = \frac{1}{1+\theta}$$

What value does Manne select for the elasticity of substitution σ between the pair of energy inputs and the other input pair? The value selected is 0.25, a relatively low elasticity. How is this figure arrived at? First, Manne argues that to a local approximation, the elasticity of substitution σ is identical to the absolute value of the price elasticity of demand for primary energy (see Hogan and Manne, 1979). Then, Manne proceeds to collect time series data on the prices of primary energy, incomes and quantities of primary energy consumed. This permits a statistically derived estimate of the long-run price elasticity of demand for primary energy to be obtained, thereby giving an approximation to the elasticity of substitution between energy and other production inputs. Manne's figure of 0.25 for this elasticity falls near the median value of recent econometric estimates of this elasticity of substitution.

Being positive, this figure suggests that energy demand will rise relative to other input demand if the relative price of other inputs to energy rises, and so the composite energy resource is a substitute for other productive inputs (a negative sign would imply the pair were complements). However, as the absolute value of the elasticity is much less than one, the degree of substitutability is very low, implying that relative input demands will not change greatly as relative input prices change.

Source: Manne (1979).

Partha Dasgupta (1993) examines these various substitution possibilities. He argues that they can be classified into nine innovative mechanism:[4]

1 An innovation allowing a given resource to be used for a given purpose. Example: the use of coal in refining pig-iron.
2 The development of new materials, such as synthetic fibres.
3 Technological developments which increase the productivity of extraction processes. For example, the use of large-scale earthmoving equipment facilitating economically viable strip-mining of low-grade mineral deposits.

[4] The examples given of each mechanism are taken from Dasgupta (1993).

4 Scientific and technical discovery which makes exploration activities cheaper. Examples: developments in aerial photography and seismology.
5 Technological developments that increase efficiency in the use of resources. Dasgupta illustrates this for the case of electricity generation; between 1900 and the 1970s, the weight of coal required to produce one kilowatt-hour of electricity fell from 7 lb to less that 1 lb.
6 Development of techniques which enable one to exploit low-grade but abundantly available deposits. For example, the use of froth-flotation, allowing low-grade sulphide ores to be concentrated in an economical manner.

7 Constant developments in recycling techniques which lower costs and so raise effective resource stocks.
8 Substitution of low-grade resource reserves for vanishing high-grade deposits.
9 Substitution of fixed manufacturing capital for vanishing resources.

In his assessment of the extent of substitution possibilities. Dasgupta argues that only one of these nine mechanisms is of limited scope, the substitution of fixed manufacturing capital for natural resources:

> Such possibilities are limited. Beyond a point fixed capital in production is complementary to resources, most especially energy resources. Asymptotically, the elasticity of substitution is less than one.

There is a constant tension between forces which raise extraction and refining costs – the depletion of high-grade deposits – and those which lower such costs – discoveries of newer technological processes and materials. What implications does this carry for resource scarcity? Dasgupta argues that as the existing resource base is depleted, profit opportunities arise from expanding that resource base; the expansion is achieved by one or more of the nine mechanisms just described. Finally, in a survey of the current stocks of mineral resources. Dasgupta notes that after taking account of these substitution mechanisms, and assuming unchanged resource stock to demand ratios:

> ... the only cause for worry are the phosphates (a mere 1300 years of supply), fossil fuels (some 2500 years), and manganese (about 130,000 years). The rest are available for more than a million years, which is pretty much like being inexhaustible.

However, adjusting for population and income growth,

> ... the supply of hydrocarbons ... will only last a few hundred years .... So then, this is the fly in the ointment, the bottleneck, the binding constraint ....

Dasgupta (1993), page 1126

Dasgupta's optimism is not yet finished. He conjectures that profit potentials will induce technological advances (perhaps based on nuclear energy, perhaps on renewables) that will overcome this binding constraint. Not all commentators share this sanguine view as we have seen previously, and we shall have more to say about resource scarcity in the next chapter. In the meantime, we return to our simple model of the economy, in which the heterogeneity of resources is abstracted from, and in which we conceive of there being one single, uniform, environmental resource stock!

Population growth

An important matter that one must confront in trying to model the long-term implications of environmental constraints is the level of human population. Over a very long period of historical time, the human population has been increasing, and most forecasts imply it will continue to do so for some considerable time to come (see Figure 5.2). Subsequently, it may attain some steady state fixed level, possibly after a prolonged period of global population decline. The United Nations 1994 forecast predicts that world population will peak at 11 billion people in the year 2100, with a substantial fall thereafter. Population trends and the process of population growth are examined in detail in Chapter 12, and we shall not anticipate that discussion any further at this point. However, it is important to devote some attention to the way in which environmental economists might take account of population growth in their analyses of resource depletion and harvesting.

Firstly, one could simply choose to ignore population growth, carrying out any analysis of resource use under the assumption that the level of population remains constant. Perhaps it is better to describe this option as one of abstracting from population growth,

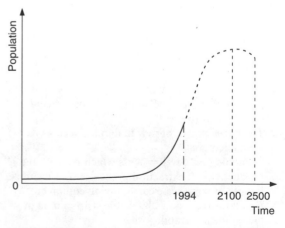

Fig 5.2 General trend of actual world population to 1994 and expected world population to 2200. Solid line: actual population; broken line: forecast.

rather than ignoring it as such. There are good reasons for following such a path. In the first place, if we wish to examine equilibrium, steady-state, or sustainable paths over time, then the only population growth rate that can logically fit that criterion is a growth rate of zero. Second, one may regard the explosion of the global population in recent historical time as a transitory state, before and after which population levels are relatively static. In this perspective, it would be inappropriate to tie our analyses of resource use too closely to historically transient phenomena.

On the other hand, whilst population growth may not be a permanent part of the human condition, it has been quantitatively of great importance for several hundred years, and will continue to be for some time to come. If resources are limited, then large population increases might have significant consequences even though they are only temporary. This implies that ignoring population growth throws away valuable information, and is likely to weaken the credibility of our conclusions. Given this perspective, the simplest way of proceeding is to assume that the growth rate of human populations is *exogenously given* – it is not affected by the levels of any of the variables in the systems we are investigating – and to build this exogenous rate of population growth into our modelling exercises. One common assumption made is that population grows exponentially at the instantaneous rate n. If the proportion of the population that participates in the labour market remains fixed over time, then this in turn implies that the labour force will grow exponentially at the rate n, so that:

$$L_t = L_0\, e^{nt} \qquad (5.5)$$

where L_t is the labour force at time t, and L_0 is a base level of the labour force in some base or reference period 0. This assumption of exponential population growth is sometimes used in analyses in which the implications of continuing population increases are being investigated. An advantage of proceeding in this way is that we can explore how our results vary with different assumptions about the rate of population growth. Furthermore, by setting $n = 0$, we obtain the special case of a constant population. Simulation techniques can be used to compare the $n = 0$ case with one in which $n > 0$, and so identify the impact of population growth itself on the variables of interest.

Notice that it is not tenable to assume that the human population will grow over very long periods at a fixed positive rate. Indeed, it is not possible for any biological population to increase in size at some fixed exponential rate indefinitely, although it may be a reasonable approximation for medium time horizons. We would expect that population growth is related, in some way, to the level and pattern of economic activity. This suggests that in models trying to characterise economic–environmental interactions over long time periods, the best way of proceeding is to regard the rate of population growth as an *endogenous* variable, determined within the system we are studying. The classical economists took this view, at least in a simple form. Malthus, for example, believed that the natural tendency was for population to grow geometrically (an equivalent assumption to exponential growth). However, as limited resource constraints began to bite, the population growth rate would decrease, and would go to zero in the stationary state. Environmental economic analyses in which population growth is an endogenous variable are daunting exercises, however, and go beyond the scope of this text.

Technical progress

Economists have often been somewhat sanguine about the consequences of resource finiteness because of a belief that continuing technical progress can partially or fully offset the cumulative extraction of exhaustible resources. On the other hand, there are those who would argue that it is not reasonable to suppose that technical progress will continue at positive rates indefinitely just because it has done so in the past. Furthermore, other writers point to the limited ability of technical progress to compensate for the degradation or losses of the services offered by natural environments. Krutilla's model of wilderness areas, examined in Chapter 10, is a classic exposition of such an argument.

Let us begin by classifying technical progress. A general way of incorporating technical progress into the production function is to introduce time (t) explicitly as an argument of the function, as in Equation 5.6 below. It is usual to assume that technical progress is always positive so that $\dot{Q}_t = \partial Q / \partial t > 0$

$$Q = Q(K, L, R, t) \qquad (5.6)$$

Alternatively, we could define the variable $A(t)$ to be the state of technology at time t, and write the function as

$$Q = Q(K, L, R, A) \qquad (5.7)$$

Equation 5.7 does not specify the manner in which technological progress affects the production function. Neutral (or Hicks neutral) technical progress exists if the production function takes the particular form

$$Q = A(t)Q(K, L, R) \qquad (5.8)$$

in which case technical progress is equivalent to an equiproportionate scaling up of the *effective* quantities of each input (even though their physical quantities had not changed). We can also envisage three other forms of technical progress – capital augmenting, labour augmenting and resource augmenting depending upon which resource is increased in terms of 'efficiency units' as a result of the technical progress. These three are given in Equations 5.9–5.11:

$$Q = Q(A(t)K, L, R) \qquad (5.9)$$

$$Q = Q(K, A(t)L, R) \qquad (5.10)$$

$$Q = Q(K, L, A(t)R) \qquad (5.11)$$

If technical progress does occur, a number of possibilities arise. As we have just seen, it might increase the effective quantities of the exhaustible resource. But technical progress can also be important in other ways. For example, it might alter the form of the production function, affecting substitution possibilities, and in some cases even rendering previously essential resources unessential. In addition, through its influence on research, exploration and extraction costs, technical progress can also alter the quantities of the exhaustible resource available for use. We investigate this aspect of technical change in the next chapter.

The social welfare function and an optimal allocation of environmental resources

The previous chapter established the meaning of the concepts of efficiency and optimality for the allocation of productive resources in general. We shall now apply these concepts to the particular case of environmental resources. Recall that we use that term in a quite general way, to include non-renewable (exhaustible) and renewable resources, and environmental assets that provide services in production and/or consumption (such as natural wilderness areas, water systems and the waste disposal capacity of the environment). For simplicity of analysis, the presen-

tation in this chapter continues to focus upon exhaustible resources. However, the ideas developed here can be readily applied to other types of environmental resource.

Our objective in this section is to establish what conditions must be satisfied for an allocation of resources to be optimal, in the sense that the allocation maximises a social welfare function. As our concern in this and following chapters is with the use of environmental resources over time, it is more accurate to say that our objective is to establish the conditions required for resource allocation to be *intertemporally* optimal.

Our first step requires that we specify the relevant social welfare function. You already know that a general way of writing the social welfare function is[5]

$$W = W(U_0, U_1, U_2, \ldots, U_T) \qquad (5.12)$$

where U_i, $i = 0, \ldots, T$, is the aggregate utility in period i. In this chapter we shall analyse optimality conditions for the particular case in which the SWF is of the utilitarian form.

Welfare maximisation and the utilitarian social welfare function

A utilitarian SWF defines social welfare as a weighted sum of the utilities of the relevant individuals. As we are concerned here with intertemporal welfare, we can interpret an 'individual' to mean an aggregate of persons living at a certain point in time, and so refer to the utility in period 0, in period 1, and so on. Then a utilitarian SWF will be of the form

$$W = \alpha_0 U_0 + \alpha_1 U_1 + \alpha_2 U_2 + \ldots + \alpha_T U_T \quad (5.13)$$

Now let us assume that utility in each period is a concave function only of the level of consumption in that period, so that

$$U_i = U(C_i) \quad \text{for all } i$$
$$U'(C) > 0$$
$$U''(C) < 0$$

[5] Writing the SWF in this form assumes that it is meaningful to refer to an aggregate level of utility for all individuals in each period. Then social welfare is a function of these aggregates, but not of the distribution of utilities between individuals within each time period. That is a very strong assumption, and by no means the only one we might wish to make. We might justify this by assuming that, for each time period, utility is distributed in an optimum way between individuals.

Notice that the function itself is not dependent upon time so that the relationship between consumption and utility is the same in all time periods. By interpreting the weights in Equation 5.13 as discount factors, related to a social utility discount rate ρ that we take to be fixed over time, the social welfare function can be rewritten as

$$W = U_0 + \frac{U_1}{1+\rho} + \frac{U_2}{(1+\rho)^2} + \ldots + \frac{U_T}{(1+\rho)^T} \quad (5.14)$$

Finally, for reasons of mathematical convenience, we switch from discrete time to continuous time notation, and assume that the relevant time horizon is infinite. This leads us to the special case of the utilitarian SWF that we shall work with often in this text:

$$W = \int_{t=0}^{t=\infty} U(C_t)\, e^{-\rho t}\, dt \quad (5.15)$$

Equation 5.15 constitutes the social welfare function that is to be maximised. It is now necessary to state the constraints that must be satisfied by any optimal solution. There are two relevant constraints. Firstly, assume that all of the resource stock is to be extracted and used by the end of the time horizon. Given this, together with the fact that we are considering an exhaustible resource for which there is a fixed and finite initial stock, the total use of the resource over time is constrained to be equal to the fixed initial stock. Denoting the initial stock (at $t = 0$) as S_0 and the rate of extraction and use of the resource at time t as R_t we can write this constraint as

$$S_t = S_0 - \int_{\tau=0}^{\tau=t} R_\tau\, d\tau \quad (5.16)$$

Expression 5.16 states that the stock remaining at time t (S_t) is equal to the magnitude of the initial stock at time zero (S_0) less the amount of the resource extracted over the time interval from zero to t (given by the integral term on the right-hand side of the equation). An equivalent way of writing this resource stock constraint is obtained by differentiating Equation 5.16 with respect to time, giving

$$\dot{S}_t = -R_t \quad (5.17)$$

where the dot over a variable indicates a time derivative, so that $\dot{S} = dS/dt$. Equation 5.17 has a straightforward interpretation, as it states that the rate of depletion of the stock, $-\dot{S}_t$, is equal to the rate of resource stock extraction, R_t. Let us call this constraint, in either of the two forms given, the exhaustible resource stock-flow constraint.

A second constraint on welfare optimisation derives from the accounting identity relating consumption, output and the change in the economy's stock of capital. The economy's output is shared between consumption goods and capital goods, and so that part of the economy's output which is not consumed results in a capital stock change. Writing this identity in continuous time form we have

$$\dot{K}_t = Q_t - C_t \quad (5.18)$$

It is now necessary to specify how output, Q, is determined. We suppose, for reasons of simplicity that output is produced through a production function involving two inputs, capital and an exhaustible resource, in which there is no technological progress:

$$Q = Q(K, R) \quad (5.19)$$

Note that because this specification of the production function does not include labour as a productive input, the rate of population growth is not relevant to our problem. It is also worth remembering that as the production function given in Equation 5.19 is in general form, it is not possible to know whether or not the exhaustible resource is essential and what particular value will be taken by the elasticity of substitution between capital and the exhaustible resource.

Substituting for Q in Equation 5.18 from the production function, the national income accounting identity can be written as

$$\dot{K}_t = Q(K_t, R_t) - C_t \quad (5.20)$$

We are now ready to find the solution for the socially optimal intertemporal allocation of the exhaustible resource. To do so, we need to solve a constrained optimisation problem: our objective is to maximise the economy's social welfare function subject to the exhaustible resource stock-flow constraint and the national income identity, written to incorporate the economy's production function. Writing this mathematically, therefore, we have the following problem:

Maximise

$$W = \int_{t=0}^{t=\infty} U(C_t)\, e^{-\rho t}\, dt$$

subject to

$$\dot{S}_t = -R_t$$

and

$$\dot{K}_t = Q(K_t, R_t) - C_t$$

The full solution to this constrained optimisation problem, and its derivation, are presented in Appendix 1. You should now try to read that Appendix. In the following section, we outline the nature of the solution, and provide economic interpretations of the results. Three equations characterise the optimal solution:

$$\dot{P}_t = \rho P_t \qquad (5.21a)$$

$$\frac{\dot{C}}{C} = \frac{Q_K - \rho}{\eta} \qquad (5.21b)$$

$$P_t = \omega_t Q_R \qquad (5.21c)$$

Before we discuss the economic interpretations of these equations, it is necessary to explain the new notation used. Q_K and Q_R, the partial derivatives of output with respect to capital and the exhaustible resource, are the marginal products of capital and the environmental resource respectively. η is the elasticity of marginal utility with respect to consumption, and so is a measure of the proportionate change in marginal utility that is associated with a small proportionate change in consumption. This concept was explained in Chapter 2 when the relationship between the utility and consumption discount rates was being explained, where it was shown to be given by

$$\eta = -\frac{C \cdot U''(C)}{U'(C)}$$

Finally, the terms P_t and ω_t are the *shadow prices* of the two productive inputs, the environmental resource and capital. The presence of time subscripts on these two shadow prices suggests that the prices will vary over time, which is precisely what they will do. So $\{P_t\}$ and $\{\omega_t\}$, $t = 0, 1, \ldots, \infty$, define two paths over time of environmental resource and capital prices. A shadow price is a price that emerges as a solution to an optimisation problem; put another way, it is an implicit or 'planning' price that a good (or in this case, a productive input) will take if resources are allocated optimally over time. If an economic planner were using the price mechanism to allocate resources over time, then $\{P_t\}$ and $\{\omega_t\}$ would be the prices he or she should establish in order to achieve an efficient and optimal resource allocation. There is one more preliminary that it is necessary to deal with. Notice that the quantity being maximised in Equation 5.15 is welfare, which is a sum of (discounted) units of *utility*. Hence, the shadow prices we derive are measured in utility, not consumption units. The prices with which we are most likely to be

familiar are money income prices – such as a car having a price of $10 000, a meal having a price of £10, and so on. But the shadow prices P_t and ω_t are in units of utility not consumption (or money income) terms.[6]

Equations 5.21a–c constitute a solution to the optimisation problem in the sense that, together with the constraints we listed above, and initial values for K and S, they can be used to find the optimal time paths for K_t and R_t and their associated prices.

Equation 5.21a is usually known as Hotelling's rule for the extraction of non-renewable resources. It is more usually expressed in the form

$$\frac{\dot{P}_t}{P_t} = \rho \qquad (5.22)$$

which states that the shadow price of the environmental resource should rise at a rate equal to the social utility discount rate, ρ. Hotelling's is, in fact, an efficiency rule – a rule which will be satisfied by any pattern of exhaustible resource extraction over time to be intertemporally efficient. We can give an economic interpretation to Hotelling's rule in the following way. First rewrite Equation 5.22 as

$$\dot{P}_t = \rho P_t \qquad (5.23)$$

Then by integration of Equation 5.23 we obtain

$$P_t = P_0 e^{\rho t} \qquad (5.24)$$

Now P_t is the current value or undiscounted price of the environmental resource. The constant value or discounted price is obtained by discounting P_t at the social utility discount rate ρ. Denoting the constant value or discounted resource price by P^*, we have

$$P_t^* = P_t e^{-\rho t} = P_0 \qquad (5.25)$$

Hotelling's rule states that the *undiscounted* shadow price of an environmental resource should rise at the social discount rate; Equation 5.25 states that the *discounted* price of the environmental resource is constant along an efficient resource extraction path. In other words, Hotelling's rule states that the present discounted value of the resource should be the same at all dates. Note the effect of changes in the social discount rate on the optimal path of resource price; the higher is ρ, the faster should be the rate of growth

---

[6] It is worth noting that if the utility function is of the special form $U(C) = C$, then the distinction between prices measured in utility versus consumption (or money income) units disappears. With suitable scaling, the units are identical. However, for other utility functions, the two measures are distinct.

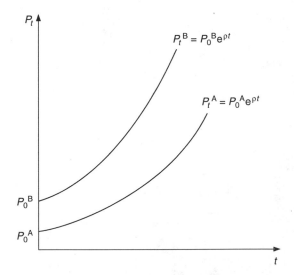

Fig 5.3 Two price paths, each satisfying Hotelling's Rule.

of prices. As we shall see in the following chapter, this implies that the initial shadow price of the environmental resource is lower, and so a greater amount is extracted in early periods. However, a proof of this assertion will be left until the following chapter.

But the Hotelling rule – requiring the growth rate of the resource price to be equal to the social discount rate – does not give rise to a unique path of resource prices over time. To see this, consider two different initial prices, say 1 util and 2 utils, which grow over time at the same discount rate, say 5%. These paths are illustrated in Figure 5.3. But it is obvious that there is an infinite quantity of such efficient price paths, each satisfying Hotelling's rule but differing in their initial prices. Only one of these price paths will be the optimal price path, and so the Hotelling rule is a necessary but not a sufficient condition for optimality. How do we find out which of all the possible efficient price paths is the optimal one? An optimal solution requires that all of the conditions listed in Equations 5.21a–c are satisfied simultaneously. So Hotelling's rule – one of these three conditions – is a necessary but not a sufficient condition for an optimal allocation of environmental resources over time.

We can also think about the nature of the optimal solution in terms of initial and final conditions that must be satisfied. There will be some initial stock of the environmental resource; similarly, we know that the resource stock must converge to zero as elapsed time passes and the economy passes towards its planning horizon. If the initial price were 'too low',

then this would lead to 'too large' amounts of resource use in each period, and all the resource stock would become depleted in finite time (that is, before the end of the planning horizon). This suggests that we might try to find the lowest possible initial price that would bring about a path of demands that is consistent with the resource stock not being depleted in finite time.

Equation 5.21b, the second of the optimality conditions, allows us to make some deductions about the optimal path of consumption over time. Note first that, by assumption, $U'(C) > 0$ and $U''(C) < 0$; it therefore follows that $\eta > 0$. Given this, Equation 5.21b implies the following relationships:

$$\dot{C}/C > 0 \quad \text{if } Q_K > \rho$$
$$\dot{C}/C = 0 \quad \text{if } Q_K = \rho$$
$$\dot{C}/C < 0 \quad \text{if } Q_K < \rho$$

Whether or not the level of consumption will be rising, constant or falling over time depends, therefore, upon the relative sizes of the marginal product of capital and the social discount rate. The first of these expressions states that if the marginal product of capital exceeds the social utility discount rate, consumption will be growing over time. Conversely, if the marginal product of capital is less than the social utility discount rate, consumption will be falling over time. In this simple economy, consumption will remain constant over time only if the marginal product of capital equals the social utility discount rate.

How may one interpret the third optimality condition (5.21c)? Dividing the resource shadow price, P_t, by the capital shadow price, ω_t, we obtain a relative shadow price of the resource. This relative price must be equal to the marginal product of the resource, Q_R, at every point in time if resource extraction is to be optimal.

PART 2
Extending the simple optimal depletion model

In our analysis of the depletion of resources up to this point, we have made several simplifying assumptions. In particular, extraction costs were taken to be zero, and the extraction and use of the resource led to no economically relevant damages. Clearly these assumptions are not likely to be satisfied in practice, and so it would be desirable to generalise the depletion model to encompass these possibilities. This is the main task of Part 2 of the chapter.

Extraction costs

We have been implicitly assuming in the analysis so far that the environmental resource can be extracted and processed for use at no cost. This will not in general be true, and it is necessary to find out how the results of our analysis change when we allow for the presence of extraction costs. Suppose that total extraction costs at time t, G_t, depend upon the amount of the resource being currently extracted, R_t, and also upon the current stock level remaining after all previous extraction, S_t. Thus we write extraction costs as

$$G_t = G(S_t, R_t) \qquad (5.26)$$

To help understand what this implies about extraction costs, look at Figure 5.4, which shows three possible relationships between total extraction costs (G) and the remaining resource stock size (S) for a fixed level of resource extraction (R). The relationship denoted (i) corresponds to the case where the total extraction cost is independent of the stock size. In this case, the extraction cost function collapses to the simpler form $G_t = g(R_t)$, in which extraction costs depend only on the quantity extracted. In case (ii), the costs of extracting a given quantity of the resource increase linearly as the stock becomes increasingly depleted. Put another way, $G_S = \partial G/\partial S$ is a constant negative number. Finally, case (iii) shows the costs of extracting a given quantity of the resource increasing at an increasing rate as S falls to zero; G_S is negative, but becomes larger in absolute value as the resource stock size falls towards zero. This third case is the most likely one for typical non-renewable resources; to see this, consider the costs of extracting oil. As the available stock more closely approaches zero, capital equipment is directed to exploiting smaller fields, often located in geographically difficult land or marine areas; these and similar reasons imply that the cost of extracting an additional barrel of oil will tend to rise very sharply as the remaining stock gets closer to exhaustion.

Appendix 2 contains the derivation of the optimal exhaustible resource depletion programme in a more general setting than that used in Part 1 of this chapter.

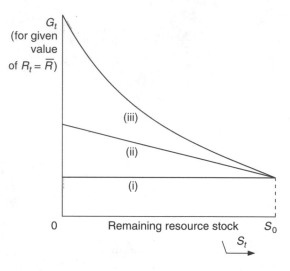

$$G_t = G(S_t, R_t)$$

Case (i) $G_t = G_1(R_t) \rightarrow \partial G_t/\partial S_t = 0$

Case (ii) $G_t = G_2(S_t, R_t)$

$$= \beta_1 R_t + \beta_2 S_t \quad (\beta_1 > 0, \beta_2 < 0)$$

$$\rightarrow \partial G_t/\partial S_t = \beta_2 < 0$$

Case (iii) $G_t = G_3(S_t, R_t)$

$$= \beta_1 R_t + \beta_2 S_t^{1/2}$$

$$\rightarrow \partial G_t/\partial S_t = \tfrac{1}{2}\beta_2 S_t^{-1/2} < 0$$

Fig 5.4 Three possible examples of the relationship between extraction costs and remaining stock for a fixed level of exhaustible resource, R.

In Appendix 2, we allow for the presence of extraction costs, population growth, the presence of labour (as well as capital and an exhaustible resource) as an input to production, technical progress in production, and the existence of environmental damages arising from the extraction and use of the exhaustible resource.

As the results in Appendix 2 demonstrate, a version of the Hotelling rule, giving a path which the shadow price of the exhaustible resource must follow over time if extraction is to be efficient, still applies when resource extraction costs are introduced into the problem. However, the Hotelling rule is now modified to

$$\dot{P} = \rho P + G_S \omega \qquad (5.27)$$

where P now denotes the *net price* of the resource, that is the resource price after subtraction of the extraction costs per unit of the resource. Note that although extraction costs do not appear explicitly, they do enter Equation 5.27 by virtue of the fact that it is the net price of the resource which enters the equation.

The 'Hotelling rule' efficiency condition now includes an extra term involving G_S, where $G_S = \partial G/\partial S$ is the rate of change of total extraction costs with respect to the stock level of the resource. So, for example, if marginal extraction costs increase as the resource becomes increasingly depleted (as might be the case if the resource stock is of varying quality, or the ore is located at varying depths) then $G_S < 0$. As ω is a shadow price (of capital) that must be positive, the term $G_S\omega$ is negative in value. This establishes the result that the rate of increase of the resource shadow price should be lower where extraction costs depend upon the resource stock size than where extraction costs are independent of the stock.

Suppose, however, that total extraction costs depend upon the flow of resource extracted, R, but not on the resource stock level itself. In this case (corresponding to (i) in Figure 5.4), $G_S = 0$, and extraction costs do not affect the rate at which the net resource price should grow.

Another interpretation of the Hotelling rule efficiency condition of Equation 5.27 is useful in understanding the result. Rearrange Equation 5.27 into the equivalent form

$$\rho P = \dot{P} - G_S\omega \qquad (5.28)$$

As we demonstrate in a moment, the left-hand side of this equation is the marginal cost of not extracting an additional unit of the resource; the right-hand side is the marginal benefit from not extracting an additional unit of the resource. Therefore, we are able to claim that, at an efficient (and at an optimal) rate of resource use, the marginal costs and benefits of resource use are balanced at each point in time.

How can this interpretation be obtained? Looking first at the left-hand side of Equation 5.28, note that P, the net price of the resource, is the value that would be obtained by the resource owner were he or she to extract and sell the resource in the current period. With ρ being the social utility discount rate, ρP is the utility return foregone by not currently extracting one unit of the resource, but deferring that extraction for one period. This is sometimes known as the holding cost of the resource stock.

The right-hand side of Equation 5.28 contains two components. The first, $\dot{P} = dP/dt$, is the capital appreciation of one unit of the unextracted resource;

the second component, $-G_S\omega$, is a return in the form of a postponement of a cost increase that would have occurred if the additional unit of the resource had been extracted. (Note that $G_S < 0$, and all other terms are positive, so $-G_S\omega$ is a positive magnitude.)

With the Hotelling rule being modified in the way indicated by Equation 5.28, the presence of a stock effect on resource extraction costs will slow down the rate of growth of the resource net price. This implies that the resource price has to be higher initially (but lower ultimately) than it would have been in the absence of this stock effect; as a result of higher initial prices, the rate of extraction will be slowed down in the early part of the time horizon, and a greater quantity of the resource stock will be conserved (to be extracted later).

Damage arising from the extraction and use of the non-renewable resource

So far in this chapter, we have implicitly assumed that no damages are associated with the extraction and use of the exhaustible resource. The results we have derived are only valid where that assumption is correct. However, this assumption is not correct in general. We must now investigate the consequences of generalising our model to the case in which resource use results in environmental damage. For simplicity in what follows, we shall assume that, in any interval of time, the amount of resource that is consumed (for example in energy production) is equal to the amount that is extracted. When referring to damages, the damages in question can arise from the process of extraction, the processes of consumption/use, or both.

Define damage, D, to be the total external costs associated with the use of the exhaustible resource (so that D does not include the internal costs of resource extraction). Suppose that these costs are an increasing function of the rate of resource extraction and of the cumulative amount of the resource extracted. That is

$$D = D(R_t, S_0 - S_t) \qquad (5.29)$$

where, as before, R_t is the rate of resource extraction in period t. Defining S_0 to be the 'initial' level of the resource stock and S_t to be the resource stock size at time t, then $(S_0 - S_t)$ can be interpreted as the cumulative total of resource extraction up to time t.

Our assumptions about damage imply that in the damage function

$$\frac{\partial D}{\partial R} > 0, \quad \frac{\partial D}{\partial (S_0 - S_t)} > 0$$

and hence

$$\frac{\partial D}{\partial S_t} < 0$$

These relationships are illustrated in Figure 5.5. Figure 5.5a shows how the total amount of environmental damages is related to the rate at which the exhaustible resource is being depleted, conditional upon the amount of cumulative depletion being held at some constant level. To imagine what this means, think about 'greenhouse gas' emissions from fossil fuel use. Suppose that the total amount of greenhouse gas stocks in the atmosphere is low, because not much cumulative extraction of fossil fuels has taken place. Now we could ask how much total damage greenhouse gas emissions would create in each period for different levels of emissions (that is, for different rates of resource extraction and use) when the stock of greenhouse gases in the atmosphere is at this low level. This is the kind of relationship· we are portraying in Figure 5.5a. Although we have drawn the relationship as a linear one, it need not necessarily be linear. Note that if damages depend upon the stock level, there will be a different relationship between damages and the rate of resource extraction for each possible level of the resource stock. Returning once again to the Greenhouse Effect example, suppose we ask about this relationship in a situation where the concentration of greenhouse gases in the atmosphere is very high (because the total cumulative extraction of fossil fuels is high). Although one would expect D and R to be positively related, the function would have a steeper slope than in the first case, as illustrated by the dotted line in Figure 5.5a.

Figure 5.5b illustrates the total damages that result from one particular fixed rate of resource extraction ($R_t = \bar{R}$) at different levels of cumulative extraction of the resource. Once again, we do not claim that the relationship will always be of this form, merely that this is one possibility. Note that this function may not go through the origin because the total damages caused by some rate of resource extraction and use could be positive even when accumulated extraction is close to zero. As with Figure 5.5a the function indicated here is not unique – there will be a different relationship between damages and

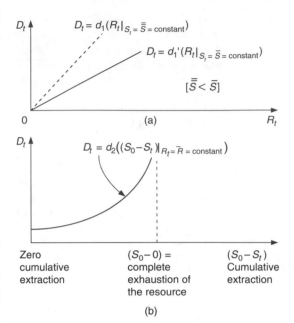

Fig 5.5 The relationships between total damage costs, D, the rate of resource extraction, R and the cumulative total of resource extraction, $S_0 - S_t$.

cumulated extraction for each feasible level of resource extraction and use.

Once our analysis is broadened in this way to incorporate the external costs of resource use, it is not surprising that the nature of the optimal solution changes. As we mentioned previously, a complete derivation of the solution for a general model incorporating external costs is presented in Appendix 2. We shall restrict our attention here to the special case in which the resource depletion problem is identical to that analysed in Part 1, save for two differences: firstly, resource extraction costs may depend upon the stock level (as we discussed above), and secondly, that exhaustible resource use incurs damages. A version of the Hotelling rule of efficient resource depletion emerges once again as one of the conditions required for efficient allocation of productive inputs over time. However, in these circumstances, the Hotelling rule efficiency condition changes to

$$\dot{P} = \rho P + G_S \omega - D_S \omega \qquad (5.30)$$

Note that the Hotelling efficiency condition in this case includes the term that allows for extraction costs to depend upon the stock size, $G_S \omega$, but now includes an additional term, $-D_S \omega$. In order to interpret this extra term, note first that $D_S \omega$ is negative (D_S is

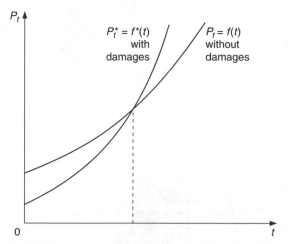

Fig 5.6 The net price of the resource with and without environmental damage.

negative, as can be deduced from Figure 5.5b, and ω is positive). Therefore $\rho P - D_S \omega > \rho P$. By dividing Equation 5.30 by P, an expression for the proportionate growth rate of the resource net price is obtained:

$$\frac{\dot{P}}{P} = \rho + \frac{G_S \omega}{P} - \frac{D_S \omega}{P} \qquad (5.31)$$

It is clear that the net resource price must grow more rapidly when pollution damages depend upon the cumulative total of resource extraction than when they do not. This is illustrated in Figure 5.6.

Two price paths through time are illustrated in Figure 5.6. The price rises more rapidly over time for the case where extraction and use of the resource results in environmental damage (the starred price path). This result is certain. However, it is not possible to say where the two net price paths will originate from at time $t = 0$. We have drawn the diagram showing the net price with damages beginning from a lower level than the price without damages, and becoming higher at some point in time later. But this is only one possibility, and it will not be possible to know the actual shapes and positions of the two price paths without knowing the actual functions that influence the solution to the problem.

If the non-renewable resource in question had no substitute and is essential in production, we expect that Figure 5.6 shows the correct general form of the relationship between the two price paths. Where damages for any given level of resource extraction are higher the greater is the cumulative total of resource extraction, there will be economic benefits to society

in extracting larger quantities in early time periods (when cumulative extraction is low) and in extracting smaller quantities in later time periods (when cumulative extraction is high). This is what one would predict from Figure 5.6. In early years, the net price is lower when damages are accounted for; the low prices encourage high rates of extraction. The opposite will happen in later years when net prices are higher than they would otherwise be.

But this is by no means the only possibility. If the resource is substitutable, is non-essential, or a backstop technology exists (see the following chapter for an explanation of this term), damages associated with use of the resource may result in the price being always higher, and the resource becoming 'economically depleted' before the stock reaches a point of physical exhaustion. We shall say more about possibilities such as these when we examine non-renewable resources in detail in Chapter 6.

Generalisation to renewable resources

We reserve a full analysis of the allocation of renewable resources until Chapter 7, but it will be useful at this point to suggest the way in which the analysis can be undertaken. To do so, first note that in this chapter so far, R has represented a fixed and finite stock of an exhaustible resource. The total use of the resource over time was constrained to be equal to the fixed initial stock. This relationship arises because the natural growth of exhaustible resources is zero except over geological periods of time. Thus we wrote

$$S_t = S_0 - \int_{\tau=0}^{\tau=t} R_\tau \, d\tau \Rightarrow \dot{S}_t = -R_t$$

However, the natural growth of renewable resources is, in general, non-zero. A simple way of modelling this growth is to assume that the amount of growth of the resource, Ω_t, is some function of the current stock level, so that $\Omega_t = \Omega(S_t)$. Given this we can write the relationship between the change in the resource stock and the rate of extraction (or harvesting) of the resource as

$$\dot{S} = \Omega(S_t) - R_t \qquad (5.32)$$

Not surprisingly, both the efficiency condition (Hotelling rule) governing the behaviour of price over time, and the set of conditions satisfied by an optimal allocation of resources, are now different from the case of exhaustible resources. However, a modified version of the Hotelling rule still applies, given by

$$\dot{P} = \rho P - P\Omega_S \qquad (5.33)$$

where $\Omega_S = d\Omega/dS$, and in which we have assumed, for simplicity, that harvesting does not incur costs, nor that any environmental damage results from the harvesting and use of the resource. Inspection of the modified Hotelling rule for renewable resources (Equation 5.33) demonstrates that the rate at which the net price should change over time depends upon Ω_S, the rate of change of resource growth with respect to changes in the stock of the resource. We will not attempt to interpret Equation 5.33 here as that is best left until we examine renewable resources in detail in Chapter 7. However, it is worth saying a few words about steady-state resource harvesting.

A steady-state harvesting of a renewable resource exists when all stocks and flows are constant over time. In particular, steady-state harvest will be one in which the harvest level is fixed over time and is equal to the natural amount of growth of the resource stock. Additions to and subtractions from the resource stock are thus equal, and the stock remains at a constant level over time. Now if the demand for the resource is constant over time, the resource net price will remain constant in a steady state, as the quantity harvested each period is constant. Therefore, in a steady state, $\dot{P} = dP/dt = 0$. So in a steady state, the Hotelling rule simplifies to

$$\rho P = P\Omega_S \qquad (5.34)$$

and so

$$\rho = \Omega_S \qquad (5.35)$$

Now it is common to assume that the relationship between the resource stock size, S, and the growth of the resource, Ω, is as indicated in Figure 5.7. This relationship is explained fully in Chapter 7. As the stock size increases from zero, the amount of growth of the resource rises, reaches a maximum, known as the maximum sustainable yield (MSY) and then falls. Note that $\Omega_S = d\Omega/dS$ is the slope at any point of the growth–stock function in Figure 5.7.

We can deduce that if the social utility discount rate ρ were equal to zero, then the efficiency condition of Equation 5.35 could only be satisfied if the steady-state stock level is $\hat{S}$, and the harvest is the MSY harvest level. On the other hand, if the social discount rate were positive (as will usually be the case), then the efficiency condition requires that the steady-state stock level be less than $\hat{S}$. At the stock level S^*, for

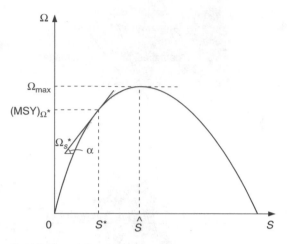

Fig 5.7 The relationship between the resource stock size, S, and the growth of the resource stock, Ω.

example, Ω_S is positive, and would be an efficient stock level, yielding a sustainable yield of Ω^*, if the discount rate were equal to this value of Ω_S.

Full details of the derivation of this and other results relating to the Hotelling rule are given in Appendix 2.

Complications

The model with which we began in this chapter was one in which there was a single, known, finite stock of an exhaustible resource. Furthermore, the whole stock was assumed to have been homogeneous in quality. In practice, of course, both of these assumptions are often false. Rather than there existing a single exhaustible resource, there are many different classes or varieties of non-renewable resource, some of which may be relatively close substitutes for others (such as oil and natural gas, and iron and aluminium).

Whilst it may be correct to assume that there exists a given finite stock of each of these resource stocks in a physical sense, the following situations are likely:

1 The total stock is not known with certainty.
2 New discoveries increase the known stock of the resource.
3 A distinction needs to be drawn between the physical quantity of the stock and the economically viable stock size.
4 Research and development, and technical progress, take place, which can change extraction costs, the size of the known resource stock, the magnitude of

economically viable resource deposits, and estimates of the damages arising from environmental resource use.

Furthermore, even when we focus on a particular kind of exhaustible resource, the stock is likely to be heterogeneous. Different parts of the total stock are likely to be uneven in quality, or to be located in such a way that extraction costs differ for different portions of the stock.

By treating all exhaustible resources as one composite good, our analysis in this chapter had no need to consider substitutes for the resource in question (except, of course, substitutes in the form of capital and labour). But once our analysis enters the more complex world in which there is a variety of different non-renewable resources which are substitutable for one another to some degree, analysis inevitably becomes more complicated. One particular issue of great potential importance is the presence of backstop technologies (see Chapter 6). Suppose that we are currently using some non-renewable resource for a particular purpose – perhaps for energy production. It may well be the case that another resource exists that can substitute entirely for the resource we are considering, but may not be used at present because its cost is relatively high. Such a resource is known as a backstop technology. For example, renewable power sources such as wind energy are backstop alternatives to fossil-fuel based energy.

Now the existence of a backstop technology will set an upper limit on the level to which the price of a resource can go. If the cost of the 'original' resource were to exceed the backstop cost, users would switch to the backstop. So even though renewable power is probably not currently economically viable, at least not on large scale, it would become so at some fossil fuel cost, and so the existence of a backstop will lead to a price ceiling for the original resource.

Each of the issues we have raised in this section, and which we have collectively called 'complications', need to be taken account of in any comprehensive account of resource use. We shall do so in the next two chapters.

Finally, note that in our analysis to this point, our utility function, $U = U(C)$, has treated utility as a function of the level of consumption alone. However, there may be circumstances in which utility is also dependent on the stock level or population of the resource. This is most likely to be relevant where the resource in question is renewable (such as whales or tropical forests) or refers to an ecological system (such

as a wilderness area) which generates amenity and other benefits. In this case the form of the utility function would need to be changed, and the results obtained from our analysis would change accordingly. Whilst we do not formally analyse this case in this book, some intuitive discussion is to be found later in Chapter 10.

Does the exhaustibility of resources pose an economic problem?

Although we have only outlined the basic elements of a model of economic growth with exhaustible resources, our discussions do provide some insight into how some of the propositions outlined at the beginning of this chapter should be assessed. In particular, given that exhaustible resources are finite, does continual use pose a 'problem'?

First note that if a resource is not essential in production, no 'problem' exists. Continued use of the resource does imply eventual exhaustion, but that does not by itself prevent future production and consumption from reaching any levels we choose (given sufficient labour and capital), as production would be possible without the use of the exhaustible resource. Nevertheless, if 'production' is viewed in a broader sense than we have used in this chapter (to include the waste processing and climate maintaining services of environmental resources for example) this conclusion may not hold. Nor has this chapter paid any attention to the direct consumption services of natural environments; potential 'problems' cannot be ruled out if we also take account of these.

If the resource is *essential* in production, we have seen that output still need not eventually decline to zero even if an economy possesses a finite quantity of the exhaustible resource. Sustainable production would be possible in the following circumstances:

1 Reproducible inputs are substitutable for exhaustible inputs. A key parameter here is the elasticity of substitution between capital and exhaustible resources.

2 Renewable resource inputs are substitutable for exhaustible inputs. Although we have not discussed this possibility in this chapter, it seems intuitively reasonable, and again we could conceive of an important parameter being the elasticity of substitution between renewable and exhaustible resources.

Once population growth and technical change are incorporated into the analysis, a large set of long-term outcomes become possible. We return to this question in Chapters 6 and 7.

A numerical application: oil extraction and global optimal consumption

In this section we present a simple, hypothetical numerical application of the theory developed above. You may find the mathematics of the solution given in Box 5.2 a little tedious; if you wish to avoid the maths, just skip the box and proceed to Table 5.1 and Figure 5.8–5.10 at the end of the section where the results are laid out. (The derivation actually uses the technique of dynamic optimisation explained in Appendix 3, but applied in this case to a discrete time model.)

Suppose that the welfare function to be maximised is

$$W = \sum_{t=0}^{t=T-1} \frac{U(C_t)}{(1+\rho)^t}$$

where C_t is the global consumption of goods and services; U is the utility function, with $U(C_t) = \log C_t$; ρ is the utility discount rate; and T is the terminal point of the optimisation period.

The relevant constraints are

$$S_{t+1} = S_t - R_t$$

$$K_{t+1} = K_t + F(K_t, R_t) - C_t$$

$$S_T = K_T = 0$$

$$S_0 \text{ and } K_0 \text{ are given}$$

S_t denotes the stock of oil; R_t is the rate of oil extraction; K_t is the capital stock; and $F(K_t, R_t) = AK_t^{0.9} R_t^{0.1}$ is a Cobb–Douglas production function, with A being a fixed 'efficiency' parameter. In this application, we assume that oil extraction costs are zero, and that there is no depreciation of the capital stock. Note that we assume that there are fixed initial stocks of the so-called 'state variables' (exhaustible resource and the capital stock), and that we specify that the state variables are equal to zero at the end of the optimisation period.

We also assume that a backstop technology exists that will replace oil as a productive input at the end (terminal point) of the optimisation period, $t = T$. This explains why we set $S_T = 0$, as there is no point

Table 5.1 Numerical solution to the oil extraction and optimal consumption problem

Welfare(p.v.)=46.67668

time	Ct	F(Kt,Rt)	Kt	Rt	St	q(t+1)	P(t+1)	dF/dK(t)
1990s	3.7342	18.0518	4.9130	2.2770	11.5000	0.2678	0.2123	3.3069
2000s	13.6819	60.8347	19.2306	1.9947	9.2230	0.0731	0.2229	2.8471
2010s	45.3301	182.8353	66.3834	1.7232	7.2283	0.0221	0.2341	2.4788
2020s	137.2777	493.8224	203.8886	1.4637	5.5051	0.0073	0.2458	2.1798
2030s	383.6060	1204.3708	560.4334	1.2167	4.0413	0.0026	0.2581	1.9341
2040s	997.9350	2654.7992	1381.1982	0.9824	2.8247	0.0010	0.2710	1.7299
2050s	2430.1080	5261.7198	3038.6624	0.7611	1.8423	0.0004	0.2845	1.5584
2060s	5584.8970	9217.1125	5870.2742	0.5525	1.0812	0.0002	0.2987	1.4131
2070s	12174.5621	13608.6578	9502.4897	0.3564	0.5287	0.0001	0.3137	1.2889
2080s	25298.4825	14361.8971	10936.5854	0.1724	0.1724	0.0000	0.3293	1.1819
2090s		0.0		0.0000	0.0000	0.0000	0.3548	

| | $\times$ 10 trillion US$ | | | | $\times$ 100 billion barrels | | | |

% Growth rates:

2000	266.3899	237.0006	291.4222	-12.4012	-19.8004	-74.0064	5.00D0
2010	231.3150	200.5443	245.1973	-13.6071	-21.6271	-71.2545	5.0000
2020	202.8399	170.0914	207.1378	-15.0607	-23.8402	-68.5517	5.0000
2030	179.4380	143.8874	174.8723	-16.8783	-26.5885	-65.9180	5.0000
2040	159.9894	120.4304	146.4518	-19.2530	-30.1053	-63.3685	5.0000
2050	143.6602	98.1965	120.0019	-22.5320	-34.7797	-60.9136	5.0000
2060	129.8209	75.1730	93.1861	-27.4081	-41.3110	-58.5599	5.0000
2070	117.9908	47.6456	61.8747	-35.4951	-51.0972	-56.3110	5.0000
2080	107.7979	5.5350	15.0918	-51.3311	-67.3996	-54.1679	5.0000

Box 5.2 Solution of the dynamic optimisation problem using the maximum principle

The current value of the Hamiltonian is

$$H_t = U(C_t) + P_{t+1}(-R_t)$$
$$+ q_{t+1}(F(K_t, R_t) - C_t) \qquad (t = 0, 1, \ldots, T-1)$$

where P_t is the shadow price of oil, and q_t is the shadow price of capital. The four necessary conditions for an optimum are:

1
$$P_{t+1} - P_t = \rho P_t - \frac{\partial H_t}{\partial S_t} = \rho P_t$$

which implies Hotelling's efficiency rule

$$P_{t+1} = (1+\rho)P_t \qquad (t = 1, \ldots, T)$$

2
$$q_{t+1} - q_t = \rho q_t - \frac{\partial H_t}{\partial K_t} = \rho q_t - q_{t+1}F_{K_t}$$

which implies

$$q_{t+1} = \frac{1+\rho}{1+F_{K_t}} q_t \qquad (t = 1, \ldots, T)$$

where

$$F_{K_t} = F_{K_t}(K_t, R_t) = \frac{\partial F(K_t, R_t)}{\partial K_t}$$

3
$$\frac{\partial H_t}{\partial R_t} = 0 = -P_{t+1} + q_{t+1}F_{R_t}$$
$$(t = 0, 1, \ldots, T-1)$$

where

$$F_{R_t} = \frac{\partial F(K_t, R_t)}{\partial R_t}$$

4
$$\frac{\partial H_t}{\partial C_t} = 0 = U'(C_t) - q_{t+1}$$
$$(t = 0, 1, \ldots, T-1)$$

where

$$U'(C_t) = \frac{dU(C_t)}{dC_t}$$

Since we know $S_T = K_T = 0$, there are 6T unknowns in this problem as given in the table below.

We have 6T equations in total to solve for these 6T unknowns:

$$P_{t+1} = (1+\rho)P_t \qquad (t = 1, \ldots, T)$$
$$(T \text{ equations})$$

$$q_{t+1} = \frac{1+\rho}{1+F_{K_t}} q_t \qquad (t = 1, \ldots, T)$$
$$(T \text{ equations})$$

$$q_{t+1} = U'(C_t) \qquad (t = 0, 1, \ldots, T)$$
$$(T \text{ equations})$$

$$P_{t+1} = q_{t+1}F_{R_t} \qquad (t = 0, \ldots, T-1)$$
$$(T \text{ equations})$$

$$S_{t+1} = S_t - R_t \qquad (t = 0, \ldots, T-1)$$
$$(T \text{ equations})$$

$$K_{t+1} = K_t + F(K_t, R_t) - C_t \qquad (t = 0, \ldots, T-1)$$
$$(T \text{ equations})$$

$(T+1)$	$+(T+1)$	$+(T-1)$	$+(T-1)$	$+T$	$+T$	$= 6T$
$\{P_t\}_1^{T+1}$	$\{q_t\}_1^{T+1}$	$\{K_t\}_1^{T-1}$	$\{S_t\}_1^{T-1}$	$\{C_t\}_0^{T-1}$	$\{R_t\}_0^{T-1}$	

---

having any stocks of oil remaining once the backstop technology has replaced oil in production. We assume that the capital stock, K_t, associated with the oil input will be useless for the backstop technology, and therefore will be consumed completely by the end of the optimisation period so $K_T = 0$.

Implicitly in this simulation, we assume that a new capital stock, appropriate for the backstop technology, will be accumulated out of the resources available for consumption. So C_t in this model should be interpreted as consumption plus new additions to the (backstop) capital stock. The question of how much

should be saved to accumulate this new capital stock is beyond the scope of our simple model.

As the notation will have made clear, this is a discrete time model. We choose each period to be 10 years, and consider a 10-period ($t = 0, 1, \ldots, 9$) time horizon of 100 years beginning in 1990 ($t = 0$). The following data are used in the simulation:

Estimated world oil reserve
= 11.5 (units of 100 billion barrels)
World capital stock
= 4.913 (units of 10 trillion $US)

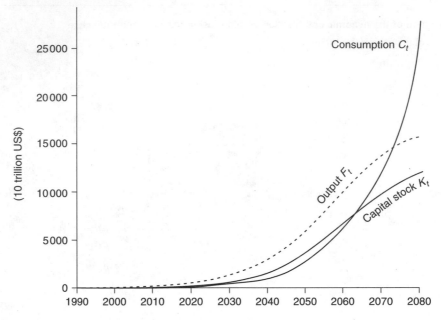

Fig 5.8 Numerical application: optimal time paths of output, consumption and capital stock.

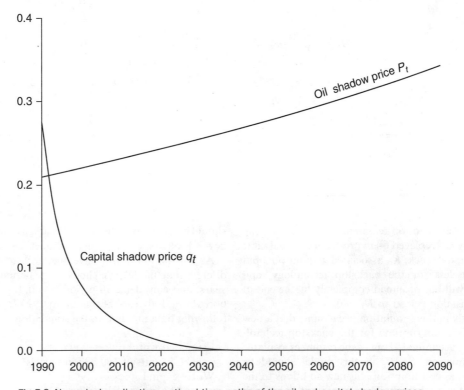

Fig 5.9 Numerical application: optimal time paths of the oil and capital shadow prices.

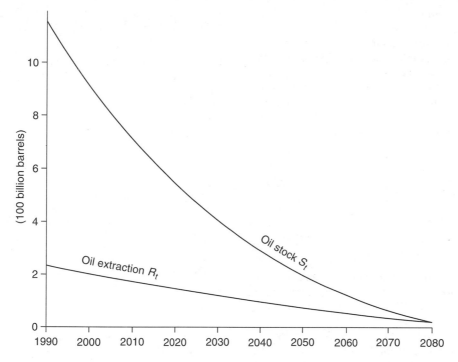

Fig 5.10 Numerical application: optimal time paths of oil extraction and the remaining oil stock.

Efficiency parameter A
  $= 3.968$
Utility discount rate
  $= 5\%$

The value of the efficiency parameter is estimated under the assumption that world aggregate output over the 1980s was $US 179.3 trillion, and aggregate oil extraction was 212.7 billion barrels.

We cannot obtain an analytical solution for this problem. But it is possible to solve the problem numerically on a computer. Table 5.1 and Figures 5.8–5.10 show the numerical solution.

Figure 5.8 shows that consumption rises exponentially through the whole of the optimisation period (the figure only shows the first part of that period, from 1990 up to 2080); output (F_t) also rises continuously, but its growth rate slows down towards the end of the period shown in the figure; this arises because at the terminal point (not shown in these figures), the capital stock has to fall to zero for the reason indicated above.

In Figure 5.9 we observe the shadow price growing over time at the rate ρ, and so satisfying Hotelling's rule; the shadow price of capital falls continuously

through time. In Figure 5.10, we see that the oil stock falls gradually from its initial level towards zero; note that as the shadow price of oil rises over time, so the rate of extraction falls towards zero. Not surprisingly, the optimal solution will require that the rate of extraction goes to zero at exactly the same point in time, t_f, that the stock is completely exhausted. Finally, note that within 100 years, the oil stock has fallen to a level not significantly different from zero; it is optimal to deplete the stock of oil fairly rapidly in this model.

What happens after the year 2090? You should now try to deduce the answer to this question!

Discussion questions

1 Are non-renewable resources becoming more or less substitutable by other productive inputs with the passage of time? What are the possible implications for efficient resource use of the elasticity of substitution between non-renewable resources and other inputs becoming

(a) higher, and
(b) lower
with the passage of time?

2 Discuss the possible effects of technical progress on resource substitutability.

3 Recycling of exhaustible resources can relax the constraints imposed by finiteness of non-renewable resources. What determines the efficient amount of recycling for any particular economy?

Problems

1 Using the relationship

$$r = \rho + \eta \frac{\dot{C}}{C}$$

demonstrate that if the utility function is of the special form $U(C) = C$, the consumption rate of discount (r) and the utility rate of discount are identical.

2 Using Equation 5.22 in the text (that is, the Hotelling efficiency condition), demonstrate the consequences for the efficient extraction of a non-renewable resource of an increase in the social discount rate, ρ.

Further reading

The mathematics underlying our analyses is presented simply and clearly in Chiang (1984, 1992). Excellent advanced level presentations of the theory of efficient and optimal resource depletion can be found in Baumol and Oates (1988), Dasgupta and Heal (1979), and Heal (1981). Dasgupta and Heal (1974) is also a comprehensive study, and is contained along with several other useful (but difficult) papers in the May 1974 special issue of the *Review of Economic Studies*.

Less difficult presentations are given in Hartwick and Olewiler (1986), Anderson (1981), and the Fisher and Peterson survey article in the March 1976 edition of the *Journal of Economic Literature*. For an application of this theory to the Greenhouse Effect, see Nordhaus (1982, 1991a). Barbier (1989a) provides a critique of the conventional theory of resource depletion, and other critical discussions are found in Common (1995) and Common and Perrings (1992).

Appendix 1

In this appendix, we derive the optimal solution to the simple exhaustible resource depletion problem discussed in Part 1 of this chapter. The technique we shall use – the Maximum Principle – is explained in Appendix 3.

We wish to maximise

$$W = \int_{t=0}^{t=\infty} U(C_t) e^{-\rho t} dt$$

subject to the constraints

$$\dot{S}_t = -R_t$$

and

$$\dot{K}_t = Q_t - C_t$$

where

$$Q_t = Q(K_t, R_t)$$

The current valued Hamiltonian for this problem is

$$H_t = U(C_t) + P_t(-R_t) + \omega_t(Q(K_t, R_t) - C_t)$$

The necessary conditions for maximum social welfare are

$$\dot{P}_t = \rho P_t \tag{5.36a}$$

$$\dot{\omega}_t = \rho \omega_t - Q_K \omega_t \tag{5.36b}$$

$$\frac{\partial H_t}{\partial R_t} = -P_t + \omega_t Q_R = 0 \tag{5.36c}$$

$$\frac{\partial H_t}{\partial C_t} = U'(C_t) - \omega_t = 0 \tag{5.36d}$$

These four conditions can be reduced to the three presented in the main text as Equations 5.21a–c in the following way. (We now drop time subscripts for notational compactness.) The elasticity of marginal utility is, by definition, the proportionate change in marginal utility that arises for a given proportionate change in consumption. That is

$$\eta = -\frac{\partial MU/MU}{\partial C/C}$$

where MU denotes marginal utility, and we have multiplied the elasticity by minus one to obtain a positive quantity. Rearranging this expression, we obtain

$$\eta = -\frac{\partial MU}{\partial C} \cdot \frac{C}{MU}$$

But noting that $MU = U'(C)$, we can also express this as

$$\eta = -\frac{U''(C) \cdot C}{U'(C)}$$

Combining Equation 5.36b and 5.36d and noting the expression for η we obtain

$$\frac{\dot{C}}{C} = \frac{Q_K - \rho}{\eta} \tag{5.37}$$

Proof: Differentiating Equation 5.36d with respect to time we obtain

$$\dot{\omega} = U''(C)\dot{C}$$

Combining Equation 5.37 with Equation 5.36b, we obtain

$$U''(C)\dot{C} = \rho\omega - Q_K\omega$$

$$\dot{C}U''(C) = \omega(\rho - Q_K)$$

$$\dot{C}U''(C) = U'(C)(\rho - Q_K)$$

Therefore

$$\frac{\dot{C}U''(C)}{C} = \frac{U'(C)(\rho - Q_K)}{C}$$

and so

$$\frac{\dot{C}}{C} = \frac{1}{\left[\dfrac{U''(C)C}{U'(C)}\right]}(\rho - Q_K)$$

or

$$\frac{\dot{C}}{C} = \frac{Q_K - \rho}{\eta}$$

as required. Equations 5.36a, 5.36c and 5.37 comprise the three necessary conditions (Equations 5.21a–c) in the main text.

The general model

Here we consider the optimal allocation of exhaustible and renewable resources in the presence of technical progress, population growth, extraction costs and damage associated with the use of the environmental resource.

We begin by defining the characteristics of the economy to be analysed. The economy's production function is

$$Q_t = Q(K_t, e^{at}L_t, e^{bt}R_t)$$

where a is a labour-augmenting technical progress parameter and b is a resource-augmenting technical progress parameter. L_t is the *physical* quantity of labour in time t, whereas $L_t e^{at}$ is the labour quantity in *efficiency units*. An equivalent interpretation applies to the exhaustible resource: R_t is the *physical* quantity of the resource in time t, whereas $R_t e^{bt}$ is the resource quantity in *efficiency units*.

The labour force grows exogenously at the rate n according to the relationship

$$L_t = L_0 e^{nt}$$

and so

$$\dot{L}_t = nL_t$$

Total extraction costs, G, are a function of the current rate of extraction R and the remaining resource stock, S:

$$G_t = G(S_t, R_t)$$

Environmental damage, D, is an increasing function of the rate of resource extraction and of the cumulative amount of the resource extracted:

$$D_t = D(R_t, S_0 - S_t)$$

and we view damage as reducing the level of consumption available from any given level of output.

The resource stock is either a renewable or a non-renewable resource. Its growth is determined according to

$$\dot{S}_t = \Omega(S_t) - R_t \tag{5.38}$$

where $\Omega(S)$ is the natural growth function of the resource, in which the amount of growth is some function of the current stock level (population) of the resource. For an exhaustible resource, $\Omega(S) = 0$ by definition.

The accounting relationship determining the growth of the capital stock is

$$\dot{K}_t = Q(K_t, e^{at}L_t e^{bt}R_t) - C_t - G(S_t, R_t) - D(R_t, S_0 - S_t)$$

That is, net investment (the addition to the capital stock) is equal to current net output, Q, less current consumption, C, less the costs of extracting the resource, G, and less the consumption foregone because of damage associated with resource use, D.

It is convenient to transform the problem by eliminating the *explicit* appearance of labour as a variable in the problem. To do this, define

$$c_t = C_t/L_t$$

$$k_t = K_t/(e^{at}L_t)$$

$$R_t^* = (e^{bt}R_t)/(e^{at}L_t)$$

$$f(k_t, R_t^*) = Q(K_t, e^{bt}R_t, e^{at}L_t)/(e^{at}L_t)$$

Using these definitions we can write the accounting relationship in a more convenient form. From the definition of k_t we have, by rearranging and then differentiating with respect to time,

$$\dot{K}_t = \dot{k}_t e^{at}L_t + ak_t e^{at}L_t + k_t e^{at}\dot{L}_t$$

and so we can rewrite the accounting relationship determining the rate of growth of the capital stock as

$$\dot{k}_t e^{at}L_t + ak_t e^{at}L_t + k_t e^{at}\dot{L}_t$$
$$= Q[K_t, e^{at}L_t, e^{bt}R_t] - C_t - G[S_t, R_t]$$
$$- D[R_t, S_0 - S_t]$$

Dividing each side by $L_t e^{at}$ we obtain

$$\dot{k}_t + ak_t + \frac{k_t\dot{L}_t}{L_t} = f(k_t, R_t^*) - c_t e^{-at} - \frac{G(S_t, R_t)}{e^{at}L_t}$$
$$- \frac{D(R_t, S_0 - S_t)}{e^{at}L_t} \qquad (5.39)$$

But since

$$\dot{L}_t = nL_t$$

we obtain

$$\dot{k}_t + ak_t + nk_t = f(k_t, R_t^*) - c_t e^{-at} - \frac{G(S_t, R_t)}{L_t e^{at}}$$
$$- \frac{D(R_t, S_0 - S_t)}{L_t e^{at}} \qquad (5.40)$$

This completes our statement of the technical relationships of the economy. Our objective is to maximise welfare which is now a function of the *consumption per worker*

$$W = \int_{t=0}^{t=\infty} U(c_t) e^{-\rho t}$$

subject to the constraints of Equations 5.38 and 5.39.

The current-valued Hamiltonian for this problem is

$$H_t = U(c_t) + P_t[\Omega(S_t) - R_t]$$
$$+ \omega_t \Big[-(a+n)k_t + f(k_t, R_t^*) - c_t e^{-at}$$
$$- \frac{G(S_t, R_t)}{L_t e^{at}} - \frac{D(R_t, S_0 - S_t)}{L_t e^{at}} \Big]$$

The necessary conditions for a maximum include (ignoring time subscripts)

$$\dot{P} = \rho P - P \cdot \Omega_S + \frac{(G_S - D_S)}{L e^{at}}\omega \qquad (5.41a)$$

$$\dot{\omega} = \rho\omega + (a+n)\omega - f_k\omega \qquad (5.41b)$$

$$\frac{\partial H}{\partial R} = -P + \omega f_{R^*}\frac{dR^*}{dR} - \omega\frac{G_R}{L e^{at}} - \omega\frac{D_R}{L e^{at}}$$
$$= 0 \qquad (5.41c)$$

$$\frac{\partial H}{\partial c} = U'(c) - \omega e^{-at} = 0 \qquad (5.41d)$$

where dR^*/dR in Equation 5.41c is $e^{bt}/e^{at}L$.

Define the elasticity of marginal utility to be

$$\eta = -\frac{U''(c) \cdot c}{U'(c)}$$

Combining Equations 5.41b and 5.41d, we obtain

$$\frac{\dot{c}}{c} = \frac{f_k - \rho - n}{\eta} \qquad (5.42)$$

Proof:

$$U'(c_t) = \omega_t e^{-at}$$
$$\omega = U'(c) e^{at}$$

Therefore, differentiating,

$$\dot{\omega} = U''(c)\dot{c} e^{at} + aU'(c) e^{at}$$

Now from Equation 5.41b,

$$\dot{\omega} = \rho\omega + (a+n)\omega - f_k\omega$$

we obtain

$$U''(c)\dot{c} e^{at} + aU'(c) e^{at} = \rho\omega + (a+n)\omega - f_k\omega$$
$$\dot{c}U''(c) e^{at} + aU'(c) e^{at} = \omega(\rho + a - f_k)$$
$$e^{at}[\dot{c}U''(c) + aU'(c)] = \omega(\rho + a + n - f_k)$$

But $\omega = U'(c)\,e^{at}$, therefore

$$e^{at}[\dot{c}U''(c) + aU'(c)] = U'(c)\,e^{at}(\rho + a + n - f_k)$$

$$\dot{c}U''(c) + aU'(c) = U'(c)(\rho + a + n - f_k)$$

$$\frac{\dot{c}U''(c) + aU'(c)}{cU''(c)} = \frac{U'(c)(\rho + a + n - f_k)}{cU''(c)}$$

$$\frac{\dot{c}}{c} + \frac{aU'(c)}{cU''(c)} = \frac{U'(c)/U'(c)(\rho + a + n - f_k)}{cU''(c)/U'(c)}$$

$$\frac{\dot{c}}{c} + a\left[\frac{1}{-\eta}\right] = \frac{(\rho + a + n - f_k)}{-\eta}$$

or finally

$$\frac{\dot{c}}{c} = \frac{f_k - \rho - n}{\eta}$$

Appendix 3

The optimal control problem and its solution, using the Maximum Principle

Optimal control theory, using the Maximum Principle, is a technique for solving constrained dynamic optimisation problems. The function to be maximised is known as the objective function, denoted $J(u)$ below. This will take the form of an integral over a time period from initial time (t_0) to the terminal point (t_f). The objective function will, in general, contain as its arguments three types of variable: x(t), a vector of state variables at time t, $u(t)$, a vector of control (or instrument) variables, and $J(u)$ the objective function, as well as time itself, t.

Underlying the optimal control problem will be some economic system, describing the initial state of a set of state variables of interest, and how they evolve over time.

Optimal control problems differ in terms of their terminal conditions. Firstly, the problem in hand may fix the values that the state variables take at the terminal point, or these values may be free (and so determined endogenously in the optimisation exercise). Secondly, either the particular problem that we are dealing with may either fix the terminal point, or that point may be free (and so, again, be determined endogenously in the optimisation exercise). The so-called transversality condition that must be satisfied in the optimisation will depend upon which of the

Table 5.2 The optimal control problem and its solution[a]

System	$\dot{x} = f(x, u, t)$, $\quad x(t_0) = x_0$			
Objective function	$J(u) = \max \int_{t_0}^{t_f} L(x, u, t)\,dt$			
Terminal state	$x(t_f) = x_f$		$x(t_f)$ free	
Terminal point	t_f fixed	t_f free	t_f fixed	t_f free
Hamiltonian	$H = H(x, u, P, t)$ $= L(x, u, t) + P^{\mathrm{T}} f(x, u, t)$			
Equations of motion	$\dot{x} = f(x, u, t)$, $\quad \dot{P} = -\dfrac{\partial H}{\partial X}$			
Max H	$\dfrac{\partial H}{\partial u} = 0$			
Transversality condition	$x(t_f) = x_f$		$P^*(t_f) = 0$	
		$H(t_f) = 0$		$H(t_f) = 0$

[a] Notation:
$x(t)$ is the vector of state variables.
$u(t)$ is the vector of control variables.
$J(u)$ is the objective function.
$P(t)$ is the vector of co-state variables or shadow prices; they give the agent's subjective valuation of the state variable in the Hamiltonian.
t_f denotes the terminal point in time for the optimisation exercise, which may be infinity.

four possibilities (generated by the two assumptions about terminal state, and the two assumptions about terminal point) is appropriate for the problem being considered.

The control variables are those instruments whose value can be chosen by the decision-maker in order to steer the evolution of the state variables over time in a desired manner. In addition to time, state and control variables, a fourth type of variable enters the problem. This is the vector of co-state variables or shadow prices, which denote the decision-maker's valuation of the state variable at each point in time along the optimum path.

Table 5.2 formally states the optimal control problem and its solution using general notation, and Table 5.3 presents the same information for the case where the objective function is a *discounted* integral (as is typical in this book).

Below Tables 5.2 and 5.3, we shall indicate briefly how the notation used and results obtained in Appendix 1 (which derives the optimal solution to the simple exhaustible resource depletion problem discussed in Part 1 of this chapter) correspond to the contents of Tables 5.2 and 5.3.

Table 5.3 The optimal control problem with a discounting factor and its solution[a]

System	$\dot{x} = f(x, u, t),$		$x(t_0) = x_0$	
Objective function[a]	$J(u) = \max \int_{t_0}^{t_f} L(x, u, t)\, e^{-\rho t}\, dt$			
Terminal state	$x(t_f) = x_f$		$x(t_f)$ free	
Terminal point	t_f fixed	t_f free	t_f fixed	t_f free
Hamiltonian	$H = H(x, u, P, t)$ $= L(x, u, t) + P^T f(x, u, t)$			
Equations of motion	$\dot{x} = f(x, u, t), \qquad \dot{P} = \rho P - \dfrac{\partial H}{\partial X}$			
Max H	$\dfrac{\partial H}{\partial u} = 0$			
Transversality condition	$x(t_f) = x_f$		$P^*(t_f) = 0$	
		$H(t_f) = 0$		$H(t_f) = 0$

[a] ρ is the discount rate.

Relationship between notation used and results obtained in Appendix 1 and the contents of Tables 5.2 and 5.3

The objective function, $J(u)$, we maximise in Appendix 1 is

$$J(C) = W = \int_{t=0}^{t=\infty} U(C_t)\, e^{-\rho t}\, dt$$

Note the following points:

1 There are two control variables (u in Tables 5.2 and 5.3) in this case, the level of consumption at each point in time, C_t, and the rate of resource extraction at each point in time, R_t. (Be careful not to confuse U and u! U in Appendix 1 denotes utility; it is what is being maximised in the objective function; u in Tables 5.2 and 5.3 is the notation used for control variables.)

2 The objective function need not contain all of the variables indicated in Tables 5.2 and 5.3 (that is state variables, control variables and time); in this case the objective function depends only on the level of the control variable; time does enter, but only through the discount factor – so Table 5.3 is relevant for this exercise.

3 There are two state variables (the x variables in Tables 5.2 and 5.3) in the model analysed in Appendix 1: the resource stock at time t, S_t and the capital stock at time t, K_t. Corresponding to these two state variables are

(a) two equations of motion

$$\dot{S} = -R_t$$

and

$$\dot{K}_t = Q_t - C_t$$

(b) two co-state variables, the shadow price of the exhaustible resource at time t, P_t, and the shadow price of a unit of capital at time t, ω_t. The term T in the Hamiltonian function means the transpose of the vector. Because there are two state variables in this exercise, there will be two shadow prices, and so the term $P^T f(x, u, t)$ in Tables 5.2 and 5.3 here consists of the two components at the end of the Hamiltonian in Appendix 1.

Finally, you should now convince yourself that Equations 5.36a–d in Appendix 1 do indeed correspond to the following two components of Table 5.3:

$$\dot{P} = \rho p - \frac{\partial H}{\partial x}$$

$$\frac{\partial H}{\partial u} = 0$$

The theory of optimal resource extraction: non-renewable (exhaustible) resources

Behold, I have played the fool, and have erred exceedingly.

1 Samuel 26:21

Introduction: the extraction of exhaustible resources

Exhaustible resources include fossil fuel energy supplies – oil, gas and coal – and non-energy minerals – copper and nickel, for example.[1] These resources are formed by geological processes that usually take millions of years, so that they can be viewed as existing in the form of fixed stocks of reserves which, once extracted, cannot be renewed. The resource will be depleted as long as the use rate is positive. One question is of central importance: what is the optimal extraction path over time for any particular exhaustible resource stock?

We have answered this question to some extent in Chapter 5. However, in that earlier analysis, we solved the optimal extraction problem for one particular, very simple, case in which it was assumed that there was only one homogeneous exhaustible resource. No differences existed between different parts of the stock according to location, and all of the stock was of uniform quality. By assuming a single homogeneous stock, we ruled out the possibility that alternative *substitute* exhaustible resources exist for the one under consideration. The only substitution possibilities we considered in Chapter 5 were between the exhaustible resource and other production inputs (labour and capital).

But in practice, exhaustible resources comprise a set of different forms of resource, differing in terms of chemical and physical type (oil, gas, uranium, coal, and the various categories of each of these) and in terms of costs of extraction as a result of differences in location, accessibility, quality and so

[1] In this chapter, we use the phrases *exhaustible resources* and *non-renewable resources* interchangeably.

on. In this chapter, we wish to analyse the optimal extraction of one component of this set of exhaustible resources, where possibilities exist for substituting other components if the price of the resource rises to such an extent that it makes alternatives economically more attractive. Consider, for example, the case of a country which has been exploiting its coal reserves, but in which coal extraction costs rise as fewer productive seams are mined. Meanwhile, gas costs fall as a result of the application of superior extraction technology. One would expect a point to be reached where electricity producers will substitute gas for coal in power generation. It is this kind of process that we wish to be able to model in this chapter.

Although the analysis that follows will employ a different framework from that used in Chapter 5, one very important result carries over to the present case. If a resource is to be optimally extracted, the Hotelling rule continues to be a necessary condition for this. As we showed in Chapter 5, the Hotelling rule is an efficiency condition which must be satisfied by *any* optimal extraction programme.

Having discussed the socially optimal extraction path for an exhaustible resource stock, we then consider how a resource is likely to be depleted in a market economy. The discussions of Chapter 4 suggest that the extraction path in competitive market economies will, under certain circumstances, be socially optimal. We demonstrate that this intuition is indeed correct. However, the competitive market is not the only market form which can exist. We shall also study the influence of one other market form, pure monopoly, upon the depletion speed of an exhaustible resource.

Our model is necessarily very simple and abstracts considerably from reality so that we can identify and examine basic concepts. The assumptions are gradually relaxed so that we can deal with increasingly complex but more realistic situations. For convenience of presentation of the arguments, it is convenient to begin with a model in which only two periods of time are considered. Even from such a simple starting point, very powerful results can be obtained, which can be generalised to analyses involving many periods. If you have a clear understanding of Hotelling's rule from Chapter 5, you might wish to skip the two-period model in the next section; we have chosen to include it to lead the reader gently into the more powerful analyses which follow.

Having analysed optimal depletion in a two-period model, we then consider a more general model in which depletion takes place over T periods, where T may be a very large number. You will notice that in our worked examples in this chapter, the demand curve we use has a maximum price: a price at which demand would be choked off to zero. Clearly, this implies either that the resource is not essential (in the sense used in Chapter 5), or that substitutes exist for the resource which become economically more attractive at that price. It is the latter interpretation we shall have in mind in this chapter. We shall have more to say on this at the appropriate place below.

There are limits to what we try and cover here. In this chapter, we do not take any account of adverse external effects arising from the extraction or consumption of the resource. It is known, however, that the production and consumption of non-renewable fossil energy fuels are the primary cause of many of the world's most serious environmental problems. In particular, the combustion of these fuels accounts for between 55 and 88% of carbon dioxide emissions, 90% of sulphur dioxide, and 85% of nitrogen oxide emissions (IEA, 1990). In addition, fossil fuel use accounts for significant proportions of trace metal emissions.

We showed earlier, in Chapter 5, that the optimal extraction path will be different if adverse externalities are present. We shall return to this matter later, in Chapters 8 and 9, in which the economics of pollution and economic policy for dealing with pollution problems are discussed. In this chapter, however, we abstract from these environmental impacts. In effect, such external effects are assumed to not exist. Any results we obtain regarding socially optimal extraction paths are conditional upon this assumption, of course. Chapter 5 has already indicated how the analysis can be generalised to take account of environmental damages, and Chapters 8 and 9 will take this matter further.

Finally, a word about presentation. A lot of mathematics is required to derive our results. The maths is not particularly difficult, but it can be tedious to go through. For this reason, we have tended to stress results and discuss them intuitively in the main text, whilst derivations (where they are lengthy) are placed in appendices. You may find it helpful to omit these on a first reading, and return to read them during a more careful second reading. The maths is presented fully and simply so you should have little difficulty in understanding the analysis. However, if you cannot cope with the appendices for any reason, do not worry; the arguments in the chapter do not *require* that they be read.

Our concern in this chapter is with the class of so-called 'non-renewable' resources. For much of our discussion, we shall assume that there exists a known, finite stock of each kind of non-renewable resource. But as we show in later sections, this assumption is not always appropriate; new discoveries are made, increasing the magnitude of known stocks, and technological change alters the proportion of mineral resources that are economically recoverable. Box 6.1 discusses the extent to which it is reasonable to claim that there are fixed and finite quantities of non-renewable resources.

A fixed stock non-renewable resource: two-period model

As explained in the Introduction, this section of the chapter can be omitted by those readers who gained a clear understanding of the Hotelling rule for efficient resource extraction and of optimal extraction from reading Chapter 5. Those readers could now turn to the next section. If your understanding is less than complete, please do read this section; some repetition of material will be found, but we feel that it will assist in your comprehension of the ideas we discuss.

Consider a planning horizon which consists of two periods, period 0 and period 1. The economy has available a fixed stock of known size of one type of an exhaustible resource. The initial fixed stock of the resource (at the start of period 0) is denoted $\bar{S}$.

Let R_t be the quantity extracted in period t and assume that for this resource, a demand[2] exists at each time, given by

$$P_t = a - bR_t$$

[2] Strictly speaking, this is an inverse demand function.

Box 6.1 Are non-renewable resources fixed and finite?

Are non-renewable resources really available in fixed and finite supply? This class of resources includes metals, oil, gases and other mineral deposits. Over sufficiently long time-scales, they are renewable, but the rate of regeneration is so slow in time-scales relevant to humans that it is sensible to label such resources non-renewable. It also seems reasonable to claim that they exist in finite quantities – albeit very large quantities indeed in some cases. But what is of most interest is whether the amounts are 'fixed' in some sense.

Table 6.1 presents some relevant information. The final column – 'Base resource' – indicates the mass of each resource which is thought to exist in the earth's crust. Most of this resource base consists of the mineral in very dispersed form, or at great depths below the surface. Base resource figures such as these are the broadest sense in which one might use the term 'resource stocks', and these quantities are, to all intents and purposes, fixed and finite. In each case, the measure is purely physical, having little or no relationship to economic measures of stocks. Notice that each of these quantities is extremely large relative to any other of the indicated stock measures.

The column labelled 'Resource potential' is arguably of more relevance to our discussions, comprising estimates of the upper limits on resource extraction possibilities given current and expected technologies. Whereas the resource base is a pure physical measure, the resource potential is a measure incorporating physical and technological information. But this illustrates the difficulty of classifying and measuring resources; as time passes, technology will almost certainly change, in ways that cannot be predicted today. As a result, estimates of the resource potential will change (usually rising), even where resource base figures are constant. Some writers are so confident of the prospects of future technological improvement as to assert that we shall never 'run out' of any resource.

An economist is interested not in what is technically feasible but in what would become available under certain conditions. In other words, he or she is interested in resource supplies, or potential supplies. These will be shaped by physical and technological factors, but will also depend upon resource market prices and the costs of extraction. Exploration and research effort will themselves be influenced by prices and costs, introducing feedbacks into the relationships. Data in the column labelled 'World reserve base' consist of estimates of the upper bounds of resource stocks (including reserves that have not yet been discovered) that are economically recoverable under 'reasonable expectations' of future price, cost and technology possibilities, whilst those labelled 'Reserves' consist of quantities that are economically recoverable under present configurations of costs and prices.

In conclusion, one might argue that whilst it might be reasonable to maintain as a working assumption the notion of fixed mineral resource stocks, in the longer term stocks are not fixed, and will vary with changing economic and technological circumstances.

Table 6.1 Production, consumption and reserves of some important mineral resources: 1991 (figures in millions of metric tons)

	Production	Reserves		World reserve base		Consumption	Resource potential	Base resource (crustal mass)
		Quantity	Reserve life (years)	Reserve base	Base life (years)			
Aluminium	112.22	23 000	222	28 000	270	19.460	3 519 000	1 990 000 000 000
Iron ore	929.754	150 000	161	230 000	247	959.6	2 035 000	1 392 000 000 000
Potassium	na	20 000	800	na	>800	25	na	408 000 000 000
Manganese	25	800	32	5000	200	22	42 000	31 200 000 000
Phosphorus	na	110	na	na	270	na	51 000	28 800 000 000
Flourine	na	2.5	na	na	12	na	20 000	10 800 000 000
Sulphur	56.87	na	na	na	na	57.5	na	9 600 000 000
Chromium	13	419	32	1950	150	13	3260	2 600 000 000
Zinc	7.137	140	20	330	46	6.993	3400	2 250 000 000
Nickel	0.922	47	51	111	119	0.882	2590	2 130 000 000
Copper	9.29	310	33	590	64	10.174	2120	1 510 000 000
Lead	3.424	63	18	130	38	5.342	550	290 000 000
Tin	0.179	8	45	10	56	0.218	68	40 000 000
Tungsten	0.0413	3.5	80	>3.5	>80	0.044	51	26 400 000
Mercury	0.003	0.130	43	0.240	80	0.005	3.4	2 100 000
Silver	0.014	0.28	20	na	na	0.02	2.8	1 800 000
Platinum	0.0003	0.37	124	na	na	0.00029	1.2	1 100 000

na denotes figure not available.
Source: Figures compiled from a variety of sources.

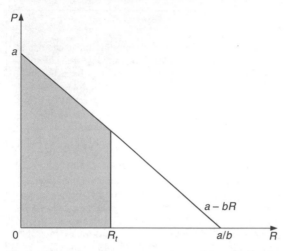

Fig 6.1 The exhaustible resource demand function for the two-period model.

where P_t is the price in period t, with a and b being positive constant numbers. So, the demand functions for the two periods will be:

$$P_0 = a - bR_0$$

$$P_1 = a - bR_1$$

These demands are illustrated in Figure 6.1.

Before we go any further, note a point made in the Introduction. A linear (and negatively sloped) demand function such as this one has the property that demand goes to zero at some price, in this case the price a. Hence, either this resource is non-essential or it possesses a substitute which becomes economically more attractive at the price a. This is not the only assumption one could make, and so you should bear in mind that the particular results we derive will, to some extent at least, be conditional upon the assumption that the demand curve is of this particular form.

Now let us return to our analysis. The shaded area in Figure 6.1 (algebraically, the integral of P over the interval $R = 0$ to $R = R_t$) shows the total benefit consumers obtain from consuming the quantity R_t in period t.[3] From a social point of view, this area

represents the gross social benefit, B, derived from the extraction and consumption of quantity R_t of the resource. We can express this quantity as

$$B(R_t) = \int_0^{R_t} (a - bR)\, dR$$

$$= aR_t - \frac{b}{2} R_t^2 .$$

where the notation $B(R_t)$ is used to make explicit the fact that the gross benefit (B) is dependent on the quantity of the resource extracted and consumed (R).

However, the total *gross* benefit obtained by consumers is not identical to the *net* social benefit of the resource, as resource extraction involves costs to society. Let us define c to be the constant marginal cost of extracting the resource ($c \geq 0$).[4] Then total extraction costs, C_t, for the extracted quantity R_t units will be

$$C_t = cR_t$$

The total net social benefit from extracting the quantity R_t is[5]

$$\mathrm{NSB}_t = B_t - C_t$$

where NSB denotes the total net social benefit and B is the gross social benefit of resource extraction and use. Hence

$$\mathrm{NSB}(R_t) = \int_0^{R_t} (a - bR)\, dR - cR_t$$

$$= aR_t - \frac{b}{2} R_t^2 - cR_t \qquad (6.1)$$

A socially optimal extraction policy

Our objective in this subsection is to identify an extraction programme which is socially optimal – in

---

[3] One way of convincing yourself that this statement is correct is as follows. We can regard a demand curve as providing information about the marginal willingness to pay (or marginal benefit) for successive units of the good in question. The area under a demand curve up to some given quantity is thus the sum of a set of marginal benefits, and is equal to the total benefit derived from consuming that quantity. This is explained in greater depth in Chapter 10, on valuing environmental resources.

[4] Constancy of marginal costs of extraction is a very strong assumption. In the previous chapter, we investigated a more general case in which marginal extraction costs are not necessarily constant. We do not consider this any further here, as little of importance would be gained, whilst it would complicate the derivations considerably. Later in this chapter, however, we do analyse the consequences for extraction of a once-and-for-all *rise* in extraction costs.

[5] Strictly speaking, social benefits derive from consumption (use) of the resource, not extraction *per se*. However, we assume throughout this chapter that all resource stocks extracted in a period are consumed in that period, and so this distinction becomes irrelevant.

other words, a programme which maximises social welfare. This will serve as a yardstick in terms of which any particular extraction programme can be assessed. Later in the chapter, we try to find out what kind of depletion programme would be undertaken in a market economy, and can then discuss whether this would be socially optimal using the criterion we develop here.

In order to find the socially optimal extraction programme, two things are required. The first is a social welfare function that embodies society's objectives; the second is a statement of the technical possibilities and constraints available at any point in time. Let us deal first with the social welfare function, relating this as far as possible to our discussion of social welfare functions in Chapters 2 and 4.

As in Chapter 4, the social welfare function that we shall use is discounted utilitarian in form. So the general two-period social welfare function

$$W = W(U_0, U_1)$$

takes the particular form

$$W = U_0 + \frac{U_1}{1 + \rho}$$

where ρ is the social utility discount rate, reflecting society's time preference. Now let us regard the utility in each period as being equal to the net social benefit in each period.[6] Given this, the social welfare function may be written as

$$W = \text{NSB}_0 + \frac{\text{NSB}_1}{1 + \rho}$$

What are the relevant technical constraints? There is only one in this case. Society has available a fixed initial stock of the non-renewable resource, $\bar{S}$. Since we are adopting a two-period model, we assume that society wishes to have none of this resource stock left at the end of the second period. Then the quantities extracted in the two periods, R_0 and R_1, must satisfy

the constraint:[7]

$$R_0 + R_1 = \bar{S}$$

We are now in a position to state precisely the optimisation problem that we wish to solve. The problem is to choose R_0 and R_1 in such a way as to maximise social welfare, subject to the constraint that total extraction of the resources over the two periods equals $\bar{S}$ exactly. Mathematically, we write the objective as

$$\max_{R_0, R_1} W = \text{NSB}_0 + \frac{\text{NSB}_1}{1 + \rho}$$

subject to

$$R_0 + R_1 = \bar{S}$$

There are several ways of obtaining solutions to constrained optimisation problems of this form. We use the Lagrange multiplier method, a technique which is explained in Appendix 1 to this chapter. The first step is to form the Lagrangian function, L

$$L = W - \lambda(\bar{S} - R_0 - R_1)$$

$$= \text{NSB}_0 + \frac{\text{NSB}_1}{1 + \rho} - \lambda(\bar{S} - R_0 - R_1)$$

$$= \left(aR_0 - \frac{b}{2}R_0^2 - cR_0\right) + \left(\frac{aR_1 - \frac{b}{2}R_1^2 - cR_1}{1 + \rho}\right)$$

$$- \lambda(\bar{S} - R_0 - R_1) \qquad (6.2)$$

in which λ is a 'Lagrange multiplier'. Remembering that R_0 and R_1 are choice variables – variables whose value we must select in order to optimise welfare – the necessary conditions for maximising this expression include:

$$\frac{\partial L}{\partial R_0} = a - bR_0 - c + \lambda = 0 \qquad (6.3)$$

$$\frac{\partial L}{\partial R_1} = \frac{a - bR_1 - c}{1 + \rho} + \lambda = 0 \qquad (6.4)$$

Since the right-hand side terms of Equations 6.3 and 6.4 are both equal to zero, this implies

$$a - bR_0 - c + \lambda - \frac{a - bR_1 - c}{1 + \rho} + \lambda$$

---

[6] In order to make such an interpretation valid, we shall assume that the demand function is 'quasilinear' (see Varian, 1987). Suppose there are two goods, X, the good whose demand we are interested in, and Y, money to be spent on all other goods. Quasilinearity requires that the utility function for good X is of the form

$$U = V(X) + Y$$

This implies that income effects are absent in the sense that changes in income do not affect the demand for good X. In this case, we can legitimately interpret the area under the demand curve for good X as a measure of utility.

[7] We could easily change the problem so that a predetermined quantity S^* ($S^* \geq 0$) be left at the end of Period 1 by rewriting the constraint as

$$R_0 + R_1 + S^* = \bar{S}$$

This would not, in any important sense, alter the essence of the conclusion we shall reach.

and so

$$a - bR_0 - c = \frac{a - bR_1 - c}{1 + \rho}$$

Using the demand function $P_t = a - bR_t$, the last equation can be written as

$$P_0 - c = \frac{P_1 - c}{1 + \rho}$$

where P_0 and P_1 are gross prices and $P_0 - c$ and $P_1 - c$ are net prices. A resource's net price is also known as the resource rent or resource royalty. Rearranging this expression, we obtain

$$\rho = \frac{(P_t - c) - (P_0 - c)}{P_0 - c}$$

If we change the notation used for time periods so that $P_0 = P_{t-1}$, $P_1 = P_t$ and $c = c_t = c_{t-1}$, we then obtain

$$\rho = \frac{(P_t - c_t) - (P_{t-1} - c_{t-1})}{P_{t-1} - c_{t-1}} \qquad (6.5)$$

which is the result we obtained previously in Chapter 5, Equation 5.21a, commonly known as Hotelling's rule. Note that in Equation 6.5, P is a gross price, whereas in Equation 5.21a of Chapter 5, P refers to a net price, resource rent or royalty. However, since $(P - c)$ in Equation 6.5 is the resource net price or royalty, these two equations are identical.

What does this result tell us intuitively? The left-hand side of Equation 6.5, ρ, is the social utility discount rate, which embodies some view about how future utility should be valued in terms of present utility. The right-hand side is the proportionate rate of growth of the resource's net price. So if, for example, society chooses a discount rate of 0.1 (or 10%), then Hotelling's rule states that an efficient extraction programme requires the net price of the resource to grow at a proportionate rate of 0.1 (or 10%) over time.

Now we know how much higher the net price should be in period 1 compared with period 0, if welfare is to be maximised; but what should be the *level* of the net price in period 0? This is easily answered. Recall that the economy has some fixed stock of the resource that is to be entirely extracted and consumed in the two periods. Also, we have assumed that the demand function for the resource is known. An optimal extraction programme requires two gross prices, P_0 and P_1 such that the following

conditions are satisfied:

$$P_0 = a - bR_0$$
$$P_1 = a - bR_1$$
$$R_0 + R_1 = \bar{S}$$
$$P_1 - c = (1 + \rho)(P_0 - c)$$

This will uniquely define the two prices that are required for welfare maximisation.

A fixed stock non-renewable resource: multi-period model

Having investigated resource depletion in the simple two-period model, let us now generalise our analysis to that of many periods. It will be convenient also to change from a discrete time framework (in which we have a number of successive intervals of time, denoted period 0, period 1, etc.) to a continuous time framework, in which we can refer to rates of extraction and use at particular points in time over some continuous time horizon.[8]

To keep the maths as simple as possible, we will push extraction costs somewhat into the background. To do this, we now define P to be the net price of the exhaustible resource, that is the price after deduction of the cost of extraction. Let $P(R)$ denote the demand function for the resource, indicating that the resource net price is a function of the quantity extracted, R.

The social utility at some point in time from consuming a quantity of the resource, R, which is equivalent to the net social benefit discussed in the previous section for the two-period case, may be defined as follows:

$$U(R) = \int_0^R P(R)\, dR \qquad (6.6a)$$

which is illustrated by the shaded area in Figure 6.2. You will notice that the demand curve we use in Figure 6.2 is non-linear, and is different from that in the previous two-period case. We shall have more to say about this particular form of the demand function shortly.

By differentiating total social utility with respect to R, the rate of resource extraction and use, we obtain

$$\frac{\partial U}{\partial R} = P(R) \qquad (6.6b)$$

[8] The material in this section, in particular the worked example investigated later, owes much to Heijman (1990).

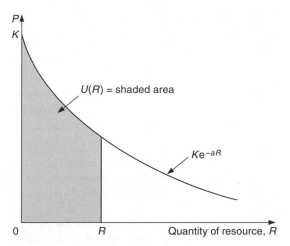

Fig 6.2 A resource demand curve, and the total utility from consuming a particular quantity of the resource.

which states that the marginal social utility of resource use equals the net price of the resource.

Assume, as we did for the two-period model, that the intertemporal social welfare function is of the utilitarian form, in which future social utility is discounted at the social utility discount rate ρ. Then the value of social welfare over an interval of time from period 0 to period T can be expressed as[9]

$$W = \int_0^T U(R(t))\, e^{-\rho t}\, dt$$

Our problem is to make social welfare maximising choices of

(i) $R(t)$, for $t = 0$ to $t = T$ (that is, we wish to choose a quantity of resource to be extracted in each period), and

(ii) the optimal value for T (the point in time at which further depletion of the resource stock ceases),

[9] It may be helpful to relate this form of social welfare function to the discrete time versions we have been using previously. We have stated that a T-period, discrete time, discounted welfare function can be written as

$$W = U_0 + \frac{U_1}{1+\rho} + \frac{U_2}{(1+\rho)^2} + \ldots + \frac{U_T}{(1+\rho)^T}$$

We could write this equivalently as

$$W = \sum_{t=0}^{t=T} \frac{U_t}{(1+\rho)^t}$$

A continuous time analogue of this welfare function is then

$$W = \int_{t=0}^{t=T} U(t)\, e^{-\rho t}\, dt$$

subject to the constraint that

$$\int_0^T R(t)\, dt = \bar{S}$$

where $\bar{S}$ is the total initial stock of the exhaustible resource. That is, the total extraction of the resource is equal to the size of the initial resource stock. Note that in this problem, the time horizon to exhaustion is being treated as an endogenous variable chosen by the decision maker, and not as a fixed, exogenous number.

We define the remaining stock of the natural resource at time t, $S(t)$, as

$$S(t) = \bar{S} - \int_0^t R(t)\, dt$$

then by differentiation with respect to time, we obtain

$$\dot{S}(t) = -R(t)$$

where $\dot{S}(t) = dS(t)/dt$, the rate of change of the remaining resource stock with respect to time.

So the dynamic optimisation problem involves the choice of a path of resource extraction $R(t)$ over the interval $t = 0$ to $t = T$ that satisfies the resource stock constraint and which maximises social welfare, W. Mathematically, we have:

$$\max W = \int_0^T U(R(t))\, e^{-\rho t}\, dt$$

subject to $\dot{S}(t) = -R(t)$. This problem is very similar to (although rather easier than) one we solved in Chapter 5 (see Appendix 1). It would be a useful exercise at this point for you to use that optimisation technique (explained in Appendix 3 of Chapter 5) to derive the solution to this problem. Your derivation can be checked against the answer given in Appendix 2 to this chapter.

Even without using formal optimisation techniques, intuition suggests one condition that must be satisfied if W is to be maximised. This is, $R(t)$ must be chosen so that the *discounted* marginal utility is equal at each point in time, that is

$$\frac{\partial U}{\partial R}\, e^{-\rho t} = \text{constant}$$

To understand this, let us use the method of contradiction. If the discounted marginal utilities from resource extraction were not equal in every period, then total welfare W could be increased by shifting some extraction from a period with a relatively low discounted marginal utility to a period with a relatively high discounted marginal utility. Rearranging the path of extraction in this way would raise welfare. It must, therefore, be the case that welfare is maximised when discounted marginal utilities are equal.

Given this result, how do we proceed? First note Equation 6.6b again:

$$\frac{\partial U}{\partial R} = P(t)$$

So the requirement that the discounted marginal utility be constant is equivalent to the requirement that the discounted net price is constant as well, a result noted previously in Chapter 5. That is

$$\frac{\partial U}{\partial R}\,e^{-\rho t} = P(t)\,e^{-\rho t} = \text{constant} = P_0$$

Rearranging this condition, we obtain

$$P_t = P_0\,e^{\rho t} \tag{6.7a}$$

By differentiation[10] this can be rewritten as

$$\frac{\dot{P}_t}{P_t} = \rho \tag{6.7b}$$

This is, once again, the Hotelling efficiency rule! It now appears in a different guise, because of our switch to a continuous time framework. The rule states that the net price or royalty P_t of an exhaustible resource should rise at a rate equal to the social utility discount rate, ρ, if the social value of the resource is to be maximised.

We now know the rate at which the resource net price or royalty must rise. However, this does not fully characterise the solution to our optimising problem. There are several other things we need to know too. Firstly, we need to know the optimal initial value of the resource net price. Secondly, over how long a period of time should the resource be extracted – in other words, what is the optimal value of T? Thirdly,

---

[10] Differentiation of Equation 6.7a with respect to time gives

$$\frac{\mathrm{d}P_t}{\mathrm{d}t} = P_0\rho\,e^{\rho t}$$

By substitution of the first of these equations into the second, we obtain

$$\frac{\mathrm{d}P_t}{\mathrm{d}t} = \rho P_t$$

and dividing through by P_t we obtain

$$\frac{\dot{P}_t}{P_t} = \rho$$

as required.

Table 6.2 The required optimality conditions

	Initial $(t = 0)$	Interim $(t = t)$	Final $(t = T)$
Royalty, P	$P_0 = ?$	$P_t = ?$	$P_T = ?$
Extraction, R	$R_0 = ?$	$R_t = ?$	$R_T = ?$
Depletion time			$T = ?$

what is the optimal rate of resource extraction at each point in time? Finally, what should be the values of P and R at the end of the extraction horizon? Table 6.2 summarises the information that is required for a full solution.

It is not possible to obtain answers to these questions without one additional piece of information: the particular form of the resource demand function. So let us suppose that the resource demand function is

$$P(R) = K\,e^{-aR} \tag{6.8}$$

which is illustrated in Figure 6.2.[11] Unlike the demand function used in the two-period analysis, this function exhibits a non-linear relationship between P and R, and is probably more representative of the form that resource demands are likely to take than the linear function used in the section on the two-period model. However, it is similar to the previous demand function in so far as it exhibits zero demand at some finite price level. To see this, just note that $P(R = 0) = K$. K is the so-called *choke price* for this resource, meaning that the demand for the resource is driven to zero or is 'choked off' at this price, presumably because at the choke price people using the services of this resource would switch demand to some alternative, substitute, exhaustible resource, or to an alternative final product not using that resource as an input.

Let us recap the argument so far. Given

- a particular resource demand function,
- Hotelling's efficiency condition,

---

[11] For the demand function given in Equation 6.8, we can obtain the particular form of the social welfare function as follows. The social utility function corresponding to Equation 6.6a will be:

$$U(R) = \int_0^R P(R)\,\mathrm{d}R = \int_0^R K\,e^{-aR}\,\mathrm{d}R = \frac{K}{a}(1 - e^{-aR})$$

The social welfare function, therefore, is

$$W = \int_0^T U(R_t)\,e^{-\rho t}\,\mathrm{d}t = \int_0^T \frac{K}{a}(1 - e^{-aR_t})\,e^{-\rho}\,\mathrm{d}t$$

Table 6.3 Optimality conditions: multi-period model

	Initial ($t = 0$)	Interim ($t = t$)	Final ($t = T$)
Royalty, P	$P_0 - K \exp(\sqrt{2\rho\bar{S}a})$	$P_t = K\,\mathrm{e}^{\rho(t-T)}$	$P_T = K$
Extraction, R	$R_0 = \sqrt{\dfrac{2\rho\bar{S}}{a}}$	$R_t = \dfrac{\rho}{a}(T - t)$	$R_T = 0$
Depletion time			$T = \sqrt{\dfrac{2\bar{S}a}{\rho}}$

- an initial value for the resource stock, and
- a final value for the resource stock,

it is possible to obtain optimal expressions for all the variables listed in Table 6.2. We do now have all this information. A particular demand curve has just been assumed, we have derived the Hotelling condition, and we know the initial stock. What about the final stock level? This is straightforward. An optimal solution must have the property that the stock goes to zero at exactly the same point in time that demand and extraction go to zero.[12] If that were not the case, some resource will have been needlessly wasted. So we know that the solution must include $S_T = 0$ and $R_T = 0$, with resource stocks being positive, and positive extraction taking place over all time up to T.

Before we proceed to obtain all the details of the solution, one important matter must be made clear. As the solution we obtain requires information about the demand function of the natural resource, the solution will vary depending upon the demand function chosen. It is important to realise that the expressions we derive below are conditional upon the particular demand function that we are assuming, and will not be valid in all circumstances. In particular, our model in this chapter assumes that the resource has a choke price, implying that a substitute for the resource becomes economically more attractive at that price.

As the mathematics required to obtain the full solution are rather tedious (but not particularly difficult), the derivations are presented in Appendix 3. You are strongly recommended to read this now, but if you prefer to omit these derivations, the results are presented in Table 6.3. You can see from Table 6.3 that all the expressions for the initial, interim, and final resource royalty (or net prices) and rate of resource extraction are functions of the parameters of the model (K, ρ, $\bar{S}$ and a) and the optimal depletion

time, T. As the final expression indicates, T is itself a function of those parameters.

Thus, given the functional forms we have been using in this section, if the values of the parameters K, ρ, $\bar{S}$ and a were known, it would be possible to solve the model to obtain numerical values for all the variables of interest over the whole period for which the resource will be extracted.

Figure 6.3 portrays in a diagrammatic form the solution to our optimal depletion model. The diagram shows the optimal resource extraction and net price paths over time corresponding to social welfare maximisation. As we show subsequently, it also represents the profit-maximising extraction and price paths in perfectly competitive markets.

In the upper right quadrant, the net price is shown rising exponentially at the social utility discount rate, ρ, thereby satisfying the Hotelling rule. The upper left quadrant shows the resource demand curve with a choke price K. The lower left quadrant gives the optimal extraction path of the exhaustible resource, which is, in this case, a linear declining function of time.

The net price is initially at P_0, and then grows until it reaches the choke price K at time T, when the demand for the resource goes to zero, and the accumulated extraction of the resource (the shaded area beneath the extraction path) is exactly equal to the total initial resource stock, $\bar{S}$. The lower right quadrant maps the time axes by a 45° line.

A worked numerical example illustrating optimal extraction is presented in Appendix 5.

Exhaustible resource extraction in perfectly competitive markets

Until this point, we have said nothing about the kind of market structure in which decisions are made. Put another way, you can imagine that we have so far

---

[12] In terms of optimisation theory, this constitutes a so-called terminal condition for the problem.

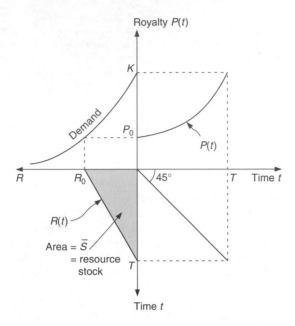

Fig 6.3 Graphical representation of solution to the optimal resource depletion model.

been imagining that a rational social planner were asked to make decisions in such a way as to maximise social welfare, given the constraints facing the economy. All of the optimality conditions listed in Table 6.3, plus the Hotelling efficiency condition, are the outcome of the social planner's calculations.

How will matters turn out if decisions are not taken by a rational and perfectly informed social planner, but are instead the outcome of profit-maximising decisions in a perfectly competitive market economy? A remarkable result we demonstrate in this section is that, *ceteris paribus*, the outcomes will be identical. We will show that Hotelling's rule and the optimality conditions of Table 6.3 are also obtained under a perfect competition assumption.

Suppose there are m competitive firms in the market. Use the subscript j to denote any one of these m firms. Assume, for simplicity, that all firms have equal and constant marginal costs of extracting the resource. Now as all firms in a competitive market face the same fixed selling price at any point in time, the market royalty will be identical over firms. Given the market royalty $P(t)$, each firm chooses an amount to extract and sell, $R_j(t)$, to maximise its profits. Mathematically

$$\max \int_0^T \Pi_j \, e^{-it} \, dt$$

subject to

$$\int_0^T \left[\sum_{j=1}^m R_j(t) \right] dt = \bar{S}$$

where $\Pi_j = P \cdot R_j$ is firm j's profit and i is the market interest rate.

Note that the stock constraint operates on all firms collectively; in other words, the industry as a whole cannot extract more than the fixed initial stock over the whole time horizon. The profit-maximising extraction rate is obtained when each firm selects an extraction $R_j(t)$ so that its discounted marginal profit will be the same at any point in time t, i.e.

$$M\Pi_j(t) \, e^{-it} = \frac{\partial \Pi_j(t)}{\partial R_j(t)} \, e^{-it} = \frac{\partial (PR_j)}{\partial R_j} \, e^{-it}$$

$$= P(t) \, e^{-it} = \text{constant}$$

where $M\Pi_j$ is firm j's marginal profit function. If discounted marginal profits were *not* the same over time, total profits could be increased by switching extraction between time periods so that more was extracted when discounted profits were high and less when they were low.

The result that the discounted marginal profit is the same at any point in time implies that

$$P_t \, e^{-it} = P_0 \quad \text{or} \quad P_t = P_0 \, e^{it}$$

Not surprisingly, Hotelling's efficiency rule continues to be a required condition for profit maximisation, so that the market net price of the resource must grow over time at the rate i. The interest rate in this profit maximisation condition is the market rate of interest. Our analysis in Chapter 4 showed that, in perfect competitive capital markets, the market interest rate will be equal to r, the consumption rate of interest, and also to δ, the rate of return on capital.

We appear now to have two different efficiency conditions,

$$\frac{\dot{P}}{P} = \rho \quad \text{and} \quad \frac{\dot{P}}{P} = i$$

the former emerging from maximising social welfare, the latter from private profit maximisation. But these are in fact identical conditions under the assumptions we have made in this chapter; by assuming that we can interpret areas under demand curves (that is, gross benefits) as quantities of utility, we in effect impose the condition that $\rho = r$. Given this result, it is not difficult to show, by cranking through the appropriate maths in a similar manner to that done in Appendix 3, that all the results of Table 6.3 would once again be produced under perfect competition, provided the private market interest rate equals the social consumption discount rate. We leave this as an exercise for the reader.

Finally, note that the appearance of a positive *net* price or royalty, $P_t > 0$, for non-renewable resources reflects the fixed stock assumption. If the resource were to exist in unlimited quantities (that is, the resource were not scarce) net prices would be zero in perfect competition, as the price of the product will equal the marginal cost (c), a result which you may recall from standard theory of long-run equilibrium in competitive markets. In other words, scarcity rent would be zero as there would be no scarcity!

Resource extraction in a monopolistic market

It is usual to assume that the objective of a monopoly is to maximise its discounted profit over time. Thus, it selects the net price $P(t)$ (or royalty) and chooses the output $R(t)$ so as to obtain

$$\max \int_0^T \Pi_t e^{-it}\, dt$$

subject to

$$\int_0^T R(t)\, dt = \bar{S}$$

where $\Pi_t = P(R).R$.

For the same reason as in the case of perfect competition, the profit-maximising solution is obtained by allocating the output $R(t)$ such that the discounted marginal profit will be the same at any time, so we have

$$M\Pi_t e^{-it} = \frac{\partial \Pi_t}{\partial R_t} e^{-it} = \text{const.} = M\Pi_0$$

i.e.   (6.9)

$$M\Pi_t = M\Pi_0 e^{it}$$

Looking carefully at Equation 6.9, and comparing this with the equation for marginal profits in the previous section, it is clear why the profit-maximising solutions in monopolistic and competitive markets will differ. Under perfect competition, the market price is exogenous to (fixed for) each firm. Thus we are able to obtain the result that in competitive markets, marginal cost equals price. However, in a monopolistic market, price is not fixed, but will depend

upon the firm's output choice. Marginal revenue will be less than price in this case.

The necessary condition for profit maximisation in a monopolistic market states that the marginal profit (and not the net price or royalty) should increase at the rate of interest i in order to maximise the discounted profits over time. The solution to the monopolist optimising problem is derived in Appendix 4. If you wish to omit this, you will find the results in Table 6.4.

A comparison of competitive and monopolistic extraction programmes

Table 6.4 summarises the results concerning optimal resource extraction in perfectly competitive and monopolistic markets. The analytical results presented are derived in Appendices 3 and 4. For convenience, we list below the notation used in Table 6.4.

P_t is the net price (royalty) of exhaustible resource with fixed stock $\bar{s}$
R_t is the total extraction of the resource at time t
R_t^j is the extraction of individual firm j at time t
i is the interest rate
T is the exhaustion time of the natural resource
K and a are fixed parameters
$h = (1.6)^2$

Two key results emerge from Table 6.4. Firstly, under certain conditions, there is an equivalence between the perfect competition market outcome and the social welfare optimum: if all markets are perfectly competitive, and the market interest rate is equal to the social consumption discount rate, the profit-maximising resource depletion programme will be identical to the one that is socially optimal.

Secondly, there is a non-equivalence of perfect competition and monopoly markets: profit-maximising extraction programmes will be different in perfectly competitive and monopolistic resource markets. Given the result stated in the previous paragraph, this implies that monopoly must be suboptimal in a social welfare-maximising sense.

For the functional forms we have used in this section, a monopolistic firm will take $\sqrt{h} = 1.6$ times longer to fully deplete the exhaustible resource than a perfectly competitive market in our model. As Figure 6.4 demonstrates, the initial net price will be higher in monopolistic markets, and the rate of price increase

Table 6.4 The comparison table: perfect competition vs monopoly

	Perfect competition	Monopoly
Objective	$\max \int_0^T P_t R_t^j \exp(-it)\,dt$	$\max \int_0^T P_t R_t \exp(-it)\,dt$
Constraint	$\int_0^T (\sum_j R_t^j)\,dt = \bar{S}$	$\int_0^T R_t\,dt = \bar{S}$
Demand curve	$P_t = K \exp(-aR_t)$	$P_t = K \exp(-aR_t)$
Optimal solution		
Exhaustion time	$T = \sqrt{2\bar{S}a/i}$	$T = \sqrt{2\bar{S}ah/i}$
Initial royalty	$P_0 = K \exp(-\sqrt{2i\bar{S}a})$	$P_0 = K \exp(-\sqrt{2i\bar{S}a/h})$
Royalty path	$P_t = P_0 \exp(it)$	$P_t = P_0 \exp(it/h)$
Extraction path	$R_t = \dfrac{i}{a}(T - t)$	$R_t = \dfrac{i}{ha}(T - t)$
	(where $R_t = \sum_j R_t^j$)	$R_0 = \sqrt{2i\bar{S}/ha}$
	$R_0 = \sqrt{2i\bar{S}/a}$	

will be slower. Extraction of the resource will be slower at first in monopolistic markets, but faster at times towards the end of the depletion horizon. Monopoly, in this case at least, turns out to be an ally of the conservationist, in so far as the time until complete exhaustion is deferred further into the future.[13] As the comparison in Figure 6.4 illustrates, a monopolist will restrict output and raise prices initially, relative to the case of perfect competition. The rate of price increase, however, will be slower than under perfect competition. Eventually, an effect of monopolistic markets is to increase the time horizon over which the resource is extracted.

Extensions of the multi-period model of exhaustible resource depletion

To this point, we have made a number of simplifying assumptions in developing and analysing our model of resource depletion. In particular, we have assumed that

- the utility discount rate and the market interest rate are constant over time;
- there is a fixed stock, of known size, of the exhaustible natural resource;

- the demand curve is identical at each point in time;
- no taxation or subsidy is applied to the extraction or use of the resource;
- marginal extraction costs are constant;
- there is a fixed 'choke price' (hence implying the existence of a backstop technology);
- no technological change occurs;
- no externalities are generated in the extraction or use of the resource.

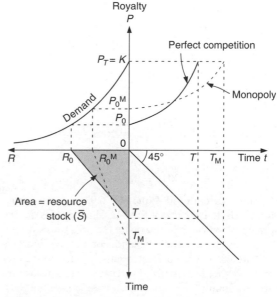

Fig 6.4 A comparison of resource depletion in competitive and monopolistic markets.

[13] Note, however, that this conclusion is not *necessarily* the case. The longer depletion period we have found is a consequence of the particular assumptions we have made. Although in most cases one would expect this to be true, it is possible to make a set of assumptions such that a monopolist would extract the stock in a shorter period of time.

We shall now undertake some comparative dynamic analysis. This consists of finding how the optimal paths of the variables of interest change over time in response to changes in the levels of one or more of the parameters in the model, or of finding how the optimal paths alter as our assumptions are changed. We adopt the device of investigating changes to one parameter, holding all others unchanged, comparing the new optimal paths with those derived above for our simple multi-period model. (We shall only discuss these generalisations for the case of perfect competition; analysis of the monopoly case is left to the reader as an exercise.)

An increase in the interest rate

Let us make clear the problem we wish to answer here. Suppose that the interest rate we had assumed in drawing Figure 6.3 was 6% per year. Now suppose that the interest rate were not 6% but rather 10%; how would Figure 6.3 have been different if the interest rate had been higher in this way? This is the kind of question we are trying to answer in doing comparative dynamics.

Since the royalty must grow at the market interest rate, an increase in i will raise the growth rate of the resource royalty, P_t. The initial price will be lower than in the base case, but the price grows more quickly, and the final price (the choke price) is reached earlier. This result follows from the fact that the change in interest rates does not alter the quantity that is to be extracted; the same total stock is extracted in each case. But this means that if the initial price is lower (and so the quantity extracted is higher), then the final price must be higher (and so the quantity extracted is lower). The resource price path will change position as shown in Figure 6.5a by the switch from the original path to the path labelled $\mathbf{c}$.[14] The initial royalty has to be lowered to increase the demand so that within a shorter time horizon, the

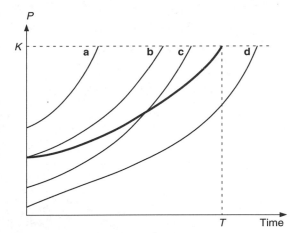

Fig 6.5a The effect of an increase in the interest rate on the optimal price of the exhaustible resource.

stock of resource is depleted completely. The implications for all the variables of interest are summarised in Figure 6.5b. This shows that a higher discount rate will tend to mean more rapid exhaustion of the exhaustible resource.

An increase in the size of the known resource stock

In practice, estimates of the size of reserves of exhaustible resources such as coal and oil are under constant revision. *Proven reserves* are those unextracted stocks that are known to exist and can be recovered at current prices and costs. *Probable reserves* relate to stocks that are known, with near certainty, to exist but which have not yet been fully explored or researched. They represent the best guess of additional amounts that could be recovered at current price and cost levels. *Possible reserves* refer to stocks in geological structures near to proven fields. As prices rise, what were previously uneconomic stocks become economically recoverable.

[14] If the rate of price increase is higher than in the initial case, this does not of itself tie down the exact position of the new price path. In Figure 6.5a, each of the price paths $\mathbf{a}$, $\mathbf{b}$, $\mathbf{c}$ and $\mathbf{d}$ shows a higher rate of price increases than the original path. However, only path $\mathbf{c}$ can be optimal.

To see this, note that paths $\mathbf{a}$ and $\mathbf{b}$ have a higher price than the original path at all times (except $t = 0$ for $\mathbf{b}$). Therefore, on paths $\mathbf{a}$ and $\mathbf{b}$, not all of the resource would be extracted before the choke price, K, is reached. These two paths cannot, therefore, be optimal ones. Case $\mathbf{d}$ is not feasible; it implies a lower price at all times than in the original case, and a longer time until the choke price is reached. But this implies, in turn, that a greater quantity is extracted over time than on the original path, which is not feasible.

Only a path such as $\mathbf{c}$ is optimal. The price is initially lower (implying more extraction early on than under the original path) but after a certain point in time, the price becomes higher and remains so (and therefore less is extracted later). If the new price path intersects the original in this manner, the optimal time to exhaustion (the time the resource price reaches K, the choke price) must be shorter.

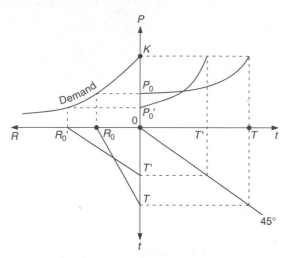

Fig 6.5b An increase in interest rates in a perfectly competitive market.

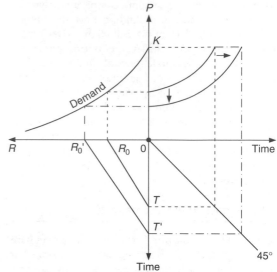

Fig 6.6 An increase in the resource stock.

Consider the case of a single new discovery of a fossil fuel stock. Other things being unchanged, if the royalty path were such that its initial level remained unchanged at P_0, then given the fact that the rate of royalty increase is unchanged, some proportion of the reserve would remain unutilised by the time the choke price, K, is reached. This is clearly neither efficient nor optimal. It follows that the initial royalty must be lower and the time to exhaustion is extended. At the time the choke price is reached, T', the new enlarged resource stock will have just reached complete exhaustion, as shown in Figure 6.6.

Now suppose that there is a sequence of new discoveries taking place over time, so that the size of known reserves increases in a series of discrete steps. Generalising the previous argument, we would expect the behaviour of the net price or royalty over time to follow a path similar to that illustrated in Figure 6.7. This hypothetical price path is one which is at least consistent with the actual behaviour of oil prices.

Changing demand

Suppose that there is an increase in demand for the resource, possibly as a result of population growth or rising real incomes. The demand curve thus shifts outwards. Given this change, the old royalty or net price path would result in higher extraction levels which will exhaust the resource before the net price has reached K, the choke price. Hence the net price must increase to dampen down quantities demanded;

as Figure 6.8 shows, the time until the resource stock is fully exhausted will also be shortened.

A fall in the price of backstop technology

In the model developed in this chapter, we have assumed there is a choke price K. If the net price were to rise above K, the economy will cease consumption of the exhaustible resource and switch to an alternative source – the backstop source. Suppose that technological progress occurs, increasing the efficiency of a backstop technology. This will tend to reduce the price of the backstop source, P_B. If P_B falls, P_0 will be too high to be optimal since the net price would reach the new backstop price, P_B, before T, leaving some of the economically useful resource unexploited. So the initial price of the non-renewable resource, P_0, must fall to encourage an increase in demand so that a shorter time horizon is required until complete exhaustion of the exhaustible resource reserve. This process is illustrated in Figure 6.9. Note that when the resource price reaches the new, reduced backstop price, demand for the non-renewable resource discontinuously falls to zero.

A change in resource extraction costs

Let us begin by considering the case of an increase in extraction costs, possibly because labour charges rise in the extraction industry. To analyse the effects of an increase in extraction costs, it is important to

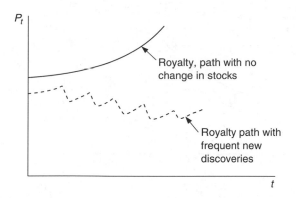

Fig 6.7 The effect of frequent new discoveries on the resource net price or royalty.

distinguish carefully between the net price and the gross price of the resource. Let us define:

$$p_t = P_t - c$$

where p_t is the resource royalty (or net price), P_t is the gross price of the exhaustible resource, and c is the marginal extraction cost, assumed to be constant. Hotelling's rule, you recall, requires that the resource *net price* grows at a constant rate, equal to the discount rate (that we take here to be constant at the rate i). Therefore, efficient extraction requires that

$$p_t = p_0 \, e^{it}$$

Now suppose that the cost of extraction, while still constant, now becomes somewhat higher than was previously the case. We suppose that this change takes place at the initial time period, period 0. Consider first what would happen if the gross price remained unchanged at its initial level. The increase in unit extraction costs would then result in the net price being lower than its initial level. However, with no change having occurred in the interest rate, the net price must *grow* at the same rate as before. It therefore follows that the net price p_t would be lower at all points in time. The gross price will be lower at all points in time, except in the original period. This is illustrated in Figure 6.10a. Note carefully that the reason why the gross price will be lower is the changed profile of the net price curve; the net price grows at the same rate as before, but from a lower starting value.

But if the gross or market price is lower at all points in time except period 0, more extraction would take place in every period. This would cause the reserve to become completely exhausted before the choke price (K) is reached. This cannot be optimal, as any optimal extraction path must ensure that demand goes to zero at the same point in time as the remaining resource stock goes to zero. Therefore, optimal extraction requires that the initial market price, P_0, must be greater than its initial level, causing less of the reserve to be extracted at each point in time, and the time to exhaustion be lengthened. This is the final

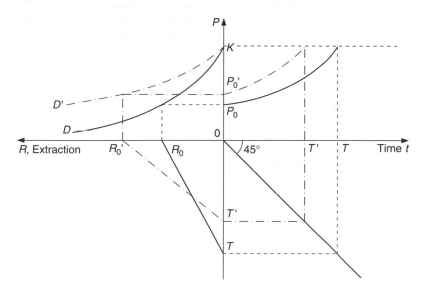

Fig 6.8 The effect of an increase in demand for the resource.

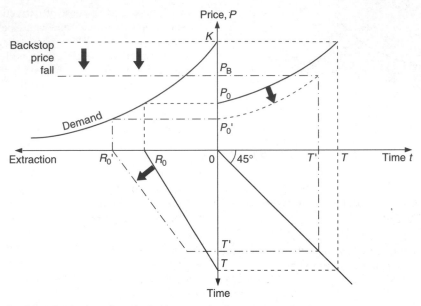

Fig 6.9 A fall in the price of a backstop technology.

outcome that we illustrate in Figure 6.10b. In conclusion, a rise in extraction costs will raise the initial gross price, slow down the rate at which the gross price increases (even though the net price or royalty increases at the same rate as before), and lengthen the time to complete exhaustion of the stock.

One other point requires our attention. If the cost increase were to be very large, then it is possible that the initial gross price, P_0, will be above the choke price. This implies that it is not economically viable to deplete the remaining reserve – it is an example of an *economic* exhaustion of a resource, even though, in

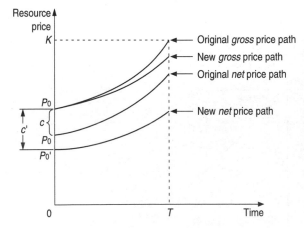

Fig 6.10a An increase in extraction costs: effects on gross and net prices.

physical terms, the resource stock has not become completely exhausted.

Let us now briefly consider the effects of a fall in extraction costs. This may be the consequence of technological progress decreasing the costs of extracting the resource from its reserves. By following similar reasoning to that we used above, it can be deduced that a fall in extraction costs will lower the initial gross price, increase the rate at which the gross price increases (even though the net price or royalty increases at the same rate as before), and shorten the time to complete exhaustion of the stock.

One remaining point needs to be considered. To this point, we have been assuming that the resource stock consists of reserves of uniform, homogeneous quality. The marginal cost of extraction was constant for the whole stock. We have been investigating the consequences of increases or decreases in that marginal cost schedule from one fixed level to another. But the stock may not be homogeneous; rather it may consist of reserves of varying quality or varying accessibility, such that marginal extraction costs differ as different segments of the stock are extracted. In this situation, there are other ways in which marginal costs can change. A fall in extraction costs may occur as the consequence of new, high quality reserves being discovered. An increase in costs may occur as a consequence of a high quality mine becoming exhausted, and extraction switching to

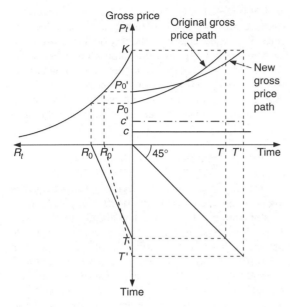

Fig 6.10b A rise in extraction costs.

another mine in which the quality of the resource reserve is somewhat lower. We do not formally analyse these cases in this text. The interested reader can find a good treatment in Hartwick and Olewiler (1986). An important dimension that is introduced into the analysis by generalising the model in this way is that we must give up the assumption that there is a known, fixed quantity of the resource. Instead, the amount of the resource 'economically' available will be a variable, the value of which depends upon resource demand and extraction cost schedules. This also implies that we could analyse a reduction in extraction costs as if it were a form of technological progress; this can increase the stock of the reserve that can be extracted in an economically viable manner.

The introduction of taxation/subsidies

Royalty tax/subsidy

A royalty tax or subsidy will have no effect on a resource owner's extraction decision in the case of a reserve that is currently being extracted. The tax or subsidy will alter the present value of the resource being extracted, but there can be no change in the rate of extraction over time that can offset that decline or increase in present value. The government will simply collect some of the mineral rent (or pay some subsidies), and resource extraction and production will proceed in the same manner as before the tax/subsidy was introduced.

This result follows from the Hotelling rule of efficient resource depletion. To see this, define α to be a royalty tax rate (which could be negative, that is a subsidy), and denote the royalty or net price at time t by p_t. Then the post-tax royalty becomes $(1 - \alpha)p_t$. But Hotelling's rule implies that the post-tax royalty must rise at the discount rate, i, if the resource is to be exploited efficiently. That is:

$$(1 - \alpha)p_t = (1 - \alpha)p_0\, e^{it}$$

or

$$p_t = p_0\, e^{it}$$

Hotelling's rule continues to operate unchanged in the presence of a royalty tax, and no change occurs to the optimal depletion path. This is also true for a royalty subsidy scheme. In this case, denoting the royalty subsidy rate by β, we have the efficiency condition

$$(1 + \beta)p_t = (1 + \beta)p_0\, e^{it} \Rightarrow p_t = p_0\, e^{it}$$

We can conclude that a royalty tax or subsidy is neutral in its effect on the optimal extraction path. However, a tax may discourage (or a subsidy encourage) the exploration effort for new mineral deposits by reducing (increasing) the expected pay-off from discovering the new deposits.

Revenue tax/subsidy

The previous subsection analysed the effect of a tax or subsidy on resource royalties. We now turn our attention to the impact of a revenue tax (or subsidy). In the absence of a revenue tax, the Hotelling efficiency condition is, in terms of net prices and gross prices:

$$p_t = p_0\, e^{it} \Rightarrow (P_t - c) = (P_0 - c)\, e^{it}$$

Under a revenue tax scheme, with a tax of α per unit of the resource sold, the post-tax royalty or net price is

$$p_t = (1 - \alpha)P_t - c$$

So Hotelling's rule becomes:

$$[(1 - \alpha)P_t - c] = [(1 - \alpha)P_0 - c]\, e^{it} \quad (0 < \alpha < 1)$$

$$\Rightarrow \left(P_t - \frac{c}{1 - \alpha}\right) = \left(P_0 - \frac{c}{1 - \alpha}\right) e^{it}$$

Since $c/(1 - \alpha) > c$, an imposition of a revenue tax is equivalent to an increase in the resource extraction cost. Similarly, for a revenue subsidy scheme, we have

$$\left(P_t - \frac{c}{1 + \beta} \right) = \left(P_0 - \frac{c}{1 + \beta} \right) e^{it} \qquad (0 < \beta < 1)$$

A revenue subsidy is equivalent to a decrease in extraction cost. We have already discussed the effects of a change in extraction costs, and you may recall the results we obtained: a decrease in extraction costs will lower the initial gross price, increase the rate at which the gross price increases (even though the net price or royalty increases at the same rate as before), and shorten the time to complete exhaustion of the stock.

The resource depletion model – some extensions and further issues

Discount rate

We showed above that resource extraction under a system of perfectly competitive markets may produce the socially optimal outcome. But this equivalence rests upon several assumptions, one of which is that firms choose a private discount rate identical to the social discount rate that would be used by a rational planner. If private and social discount rates differ, however (and Chapter 2 showed several reasons why this may happen), then market extraction paths may be biased toward excessive use or conservation relative to what is socially optimal.

Forward markets and expectations

The Hotelling model is an abstract analytical tool; its operation in actual market economies is, as we have seen, dependent upon the existence of a set of particular institutional circumstances. In many real situations, these institutional arrangements do not exist, and so the rule lies at a considerable distance from the operation of actual market mechanisms. In addition to the discount rate equivalence mentioned in the previous section, two very strict assumptions are required to ensure a social optimal extraction in the case of perfect competition, Firstly, the resource must be *owned* by the competitive agents. Secondly, each agent must know at each point in time all current and future prices. One might just assume that agents have

perfect foresight, but this hardly seems tenable for the case we are investigating. In the absence of perfect foresight, knowledge of these prices requires the existence of both spot markets and a complete set of forward markets for the resource in question. But no resource does possess a complete set of forward markets, and in these circumstances there is no guarantee that agents can or will make rational supply decisions.

Optimal extraction under uncertainty

Uncertainty is prevalent in decision-making regarding non-renewable resource extraction and use. There is uncertainty, for example, about stock sizes, extraction costs, how successful research and development will be in the discovery of substitutes for exhaustible resources (thereby affecting the cost and expected date of arrival of a backstop technology), pay-offs from exploration for new stock, and the action of rivals. It is very important to study how the presence of uncertainty affects appropriate courses of action. For example, what do optimal extraction programmes look like when there is uncertainty, and how do they compare with programmes developed under conditions of certainty?

Let us assume an owner of a natural resource (e.g. a mine) wishes to maximise the net present value of utility over two periods:[15]

$$\max U_0 + \frac{U_1}{1 + \rho}$$

If there is a probability (π) of a disaster (e.g. the market might be lost) associated with the second period of the extraction programme, then the owner will try to maximise the *expected* net present value of the utility (if he is risk-neutral):

$$\max U_0 + \pi.0 + (1 - \pi) \frac{U_1}{1 + \rho}$$

$$= \max U_0 + (1 - \pi) \frac{U_1}{1 + \rho}$$

$$\Rightarrow \max U_0 + \frac{U_1}{1 + \rho^*}$$

where

$$\frac{1}{1 + \rho^*} = \frac{1 - \pi}{1 + \rho}$$

[15] This argument follows very closely a presentation in Fisher (1981).

To solve ρ^*:

$$(1 + \rho^*)(1 - \pi) = 1 + \rho$$

$$\Rightarrow 1 + \rho^* - \pi(1 + \rho^*)(1 - \pi) = 1 + \rho$$

$$\Rightarrow \rho^* - \rho = \pi(1 + \rho^*) > 0$$

$$(\text{if } 1 \geq \pi > 0)$$

$$\Rightarrow \rho^* > \rho$$

Therefore, in this example, the existence of uncertainty is equivalent to an increase in the discount rate for the owner, which implies as we have shown before that the price of the resource must rise more rapidly and the depletion is accelerated.

Natural resource scarcity

Concern with the supposed increasing scarcity of natural resources, and the possibility of running out of strategically important raw materials or energy sources, is by no means new. As Chapter 1 indicated, worries about resource scarcity can be traced back to at least medieval times in Britain, and have surfaced periodically ever since. The scarcity of land was central to the theories of Malthus and the other classical economists. In the twentieth century, fears about timber shortages in several countries led to the establishment of national forestry authorities, charged with rebuilding timber stocks. As we have seen earlier, pessimistic views about impending resource scarcity have been most forcibly expressed in the *Limits to Growth* literature; during the 1970s, the so-called oil crises further focused attention on mineral scarcities.

What do we mean by resource scarcity? One use of the term – what might be called absolute scarcity – holds that all resources are scarce, as the availability of resources is fixed and finite at any point in time, whilst the wants which resource use can satisfy are not limited. Where a market exists for a resource, the existence of any positive price is viewed as evidence of absolute scarcity; where markets do not exist, the existence of a positive shadow price – the implicit price that would be necessary if the resource were to be used efficiently – similarly is an indicator of absolute scarcity for that resource.

But this is not the usual meaning of the term in general discussions about natural resource scarcity; in these cases, scarcity tends to be used to indicate that the natural resource is becoming harder to obtain, and requires more of other resources to obtain it. The relevant costs to include in measures of scarcity are both private and external costs; it is important to recognise that if private extraction costs are not rising over time, social costs may rise if negative externalities such as environmental degradation or depletion of common property resources are increasing as a consequence of extraction of the natural resource. Thus, a rising opportunity cost of obtaining the resource is an indicator of scarcity – let us call this use of the term *relative scarcity*. In the rest of this section, our comments shall be restricted to this second form.

Before we take this matter any further, it is necessary to say something about the degree of aggregation used in examining resource scarcity. To keep things as simple as possible, first consider only exhaustible (non-renewable) natural resources. There is not one single resource but a large number, each distinct from the others in some physical sense. However, physically distinct resources may be economically similar, through being substitutes for one another. Exhaustible resources are best viewed, then, as a structure of assets, components of which are substitutable to varying degrees. In Chapter 5, when we discussed the efficient extraction of a single exhaustible resource, this suggests that the 'resource' might be viewed as an aggregate set of resources in this particular sense. Moreover, when the class of resources is extended to incorporate renewable resources, so the structure is enlarged, as are the substitution possibilities.

Except for resources for which no substitution possibilities exist – if indeed such resources exist – it is of limited usefulness to enquire whether any individual resource is scarce or not. If one particular resource, such as crude oil, were to become excessively costly to obtain for any reason, one would expect resource use to substitute to another resource, such as natural gas or coal. A well-functioning price mechanism should ensure that this occurs. Because of this, it is more useful to consider whether natural resources in general are becoming scarcer – is there any evidence of increasing generalised resource scarcity?

What indicators might one use to assess the degree of scarcity of particular natural resources, and natural resources in general? There are several candidates for this task, including physical indicators (such as reserve quantities or reserve-to-consumption ratios), marginal resource extraction cost, marginal exploration and discovery costs, market prices, and resource rents. We shall now briefly examine each of these.

Physical indicators

A variety of physical indicators have been used as proxies for scarcity, including various measures of reserve quantities, and reserve-to-consumption ratios. Several such measures were discussed earlier in this chapter and appropriate statistics listed (see Box 6.1 and Table 6.1). Inferences drawn about impending resource scarcity in the *Limits to Growth* literature were drawn on the basis of such physical indicators. Unfortunately, they are severely limited in their usefulness as proxy measures of scarcity for the reasons discussed in Box 6.1. Most importantly, most natural resources are not homogeneous in quality, and the location and quantities available are not known with certainty; extra amounts of the resource can be obtained as additional exploration, discovery and extraction effort is applied. A rising resource net price will, in general, stimulate such effort. It is the absence of this information in physical data that limits its usefulness.

Real, marginal resource extraction cost

We argued earlier that scarcity is concerned with the real opportunity cost of acquiring additional quantities of the resource. This suggests that the marginal extraction cost of obtaining the resource from existing reserves would be an appropriate indicator of scarcity. The classic study by Barnett and Morse (1963) used an index of real unit costs, c, defined as

$$c = \frac{(\alpha L + \beta K)}{Q}$$

where L is labour, K is capital, and Q is output of the extractive industry, and α and β are weights to aggregate inputs. Rising resource scarcity is proxied by rising real unit costs. Note that ideally marginal costs should be used, although this is rarely possible in practice because of data limitations. An important advantage of an extraction costs indicator is that it incorporates technological change. If technological progress relaxes resource constraints by making a given quantity of resources more productive, then this reduction in scarcity will be reflected in a tendency for costs to fall. However, the measure does have problems. Firstly, the measurement of capital is always difficult, largely because of the aggregation that is required to obtain a single measure of the capital stock; similarly, there are difficulties in obtaining valid aggregates of all inputs used. Secondly, the indicator is

backward-looking, whereas an ideal indicator should serve as a signal for future potential scarcity. Finally, it may well be the case that quantities and/or qualities of the resource are declining seriously, whilst technical progress that is sufficiently rapid results in price falling. In extreme cases, sudden exhaustion may occur after a period of prolonged price falls. Ultimately, no clear inference about scarcity can be drawn from extraction cost data alone.

Barnett and Morse (1963) and Barnett (1979) found no evidence of increasing scarcity, except for forestry. They concluded that agricultural and mineral products, over the period 1870 to 1970, were becoming more abundant rather than more scarce, and explained this in terms of the substitution of more plentiful lower-grade deposits as higher grades were depleted, the discovery of new deposits, and technical change in exploration, extraction and processing. References for other, subsequent studies are given at the end of the chapter.

Marginal exploration and discovery costs

An alternative measure of resource scarcity is the opportunity cost of acquiring additional quantities of the resource by locating as yet unknown reserves. Higher discovery costs are interpreted as indicators of increased resource scarcity. This measure is not often used, largely because it is difficult to obtain long runs of reliable data. Moreover, the same kinds of limitations possessed by extraction cost data apply in this case too.

Real market price indicators and net price indicators

The most commonly used scarcity indicator is time series data on real (that is, inflation-adjusted) market prices. Such data are readily available, easy to use, and like all asset prices are forward-looking, to some extent at least. Use of price data is beset by three main problems. Firstly, prices are often distorted as a consequence of taxes, subsidies, exchange controls and other governmental interventions; reliable measures need to be corrected for such distortions. Secondly, the real price index tends to be very sensitive to the choice of deflator. Should nominal prices be deflated by a retail or wholesale price index (and for which basket of goods), by the GDP deflator, or by some input price index such as manufacturing wages? There is no unambiguously correct answer to this question, which is unfortunate as very different conclusions can be arrived at about resource scarcity with different choices of deflator. Some evidence on this is given in the chapter on resource scarcity in Hartwick and Olewiler (1986); these authors cite an analysis by Brown and Field (1978) which compares two studies of resource prices using alternative deflators. For eleven commodities, Nordhaus (1973) uses capital goods prices as a deflator and concludes that all eleven minerals were becoming less scarce. However, Jorgensen and Griliches (1967) use a manufacturing wages deflator and conclude that three of the minerals – coal, lead and zinc – were becoming more scarce over the same period. The third major problem with resource price data is that they may not be measuring the right thing; an ideal price measure would reflect the net price of the resource (otherwise known as the resource rent or royalty). Hotelling's rule shows that it is this which rises through time as the resource becomes progressively scarcer. Unlike gross market prices, however, net resource prices are not directly observed variables, and so it is rather difficult to use them as a basis for empirical analysis.

Despite the limitations of market price data, there does appear to be broad agreement between this measure and the others discussed in this section. One illustration is given in Figure 6.11, taken from Brown and Field (1979), which suggests that, for an aggregate index of all metals, scarcity was decreasing over the period 1890 to 1970.

Can any general conclusions about resource scarcity be obtained from the literature? The majority of economic analyses conducted up to the early 1980s concluded that few, if any, non-renewable natural resources were becoming more scarce. Paradoxically, these studies also suggested it was in the area of renewable resources that problems of increasing scarcity were to be found, particularly in cases of open access. The reasons why scarcity may be particularly serious for some renewable resources will be examined in the following chapter. In the last 15 years, concern about increasing scarcity of renewable resources has increased; as far as non-renewable resources are concerned, the evidence has become less clear-cut, with widely differing conclusions being reached in different studies.

Discussion questions

1 Discuss the merits of a proposal that the government should impose a tax or subsidy where an exhaustible resource is supplied monopolistically in order to increase the social net benefit.
2 'An examination of natural resource matters ought to recognise technical/scientific, economic, and socio-political considerations.' Explain.
3 'The exploitation of resources is not necessarily destructive... need not imply the impoverishment of posterity.... It is the diversion of national income from its usual channels to an increased preservation of natural wealth that will harm posterity.' (Anthony Scott) Explain and discuss.
4 The notion of sustainability is used differently in economics than in the natural sciences. Explain the meaning of sustainability in these two frameworks, and discuss the attempts that have been made by economists to make the concept operational.

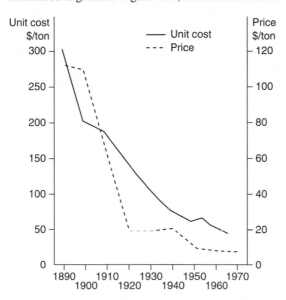

Fig 6.11 Price and unit cost for all metals, 1890–1970. *Source:* Brown and Field (1979). Copyright, Resources for the Future, Inc.

Problems

1 The version of Hotelling's rule given in Equation 6.5 requires the net price to grow proportionately at

the rate ρ. Under what circumstances would this imply that the gross price also should grow at the rate ρ?

2 In Equation (6.5), If $\rho = 0$, what are the implications for
  (a) P_0 and P_1?
  (b) R_0 and R_1?
  (Problems 3, 4 and 5 are based on Table 6.4 in the text of this chapter.)

3 Explain, with diagrams, why a monopolistic exhaustible resource market is biased towards conservation and therefore will increase the 'life' of the resource.

4 In the case of perfect competition, if the private discount rate is higher than the correct social discount rate, explain, with diagrams, why the market will exhaust the resource too quickly.

5 Discuss, with diagrams, the consequences of the discovery of North Sea oil for
  (a) the price and output levels for the oil market;
  (b) the date of exhaustion of oil reserves.
  What will be the probable path over time of oil prices if there are frequent discoveries of oil?

Further reading

The references for further reading given at the end of Chapter 5 are all relevant for further reading on the material covered in this chapter. In particular, the best advanced level presentations of the theory of efficient and optimal resource depletion can be found in Baumol and Oates (1988), Dasgupta and Heal (1979), Heal (1981) and the collection of papers in the May 1974 special issue on resource depletion of the *Review of Economic Studies*. As stated previously, less difficult presentations are given in Hartwick and Olewiler (1986), Anderson (1981) and Fisher (1981).

Good general discussions of resource scarcity can be found in Hartwick and Olewiler (1986, Chapter 6), which provides an extensive discussion of the evidence, Fisher (1981) and Harris (1993). Important works in the field of resource scarcity include Barnett (1979), Barnett and Morse (1963), Brown and Field (1979), Deverajan and Fisher (1982), Fisher (1979), Jorgensen and Griliches (1967), Leontief *et al.* (1977), Nordhaus (1973), Norgaard (1975), Slade (1982), Smith (1979) and Smith and Krutilla (1979).

An excellent discussion on natural resource substitutability can be found in Dasgupta (1993).

Appendix 1

The Lagrange multiplier method of solving constrained optimisation problems

In this appendix, we state one method for solving maximisation problems with equality constraints. Suppose we have the following problem:

$$\max f(x_1, x_2, x_3)$$

subject to

$$g(x_1, x_2, x_3) = 0$$
$$h(x_1, x_2, x_3) = 0$$

The Lagrangian (L) is

$$L(x_1, x_2, x_3, \lambda_1, \lambda_2) = f(x_1, x_2, x_3) + \lambda_1 g(x_1, x_2, x_3) + \lambda_2 h(x_1, x_2, x_3)$$

The necessary first-order conditions for a maximum are

$$\frac{\partial L}{\partial x_1} = f_1 + \lambda_1 g_1 + \lambda_2 h_1 = 0$$

$$\frac{\partial L}{\partial x_2} = f_2 + \lambda_1 g_2 + \lambda_2 h_2 = 0$$

$$\frac{\partial L}{\partial x_3} = f_3 + \lambda_1 g_3 + \lambda_2 h_3 = 0$$

$$\frac{\partial L}{\partial \lambda_1} = g(x_1, x_2, x_3) = 0$$

$$\frac{\partial L}{\partial \lambda_2} = h(x_1, x_2, x_3) = 0$$

where

$$f_i = \frac{\partial f}{\partial x_i}, \ g_i = \frac{\partial g}{\partial x_i}, \ h_i = \frac{\partial h}{\partial x_i} \qquad \text{for } i = 1, 2, 3$$

The second-order conditions for a maximum require that the following determinant be positive:

$$\begin{vmatrix} L_{11} & L_{12} & L_{13} & g_1 & h_1 \\ L_{21} & L_{22} & L_{23} & g_2 & h_2 \\ L_{31} & L_{32} & L_{33} & g_3 & h_3 \\ g_1 & g_2 & g_3 & 0 & 0 \\ h_1 & h_2 & h_3 & 0 & 0 \end{vmatrix} > 0$$

where

$$L_{ij} = \frac{\partial^2 L}{\partial x_i \, \partial x_j}$$

The first- and second-order conditions are sufficient for a constrained maximum.

Appendix 2

Solution of the multi-period resource depletion model

In this appendix, we derive the optimal solution to the multi-period exhaustible resource depletion problem discussed in the third section of this chapter. The technique we shall use – the Maximum Principle – is explained in Appendix 3 to Chapter 5.

We wish to maximise

$$W = \int_{t=0}^{t=T} U(R_t) e^{-\rho t} dt$$

subject to

$$\dot{S} = -R_t$$

The current-valued Hamiltonian for this problem is

$$H = U(R_t) + P_t(-R_t)$$

The necessary conditions for maximum social welfare are

$$\dot{P}_t = \rho P_t \qquad (6.10)$$

$$\frac{\partial H}{\partial R} = -P_t + \frac{dU}{dR} = 0 \qquad (6.11)$$

Rearranging Equation 6.11 we obtain

$$P_t = \frac{dU}{dR}$$

so that the resource shadow price (P_t) is equal to the marginal utility of the exhaustible resource, an equality used in the main text. Equation 6.10 is, of course, the Hotelling efficiency condition, given as Equation 6.7b in the chapter.

Appendix 3

As we noted in the chapter, an optimal solution must have the property that the stock go to zero at exactly the point that demand goes to zero. In order for demand to be zero at time T (which we determine in a moment) the net price must reach the choke price at time T. That is

$$P_T = K$$

This, together with Equation 6.7 in the main text, implies

$$K = P_0 e^{\rho T} \qquad (6.12)$$

To solve for $R(t)$, it can be seen from Equations 6.7 and 6.8 in the main text that

$$P_0 e^{\rho T} = K e^{-aR}$$

Substituting for K from Equation 6.12 we obtain

$$P_0 e^{\rho T} = P_0 e^{-(aR - \rho T)}$$

$$\Rightarrow \rho t = -aR + \rho T$$

$$\Rightarrow R(t) = \frac{\rho}{a}(T - t) \qquad (6.13)$$

This gives an expression for the rate at which the resource should be extracted along the optimal path. To find the optimal time period, T, over which extraction should take place, recall that the fixed stock constraint is:

$$\int_0^T R(t) \, dt = \bar{S}$$

and so by substitution for $R(t)$ from Equation 6.13 we obtain:

$$\int_0^T \left[\frac{\rho}{a}(T - t) \right] dt = \bar{S}$$

Therefore

$$\frac{\rho}{a} \left[Tt - \frac{t^2}{2} \right]_0^T = \bar{S}$$

$$\frac{1}{2} \frac{\rho}{a} \cdot T^2 = \bar{S}$$

or

$$T = \sqrt{\frac{2\bar{S}a}{R}}$$

Next we solve, using Equation 6.12, for the initial royalty level, P_0:

$$P_0 = K e^{-\rho T} = K e^{-\sqrt{2\rho \bar{S} a}}$$

To obtain an expression for the resource royalty at time t, we use the demand function (Equation 6.8) together with Equation 6.7. Substituting Equation 6.7 into 6.8 we obtain the required condition:

$$P_t = K e^{\rho(t - T)}$$

The optimal initial extraction level is, from Equation 6.13,

$$R_0 = \frac{\rho}{a}(T - 0) = \frac{\rho T}{a} = \sqrt{\frac{2\rho \bar{S}}{a}}$$

Appendix 4

To solve for the monopolist's profit-maximising extraction programme, we need to do some additional calculation.[16] First let us derive an expression for the firm's marginal profit function, $M\Pi$:

$$M\Pi_t = \frac{\partial \Pi_t}{\partial R_t} = \frac{\partial(P(R_t)R_t)}{\partial R_t} = \frac{\partial P_t}{\partial R_t}R_t + P(R_t) \quad (6.14)$$

Now, substituting for $P(R_t)$ from the resource demand function (Equation 6.8) we can express this equation as

$$M\Pi_t = -aR_tKe^{-aR_t} + Ke^{-aR_t}$$
$$= K(-aR_t + 1)e^{-aR_t} \approx Ke^{-ahR_t} \quad (6.15)$$

Notice the approximation here: why do we do this? Because if this is not done, it is not possible to obtain an analytical solution, given the double appearance of R_t.

But since resource extraction at the end of the planning horizon must be zero $(R(T) = 0)$ we have

$$M\Pi_T = Ke^{-ahR(T)} = K \quad (6.16)$$

To obtain $M\Pi_0$, using Equation 6.9 we obtain

$$M\Pi_0 = M\Pi_T e^{-iT} = Ke^{-iT} \quad (6.17)$$

To obtain an expression for $M\Pi_t$, using Equations 6.9 and 6.17 we have

$$M\Pi_t = M\Pi_0 e^{it} = Ke^{i(t-T)} \quad (6.18)$$

Now we may obtain a solution equation for R_t, using Equations 6.15 and 6.18:

$$Ke^{-ahR_t} = Ke^{i(t-T)}$$
$$\Rightarrow i(t-T) = -ahR(t)$$
$$\Rightarrow R(t) = \frac{i}{ha}(T-t) \quad (6.19)$$

In order to obtain the optimal depletion time period T we use the fixed stock constraint together with Equation 6.19, the result we have just obtained:

$$\int_0^T R(t)\,dt = \bar{S}$$

$$\Rightarrow \int_0^T \frac{i}{ha}(T-t)\,dt = \bar{S}$$

$$\frac{i}{ha}\left[Tt - \frac{t^2}{2}\right]_0^T = \bar{S}$$

$$\frac{1}{2} \cdot \frac{i}{ha}T^2 = \bar{S}$$

[16] This appendix is based on Heijman (1990).

Therefore

$$T = \sqrt{\frac{2\bar{S}ha}{i}}$$

To solve the initial extraction R_0, from Equation 6.19:

$$R_0 = \frac{i}{ha}(T-0) = \frac{iT}{ha} = \sqrt{\frac{2i\bar{S}}{ha}}$$

Finally, to solve the initial net price P_0, from Equation 6.8 (the demand curve)

$$P_0 = Ke^{-aR_0} = K\exp\left(-\sqrt{\frac{2i\bar{S}a}{h}}\right)$$

Appendix 5

A worked numerical example.

Let us take 1990 as the 'initial year' of the study. In 1990, the oil price was $P_0 = \$20$ per barrel, and oil output was $R_0 = 21.7$ billion barrels. From our demand function (Equation 6.8 in the main text)

$$P_0 = Ke^{-aR_0} = K\exp(-aR_0)$$

we obtain

$$R_0 = \frac{\ln K}{a} - \frac{1}{a}\ln P_0$$

The price elasticity of the initial year is, therefore:

$$\epsilon_0 = \frac{dR_0}{dP_0} \cdot \frac{P_0}{R_0} = \left[-\frac{1}{aP_o}\right] \cdot \frac{P_0}{R_0} = -\frac{1}{aR_0}$$

Assume that $\epsilon = -0.5$, then we can estimate a:

$$a = -\frac{1}{\epsilon R_0} = \frac{1}{0.5 \times 21.7} \approx 0.1$$

We can also estimate the parameter K as follows:

$$K = P_0\exp(aR_0) = 20\exp(0.1 \times 21.7) \approx 175$$

The global oil reserve stock is $S = 1150$ billion barrels. The optimal oil extraction programme under the assumptions of a discount rate $\rho = 3\%$ and perfect competition are given by the following. The optimal exhaustion time is:

$$T^* = \sqrt{\frac{2Sa}{\rho}} = \sqrt{\frac{2 \times 1150 \times 0.1}{0.03}} = 87.5\,\text{years}$$

The optimal initial oil output is

$$R_0^* = \sqrt{\frac{2\rho S}{a}} = \sqrt{\frac{2 \times 0.03 \times 1150}{0.1}}$$

$$= 26.26 \text{ billion barrels}$$

The corresponding optimal initial oil price is

$$P_0^* = K \exp(-aR_0^*) = 175 \exp(-0.1 \times 26.26)$$

$$= \$12.7/\text{barrel}$$

The optimal oil output is obviously higher than the actual output in 1990, and the optimal price is lower than the actual one. So there is apparent evidence of distortion (inefficiency) in the world oil market.

The theory of optimal resource extraction: renewable resources

It will appear, I hope, that most of the problems associated with the words 'conservation' or 'depletion' or 'overexploitation' in the fishery are, in reality, manifestations of the fact that the natural resources of the sea yield no economic rent. Fishery resources are unusual in the fact of their common-property nature; but they are not unique, and similar problems are encountered in other cases of common-property resource industries, such as petroleum production, hunting and trapping, etc.

H. Scott Gordon (1954)

Renewable resources: an introduction

The main class of renewable resources comprise living organisms such as fish, animals, birds, and forests. Unlike the non-renewable mineral resources we investigated in the previous chapter, these forms of renewable resources consist of populations of individual organisms that reproduce, grow and die. This is, of course, what is usually meant by a renewable resource.

There is another way of thinking about these resources which may be more illuminating from an economics point of view. Consider stocks of fish. There may be a limit to the number of fish that can be supported in a particular habitat at any point in time, but harvesting a fish and removing it from the population does not mean that the total stock of fish at the next instant in time will necessarily be smaller.

A broad definition of renewable resources would not only include renewable *stock* resources of the kind to which we have just been referring, but would also include renewable *flow* resources, such as solar, wave, wind and geothermal energy. These share with biological stock resources the property that harnessing some units of the flow does not mean that the total magnitude of the flow at the next instant in time will be smaller. Indeed, for such resources, the total size of the available flow is unaffected by the amount of the flow that is harnessed at any point in time. We may also choose to extend the class of renewable resources in two further directions. First, arable and grazing lands can be regarded as renewable resources, with fertility levels naturally regenerating so long as the demands made on the soil are not excessive. Secondly, renewable resources include water systems and atmospheric processes; whilst these do not possess any *biological* growth capacity, water and atmospheric stocks do have some ability to assimilate and cleanse themselves of pollution inputs, and, at least in the case of water resources, can self-replenish as stocks are run down.

We wish to conduct our analysis of renewable resources at a general level, developing a framework which can, in principle at least, be applied to all forms of renewable stock resources. However, it will be convenient to exemplify the analysis by considering one particular case in some detail. The example of fisheries will be used for this purpose. Although our general framework can be used to analyse harvesting and depletion processes for most forms of renewable resource, the reader should note that important differences do exist between fisheries, forests, wilderness areas, water systems and other kinds of renewable resource. These differences are important, and will be pointed out (and their consequences discussed) at appropriate places in the chapter.

As with non-renewable resources, it is important to distinguish between stocks and flows of the renewable resource. The stock, or population, is a measure of the quantity of the resource existing at a point in time, measured either as the aggregate mass of the biological material (the biomass) in question (such as the total weight of fish of particular age classes or the cubic metres of standing timber), or in terms of population numbers.[1] The flow is the change in the stock over an interval of time, where the change results either from biological factors, such as the entry of new fish into the population through birth (called recruitment) or the exit from the population due to

---

[1] In this chapter, the terms *mass* and *population* of a resource stock are used synonymously. This is a simplification which makes little difference to the validity of the subsequent arguments.

natural death, or from economic factors such as harvesting of the species in question.

One similarity between renewable and non-renewable resources is that both are capable of being fully exhausted (that is, the stock is driven to zero) if too much harvesting and extraction activities are carried out over some time period. In the case of non-renewable resources, exhaustibility is a consequence of the finiteness of the stock. For renewable resources, although the stock can grow, it can also be exhausted if conditions interfere with the reproductive capability of the renewable resource, or if rates of harvesting continually exceed natural growth. As a result of this similarity, some writers use the term 'exhaustible resources' to describe both renewable and non-renewable resources. To avoid confusion, we follow conventional usage by limiting our use of that phrase to non-renewable resources only.

As the analysis in this chapter will make clear, for many forms of renewable resource, private property rights do not exist. In the absence of government regulation or some other form of collective control over harvesting behaviour, the resource stocks are subject to open access. Open access resources tend to be overexploited, in a precise sense to be made clear later, and the likelihood of the resource being harvested to the point of exhaustion is higher than in situations where private property rights are established and access to harvesting the resource can be restricted. We begin our analysis by examining how an open access, renewable resource stock tends to be harvested. We then identify a privately optimal (that is, profit-maximising) harvesting programme for a renewable resource, and compare this with the behaviour expected under conditions of open access. In doing this, a matter of particular importance will be the relationship between harvesting behaviour and the discount rate used by potential or actual harvesters. Open access harvesting is then revisited and socially optimal harvesting programmes discussed. Under certain conditions, a perfectly competitive industry in which private property rights to the resource stocks are established and enforceable will follow a harvesting programme which is socially optimal. This is not the case if the resource is in monopolistic ownership, discussed in a section to itself. We then examine a set of policy instruments that could be introduced, in conditions of open access to the resource, in an attempt to move harvesting behaviour closer to a socially optimal programme. The final section presents an outline of the economics of forestry.

Biological growth processes for renewable resources

Our analysis begins with the concept of a growth function for a biological renewable resource.[2] This function describes the growth process of one species at a particular location, in the absence of any human predation. The resource stock exists within a certain environmental milieu, which determines the population's growth possibilities. We assume that the ecological characteristics of this environmental milieu remain constant (except for the part played by humans).

Let S_t denote the mass of the resource stock at time t. The amount of growth of the resource stock, G, is a function of the size of the resource stock itself. This is known as 'density dependent growth'. Hence the biological growth function may be written as

$$G_t = G(S_t)$$

In the absence of human predation, the following identity relates stocks and flows of the renewable resource:

$$\frac{\mathrm{d}S_t}{\mathrm{d}t} = G(S_t) \qquad (7.1)$$

A form of biological growth function which appears to approximate very well to the natural growth processes of many fish, animal and bird populations (and indeed to some physical systems such as the quantity of fresh water in an underground reservoir) is the logistic growth function, which is illustrated in Figure 7.1. The logistic growth model is examined and explained in Box 7.1.

The logistic growth model implies that an environmental system will have a maximum carrying capacity for a particular species, indicated by the stock level S_{MAX} in Figure 7.1. Unless environmental characteristics become more favourable for the species in question, this is the maximum size to which the biomass can grow. Secondly, there will be a particular stock size at which the quantity of net growth is at a maximum. This will be of interest to us in subsequent sections, for a resource management programme could be devised in which a yield (or harvest) of a

---

[2] This is not so restrictive as it may first appear. If we wish to consider renewable resources that are not biological in form, the resource must (by definition) possess some capacity for replenishment, in either quality of quantity terms, that could be modelled in a similar if not identical way.

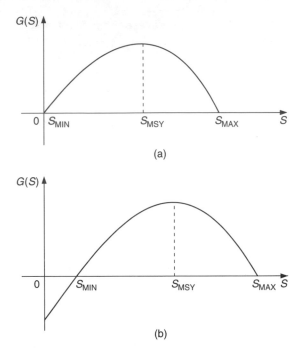

Fig 7.1 The logistic growth process.

certain size could be taken in perpetuity whilst maintaining the stock size at the fixed level, S_{MSY}. As this is the largest perpetual yield that could be obtained from the resource, this is denoted the *maximum sustainable yield* (MSY) and the stock size associated with it is denoted S_{MSY}. Many people regard it as being self-evident that a fishery, forest or other renewable resource should be managed so as to produce its maximum sustainable yield. We shall see later in this chapter whether this suggestion finds any support in economic theory.

Finally, there may be some critical level of the stock, S_{MIN}, which is essential for survival of the species, or more precisely, survival of a particular population of the species in one environment. If the stock (or population) falls below S_{MIN}, reproduction is less than natural mortality, and the species gradually dies out.

In Figure 7.1a, the minimum sustainable population stock, S_{MIN}, is shown as occurring at a zero stock size. Any positive population stock is capable of being maintained in perpetuity. Figure 7.1b differs in that the minimum sustainable population stock, S_{MIN}, is some positive quantity. If the stock were to fall below that level, it would subsequently and inevitably collapse to zero, and the stock in question would

disappear. If the stock portrayed in the diagram refers to the whole population of a particular species, then the species itself would become extinct.

It appears likely that many populations will exhibit growth processes resembling that shown in Figure 7.1b rather than 7.1a. This has important implications for resource management and conservation policy, particularly where there is also uncertainty about the level of S_{MIN}, about the actual size of the stock existing at some point in time, or about the actual level of resource harvesting. We discuss this issue further later in this chapter.

Some examples of animal populations which have been driven to zero, or appear to be in danger of becoming extinct, at least partially as a consequence of harvesting rates being high relative to natural rates of regeneration, are presented in Box 7.2.

The economics of harvesting a renewable resource

The next step in our analysis is to introduce human predators into the resource model. Denote by R_t the total catch or *harvest* in period t. We use the symbol R for harvest to stress the fact that the harvest in a renewable resource model is an equivalent concept to the quantity extracted in a non-renewable resource model, which we earlier denoted as R.

What determines the quantity of the harvest in any given period? Firstly, the harvest will depend upon the amount of 'effort' devoted to harvesting. In the case of marine fishing for example, harvesting effort describes the number of boats deployed and their efficiency, the number of days when fishing is undertaken and so on. Let us assume, for simplicity, that all the different dimensions of harvesting activity can be aggregated into one magnitude called effort, E. Secondly, it seems likely that the harvest will also depend upon the size of the resource stock; the larger the stock, the greater the harvest, other things being equal. The size of harvest will also depend upon other factors, including random influences, but we abstract from these in our analysis, and take harvest to depend upon the effort applied and the stock size. That is

$$R_t = R(E_t, S_t) \qquad (7.5)$$

This relationship can take a variety of particular forms. One very simple form appears to be a good

---

Box 7.1 The logistic form of the biological growth function

Logistic growth is one example of the general class of density dependent growth processes. This model was first applied to fisheries by Schaeffer (1957). The equation for the logistic growth function of one species or type of renewable resource at a particular location is

$$G(S) = gS - \frac{gS^2}{S_{MAX}} \qquad (7.2)$$

This is illustrated in Figure 7.1a. The coefficient g is a growth rate parameter, and S_{MAX} is the maximum stock size that can be supported in the environmental milieu. Given that these are constant numbers, the logistic Equation 7.2 shows that the amount of growth, G, is a quadratic function of the resource stock size. Equation 7.2 is more commonly written in the form

$$G(S) = gS\left(1 - \frac{S}{S_{MAX}}\right) \qquad (7.3)$$

Equation 7.2 or 7.3 defines a logistic growth function for the case where the species does not possess any (non-zero) lower threshold population level. However, suppose there is some positive population threshold level, S_{MIN}, such that the population would inevitably and permanently decline to zero if the actual population were ever to fall below that threshold.

Then the logistic growth function would need to be generalised to

$$G(S) = g(S - S_{MIN})\left(1 - \frac{S}{S_{MAX}}\right) \qquad (7.4)$$

as illustrated in Figure 7.1b. The logistic growth model should be thought of as a stylised representation of the population dynamics of renewable resources. A number of factors which influence the actual growth patterns are ignored in this model, including the age structure of the resource (which is particularly important when considering long-lived species such as trees or whale stocks) and random or chance influences. At best, therefore, it can only be a good approximation to the true population dynamics.

The model is particularly suited to non-migratory species at particular locations. Among fish species, demersal or bottom-feeding populations of fish such as cod and haddock are thought to be well characterised by this model. The populations of pelagic or surface feeding fish, such as mackerel, are less well explained by the logistic function, as these species exhibit significant migratory behaviour.

Brown and McGuire (1967) argue that the logistic growth model can also be used to represent the behaviour of a freshwater stock in an underground reservoir.

---

approximation to actual relationships in many cases (see Munro, 1981, 1982), and is given by

$$R = e \cdot E \cdot S \qquad (7.6)$$

where e is a constant number, often called the catch coefficient. Dividing each side by E, this relationship states that the quantity harvested per unit effort is equal to some multiple (e) of the stock size.

We are now in a position to state the renewable stock growth function taking into account human predation. It is simply the biological growth function, less the quantity harvested, that is

$$\frac{dS_t}{dt} = G(S_t) - R_t \qquad (7.7)$$

The costs and benefits of harvesting the renewable resource can now be described. Assume, for simplicity, that the costs of harvesting the resource are a linear function of effort,

$$C_t = w \cdot E_t \qquad (7.8)$$

where C is the total cost of harvesting, and w is the cost per unit of harvesting effort, taken to be a constant. Let B denote the total gross benefit from harvesting a given quantity of the renewable resource. In general, the gross benefit will depend upon the quantity harvested, so we have

$$B_t = B(R_t)$$

As we wish to begin our analysis by looking at the commercially chosen levels of renewable resource harvesting, the appropriate measure of gross benefits is the total revenue which accrues to firms. Denoting the revenue obtained from the harvest as V, by definition

$$V_t = P_t \cdot R_t$$

where P is the gross (market) price of the resource. At this point, it is necessary to make an assumption about the determination of this gross price. We will continue to assume, as was done for non-renewable resources in Chapter 6, that a market demand

Box 7.2 Biological growth and extinction

As we show elsewhere in this chapter, the probability of a species becoming extinct can be high when high interest rates, in conjunction with low growth rates, low costs of harvesting and high value of the harvested resource, lead to a low stock size. In some cases, economically efficient stock sizes can be zero, although Clark (1990) demonstrates that this is a very unlikely possibility. Of greater likelihood is extinction resulting not from 'planned' harvesting programmes but, instead, from environmental perturbances when stock sizes are close to minimum threshold population levels. The important point to note here is that even where harvesting is economically efficient, extinction is possible. The likelihood of extinction is increased where extraction is inefficient (as in conditions of open access) or where environmental conditions undergo random variation, particularly where stock levels are already low. Although blue whales (and other whale species) and African elephants are not extinct, there have been fears that they could easily become so. The reasons for these fears can be seen by noting that many of the conditions favouring extinction seem to be present in these cases.

Unlike most fish species, the biotic growth potential of large mammals is sufficiently low to mean that heavy harvesting can drive the stock to zero. A well-known example is the American plains buffalo. Hunting and trapping have left many land creatures perilously close to or beyond the point of extinction. In the case of African elephants, it has long been the case that these animals have been regarded as common property. In recent decades, elephant stocks have fared quite differently in different countries, in part at least in response to the way in which governments have managed stocks, arranged economic incentives and controlled access. Several southern African states (e.g. Zimbabwe, Botswana and South Africa) manage the stocks as capital assets, strictly limiting access and allowing limited high-income-generating hunting. The most successful conservation programmes seem to have taken place where local people have had strong financial incentives for participating in these programmes, and so support strong anti-poaching measures. Kenya has experienced serious falls in its elephant population, not having established strong economic incentives for local people to participate in elephant protection.

Two large Asian countries – China and India – are threatened with substantial losses of species in the near future. Threatened species in China include a number of large mammals, including the giant panda, tiger, snow leopard, white-lip deer and golden monkey (see *World Resources 1994–95*, page 79). The main influences appear to be general habitat change arising from population growth and the associated pressures for increasing food output. Other contributory factors are hunting, and collection of specimens for taxidermy and for preparation of medicines (particularly in the case of plants). Similarly, many large mammal populations are threatened in India, including the tiger, elephant and some apes.

Both China and India have recognised these threats for at least two decades, have instituted systems of protected areas, and have plans to increase the protected land area by large quantities over the next two decades. These schemes show many interesting qualities; for example, Chinese plans include attempts to create corridors, providing natural links between nature reserves within the country and to reserves outside China.[3] However, the limited success to date of these protected areas in attaining conservation objectives demonstrates the importance of providing appropriate economic incentives to local populations. In India, for example, local tribespeople displaced from land devoted to tiger reserves have no incentive to conserve the animal, and their poaching has added to the pressures on tiger numbers (*World Resources 1994–95*, page 99). As we remarked earlier, the designation of protected status is of little use in itself unless there are concomitant changes in human behaviour; these can only be expected if local people are granted secure land tenure, property rights are firmly established, and the enforcement of those rights is supported by the state.

This brings us back to the question of open access, which we shall investigate in depth later in this chapter. Blue whale stocks have suffered from open access, together with very slow rates of natural growth. Efforts by the International Whaling Commission to conserve blue whale stocks have been largely ineffective. The passenger pigeon, which effectively became extinct through hunting in the late nineteenth century, also shows the dangers of extinction associated with open access.

[3] Similar proposals to construct corridors have been mooted for the former socialist countries of Central and Eastern Europe. Previous no-go areas along national boundaries offer the prospects of providing, at little real cost, very ecologically diverse nature reserves connected to one another by ecological corridors following the national boundaries.

Box 7.2 Continued

Whilst hunting or harvesting has been a major cause of extinction (or threats to extinction) of many large animal species, there are strong grounds for believing that most cases of species extinction do not result directly from excessive harvesting of the resource. Indeed, very often, species becoming extinct were never harvested at all. Most species extinction results from habitat change. Habitats do evolve naturally, of course, and so extinction is not only the result of human activity. But economic activity imposes very rapid and substantial changes to environmental systems, and it is this which is the cause of most species loss. We shall look at this in a little more depth later in this Chapter in Box 7.4.

---

function exists for the renewable resource in which the resource gross price is negatively related to the quantity harvested. That is

$$P_t = P(R_t), \qquad \frac{\mathrm{d}P}{\mathrm{d}R} < 0$$

Harvesting a renewable resource under open access conditions

In this section, we investigate the consequences of harvesting a renewable resource under a particular set of institutional arrangements, in which the resource in question is either commonly owned or is not owned at all, and is exploited under conditions of individualistic competition. Such resources are often described as *open access resources*. We will demonstrate that such institutional circumstances tend to result in 'overharvesting', in a precise sense to be made clear later. Overfishing and the like are shown to be consequences of these particular institutional arrangements, and not the result of ecological problems *per se*.

Our focus in this section shall be on steady-state equilibria, although Appendix 2, which more formally analyses the model discussed here, also contains some analysis of non-steady-state situations. We use the term *steady-state equilibrium* to refer to a path over time in which relevant variables of interest remain at constant levels (hence steady state) and from which appropriate decision makers have no desire to change (hence equilibrium). So in a steady state, it will be the case, for example, that the harvest rate equals the rate of net resource growth (so that the stock neither increases nor decreases) and that these equalised rates are constant over time. That is, in a steady state

$$G(S_t) = R_t = R, \qquad \text{for all } t$$

The fundamental property of an open access equilibrium is that it is characterised by all 'firms' (more generally, resource harvesters) earning zero economic rent. Equivalently, we could say that open access equilibria are characterised by zero royalties, or that the net price is, on average, zero. Economic rent is defined as the difference between the total revenue from the sale of harvested resources (V) and the total cost (C) incurred in resource harvesting. The zero rent condition applies to each harvester and to the industry as a whole.

Why does this occur? For an open access resource, there is no method of excluding incomers into the industry, nor is there any way in which existing firms can be prevented from changing their level of harvesting effort. If we assume that markets in the rest of the economy are perfectly competitive and so economic profit is zero in long-run equilibrium in each market, then the existence of positive rent in fishing will attract new firms into the industry, or cause existing firms to increase their fishing effort, in an attempt to appropriate part of these rents. An open access equilibrium is only possible when rents have been driven down to zero, so that there is no longer an incentive for entry into or exit from the industry, nor for the fishing effort on the part of existing fishermen to change. The essence of the argument here is that the resource is subject to free or open access. This is equivalent to saying that property rights do not exist in the resource, or, more precisely, that *enforceable* property rights are not in existence. If they were, then the holder of the property rights could extract compensation from the harvesters and, as we shall see subsequently, a very different outcome would emerge.

An alternative perspective on open access resources comes from considering the incentives that face individual harvesters. Let us consider incentives in the case of a commercial fishery in which there are no access restrictions and no entry charges to fishermen. Firms will exploit the fishery as long as profit opportunities are available. Each fishing vessel has an incentive to maximise its catch. Although reducing the total catch today may be in the collective interest (by allowing fish stocks to recover and grow, for example), it is not rational for any individual fisherman to restrict his fishing effort, as there is no guarantee that he will receive any of the rewards that this may generate in terms of higher catches later. Indeed, for some fisheries, there is no certainty that the stock will even be available tomorrow. In such circumstances, each firm will exploit the fishery today to its maximum potential, subject only to the constraint that its revenues must at least cover its costs.

We will see in the following section that extinction of renewable resource stocks is a possibility in conditions of open access. However, that is all we can legitimately argue in general. Contrary to what is sometimes thought, open access conditions do not necessarily result in extinction of species, although they may in certain circumstances.

Our task now is to find out what the steady-state stock level and harvest rate will be in an open access equilibrium. To do this, recall the assumptions we have made about the costs and revenues associated with resource harvesting. The total cost function is taken to be

$$C = w \cdot E \qquad (7.8)$$

and we choose the special form of the relationship between the harvest rate, effort and stock size proposed by Munro (1981, 1982):

$$R = e \cdot E \cdot S \qquad (7.6)$$

As we are concerned at this point only with steady state equilibria, in which variables are at constant levels over time, we have here omitted time subscripts for brevity of notation. Substituting Equation 7.6 into Equation 7.8 we obtain

$$C = w\left(\frac{R}{eS}\right) \qquad (7.9)$$

so that total fishing costs are a function of the harvesting rate and stock level. Note carefully that we are here regarding the cost per unit effort (w) and the catchability coefficient (e) as *constant* parameters. In many circumstances, these will be untenable assumptions. However, we proceed for the moment by assuming they are valid. Now suppose that the logistic function describes the biological growth process of the species (see Equation 7.3).

That is

$$G(S) = gS\left(1 - \frac{S}{S_{\text{MAX}}}\right)$$

But as we are considering only steady-state equilibria, it must be the case that $R = G(S)$, and so we can substitute for R in Equation 7.9 to obtain

$$C = \frac{w}{eS} \cdot gS\left(1 - \frac{S}{S_{\text{MAX}}}\right) = \frac{wg}{e}\left(1 - \frac{S}{S_{\text{MAX}}}\right) \quad (7.10)$$

Therefore C, the total cost, is a linear function of the resource stock, S, as illustrated in Figure 7.2.

On the income side, it is true by the definition of total revenue, V, that

$$V = R \cdot P(R) \qquad (7.11)$$

Now we are particularly interested in the relationship between V and S, in order to derive the equilibrium resource *stock* level under open access. The precise relationship between V and S will depend upon the specific forms taken by the resource demand function and by the growth function of the resource. Under plausible and likely conditions, we can show that the relationship will be of the form shown by the curve labelled V in Figure 7.2, with the revenue to the industry being at a maximum at S_{MSY}. (See Appendix 1 for further discussion of this assertion.)

Given the set of assumptions made, a unique open access equilibrium will occur at a stock level where total cost equals total revenue for a positive steady-state level of fishing. Such an equilibrium is shown by point A in Figure 7.2, corresponding to the stock level S_{OA}.[4] At this point, a double 'bio-economic' equilibrium is attained:

1 economic equilibrium: the industry is in an open access zero rent equilibrium, as $V = C$,
2 biological equilibrium: the resource stock is constant through time, as $G(S) = R$.

It is clear that, under the assumptions we have made and for the functions drawn in Figure 7.2, the open access steady state is unique, and is also a *stable* equilibrium. If the resource stock were to fall below S_{OA}, costs would exceed revenues and harvesting rents would become negative, leading to less harvesting activity and a recovery of stocks towards S_{OA}. By a similar argument, a rise in stocks above

---

[4] We should stress the point that our assertion than an open access equilibrium exists and is unique depends upon the assumptions made here. There is no guarantee that this will be true in general.

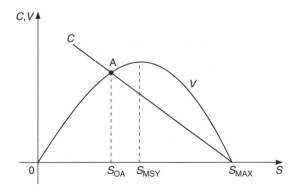

C = Total harvesting costs $(C = wE)$

V = Total harvest revenue $(V = R.P(R))$

S_{OA} = Open access steady state equilibrium

Fig 7.2 A simple model of fish harvesting.

S_{OA} would set in motion an adjustment process leading, once again, to the open access equilibrium at point A.

Further analysis of open access equilibria

In our illustration of an open access equilibrium, the steady state stock, S_{OA}, is less than the stock size at which the sustainable yield is maximised. However, such an outcome is not inevitable. The level of S_{OA} will depend on several factors, including the cost of a unit of harvesting effort, w, and the form and parameters of the demand function (which will influence the steady-state price). Consider, for example, the consequence of an increase in w. The cost function will rotate clockwise from a fixed point at $S = S_{MAX}$. In so doing, the open access equilibrium would correspond to an increasingly large steady state stock. Clearly, for a sufficiently large w, the intersection of C and V will occur at a point where the revenue curve had a negative slope, and so the open access stock level will exceed S_{MSY}, as shown in Figure 7.3. Two particular cases are of special interest. If the cost function intersected the revenue function at its maximum point, the open access equilibrium stock level would be the one generating the maximum sustainable yield. Clearly, open access is not necessarily anti-conservationist. The second case of interest arises when harvesting costs are so high (relative to fishing revenues) that no level of steady-state fishing is commercially viable. In this case, stocks would rise to S_{MAX}.

It can also be shown (see Appendix 1) that if the parameters of the demand function shift so that demand increases and the resource price becomes higher at any harvested quantity, the revenue function shown in Figure 7.3 will have a higher maximum value. In this case, the open access equilibrium will exist at a lower resource stock level. This is illustrated in Figure 7.4 by the shift of the revenue function from V to V', and the associated change in the open access equilibrium from A to A', at a lower stock level.

Private property equilibrium

The main characteristic of an open access equilibrium is zero long-run rent or profit. Price equals average cost, including a normal return on capital. The zero rent condition is a consequence of non-excludability – under open access arrangements, no institutional barriers exist to exclude those seeking to harvest the resource. The process of unrestricted individualistic competition drives rents to zero.

But if the fishery were organised into private ownership, and owners could enforce exclusion (or could charge a rent for entry), then it can be shown that an open access equilibrium would not be privately profitable to the resource owners.

The key to understanding private profit-maximising behaviour when access to the resource can be controlled lies in capital theory. A renewable resource is a capital asset. To fix ideas, think again about a fishery. The owner (or owners) of the fishery own a capital asset. Investment can be made in the capital stock by the decision to not harvest some fish. Biological growth processes will then result in a stock increase greater than the original investment – in other words, the asset is productive. Economic theory assumes that the owner takes decisions in any period so as to maximise the present value of his profits over some long period of time. Suppose that the owner of the fishery could invest his capital elsewhere in the economy at the rate of return i. Then the resource owner will require to obtain that return in the fishery, and so will manage the resource in such a way that it too produces a return equal to i.

An attempt to demonstrate the validity of this claim might be based on the following reasoning. Compare the open access equilibrium (point A in Figure 7.4) with another steady-state equilibrium, indicated by

---

Box 7.3 A story of two fish populations

One species of fish – the Peruvian anchovy – and one group of commercial fish – New England groundfish – present case studies of the mismanagement and economic inefficiency which often characterise the world's commercial fisheries. In this box, we summarise reviews of the recent historical experiences of these two fisheries; the reviews are to be found in Chapter 10 of *World Resources 1994–95*.

Peruvian anchovy are to be found in the Humboldt upswelling off the west coast of South America. Upswellings of cold, nutrient-rich water create conditions for rich commercial fish catches. During the 1960s and 1970s, this fishery provided nearly 20% of the world's fish landings. Until 1950, Peruvian anchovy were harvested on a small scale, predominantly for local human consumption, but in the following two decades the fishery increased in scale dramatically as the market for fish-meal grew. The maximum sustainable yield (MSY) was estimated as 9.5 million tonnes per year, but that figure was being exceeded by 1970, with harvests beyond 12 million tonnes. In 1972, the catch plummeted. This fall was partially accounted for by a cyclical natural phenomenon, the arrival of the El Niño current. However, it is now recognised that the primary cause of the fishery collapse (with harvest down to just over 1 million tonnes in the 1980s) was the conjunction of overharvesting with the natural change associated with El Niño. Harvesting at rates above the MSY can lead to dramatic stock collapses that can persist for decades, and may be irreversible (although, in this case, anchovy populations do now show signs of recovery).

The seas off the New England coast have been among the most productive, the most intensively studied and the most heavily overfished in the world since 1960. The most important species in commercial terms have been floor-living species including Atlantic cod, haddock, redfish, hake, pollock and flounder. Populations of each are now near record low levels. Although overfishing is not the only contributory factor, it has almost certainly been the principal cause of stock collapses. The New England fisheries are not unusual in this; what is most interesting about this case is the way in which regulatory schemes have failed to achieve their stated goals. In effect, self-regulation has been practised in these fisheries and, not surprisingly perhaps, regulations have turned out to avoid burdening current harvesters. This is a classic example of what is sometimes called 'institutional capture'; institutions which were intended to regulate the behaviour of firms within an industry, to conform with some yardstick of 'the common good', have in effect been taken over by those who were intended to be regulated, who then design administrative arrangements in their own interest. The regulations have, in the final analysis, been abysmal failures when measured against the criterion of reducing the effective quantity of fishing effort applied to the New England ground fisheries.

Long-term solutions to overfishing will require strict quantity controls over fishing effort, either by direct controls over the effort or techniques of individual boats, or through systems of transferable, marketable quotas. We investigate each of these classes of instruments later in this chapter, and in Chapter 9.

---

point B. Whereas rents are zero at point A, they are positive at point B. Therefore, an open access equilibrium cannot be a rent (profit) maximising equilibrium.

We might continue our reasoning as follows. Point B is not only superior to A in that it has positive rent, it is also the point at which the steady-state profit level (the difference between V and C) is maximised. The steady-state equilibrium for resource extraction under conditions of private ownership, in which excludability is possible, will therefore exist at a point such as B. Under the assumptions we have made, this will correspond to a resource stock level which exceeds that under open access.

Unfortunately, there is an important deficiency in this argument, and it turns out to be the case that the

conclusion we have just reached is *only* valid in the special circumstance that the private discount rate is zero. It is to this deficiency that we now turn our attention.

The dynamics of resource harvesting

Consider for a moment what precisely it is that a 'profit maximising' firm tries to maximise. If a firm exists over many periods of time, and acts rationally, it will aim to maximise the *present value* of the stream of profits earned over its lifetime. Assume that a market interest rate, i, exists, and the firm can lend money on the capital market at this rate of return. The present value of a series of discrete returns, each

---

Box 7.4 Genetic diversity

As Fisher (1981, page 75) argues, much of the concern about resource exhaustion appears to involve renewable resource use and the endangerment of species. He quotes one early assessment by a biologist:

> The worst thing that can happen – will happen [in the 1980s]- is not energy depletion, economic collapse, limited nuclear war, or conquest by a totalitarian government. As terrible as these catastrophes would be, they can be repaired within a few generations. The one ongoing process in the 1980s that will take millions of years to correct is the loss of genetic and species diversity by the destruction of natural habitats. This is the folly our descendants are least likely to forgive us.
>
> *Wilson (1980)*

This prognosis is supported by the following assessment which introduces the discussion of diversity found in Chapter 8 of the 1994–95 edition of *World Resources*:

> By some accounts, the world is on the verge of an episode of major species extinction, rivalling five other documented periods over the past half billion years during which a significant portion of global flora and fauna were wiped out . . . . Unlike previous die-offs, for which climatic, geologic and other natural phenomena were to blame, the current episode is driven by anthropogenic factors: the rapid conversion and degradation of habitat for human use; the accidental and deliberate introduction of exotic species; overharvesting animals, fish and plants; pollution; human-caused climate change; industrial agriculture and forestry; and other activities that destroy or

impair natural ecosystems and the species within them.

> *World Resources 1994–95*, page 147

The important point that emerges from this is the potential for *irreversible* effects of resource use. This characteristic of irreversibility suggests that there may be benefits from cautious or conservative use of resources, especially when there is uncertainty about the role and functions of species that might be lost by development. We investigate this issue further in Chapter 10. Ehrlich and Ehrlich (1981) provide the following statistics regarding species loss:

> Reduction in the number of species is occurring at record rates, mainly as a result of habitat takeover. A twenty percent reduction in the total number of species is projected by the year 2000.

We often think of land-based organisms when discussing loss of biodiversity. However, there is evidence that the biodiversity of freshwater lakes, streams and rivers may be the most threatened terrestrial ecosystem. Furthermore, marine waters, which contain over 90% of the world's living biomass, may be experiencing substantial loss of biodiversity (see *World Resources 1994–95*, pages 184 and 192).

These losses have their origins in behavioural patterns which reflect the fact that biodiversity is predominantly a public good (see Chapter 4), and also in the fact that the option and quasi-option values which biodiversity carries are not typically reflected in market values of these resources (see Chapter 10).

---

of which is Z_t, over $n + 1$ periods is

$$PV = \sum_{t=0}^{t=n} \frac{Z_t}{(1+i)^t}$$

or in the continuous time analogue

$$PV = \int_{t=0}^{t=n} Z_t e^{-it} dt$$

There were two limitations in the previous analysis. The first was that it only considered steady-state situations. The second limitation arises from the fact that it took no account of the present value of the steady-state rent flow. It may well be the case that the present value of the steady-state rent flow at point B in Figure 7.4 is less than the present value of some other harvesting regime, steady-state or otherwise. Before we go further, note that this problem does not arise in the case of the open access

equilibrium. Under open access, rents are zero in each period in steady-state equilibria, irrespective of the discount rate used. This is not the case in a private property equilibrium where positive rents can exist; discounting does make a difference in that case.

Let us for a moment turn our attention away from steady-state situations to the more general case where the levels of variables may be changing over time. We shall also assume, from this point onwards in our analysis, that total harvesting costs depend positively on the amount harvested, R, and negatively on the size of the resource stock, S. That is

$$C_t = C(R_t, S_t) \qquad C_R > 0, C_S < 0$$

Understanding the dynamics of resource harvesting is helped if we view the problem in the following way. Imagine that the owner of a fishery wishes to

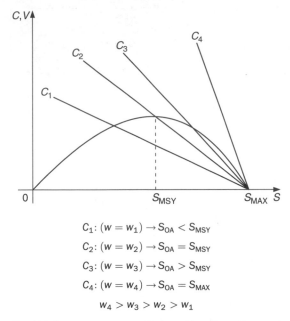

$C_1: (w = w_1) \rightarrow S_{OA} < S_{MSY}$

$C_2: (w = w_2) \rightarrow S_{OA} = S_{MSY}$

$C_3: (w = w_3) \rightarrow S_{OA} > S_{MSY}$

$C_4: (w = w_4) \rightarrow S_{OA} = S_{MAX}$

$w_4 > w_3 > w_2 > w_1$

Fig 7.3 Open access equilibria with alternative cost functions.

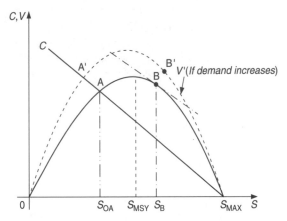

$C = $ Total cost $(= w(R/eS))$

$V = $ Total revenue $(= P(R) \cdot R)$

$A = $ Open access equilibrium

$A' = $ New open access equilibrium if demand increases

Fig 7.4 The effects of an increase in demand in open access.

maximise the present value of his or her resource. A decision is to be taken about whether to harvest a little extra of the fish stock today, or to defer that additional harvesting until a later period. The owner compares the additional costs and benefits of adding one more unit to the stock (that is, refraining from harvesting a marginal unit). By choosing *not* to harvest an incremental unit, the fisher incurs an opportunity cost in holding a stock of unharvested fish whenever the stock is valued at a positive net price. Holding these units sacrifices an available return, as sale of the harvested fish would have led to a revenue which can be invested at the prevailing rate of return on capital, i.

So the cost involved in this choice derives from the foregone current return, the value of which is the net price of the resource, p. Note that $p = P - c$, where P is the market price of the resource and $c = C/R$ is the *marginal* cost of one unit of the harvested resource. However, since we are considering a decision to defer this revenue by one period, the present value of this sacrificed return is ip.

The owner compares this cost with the benefits obtained by the resource investment. There are three categories of benefit:

1 The unit of stock may appreciate in value by the amount dp/dt.

2 As a consequence of an additional unit of stock being added, *total* harvesting costs will be reduced by the quantity $\partial C/\partial S$ (note that $\partial C/\partial S < 0$).

3 The additional unit of stock will grow by the amount dG/dS. The value of this additional growth is the amount of growth valued at the net price of the resource, that is $(dG/dS)p$.

A present value-maximising owner will add units of resource to the stock provided

$$ip < \frac{dp}{dt} - \frac{\partial C}{\partial S} + \frac{dG}{dS} \cdot p \qquad (7.12a)$$

That is, a unit will be added to stock provided its holding cost is less than the sum of its current capital appreciation, harvesting cost reductions and growth benefits. Conversely, a present value-maximising owner will harvest additional units of the stock if

$$ip > \frac{dp}{dt} - \frac{\partial C}{\partial S} + \frac{dG}{dS} \cdot p \qquad (7.12b)$$

These imply the *asset equilibrium condition*:

$$ip = \frac{dp}{dt} - \frac{\partial C}{\partial S} + \frac{dG}{dS} \cdot p \qquad (7.13)$$

A formal derivation of this condition using dynamic optimisation techniques is provided in Appendix 2. What is important to understand at this point is the interpretation of the asset equilibrium condition stated in Equation 7.13. When this equation is satisfied, the rate of return the resource owner obtains from the fishery is equal to the rate of return that could be obtained by investment elsewhere in the economy – that is, the return i. To see this, divide both sides of Equation 7.13 by the net price p to give

$$i = \frac{\left(\dfrac{\mathrm{d}p}{\mathrm{d}t}\right)}{p} - \frac{\left(\dfrac{\partial C}{\partial S}\right)}{p} + \frac{\mathrm{d}G}{\mathrm{d}S} \qquad (7.14)$$

This shows that Equation 7.13 is actually Hotelling's rule of efficient resource depletion/harvesting, albeit in a modified form. The left-hand side of Equation 7.14 is the rate of return that can be obtained by investing in assets elsewhere in the economy. The right-hand side is the rate of return that is obtained from the renewable resource: the proportionate growth in net price, plus the growth in the stock, less an adjustment for the dependence of total costs on stock level.[5]

We are now in a position to make some deductions about the nature of the stock level which will be associated with a privately optimal outcome. Let us switch our attention back once again to steady-state situations only, so as to compare our present results with those we obtained in the previous two sections. In a steady-state equilibrium, the net price does not change over time. Therefore, Equation 7.14 simplifies to

$$i = -\frac{\left(\dfrac{\partial C}{\partial S}\right)}{p} + \frac{\mathrm{d}G}{\mathrm{d}S} \qquad (7.15)$$

It will also be helpful in obtaining results if we temporarily assume that total harvesting costs do *not* depend on the stock size. In that case, $\partial C/\partial S = 0$, and so Equation 7.15 simplifies further to

$$i = \frac{\mathrm{d}G}{\mathrm{d}S} \qquad (7.16)$$

This is an interesting result. It tells us that a private profit-maximising steady-state equilibrium, where access can be controlled and costs do not depend upon the stock size, will be one in which the resource stock is maintained at a level where the rate of growth ($\mathrm{d}G/\mathrm{d}S$) equals the market rate of return on investment – exactly what standard capital theory

[5] It is instructive to compare this version of Hotelling's rule with other versions that we have derived previously. See, for example, Equation 5.41a of Chapter 5 and Equation 6.7b of Chapter 6.

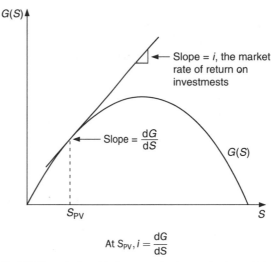

$$\text{At } S_{\mathrm{PV}}, i = \frac{\mathrm{d}G}{\mathrm{d}S}$$

Fig 7.5 The relationship between the interest rate and the present value-maximising stock size in steady-state equilibrium.

suggests should happen. This is illustrated in Figure 7.5. At the present value maximising resource stock size (which we denote by S_{PV}), $i = \mathrm{d}G/\mathrm{d}S$. It is also clear from this that as the interest rate rises, the profit-maximising stock size will fall.

The second deduction is straightforward. In open access equilibrium, the resource net price is zero, as all rents are dissipated by entry into the fishery. However, in a present value-maximising steady-state equilibrium, the net price, p, is greater than zero, as access restrictions allow positive rents to be earned. This requires that the present value-maximising resource stock is greater than the open access stock. To check this, look again at Figure 7.2. At S_{OA}, p is zero. For p to be positive, the stock size must be larger than S_{OA}. The open access stock is certainly 'sub-optimal' from the private viewpoint of the fishing industry, leading to too low a stock level for industry profits over time to be maximised.

A third deduction follows from Equation 7.16. If a zero discount rate were used (which is not likely in commercial enterprises, but is sometimes advocated as a rate that should be used – see Chapter 2) then the rate of growth ($\mathrm{d}G/\mathrm{d}S$) should be zero, and so the stock level should be S_{MSY}.

The three results we have just derived were under the assumption that costs are not dependent on the stock size. But they usually will be so dependent; in general, the total costs of harvesting a given quantity will rise as the stock size falls. When we allow for this dependency, Equation 7.16 is the relevant condition, not Equation 7.15. Not surprisingly, the results will then be somewhat different. The key point is that when costs depend (negatively) on the stock size, the present value-maximising stock will be higher than it would be otherwise. This arises because benefits are available by allowing the stock size to rise, and so reducing total harvest costs. We illustrate this in Figure 7.6, which compares the present value optimal stock levels with and without the dependence of costs on the stock size, S_{PV}^* and S_{PV}.

An analytical expression for the present value-maximising stock level is derived and presented in Appendix 3. Unfortunately, it is not possible to translate this result into one that can be shown in terms of Figure 7.2. The reason we cannot do this is that the cost curve there assumes no dependence of harvesting cost on stock size.

However, $S_{PV} = S_{MSY}$ if $i = 0$ and $\partial C/\partial S = 0$. That is, it makes sense to pick the stock level which gives the highest yield in perpetuity if costs are unaffected by stock size. To see the reasoning behind this, look at the main text of this chapter and in Appendix 2. More specifically, in the appendix we use r (rather than i) to denote the interest rate, and, secondly, we use $-\lambda$ (rather than P) to denote the resource net price. Bearing in mind these notational differences, if $i = 0$ and $\partial C/\partial S = 0$, this becomes in steady state

$$0 = 0 \cdot P - P \cdot \frac{\partial G}{\partial S} + 0$$

which implies that

$$P \cdot \frac{\partial G}{\partial S} = 0 \quad \text{and so} \quad \frac{\partial G}{\partial S} = 0$$

a condition which can only occur at S_{MSY}.

Also note that if > 0 and $\partial C/\partial S = 0$, then $S_{PV} < S_{MSY}$. The stock is drawn down below MSY as future losses in income from higher harvests are discounted and there is no penalty from harvest cost increases.

Open access revisited and the extinction of species

Our earlier discussion of resource harvesting under conditions of open access showed that there is not an inevitable conflict between a resource being harvested under open access conditions and the sustainability or conservation of the stock or species. Steady-state equilibria in which both harvests and stocks are

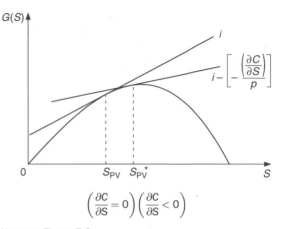

$$\left(\frac{\partial C}{\partial S} = 0\right)\left(\frac{\partial C}{\partial S} < 0\right)$$

Notes to Figure 7.6

No dependence of C on S	Dependence of C on S
$i = \dfrac{\partial G}{\partial S}$	$i = \dfrac{-\left(\dfrac{\partial C}{\partial S}\right)}{p} + \dfrac{\partial G}{\partial S}$
	$\dfrac{\partial C}{\partial S} < 0$
$\therefore i = \dfrac{\partial G}{\partial S}$	$\therefore i > \dfrac{\partial G}{\partial S}$
is required in equilibrium	is required in equilibrium

As i is a contrast, this implies

Fig 7.6 Present value-maximising fish stocks with and without the dependence of costs on stock size.

positive, constant amounts over indefinite periods of time are possible and likely. Open access does *not* necessarily result in renewable resource stock exhaustion. It is, of course, also possible that open access conditions do lead to the stock levels being driven to zero. But this is not only true under open access – even with private property rights established and enforceable, it can be commercially optimal to harvest a resource stock to extinction.

The proof of this assertion lies beyond the scope of this text; the reader who is interested in finding a proof of this result should consult one or more of the references given in the list of additional reading at the end of this chapter. A good point at which this additional reading might begin is the relatively simple, non-technical account given in Conrad (1995). For a more rigorous and complete account, see Clark (1990). Some of the results which emerge from this literature can be easily summarised, however. Some conditions will increase the likelihood of extinction, irrespective of whether the resource is harvested under conditions of open access or private property. Species extinction is more likely:

- the higher is the market (gross) resource price,
- the lower is the cost of harvesting a given quantity of the resource,
- the more that market price rises as the catch costs rise or as harvest quantities fall,
- the lower the natural growth rate of the stock, and
- the lower the extent to which marginal extraction costs rise as the stock size diminishes.

Thus, even under private property conditions, it may be the case that optimal harvesting programmes drive a stock to extinction if fish are very easy to catch as the stock diminishes towards its critical minimum threshold level and if it is very valuable. In this case, the optimal harvest level could exceed biological growth rates at all levels of stock. Furthermore, the higher is the discount rate, the more likely is a catch programme that drives the stock to zero.

Extinction is also made more probable, other things being equal, where the critical minimum threshold population size is relatively large. In this case, a greater proportion of possible harvesting programmes will lead to harvest rates that cannot be maintained over time. The existence of uncertainty also plays a very important role. Uncertainty may relate to the size of the minimum threshold population, to the actual stock size, or to the current and forecast harvesting rates. If errors are made in estimating any of these magnitudes, then it is clear that the likelihood of stock extinction is increased.

Another important consideration refers to the role of chance or random factors. Our presentation has assumed that all functions are deterministic – for given values of explanatory variables, there is a unique value of the explained variable. But many biological and economic processes are stochastic, with chance factors playing a role in shaping outcomes. In these circumstances, there will be a distribution of possible outcomes rather than one single outcome for given values of explanatory variables. This is what is meant by saying that outcomes are risky; uncertainty *per se* exists whenever it is not possible to assign known probabilities to each of the possible outcomes. Once again, an analysis of risk and uncertainty is beyond our scope in this text – you are recommended to pursue these matters by following up some of the references given in the Further reading section.

Having said all this, it still remains true that any given resource stock is more likely to be harvested to exhaustion, or a species driven to extinction, when it is harvested under conditions of open access than under a system in which property rights have been established and are enforceable. Why is this? The main reason is that harvest rates are typically higher under conditions of open access; other things being equal, the greater are harvesting rates, the higher is the likelihood of extinction.

Another way of thinking about this is in terms of economic efficiency. Open access harvesting programmes are inefficient because the resource harvesters are unable to appropriate the benefits of investment in the resource. If a single fisher were to defer the harvesting of some fish until a later period, all fishers would benefit from this activity. It would be in the interests of all if a bargain were made to reduce fishing effort by the industry. However, the conditions under which such a bargain could be made and not reneged upon are very unlikely to exist. Each potential bargainer has an incentive to free-ride once a bargain has been struck, by increasing his or her harvest whilst others reduce theirs. Moreover, even if all existing parties were to agree among themselves, the open access conditions imply that others could enter the market as soon as rents became positive. Open access resources thus have one of the properties of a public good – non-excludability – and this alone is sufficient to make it likely that markets will fail to reach efficient outcomes.

An important externality also arises in open access situations; this is often known as a crowding diseconomy. Under conditions of open access, there will be a tendency for the industry to consist of more harvesters and harvesting capital than is economically efficient. In the case of a fishery, for example, each boat's catch imposes an external cost on every other boat; by taking fish from the water, the costs of harvesting a given quantity of fish become higher for all other boats, provided fishing costs are related to stock size. In effect, each fisherman imposes an external cost on all others. This externality drives the average costs of fishing for the fleet as a whole above the marginal costs of an individual fisher.

There is no way that such external effects can be avoided, in the case of fishing at least. The crowding diseconomy is a technical effect that will operate whenever more than one vessel harvests from a particular fish population. However, if the fishery were in private property ownership and access were regulated, it would be feasible for the size of the

Box 7.5 Overcapacity in fishing fleets

Our discussions of open access resources implied that rents will be driven down to zero in an open access equilibrium. Recent UNFAO calculations suggest that the global fishing fleet did not even succeed in attaining zero rent. In 1989, the fleet was operating at a loss of $22 million; the loss including capital costs was $54 million. Summary statistics, taken from *World Resources 1994–95*, are presented in Table 7.1.

The industry is able to survive on such a loss-making basis partly as a result of government

Table 7.1 Operating costs and revenues for the global fishing fleet, 1989

Annual operating costs	Amount (millions of US$)
Routine maintenance	30 207
Insurance	7 193
Supplies and gear	18 506
Fuel	13 685
Labour	22 587
Total annual operating costs	92 178
Gross revenue from 1989 catch	69 704
1989 deficit (excluding debt servicing)	22 474

Source: Food and Agriculture Organization of the United Nations (FAO), *Marine Fisheries and the Law of the Sea: A Decade of Change* (FAO), Rome, 1992), pp. 20 and 58. Printed in *World Resources 1994–95*, page 187.

subsidies. For example, some governments pay entry fees for their nation's boats to enter foreign fisheries, whilst allowing domestic boats free access to their own territorial waters. The losses referred to above also reflect chronic overcapitalisation in the fishing industry; far more fishing capacity is actually available and used than is necessary to catch at current levels. As a result, the industry is, overall, massively inefficient.

To some extent overcapacity is a result of government and commercial responses to fluctuations in fish populations. As stocks rise, perhaps as a result of unusually beneficial environmental conditions, the industry installs new capital, often with government support. Subsequently, as stocks fall, either because of natural changes in environments or because of excessive harvesting, the industry is left heavily overcapitalised. Normal market mechanisms, driving firms out of loss-making industries, commonly work slowly or not at all, as government protective subsidies are introduced to maintain employment in areas where fishing activity is heavily concentrated.

Huppert (1990) presents some evidence on over-capitalisation in a fishery in the Bering Sea and Aleutian Islands. The efficient number of mother ships – those required to process the catches of fish from the fishing vessels – was estimated to be nine for the whole fishery. In fact, the number of mother ships was 140. A financial measure of this inefficiency is given by Huppert's calculation of $124 million per annum in lost benefits to the fishery.

fishing fleet to be chosen at an optimal size. The optimal size of fleet would balance the additional benefits of extra boats against the additional external costs of extra boats – what we have called crowding diseconomies. The negative effects become internalised in this way, leading to efficient outcomes. There is ample evidence that fishing effort is massively excessive and inefficient in many open access fisheries throughout the world. We give some evidence on this in Box 7.5.

Socially optimal resource harvesting

Appendix 2 derives the socially optimal harvesting programme under the most general set of conditions we have considered in this chapter. To derive the socially optimal programme, we assume that the

objective is to maximise a net benefits function over an infinite time horizon, where net benefits are discounted at a social consumption discount rate r. The socially optimal harvesting programme is shown to be identical to the privately optimal programme (assuming enforceable property rights exist) provided $r = i$.

Harvesting by a monopolist owner

It is important to be clear in what sense we are referring to monopoly in this section. Firstly, we are restricting attention to a renewable resource for which enforceable property rights exist and so access can be controlled by the owners. If an individual harvester makes positive profits, or if this is achieved by the industry as a whole, these controls over access prevent the rents being dissipated by new entry. In this sense, any private property resource could be said to have monopolistic characteristics, in so far as an important component of a monopolistic market is the ability of an established producer to prevent the entry of rivals into the market.

But this is not the meaning that we wish to ascribe to a 'monopolistic market' in this section. Rather, a resource market is monopolistic if there is one single harvester or a small number of harvesters that dominate the industry and are price setters. As is well known from standard micro economic theory, marginal revenue will exceed marginal cost at a monopolistic market equilibrium. A competitive market, on the other hand, has a large number of producers each of which is a price taker, with no individual control over market price. In the fishing case, a competitive industry in which access is restricted is a form of cartel, in which the cooperation among the members of the cartel is restricted to one thing: action to restrict access to the fishery by non-members of the cartel. In competitive market equilibrium, marginal revenue will equal marginal cost, as is the case for a competitive (but limited access) fishing industry.

As shown in Appendix 2, if a renewable resource were harvested under monopolistic market conditions rather than competitive conditions, then an economically inefficient harvesting level may result. A monopoly owner would tend to harvest less each period, and sell the resource at a higher market price, than is socially optimal. If we define a 'conservationist' as someone who regards high stock sizes as intrinsically desirable (and perhaps as someone who does not accord economic efficiency arguments much weight), then he or she may regard monopoly as more desirable than competition in renewable resource markets, however.

Renewable resources policy

What goals might one reasonably expect governmental policy towards the use of renewable resources to take? Firstly, there are efficiency goals; when the use of resources is economically inefficient, there are potential welfare benefits to the community from policy which leads to efficiency gains. This suggests that policy may be directed towards removing externalities. improving information, developing property rights, removing monopolist industrial

structures, and using direct controls or fiscal incentives to alter rates of harvesting whenever there is reason to believe that harvesting programmes are inefficient. Chapter 9 examines economic policy towards the environment and the instruments it has available to attain policy targets, so we shall defer a full consideration of how these objectives might be attained until then. However, some comment is warranted at this stage.

A key issue in renewable resource exploitation, as you have seen, is the adverse consequences of open access to many resources. This is a particularly significant problem in the case of ocean fisheries, but also applies to water and land resources, primary forests, and many other environmental systems. The simplest way of dealing with this may be to define and allocate property rights to the resource. Many nations have done something similar to this by extending their limits of national jurisdiction to 200 miles over their coastal waters. However, in order for this approach to yield efficient outcomes, two conditions must be satisfied. First, the access restriction must be enforceable. Secondly, the individual boats and their crews should harvest the resource in a collectively efficient manner. This latter condition is not likely to be satisfied purely as a consequence of extended national jurisdiction.

Secondly, given that uncertainty is so great in matters relating to natural resources, the government's role in the provision of information is likely to be crucial. In the case of commercial fisheries, for example, individual fishermen will not be in a position to know, in quantitative terms, how previous and current behaviour has affected and is likely to affect the population levels of relevant species. The consequences of cyclical natural phenomenon, such as the El Niño current mentioned in Box 7.3, will similarly be largely unpredictable by individual agents. Obtaining this kind of information requires a significant monitoring and research effort which is unlikely to be undertaken by the industry itself. Even if it were obtained privately, the dissemination of such information would probably be sub-optimal, as those who devote resources to collecting the information may well seek to limit its availability to others.

Efficiency gains, in the form of improved intertemporal resource extraction programmes, may also be obtained if government assists in the establishment of forward or futures markets. As we saw in Chapter 4, efficient outcomes are not possible in general unless all relevant markets exist. The absence of forward markets for most exhaustible and renewable resources suggests that it is most unlikely that extraction and harvesting programmes will be intertemporally efficient.

As far as the use of fiscal incentives is concerned, one way in which the fishing industry might be led into efficient resource harvesting is through the use of a tax levied at a fixed rate per unit of the resource landed. How should the level of such a tax be set? Look at Equation 7.23 in Appendix 2: this states that in an optimal harvesting regime, the market price (P) should equal the net price or royalty (p) plus the *marginal* cost of harvesting the resource. On the other hand, under open access, the zero rent result means that market price equals the *average* cost of harvesting. To bring about an optimal outcome, a two-part tax is therefore required. The first component of the tax rate is equal to the net price or royalty, p; the second component is the difference between marginal and average extraction costs. If a tax is levied at a rate equal to the sum of these two components, harvesting will take place at the optimal level. The royalty component corrects for the fact that fishermen in open access take no account of the future benefits to be obtained by refraining from harvesting. The second component internalises the crowding externalities referred to earlier.

Tax systems of this kind are very uncommon; an alternative to a tax regime is a system of transferable or marketable catch permits to harvest the resource. Let us call these catch permits 'individual transferable quotas' (ITQ). The ITQ system operates in the following way. Scientists assess fish stock levels, and determine maximum total allowable catches (TAC) for controlled species. The TAC is then divided among fishers. Each fisher can catch fish up to the amount of the quota it holds, or the quotas can be sold to other fishers. No entitlement exists to harvest fish in the absence of holding ITQs. In principle, the ITQ system can ensure that a given target quantity of fish can be harvested in a cost-efficient manner. To see how this operates, consider the following hypothetical example.

Suppose that a fishing industry consists of two groups of fishers – low cost ($2 per tonne) and high cost ($4 per tonne) – and assume that a tonne of fish can be sold for $10. Each group has historically caught and sold 100 tonnes of fish each period. Now consider what will happen if the government imposes a TAC of 100 tonnes.

In the first case, suppose that a non-transferable quota of 50 tonnes is imposed on each fisher. The total catch will be 100 tonnes, at a total cost of $300 (that is, $50 \times 4 + 50 \times 2$). Next, suppose that a transferable quota of 50 tonnes is allocated to each fisher; what will happen in this case? Given that the low-cost fishers make a profit (net price) of $8 per tonne, while high-cost fishers make a profit (net price) of $6 per tonne, a mutually advantageous trade opportunity arises. Suppose, for example, that an ITQ price is $7. High-cost producers will sell quotas at this price, obtaining a higher value per sold quota ($7) than the profit foregone on fish they could otherwise catch ($6). Low-cost producers will purchase ITQs at $7, as this is lower than the marginal profit ($8) they can make from the additional catch that is permitted by possession of an ITQ. A Pareto gain takes place, relative to the case where the quotas are non-transferable. This gain is a gain for the economy as a whole as can be seen by noting the total costs after ITQ trading. In this case, all 50 ITQs will be transferred, and so 100 tonnes will be harvested by the low-cost fishers, at a total cost of $200.

Although this example is unrealistically simple, the underlying principle is correct and applies to all marketable permit or quota systems. Transferability ensures that a market will develop in the quotas. In this market, high-cost producers will sell entitlements to harvest, and low-cost producers will purchase rights to harvest. The market price will be set at some level intermediate between the net prices or profits of the different producers. (We will demonstrate in Chapter 9 that this efficiency property is also shared by a tax system; indeed, a tax rate of $7 per tonne of harvested fish would bring about an identical outcome to that described above. Why is this so?) The transferable quota system has been used successfully in several fisheries, including some in Canada and New Zealand, and is examined in Box 7.6.

However, most regulatory policy has not used a tax/subsidy or marketable catch quota instrument. A common approach is to impose technical restrictions on the capital equipment used by fishermen – for example, restrictions on fishing gear, mesh or net size, boat size and so on. Such controls deliberately impose economic inefficiency on the industry, in an effort to reduce harvest sizes, and so cannot be cost-efficient methods of attaining harvest reduction targets. An alternative approach is to restrict the amount of fishing effort taking place by limitations on the times at which fishing may take place. Like the previous instrument, such restrictions fail to tackle at its root the excess fishing capacity that tends to be a consequence of open access.

Box 7.6 The individual transferable quota system in New Zealand fisheries

New Zealand introduced in 1986 an individual transferable quota (ITQ) system for its major fisheries. The ITQ management system operates in the way we described earlier. Government scientists annually assess fish stock levels, and determine maximum total allowable catches (TAC) for controlled species. New Zealand legislation requires that the TAC levels are consistent with the stock levels that can deliver maximum sustainable yields (although that is not the only way in which TAC levels could be set). The TAC is then divided among fishers, with the shares being allocated on the basis of individual catches in recent years. Each fisher can catch fish up to the amount of the quota it holds, or the quotas can be sold or otherwise traded.

The ITQ system has a number of desirable properties. First, fishermen know at the start of each season the quantity of fish they are entitled to catch; this allows effort to be directed in a cost-minimising efficient manner, avoiding the mad dash for catches that characterises free access fishery. Secondly, as a market exists in ITQs, resources should be allocated in such a way that fishing effort is undertaken by those firms who have the lowest harvesting costs. The reasoning behind this assertion is explained in the main text.

The ITQ system operates in conjunction with strictly enforced exclusion from the fishery of those not in possession of quotas. This access restriction generates appropriate dynamic incentives to conserve fish stocks for the future whenever the net returns of such 'investments' are sufficiently high.

The evidence of the ITQ system in operation suggests that, in comparison with other alternative management regimes that might have been implemented, it has been successful both as a conservation tool and in terms of reducing the size of the uneconomically large fleets. The ITQ system has not eliminated all problems, however. The fishing industry creates continuous pressure to push TAC levels upwards, and great uncertainty remains as to the levels at which the TAC can be set without jeopardising population numbers. The ITQ system has failed to find a clear solution to the problems of bycatch – the netting of unwanted, untargeted species – and highgrading – the discarding of less valuable species or smaller-sized fish, in order to maximise the value of quotas set in terms of fish quantities.

The ITQ system now operates, to varying extents, in the fisheries of Australia, Canada, Iceland and the United States.

Source: World Resources 1994–95, Chapter 10.

The restrictions we have just discussed all attempt to reduce fishing effort, or to reduce the catch coefficient (the catch rate per unit effort). However, they cannot be cost-effective relative to a scheme which reduces the fishing industry capital stock to an optimal level. Governments might try to attain this by incentives for firms to leave the industry, but this will be useless if the reduced effort that results is just matched by increased effort from other firms, as seems very likely.

Another approach that is often used is to impose controls in the form of quantity restrictions on catches. This is the centrepiece of fishing regulation in the European Community, for example, in the Total Allowable Catch system. This often has the perverse effect of increasing fishing effort; individual firms buy larger boats, or more boats, or install more sophisticated harvesting technology in order to win a larger share of the fixed quota for themselves. This results in shorter fishing seasons (often imposed by regulation), and the larger capital stock either lying idle for even longer periods, or turning to exploit other fisheries, thereby imposing stock depletion problems elsewhere.

For example, the season for eastern Pacific yellowfin tuna fell from 9 months prior to catch quotas being introduced to just three months after a quota restriction was imposed. Gordon (1954) provides an interesting account of the use of quota restrictions in the Pacific halibut fishery. During the 1930s, Canada and the USA agreed to fixed-catch limits. For many years, the scheme was hailed as an outstanding success, with catch per unit effort quantities rising over two decades, one of the few quota schemes to have achieved this goal. However, Gordon shows that the improvements were not the result of quotas, but of a natural cyclical improvement in Pacific halibut stocks; catches rose rather than fell during the period when quotas were introduced, yet the total catch taken was only a small fraction of the estimated population reduction prior to regulation. Furthermore, the efficiency loss of the regulations was enormous, with the fishing season before quotas were met falling from six months in 1933 to between one and two months in

1952. Despite their widespread use, these quantitative restrictions on either effort or catch have very little justification in either economic or biological terms.

You may wonder at this point why aggregate catch quotas have inefficient (or even counterproductive) outcomes, whereas we argued earlier that marketable or transferable quota regimes lead to efficient outcomes. The difference arises precisely because of marketability. Where quotas are marketable, an economic incentive exists to reduce fishing – such an incentive does not exist in non-transferable, non-marketable quota regimes. We shall explore the implications of this in depth in Chapter 9.

Finally, it is important to note that many writers (particularly non-economists) would argue that correcting market failure and eliminating efficiency losses is not *sufficient* as an objective for government. They would argue that policy should be directed to prevention of species extinction or the loss of biological diversity whenever that is reasonably practical. This introduces the principle that policy should satisfy a criterion of safe minimum standard of conservation. It is to this matter that we turn in the next section.

A safe minimum standard of conservation

Our discussion of the 'best' level of renewable resource harvesting and policy has placed emphasis very heavily upon the criterion of economic efficiency. However, if harvesting rates pose threats to the survival or sustainability of some renewable resource (such as North Atlantic fisheries or primary forests) or jeopardise an environmental system itself (such as a wildlife reserve containing extensive biodiversity) then the criterion of efficiency may not be appropriate by itself. We have seen that the pursuit of an efficiency criterion is not sufficient to guarantee the survival of a renewable resource stock or an environmental system in perpetuity, particularly when resource prices are high, harvesting costs are low, discount rates are high, and uncertainty pervades the relevant functions.

When a renewable resource or environmental system is of high intrinsic value, so that we would be strongly averse to outcomes that involve the resource being driven to extinction or being unable to yield valuable environmental services, constraints on harvesting behaviour may be deemed appropriate. The notion of a Safe Minimum Standard of Conservation (SMC), has been advocated as a response to

this set of circumstances, and we shall now examine this principle, and see how it can be applied to renewable resource policy.

A strict version of SMC would involve imposing constraints on resource harvesting and use so that all risks to the survival of a renewable resource are eliminated. This is unlikely to be of much relevance, however. Virtually all conceivable human behaviour entails some risks to species survival, and so strict SMC would appear to prohibit virtually all economic activity. In order to obtain a useful version of SMC, it would appear to be necessary to impose weaker constraints, so that the adoption of an SMC approach will entail that, under *reasonable* allowances for uncertainty, threats to survival of *valuable* resource systems are eliminated, provided that this does not entail *excessive cost*. For decisions to be made that are consistent with such a weaker SMC criterion, judgements will be necessary about each of the italicised words or phrases in the previous sentence; decisions will be required as to what constitutes 'reasonable uncertainty' and 'excessive cost', and which resources are deemed 'sufficiently valuable' for application of the SMC criterion.

Let us explore the concept of SMC a little further by following the exposition of this concept given in a recent paper by Randall and Farmer (1995). Suppose there is some renewable resource that grows over time in a particular way, illustrated by the curve labelled 'Regeneration function' in Figure 7.7. The function shows the resource stock level that will be available in period $t + 1$ for any level of stock that is conserved in period t. Resource stock levels are denoted by the letter S. Notice that the greater is the level of current stock conservation, the higher will be the stock level available in the next period.[6]

Randall and Farmer restrict their attention to sustainable resource use, interpreting sustainability to mean a sequence of states in which the resource stock does not decline over time. Therefore, only those levels of stock in period t corresponding to segments of the regeneration function that lie on or above the 45° line (labelled 'Slope = 1') constitute sustainable stocks. The minimum sustainable level of stock conservation is labelled S_{MIN}.

The efficient level of stock conservation is S_t^*. To see this, construct a tangent to the regeneration function with a slope of $1 + r$, where r is a

---

[6] The relationship is non-linear due to the characteristics of the resource stock–growth relationship for the renewable resource in question.

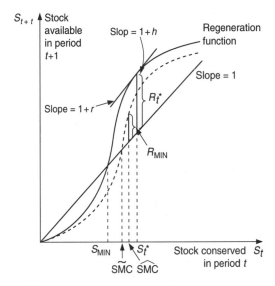

Fig 7.7 A safe minimum standard of conservation.

(consumption) social discount rate, and let h denote the rate of growth of the renewable resource. At any point on the regeneration function, a tangent to the function will have a slope of $1 + h$. For the particular stock level S_t^* we have

$$1 + r = 1 + h \quad \text{or} \quad r = h$$

and so the rate of growth of the renewable resource (h) is equal to the social discount rate (r). This is an efficiency condition for steady-state renewable resource harvesting, as we have seen previously in Equation 7.16. Note also that at the efficient stock level, the amount of harvest that can be taken in perpetuity is R_t^*. By harvesting at this rate, the post-harvest stock in period $t + 1$ is equal to that in period t, thus satisfying the sustainability requirement.

Now suppose that the regeneration function is subject to random variation. For simplicity, assume that the worst possible outcome is indicated by the dotted regeneration function in Figure 7.7; at any current stock, the worst that can happen is that the available future stock falls short of the expected quantity by an amount equal to the vertical distance between the solid and dotted functions.

Now even in the worst outcome, if $\widetilde{\text{SMC}}$ is conserved in each period, the condition for perpetual sustainability of the stock will be maintained. We might regard $\widetilde{\text{SMC}}$ as a stock level that incorporates the safe minimum standard of conservation, reflecting the uncertainty due to random variability in the

regeneration function. Put another way, whereas S_{MIN} is an appropriate minimum stock in the absence of uncertainty, $\widetilde{\text{SMC}}$ takes account of uncertainty in a particular way.

In fact, $\widetilde{\text{SMC}}$ is not what Randall and Farmer propose as a safe minimum standard of conservation. They argue that any sustainable path over time must involve some positive, non-declining level of resource harvesting and consumption in every period. Suppose that R_{MIN} is judged to be that minimum required level of resource consumption. Then Randall and Farmer's safe minimum standard of conservation is $\widehat{\text{SMC}}$. If the stock in period t is kept from falling below this level then, even in the worst possible case, R_{MIN} can be harvested without interference with sustainability.

The SMC principle implies maintaining a renewable resource stock at or above some safe minimum level such as $\widehat{\text{SMC}}$. In Figure 7.7, there is no conflict between the conservation and efficiency criteria. The safe minimum standard of conservation actually implies a lower target for the resource stock than that implied by economic efficiency. This will not always be true, however, and one can easily imagine circumstances where an SMC criterion implies more cautious behaviour than the economically efficient outcome.

Finally, what can be said about the qualification that the SMC should be pursued only where it does not entail excessive cost? Not surprisingly, it is difficult to make much headway here, as it is not clear how one might decide what constitutes excessive cost. Randall and Farmer suggest that no society can reasonably be expected to decimate itself; therefore, if the SMC conflicted with the survival of human society, that would certainly entail excessive cost. But most people are likely to regard costs far less than this, such as extreme deprivation, as being excessive. Ultimately, the political process must generate views as to what constitutes excessive costs.

The economics of forestry

Although the analysis in this chapter has been concerned with the general category of renewable resources, much of the detail of the arguments, and most of the examples we have used, have related to one kind of renewable resource – ocean fisheries. We now turn our attention to forestry resources. Forests and woodlands can be thought of as comprising two types; commercial forests, managed primarily for timber revenues, and native or natural woodlands or forest, some of which are managed for purposes other than timber revenues, such as a number of American national parks, and others which are not managed according to any coordinated policy, as is the case in large areas of tropical forest.

Let us begin by summarising some of the key characteristics of forest resources, noting in which ways forests differ from other renewable resources.

1 Forests are multi-functional, providing a wide variety of goods and services, including raw materials and fuels, habitats for wildlife, watershed maintenance, regulation of atmospheric quality, recreational facilities and other amenities. Because of the wide variety of functions that forests perform, timber managed for any single purpose generates a large number of important external effects. We would expect that the management of woodland resources is often economically inefficient because of the presence of these external effects.

2 As one kind of renewable resource, woodlands are capital assets which are intrinsically productive. In this, they are no different from fisheries, and so the techniques we developed earlier for analysing efficient and optimal exploitation should also be applicable (albeit with amendments) to the case of forest resources.

3 Trees typically exhibit very long lags between the dates at which they are planted and the date at which they attain biological maturity. The length of time between planting and harvesting is usually at least 25 years, and can sometimes be as large as 100 years. This is considerably longer than for most species of fish.

4 The growth of a single stand of timber, planted at one point in time, resembles that illustrated for fish populations earlier in this chapter. Figure 7.8, based on data in Tietenberg (1992), represents a typical profile for the volume (usually measured in cubic feet) of standing timber in such a stand at various times after planting.[7] The data for the

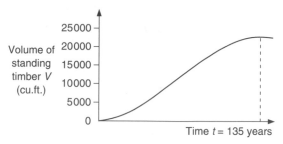

Fig 7.8 The growth of a single stand of timber.

example we use in this section are listed in the first two columns in Table 7.2. An early phase of slow growth in volume (although not in height) tends to give way to a period of rapid volume growth, after which a third phase of slow growth takes place as the stand moves towards maturity. Eventually, positive growth ceases altogether (and in some cases becomes negative, as in our diagram). As explained above, the amount of time until maturity can exceed a century.

Commercial forestry

A huge literature exists analysing timber extraction. We attempt to do no more than present a flavour of some basic results, and refer the reader to specialist sources of further reading at the end of the chapter. An important biological criterion used in making prescriptions about forest management is Mean Annual Increment (MAI) maximisation. The MAI of a stand of timber is defined as the ratio of the volume of timber in the stand to the age of the stand. The MAI criterion for felling a single stand of timber of uniform age is to fell at the age where MAI is at its maximum value. This is illustrated in Figure 7.9. For the data used in our illustrative example, the MAI is at its maximum value when the stand has been growing for 97 years.

Despite having attractions because of simplicity and plausibility, most economists regard the MAI criterion as being arbitrary, ignoring as it does the costs and revenues of harvesting (and when these occur), and giving no attention to the role that might be played by discounting. Economic criteria for efficient felling derive from simplified models of the timber growth and harvesting process, in which an answer is sought to the following question:

What harvest programme is required in order that the present value of the net benefits from the stand of timber is maximised?

---

[7] The age–volume relationship used in Figure 7.8 is derived from the equation

$$V = 40t + 3.1t^2 - 0.016t^3$$

where V is the volume in cubic feet of timber in a stand of US north-west Pacific region Douglas firs, and t is the age in years of the stand since planting. The equation is reported in Tietenberg (1992), page 280, which is taken in turn from Clawson (1977).

Table 7.2 Present values of revenues, costs and net benefit undiscounted and discounted at 3%

Age of stand *t* (years)	Volume of timber *V* (cu. ft.)	MAI $(= V/t)$	Interest rate $i = 0$			Interest rate $i = 0.03$		
			Revenue R1	Cost C1	Net benefit NB1	Revenue R2	Cost C2	Net benefit NB2
1	43	43	431	5 086	−4 655	418	5 084	−4 666
10	694	69	6 940	6 388	552	5 141	6 028	−887
20	1 912	96	19 120	8 824	10 296	10 493	7 099	3 395
26	2 854	110	28 544	10 709	17 835	13 085	7 617	5 468
30	3 558	119	35 580	12 116	23 464	14 466	7 893	6 573
31	3 742	121	37 424	12 485	24 940	14 766	7 953	6 813
38	5 118	135	51 184	15 237	35 948	16 370	8 274	8 096
40	5 536	138	55 360	16 072	39 288	16 674	8 335	8 339
50	7 750	155	77 500	20 500	57 000	17 293	8 459	8 834
60	10 104	168	101 040	25 208	75 832	16 702	8 340	8 361
68	12 023	177	120 235	29 047	91 188	15 634	8 127	7 507
70	12 502	179	125 020	30 004	95 016	15 310	8 062	7 248
80	14 848	186	148 480	34 696	113 784	13 470	7 694	5 776
90	17 046	189	170 460	39 092	131 368	11 456	7 291	4 165
98	18 633	190	186 333	42 267	144 067	9 851	6 970	2 881
100	19 000	190	190 000	43 000	147 000	9 460	6 892	2 568
110	20 614	187	206 140	46 228	159 912	7 603	6 521	1 082
120	21 792	182	217 920	48 584	169 336	5 954	6 191	−236
130	22 438	173	224 380	49 876	174 504	4 542	5 908	−1 366
135	22 532	167	225 315	50 063	175 252	3 926	5 785	−1 860
140	22 456	160	224 560	49 912	174 648	3 367	5 673	−2 306
145	22 200	153	221 995	49 399	172 596	2 865	5 573	−2 708

Let us consider briefly one of the most simple forest models; despite its lack of realism, this model does offer useful insights into the economics of timber harvesting.

Suppose there is a stand of timber of uniform age. All trees in the stand are to be cut at one point in time, and once felled will not be replanted. What is the optimum time at which to fell the trees? The answer is obtained by choosing the age of trees at which the present value of the net benefits from the stand of timber is maximised. The present value of net benefits from felling the stand at a particular age of trees is obtained by subtracting the present value of planting and harvesting costs from the present value of timber at that stand age. We present some illustrative calculations for this simple model in Table 7.2. The three columns labelled R1, C1 and NB1 refer to the present values of revenues, costs and net benefits when the interest rate is zero. The three columns labelled R2, C2 and NB2 refer to the present values of revenues, costs and net benefits when the (continuous) interest rate is 3%. In these calculations, we assume that the market price per cubic foot of felled timber is £10, planting costs are £5000, incurred immediately the stand is established, and harvesting costs are £2 per

cubic foot, incurred at whatever time the forest is felled.

When a discount rate of zero is used (that is, when there is no consumption discounting) the present (or discounted) value of net benefits is equal to the actual (or undiscounted) value of net benefits. This variable is listed in Table 7.2 under the title NB1, and is shown in Figure 7.10 by the curve labelled by that name. These net benefits are maximised at 135 years, the point at which the biological growth of the stand becomes zero. With no discounting, the profile of net *value* growth of the timber is identical to the profile of net *volume* growth of the timber, as can be seen by comparing Figures 7.9 and 7.10.

It is also useful to look at this problem in another way. The interest rate to a forest owner is the opportunity cost of the capital tied up in the growing timber stand. In this case, that opportunity cost is zero. It will, therefore, be in the interests of the owner to *not* harvest the stand as long as the volume (and value) growth is positive, as it is up to an age of 135 years.

Now let us consider the case where a discount rate of 3% is used. The present value of net benefits is now given by the column of Table 7.2 labelled NB2, and is plotted under that legend in Figure 7.11a. When the interest rate is 3%, the present value of net benefits is

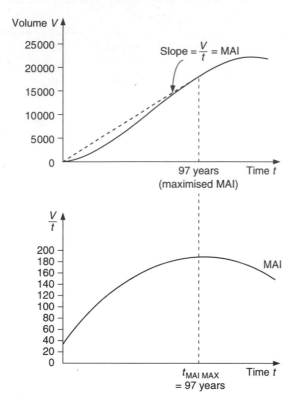

Fig 7.9 Mean annual increment (MAI) maximisation.

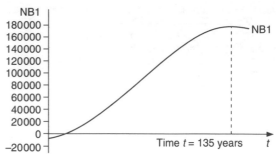

Fig 7.10 Undiscounted net benefits and discounted net benefits if zero discount rate is used.

maximised at only 50 years stand age. That is the age of the stand at which the timber should be felled if the owner's objective is to maximise his or her wealth. Expressed another way, the growth of the *undiscounted* net value falls to 3% at year 50, and is less than 3% thereafter, as shown in Figure 7.11b. If the interest rate is 3%, the timber should be harvested at age 50 years – up to that point, the return from the forest is above the interest rate, and beyond that point the return to the forest is less than the interest rate.

In conclusion, we can think of the forest felling problem in either of two equivalent ways. Firstly, the stand should be harvested when the rate of growth of the undiscounted net benefits falls to a rate at which it becomes equal to the interest rate. Alternatively, the stand should be harvested when the rate of growth of the discounted net benefits falls to zero – at this point, the present value of net benefits is maximised. The equivalence of the two conditions is proved mathematically in Appendix 4. It is worth noting at this point that this is exactly equivalent to a result we obtained earlier when discussing optimal harvesting

in a fishery. If you look back to Equation 7.16 and the discussion surrounding it, you will see that is so.

The model we developed and explored above makes it clear that the optimal time for felling will depend upon the discount rate used. Whenever the costs of planting, management, and harvesting occur at different times from the revenues derived from sold timber, the introduction of discounting (at non-zero rates) will in general make a difference. We saw earlier that felling should take place when the rate of change of undiscounted net benefits is equal to the discount rate. As the discount rate rises, it is clear from Figure 7.11b that the age at which the stand is felled will have to be shortened in order to bring about an equality between the rate of change of undiscounted net benefits and the discount rate.

This sensitivity of the optimal felling age on the level of the interest rate can be very great. In Figure 7.12, we illustrate how the optimal felling age varies with the interest rate. Be careful not to read too much into this; the relationship shown is valid only for the growth model used here, and the various assumptions we made about growth parameter values, prices and costs. However, it does indicate that under quite plausible circumstances, small changes in interest rates can dramatically alter privately optimal harvesting programmes.

Extensions to the simple forest model

The forestry model we investigated in the previous section is unrealistic in many ways. One serious limitation of that model was its assumption of a single harvest, after which replanting does not occur. Many forestry enterprises are planned to operate on a perpetual basis, however, with replanting taking place after each felling. This suggests that we should also model forests in which there is an infinite sequence of

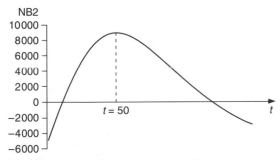

Fig 7.11a Net benefits, discounted at 3%.

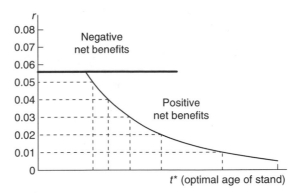

Fig 7.12 The variation of optimal felling age with the interest rate.

harvesting and replanting. Moreover, it is often the case that a forest will consist of sets of trees of various ages, each age group being felled at an optimal time, and replanting taking place to replace those felled trees. In this way, a forest can yield a continuous sustained yield, rather than bursts of felled timber at discrete intervals of decades.

In the previous section, an important result about optimal felling was established. Felling should take place when the rate of change of undiscounted net benefits from the growing timber is equal to the discount rate. We could write this in the form of the following equality:

$$i = \frac{\left(\dfrac{d(NB)}{dt}\right)}{NB}$$

When harvesting of a stand (or part of a stand) is to be followed by the establishment of another stand, an additional element enters into the calculations. In this case, a decision to defer harvesting for a while incurs an additional cost over that in the previous model. Not only is there an opportunity cost in the form of the delayed rate of return on the revenues from harvesting, i, but also there is an opportunity cost arising from the delay in establishing the next planting in the cycle. Timber that would have been

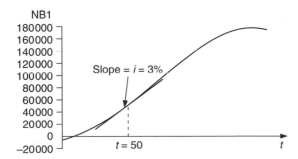

Fig 7.11b Undiscounted net benefits.

growing in the next cycle will have a delayed start to its growth. So an optimal harvesting and replanting programme must equate the benefits of deferring harvesting – the rate of growth of the undiscounted net benefit of the timber stand – with the costs of deferring that planting – the interest rate and the return lost from the delay in establishing the next planting in the cycle. Denoting by w the rate of growth of value from this next cycle, the equality condition is amended to

$$i + w = \frac{\left(\dfrac{d(NB)}{dt}\right)}{NB}$$

As a higher rate of growth of the net benefits of the stand of timber is required to satisfy this equality, each stand will be harvested at an earlier tree age than was the case in our original model. Trees will be felled when they are younger in these so-called 'infinite rotation' models. A second important difference exists between single and infinite rotation harvest models: in the single rotation model, the level of planting and the level of harvest costs have no effect on the optimal harvest age; changes in these levels merely shift up or down the net benefits profile. However, the levels of planting and harvesting costs do 'matter' in infinite rotation models. Without proof, we just state a result: an increase in planting or harvesting costs reduces the opportunity cost of delaying the establishment of following plantings, and so lengthens the optimal period of any rotation (that is, the age of trees at harvesting). It also follows that taxes can affect the choice of rotation time; a tax per unit of felled timber is equivalent to an increase in harvesting costs. The introduction of such a tax will, therefore, tend to increase the length of each rotation in the cycle. The effect of prices is examined in Problem 1.

Privately and socially optimal felling programmes

Our discussions of forestry have looked at optimality in the sense of what is profit-maximising (more precisely, present value-maximising) from the point of view of an individual private forester. Will privately present value-maximising choices also be socially efficient or optimal? The answer to this question should be clear to you by comparison with the equivalent question in the case of renewable resources in general. If all markets exist, all the conditions described in Chapter 4 for efficient allocation of resources are satisfied throughout the economy, and if the interest rate used by private foresters is identical to the social consumption discount rate, privately optimal choices in forestry will be socially efficient, and, given appropriate distributions of initial endowments of property rights, could be socially optimal too. Unfortunately these conditions are not likely to be satisfied. Apart from the fact that the 'rest of the economy' is unlikely to satisfy all the necessary efficiency conditions, there are particular aspects of forestry that imply a high likelihood of private decisions not being socially efficient. What are these aspects?

The main reason for a probable difference between privately and socially efficient outcomes arises from the prevalence of externalities to which reference was made earlier. Forests are multi-functional, providing a wide variety of economic and other benefits. Private foresters are unlikely to incorporate all these benefits into their private net benefit calculations, as they often have very weak or no financial incentives to do so. Forest amenity benefits may be very substantial, and should increase the length of socially optimal rotations. But foresters will find it difficult or impossible to extract the monetary value of these amenity benefits. These externality problems are particularly acute in the case of tropical forests and other open access woodlands, and so we shall briefly investigate these now.

Tropical forests and other open access woodlands

Tropical forests are typically *de facto* open access resources. In discussing fisheries, we argued that whilst it is possible that stocks will be driven down to zero under open access, this is rather unlikely. As stocks decline to low levels, the marginal costs of catching fish usually rise very sharply. This means that it usually becomes uneconomic to harvest fish before their stock levels have reached critical minimum levels. This does not apply in the case of woodland, however. Unlike fish, trees are not mobile, elusive creatures; harvesting costs tend to be affected very little by the stock size, unlike the case of fisheries where harvest costs tend to be inversely related to stock levels. So, provided timber values are high (or the return from other uses of the land is sufficiently attractive), there is no in-built mechanism stopping stock declines to zero. This is reflected in the rates of deforestation observed in tropical forests, described in the second section of this chapter.

The lack of access restrictions also explains why less than 0.1% of tropical logging is currently being done on a sustainable yield basis (International Tropical Timber Organisation: 1989 study). Open access ensures that few individuals are willing to incur the large capital costs in restocking felled timber, particularly when returns are so far into the future. It also explains why so much of the use of tropical forests is best characterised by a process of conversion of capital assets into current income.

In addition to the losses which arise from inefficient harvesting of the timber itself, tropical deforestation has other important external consequences. Extensive and rapid felling has increased global warming (see Chapter 12), contributed to losses of soil fertility and declines in agricultural productivity, and significantly decreased biodiversity. Tropical forests exemplify the absence of clearly defined and enforceable property rights *par excellence*. In addition, the pressure to fell, or merely to clear trees so that land may be used for other purposes, has been and remains acute in many countries that face widespread poverty or severe debt.

Many of the externalities associated with tropical deforestation cross national boundaries, making internationally concerted action a prerequisite of efficient policy. We discuss the use of internationally organised tax or subsidy instruments, debt for nature swap arrangements and international conservation funds in Chapter 12.

Discussion questions

1 Would the extension of territorial limits for fishing beyond 200 miles from coastlines offer the prospect of significant improvements in the efficiency of commercial fishing?

2 Discuss the implications for the harvest rate and possible exhaustion of a renewable resource under circumstances where access to the resource is open, and property rights are not well defined.

3 To what extent do environmental 'problems' arise from the absence (or unclearly defined assignation) of property rights?

Problems

1 Demonstrate that a tax imposed on each unit of timber felled will increase the optimal period of any rotation (that is, the age of trees at harvesting) in an infinite rotation model of forestry. What effect will there be on the optimal rotation length if the expected demand for timber were to rise?

2 Analyse the relationship between the market discount rate and the likelihood of extinction of a commercially harvested animal species.

Further reading

Excellent reviews of the state of various renewable resources in the world economy, and experiences with various management regimes are contained in the biannual editions of *World Resources*. See, in particular, the sections in *World Resources 1994–95* on biodiversity (Chapter 8), marine fishing (Chapter 10) and forestry (Chapter 7). Various editions of the *United Nations Environment Programme, Environmental Data Report* also provide good empirical accounts.

Clark (1976), Conrad and Clark (1987) and Dasgupta (1982) provide graduate-level accounts, in quite mathematical form, of the theory of renewable resource depletion, as does Wilen (1985). Good undergraduate accounts are to be found in Fisher (1981, Chapter 3), the survey paper by Peterson and Fisher (1977), Hartwick and Olewiler (1986) and Tietenberg (1992).

Gordon (1954) is a classic paper developing the idea of open access resources. Munro (1981, 1982) provides rigorous accounts of the theory of resource harvesting. Anderson (1985, Chapter 7) gives a very thorough and readable analysis of policy instruments that seek to attain efficient harvesting of fish stocks, using evidence from Canadian experience. That book also provides a good account of models of fluctuating fish populations, an issue of immense practical importance.

Excellent accounts of the notion of a Safe Minimum Standard of Conservation are to be found in Randall and Farmer (1995) and Bishop (1978). Other good references in this area include Ciriacy-Wantrup (1952), Norgaard (1984, 1988), Ehrenfeld (1988) and Common (1995).

Appendix 1

The revenue from resource harvesting

As stated in the text, the precise relationship between total revenue from resource harvesting, V, and the resource stock size, S, will depend upon the specific form taken by the resource demand function. Under plausible and likely conditions, we can show that the relationship will be of the form shown in Figure 7.2, with the revenue to the industry being at a maximum at S_{MSY}.

Assume that the intrinsic growth function is given by

$$G(S) = gS\left(1 - \frac{S}{S_{MAX}}\right) \qquad (7.17)$$

where $g > 0$, and the demand for the renewable resource has a constant price elasticity ϵ_d:

$$P = aG(S)^{1/\epsilon_d} \qquad \text{where} \quad a > 0 \qquad (7.18)$$

The revenue function is then

$$V(S) = PG(S) \qquad (7.19)$$

By substituting Equations 7.18 into 7.19 we have

$$V(S) = PG(S) = aG(S)^{1 + 1/\epsilon_d}$$

Hence

$$\frac{dV(S)}{dS} = \left(1 + \frac{1}{\epsilon_d}\right)aG(S)^{1/\epsilon_d}\frac{dG(S)}{dS}$$

$$= agG(S)\left(1 - \frac{2S}{S_{MAX}}\right) \cdot \left(1 + \frac{1}{\epsilon_d}\right)$$

If $\epsilon_d < -1$, then

$$\frac{dV(S)}{dS} > 0 \quad \text{for} \quad S < S_{MAX}$$

and

$$\frac{dV(S)}{dS} < 0 \quad \text{for} \quad S > S_{MAX}$$

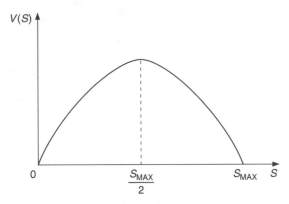

Fig 7.13 The relationship between the revenue from harvesting and the resource stock size.

So when $S = S_{MAX}/2$, revenue $V(S)$ reaches its maximum as indicated in Figure 7.13.

It can also be shown (although we do not do so here) that, in these circumstances, if the parameters of the demand function shift so that demand increases and the resource price becomes higher at any harvested quantity, the revenue function shown in Figures 7.2 and 7.13 will have a higher maximum value. In this case, the open access equilibrium will exist at a lower resource stock level.

Note that the results we have obtained here depend upon the assumptions we made about functional forms of demand and growth functions. They will not necessarily be true in other cases.

Appendix 2

We begin by deriving the socially optimal harvesting programme, in which the parameter r is taken to be the social consumption discount rate. The objective is to maximise discounted social net benefits over an infinite horizon, subject to a resource growth constraint. We may state the problem as

$$\max \int_0^\infty \{B(R_t) - C(R_t, S_t)\} e^{-rt} \, dt$$

subject to

$$\frac{dS}{dt} = G(S_t) - R_t$$

The current-valued Hamiltonian for this problem is

$$H_t = B(R_t) - C(R_t, S_t) + \lambda_t \cdot (G(S_t) - R_t)$$

where λ is a Lagrange multiplier, interpretable as the net price of the renewable resource, and denoted as p in the main body of the text.

The necessary conditions for a maximum are

$$\frac{\partial H_t}{\partial R_t} = 0 = \frac{dB}{dR_t} - \frac{\partial C}{\partial R_t} - \lambda_t \qquad (7.20)$$

$$\frac{d\lambda_t}{dt} = r \cdot \lambda_t - \lambda_t \frac{dG}{dS_t} + \frac{\partial C}{\partial S_t} \qquad (7.21)$$

$$\frac{dS}{dt} = G(S_t) - R_t \qquad (7.22)$$

Note that Equation 7.20 defines the relationship between net price or royalty, gross price and marginal cost; Equation 7.21 is the Hotelling efficient harvesting condition for a renewable resource in which costs depend upon the stock level, and Equation 7.22 is the biological growth equation, taking account of resource harvesting.

We assume that there is an inverse demand function for the resource given by $P_t = P(R_t)$. This implies (see the explanation given in Chapter 10) that $dB/dR_t = P_t$, and so Equation 7.20 can be rewritten as

$$\lambda_t = P_t - \frac{\partial C}{\partial R_t} \qquad (7.23)$$

which states that the net price (marginal rent, or marginal royalty) is equal to the gross (market) price minus the marginal cost of a unit of resource harvested.

Equation 7.21 is often called the asset equilibrium condition. It is a generalised version of the *Hotelling rule efficiency condition* (compare with Equations 7.14).

Initial and terminal conditions

This problem has a single initial condition, namely that there exists a fixed, positive initial stock level, S_0. Let $\{R_T, S_T\}$ denote the terminal, steady-state values of the harvest rate and resource stock, such that

$$\frac{dR}{dt} = 0 \quad \text{and} \quad \frac{dS}{dt} = 0$$

When $S_t < S_T$, R_t should be set at a level such that $R_t < G(S_t)$, so that S_t grows over time and gradually converges to its steady-state value, S_T. Then, as dR/dt gradually converges to zero, the process converges to the terminal steady-state equation

$$r \cdot \lambda = \lambda \frac{dG}{dS} - \frac{\partial C}{\partial S}$$

which upon using the notation p for the net price, can be rewritten as

$$r \cdot p = p\lambda \frac{dG}{dS} - \frac{\partial C}{\partial S}$$

which is identical to Equation 7.15 in the text, with i replaced by r and the equation then multiplied through by r.

Private present value maximising harvesting in a competitive market with enforceable property rights

Let i be the appropriate private discount rate. In this case, the problem is defined as

$$\max \int_0^\infty \{V(R_t) - C(R_t, S_t)\} e^{-it} \, dt$$

subject to

$$\frac{dS}{dt} = G(S_t) - R_t$$

The current-valued Hamiltonian for this problem is

$$H_t = V(R_t) - C(R_t, S_t) + \lambda_t(G(S_t) - R_t)$$

The necessary conditions for a maximum are the same as in the previous case (with i replacing r) except for Equation 7.20 which is now

$$\frac{\partial H_t}{\partial R_t} = 0 = \frac{dV}{dR_t} - \frac{\partial C}{\partial R_t} - \lambda_t \qquad (7.24)$$

Now $V = P.R$. In a competitive market, each firm is a price-taker and so we have $dV/dR = P$ in equilibrium. Given this, the profit-maximising conditions for a perfectly competitive industry in which the resource is privately owned and excludable will be identical to that for the social optimum, provided the social discount rate, r, equals the private discount rate, i.

Private present value-maximising harvesting in a monopolistic market with enforceable property rights

For a monopolistic industry, $V = P(R).R$ and so

$$\frac{dV}{dR} = \frac{d}{dR}(P(R) \cdot R) = \frac{dP}{dR} \cdot R + P(R)$$

and so $dV/dR < P$, as $dP/dR < 0$. Hence the monopolistic profit-maximising solution is different from the socially optimal solution. To see precisely how it is different, look at Equations 7.20 and 7.24 under the two alternative market structures.

Monopoly:

$$P(R) = \frac{\partial C}{\partial R} + \lambda_T - \frac{dP}{dR} \cdot R$$

Competition:

$$P(R) = \frac{\partial C}{\partial R} + \lambda_T$$

Now as dP/dR is negative, this implies that the market price is higher in monopolistic than in competitive markets, and so less is harvested and sold. One would expect the stock size to be larger in monopolistic than in competitive markets.

Appendix 3

As we are considering steady states only, the stock level S and the harvest rate R are each constant. So, provided the demand function does not change over time, dp/dt is zero in a steady state. Imposing this on the Hotelling rule, Equation 7.13, we obtain

$$ip = -\frac{\partial C}{\partial S} + \frac{dG}{dS} \cdot p \qquad (7.25)$$

Now if $i = 0$, then from Equation 7.25 we would have

$$\frac{\partial C}{\partial S} = \frac{dG}{dS} \cdot p \qquad (7.26)$$

But as $p = P - c$ (where $c = \partial C / \partial R$) then

$$\frac{\partial C}{\partial S} = \frac{dG}{dS} \cdot (P - c)$$

$$\frac{\partial C}{\partial S} = \frac{dG}{dS} \cdot P - \frac{dG}{dS} \cdot c$$

or

$$\frac{\partial G}{\partial S} \cdot P = \frac{dG}{dS} \cdot c + \frac{\partial C}{\partial S}$$

This is the condition for maximising the net present value of the renewable resource. The left-hand side can be interpreted as the steady-state marginal revenue of harvesting, the right-hand side the steady-state marginal cost of harvesting, taking account of the dependence of costs on effort, the cost per unit effort *and* the dependence of cost on the size of the resource stock.

Appendix 4

Suppose the objective is to maximise the present value of discounted net benefits, where $NB = B - C$. That is, we wish to maximise $Z = NB(t) e^{-rt}$. This requires that $\partial Z/\partial t = 0$. Obtaining this derivative we have

$$-r(B_t - C_t)\,e^{-rt} + e^{-rt}\left(\frac{\mathrm{d}B_t}{\mathrm{d}t} - \frac{\mathrm{d}C_t}{\mathrm{d}t}\right) = 0$$

Rearranging this condition, we obtain

$$r = \frac{\left(\dfrac{\mathrm{d}B_t}{\mathrm{d}t} - \dfrac{\mathrm{d}C_t}{\mathrm{d}t}\right)}{B_t - C_t}$$

or

$$r = \frac{\dfrac{\mathrm{d}}{\mathrm{d}t}(\mathrm{NB}_t)}{\mathrm{NB}_t}$$

So the maximisation of the present value of net benefits (the initial equation) is equivalent to the rate of growth of undiscounted net benefits being set equal to the discount rate, r (the last equation).

CHAPTER 8

The economics of pollution

The use of coal was prohibited in London in 1273, and at least one person was put to death for this offence around 1300. Why did it take economists so long to recognise and analyse the problem?

Fisher (1981), page 164

Pollution: physical and economic meanings

Pigou (1920) appears to have been the first writer to have presented a systematic economic analysis of pollution. This arose from his development of the concept of externalities. Despite Pigou's original work, little further attention was given either to externalities or to the economics of pollution prior to 1950. During the 1950s, the theory of externalities was extended and developed, and in the 1960s economists began to turn their attention to the economics of pollution.

Important early work was done by Boulding (1966) who demonstrated that residual materials are not unusual or unimportant local difficulties. On the contrary, residuals are an intrinsic part of economic activity, and will be with us increasingly as activity levels rise. The earth is a closed materials system, in which materials flows must satisfy the laws of thermodynamics; residuals will be equal in mass to the total amounts of fuels, food and raw materials entering the economy, after deduction of materials accumulated as inventories and quantities recycled. Pollution is a pervasive phenomenon in a materially growing economy.

Let us now make clear precisely what we mean by pollution. To a natural or environmental scientist, pollution refers to those residual flows, arising from human behaviour, that enter environmental systems. These residuals may then have effects upon the environmental systems into which they flow. These flows will often have a material form, such as emissions of carbon monoxide from coal and oil combustion. In this case the word *residual* is apposite as the pollutant results from a production or consumption process in which the conversion of inputs into outputs is less than fully efficient in a physical sense. That is, not all of the mass of inputs is combined into useful output; some of the input is converted into unwanted or residual outputs.

One way of thinking about pollution was outlined in Chapter 1, where we outlined a materials balance model representing flow interactions between the economy and the environment. Residuals, in the form of mass or energy, from economic processes enter environmental media (air, soils, biota and water sub-systems), imposing waste or emissions loads upon the environment. The extent to which these waste loads cause subsequent damage depends upon the absorptive capacity of the relevant environmental media. This idea is illustrated in Figure 8.1. Some proportion of the emission flows from economic activity is quickly absorbed and transformed by environmental media into harmless forms. The remaining pollution flows may cause damage directly and instantaneously, and may also, by accumulating as pollutant stocks, cause additional damage over future periods of time. Stocks of pollutants will usually decay into harmless forms over time, but in some cases (infinitely persistent pollutants) the rate of decay will be approximately zero.

In some cases, the absorptive capacity of environmental media is sufficiently high to ensure that the whole amount of waste is naturally processed, so that no pollutants remain to accumulate and cause damage. In other cases, the quantity of emissions is too large to be fully processed, and so the waste flows may accumulate and cause damage to ecosystems and, perhaps, to human welfare.

To form an appropriate framework for economic analysis, two additional points should be noted. Firstly, pollution flows may not exist as material wastes from economic activities; put another way,

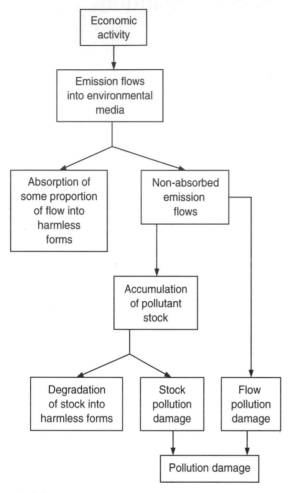

Fig 8.1 Economic activity, residual flows and environmental damage.

economy–environment interactions. We return to this point below.

The second point to note is that the economist is ultimately interested in the impacts of production and consumption processes upon welfare. Not all residual flows have impacts upon human welfare, and nor do all residual flows have adverse impacts upon ecological systems. If a waste flow is processed completely and instantaneously by the environment, or, even when unprocessed, has no impact upon environmental quality, then no damage is associated with the waste flow. The economist is particularly concerned with those flows which have damaging consequences (directly or indirectly), and so we reserve the term *pollution* to refer to the net flows – those exceeding the absorptive capacity of the environment, and which have damaging effects upon human welfare or upon ecological systems in general.[1]

Pollution and the depletion of the quality or quantity of environmental resources

The first section has offered an interpretation of pollution as waste flows from the economic system into the environmental system, which have damaging effects upon human welfare or ecological systems. If we turn our attention to the consequences of pollution (that is, the pollution damage), it turns out to be useful to view pollution damage in terms of its impact upon environmental resources.

In some cases, pollution affects the *quantity* of an environmental resource. One can easily find examples where the magnitude of residuals flows can affect the quantity of an environmental resource. Pollutant levels certainly affect the magnitudes of plant and timber growth, and the size of marine populations. But effects of pollution on the growth rates of renewable resources by no means exhaust the possibilities. Suppose that we choose to regard the quantity of the absorptive capacity of the environment as an environmental resource. This capacity often seems to depend upon the emissions load to

they may not be residuals in the sense in which we have just used that word. For example, the production of noise or light may have negative effects upon some people's welfare, but such emissions are not necessarily unwanted by-products of production processes. Consider the case of noise generated by an open-air pop concert; this is the intended product of the concert, and presumably gives utility to those who choose to be in the audience. But for some persons living nearby, the noise may be an undesirable intrusion, and they may well refer to it as 'noise pollution'. Similar arguments could be made about light pollution arising from urban lighting. These examples suggest that pollution may arise as production or consumption externalities, in ways which do not appear in materials-balance models of

[1] Note, however, that we *may* choose to define human welfare in a broad sense, and regard human welfare as being affected by the conditions of existence of non-human lives. In the final analysis, the choice of what constitutes 'human welfare' for any particular society is essentially a political choice (and is outside the realms of economics).

which the relevant environmental media are exposed. This appears to be the case, for example, with water systems. The case of greenhouse gas emissions provides another illustration of this relationship. The stock of greenhouse gases (GHG) in the atmosphere does not in general rise each period by an amount equal to the gross emission flow of GHG emissions. Part of the reason for this is that the oceans absorb some proportion of the emissions. However, that proportion is not a constant over time, but varies with ocean temperature and also, possibly, with the total quantity of the GHG emitted in previous time. Here we have a case, then, where the quantity of the cleaning capacity of the environment is affected by the quantity of waste emissions into the environment.

In other cases, pollution affects the *quality* of environmental resources, such as the extent of biological diversity, the health of animal or plant populations, the degree of peace or solitude in a wilderness area, or the quality of the air we breathe. Changes in the quality of environmental resources may have effects upon welfare even more profound than changes in quantity, as exemplified by the health damages associated with air pollution (see the Case Study in Chapter 4 for some evidence on this matter). Throughout the present chapter, our analysis assumes for simplicity that pollution damages are measurable in quantitative terms. It would not be difficult, though, to recast the discussions which follow in terms which correspond to qualitative damage effects, or, more generally, to model pollution flows as affecting both the quality and quantity of environmental resources.

Classification of forms of pollution

In this section we classify pollution into stationary source and mobile source air pollution, water pollution, and persistent toxic pollution, and also into local, regional and global pollution; and we examine the degree of mobility and mixing of pollutants. For some purposes, it is useful to think about pollution as a single-dimensional homogeneous quantity. However, for many other purposes, it is preferable to recognise the heterogeneous nature of pollution flows and stocks. In the following chapter, we shall demonstrate that the best policy instruments for dealing with pollution problems are likely to be quite different for different types of

pollutant. There are many ways in which one might classify pollutants. We shall focus in this text on four dimensions of pollution, having the greatest bearing upon the economic analysis of pollution and pollution control.

Dimension 1: The nature of the emissions–damage relationship

Here we look at pollution damage arising from residual flows and pollution damage arising from residual stocks. It is useful to distinguish between these two forms of pollution, in terms of the manner in which pollution damage takes place.

Flow pollution occurs when damages result from the level of the flow of residuals, that is the rate over time at which they are being discharged into the environmental system. The 'purest' example of flow pollution is noise pollution. By definition, for pure cases of flow pollution, the damage will instantaneously drop to zero if the polluting flow becomes zero. This is only likely to occur when the pollutant exists in an energy form such as noise, so that when the energy emission is terminated, no residuals remain in existence. However, many forms of pollution are such that the damage done at some point in time depends almost entirely upon the current rate of emissions. Whilst the wastes are not instantly reprocessed or do not have infinitely short lives, processing is sufficiently quick to prevent the build-up of a damaging stock of the pollutant. Emissions such as these may be regarded as approximately fitting the description of a flow pollutant.

We define *stock pollution* as occurring when damages are a function of the stock of the residual in the relevant environmental system at any point in time. Damages result from the concentration rate of the pollutant in the environmental medium, rather than from the flow level itself. For a stock of the pollutant to accumulate, it is necessary that emissions are being produced at a rate which exceeds the absorptive capacity of the environment. An extreme case is that in which the absorptive capacity is zero, as seems to be the case for some synthetic chemicals and a number of heavy metals. Metals such as mercury or lead accumulate in soils, aquifers and biological stocks, and subsequently in the human body, causing major damage to human health. Persistent synthetic chemicals, such as PCBs (polychlorinated biphenyls), DDT and dioxins, have similar cycles and effects. Rubbish which cannot biodegrade is another case. Strongly radioactive elements such as plutonium with extremely long radiation half-lives are close to but not identical with the pure stock pollution case, as the radiative flows do decay gradually, but only over very long periods of time.

Pollution damage may also result from a mixture of these flow and stock effects. Indeed, the majority of pollutants are probably mixed cases, with the nature of the mixture varying over time and space. Organic and inorganic waste emissions into water systems are examples of mixed stock/flow pollutants, as are damages arising from the emissions of compounds of carbon, sulphur and nitrogen; their effects depend upon relevant stock levels (for example, the atmospheric concentration of GHG determines the long-run impact upon temperature) and upon flow levels (for example, the magnitudes of the GHG flows influence how rapidly temperature will rise).

Dimension 2: Horizontal zone of influence

Local pollution damage is experienced only near the emission source. This characterises sound, light, and visual pollution flows. *Regional* damage is experienced near the emission source and also at greater distances. For example, sulphur and nitrogen oxides generate (at least) regional damage. *Global* damage is experienced throughout the whole global economy, although not necessarily equally at all points in space.

Dimension 3: Degree of atmospheric mixing of pollutant

Surface pollutant damage is related to pollution flows or concentrations at or near the surface level. This includes all forms of water pollution, and many categories of air pollution, such as carbon monoxide and ozone smogs. *Global* pollutant damage is related to pollutant concentrations in the upper atmospheric levels. This characterises, for example, carbon dioxide (CO_2) and CFCs in their roles as greenhouse gases, and also CFC emissions in their roles as destroyers of the ozone layer in the upper atmosphere.

Dimension 4: Mobility of emission sources

We distinguish between *stationary* source and *mobile* source pollution. Many pollutants derive from sources which have stationary locations in space, such as power stations and pesticide use in agriculture. Others are associated with geographically mobile sources, the most important example of which is vehicle traffic pollution.

The efficient level of pollution

In this chapter, our primary objective is to show how one could identify an efficient level of pollution (or, equivalently, pollution abatement or control). We shall do this first of all for the relatively simple case where the pollutant in question is a flow pollutant. Then we establish some results for the more complex case in which a pollutant is a pure stock pollutant or is of a mixed form, in which damage is caused by both the current flow and the current stock levels.

At some points in the presentation, we shall make use of an objective (or welfare) function, which decision-makers aim to maximise. When this is done, we can then claim that any solution which maximises such an objective function is *optimal* (as well as efficient) with respect to that objective function. This will enable us to make statements about how much pollution there should be, or how much pollution control should take place, because the objective function will embody the preferences of the affected parties.

However, a note of caution should be introduced. Many forms of pollution affect only subsets of people living in a particular society. Sometimes, it is convenient to look at cost and benefit functions for only that subset of people affected by the pollutant in question. Whenever this is done, we can claim that a solution to the problem is efficient for the persons concerned. But it is not correct in these circumstances to argue that such an outcome is socially optimal, as we will not necessarily have maximised a welfare function embodying preferences for the whole community.

The key principle lying behind efficiency concepts, you will remember, is that of Pareto improvements. If a given allocation of resources is one in which a Pareto improvement is possible, that allocation cannot be an efficient one. Put another way, an efficient allocation is one in which no Pareto gains are possible. In this chapter, we interpret a pollutant as a good produced, along with other goods, by the use of resources. Of course, this good is different from many others in so far as its consumption confers negative utility; for this reason, such goods are sometimes described as 'bads'. We could describe a pattern of resource use at some point in time (a static allocation) or a pattern of resource use over time (an inter-temporal allocation) as inefficient if, for example, we are able to show that Pareto gains are possible. To keep matters simple, our discussions throughout this chapter will be carried out treating the economy as a single aggregate unit, that will usually be referred to as 'society'. Thus, for example, we shall discuss society's costs or damages of pollution, and the social cost of controlling or abating pollution.

How can we set about trying to identify the efficient level of pollution? Pollution flows are clearly undesirable in themselves as they are damaging, either to us humans, or to some biological or physical systems. Looking at costs in isolation, we should like these costs to be as low as possible. But there is a trade-off here, which lies at the heart of the problem. Existing technology does not allow us to produce or consume goods or services without generating residuals of one form or another. Indeed, fundamental principles from physics suggest that this will never be possible; mass cannot be destroyed and ultimately everything we produce must be returned to the environment in some residual forms. So the production of goods and services is desirable; looking at output benefits in isolation, we should like these to be as high as possible. The trade-off, then, arises from the fact that production creates some desirable outputs but also some undesirable outputs.

An efficient output level would be one that maximises the net output, the difference between the desirable components of output generating positive utility and the undesirable components, pollutants, yielding negative utility. For reasons that will become clear shortly, however, it is more useful to us to visualise this trade-off in terms of pollution rather than output. The efficient level of pollution will be the level which maximises the net benefit of the pollution flow, where

$$
\begin{aligned}
\text{Net benefit of} \\
\text{pollution (NB)}
\end{aligned}
=
\begin{aligned}
&\text{Benefit of the output with} \\
&\text{which the pollution is} \\
&\text{associated } (B) \\
&-\text{Damages resulting from} \\
&\text{the pollution } (D)
\end{aligned}
$$

The efficient level of flow pollution

We begin by considering the case where the current pollution damage is related to the current flow of pollution:

$$D_t = D(\Psi_t)$$

Notice that this function is one in which the functional relationship between damage and pollution is not time-dependent. Although the level of damage can change because the pollution level changes, the relationship between the two is constant through time. Such a relationship is possible in the case of flow pollution, but, as we shall see in the following section, cannot be correct for stock pollutants, where the damage is not just a function of current levels of pollution but also depends upon the whole history of previous flows.

However, even when attention is restricted to flow pollution, it is not necessarily correct to argue that the value of damages is a time-invariant function of the current level of pollution. For example, the damage associated with a particular level of noise pollution may change over time if our preferences for a noise-free environment change. We shall see in Chapter 10 that Krutilla has hypothesised that the value of wilderness areas will tend to rise over time because of rising living standards and the asymmetric implications of technical progress. If this is true, the value of a constant physical quantity of damage will not be independent of time. Nevertheless, for reasons of simplicity, we begin with the special case of a time-invariant damage function.

In these circumstances, the value of damage in any period relates only to the pollutant flow in that period. We can select any one time period in isolation from all others and calculate the efficient level of pollution from knowledge of damages and benefits associated with pollution in that period alone, using the definition of net benefit given at the end of the preceding section.

How are damages and benefits related to the flow of pollution? The answer to this question will depend upon a number of things, including the type of pollutant and the place and time we are considering. However, it is probable that most damage and benefit functions will have the general forms shown in Figure 8.2. Note that this diagram employs marginal rather than total functions. The marginal damage arising from a pollutant is likely to rise with the size of the pollution flow, as shown in the diagram.

It may appear paradoxical to refer to the 'benefits' of pollution. What are these benefits? The relevant measure of benefits of pollution is the benefit that is derived from the output of goods and services with which the pollution is associated, net of the costs of

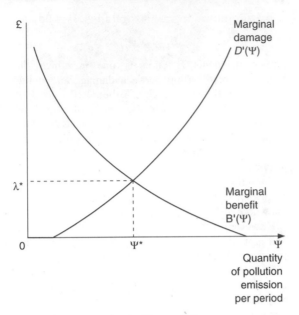

Fig 8.2 The efficient level of flow pollution.

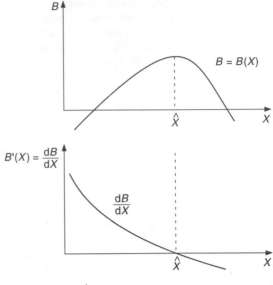

Key:

 B = Total benefit
 $B'(X) = \mathrm{d}B/\mathrm{d}X$ = Marginal benefit (per unit of output)
 $B'(\Psi) = \mathrm{d}B/\mathrm{d}\Psi$ = Marginal benefit (per unit of pollution)

Fig 8.3 Total and marginal pollution benefits.

production (that is, value added). Let us explain this idea more carefully. Suppose that the quantity of pollution emitted in production, Ψ, is proportional to the output of some useful good or service, X. That is

$$\Psi = kX$$

where k is a constant number. Then the benefit (B) of one unit of emission is the benefit from $1/k$ units of good X. Now suppose the relationship between total benefits and output is as shown in the top part of Figure 8.3.[2] By differentiation, one can obtain from this the relationship between marginal benefits and output as shown in the central diagram. Given the constant proportional relationship between pollution and output, we can then obtain the marginal benefits–pollution relationship as shown in the lower diagram of the figure, where, for simplicity, we have assumed $k = 1$. More generally, pollution may be functionally related (but not necessarily proportional) to output; if so, a mapping is possible from output to pollution, which allows us to construct the marginal benefits–pollution relationship. Standard microeconomic theory leads one to expect the marginal net benefits function to be a declining function of pollution, as

[2] The shape of the benefits in Figure 8.3 is, of course, just one possibility out of many. It could be justified, however, using the conventional assumption of diminishing marginal utility.

shown in the bottom part of Figure 8.3. This relationship generates the curve labelled 'Marginal benefit' in Figure 8.2.

The story we have just told is misleading in one very important way, as it assumes that a functional relationship exists between output and pollution. But a unique relationship may not exist. As we show in the following chapter, environmental policy itself will alter this relationship; indeed, one could argue that the main purpose of environmental policy is to do exactly that. If, for example, a pollution tax is applied to industrial emissions, firms are likely to change production techniques in such a way as to reduce the amount of emissions for any given level of output. So in general, it is difficult to establish the linkages between pollution benefits and the level of pollution, as that requires that we incorporate substitution effects and technology changes by producers. Nevertheless, it is possible to obtain such a relationship, and you should interpret the marginal benefit function in Figure 8.2 and at all subsequent places in this chapter as showing the relationship between the marginal benefits of pollution and the level of pollution, *incorporating any behavioural adjustments that take place as the pollution level is varied*.

Now let us return to the main line of argument. We have previously defined the social net benefit of pollution, NB(Ψ), as the benefits of pollution, $B(\Psi)$, less the social damages of pollution, $D(\Psi)$. That is

$$\text{NB}(\Psi_t) = B(\Psi_t) - D(\Psi_t)$$

To maximise the net benefits of economic activity, we require that the pollution flow, Ψ_t, be selected so that

$$\frac{d\text{NB}(\Psi_t)}{d\Psi_t} = \frac{dB(\Psi_t)}{d\Psi_t} - \frac{dD(\Psi_t)}{d\Psi_t} = 0$$

or equivalently that

$$\frac{dB(\Psi_t)}{d\Psi_t} - \frac{dD(\Psi_t)}{d\Psi_t} = 0$$

which states that the *net* benefits of pollution are maximised where the marginal benefits of pollution equal the marginal damage of pollution.

The equilibrium 'price' of pollution, denoted as λ^* in Figure 8.2, is a shadow price and has a particular significance in terms of an optimal rate of emissions tax, as we shall discover in the following chapter. There is no market for pollution, and so this 'price' is not an existing market price. Rather, it is a hypothetical price, implied by the solution to a problem in which we are interested. In this case, λ^* is the implied price of a unit of pollution at the socially optimal level of pollution, and is equal to the marginal damage of pollution at that level. If a market were, somehow or other, to exist for the pollutant itself so that firms had to purchase rights to emit units of the pollutant, λ^* would be the efficient market price.

The economically efficient level of pollution is Ψ^*, as pollution levels lower or higher than that would yield a smaller quantity of net benefits than that attainable at Ψ^*. If pollution is less than Ψ^*, the marginal benefits of pollution are greater than the marginal damage from pollution, so higher pollution will yield additional net benefits. Conversely, if pollution is greater than Ψ^*, the marginal benefits of pollution are less than the marginal damage from pollution, so less pollution will yield more net benefits.

An alternative exposition in terms of pollution abatement

Discussion and analysis of policy relating to pollution is often conducted in terms of the amount of control or abatement which is implied by efficiency considerations. To set the framework for this in the following chapter, we can reinterpret the information in Figure 8.2 in a way that explicitly incorporates abatement costs. Figure 8.4a contains the same marginal pollution damage function, but contains a marginal abatement cost function instead of a marginal pollution benefit function. Assume that $\hat{\Psi}$ is the uncontrolled pollution level, the level of pollution that would take place in a market economy where government took no steps to abate pollution. Notice that the amount of abatement increases as one moves *leftwards* along the horizontal axis, with complete abatement (that is, zero pollution) at the origin in Figure 8.4a. We have drawn the marginal abatement cost (MAC) function to show marginal abatement costs as an increasing function of the amount of abatement undertaken in any period.

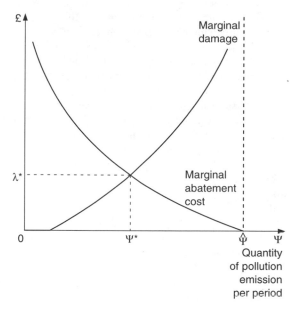

Key:

$\hat{\Psi}$ = Uncontrolled level of pollution per period
Ψ^* = Efficient level of pollution per period
$(\hat{\Psi} - \Psi^*)$ = Efficient level of pollution abatement per period

Fig 8.4a The efficient level of pollution and pollution abatement.

How do the abatement cost and the pollution benefit functions in Figures 8.2 and 8.4a relate to one another? If the only way of abating pollution is by reducing output, the cost of abatement would be equal to the value added foregone, and so the abatement cost function would be identical to the marginal benefits of pollution function illustrated in Figure 8.3. But in general, pollution can be abated in many ways, some of which may be more cost-effective than by reducing output. You will recall that we have chosen to interpret the marginal benefit function in Figure 8.2 as *incorporating* behavioural adjustments by firms as pollution levels change. This means that it is identical to the marginal abatement cost function shown in Figure 8.4a, and explains why the shapes and positions of the functions in the two diagrams are identical.

We are now in a position to be able to identify the efficient level of pollution abatement. Looking at Figure 8.4a, it is evident that the *efficient level of pollution abatement* is the distance $\hat{\Psi} - \Psi^*$, where $\hat{\Psi}$ is the uncontrolled pollution level, and Ψ^* is the *efficient level of pollution*. The shadow price λ^* shown in Figure 8.4a has the same interpretation we offered in the previous section – it is the value of the damage caused by pollution (or equivalently, the value of pollution abatement) at the efficient level of pollution abatement.

An examination of Figure 8.4b shows that the efficient level of pollution is the one that minimises the sum of total abatement costs plus total damage costs. Exactly the same, of course, is true for the efficient level of pollution abatement. To see this, note that at the efficient pollution level, the sum of total damage costs (the area C_2) and total abatement costs (the area C_1) is $C_2 + C_1$. Any other level of pollution yields higher total costs. If, for example, 'too much' abatement is undertaken and the pollution flow is reduced to Ψ_A, it can be deduced that total costs rise to $C_1 + C_2 + C_3$, so C_3 is the efficiency loss arising from the excessive abatement. If you cannot see how this conclusion is reached, please look now at Problem 2 at the end of this chapter. You should also convince yourself that too little abatement results in higher costs than $C_1 + C_2$.

It can also be deduced from Figures 8.2 and 8.4b that the economically efficient level of pollution will not, in general, be zero. (By implication, the economically efficient level of pollution abatement will not, in general, correspond to that level which fully eliminates pollution.) Problem 1 examines this matter.

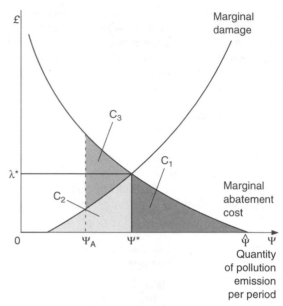

Fig 8.4b The economically efficient level of pollution minimises the sum of abatement and damage costs.

Stock pollution

Stock pollution is pollution in which damages are determined by the stock size of the persistent pollutant. The analysis of the efficient level of a stock pollutant is more complex than was the case for a flow pollutant. Where a flow pollutant is concerned, the fact that damages in any period relate only to the emission level in that period means that time periods may be treated as independent. The researcher can, in principle, establish the efficient level of flow emission in 1995 without reference to any other year. Furthermore, *ceteris paribus*, the solution for any one period is also the solution for every other period.

However, the essential nature of a stock pollutant leads to a breakdown of this independence between time periods. Stock pollutants persist through time, and so current emissions add to the current *and future* stock levels, causing damage which will persist through time, even if the emission were to be stopped immediately. In extreme cases where the pollutant is perfectly persistent, the stock of the pollutant will be the sum of all previous emission flows, and the damages which arise will last indefinitely. This is approximately true for some synthetic chemicals, such as heavy metal residuals, and toxins such as DDT and dioxin. More generally, the pollutant stock will gradually decay over time, being converted into relatively harmless elements or compounds. Greenhouse gases, for example, are not perfectly persistent, but do nevertheless have very slow rates of decay (see Chapter 12 for further details).

A consequence of these observations is that in determining the efficient level of stock pollution, we must take into account the fact that the pollutant accumulates over time, often generating a sequence of damages that become increasingly large. Even if the flow of pollution emissions were constant, the damage associated with that flow will rise over time. Furthermore, an efficient allocation of the pollutant must refer now to a path of pollution flows through time, rather than to the flow in just one time period. In this section, we shall describe the nature of an efficient allocation of a stock pollutant, without attempting to present a formal derivation. A formal exposition of the argument is presented in Appendix 1.

The general principle which underlies the analysis of this problem is identical to that for a flow pollutant; an efficient quantity of pollution is one which maximises net benefits to society. The differences arise because

- we need to maximise the net benefit over some relevant time horizon when considering stock pollutants, and
- the way in which damages enter the problem is more complex.

Let us begin by specifying the benefit and damage functions for stock pollutants. The benefit function is identical to that in the flow pollution case; that is, gross benefits B are assumed to be a function of the flow level of pollution Ψ:

$$B_t = B(\Psi_t)$$

Now let us consider damages. To keep matters as general as possible, we assume that damages arise both from the level of the pollution flow at some point in time:

$$D_t = D(\Psi_t)$$

and from the size of the pollution stock Q:

$$D_t^\Delta = D^\Delta(Q_t)$$

Notice that we are using different notation for the two types of damage relationship. D is damage resulting from the current flow of pollution, whilst D^Δ is damage resulting from the current level of the pollution stock.

How is the size of the pollution stock determined? For the case of a perfectly persistent pollutant, the stock level at time t is simply the sum of all previous pollution flows:

$$Q_t = \int_0^t \Psi(\tau)\, d\tau$$

However, most stock pollutants do not persist perfectly, as the pollutant has a limited 'life'. During its existence, the pollutant decays or is otherwise transformed into harmless forms. In this case, part of the stock disappears in each period through natural processes. For simplicity, let us assume that θ denotes a fixed proportion of the pollution stock which decays in each period. Then the stock at time t will be the sum of all previous pollution emissions *less* the sum of all previous pollution decay. That is

$$Q_t = \int_0^t (\Psi(\tau) - \theta Q(\tau))\, d\tau$$

Let us now define the objective function for this problem. The net benefit (NB) from economic activity at a point in time t is the benefit from consumption of goods net of the private or internal production costs (B), less

- D, the damages resulting from the emission flow at t, and
- D^Δ, the damages arising from the stock level at time t.

Thus we have

$$NB_t = B[\Psi_t] - D[\Psi_t] - D^\Delta[Q_t]$$

Assuming that our objective function discounts net benefits at a social consumption discount rate r, the efficient path of pollution flows over time is the one which maximises the discounted (or present) value of net social benefits. That is, our objective is to choose a sequence of pollutant emission flows, $\Psi(t)$, $t = 0$ to $t = \infty$, to maximise

$$\int_{t=0}^{t=\infty} e^{-rt} NB_t\, dt$$

or expressed in full

$$\int_{t=0}^{t=\infty} \{B[\Psi_t] - D[\Psi_t] - D^\Delta[Q_t]\} e^{-rt}\, dt$$

subject to the constraint

$$\frac{dQ_t}{dt} = \Psi_t - \theta Q_t$$

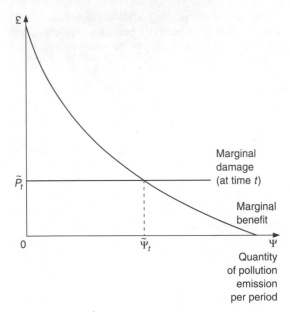

Key:

$$\text{Marginal benefit} = \frac{\mathrm{d}B}{\mathrm{d}\Psi} - \frac{\mathrm{d}D}{\mathrm{d}\Psi}$$

= current (period t) marginal benefit of allowing pollution to rise by one unit

Marginal damage = P_t = the foregone future benefit arising from the increased pollution stock that results from allowing the current level of pollution to rise by one unit

The symbol ~ denotes an efficient level for a variable at the given point time, t

Fig 8.5 The (temporary) efficient flow level of pollution, at time t, for a stock pollutant.

where P is the shadow price of a unit of the pollutant, or the marginal social value of a unit of emissions. For notational simplicity, we have omitted time period subscripts; all variables refer to time period t, except where otherwise stated. Let us interpret these two equations.

Equation 8.1 corresponds to Equation 8.6 in Appendix 1, with one difference in that P in 8.1 is equal to $-\lambda$ in 8.6. The term on the right-hand side of Equation 8.1, P, is a shadow price. It is the shadow price of a unit of the pollutant, equal to the loss in future net benefit that arises when the output of the pollutant is allowed to rise by one unit. The term on the left-hand side of Equation 8.1 is the increase in the current net benefit that arises when the output of the pollutant is allowed to rise by one unit. Clearly, an efficient solution requires that the current net benefit of a marginal unit of pollution equals the loss in future net benefit that arises from the marginal unit of pollution. This marginal balancing is illustrated in Figure 8.5.

It is very important to note that the functions drawn in Figure 8.5 refer to only one point in time. Although for a given value of Ψ, $\mathrm{d}B/\mathrm{d}\Psi$ and $\mathrm{d}D/\mathrm{d}\Psi$ may be constant over time, $\tilde{P}_t$ will not be constant over time. The reason is simple; we are dealing here with stock pollutants. As the stock accumulates through time, the stock damage D^Δ rises, and so $\tilde{P}_t$ rises too, as shown in Figure 8.6a. This implies that the efficient pollution flow level will fall through time, as shown in Figure 8.6b.

What is the eventual outcome of this process? For a perfectly persistent pollutant, each emitted unit will permanently raise the stock by one unit. In this case, $\tilde{P}_t$ will rise indefinitely, provided that pollution is

This constraint is obtained by differentiating the previous expression for Q with respect to time, and states that the rate of change of the pollution stock is equal to the pollution flow minus the rate of pollution stock decay. The derivation of the solution to this problem is presented in Appendix 1. Here, we just state the solution, interpret that solution intuitively, and discuss some of its characteristics.

The solution involves the following two necessary conditions:

$$\frac{\mathrm{d}B}{\mathrm{d}\Psi} - \frac{\mathrm{d}D}{\mathrm{d}\Psi} = P \qquad (8.1)$$

$$rP = \frac{\mathrm{d}P}{\mathrm{d}t} - \frac{\mathrm{d}D^\Delta}{\mathrm{d}Q} - \theta P \qquad (8.2)$$

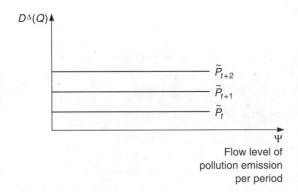

Fig 8.6a Rising stock damage over time for a persistent pollutant.

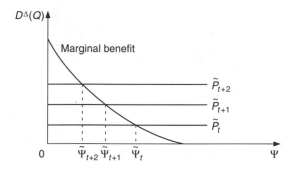

Fig 8.6b The efficient level of pollution falling over time for a persistent (stock) pollutant.

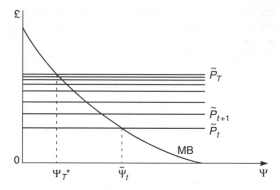

Fig 8.7b A finite but positive efficient level of pollution flow for an imperfectly persistent stock pollutant.

positive in each period. The sequence will end as shown in Figure 8.7a; at some point in time (say period T) stock damage will have become so great that it will exceed the marginal net benefits of pollution for any level of Ψ. Optimal pollution, and so optimal output, will fall to zero at time T. This is a very strong result – any activity that generates perfectly persistent pollutants that lead to *any* positive level of damage cannot be carried on indefinitely. At or before time T, a technology switch is required so that the pollutant is not emitted; if that is not possible, the activity itself must cease. The policy implications of this result are discussed further in the following chapter. However, from the analysis we have undertaken, one can deduce that to cope with the rising social cost of producing the final output, the quantity of resources devoted to abating the pollution, recycling the residuals, or processing the residuals into harmless forms should rise.

However, for a pollutant that decays over time, a sustainable and positive level of pollution is feasible.

Recall the stock evolution equation

$$\frac{\mathrm{d}Q_t}{\mathrm{d}t} = \Psi_t - \theta Q_t$$

Now consider a situation in which Ψ_t exceeds θQ_t. This must result in an increase in the pollution stock level. Eventually, Q_t will have risen to the point where $\theta Q_t = \Psi_t$, at which point the stock remains at a constant steady-state level. Such a steady state is illustrated in Figure 8.7b. At time T and thereafter, the pollution flow level attains a constant, positive, steady state level, Ψ_T, and the following equalities are satisfied:

$$\theta Q_T = \theta Q^* = \Psi_T = \Psi^*$$

where asterisks indicate constant steady-state levels of a variable. Some additional analysis of the steady state for this problem is given in Appendix 2.

Now let us interpret the second necessary condition, Equation 8.2, that corresponds to Equation 8.7 in Appendix 1. Once again, P in Equation 8.2 is the exact counterpart of $-\lambda$ in Equation 8.7. It is the marginal social value of a unit of emissions. The best way of thinking about Equation 8.2 is as an asset equilibrium condition. Think of the 'environment' as being a depletable natural resource stock. Pollution

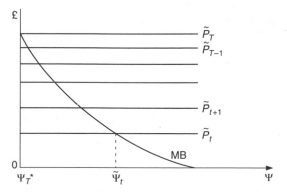

Fig 8.7a The efficient level of pollution flow is eventually zero for a perfectly persistent stock pollutant.

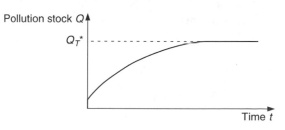

Fig 8.7c The efficient size of the pollution stock over time for a persistent pollutant.

emissions use up units of this depletable environmental stock. Now suppose we decide to defer the extraction of one unit of the resource by one period. This is equivalent to deferring a unit of pollution until one period into the future.

Now P is the marginal social value of a unit of emissions. By deferring the benefits of pollution by one period, a loss of P times the discount rate r is incurred (in the same way as being given £1 one period later when the interest rate is r involves a loss to an individual of £r). So the component on the left-hand side of the equation, rP, is the *cost* of reducing pollution (and so adding to the environmental resource stock) by one unit for one period. This is also known as the holding cost or the carrying cost of the pollution.

The *benefits* of less pollution (that is, adding to the environment stock) are given by the components on the right-hand side of Equation 8.2. These benefits consist of (i) the increased benefit by polluting one period later (dP/dt) and (ii) the stock damage that is avoided by polluting later (dD^Δ/dQ). The presence of the third term, θP, arises because if the pollutant had been emitted during this period, a proportion θ of it would have decayed by the next period; this 'benefit' is lost when the emission is deferred. In the case of a perfectly persistent pollutant, of course, this term disappears from Equation 8.2 as the natural decay rate of the pollutant, θ, is zero. This interpretation of Equation 8.2 is illustrated in Figure 8.8.

We can also write Equation 8.2 in a form that will be more familiar. Dividing Equation 8.2 by P, we obtain

$$r = \frac{\left(\dfrac{dP}{dt}\right)}{P} + \frac{\left(\dfrac{dD^\Delta}{dQ} - \theta P\right)}{P}$$

which is just a version of Hotelling's rule. More precisely, it is Hotelling's rule for the efficient intertemporal allocation of an environmental resource, generalised to the case of a resource which is diminished in quantity as pollution takes place, and where the pollutant has stock as well as flow effects. The resource which is being extracted here is 'the natural environment'; we are regarding this as being reduced as pollution rises.

Convexity and non-convexity in damage and abatement cost functions

In the conventional exposition of the theory of efficient pollution, an assumption is made about the

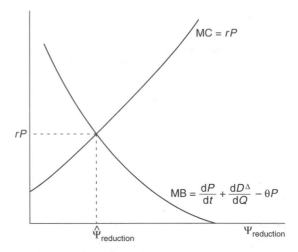

MC: rP = the cost of reducing pollution (and so adding to the environmental resource stock) by one unit for one period.

MB: $\dfrac{dP}{dt} + \dfrac{dD^\Delta}{dQ} - \theta P$ = the benefit of reducing pollution by one unit for one period

Fig 8.8 The efficient level of pollution flow for a stock pollutant balances the carrying cost with the benefits of pollution at the margin.

form of the *total* damage cost and *total* abatement cost functions. These functions are each assumed to be strictly convex. We will first define the concept of a strictly convex function, and then show how the analysis in this chapter incorporates that assumption. Having done this, we explain why these functions may not be convex in practice.

When one or both of the total damage or total abatement cost functions are non-convex, the marginal analysis of efficient pollution can be misleading. At the least, the investigator must check to see whether equalising marginal damages and marginal abatement costs does, in fact, correspond to an efficient level of pollution (or pollution abatement). The last part of this section explains this point carefully.

Consider a function, $f(x)$, of a single variable x. The function is strictly convex if its graph, when viewed from the horizontal axis, has a smooth and continuous U shape, so that its graph is of the form indicated in Figure 8.9.

More precisely, a strictly convex function requires that if we choose any two distinct points on the function (such as **a** and **b**), the line segment connecting those two points lies everywhere above

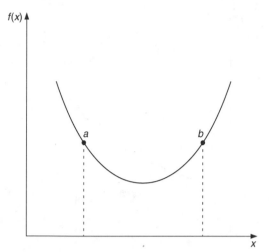

Fig 8.9 A strictly convex function.

the function $f(x)$, except at the points **a** and **b** themselves. A function is convex (as opposed to strictly convex) if the line segment lies everywhere above or on the function $f(x)$, but not below it.

Conventional environmental economics theory assumes that the total damage costs function

$$D = D(\Psi)$$

and the total abatement costs function

$$C = C(Z)$$

are strictly convex functions (where Ψ is the level of pollution, and Z is the amount of pollution abatement, equal to $\hat{\Psi} - \Psi$, where $\hat{\Psi}$ is the uncontrolled level of pollution and Ψ is the actual level of pollution). In graphical terms, this implies that the functions have the shapes shown in Figures 8.10a and b.

However, as $Z = \hat{\Psi} - \Psi$, the abatement function can be redrawn in terms of pollution as illustrated in Figure 8.10c. The functions drawn in Figures 8.10a and b are for total functions – we have used marginal functions in the analysis in this chapter. So what do the marginal damage cost and marginal abatement cost functions look like when the total functions are convex? They will be of the form indicated in Figure 8.10d–f. Let us look at this relationship in more detail for the total and marginal damage functions. In order for the quantity of total damages to rise at an increasing rate (as in Figure 8.10a) the marginal damage function (in 8.10d) must be continuously increasing. The marginal damage function will not necessarily have the same shape as that shown in the diagram, but it must be continuously rising.

Gathering the threads of our argument together, the conventional convexity assumptions imply that, as functions of pollution, marginal damages are continuously increasing, and marginal costs of abatement are continuously decreasing, as shown in Figure 8.11.

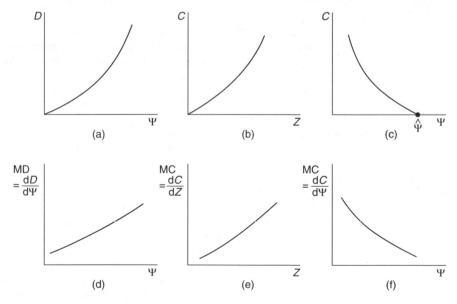

Fig 8.10 Strictly convex pollution abatement and pollution damage functions, and the counterpart marginal functions.

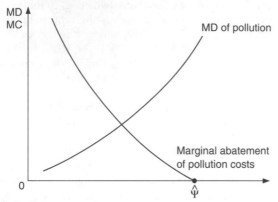

Fig 8.11 The unique efficient level of pollution when damage and abatement cost functions are convex.

If you compare this diagram with Figure 8.4 that we used in our analysis of the efficient level of pollution (or pollution abatement), you will see that they are essentially identical. We have been assuming convexity in drawing the functions used in this chapter (and, indeed, throughout the book as a whole).

Convexity and efficiency

If total cost and total damage functions are convex, it is clear from Figure 8.11 that there can be only one level of pollution at which the marginal costs of pollution abatement are equal to the marginal damage of pollution. This implies that marginal analysis is sufficient for identifying the efficient level of pollution – that level occurs at the unique pollution level at which those two marginal quantities are equalised. As you will see shortly, this is no longer necessarily true when one or both of the functions is non-convex.

Non-convexity of the damage function

There are many reasons why the total damages of pollution function may be non-convex, giving rise to a marginal damage function which is not continuously increasing. We will look at two such cases. First, assume that pollution can reach a saturation point, at which no further damage is done as pollution levels rise beyond that saturation point. This may be the case with acidic pollution of rivers and lakes; at a saturation level of pollution, the lake may become biologically dead, unable to support animal or plant life. The total and marginal damages function in this case will be of the form shown in Figure 8.12.

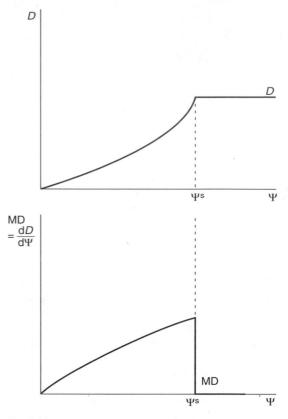

Fig 8.12 A non-convex damage function arising from pollution reaching a saturation point.

A second example, discussed in Fisher (1981), is non-convexity of damages arising from aversive behaviour by an individual. Suppose a factory emits particulate emissions that create external damages for an individual living in the neighbourhood of the factory. The marginal damage initially rises with the amount of the pollution. However, at some critical level of pollution flow, the affected individual can no longer tolerate living in the neighbourhood of the factory, and moves to live somewhere else where the damage to him or her becomes zero. As far as this particular individual is concerned, his or her marginal damage function is also of the form shown in Figure 8.12. However, if there are many individuals living in the neighbourhood, with varying tolerance levels, many of whom are prepared to move at some level of pollution, the aggregate marginal pollution damage function will be the sum of a set of individual functions, each of which has the same general form but with differing pollution tolerance levels Ψ^s. The aggregate function will be of the form shown in Figure 8.13, a

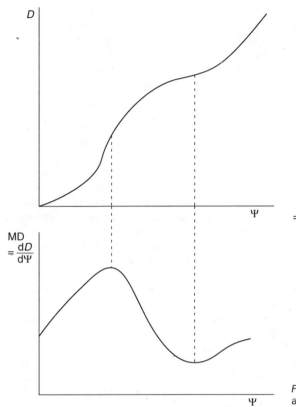

Fig 8.13 A non-convex damage function arising from behavioural adjustments of individuals.

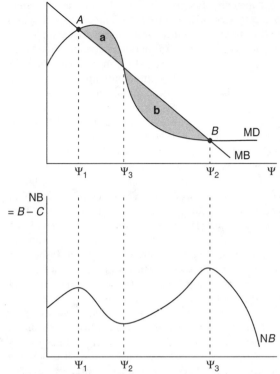

Fig 8.14 The case of a convex abatement cost function and a non-convex damage function.

'smoothed' version of an individual counterpart. Clearly, the two damage functions are non-convex.

Implications of non-convexity

Suppose the marginal damage function is of the form shown in Figure 8.14, and that the abatement cost function is of a conventional shape. Marginal costs and benefits are equalised here at three pollution levels. To ascertain which is the best (that is, the efficient) level of pollution, it is necessary to inspect the level of total net benefits at these three points, *and* at all other levels of pollution. The two points labelled A and B are 'local optima', as they satisfy the second-order conditions for a local maximum of net benefits, as shown in the lower half of Figure 8.14. In this case Ψ_3 is a global net benefits-maximising pollution level. Note that in moving from Ψ_1 to Ψ_3, net benefits at first fall (by the area labelled **a**) and then rise (by the area labelled **b**).

A more serious consequence of non-convexity for policy-making may be its implications for

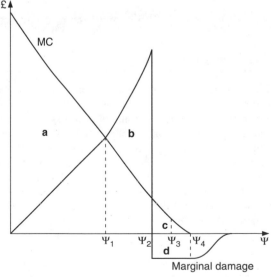

Fig 8.15 A non-convex damage function arising from pollutants harmful at low concentrations but beneficial at higher concentrations.

cost–benefit analysis-based calculations of small projects. Consider Figure 8.15. The damage function in this diagram is a little unusual, but an example that would generate such a function is given in Goodstein (1995). Nitrogen oxides (NO_x), in combination with some volatile organic compounds and sunlight, can produce damaging lower atmosphere ozone smogs. Initially, the damage rises at an increasing rate with NO_x emissions. However, high levels of NO_x act as ozone inhibitors, and so beyond Ψ_2 higher levels of NO_x reduce ozone damage; hence the negative part of the marginal damage function.

Suppose an economy was at a point such as Ψ_3. A cost–benefit analysis of small changes in NO_x emissions would suggest that the pollutant flow should be increased, as this will both reduce abatement expenditures and result in lower total damage. But this would be a misleading conclusion. Inspection of the areas **a**, **b**, **c** and **d** shows that the economically efficient pollution level (over the whole range of possible pollution levels) is in fact Ψ_1. The cost–benefit analysis prescription would lead the economy further away from the efficient allocation of resources.

There are many other reasons why damage functions may be non-convex. Furthermore, it is possible (although less likely) that abatement costs exhibit non-convexities too. Space prevents us continuing the analysis any further. An excellent survey of the non-convexity issue can be found in Burrows (1995).

Further issues in the economics of pollution

Technological progress

Technological progress could be manifested in a variety of ways: firstly, it might take the form of a lower level of emissions per unit of output; secondly, it could reduce the cost of recycling residuals, or thirdly, it may lead to a reduction of the magnitude of damages corresponding to any stock level of the pollutant.

In each case, as damages become less for any pattern of output production, one would expect these forms of technological progress to result in a higher steady-state output level. We leave this as an exercise for the reader.

Pollution, externalities and market economies

We do not expect pure market economies to deliver optimal or efficient outcomes in terms of pollution.

One reason for this has been discussed at length in earlier chapters: pollution tends to be an externality to the market process, and as a result is not adequately reflected in private market decisions. Put another way, whilst the costs of controlling or abating pollution would be met by firms, the benefits of abatement would not be received by firms (although they would by society). Hence, in considering pollution abatement, the control level which maximises net benefits to firms is different from the level which maximises social net benefits.[3]

We have discussed the concept of externalities at length in Chapter 4. Recall the essential point: an externality occurs where one person's utility function is affected by the production or consumption activities of another person or persons, and where no compensation is made to the affected party by the generator of the external effect.

Now, clearly, much of what we understand by the notion of pollution can be understood and interpreted within the framework of the theory of externalities. In the following chapter, we demonstrate the application of externalities theory to noise and light pollution, various forms of airborne pollution (for example, tobacco smoke, industrial emissions, particulate emission from diesel traffic), ground pollution (dumping of toxic waste, accumulation of chemicals in agricultural soils) and water pollution (for example, river pollution, contamination of aquifers). We also show that the literature on obtaining efficient allocations of resources where external effects are present points to a policy framework for an economically efficient approach to pollution control.

A safe minimum standard of conservation

In our discussions of the 'best' level of pollution, emphasis has been placed almost exclusively upon the single criterion of economic efficiency. However, if pollution levels pose threats to the survival or sustainability of some renewable resource (such as European marine fisheries or tropical forests) or jeopardise an environmental system itself (such as a wilderness area characterised by extensive biodiversity) then the criterion of efficiency may be regarded

---

[3] This is not, of course, the *only* reason why market outcomes are inefficient. Several other reasons were given in earlier chapters. One other should be mentioned now. Markets are very unlikely to pay adequate regard to the preferences and welfare of unborn future generations. We return to this point in the next chapter.

as inappropriate. Our analyses in Chapter 7 demonstrated that the efficiency criterion is not sufficient to guarantee the survival of a renewable resource stock or environmental system in perpetuity, particularly under conditions of uncertainty. When a renewable resource or environmental system is thought to be of high intrinsic value, so that we would be strongly averse to allowing pollution to reach levels at which that resource is driven to extinction or that system is unable to yield valuable environmental services, constraints on behaviour may be deemed appropriate. In Chapter 7 we introduced the notion of a Safe Minimum Standard of Conservation (SMC), and explained why this criterion is sometimes proposed as a means of formulating policy concerning renewable resource harvesting and use. The SMC was seen to be appropriate under precisely the circumstances we are discussing here in which there are grounds for believing that an efficiency criterion may be insufficient to ensure sustainability of valuable or potentially valuable resources.

When applied to pollution policy, the adoption of an SMC approach to policy entails that, under reasonable allowances for uncertainty, threats to survival of valuable resource systems from pollution flows are eliminated, provided that this does not entail excessive cost. Alternatively, one may view the SMC criterion in terms of constraints – pollution policy should in general be determined using an efficiency criterion, but subject to the overriding constraint that an SMC is satisfied. This formulation of pollution policy recognises the importance of economic efficiency but accords a lower priority than conservation when the two conflict, provided that the opportunity costs of conservation are not excessive.

This compromise between efficiency and conservation criteria implies that 'correct' levels of pollution cannot be worked out analytically. Instead, judgements will need to be made about what is reasonable uncertainty, what constitutes excessive costs, and which resources are deemed sufficiently valuable for application of the SMC criterion.

Discussion questions

1 'Only the highest standards of environmental purity will do'. Discuss.
2 'A clean environment is a public good whose benefits cannot be privately appropriated. Therefore private industry which is run for private

gain will always be the enemy of a clean environment'. Examine this proposition.
3 Describe the nature of the externalities arising in environmental situations, and comment on the relevance of Coase's Theorem.
4 Discuss the relevance and application of the concept of externalities in environmental economics.

Problems

1 Under which circumstances will the economically efficient level of pollution be zero? Under which circumstances will it be economically efficient to undertake zero pollution abatement?
2 We have seen that the efficient level of pollution is the one that minimises the sum of total abatement costs plus total damage costs. Refer now to Figure 8.4b. Show that if pollution abatement takes place to the extent $\hat{\Psi} - \Psi_A$ the sum of total damage costs and total abatement costs is $C_1 + C_2 + C_3$. Prove that 'too little' abatement (relative to the efficient quantity) results in higher costs than $C_1 + C_2$.
3 Explain the concept of the 'economically optimal level of pollution'. What information is required in order to identify such an optimal quantity?
4 Discuss the relative merits of alternative policy instruments that could be used to attain particular pollution targets.

Further reading

Excellent and extensive presentations of the economics of pollution are to be found in Anderson (1985), Hartwick and Olewiler (1986) and Fisher (1981, Chapters 5 and 6). Tietenberg (1992) gives little attention to the economic analysis of pollution in general, but gives a very extensive, descriptive coverage of specific types of pollution. Baumol and Oates (1988) is a classic source in this area, although the analysis is formal and quite difficult. Other useful treatments which complement the discussion in this chapter are Dasgupta (1982, Chapter 8), and Fisher and Peterson (1976). Smith (1972) gives a mathematical presentation of a very interesting application of the theory.

Some economics journals provide regular applications of the economic theory of pollution. Of particular interest are the *Journal of Environmental Economics and Management* and *Natural Resources Journal*.

Appendix 1

Dynamic optimisation with persistent pollutants

This presentation follows quite closely, and owes a debt to, the analysis of stock pollution given in Anderson (1985).

The objective is to choose a sequence of pollutant emission flows, $\Psi(t)$, $t = 0$ to $t = \infty$, to maximise

$$\int_{t=0}^{t=\infty} \{B[\Psi(t)] - D[\Psi(t)] - D^{\Delta}[Q(t)]\}\, e^{-rt}\, dt \quad (8.3)$$

subject to the constraint

$$\frac{dQ(t)}{dt} = \Psi(t) - \theta Q(t) \quad (8.4)$$

The current-valued Hamiltonian for this problem is

$$H(t) = B[\Psi(t)] - D[\Psi(t)] - D^{\Delta}[Q(t)]$$
$$+ \lambda(t)\{\Psi(t) - \theta Q(t)\} \quad (8.5)$$

The necessary conditions for a maximum are

$$\frac{\partial H}{\partial \Psi} = 0 \Rightarrow \frac{dB}{d\Psi} - \frac{dD}{d\Psi} + \lambda = 0 \quad (8.6)$$

$$\frac{d\lambda}{dt} = r\lambda + \frac{dD^{\Delta}}{dQ} + \theta\lambda \quad (8.7)$$

To obtain the dynamics of the control variable, $\Psi(t)$, we take the time derivative of Equation 8.6:

$$\frac{d\lambda}{dt} = -\left(\frac{d^2B}{d\Psi^2} - \frac{d^2D}{d\Psi^2}\right)\frac{d\Psi}{dt} \quad (8.8)$$

Substituting Equation 8.8 into Equation 8.7 we have:

$$(r+\theta)\lambda + \frac{dD^{\Delta}}{dQ} = -\left(\frac{d^2B}{d\Psi^2} - \frac{d^2D}{d\Psi^2}\right)\frac{d\Psi}{dt} \quad (8.9)$$

Substituting Equation 8.6 into Equation 8.9 we have:

$$\frac{d\Psi}{dt} = \frac{(r+\theta)\left(\dfrac{dB}{d\Psi} - \dfrac{dD}{d\Psi}\right) - \dfrac{dD^{\Delta}}{dQ}}{\dfrac{d^2B}{d\Psi^2} - \dfrac{d^2D}{d\Psi^2}} \quad (8.10)$$

We can then solve Equation 8.10 together with Equation 8.4 to obtain the efficient values of $\{\Psi(t), Q(t)\}$.

The terminal conditions for pollution emissions are

$$\Psi(T) = \theta Q(T)$$

from Equation 8.4, and

$$(r+\theta)(B'(\Psi(T)) - D'(\Psi(T)) - D^{\Delta'}(Q(T)) = 0$$

where we use notation of the form $Y'(X) = dY/dX$. If the initial pollution stock $Q(0) < Q(T)$, then the pollution flows are positive and moving towards the steady-state terminal condition. If $Q(0) > Q(T)$, then the pollution flows are kept to $\Psi(t) < \theta Q(t)$ so that $dQ/dt < 0$, and the pollution stock will decline to $Q(T)$. If $Q(0) = Q(T)$, then we can set $\Psi(t) = \Psi(T) = \theta Q(T)$ so that $dQ/dt = 0$, and the pollution stock remains at the steady-state level.

Appendix 2

The steady state

Let us draw together the threads of this discussion by carefully examining the pollution steady states. Recall first the two necessary conditions for an efficient outcome:

$$\frac{dB}{d\Psi} - \frac{dD}{d\Psi} = P \quad (8.11)$$

$$rP = \frac{dP}{dt} + \frac{dD^{\Delta}}{dQ} - \theta P \quad (8.12)$$

In a steady state, P is constant and so dP/dt is zero. So these two equations collapse to

$$\frac{dB}{d\Psi} - \frac{dD}{d\Psi} = P^* \quad (8.13)$$

$$rP^* = \frac{dD^{\Delta}}{dQ} - \theta P^* \quad (8.14)$$

Also, in steady state

$$\frac{dQ_t}{dt} = \Psi_t - \theta Q_t$$

collapses to

$$\Psi^* = \theta Q^* \quad (8.15)$$

which implies that the inflow of pollutants to the stock is balanced by the amount of stock decay.

Perfectly persistent pollutants

A steady state requires zero emissions so

$$\Psi^* = \theta Q^* = 0$$

Given that, by definition, θ is zero for perfectly persistent pollutants, the steady state will be characterised by a constant stock and zero emissions of the pollutant. Also, from Equation 8.14 we obtain

$$P^* = \frac{dD^\Delta/dQ^*}{r}$$

Imperfectly persistent pollutants

A steady state will be characterised by positive emissions

$$\Psi^* = \theta Q^* = k$$

where $k > 0$. The decay rate θ is positive for imperfectly persistent pollutants. The steady state will be characterised by a constant stock and positive emissions of the pollutant. As before, in steady state the pollutant price will be

$$P^* = \frac{dD^\Delta/dQ^*}{r}$$

CHAPTER 9

Pollution control policy

One reason why environmentalists' writings frequently appear quaint to the hard-nosed economist is the draconian measures they often advocate for curbing aggregate activities. It is one thing to claim that short-term gains from an increased growth in output can often be at the expense of output in the long run (e.g. via the degradation of soil). It is quite another to demand that economic growth ought to be curbed forthwith. One finds it difficult to believe that environmental problems have in recent years grown as rapidly as the concern that environmentalists have shown about them. Nevertheless, this growth in concern has had one important salutary effect; it has forced such issues to be included on the agenda of public debate.

Partha Dasgupta (1982), page 203

Pollution and economic policy

We have argued throughout this volume that all economic activity involves the production of waste residuals, in either energy or mass forms. Fundamental physical principles, moreover, imply that it is not possible, through economic processes, to convert these residuals completely into useful forms. The perfect recycling of wastes is impossible. We know, also, that waste residuals can become damaging pollutants if their flows into environmental sinks exceed the carrying capacity of these environmental media. What role should government take with regard to environmental pollution? Indeed, should it have any role at all, other than just creating and sustaining the conditions for competitive market behaviour?

We begin our attempt to answer these questions by outlining in the next section some insights developed by Ronald Coase, the most important of which draws attention to the possibility that bargaining between affected parties can lead to efficient solutions to externality problems. Coase's work points to the importance of property rights and transactions cost in determining the extent to which bargaining will take place. If circumstances are favourable for the existence of bargaining, external effects will often be efficiently dealt with by private bargaining. Under these conditions, no public intervention is necessary to secure an efficient allocation of resources. This is a very powerful insight, and should lead one to be wary of assertions that government corrective action is necessary whenever external effects are present in economic activity. However, for a very large class of external effects, the circumstances required for bargaining solutions to be applicable will not be met. Market allocations will then be inefficient, and

gains may be possible through government intervention. The source of these potential efficiency gains, and insights into how one can design policy instruments to secure them, can be found using the economic theory of externalities developed in Chapter 4.

In the third section of this chapter, after briefly reviewing the concept of an economically efficient level of pollution, attention turns to what this implies for an economically efficient pollution abatement programme. The main emphasis of our arguments throughout this chapter is on the efficiency properties of various pollution abatement programmes. However, it is always important to remember that efficiency is not the only relevant criterion when assessing alternative choices, nor necessarily the most important one. So it may not be always be desirable to construct policy in terms of a full economic efficiency criterion. Human communities appear to be unwilling to allow all policy targets to be decided using economic criteria, and may instead press for some to be chosen using other criteria. This often seems to be the case where health issues are under consideration; many people think it wrong for the size of the health care budget to be decided on economic grounds. When environmental matters are being discussed, similar views are often expressed, and it is common to find criticisms of economists for attempting to 'reduce everything to monetary considerations' and ignoring our responsibilities towards non-humans. So whilst the economist is inclined to stress the usefulness of decision frameworks based around the idea of economic efficiency, there is no ground for believing that policy targets either should be set or actually will be set in this way.

A second reason why targets may not be set using a full economic efficiency criterion is that this may not be possible because of limitations in the information available to decision makers. Suppose that government knows the costs of controlling a particular kind of pollutant, but does not know the pollution damage costs; it will then not be possible to identify an economically efficient pollution level. In that case, pollution targets must be chosen using some other criterion. However, once a pollution control target has been selected, whether on the basis of an economic or a non-economic criterion, economic reasoning still has a role to contribute in designing a programme to achieve that target. In particular, we might wish to adopt the criterion that any target should be achieved at least cost. This is known as the cost-efficiency criterion, and is discussed at length in the third section. As you will see, the criterion of cost-efficiency is not an alternative criterion to that of economic efficiency – rather, it is a weaker condition. An economically efficient pollution control programme achieves a particular target – the economically efficient pollution level – at the minimum overall cost to society. A cost-effective programme merely attains *some* target, but not necessarily the best one, at minimum cost to society.

In the last chapter we viewed pollution within the framework of the economic theory of externalities. It follows from such a perspective that if a polluting externality can be internalised, market behaviour should (under the conditions discussed in Chapter 2) lead to an efficient outcome. This suggests that we should investigate how externalities can be internalised in a market economy. As we will have seen, Coase's work shows one way in which externalities can be internalised, through private bargains. We show in the fourth and fifth sections that some forms of economic policy instrument, including pollution taxes and pollution abatement subsidies, also have this property, and so offer the prospect of being used to obtain an efficient allocation of resources where unregulated markets would fail to do so.

We have already noted that government may have incomplete information about either the costs or the benefits of various types and levels of intervention. It turns out to be the case that incomplete information has important implications for the design and choice of policy instruments. The type of instrument which is 'best' for achieving some particular goal will depend upon the form which uncertainty takes. These matters are analysed in the sixth section.

Our preliminary analysis of pollution control programmes is set in the context of a particular class of pollutants – those which we define to be uniformly mixing flow pollutants. The meaning of

this phrase will become clear as you read through the chapter. In the seventh section of this chapter, we turn our attention to flow pollutants that do not mix uniformly, and so have localised or regional effects that can vary with the time of the emission. Then we investigate pollution control programmes for stock pollutants.

The last section of this chapter deals with a miscellany of other relevant matters. Although it is desirable that, other things being equal, an economic instrument should be efficient, it is important to realise that different instruments can have very different implications for the way in which the gains and costs of policy intervention are distributed. The political choice of instrument is likely to be influenced by distributional issues at least as much as by efficiency criteria.

Whilst we argue in this chapter that markets sometimes fail to deliver efficient outcomes, there is no guarantee that government intervention will not be subject to efficiency losses also. It would be quite wrong to assume that a potential efficiency gain will inevitably be achieved by government intervention. In some circumstances, the efficiency losses of intervention might exceed those arising from the market failure which prompts that intervention, and so public sector involvement may not be warranted.

Bargaining and the work of Ronald Coase

We argued in Chapter 4 that one situation in which environmental 'problems' tend to arise is where property rights are ill-defined or do not exist. Let us now investigate this claim. To fix ideas, consider two people living as neighbours, one who plays a saxophone for his own enjoyment, the other who finds the sax noise disturbing. Figure 9.1 represents these two effects of the music, the curve MB denoting the marginal benefits to the musician derived from playing his instrument, and MC denoting the marginal cost of sax playing to the disturbed neighbour. The horizontal axis is measured in units of noise, labelled Ψ, to indicate that we treat this case as an example of a pollution externality.

If the musician behaved without any regard for his neighbour, and were not subject to any external control, he would maximise his private benefit at the output Ψ_3, where all additional benefits to him from sax playing have been exhausted. This would clearly not be an efficient outcome, however. The efficient

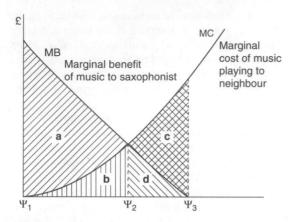

Fig 9.1 The bargaining solution to an externality.

solution is found at the output level Ψ_2. How might such an outcome be achieved?

One method is via bargaining between the affected parties. Starting from the noise level Ψ_3 a mutually beneficial bargain (a Pareto improvement) is possible. If a bargain were struck such that the musician reduced his noise output to the level Ψ_2, the gains to the disturbed neighbour would be shown by the areas **c + d**. The loss to the musician is represented by the area **d**.[1] Thus provided the neighbour compensated the musician by some payment greater than **d** but less than **c + d**, both individuals would be in a superior position than they were initially. A Pareto improvement would have taken place, and an efficient outcome would have been achieved. Potentially inefficient outcomes can be avoided if the affected parties can bargain with one another to establish mutually beneficial outcomes. Putting this argument another way, inefficiencies create the basis for mutually beneficial bargains, which may, depending on the circumstances, take place.

So far, we have deliberately remained silent about how rights to emit noise pollution (or equivalently, rights to use the medium in which sounds can travel) are allocated; we have said nothing about property rights. As we show shortly, a bargaining solution is only likely to take place if enforceable property rights exist. But does the manner in which these rights are distributed matter in any way? Continuing our example, let us focus on two of the ways in which such rights could be distributed. Firstly, producers

may be given unconstrained rights to produce noise (or to make use of the relevant environmental medium). Secondly, individuals may be granted the right to noise-free environments. In a classic article (Coase, 1960) Ronald Coase reached two conclusions. First, he argued that where bargaining is free to take place, and the costs of bargaining are negligible, efficient outcomes will be achieved through bargaining between affected parties. Second, he claimed that the same, efficient outcome will be attained irrespective of the way in which property rights are distributed. The manner in which property rights are distributed does matter, but only in determining the distribution of the net gains which arise from the bargain. They do not matter in terms of the final way in which real resources are allocated. This second result is commonly known as Coase's Theorem.

To see the basis for the Coase Theorem, look again at Figure 9.1. If property rights were vested in the producer of noise, the producer would have no legal liability for any noise he produced, and the pre-bargaining level of noise output would be Ψ_3. However, for the reason we gave above, one would expect bargaining to take place between the affected parties, leading to the final outcome Ψ_2. If, on the other hand, legislators granted residents the right to a noise-free environment, the producer would not be entitled to generate any noise, and so the pre-bargaining pollution level would be Ψ_1. However, the two parties are still confronted by the possibility of a mutually beneficial transaction. That transaction would take the form of the neighbour allowing the musician to produce Ψ_2 without seeking redress through the courts. In return for this entitlement, the musician would compensate the neighbour by an amount greater than **b** but less than **a + b** in terms of the areas in Figure 9.1. You should convince yourself that such a deal would be of benefit to both persons.

Coase's first argument was that the likelihood of such a bargain taking place will be low unless enforceable property rights exist. Enforceability refers to the fact that the judicial system would impose punitive penalties on any individual infringing another's property right. A bargain can be thought of as a contract between individuals whereby the holder of property rights agrees to waive any claim for damages resulting from the other party, in exchange for some compensation. If enforceable property rights do not exist, contractors could renege on contracts after compensations have been paid without fear of redress. This is known as opportunistic recontracting. The existence of property rights, and the existence of a

---

[1] If the reasoning behind interpreting areas under marginal cost and benefit curves in this way is not clear, you may find it useful to read the first section of Chapter 10 now.

legal system which guarantees the enforcement of contracts and of property rights, appear to be necessary conditions for bargaining solutions.

Coase's results are of immense importance. Firstly, they show that bargaining between affected parties may allow *potentially* inefficient outcomes to be avoided without the need for any government regulation. Self-interested behaviour may ensure that resources will be deployed efficiently, even where external or spillover effects take place. If bargaining solutions to externalities do in fact take place widely, or could easily do so, the proper scope for government intervention in the economy is greatly reduced. Secondly, the manner in which property rights are initially distributed has no effect as far as the efficient allocation of resources is concerned. If efficiency were the only thing that mattered, then this means that as long as property rights do exist, it is irrelevant how they are distributed. However, efficiency is not the only thing that 'matters'. If one believes that distributional issues deserve consideration, then the initial distribution of property rights is clearly relevant. As Problem 1 demonstrates, the distribution of gains and benefits from bargaining will depend upon property rights distributions.

We have argued that bargaining is unlikely to take place if property rights do not exist. However, two other conditions will also affect the probability of bargaining solutions taking place. First, the number of affected parties must be relatively small; if not, the costs and difficulties of bargaining may prevent the outcome being realised. Secondly, the affected parties should be identifiable. Once again, it is difficult to conceive of efficient bargains being conducted if it were not possible to identify and organise all parties affected by the activity.

Theoretical limitations of bargaining solutions to externalities and the applicability of Coase's results to environmental pollution issues

There are a number of limitations which reduce the extent to which bargaining is likely to be an effective means of dealing with inefficiencies arising from external effects, particularly where the environment is concerned. The most important limitation concerns the possibility of efficient bargaining in the context of choices about the use of public goods. Externalities may be either private or public. A private externality occurs where the external effect in question has the characteristics of a private good. In our hypothetical example, this condition is satisfied, as by assumption

the noise pollution spillover affects no third party. However, if other people lived close by, and they were also irritated by the noise, the example would not satisfy the criteria of a private good. A public externality exists where the external effect in question has the characteristics of a public good. In this case, consumption of the externality by one person does not prevent another person also consuming the externality. Whilst bargaining may well be viable in the case of private externalities, the free-rider problem and the incentive to misrepresent preferences which arise in the case of public goods (see Chapter 4 for details) leads one to suppose that bargaining will not yield efficient outcomes where public goods externalities are present.

A second reason why bargaining solutions are likely to be of limited relevance to most environmental problems concerns the numbers of affected parties. Typically, environmental pollution affects a large number of people. It is often very difficult to identify all the affected parties, and the costs of organising these people for the purpose of undertaking a bargaining exercise can be enormous. If the large numbers characteristic operates in conjunction with the externality being public, there will be strong incentives on producers of pollution to act covertly so as to avoid bargaining payments where property rights imply that polluters pay, or strong incentives on victims of pollution to not disclose their identity if property rights imply that victims must compensate polluters. The scope for efficient bargaining behaviour seems very restricted in these circumstances.

A third issue of particular interest to us is the possibility of intertemporal bargaining, including bargaining between current and future generations. Many environmental externalities cut across generations – our behaviour today imposes externalities on future persons. Whilst bargaining between affected individuals at one point in time seems feasible, it is difficult to imagine that this could happen between representatives of the present generation and those not yet living.

Finally, the Coase Theorem itself claims that, given certain conditions, the manner in which property rights are initially distributed has no implications for the real allocation of resources; the same final efficient outcome would emerge through bargaining however that initial distribution were made. But this claim has been disputed. We know that the initial distribution of property rights affects the gains from bargains, and so it will affect the net wealth of affected parties. If net wealth changes (as it would if property rights were reallocated) then the real allocation of resources will in general change. The independence Coase established between distributional and real resource allocation matters is only valid if wealth has no affect on consumption preferences, which is very unlikely to be true in most cases. Secondly, bargaining power probably matters too. In general, once wealth effects are introduced into the analysis, the final outcome will depend upon the bargaining powers of the respective parties, and will not necessarily be the economically efficient outcome shown in Figure 9.1. So a claim that bargaining will always lead to efficient outcomes is not valid in all circumstances.

Even if one took a highly optimistic view about the likelihood and efficacy of bargaining behaviour, a role for government is still implied by these arguments. Government should aim to develop and sustain an institutional structure which maximises the scope for bargaining behaviour. Some policy implications might be derived from our analysis of Coase's results:

1 Wherever practicable, property rights should be defined and allocated in a clearly defined manner.
2 If there are efficiency gains to be had from a centralised information gathering and processing system, then government should take responsibility for environmental monitoring, so as to identify pollution producers and recipients. Information from such monitoring exercises can then be made available to affected parties.
3 There are major advantages to be obtained in establishing, quantifying and publicising legal liability for the damaging consequences of behaviour, in order to facilitate future bargaining.
4 Access to the judicial system should be easy and cheap. If the legal system works to allow redress of grievances for damages caused by others, then these other parties will face a potential charge for any damages they cause. This may be sufficient in some situations for efficient outcomes to be achieved.

Economically efficient pollution abatement programmes and cost-effective pollution abatement programmes

It is not easy to find rules which apply in all circumstances, and this is certainly true when it comes to environmental policy. Because pollutants take a variety of forms, and lead to damages in a variety of ways, one should not be surprised to learn that the nature of an economically efficient pollution abatement programme depends on the type of pollutant under consideration. We deal in this and the next three sections with a particular class of pollutant, namely *uniformly mixing flow pollutants*. This analysis will, nevertheless, lead to a number of principles which apply quite generally.

Uniformly mixing flow pollutants have the property that the damage attributable to the pollutant is independent of the location of the emission source and the timing of the emission (within some period such as a day). Because of this, we can analyse this form of pollutant without needing to consider the spatial or temporal dimensions. This is the most straightforward case to analyse, and will enable us to derive some general principles which apply to all classes of pollutants. Subsequently we investigate the ways in which these general principles may need to be amended when dealing with other classes of emissions.

Now consider the following question: what are the characteristics of an economically efficient pollution abatement programme? The answer is straightforward; for a pollution abatement programme to be economically efficient, two criteria should be satisfied:

1 The total quantity of pollution which is abated should be the economically efficient level of abatement. A key result we obtained in Chapter 8 identified an efficient pollution level to be one at which the marginal cost of pollution abatement equals the marginal damage of the pollutant. In this circumstance, no efficiency gains are possible by changing the level of pollution.
2 The abatement level selected should be achieved at minimum cost.

To see what this second condition implies, let us look at a simple hypothetical example shown in Table 9.1. Suppose government wishes to reduce the emission of a particular pollutant from 90 units per period (the uncontrolled level) to 50 units per period. We regard 50 units of emission per period as Ψ^*, the economically efficient level of pollution. This information implies that the efficient abatement target is 40 units of pollutant per period, as indicated in the final column of Table 9.1. Now suppose that the pollutant arises from the production activities of just two firms, A and B, and that the marginal cost of abatement schedules for each firm are as indicated in

Table 9.1 Pollution abatement data for firms A and B

	A	B	A + B
Uncontrolled emissions $\hat{\Psi}$	40	50	90
Uncontrolled abatement $\hat{Z}$	0	0	0
Efficient emissions Ψ^*	15 (Ψ_A^*)	35 (Ψ_B^*)	50
Efficient abatement Z^*	25 (Z_A^*)	15 (Z_A^*)	40
Initial permit allocation	25	25	50
Final permit allocation	15	35	50

Figure 9.2. We use Z to denote a quantity of pollution abatement.

Firm A has a lower marginal abatement cost schedule. Does this imply that firm A should undertake all 40 units of abatement? If we wish to achieve the target at minimum cost, the answer is no. To see why, look at Figure 9.3, which presents the identical information to Figure 9.2, but in a slightly different form. Firm B's abatement cost schedule is shown as before, so going from left to right corresponds to more abatement being done by B. But we have reversed the abatement cost schedule for A. Moving leftwards in the diagram corresponds to increasing abatement by A.

The least cost abatement of 40 units is attained where Firm A undertakes 25 units and Firm B 15 units. The firm we labelled 'low cost' undertakes most of the abatement, but not all of it. Minimised total abatement costs can be read off from the diagram. The area denoted β shows B's total abatement costs, while the area denoted α represents A's total abatement costs. There is no other combination of abatement efforts, adding up to 40 units in total, which can be attained at lower cost than $\alpha + \beta$. You should verify that this is correct.

Notice a very important result here. At the minimised pollution control cost point, the marginal cost of abatement is identical for each abater. It is

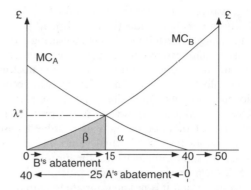

MC$_A$ = Marginal cost of pollution abatement for firm A.
MC$_B$ = Marginal cost of pollution abatement for firm B.

Fig 9.3 Cost-effective pollution abatement.

easy to see why this should be so. If some total level of abatement were being achieved at differing marginal costs, it would be possible to switch some control effort from a high marginal cost firm to a low marginal cost firm, and attain the same outcome at lower cost.

In a world in which policy makers had perfect information, economists generally advocate that pollution (or pollution abatement) targets should be chosen to be economically efficient targets. However, identifying the economically efficient level for a particular pollutant requires knowledge of its control cost (abatement) function and of its damage function. This information would be available in a world in which policy makers had perfect knowledge, but in practice policy makers may have little information about the magnitudes of the damage resulting from the pollutant, or about the abatement cost function. In such a case, an efficient target cannot be identified.

To see this, let us consider an example. The generation of power by means of nuclear fission generates a number of potential damages. Firstly, low level but continual escape of radioactive particles poses health risks, almost certainly increasing the incidence of leukaemia in surrounding areas. Transportation and storage of radioactive material, and the decommissioning of nuclear plant similarly lead to flows of harmful radiation into environmental media. Furthermore, whilst the probability of serious calamities is very low, the damages that would be associated with such incidents would be enormous. There are two important points in this. First, many people are sceptical about whether some of these damages are even quantifiable. Is it possible to place a value on the loss of a human life, for example? If a

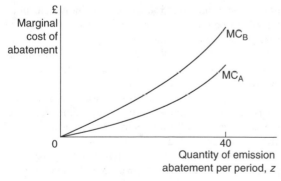

Fig 9.2 Marginal cost of pollution abatement functions for two firms A and B.

damage was regarded as being unquantifiable, then it is clearly impossible to identify an 'efficient' target. Secondly, huge uncertainties exist in measuring dose–response relationships for many environmental effects, and this is certainly true in the case of nuclear radiative effects. Whilst we know damage will occur, we do not know its value with any precision. If all possible outcomes are known, as is the probability distribution of these outcomes, it is possible to use expected values instead of actual values in calculations. But in some circumstances, these probabilities are not known or are not knowable. Such uncertainties may mean that it is not appropriate to search for an efficient target. Similar comments also apply, of course, to the abatement cost function, although it is likely that decision makers will have much more information about this than about damages.

Where a pollution target cannot be set on grounds of economic efficiency, it has to be chosen on the basis of some other criterion. Continuing the nuclear fission example, we may choose to establish a radiation pollution target with reference to a maximum level that is considered to be acceptable in terms of the likely health risks implied, although this does rather beg the question of what criterion might be employed in judging what are felt to be 'acceptable' levels of health effects. Standards of ambient air pollution are sometimes set by reference to perceptions of tolerable health risks.

The previous argument presupposed that we wished to establish targets on economic grounds alone; the problem was that this objective is sometimes not feasible because of information limitations. However, it may not be *desirable* to devise policy targets using an economic criterion. Decisions about the use of resources are taken through political processes. Whilst economic principles have some input into such processes, they are by no means the only inputs. In many areas of social policy, including health care and educational provision, decisions about the use of resources are shaped and influenced by ethical principles relating to perceptions of fairness and justice. It is quite possible that policy targets derived from economic principles may conflict with those derived from some ethical standpoints, and the community may choose the latter. In Box 9.1, we present some examples of existing environmental targets, and the principle used in establishing each target.

Nevertheless, even where a target is chosen on non-economic grounds, economic principles may still be useful in identifying the best way in which that target could be achieved. In particular, a criterion we might wish to use in selecting policy instruments is that the target be achieved at minimum or least cost. A least-cost control regime implies that the marginal cost of abatement is equalised over all firms undertaking pollution control. An instrument which attains a pollution target at least cost is known as a cost-effective instrument.

The requirement of cost-effectiveness is weaker than that of economic efficiency. A corollary of this is that the search for, and use of, cost-effective instruments considerably reduces the information that the policy maker and administrator is required to possess. Once a policy target is set, a cost-effective policy instrument achieves that target at minimum cost. For example, suppose that a pollution control authority wished to reduce river pollution to a predetermined level. The use of a marketable emission permits system is a cost-effective instrument for this purpose. The control authority could issue (or sell) marketable emission permits up to the target emission level. To operate the scheme, it needs to know neither the damage function of the pollutant nor the abatement cost function. As we show below, the marketable permit scheme will attain the target at minimum cost. It does so because a market in permits will develop in which a single price becomes established for each permit. Polluters will reduce emissions whenever the cost of doing so is less than the permit price. In this way, marginal abatement costs will be equalised over firms, at the level of the permit price.

In this example, the pollution control instrument is cost-effective whether or not the environmental protection agency knows the abatement cost function of each polluter. However, it is sometimes the case that an instrument can only be cost-effective if abatement cost functions are known. For example, non-transferable emission quotas on individual polluters can be cost-effective instruments if the quotas are set so that the marginal abatement costs are equalised over all pollution abaters. This does, of course, presuppose that the control authority has information about abatement costs.

But the conclusion we wish to stress here is that an instrument can be cost-effective without knowledge of the damages of pollution. Sometimes, knowledge of abatement costs will also not be required. Thus cost-effectiveness is likely to be an attractive property of a policy instrument when knowledge is limited, and is applicable in a wider class of situations than a full economic efficiency criterion.

Box 9.1 Environmental targets

Pollutant	Target	Relevant criterion
United Kingdom		
Grains emitted in cement production	0.1–0.2 grains per cubic foot	Best practicable means
Sewage concentration	Max. 30 mg/litre suspended solids, Max. BOD 20 mg/litre	1976 National Water Council: Precautionary principle, perceived health risks
Cadmium/lead	Discharges into North Sea to fall by 70% between 1985 and 1995	Health criterion
PCBs	Phase out by 1999	Strict precautionary principle - health risks
Waste recycling	50% domestic waste to be recycled	Political target?
United States		
Particulates	Ambient air concentration of TSP to not exceed 50 $\mu g/m^3$ average annual or 150 $\mu g/m^3$ average 24 hours	Health risks
Sulphur dioxide	Ambient air concentration of SO_2 to not exceed 80 $\mu g/m^3$ average annual or 365 $\mu g/m^3$ average 24 hours	Health risks/significant respiratory problems
Lead	Concentration to not exceed 1.5 $\mu g/m^3$ maximum in any quarter	
International		
CFCs	CFC production to fall to 80% and 50% of 1986 levels by 1994 and 1999 respectively	Political feasibility, with final targets set in terms of critical load

[a] BOD = Biochemical oxygen demand, TSP = total suspended particulate matter.
[b] The concepts of 'best practicable means', 'critical load', and 'precautionary principle' will be explained later in the chapter.

Alternative instruments for achieving pollution abatement targets

So far, we have considered how target levels of pollution or pollution abatement could be established, and have outlined the principle of cost-efficiency. We have not yet investigated the methods which could be used to attain some target level of pollution, nor identified which instruments are cost-efficient. It is to these matter that we now turn. In this text, the term *policy instrument* will be used to denote a set of arrangements, introduced by government, which could be used to attain some target of policy.

For each instrument discussed in this section, we attempt to answer the following questions: What is the nature of the instrument? How does it work? Is it, or can it be, cost-efficient? Other than its efficiency properties, what advantages and disadvantages does the use of the instrument confer? A number of criteria are relevant here. They include

1 Dependability: to what extent can the instrument be relied upon to achieve the pollution target?
2 Information requirements: how much information does the instrument require that the control authority have, and what are the costs of acquiring it?
3 Enforceability: how much monitoring is required for the instrument to be effective, and can compliance be enforced?
4 Long-run effects: does the influence of the instrument strengthen, weaken or remain constant over time?

5 Dynamic efficiency: does the instrument create continual incentives to improve products or production processes in ways that reduce the extent of pollution for given values of output?

6 Flexibility: is the instrument capable of being adapted quickly and cheaply as new information arises, as conditions change, or as desired targets are altered?

The importance attached to each of these criteria by the pollution control authority, by the policy maker, and perhaps by the general public will influence the choice of instrument for any desired control programme. It is likely that the weights attached to these will vary with different types of pollution. For example, where a dangerous and persistent toxin is concerned, certainty or dependability of control is of great importance, and will dominate instrument choice. No single instrument is 'best' for all types of pollution in all circumstances.

Finally, we must take account of the equity of policy instruments. What implications does the use of an instrument have for the distribution of income or wealth? The moral and political acceptability of an instrument will certainly be influenced by perceptions of its fairness or equity. We shall have more to say on this in the final section.

Control over the permissible quantity of emission

As pollution targets are often specified in terms of a total quantity of allowed emissions (or, equivalently, in terms of a quantity of required abatement), it follows that one instrument for implementing such a target is direct regulation of the quantity of pollution emitted by all sources collectively. In almost all cases of interest, there will be multiple sources of emissions, and so some apportioning of the total quantity will need to be made among the various sources. Once this apportioning has been done, however, a quota or permitted emission licence can be allocated to each source, such that the aggregate target is met. Successful operation of quota schemes is unlikely if polluters believe their actions are not observed, or if the costs to the polluters of not meeting quota restrictions are low relative to the cost of abatement. Quota schemes will have to be supported, therefore, by effective pollution monitoring systems and by sufficiently harsh penalties for non-compliance.

Quantitative controls of this form – often called 'command and control' instruments – are the most prevalent method of pollution control. The extent to which quantity regulations succeed in attaining pollution abatement targets depends upon the magnitude of penalties for non-compliance and the efficacy of the associated monitoring procedures, which determines the probability that non-compliance will result in the imposition of those penalties. It is common for penalties to be relatively low, and monitoring to be fairly weak, thereby reducing the effectiveness and dependability of the control programme.

The use of regulatory, or command and control, instruments *can* be efficient, as it is possible in principle to choose emission standards for each firm that will correspond to an efficient abatement programme. As we saw in the last section, this requires that the marginal cost of abatement be equal over all firms undertaking abatement. However, this is very unlikely to be achieved in practice. To do so, the control authority would need to know the abatement cost function for each firm, as shown in Figure 9.3.

Control authorities are very unlikely to be in possession of the information required to set standards for each polluter in this way. If they tried to acquire information about abatements costs for each emitter, the costs of collecting that information could well be prohibitive, and may outweigh the potential efficiency gains arising from intervention. An additional complication arises from information symmetries and weak or perverse incentives to disclose information. The asymmetry arises from the fact that whilst firms may know their control cost functions, the regulator will not do so. Firms can have strong incentives to not disclose information, or worse, to provide misleading information.

A consequence of these observations is that quantitative controls are likely to be applied using some arbitrary method of distributing an abatement burden over firms. As a result, they will be inefficient (relative to some other instruments we shall look at shortly, including tax or subsidy schemes) in that they will tend to attain any given level of pollution reduction at a greater cost than is necessary. Another problem associated with command-and-control quantity restrictions is that they embody very weak incentives to promote dynamic efficiency. We investigate these matters further in Box 9.2 and in the next section.

It is often the case (as is evident from Box 9.1) that environmental targets are specified in terms of maximum permitted concentrations of pollutants in

---

Box 9.2 Quantitative emissions and technology controls in practice

Regulations mandating the use of particular control technologies or requiring the attainment of given standards are still the most prevalent form of policy instrument in Europe, North America and the other OECD countries. In the UK, the basis for pollution control has been that of 'best practicable means'. The adjective *practicable* has never been given a precise legal definition, but the 1956 Clean Air Act stated that

> Practicable means reasonably practicable having regard, amongst other things, to local conditions and circumstances, to the financial implications and the current state of technology.

Despite a clear element of tautology in this statement, it can be interpreted as meaning that a practicable control technology should be technologically effective, subject to the constraint that it is not excessively costly. In recent years, the cost qualification has been given greater priority, and has been enshrined in the principle of BATNEEC: the best available technology not entailing excessive cost. This puts the instrument closer to the kind advocated by economists, as the excessive cost condition implies part of a cost-benefit calculation in the administration of the instrument. But as BATNEEC (and all quantitative control schemes) do not require any assessment of the benefits of the control programme, they fall short of instruments that satisfy a full economic criterion.

The manner in which technology-based instruments has been implemented varies considerably between countries. In the UK, officials of Her Majesty's Inspectorate of Pollution (successors to the old Alkali Inspectors) negotiate controls with plant managers (but have the right, in the last instance, to require the adoption of certain control technologies). In the USA, the Environmental Protection Agency (EPA) promotes a rather more uniform control programme; in 1990, Congress required the EPA to establish technology-based standards for about 200 specific pollutants.

Although they can be 'best' instruments in some circumstances, such direct controls are often extremely costly. Tietenberg (1984) finds that the 'command-and-control' approach costs from twice to 22 times the least-cost alternative for given degrees of control, and his 1990 paper reports estimates that compliance to the US Clean Air Act through market instruments has led to accumulated capital savings of over $10 billion. Thus market-based incentive approaches are likely to be more efficient than regulation and control. Three arguments underlie this tenet. First, markets are effective in processing information; secondly, market instruments tend to result in pollution control being undertaken where that control is least costly in real terms; and thirdly, market-based approaches generate dynamic gains through responses over time to their patterns of incentives. Whereas quantity and technology controls give no incentive to improve upon some standard once it is attained, market-based instruments – emissions charges, abatement subsidies, and marketable emissions permits – create continual incentives to innovate and reduce pollutant emissions.

However, as you will see later in the chapter, stringent conditions are necessary for markets to guarantee efficient outcomes. Policy instrument choice takes place in a 'second-best' world, where results are much less clear. The absence of markets (including those for externalities and public goods), asymmetric information, moral hazard and other instances of market failure, all point to possible benefits of command-and-control based public intervention or to the inappropriateness of complete reliance on markets and market instruments. (See Fisher and Rothkopf (1989) for an excellent survey.) Even where we do wish to use markets, however, government still has an important and inescapable role to play, not least in acquiring and processing the information necessary for choice of the level or rate at which the instrument is to be applied.

You will also see below that quantitative emissions controls, technology requirements and the standard-setting approach may be inadequate where uncertainties exist and new information is continually being obtained. Marketable permits, where control agencies have the flexibility to vary the stock of licences (as in the manner of open-market operations for short-term debt), or pollution tax instruments where tax rates can be altered as new information becomes available, offer attractive alternatives, as we shall see shortly (see also Barbier and Pearce, 1990).

---

environmental media. In the United States, for example, the federal Environmental Protection Agency has in recent decades established national ambient air quality and water quality standards with respect to a specified set of pollutants. Ambient air quality standards cover, among other pollutants, sulphur dioxide, particulates, carbon monoxide, nitrogen oxides, hydrocarbons and petrochemical oxidants. However, it is important to recognise that, unlike quantity controls on permitted *emissions* levels, targets specified in terms of maximum permitted *concentrations of pollutants in environmental media* are not control instruments; they are targets, to the satisfaction of which instruments are directed. In the USA and the UK, as we shall see later, the main instrument used to attain such targets has been mandatory emissions control technology.

Other forms of direct regulation

Another variety of the command-and-control approach to pollution control involves specifying required characteristics of production processes or capital equipment used. In other words, minimum technology requirements are imposed upon potential polluters. Examples include requirements to use flue gas desulphurisation equipment in power generation, regulation of minimum stack heights, the installation of catalytic converters in vehicle exhaust systems, and maximum permitted lead content in engine fuels. These instruments are easy and cheap to administer, and can be very effective in the sense of achieving large reductions in emissions quickly, particularly when technological 'fixes' are available but not widely adopted. As shown in Box 9.2, the required use of specified pollution control technology has been the dominant instrument for environmental protection in most OECD economies.

Such controls are dependable in their effects, and have almost certainly resulted in huge reductions in pollution levels compared with what would be expected in their absence. However, they are usually not cost-efficient, as the instrument contains no intrinsic mechanism whereby abatement effort is concentrated on polluters which are able to abate at least cost. Technology regulation instruments also suffer from two other disadvantages; they tend to be inflexible, and they have very poor incentives to promote dynamic efficiency.

Tax or subsidy schemes to internalise marginal damage

Taxes and subsidies can be thought of as instruments that control pollution levels through economic incentives created by the modification of relative prices. Taxation may be imposed either on the levels of certain inputs, or on the levels of pollution discharges. We concentrate on the latter type. Subsidies can be paid for pollution abatement. Clearly, the selective use of taxes or subsidies can change relative prices in any manner desired by the policy maker. In this section, taxes on pollutant emissions and subsidies for pollution abatement are

treated as if they were one type of instrument, rather than two distinct instruments. This is done because we wish to stress a fundamental symmetry between them. As will become apparent, the incentive effects of an emissions tax and an abatement subsidy are essentially the same. References below to tax schemes, therefore, apply equally well to abatement subsidy programmes. However, the long-run effects of subsidies may be different from the long-run effects of taxes, given their different distributional implications.

A tax on pollutant emissions is the standard form of instrument advocated by economists to achieve some preset pollution target. It eliminates the wedge (created by the external pollution damage) between private and socially efficient prices, by imposing a tax that brings private prices into line with social prices. In order to achieve an economically efficient level of pollution, the tax should be applied on each unit of pollution emitted, at a rate equal to the monetary value of marginal pollution damage at the optimal level of pollution. Such a tax will 'internalise the externality' in the sense that the generator of the (previously) external effect will now be taking decisions using cost functions which incorporate the pollution costs to society. The decision will then take account of all relevant costs, rather than just the producer's private costs, and so the profit maximising pollution level will coincide with the socially efficient level.

In Figure 9.4, we illustrate the effects of the imposition of a tax per unit of pollution. You will notice that in this diagram, the functions we are using are the marginal benefit firms derive from pollution and the marginal damage society incurs as a result of pollution. If firms behave without regard to the social damage of any pollution they generate, they will produce output (and so emissions) up to the point where they derive no additional profit from extra units of pollution. This is shown as $\hat{\Psi}$ in Figure 9.4, and is what we shall now call the uncontrolled level of pollution.

Now suppose an emissions tax were to be introduced, such that at each level of pollution, the tax rate per unit of pollution is equal to the level of marginal damage at that pollution level. Given this, the post-tax marginal benefit schedule differs from the original (pre-tax) marginal benefit schedule by the value of marginal damage. It can be seen that private profit-maximising behaviour by firms leads, once the tax is operative, to a pollution choice of Ψ^* (where the private post-tax marginal benefits of additional pollution are zero) rather than $\hat{\Psi}$, as was the case

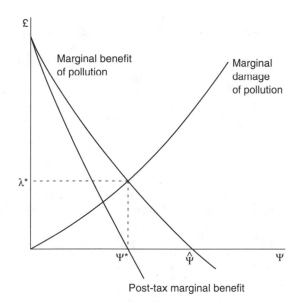

Fig 9.4 The effect of introducing an efficient emissions tax.

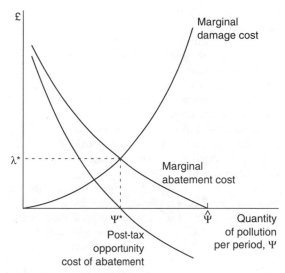

Prior to the emissions tax being levied, profit-maximising producers choose as emissions level $\hat{\Psi}$. This corresponds to an output level at which marginal benefits, *net of private production costs*, equal zero. At $\hat{\Psi}$, profits are maximised. After the efficient tax is introduced, levied at the rate λ^* per unit of emission of the pollutant, the maximising producers select emission level Ψ^*, as this is now where post-tax marginal benefits are zero. Note that Ψ^* is the socially efficient pollution level.

before the tax. Finally note that at the optimal pollution level, the tax rate per unit of pollutant is equal to λ^*, the value of marginal external damage per unit of pollution at the efficient outcome. Our analysis so far has dealt with pollution taxes, but a subsidy on units of pollution reduced (or abated) would have an equivalent effect. This equivalence arises from the fact that the incentives offered by tax and subsidy schemes are identical. A pollution tax scheme imposes a cost of λ^* on each unit of pollution it does not abate at the margin; a subsidy scheme also imposes a cost of λ^* on each unabated unit of pollution.

It is often useful to analyse pollution control in terms of abatement rather than the level of pollution itself, as shown in Figure 9.5. To change emphasis in this way, we replace the marginal benefit of pollution function with a marginal abatement cost function. (You will recall from our discussions in Chapter 8 that, given a proper interpretation of the marginal benefit of pollution and marginal abatement cost functions, the two ways of viewing the pollution

Is it worth a firm undertaking any pollution abatement? *Before* any tax or subsidy exists, the abatement cost schedule will be as shown above, as the curve labelled 'Marginal abatement cost'. As abatement costs the firm money, but it receives no additional market income from reducing pollution, profit maximisation implies it should undertake zero abatement, so pollution would be at the uncontrolled level $\hat{\Psi}$. In the presence of either a tax penalty per unit of emission or a subsidy payment per unit of emission abated equal to λ^*, the value of marginal damage at the socially efficient pollution level, the real (opportunity) cost of marginal abatement will be that indicated by the function labelled 'Post-tax opportunity cost of abatement'. In this case, a profit-maximising firm will abate pollution up to the socially efficient level, Ψ^*. That is, the firm achieves a net gain (rather than a net loss), as it *avoids* the payment of a tax *or* it receives the payment of a subsidy. Note that the post-tax opportunity cost of abatement is defined as the marginal abatement cost less the marginal damage cost (pollution tax).

Fig 9.5 The effect of an emissions tax on marginal abatement cost.

abatement are equivalent.) The marginal abatement cost function should be 'read' from right to left – beginning from no abatement, at pollution level, marginal costs rise as, moving from right to left, abatement effort increases.

In the absence of an emissions tax (or an abatement subsidy), firms have no financial incentive to abate pollution. Whilst the firm would have to incur costs if it undertook pollution abatement, it would receive no additional income corresponding to the social gains from a less polluted environment. In these circumstances, private profit-maximising behaviour implies that firms will undertake zero abatement, corresponding to the point $\hat{\Psi}$ in Figure

9.5. However matters are quite different when an emissions tax is levied (or when an abatement subsidy is available). In these circumstances, an incentive to abate does exist, taking the form of either the avoidance of a tax or the gain of subsidy payments. Firms will then find it privately profitable to abate pollution as long as their marginal abatement unit costs are less than the absolute value of the tax rate per unit of pollution (or less than the subsidy per unit of emission abated). Provided the tax/subsidy is levied at the efficient rate, λ^*, abatement takes place up to the efficient pollution level Ψ^*.

This argument reflects, once again, the equivalence between a pollution tax on emissions and a subsidy to output producers for each unit of pollution reduction. If the rates of subsidy were identical to the pollution tax rate, then the outcome in terms of levels of output and pollution would be the same under each scheme. However, the distribution of gains and losses will usually differ, and this could affect the long-run level of pollution abatement under some circumstances.

For the simple special case of a uniformly mixing flow pollutant, in which the value of the damage created by the emission is independent of the location of the emission source or the time of the emission, several points about pollution taxes are worth stressing.

1 For the tax to be an efficient instrument, the tax rate should be uniform over all polluters. That is, it will be applied at the same rate per unit of pollution on all units of the pollutant. As a consequence of this, a pollution tax control scheme will automatically be cost-effective. This property of uniformity of the tax rate follows from the fact that we are dealing here with uniformly mixing pollutants, where the damage done by each unit of emissions is independent of time and place. Where pollution is not uniformly mixing, and so damage depends upon the location or timing of the emission, an optimal tax rate will no longer be uniform. See the later sections on surface and stock pollutants, and Problem 4, for more on this matter.

2 The magnitude of the economically efficient tax rate will be equal to the magnitude of the marginal external damage of the pollutant *at the socially optimal level of pollution*.

3 The tax is not a tax on output; it is a tax on pollutant emissions. This encourages economically efficient substitution effects to take place, as the introduction of the tax leads to changes in relative prices. Consider the example of two fuels currently selling at a single price per unit of thermal energy, one generating a higher amount of pollutant per unit of produced energy than the other.[2] Suppose that a tax is applied on each fuel proportional to their relative pollutant emissions per unit of energy. The price of the more polluting fuel will then be higher relative to that of the cleaner fuel, and so consumers of fuel will substitute away from the more polluting fuel. Further substitution effects will take place if relative prices of consumer goods alter in response to changes in energy prices. If the tax changes alter the net prices or royalties of the two fuels, substitution effects will also take place on the supply side as the degree of exploration effort into searching for new reserves changes in response to changing royalties.

Our discussion in this section so far has been premised on the assumption that government wishes to attain an economically efficient level of pollution, and has sufficient information for this to be feasible. But we have seen that if the control authority does not know the marginal damage function, it will not be able to identify the economically efficient level of pollution abatement, nor the efficient tax or subsidy level. However, knowledge of the pollution abatement schedule alone means that it can calculate the required rate of tax to achieve any target level it wishes. The tax would attain that target at minimum feasible cost, and so would be cost-efficient for that level of pollution abatement. If it knew neither the marginal damage nor the marginal abatement cost schedules, then it could arbitrarily set a tax rate, confident in the knowledge that whatever level of abatement this would generate would be attained at minimum feasible cost. Taxes and subsidies are, therefore, cost-efficient policy instruments, and could also, given sufficient information, achieve the efficient level of pollution.

We illustrate these observations in Figure 9.6. Diagram (a) shows a situation in which the control authority knows the marginal damage and abatement cost functions, and so can identify a tax rate, λ^*, which will yield an economically efficient level of pollution, Ψ^* (or equivalently, pollution abatement, $\hat{\Psi} - \Psi^*$). Case (b) illustrates a situation in which the

[2] Coal and natural gas provide a good example. In terms of CO_2 emissions, coal produces 1.8 times as much emission as gas per unit of produced energy.

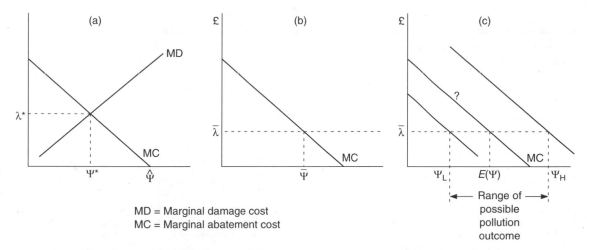

MD = Marginal damage cost
MC = Marginal abatement cost

Fig 9.6 Emissions control under uncertainty.

authority knows only the marginal abatement cost function; if it wished to restrict pollution to the level $\bar{\Psi}$, it could do so by setting the tax rate at $\bar{\lambda}$. In the third case, the control authority only knows that the MC function lies in the shaded interval. If it were to set a tax rate at the level $\bar{\lambda}$, the amount of pollution that actually takes place lies in the interval Ψ_H to Ψ_L. Whatever the outcome, it is nevertheless achieved cost-efficiently.

Transferable (marketable) emissions permits

A marketable permit scheme involves:

1 A decision as to the total quantity of pollution that is to be allowed. If an efficient programme is to be attained, the total quantity of emission permits issued (measured in units of pollution) should be equal to the efficient level of pollution, Ψ^*. If knowledge does not allow the control authority to identify Ψ^*, or if it is felt inappropriate to choose pollution levels using an efficiency criterion, then the number of permits to be issued must be decided on some other basis.
2 A rule which ensures that any firm is allowed to produce pollution (of a certain designated type) only to the quantity of emission permits it possesses. Any emission beyond that level by a firm is subject to a prohibitively expensive fine or other penalty.
3 A choice by the control authority over how the total quantity of emission permits is to be initially allocated between procedures.
4 A guarantee that emission permits can be freely

traded between firms at whichever price is agreed for that trade.

Looking at Figure 9.5 once again, we can note the basis for a system of transferable emission permits as an instrument for controlling pollution. Efficient control could be achieved by imposing either a tax at the rate λ^* per unit of pollutant, or a permitted quantity of pollutant, Ψ^*. Transferable permit schemes differ from tax or subsidy schemes by working in terms of quantities rather than prices. But this feature is also true for quantity controls such as quotas, licences and standards. Wherein lies the difference between this set and a transferable permit scheme? The difference arises because of the transferability (or marketability) of the permits in the latter case. A market will become established for transferable permits, in which the market permit price will be λ^* if the total quantity of permits issued is Ψ^*. This characteristic of the permit system leads to the transferable permit instrument having essentially similar effects to a tax levied of the rate λ^*.

Consider again the information shown in Table 9.1, in which we suppose that a total permit allocation of 50 units is selected. Suppose that the pollutant is emitted by just two firms, A and B, and that pollution abatement can only be undertaken by these firms. The government decides arbitrarily to allocate half to each firm, so A and B are allocated 25 permits each, allowing them to emit 25 units of the pollutant. We assume that in the absence of any control system, A would emit 40 units and B 50 units. Given the permit allocations, A must reduce pollution by 15 units and

Box 9.3 The equivalence of pollution taxes and emissions abatement subsidies

We have argued that an emission tax levied at the rate λ per unit of pollutant is equivalent to an abatement subsidy paid at the rate λ per unit of pollution abated. This statement needs some qualification, however. Let us clarify, first of all, the sense in which the two are equivalent. The claim made is that, for an industry of a given size, the two would result in an equal amount of emissions abatement. Thus, looking at Figure 9.5, a subsidy at the rate λ^* per unit of emission abatement and a tax at the rate λ^* per unit of emission will both reduce emissions from $\hat{\Psi}$, the uncontrolled level, to Ψ^*, the efficient level. However, the two instruments are certainly not equivalent in all respects. One difference lies in the implications they suggest for income distribution. In terms of income, a firm will benefit from an abatement subsidy, as it will undertake abatement wherever the subsidy it receives per unit of abatement exceeds the marginal abatement cost. A tax on the other hand will result in a loss of income to the firm. The firm must pay the tax on all units of the pollutant it emits. To make this comparison more precise, look at Figure 9.7, the functions in which reproduce those in Figure 9.5.

An emissions abatement subsidy will result in a payment to the firm equal to the areas $S_1 + S_2$ (that is, λ^* multiplied by $(\hat{\Psi} - \Psi^*)$). However, by reducing pollution from $\hat{\Psi}$ to Ψ^*, the firm loses S_2 in profit on

final output. The net gain to the firm is equal, therefore, to the area S_1. An emission tax levied at the rate λ^* on pollution of Ψ^* will cost the firm $\lambda^*\Psi^*$, that is, the sum of the areas S_3, S_4, S_5 and S_6. However, by reducing pollution from $\hat{\Psi}$ to Ψ^*, the firm also loses the area S_2, the profit on lost output. So the income effects are entirely different.

Let us explore this difference a little further. Recall that the tax paid is equal in value to $\lambda^*\Psi^*$, whilst the subsidy received is $\lambda^*(\hat{\Psi} - \Psi^*)$. But $\lambda^*(\hat{\Psi} - \Psi^*) = \lambda^*\hat{\Psi} - \lambda^*\Psi^*$. The second term on the right-hand side, $\lambda^*\Psi^*$, is identical to the tax paid, and will depend on the amount of abatement undertaken. It is this second component which gives the firm an incentive to abate pollution. Recalling that λ is a negative quantity in a tax scheme and a positive quantity in a subsidy scheme, $\lambda^*\Psi^*$ with a tax is identical to $-\lambda^*\Psi^*$ with a subsidy. The two incentive effects are identical, and it is this which forms the basis for the claim that the instruments are equivalent. However, the subsidy differs from the tax by the presence of the additional term, $\lambda^*\hat{\Psi}$, a fixed or lump sum payment, independent of the amount of abatement the firm actually undertakes. In the long-run such payments may alter industry profitability, and so alter the size of the industry itself. This lump sum payment component of the subsidy may destroy the equivalence between the two instruments in terms of their effects on pollution abatement.

We are thus faced with the possibility, at least, that a subsidy might enlarge the industry, partially or wholly offsetting the short-run pollution reduction. It is not possible to be more precise about the final outcome, as that would depend upon many other factors. A general equilibrium analysis would be necessary to obtain clear results. This is beyond our scope in this text, so we just note that the equivalence asserted above is by no means valid in all cases.

Finally, note another aspect of an abatement subsidy scheme. As one component of the subsidy received depends upon the uncontrolled level of emissions, $\hat{\Psi}$ (i.e. the component $\lambda^*\hat{\Psi}$), a firm has an incentive to misrepresent the uncontrolled level of emissions in order to obtain a favourable benchmark in terms of which the subsidy payments are calculated. Whether or not a firm can succeed in doing this depends upon whether or not $\hat{\Psi}$ is observed for each firm.

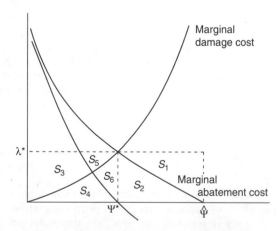

Fig 9.7 Emissions tax and abatement subsidy schemes: a comparison.

B by 25 units. This is the initial position, indicated by the point Z_1 in Figure 9.8. Note that the functions portrayed in Figure 9.8 reproduce exactly those previously employed in Figure 9.3.

But we can see that Firm A has lower marginal abatement costs (λ_A) than Firm B (λ_B) at the point where Firm A undertakes 15 units of abatement and Firm B undertakes 25 units of abatement. The total

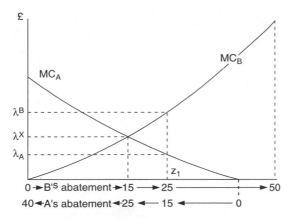

Notes: MC_A = Marginal cost of pollution abatement for firm A
          MC_B = Marginal cost of pollution abatement for firm B
          Numbers along the horizontal axis refer to amount of
          abatement undertaken by each firm

Fig 9.8 Cost-effectiveness and marketable emissions permits.

cost of abating pollution by 40 units would be reduced if Λ were to do more abatement, and B less. But this is exactly what will happen. Notice there is a basis for a mutually advantageous trade here. Suppose that A were to sell an emission permit to B at some price above λ_A but below λ_B. A would be required to do more abatement, but would benefit in net terms as the price it received from selling permits would exceed its additional control costs. Firm B would also benefit; whilst it must pay A to acquire extra permits, this would be more than compensated for by the abatement costs it can now avoid.

Trading would cease only where marginal control costs are equalised across polluters. This requires that the market price of the permit be λ^*, at which point all firms would be abating pollution to the efficient level. If the total quantity of permits were set at the level corresponding to the economically efficient level of pollution, it can be shown that *transferability* will result in the establishment of a market in permits, in which the equilibrium market price will equal λ^*, the shadow price of pollution at the social optimum level. The permit system will, therefore, have identical effects on output and pollution as an optimal tax or subsidy system, and will be identical in terms of its cost-effectiveness property.

Although taxes and subsidies on the one hand, and marketable permits on the other hand, have equivalent effects upon the levels of pollution abatement, their *distributional* effects may well be very different. We shall investigate these matters in the following section.

A comparison of emissions tax and marketable permit instruments

Dependability of the control instrument

If the aggregate abatement cost function is known with certainty, then the control authority can determine what emissions tax rate is needed to achieve any given level of abatement. Once that tax rate is introduced, abatement is attained at the desired level – the instrument is completely dependable. A similar result holds in this case for marketable permits; the control authority sets the amount of permits issued, and trading on the permits market will lead to a permit price that can be perfectly predicted by the policy maker. So knowledge of abatement costs leads to dependability of the quantity of emission abatement (and of the tax or permit price) for both tax and permit systems.

However, where the abatement function is not known with certainty, the two instruments differ. In the case of the tax instrument, a tax rate will be decided upon by the control authority, but the amount of abatement that results from this will not be certainly known, as it will depend upon the actual (but unknown) position of the abatement cost function. Similar comments apply to a subsidy system. Marketable emission permits always achieve dependability in terms of quantities of abatement, and in this respect nothing is altered from the first case. But where uncertainty exists about control costs, the price of pollution permits cannot be predicted with certainty.

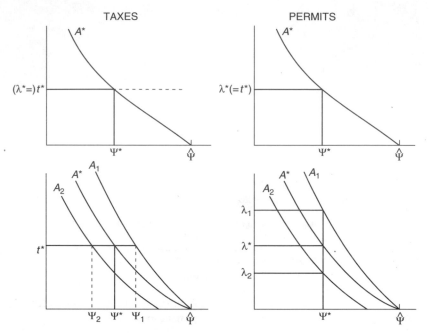

Fig 9.9 A comparison of taxes and marketable permits when control costs are uncertain.

The differing way in which abatement cost uncertainty affects these two instruments is illustrated in Figure 9.9. In the upper half of the figure, a single abatement cost function is drawn, assumed to be known by the authority. Tax and permit regimes are identical in outcomes. Abatement cost uncertainty (shown in the lower half, with three different possible realisations of abatement costs) affects the amount of abatement under a tax system, whilst it affects the permit price under a marketable permits system.

Distributional issues

As far as permit schemes are concerned, the distributional effects will depend primarily upon which method of initial permit allocation is chosen. An initial choice the control authority must make is whether to sell the permits, or allocate them freely in the first instance. If the permits are sold, one way of doing so is through a competitive auction market. The equilibrium permit price in such a market will be determined by the marginal abatement cost (MAC) function; it will be equal to the marginal abatement cost at the level of pollution abatement which is implied by the total number of permits that are issued.

Suppose, for example, that the MAC function is given by

$$MC = 10 + 0.1(\hat{\Psi} - \bar{\Psi})$$

or

$$MC = 10 + 0.1\bar{Z}$$

where $\bar{Z} = \hat{\Psi} - \bar{\Psi}$ is the quantity of emissions abatement undertaken. If the uncontrolled level of emissions ($\hat{\Psi}$) is 200 and the target level ($\bar{\Psi}$) 150, then 150 permits will be issued and the required abatement ($\bar{Z}$) is 50 units. Marginal abatement costs will be

$$MC = 10 + 0.1(200 - 150) = 15$$

There is no reason why the pollution control authority need sell the permits at their first allocation – an alternative is to initially distribute the permits at no charge, but to allow them to be subsequently traded in a free market. Given the abatement costs we have just been considering, the market price would still be 15 if 150 permits were issued. This illustrates one of the advantages claimed for a permits system; any desired level of pollution abatement can be achieved at the same real economic cost irrespective of how the permits are initially allocated. This is easily understood once it is remembered that the amount of abatement will depend upon the number of permits issued; whether they are initially sold or given away freely, and who initially receives them, will have no bearing on that – if permits to pollute up to one million tons are available, that will be how much pollution takes place (assuming the permit scheme is enforced effectively).

However, the manner in which the initial allocation is made will have effects on the *distribution* of gains and losses associated with the scheme. We have already seen that a single price will become established in the permit market. Those who hold permits but can abate pollution at lower cost than the permit price will sell permits, and gain from that sale. Polluters who do not hold permits will purchase them if their costs of abatement exceed the permit price.

If permits are issued freely in the first instance, there will be no net financial burden on polluting firms (although they will experience costs in the sense that they have to abate pollution). Trades of permits between firms, however, mean that some gain financially whilst others lose, even though net transfers between firms are zero.

On the other hand, if the pollution control agency decides to initially sell permits by competitive auction, then there will be a net transfer of income from polluters to the control agency equal to $\bar{\lambda}\bar{\Psi}$, the price per permit times the number of permits auctioned.

What kind of distributional implications do pollution taxes have? Clearly taxes will result in a transfer of income from polluters to the tax authority, equal to $\bar{\lambda}\bar{\Psi}$, the tax rate times the amount of pollution that takes place. Thus the distributional effects of a pollution tax scheme and a permits scheme in which permits are initially auctioned are identical. We have already seen that an abatement subsidy scheme will be of net benefit to polluters.

Different instruments for pollution control have different implications, therefore, for the distribution of income within an economy. It is important to realise that gains and losses to the business sector are not necessarily gains or losses to the economy as a whole. The income shifts we have been describing in this section are redistributive, and do not correspond to any real economic gains and losses to the economy. Indeed, it should be clear that any economically efficient pollution control instrument will bring net economic gains – what has been at issue in this section is how these gains are distributed. Note also that even where a particular instrument adversely affects one sector of the economy, it is open to the government to use compensating fiscal changes to offset those 'losses'. For example, if a pollution tax scheme would result in a net transfer of £1 billion from business to government, the latter could compensate firms by lump sum payments of £1 billion, and (at least in principle) these payments could be financed by lump-sum charges on the beneficiaries of pollution control.

Finally, it should be noted that taxes, for example on carbon content or on pollutant emissions more generally, have important implications for the tax structure within economies and the competitiveness of economies in relative terms. Some analysts have advocated a switch from taxes on labour and capital to taxes on pollution to avoid excessive tax burdens, and schemes have been proposed to penalise nations who attempt to gain competitive advantage by not introducing emissions taxes. Good discussions of these issues are to be found in Grubb (1989a), Bertram *et al.* (1989), Weizsacker (1989), Hansen (1990), Brown (1989), and Kosmo (1989).

Other forms of pollution control instrument

In this chapter, we have focused on command-and-control instruments, and three market based instruments: pollution taxes, abatement subsidies, and marketable permit schemes. These are by no means the only instruments available to pollution control agencies and to government.

Another option available is to move affected persons to areas not located near the source of pollution. There have been examples when people have been removed from heavily contaminated areas, including movements away from irradiated sites such as Chernobyl, Times Beach (Missouri), and Love Canal (New York). However, it has been far more common to move pollution sources away from areas where people will be affected, or to use planning regulations to ensure separation.

A number of legal instruments are also available to governments, the most important of which is the establishment of legal liability of polluters for the damages that they are responsible for. An interesting recent development is the moves in several countries to establish legal liability throughout the life cycle of a product, by attempting to develop the principle that original producers are responsible for damage from 'cradle to grave'.

Finally, educational and cultural measures may be appropriate in some circumstances. Government can encourage the education of individuals who may be affected by pollution, develop awareness of the environmental impacts of economic activity, and try to foster a business environment in which public opinion and market pressure demand environmentally responsible behaviour.

Box 9.4 Emissions permits in practice

The USA has had nearly two years' experience with a variety of emissions permit trading programmes, and we review and assess the success of these programmes in this section. The material presented in this box draws very heavily on – Tietenberg (1990) and Goodstein (1995).

The nature of emissions permits in the USA is similar to that described in the text of this chapter, but differs in some important details. American tradable permit systems operate in conjunction with more conventional standards or quota schemes. In essence they operate as follows. Suppose some particular pollutant is to be controlled. The United States Environmental Protection Agency (EPA) or other relevant regulatory agency establishes national standards, in terms of ambient air quality, permissible pollutant concentrations in water systems, and the like. To attain these standards, controls are imposed on individual polluting sources, usually taking the form of required abatement technologies and upper limits on flows of pollutants. In all of this there is nothing novel – this is simply the conventional command-and-control (CAC) approach that has characterised pollution control in most countries in the twentieth century. The novelty arises in the next component of the programme.

If any polluter succeeds in reducing emissions by a greater amount than is required by the standard it must satisfy, it obtains *emission reduction credits* (ERC) of that quantity. The firm which acquires these emission reduction credits can engage in trades, selling some or all of its ERCs to other firms, which then obtain a legal entitlement to emit pollutants beyond the standard which the EPA has imposed on them. Put another way, each firm is legally entitled to emit a quantity of pollutants up to the sum of its standard entitlement plus any ERC it has acquired. Each ERC is, thus, a transferable or marketable emissions permit in the sense we used in the text. However, the number of permits being traded will be much less than we indicated in that earlier discussion. To explain this, suppose that the US EPA decided that no more than 100 million tons of SO_2 emissions will be permitted, and allocated quotas to firms that added up to this total quantity. Suppose, also, that one set of firms chose to emit 25 million tons of SO_2 less than their allowed quotas; they will then acquire ERC to the amount of 25 million tons, and that is the maximum amount of permits that can be traded on the market. In the alternative method of implementing the scheme that we outlined in the text, permits would be issued to the amount of 100 million tons in this example.

The American ERC trading system has a number of other distinctive features:

- The *offset policy* allows existing firms to expand, or new firms to enter, areas in which emission standards have not been met in the aggregate provided that they acquire sufficient quantities of ERC. In other words, growth can take place provided corresponding emissions reductions take place by existing firms within that area.
- The *bubble policy* treats an aggregate of firms as one polluting source (as if they were enclosed in a single bubble) and requires that the bubble as a whole meets a specified standard. If that is achieved, it does not matter whether an individual source within the bubble fails to meet the firm-specific standard imposed on it.
- *Emissions banking* allows firms to store ERC for subsequent use or sale to others.

The actual extent to which marketable pollution permit programmes have been used is limited, but has undergone considerable growth in recent years. It has been used to reduce the lead content in petrol, to control production and use of chlorofluorocarbon ozone-depleting substances, and in the 'Emissions Trading Program' for the control of volatile organic compounds, carbon monoxide, sulphur dioxide, particulates and nitrogen oxide. Details of the programmes which exist in the USA can be found in recent surveys by Cropper and Oates (1992), Tietenberg (1990), Hahn (1989), Hahn and Hester (1989a, b), Opschoor and Vos (1989) and Goodstein (1995). The passage of the 1990 Amendments to the Clean Air Act has seen the United States introduce a major system of tradable permits to control sulphur emissions.

Most economists expect emissions trading to confer large efficiency gains relative to the use of command and control instruments alone. These gains arise from the reductions in overall abatement costs that trading permits; recall from our previous discussions that high cost abaters do less abatement and low cost abaters do more abatement when trading of permits or ERC is allowed. Tietenberg's assessment of the performance of the emissions permit trading schemes is

- The programme has unquestionably and substantially reduced the costs of complying with the Clean Air Act. Most estimates place the accumulated capital savings for all components of the programme at over $10 billion. This does not include the recurrent savings in operating costs. On the other hand the programme has not

Box 9.4 Continued

produced the magnitude of cost savings that was anticipated by its strongest proponents at its inception.

- The level of compliance with the basic provisions of the Clean Air Act has increased. The emissions trading programme increased the possible means for compliance and sources have responded accordingly.
- The vast majority of emissions trading transactions have involved large pollution sources.
- Though air quality has certainly improved for most of the covered pollutants, it is virtually impossible to say how much of the improvement can be attributed to the emissions trading programme.

Tietenberg (1990), pages 269–270 in the Markandya and Richardson (1992) reprint

The Cropper and Oates survey confirms the view that the use of transferable permit programmes, and other market incentive schemes based on taxes or subsidies, has been very limited in scale, but they assess interest in and acceptability of market-based incentive instruments to be growing:

... effluent charges and marketable permit programs are few in number and often bear only a modest resemblance to the pure programs of economic incentives supported by economists .... As we move into the 1990s, the general political and policy setting is one that is genuinely receptive to market approaches to solving our social problems. Not only in the United States but in other countries as well, the prevailing atmosphere is a conservative one with a strong predisposition towards the use of market incentives wherever possible, for the attainment of our social objectives.

Cropper and Oates (1992), pages 729 and 730

Command-and-control and market instruments: a comparison

We shall use the term 'command-and-control' to denote pollution control schemes that are based on legislative or administrative regulations directly relating to some relevant *quantity* (usually final output or permitted pollutant level or concentration rate) or to the *quality* of technology applied. The term 'market instrument' shall be used to denote a device which either alters the prices agents face (via tax or subsidy schemes, for example) or which generates price incentives to influence private behaviour (as with marketable permit schemes).

Market instruments have a number of desirable properties. In what follows, we discuss these with reference to a pollution tax scheme, but the results will also be valid for other market instruments, such as subsidy and permit schemes. The most important properties are:

1 An emissions tax can achieve an efficient pollution target at least cost among all feasible forms of control.
2 An emissions tax can achieve any given pollution target (not necessarily an efficient one) at least cost among all feasible forms of control.

3 An emissions tax set at any level can achieve some level of pollution control; that level of control will be achieved at least cost among all feasible forms of control.
4 An emissions tax will generate a dynamically efficient pattern of incentives on corporate and consumer behaviour.

Properties (1) to (3) here relate to cost-efficiency of pollution tax instruments. The reason why a pollution tax has this property is that tax will ensure that all pollution abaters face the same marginal cost of abatement, equal to the tax rate selected. The distribution of the burden of overall abatement between firms will result from the profit-maximising decisions of firms. A cost-efficient outcome does not require that the government have any knowledge of control costs of individual firms.

In contrast, a command-and-control regulation instrument may, but will not necessarily, be cost-efficient. Consider Figure 9.10, which represents an industry with two producers, A and B. Associated with each firm's output is the production of a damaging residual. The curves labelled MC_A and MC_B describe the marginal costs of abating the residual for firms A and B respectively. Note that these marginal costs differ between the two firms. The combined or industry marginal cost of abatement schedule, MC_{A+B}, is obtained by horizontal summation of the firms' marginal cost schedules.

Box 9.5 Pollution tax and abatement subsidies in practice

Emissions taxes (or emissions charges) are currently used in Japan and a number of European countries. Effluent charges to control water pollution are used in France, Italy, Germany and the Netherlands; in some cases, charge revenues are earmarked for purposes of water quality improvement. In the cases of Germany and Italy, charges are used in conjunction with effluent standards; those firms which meet or better the standards are taxed at a lower rate per unit effluent than others.

France and Japan operate systems of air pollution emissions taxes. France has used charges as an incentive to install pollution abatement technology, with charges being repaid in the form of capital subsidies to firms adopting recommended control technologies. The Japanese system levies taxes in order to maintain a fund for compensation for victims of air pollution; charge levels are dependent upon amounts of compensation paid out in previous years. Differential tax rates on leaded and unleaded petrol in the United Kingdom serve as an indirect charge on lead emissions, and Sweden has used differential charges and subsidies on cars and heavy vehicles to encourage the purchase of low pollution engines and the adoption of catalytic converters. Mention should also be made of the relatively high rates of tax on electricity and primary energy sources throughout Western Europe; whilst not being examples of pollution taxes as such, they do have similar incentive effects by encouraging energy conservation and enhancing energy efficiency.

The Commission of the European Union has for some time been studying the possibility of introducing a Europe-wide carbon tax to moderate greenhouse gas emissions, and to meet the EC objective of stabilising carbon dioxide emissions at the 1990 level by the year 2000. Initial plans were for the tax to be introduced in 1993 at the rate of $3 per barrel, and to be raised by $1 per year until it reached the level of $10 in 2000. Revenues would accrue to member states to be used exclusively for environmental improvement. The Commission's plan had been rejected by the EC Council of Ministers, and is unlikely to be implemented in the near future.

The USA makes very little use of emissions taxes or charges, the exceptions being fees on sewage and solid and hazardous waste at landfills (Goodstein, 1995); households typically pay by the gallon for sewage disposal, and waste haulage firms pay by the ton for solid waste disposal. Unfortunately, from an efficiency perspective, these marginal disposal costs are not passed on to the initial producers of waste; household and business enterprises typically pay lump sum disposal charges. The United States has, though, made more extensive use of marketable emission permit instruments than European economies (see Box 9.4).

In our analysis of emissions taxes in this chapter, we discussed taxes used to achieve fully efficient outcomes (by internalising pollution costs at the socially efficient pollution level) and taxes designed to achieve cost-effective (that is, least-cost) attainment of targets for a level of pollution abatement that may or may not be socially efficient. No existing system of taxes fits either of these criteria perfectly. Taxes or subsidies, where they have been used, have typically been set at low levels, with correspondingly low levels of impact, although the Netherlands, with relatively high rates, has shown large improvements in water quality. Sweden's use of differential taxes and subsidies, and the differential tax on unleaded petrol in the UK have been very effective in causing substitution in the intended directions.

Sources: Tietenberg (1990), reprinted as Chapter 21 in Markandya and Richardson (1992), and Goodstein (1995).

The government seeks a total quantity of pollution abatement in each period of Z^*. Suppose that it implements this target by means of imposing a ceiling on the quantity of pollutant each firm is permitted to make. Knowledge of the uncontrolled emissions level of each firm would allow us to translate these ceilings into minimum quantities of abatement that must be undertaken by each firm. For simplicity, we assume in our example that each firm is required to achieve the same level of abatement, so to reach the target, each firm must achieve $Z^*/2$ units of pollution reduction per period. The total costs of pollution abatement in this case will be equal to the sum of the areas under each firm's marginal cost schedule over the interval zero to $Z^*/2$.[3]

Next, suppose that a tax per unit emission of λ^* is imposed. Firm A will then undertake abatement to the level Z_A^*, firm B to the level Z_B^*. Note that $Z_A^* + Z_B^* = Z^*$. Total abatement costs will be the sum of the areas under the firms' marginal cost curves, up to the levels Z_A^* and Z_B^* respectively. It is

---

[3] This statement is not strictly valid, as it ignores the possible presence of fixed costs.

easy to show that abatement costs under the tax regime will be less than those under quantity controls in this example.[4] The reason for this is that the two producers will face different marginal costs of abatement under the quantity control. This cannot be a cost-effective way of achieving the target, as the same target could be achieved at lower cost by switching some abatement effort from A (where the marginal cost is high) to B (where the marginal cost is low). For the tax approach, the target is being achieved in a cost-effective manner, as marginal abatement costs have been equalised.[5]

The conclusion we can draw from this example is that the quantity regulation approach is inefficient relative to the tax scheme, as it achieves the specified target at a higher real cost. Some empirical evidence on this is presented in Box 9.6. Note, however, that if the environmental protection agency knew the control cost function of each polluter, it could establish a pollution limit for each firm such that marginal abatement costs were equalised across all firms. In that case, the command-and-control instrument would also be cost-efficient.

So far, we have said nothing about the costs associated with monitoring, administering and enforcing compliance with the instruments. These costs could be quite substantial, and if they are

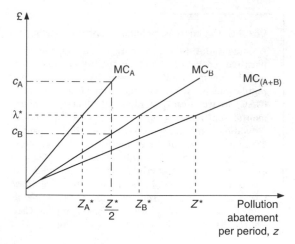

MC_A = Marginal cost of abatement of firm A
MC_B = Marginal cost of abatement of firm B
MC_{A+B} = Combined marginal cost of abatement for industry, A + B

$$Z_A^* + Z_B^* = Z^*$$

$$2\left(\frac{Z^*}{2}\right) = Z^*$$

Fig 9.10 A comparison of abatement costs under a pollution tax scheme and an emission quantity control scheme.

---

[4] A proof of this assertion is as follows. Let two pollution abaters have total costs of abatement functions given by

$$C_1 = f_1(Z_1)$$
$$C_2 = f_2(Z_2)$$

where Z_1 and Z_2 are the quantities of abatement undertaken by firms 1 and 2. The total cost of abating pollution, C, is the sum of the abatement costs of the two firms, C_1 and C_2. That is

$$C = C_1 + C_2$$

Suppose that we seek to attain some target level of total pollution abatement, Z^*, at minimum cost. Noting that $Z^* = Z_1 + Z_2$, the Lagrangian for this problem is

$$L = f_1(Z_1) + f_2(Z_2) + \lambda(Z^* - Z_1 - Z_2)$$

The necessary conditions for a minimum (of this constrained cost function) include

$$\frac{df_1}{dZ_1} - \lambda = 0$$

$$\frac{df_2}{dZ_2} - \lambda = 0$$

and so

$$\frac{df_1}{dZ_1} = \frac{df_2}{dZ_2}$$

which states that the marginal costs of abatement are equalised over the two firms.

[5] Exactly the same result will occur where a permit scheme issues permits such that Z^* abatement must take place. In this case, λ^* will be the market price per permit, and the result is identical to that just described.

Box 9.6 The costs of pollution abatement using command-and-control and market based instruments

A substantial literature now exists on the comparative costs of attaining pollution abatement targets using traditional quantity or technology regulations – what we call command-and-control (CAC) instruments – and so-called market instruments (particularly emissions taxes, abatement subsidies, and marketable/transferable emissions permits). Much of this literature derives from experience in the USA with these two categories of instrument. Tietenberg (1990) provides an admirable account of recent evidence on these costs. Table 9.2 reproduces one of Tietenberg's tables, showing the ratio of costs under CAC approaches to the least-cost controls (using market instruments) for air pollution control in the United States.

It should be pointed out that these studies compare actual CAC costs with those theoretically expected under least-cost market-based instruments. In practice, one would not expect market instruments to operate at these theoretical minimum costs, and so the ratios overstate the cost savings that would be obtained in practice by switching CAC techniques. However, the ratios – varying from 1.07 to 22.0, the latter figure implying that CAC may be 22 times more expensive than is necessary – suggest that massive cost savings might be available if market instruments were to be used in place of CAC.

Table 9.2 Empirical studies of air pollution control

Study	Pollutants covered	Geographic area	CAC benchmark	Ratio of CAC cost to least cost
Atkinson and Lewis	Particulates	St Louis	SIP regulations	6.00[a]
Roach et al.	Sulphur dioxide	Four corners in Utah	SIP regulations Colorado, Arizona, and New Mexico	4.25
Hahn and Noll	Sulphates standards	Los Angeles	California emission	1.07
Krupnick	Nitrogen dioxide regulations	Baltimore	Proposed RACT	5.96[b]
Seskin et al.	Nitrogen dioxide regulations	Chicago	Proposed RACT	14.40[b]
McGartland	Particulates	Baltimore	SIP regulations	4.18
Spofford	Sulphur dioxide	Lower Delaware Valley	Uniform percentage regulations	1.78
	Particulates	Lower Delaware Valley	Uniform percentage regulations	22.0
Harrison	Airport noise	United States	Mandatory retrofit	1.72[c]
Maloney and Yandle	Hydrocarbons	All domestic DuPont plants	Uniform percentage reduction	4.15[d]
Palmer et al.	CFC emissions from non-aerosol applications	United States	Proposed standards	1.96

Notes:
CAC = command and control, the traditional regulatory approach.
SIP = state implementation plan.
RACT = reasonably available control technologies, a set of standards imposed on existing sources in non-attainment areas.
[a] Based on a 40 $\mu g/m^3$ at worst receptor.
[b] Based on a short-term, one-hour average of 250 $\mu g/m^3$.
[c] Because it is a benefit–cost study instead of a cost-effectiveness study the Harrison comparison of the command-and-control approach with the least-cost allocation involves different benefit levels. Specifically, the benefit levels associated with the least-cost allocation are only 82% of those associated with the command-and-control allocation. To produce cost estimates based on more comparable benefits, as a first approximation the least-cost allocation was divided by 0.82 and the resulting number was compared with the command-and-control cost.
[d] Based on 85% reduction of emissions from all sources.

Source: Tietenberg (1990), Table 1.

Box 9.6 Continued

Table 9.3 Andreasson's real economic (resource) costs and effects on farm incomes

Policy instrument	Resource costs (million kronor)		Farm income (% of total income)	
	Scenario A	Scenario B	Scenario A	Scenario B
Quotes	24.1	34.2	−10.0	−15.4
Tax	18.7	21.2	−13.9	−12.4
Tradable permits	18.7	21.2	−7.6	−9.0

Source: Hanley and Spash (1993), page 202.

We shall now consider a European example Andreasson (1990) examines the costs of policies for reducing nitrate fertiliser use on the Swedish island of Gotland. This study is discussed at length in Hanley and Spash (1993), in a chapter devoted to analysing the costs and benefits of nitrate pollution control. Andreasson investigates three policies for achieving the Swedish government's upper limit of 30 milligrams per litre nitrates in drinking water. Model calculations suggest the need for a 50% reduction in nitrogenous fertiliser application to meet that target (scenario B). However, uncertainty exists about the rate at which nitrate leaches from manure and fertiliser, and it is possible that a more modest reduction in fertiliser application (14%) would be sufficient to achieve the target (scenario A).

The three policy instruments investigated by Andreasson are (non-tradable) quotas on fertiliser use, a tax on nitrogenous fertiliser, and a tradable permit system. Table 9.3 presents the real economic (resource) costs of achieving the pollution target under the two scenarios for each of the three policy instruments. In addition, Andreasson estimates the effects on farm incomes of the alternative policies;

these farm income effects are also shown in Table 9.3.

These results are consistent with the conclusions suggested by our analysis in this chapter. Look first at the real economic costs (called resource costs in Table 9.3). As both taxes and tradable permits are fully efficient, their theoretical costs are identical. Costs under non-tradable quota controls are higher − here by about a third in scenario A and a half in scenario B. These higher costs arise from the fact that non-tradability means that marginal pollution control costs are not being equalised between different users of fertilisers. Secondly, the effects on farm incomes differ widely between the three policies. Taxes cause the largest loss of farm income under the lower reduction scenario, whereas quotas hit farm incomes most harshly when a high reduction is sought. Tradable permits are the least costly from the viewpoint of farmers in each case. This arises from the fact that Andreasson's simulations assume that the permits are initially allocated free of charge; if they were auctioned on a free market initially, losses to farm incomes would, of course, by higher than those indicated in the table.

significantly different between instruments could affect which type of instrument is the least-cost one for achieving a particular target. One reason for the prevalence of minimum technology requirements as a pollution control instrument may be that these costs are low relative to those of instruments which try to regulate pollution output levels.

Can we say anything in general about Property (4), relating to the dynamic incentives under the alternative control regimes? The key question we seek to answer here is what incentives firms face in developing pollution-saving technology or developing new, environmentally cleaner products. Under a pollution tax scheme, these incentives are very strong, as we show in Figure 9.11.

Area Ω is the saving that would result if marginal costs were lowered from MC_1 to MC_2 and the pollution level were unchanged. But if marginal cost were lowered in this way, the firm's profit-maximising pollution abatement level would rise from Z_1^* to Z_2^*, and so an additional saving of Λ would accrue to the firm. The firm has an incentive to develop new technology to abate emission if the total costs of developing and applying the technology are less than the present value of the savings $\Omega + \Lambda$ accumulated over the life of the firm.[6]

---

[6] Note that the optimal tax rate would change as new technology lowers control costs. So matters are a little more complicated!

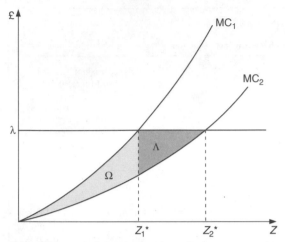

Fig 9.11 Dynamic incentives under pollution tax controls.

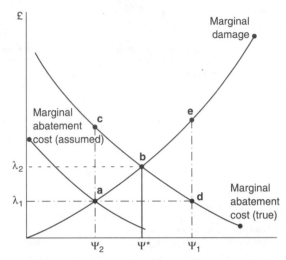

Area **abc** = efficiency loss under an 'incorrect' standard
Area **bde** = efficiency loss under an 'incorrect' emission tax

Fig 9.12 Uncertainty and the choice of pollution control instrument.

The loss of dynamic incentives in regulatory systems is easy to understand. If a target is set in quantitative terms, then once that target has been met there is little or no *further* incentive on the polluter to reduce pollution. In a market-based scheme, such an incentive is always present as every unit of pollution reduction is rewarded by a tax saving.

The consequences of uncertainty for the design of pollution control programmes

In a situation of certainty, decision makers know the pollution abatement cost and pollution damage functions, and can therefore determine the efficient level of pollution abatement. In such circumstances, economic arguments of the kind used in the previous section suggest that market-based control instruments (taxes, subsidies and marketable permits) are in general the best means of achieving control targets.

However, where decision makers have uncertain knowledge of these functions, market instruments are no longer necessarily best. Under conditions of uncertainty, the government can overestimate or underestimate marginal abatement costs or benefits. Therefore, both a market-based instrument and a regulatory control system can lead to non-efficient amounts of pollution. One example of this is shown in Figure 9.12 for the case in which government underestimates the marginal costs of abatement.

Both types of instrument will result in an 'efficiency loss', in the sense that total net benefits are less than they could be if the efficient level of control had been implemented. Consider first a pollution tax instrument. Using its incorrect information, government imposes a pollution tax at the rate λ_1 (as opposed to the value it should have been, λ_2). Firms will abate pollution as long as marginal abatement costs are below the tax, and so will emit Ψ_1 units of pollution, a quantity in excess of the efficient level. The efficiency loss which corresponds to this is indicated by the area **bde**, the sum of the excess of marginal damage over marginal abatement costs for the excessive units of pollution.

Now consider the case of an emissions quota. Using its incorrect information, the government calculates its pollution target to be Ψ_2, which is lower than the efficient level Ψ^*. Put another way, incorrect information has led the government to impose too much abatement. In this case, the efficiency loss is indicated by the area **abc**, corresponding to the excess of marginal abatement costs over marginal damage for those excessive units of abatement.

What conclusions can we draw from this analysis? If the government makes mistakes in estimating the form of one or both functions, the result will be an efficiency loss; abatement will be either too low or too high. To know which system gives the greater efficiency loss will require a comparison of the areas **abc** with **bde**. In general, we cannot say in advance which of these two will be greater. But at the very least, we can say that it is no longer true that market instruments are more efficient than quantitative

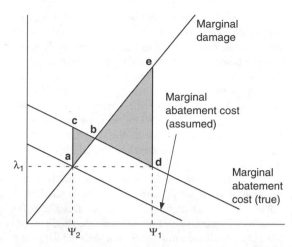

Fig 9.13 The efficiency loss when an error is made about the magnitude of abatement costs.

regulations. They may be in some circumstances but not in others.

You can probably see that the relative sizes of the losses will depend upon the parameters of the respective marginal functions. To illustrate this point, look at Figure 9.13 in which the marginal benefit function is very 'flat' relative to the marginal damage function. As before, the government underestimates the true value of marginal abatement costs. In this case, the efficiency loss is less under a quantitative control (**abc**) than under an emissions tax (**bde**). As Problem 5 shows, the opposite would be true if the marginal damage function had a slope lower in absolute value than the marginal abatement cost function.

We have looked at only two of the many possibilities here. Other possibilities arise when the marginal damage function is incorrectly estimated, or when mistakes are made with respect to both functions. Our conclusion must be that, once uncertainty is introduced into the analysis, it is not possible to claim superiority for one instrument in all circumstances.[7]

The safe minimum standard of conservation

Where markets exist and are competitive, and agents have perfect foresight, we have seen that powerful forces for conservation exist. Even in these circumstances, Chapter 7 demonstrated that efficiency cannot guarantee the survival of species, particularly where biological growth functions are slow, and initial quantities of the species are limited. Conservation becomes more unlikely where markets are incomplete, access to a resource is open, functions are not known with certainty, and decision-makers do not have perfect foresight.

Some writers have argued that a constraint should be imposed upon economic behaviour: a safe minimum standard of conservation should be maintained unless the costs of doing so were intolerably high. This is sometimes proposed in the context of a critique of cost–benefit analysis (CBA) techniques of decision making. The CBA approach calculates expected costs and benefits of proposed actions, and derives an expected net present value. If this is positive, the project is recommended as worthwhile (see Chapter 2 for a discussion of this). In order to make the concept of a safe minimum standard of conservation operational, two questions require answers: what principles should be used in identifying a safe minimum standard; and what constitutes an intolerably high cost?

Three conditions underpin arguments for a safe minimum standard of conservation (SMSC). As the concept was first developed in the context of discussions about biodiversity, we shall illustrate the arguments using that example. The first is the existence of uncertainty; humans do not know the full consequences of all their actions. Ecological systems and processes are characterised by pervasive uncertainties, and it is seems difficult to deny that we simply do not know the consequences of major changes to ecosystems, such as widespread loss of species arising from habitat change. Secondly, the environmental consequences of economic activity are often irreversible, a matter discussed at more length in Chapter 10.

---

[7] The analysis in this section follows very closely that presented in Hartwick and Olewiler (1986). For further analysis of the design of policy under conditions of uncertainty, see page 422 in that reference. It is worth noting two further conclusions that Hartwick and Olewiler reach:

1 When the government has imperfect information about the marginal abatement cost (MA) or marginal damage (MD) cost functions, it should use a quantity policy if MA is flatter than MD, and a tax if the reverse is true, if it wishes to minimise the efficiency losses arising from incorrect information.

2 When the government is uncertain about the shape and location of both functions, a programme that combines a tax with a quantity control will minimise the expected losses arising from incorrect information (and will also minimise pollution control costs).

Thirdly, the losses involved in these irreversible changes can be very large (although not known with certainty because of the first condition). Given these conditions, it seems sensible to adopt a risk-averting approach; even where it seems likely that an action does not threaten adverse consequences, we may wish to build some safeguard into behaviour, reducing the risk of serious adverse consequences even further. Of course, the complete elimination of such risk may be impossible, or at the very least extremely costly, possibly prohibiting large areas of human action. Hence the role of the qualification that the SMSC constraint should not be at intolerable cost.

It would be desirable if the notion of an SMSC could be given a more rigorous foundation than the intuitive ideas we have just outlined. This is what Randall and Farmer (1995) try to do in an excellent review of the arguments for an SMSC. They consider a situation in which it is agreed that preserving biodiversity and enhancing the life prospects of poor people are both moral goods. However, the claim of humans trumps that of non-humans. Randall and Farmer (1995, page 34) show that

> From these moral principles, it can be deduced that humans should make some, but not unlimited, sacrifices for biodiversity. This result endorses the basis of a safe minimum standard (SMS) rule: a sufficient area of each unique habitat should be preserved to ensure the survival of each unique species, subspecies or ecosystem, unless the costs of doing so are intolerably high (Ciriacy-Wantrup, 1952; Bishop, 1978) ... The SMS rule places biodiversity beyond a reach of routine tradeoffs where to give up 90 cents worth of biodiversity to gain a dollar's worth of ground beef is to make a net gain. It also avoids claiming trump status for biodiversity, permitting some sacrifice of biodiversity in the face of intolerable costs. But it takes intolerable costs to justify relaxation of the SMS.

Clearly, if governments choose to pursue an SMSC objective, the instruments discussed in this chapter can still be used, but it is likely that the degree of control required would be considerably stronger than that implied in many of the diagrams used in this chapter (in which we have focused primarily on efficiency targets).

Non-uniformly mixed (surface) pollutants

In our analysis so far, we have been dealing with the special case of pollutants which are uniformly mixed by physical processes such as air flows in the upper atmosphere. Gaseous pollutants in the upper atmosphere such as carbon dioxide are good examples, with atmospheric concentrations varying very little from place to place. In such circumstances, the location of the source is irrelevant to the magnitude of the damage which results from a given quantity of emissions. We have also been restricting our attention so far to flow emissions. When these two conditions, *uniform mixing* and *flow* pollution, are satisfied, damage is also unrelated to the timing of the emission and to the extent to which emission flows over some period of time are clustered or smoothed. In these circumstances, analysis is relatively simple as all that matters as far as damage is concerned is the total quantity of an emission flow in some specified period. But these conditions are clearly not satisfied for many forms of pollution with which we need to be concerned. We now turn our attention to a brief analysis of policy for some other forms of pollution.

Stationary source local air, water and ground flow pollution

Many forms of air, water and ground pollution have impacts which are felt predominantly within some geographically defined local or regional area surrounding an emissions source or cluster of sources. This arises because the pollutant does not mix uniformly or perfectly; more precisely, the pollutant might eventually mix through a variety of physical processes, but the incidence of its damage takes place before a high degree of mixing has occurred. Whilst it may not be possible to delineate a precise boundary separating areas subject to zero damage from those subject to positive damage, we might wish to think in terms of some boundary separating, to a reasonable degree of approximation, areas in which damages are significant from those in which they are insignificant. Furthermore, within the latter area, we might expect damage to be related to proximity to an emissions source. Clearly, many types of air pollution tend to fall into this category, including lower atmospheric ozone emissions, particulate pollutants from diesel engines, and trace metal emissions (although this last example is better regarded as a form of stock pollution). Some problems of water and ground pollution also fit this description too.

Rather than talking about the environment as a single, homogeneous medium, it is now appropriate to think of the environment (the low-level atmosphere, for example) as a series of spatially distinct reception areas. The damage resulting from a unit of pollution will now depend upon the following factors.

The extent to which emissions are geographically clustered

Clustering tends to force a given mass of residuals into localised sinks, giving higher total damage for a given mass of residuals.

The extent to which emissions are temporally clustered

The extent of urban air pollution, for example, varies by time of day, and depends upon other temporally varying conditions, such as humidity, wind speed and wind direction. This is true to an even greater extent for the damage associated with any degree of pollution. Furthermore, the dose–response relationship between physical quantities of pollutant and its associated damage can be highly non-linear, and subject to important threshold effects. These properties destroy the 'homogeneity' of pollution that characterises uniformly mixing pollutants: location and timing do matter in this case, and so presumably it is not appropriate to impose the same degree of control over each unit of pollutant irrespective of timing or location.

The economic, cultural and ecological characteristics of areas surrounding an emissions source

Different locations for emission mean different locations for damage. Clearly, damage is likely to depend upon the proximity of the source to big population centres, to wilderness areas or sites of recreational amenities, and so on. Timing and peak loads of emissions can have large impacts upon the extent of damages.

The mixing qualities of the receptor environmental media

These are especially relevant to water pollution, but are also important in cases of localised air pollution effects.

Policy instruments

A common first step in any programme of pollution control is the specification by the environmental protection agency of ambient standards of air quality, permitted concentration rates of pollutants in water or ground soils, and so on. However, ambient standards are not policy instruments as such, merely official statements of what the control authority deems to be acceptable. Instruments are required in order that these targets or standards are attained. The set of instruments available to the control authority is no different in principle from those we have already discussed; any differences relate to the manner in which the instruments are used in conjunction with local pollution. These differences arise because, given the characteristics of local pollutants that we have just listed, space and time do matter. This means that the magnitude of the control should not be homogeneous for all emission sources, but should be dependent on the particular temporal and spatial conditions in question. Efficient instruments are likely to be harder to construct in this case, as they will need to be related to the particular circumstances in question.

Planning controls and other forms of direct regulation have a large role to play in the control of pollution with localised impacts. First of all, location of the source is important and policy may be directed to influencing location decisions, either of the polluter or of those who might potentially locate in the proximity of pollution sources. Planning controls may be used to prevent harmful spatial clustering of emission sources. Similarly, industrial planning regulation might attempt to avoid temporal clustering of emissions. Where particularly serious damage is associated with pollutants being emitted under special atmospheric conditions, the environmental protection agency can limit or prohibit the quantity of permitted emissions at particular times or in particular places.

One would expect much less use to be made of pollution tax or subsidy instruments in the case of stationary source local air, water and ground pollution. Whilst tax levels can in principle be adapted to particular conditions and changed over time, this is likely to be extremely costly to administer. Marketable permits offer better prospects of success as low-cost instruments, but it may be desirable to regulate the conditions under which the permits can be transferred. To explain this point, consider two firms that agree to exchange a permit. Suppose that the buyer of the permit is located in an area where one unit of pollution results in a high level of damage, whilst the seller is located where marginal damage is relatively low. Trades of permits make no difference in the case of perfectly mixing pollutants – the same quantity of abatement takes place however the permits are finally distributed, and the damages averted are not affected by that distribution. But this is no longer true where damages depend upon time and space. Although trading does not affect the overall level of abatement, it does affect the extent of averted damages, as our simple example makes clear. Therefore, a fully efficient transferable permit system would need to ensure that conditions are attached to the trades. For example, if one permit is purchased by a more damaging polluter, it will correspond to a smaller quantity of permitted pollution than if purchased by a less damaging polluter. The difficulties in design and implementation of a fully efficient permit marketable system are immense.

Mobile source air pollution

Emissions from mobile sources, the main examples of which are land, air and sea vehicles, pose considerable problems in the design of appropriate policy instruments. Vehicle fuel combustion is the major source of three types of airborne pollutant – carbon monoxide, hydrocarbons (often in particulate form), and nitrogen oxides. It is also a significant source of other harmful emissions, including lead and other trace metals, and carbon dioxide. With the exception of carbon dioxide, all the pollutants listed here are primarily surface pollutants, their effects being concentrated at or near to ground level. In terms of the classification we adopted earlier by geographical scale of damages, they are mainly local pollutants. While it is usual to regard mobile source air pollution as forms of flow pollutant, they are better thought of as mixed flow–stock pollutants; in particular, the most acute damages (see Box 9.7) tend to occur when atmospheric conditions lead to localised, temporary high concentrations of the pollutants, in the form for example of the smogs associated with Athens, London, Los Angeles, Mexico City and Tokyo. These substances are damaging to human and other forms of life, although the extent of the damage is not yet known with accuracy (Royal Commission on Environmental Pollution, 1994).

The design of policy instruments which are dependable, cost-effective and satisfactory on other criteria that we discussed earlier poses considerable problems, and seems to be more difficult than the design of policy instruments for uniformly mixing stationary source pollutants. Among the reasons for these difficulties are the following characteristics of mobile source pollution.

1 The extent of pollution damage depends upon the location of the emitting source: a particular quantity of nitrogen dioxide released in a heavily populated residential area, for example, will be more damaging than that quantity released in a thinly populated rural area. This is also true to some extent for uniformly mixing pollutants, if only because more damage will be done where there are more people who can be damaged. But the locational effect is more important here, and arises largely from the fact that the pollution is not uniformly mixing, and is mainly local in effect. This much applies to all local pollutants, of course. What is unusual about vehicles is that the place in which they happen to be can change, and the damage for which they are responsible will change accordingly. Efficient pollution-charging systems for vehicle emissions require a tariff that is adjustable in quite subtle ways, a very difficult property to achieve.

2 Pollution damage depends upon the timing of the emission. Again, in some sense, this is probably true for all forms of emission. But the localised nature of most important forms of mobile source pollution gives this a particular importance in this instance. It is easy to find examples; car exhaust emissions will be at their worst in situations of heavily congested traffic, particularly in conjunction with special atmospheric conditions as shown in Box 9.7. Damage is probably less acute for night rather than day travel, and so on. As in point (1), this suggests that imagination will be required if efficient or cost-effective instruments are to be found. Furthermore, both points (1) and (2) suggest that emission controls on vehicles at the point of manufacture – a very important component of policy in practice – are likely to be of little use in targeting effort efficiently.

3 The monitoring, control and enforcement of regulations can be very difficult and costly because of the large numbers of individual pollution sources, and because of the mobility of the sources. Regulations stipulating minimum standards for exhaust emissions can easily be implemented for new vehicles, but less easily for existing vehicle stocks.

4 It is the use of vehicles, not their production, which is the predominant source of pollution. A significant proportion of an economy's stock of vehicles is modernised or updated very infrequently. Hence there is an inertia effect or vintage effect – incentives or regulations designed to reduce environmental impacts of new vehicles have limited short-term effects. Users of cars, for example, can easily change the rate of use of their vehicles, but often cannot easily or cheaply introduce efficient technical substitutions.

Box 9.7 The health effects of vehicle pollution

In this box, we present two items from the British press published in the summer of 1994, at the end of a period of weather which, in conjunction with air pollution, had caused unusually large damage to health. The ozone smog of that summer led to high media interest in air pollution. The two pieces illustrate many of the points we make in our analysis of mobile source air pollution. We begin with some extracts from an article that appeared in *The Independent* newspaper on 23 June, at the height of the ozone smogs:

Pollution from car exhausts probably killed up to 160 Londoners in less than a week of foggy weather during December 1991.... Scientists found that deaths increased by 10% in the London area during a period when unusually still weather caused a build-up of toxic exhaust gases.... Nitrogen dioxide emitted from car exhausts reacts with water droplets in the air and the moist tissues lining the lungs to form an acid which can cause intense irritation, induce asthmatic attacks and put extra stress on the heart by making breathing more difficult.... Cold, static weather trapped air pollutants from traffic fumes. Nitrogen dioxide reached record levels, peaking at 423 ppb, considerably higher than the level of 300 ppb which the Department of Health believes is serious enough for it to issue health warnings aimed at people with respiratory problems.... The research is the strongest evidence since the London smogs of the 1950s that air pollution causes increased death rates.... The new nitric acid smogs are less dangerous than the sulphurous smogs of the 1950s, caused by burning coal and culminating in a thick pea-souper of December 1952 which it is estimated caused about 4,000 deaths.... The research is expected to lead to a review of the safety levels for nitrogen dioxide, the main contributor to respiratory problems from car exhausts.

The Independent, 23 June, 1994.

This extract illustrates the fact that pollution control faces the difficulty of dealing with significant, and sometimes quite rapid, changes in the types and patterns of pollutants. Moreover, the impact of emission flows varies in marked ways as atmospheric conditions change. This creates immense difficulties in designing emissions targets, and in constructing control programmes that are flexible enough to cope with changing circumstances.

The second item reproduces extracts from an article written by Walter Ellis in *The Times* on 5 July, 1994, when weather conditions had eased the ozone smog problem described in the first piece. Whilst economists typically advocate the use of market-based instruments to control pollution, the article shows that command-and-control instruments can be extremely powerful and fact acting – although at what cost relative to other techniques one cannot say from this information.

Those who argue that legislation alone cannot change the environment should consider the impact of the 1956 Clean Air Act which banned the use of untreated domestic coal. Before the Bill's passage, Britain's towns and cities were caked in grime, and bronchitis was one of the principal causes of death among the elderly.... Yet within a week of the new legislation passing into law, the transformation was magical. Urban dwellers regained their sight.... More importantly, their health was transformed.

Similar measures may be required today. Until the weather broke in much of the country in the early hours of yesterday, Britain was in the grip of a worsening ozone crisis, caused by vehicle emissions, that could well have caused a number of people to lose their lives.... The new threat, like much that is least attractive in the late 20th century, derives directly from the automobile. In the five years from 1987 to 1992, the number of cars and taxis alone on British roads rose by 15 per cent. By 2010, according to the lowest estimate from the Department of Transport, there will have been a further increase, on 1992, of 36 per cent. Traffic is not simply running slower and slower, it has become our principal environmental menace.

New cars, by law, must have catalytic converters fitted to reduce exhaust emissions and must run on lead-free petrol. Yet while the production of dangerous hydrocarbons is thus considerably reduced per vehicle, the remorseless rise in vehicle numbers ensures that the improvement overall is only gradual. Working in the opposite direction, the surge in popularity of diesel-engined cars has caused a steady increase in particle emission – an entirely separate form of pollution – which so far no amount of technological refinement has been able to remedy.

Water Ellis, 'Britain fights for breath', *The Times*, 5 July 1994

Policy in practice

In most countries, controls relating to mobile source pollution are predominantly confined to regulation at point of production, not use. These tend to take the form of mandatory technology standards, required capital equipment, or emissions standards required from engine units of given sizes. Such controls are imposed on the producer, and aim to achieve target levels of emissions per unit of distance driven.

Examples include requirements to install catalytic converters, particulate emission standards for new diesel engines, requirements that engines be operable using unleaded fuel, or the more stringent regulations of environmental impact adopted in California. A standards-based approach is the main component of control programmes in the United States and Europe. Economists tend to be sceptical of the impact that standards will have. They will certainly reduce the quantity of emissions per mile driven for given types of vehicle, but will only affect new sources; considerable time delays exist before such standards permeate the whole fleet. But most importantly, they fail to create the right incentives at the margin; such regulations will not affect user choices about total mileage driven, nor about its timing or location. A good summary of these drawbacks can be found in the eighteenth report of the Royal Commission on Environmental Pollution (1994).

The essence of the problem here is that when pollutants are not uniformly mixing, the use of uniform standards cannot be efficient. Even if the instrument were able to result in an equalisation of marginal abatement costs over all polluters, a necessary condition for efficiency, that would not be sufficient for efficiency in this case, as the marginal damage will vary in the ways we indicated above. The control should, ideally, bite more or less strongly in accordance with the extent of the damage. Moreover, standards or regulations at the point of manufacture do not generate financial incentives to improve technology. Indeed, they may even lead to perverse incentives as manufacturers may wish to hide potential technology improvements for fear of these becoming built into a tightened future standard. Not all is as bleak as this might suggest, however. If a control authority announces a programme of credible targets over time, where standards are progressively tightened in a planned manner, rational firms may try to anticipate these gradually tightening constraints. The programme may, therefore, generate appropriate dynamic incentives.

Regulations or other quantitative controls may be over use rather than build standard. Such instruments are becoming increasingly pervasive, and much discussion of car pollution is couched in terms of where and when cars should be permitted to travel and so on. Simple access restrictions (such as those on car use in some US National Parks, to city centres in several European countries, or those mooted for the English Lake District) may be necessary where congestion problems become intolerable, or where

road traffic volume has risen to levels at which valuable environmental amenities are being destroyed.

Future policy options

The preference of economists for price-based incentive policies carries over to mobile source pollution too. Obvious candidates are fuel taxes and congestion-related parking charges. The former partially takes account of spatial and temporal aspects, in so far as urban fuel use is higher than rural use, especially in busy periods. However, neither of these completely addresses the problems of spatial and temporal variation we described earlier. A number of schemes have been proposed that make use of modern electronic monitoring equipment. It is feasible (although perhaps not economically viable) to install in each vehicle a recording system that embodies the history of its movements. A flexible charging system could then extract appropriate payments from each user.

There is no uniquely best instrument for all circumstances. It is probably desirable to select a range of instruments, and operate these in a flexible manner. However, a good incentive system is a simple, transparent system, and so it is important to avoid over-elaboration and excessive complexity in the chosen set of policy instruments.

Stock pollution

The previous chapter accorded a central role to the analysis of stock pollution. The main reason for doing so was that, in the judgement of the authors of this text, most important forms of pollution belong to that class. For stock pollutants, damage is, at least in part, related to the stock level or concentration of the pollutant. Some support for our judgement concerning the prevalence and importance of stock pollutants can be found by looking at how environmental targets have been set by governmental agencies. In very many cases, the targets are specified in terms of maximum permissible concentration rates of the pollutant in some medium of interest. Environmental targets for air pollution rarely limit the flow of emissions, but are usually set in terms of standards of ambient air quality – these prescribe maximum limits to the concentrations of various pollutants in the atmosphere. Similar comments apply to water and ground pollution; targets typically define permissible concentration rates.

Despite the great importance of stock pollution, it is largely neglected in the introductory environmental economics literature, which tends to deal only with the more simple case of flow pollution. In many analyses, an assumption is made (either explicitly or implicitly) that the relevant functions – the marginal damage cost and marginal abatement cost functions – are constant over time, permitting the analyst to identify efficient control for an arbitrary period and then to argue that the results of such analysis apply to any period.

The starting point of any investigation of stock pollution should be the recognition that the relevant functions, and in particular the marginal damage function, will not be constant through time. This clearly emerged in our discussion of efficient stock pollution in the previous chapter, and was shown clearly in Figure 8.5 of that chapter. As pollution stock levels rise over time, environmental damage becomes higher, and the marginal damage associated with additional units of pollution becomes larger. This suggests that an efficient control programme will need to involve a progressive tightening of the pollution restrictions for as long as the stock level continues to increase.

Because of the nature of stock pollution, it is important that pollution control programmes are designed in such a way that stocks and flows attain steady state, sustainable outcomes. By definition, a steady-state is characterised by the flows and the stocks of pollution remaining constant through time. This requires that the flow of pollutants into relevant environmental media is equal to the flow of pollution stock decay.

Consider first the case of perfectly persistent pollutants, and suppose also that total damages become larger, the larger is the stock of the pollutant. If stock levels are allowed to rise over time, damage levels will eventually become catastrophic, even if damages are fairly modest at low or moderate concentrations. Perfect persistence means that the rate of decay of the pollutant is zero. A steady state is only possible, therefore, if the flow of emissions is zero. Any efficient control programme should have this as its objective.

One instrument that might be used with such a pollutant is total prohibition, supported by an effective monitoring regime and very large penalties for non-compliance. It is not necessarily the case that emission levels should be set to zero immediately; it

may well be the case that costs of adjustment can be reduced substantially if total prohibition is the final stage of a programme of gradually more restrictive controls. Whether deferring the time at which the ban is introduced is socially beneficial or not depends upon how much larger the stock damages will become compared with the benefits gained by slow adjustment. A good example of a phased abolition of a stock pollutant relates to CFC emissions, details of which are provided in Chapter 12.

Now let us turn our attention to the more general case in which the pollutant persists over time but does decay at some positive rate. If the pollutant in question were massively damaging even in very low concentrations, an efficient flow level might be zero in this case too, particularly if the rate of pollution decay is slow. In most cases, the efficient steady-state stock and flow levels will not be zero, and the environmental protection agency of a country might seek to identify an economically efficient steady state in which emission inflows into environmental media are equal to rates of pollutant decay and transformation. The theory behind this was covered in the previous chapter, so need not be repeated here. Suffice it to say that the steady-state pollution flow level will tend to be lower

- the lower is the rate of decay;
- the higher is the level of damage;
- the less costly it is to find alternative technologies or substitutes that permit the pollutant to be reduced.

Most of our previous discussion of instruments for flow pollution control apply to stock pollutants, provided we remember that the level of control will have to be altered over time until a steady-state pollution stock and flow is achieved. If tax or subsidy instruments are to be used for stock pollutants, the analysis of Chapter 8 implies that an efficient tax rate should contain two components. The first component is designed to price the pollution *flow* externality, the other to price the pollution *stock* externality.

Finally, it is likely to be the case that uncertainty is at its most acute when pollution is of the stock-damage form. Chapter 8 argued that where uncertainty exists and the costs of adverse outcomes might be very large, one might wish to amend conventional efficiency-based approaches to pollution control by incorporating the principle of a Safe Minimum Standard of Conservation. This implies a more cautious, risk-averse approach to pollution control than we have been taking in this chapter, so ensuring that pollution stocks and flows are regulated to much lower levels than those suggested by conventional economic analyses. Some writers argue that in these circumstances, certainty or dependability of the chosen control instruments becomes of utmost importance. If this is so, then tax and subsidy instruments may be less appropriate than quantity controls.

Some final considerations

Our evaluation and comparison of pollution control instruments has concentrated principally on efficiency properties. However, the distributional consequences of pollution control policy instruments will be very important in determining which instruments are selected in practice. There are two issues here. Firstly, if a particular instrument is used, what are its consequences for income and wealth distribution? One could compare different possible instruments using this criterion. Notice that it is important to distinguish between the costs of an instrument to particular groups or individuals, and the real resource costs to society as a whole. Thus, subsidies will be beneficial to polluters, whereas taxes will be costly to producers. But the real resource costs – the opportunity costs of the scheme, if any, from the point of view of society as a whole – may well be identical.

A second, but related, question concerns the possibility of compensation. Can government design a package of measures such that the chosen instrument achieves its intended efficiency goal but without the distribution of income and wealth being altered between individuals? The answer is that this is usually possible, at least in principle. For example, a pollution tax imposed upon fossil fuels will tend to impose private costs on some firms, and indirectly upon final consumers who purchase goods that have a large energy input. Individuals for whom heating comprises a large proportion of their budget may well experience quite large falls in real income. However, additional tax revenues are received by government, and these could be earmarked to be redistributed to groups adversely affected by the initial policy change. It cannot be denied that the difficulties in designing 'distributionally neutral' packages are immense. Where compensation is paid to individuals or groups for whom the tax incidence is considered excessive, the form of compensation should be designed to not alter behaviour, otherwise the efficiency properties of the instrument will be adversely affected. This implies that lump sum compensation should be used where

possible. Neither can it be denied that compensation schemes of this form rarely happen in practice. But the point we wish to stress is that decision makers do have this option: whether they choose to exercise it is another matter.

We analysed in Chapter 8 some of the implications of non-convexities in either or both of the abatement cost and damage cost functions for pollution control policy. It is generally correct that the efficient policy is one that minimises the sum of abatement and damage costs. However, non-convexities imply that one cannot be assured that any pollution level at which marginal damage costs and marginal abatement costs are equalised corresponds to such an efficient point. Multiple 'equilibria' (in the sense of equalised marginal damage and abatement costs) can exist once functions are non-convex. This implies that care must be taken in using cost–benefit calculations in setting targets (as we explained in Chapter 8), and in selecting appropriate tax or subsidy rates.

Finally, whilst we argue in this chapter that markets sometimes fail to deliver efficient outcomes, there is no guarantee that government intervention will not be subject to efficiency losses also. It would be quite wrong to assume that a potential efficiency gain will inevitably be achieved by government intervention. In some circumstances, the efficiency losses of intervention might exceed those arising from the market failure which prompts that intervention, and so public sector involvement may not be warranted.

The astute reader may have noticed that nearly all our discussion of policy instruments in this chapter has taken place in the context of pollutants that were either local or regional in scale, or where it was assumed that some single authority has the ability and the responsibility to appoint an agency, which can then implement and administer a single control programme. We implicitly assumed this, even in the context of uniformly mixing, global pollutants. But there is a problem here. The world economy does not have a single government, yet global pollutants affect all countries, albeit in different ways. How, then, can policy targets and instruments be devised, introduced, administered and monitored for global pollutants in an interdependent world economy consisting of a large number of sovereign states? This question is of great practical importance, but raises so many new problems that it warrants separate attention. We have, therefore, allocated a separate chapter (Chapter 12) to this set of issues, which some readers may prefer to read immediately after completing this chapter.

Discussion questions

1 Consider a good whose production generates pollution damage. In what way will the effects of a tax on the output of the good differ from that of a tax on the pollutant emissions themselves? Which of the two is likely to be economically efficient?

2 Discuss the distributional implications of different possible methods by which marketable permits may be initially allocated.

3 Distinguish between private and public goods externalities. Discuss the likelihood of bargaining leading to an efficient allocation of resources in each case.

4 Use diagrams to contrast pollution tax instruments with marketable emission permit systems, paying particular attention to the distributional consequences of the two forms of instrument. (Assume a given, target level of pollution abatement, and that permits are initially distributed through sale in a competitive market.)

5 Discuss the efficiency properties of a pollution tax where the tax revenues are earmarked in advance for the provision of subsidies for the installation of pollution abatement equipment.

6 Suppose that a municipal authority hires a firm to collect and dispose of household waste. The firm is paid a variable fee, proportional to the quantity of waste it collects, and is charged a fee per unit of waste disposed at a municipal waste landfill site. Households are not charged a variable fee for the amount of waste they leave for collection, instead paying an annual fixed charge. Comment on the economic efficiency of these arrangements and suggest how efficiency gains might be obtained.

Problems

1 The Coase Theorem claims that a unique and efficient allocation of resources would follow from rational bargaining, irrespective of how property rights were initially allocated. Demonstrate that the distribution of net gains between bargaining parties will, in general, depend upon the initial distribution of property rights.

2 Show that a pollution tax on emissions and a subsidy to output producers for each unit of pollution reduction would, if the rates of subsidy were identical to the pollution tax rate, lead to identical outcomes in terms of the levels of output and pollution for a given sized industry. Explain why the distribution of gains and losses will usually differ, and why the long-run level of pollution abatement may differ when the industry size may change.

3 In all discussions of pollution abatement costs in this chapter, the fixed costs of pollution abatement were implicitly taken to be zero. Do any conclusions change if fixed costs are non-zero?

4 Demonstrate that in the simple special case of a uniformly mixing flow pollutant, in which the value of the damage created by the emission is independent of the location of the emission source or the time of the emission, the tax rate should be uniform over all polluters for the tax to be an efficient instrument (that is, it will be applied at the same rate per unit of pollution on all units of the pollutant).

5 Our discussion in this chapter has shown that if the control authority does not know the marginal damage function, it will not be able to identify the economically efficient level of pollution abatement, nor the efficient tax or subsidy level. Demonstrate that

   (a) knowledge of the pollution abatement schedule alone means that it can calculate the required rate of tax to achieve any target level it wishes,

   (b) if it knew neither the marginal damage nor the marginal abatement cost schedules, then it could arbitrarily set a tax rate, confident in the knowledge that whatever level of abatement that would generate would be attained at minimum feasible cost.

6 You are given the following information

   (a) A programme of air pollution control would reduce deaths from cancer from 1 in 8 000 to 1 in 10 000 of the population.

   (b) The cost of the programme is expected to lie in the interval £2 billion (£2 000 million) to £3 billion annually.

   (c) The size of the relevant population is 50 million persons.

   (d) The 'statistical value' of a human life is agreed to lie in the interval £300 000 to £5 million.

If the only benefit from the programme is the reduced risk of death from cancer, can the adoption of the programme be justified using an economic efficiency criterion?

Further reading

Baumol and Oates (1988) is a classic source in this area. The whole book is relevant but it is quite difficult and formal. Tietenberg (1992, Chapters 14 to 20) provides an extensive and primarily descriptive coverage of specific types of pollution and the control techniques applied to each. Other good general accounts of pollution control policy are to be found in Fisher (1981, Chapter 12) which discusses the work of Ronald Coase and the roles of wealth and bargaining power, Common (1995), Hartwick and Olewiler (1986) and Goodstein (1995). Portney (1990) analyses air pollution policy in the USA, and Portney (1989) carefully assesses the US Clean Air Act. Fisher and Rothkopf (1989) consider the justification for public policy in terms of market failure.

For a detailed analysis of issues concerning compensation in connection with distribution effects of tax changes, see Hartwick and Olewiler (1986), Chapter 12. These authors also analyse the consequences of subsidies and taxes in the short run and the long-run. The role and importance of non-convexities are discussed in Fisher (1981, page 177), Portes (1970) and Baumol and Oates (1988).

Discussion of the idea of a safe minimum standard of conservation can be found in Bishop (1978) and Randall and Farmer (1995). For analysis of the use of market-based pollution control instruments see Hahn (1984, 1989), Hahn and Hester (1989a, b), Opschoor and Vos (1989), and Tietenberg (1990, 1992). Jorgensen and Wilcoxen (1990a, b, c) analyse the impact of environmental regulation upon economic growth in the United States (but note that these papers are relatively difficult).

The 'Blueprint' series (see, for example, Pearce, 1991a) provides a clear and simple account of the new environmental economics policy stance, in a rather ideological style. Finally, a number of texts provide collections of papers, several of which are relevant to pollution control policy: these include Bromley (1995) and, at a more rigorous level, the three 'Handbooks' edited by Kneese and Sweeney (1985a, b, 1993).

CHAPTER 10

The valuation of environmental resources

If the environment is one of the world's bloodiest political battlefields, economics provides many of the weapons. Environmental lawsuits and regulatory debates would be starved of ammunition if economists did not lob their damage estimates into the fray. The trouble with these number wars is that the estimate's accuracy is often more akin to that of second-world-war bombers than precision-guided missiles.

The Economist, 3 December, 1994, page 106

Introduction

Throughout this book, we have assumed that it is possible to attach monetary values to all stocks and flows of environmental resources, irrespective of whether the stocks or flows are the subject of market transactions. Environmental resources are sometimes the subject of market transactions, and will then have observable prices that we might take to contain information about their social value. We will show, though, that market prices do not necessarily give correct indications about the social value of a resource. Environmental resources often have the characteristics of public goods, either partially or completely. In these cases, markets (and so market prices) will rarely exist, and any attempt to estimate the social value of such a resource will require that we obtain information about individual and social preferences in some other way. A second situation in which prices are 'missing' concerns externalities associated with the production or consumption of resources. By definition, externalities refer to real effects upon utility (and so do have implications for value) which find no reflection in market transactions. We may need to obtain estimates of the values associated with these externalities, as for example where one seeks to identify a socially optimal pollution tax rate.

Our objectives in this chapter are to

1 clarify and explain the meaning of the value of a resource, or the services derived from the resource;
2 survey the techniques used by economists to attach monetary values[1] to stocks or flows of environmental resources, and to changes in these stocks and flows;
3 critically assess existing techniques for the evaluation of environmental resources; and
4 show how these valuation techniques can be used to estimate the losses associated with reductions in the quality or quantity of environmental resources.

Dimensions of value

In this book, we are concerned with the *economic* value of a resource or service, albeit an economic value defined in a broad sense. In general, economists regard individual preferences as the basis of value, as we shall show in the next section. Nevertheless, economists do not argue that this way of conceptualising value is the only legitimate one, nor even the one that is most useful. The claim being made in this book is a much weaker one – merely that a measure of economic value is often useful, and may indeed be the only one that can be used in the context of an economic analysis of environmental issues.

We begin from the premise that individuals have needs, wants, and wishes, the satisfaction of which gives utility to the individual. Individual preferences for goods and services reflect the utilities that are expected to be derived from their consumption (or existence, as we shall see below). Many of the 'goods and services' which confer utility will no doubt be of a material kind, and will be consumed largely for self-interested reasons. We would expect that, for many

[1] In order to facilitate good decision taking, it is desirable to identify all the benefits and costs of a 'project'. Having done this (to the best of our ability), it would then be useful to evaluate all costs and benefits using a single metric (measuring framework). Such a metric could take many forms; traditionally, economists use a *money metric* (presumably because this permits easy comparison with other magnitudes that are of interest to decision takers). There is, however, no reason why this metric *need* be a monetary one.

(or perhaps all) people, valuable goods will include environmental goods and services, such as clean air and the visual amenities that derive from unspoilt landscapes.

There is no reason, of course, why utility need only derive from directly self-interested consumption. It is quite possible that individuals get utility by actions which benefit others, whether these 'others' are other humans or non-humans. Nothing new is introduced into our analysis by recognising the possibility of altruistic behaviour, if we are prepared to explain that behaviour within a utility-maximising framework.

However, we argued in Chapter 2 that 'resources' may possess values quite independently of any use that humans may make of them, or independently of any effect that the use or existence of these resources has on humans. Ethical arguments may also suggest that resources have intrinsic rights, and that the existence of these rights imposes constraints on the way in which these resources should be used by humans. There is no way in which such rights and values can be incorporated in the economic utility-maximising framework. These values and rights should be taken account of when decisions are made which have potential environmental impacts, but they cannot be handled within an economic framework as such. Clearly, this implies that the information and valuations provided by economists will only provide part of the relevant information that should be considered in the decision making process.

The values with which we shall be concerned in this chapter are the class of use values. These denote the values derived from actual or potential future consumption of a good or service. We may sub-divide this class of values into current use values, option values and quasi-option values. Current use value derives either from the utility gained by an individual from the consumption of a good or service, or vicariously from the consumption of others (for example, parents may obtain utility from their children's consumption).

Option value refers to the value that arises from retaining an option to a good or service for which future demand is uncertain. The option value is an additional value to any utility that may arise if and when the good is actually consumed. If we are certain as to our future preferences and the future availability of the resource, option value will be zero. But if we are not certain about either our future preferences or about future availability, we may be willing to pay a premium (the option value) to keep the option of future use open. We shall examine the nature of option value more thoroughly.

Quasi-option value refers to the utility gains expected to be realised from not undertaking irreversible decisions, and so maintaining options for future use of some resource, given expectations of future technological advance and/or the growth of knowledge. Once again, we shall examine quasi-option value, and its relationship to option value, later in this chapter.

However, individual preferences may exist for maintaining resources in their present forms even where no actual or future 'use' is expected to be made of the resource. These preferences are the basis for what could be called existence value. Existence value derives from human preferences for the existence of resources as such, unrelated to any use to which such resources may be put.

Let us use the term *total economic value* to refer to the whole class of values that have a basis in human preferences, and so are amenable to analysis within an economics framework. Total economic value is, then, the sum of current use value, option value, quasi-option value, and existence value.

The economic valuation of environmental resource stocks and flows

We begin by considering the *individual's* valuation of a good or service. The issue of how we may move from individual valuations to a community or social value is left until the section after next. It will also be convenient to start our analysis by ignoring any particular characteristics of *environmental* goods or services, and consider valuation of goods in general. The particular difficulties in valuing environmental goods can be introduced as we proceed. Let us follow the conventional practice in economics and regard value as the utility that an individual derives from the use of a good.

Suppose that the total utility (U) an individual obtains is some function of the quantity of a good he or she consumes in a given period of time. That is

$$U = U(C)$$

with marginal utility (MU) denoted by

$$MU = U'(C) = \frac{dU(C)}{dC}$$

Box 10.1 Total economic value

David Pearce has popularised the concept of total economic value. In one recent application in which he explores the valuation of forest benefits, Pearce decomposes the total economic value of forests into the components listed in Table 10.1. The key beneath the table defines the forest benefit which corresponds to each of the letters in Table 10.1.

Notice that David Pearce uses, in this table, an additional category of value to those discussed in the text. By bequest value, Pearce means the utility derived from individuals from the knowledge that an environmental asset will be conserved for the benefit of future generations. One might argue with Pearce's exclusion of bequest values from the class of use values, as the conserved resources will confer utility to individuals at some future times (and perhaps the conserver will derive utility from his or her act of bequest itself). Note also that Pearce draws a distinction between direct and indirect use values of forests, presumably the former referring to utility contemporaneously derived from timber products or woodlands in themselves, and the latter referring to benefits that derive from consumption of other goods and services whose provision is supported by the existence of forests and woodlands.

As far as the particular types of forest benefit are concerned, moth of those listed in the table are self-explanatory, or have been explained elsewhere in the text. *Economic security* consists of the advantages an economy may derive through having supplies of a basic raw material readily available and under its own control. This was once regarded as a principal benefit of forests, particularly in times when the probability of war was high, and indeed was a contributory factor in the establishment of national forestry authorities in a number of countries. Its importance is now generally regarded as rather low. *Community integrity benefits* have their basis in the possibility that woodlands may support the maintenance of communities with cultures that are regarded as being of intrinsic worth, or that contribute to cultural diversity. In extreme cases, such as indigenous cultures in some areas of tropical forest, deforestation can eliminate an entire culture.

Forests also have very important ecological implications. They serve as vital components of a variety of complex water and climate systems, operate as natural scrubbers or processors of water and air pollutants, and may serve as habitats that support highly diverse biological communities. The benefits labelled as microclimate, biodiversity, greenhouse impact, air pollution and water pollution all relate to this set of woodland functions. (A detailed analysis of tropical deforestation, looking principally at its causes, but also considering the losses associated with that process, can be found in Brown and Pearce, 1994.)

Table 10.1 Components of total economic value of forests

	Direct use values	Indirect use values	Option values	Existence values	Bequest values
Types of benefits	T	D	D	D	D
	R	W	R	L	
	D	M	I		
	S	G	L		
	L	I			
		A			
		P			

Key:
T = Timber
R = Recreation
D = Biodiversity
S = Economic security
I = Community integrity
L = Landscape
W = Watershed/ecosystem function
M = Microclimate
G = Greenhouse impact
A = Air pollution
P = Water pollution

Source: Adapted from Pearce, in Layard and Glaister (eds), 1994, page 473.

For a typical good, the relationships between total utility, marginal utility, and the quantity consumed in one time period are typically represented as in Figure 10.1.

The additional utility that a consumer would derive by increasing his or her rate of consumption from C_1 to C_2 is shown by the quantity $U_2 - U_1$, and also by the area under the marginal utility curve between consumption levels C_1 and C_2, the shaded area in the lower part of the diagram. Unfortunately, we cannot use this approach in practice to obtain measures of

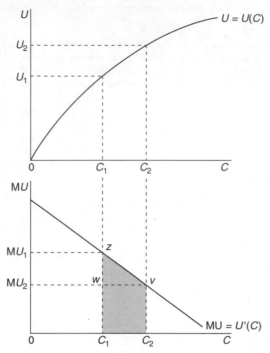

Fig 10.1 Total and marginal utility functions.

conditions. One of these necessary conditions is constancy of the marginal utility of money income (MU_Y). In particular, MU_Y should not change as either prices change or income changes. To demonstrate how restrictive these conditions can be, constancy of MU_Y requires, among other things, that the price elasticity of demand for the good in question is unity, and that quantity changes do not affect the marginal utilities derived from other goods. Clearly, such conditions are very unlikely to be satisfied in general.

An additional dilemma which is posed by the Marshallian measure of individual utility changes is that the measure will, in general, not be invariant to the direction in which the change occurs. A number of other (very restrictive) conditions are necessary for invariance of the Marshallian measure to the direction of change. Most, if not all, of the conditions required to obtain invariant measures of utility change from the consumer's demand function are highly implausible in general. In addition, the Marshallian apparatus requires that money serve as a cardinal index of utility, and many economists refuse to accept the whole conceptual framework of cardinal utility theory.

utility change as utility is unobservable. Some other approach is required if we are to measure the welfare impacts of quantity changes.

One way in which we might proceed is to follow a method developed by Alfred Marshall. Marshall's approach involved using money as a cardinal index of utility and interpreting the consumer's demand curve for a good as his or her marginal utility function for that good. In this way, changes in the area under a consumer's demand curve as the quantity is changed may be interpreted as changes in the individual's utility. Marshall's money measure of utility change involves assuming that a constant relationship exists between units of utility and units of money, and so the marginal utility of money income is constant. Let us express this relationship as

$$MU = \alpha P$$

where P denotes price (and so is in monetary units). If units are chosen so that $\alpha = 1$, then the marginal utility curve in Figure 10.1 can be re-expressed as the individual's demand curve, showing the relationship between price and quantity demanded.

Unfortunately, this equation of the area under a consumer's demand curve with the (true) change in utility is valid only under a very restrictive set of

Ordinal utility analysis and Hicksian utility measures: compensating variation and equivalent variation

Fortunately, an alternative framework is available for obtaining money measures of utility changes without invoking cardinal utility theory. This framework makes use of ordinal utility, which merely requires that consumers be able to preferentially rank alternative bundles of goods in a manner consistent with certain axioms of rational behaviour. John Hicks (1941) developed a set of money measures of utility change. We can make use of these to provide a sound theoretical foundation for the valuation of environmental resources.

Suppose, for example, that we wish to obtain a measure of an individual's welfare change that would arise from a reduction in airborne pollution which reduces the price of some good (say C_1) from P_1' to P_1''. Our objective is to obtain a money measure of the benefit that the individual gains from this price fall. Define a second good (C_2) as the composite good which is all goods other than C_1, let the price of C_2 be unity, and suppose that the individual has a fixed money income, Y_0. The consumer's budget constraint, prior to the price

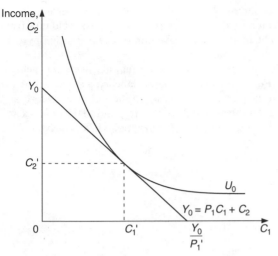

Fig 10.2a Utility maximisation subject to a budget constraint.

fall, can then be written as

$$P'_1 C_1 + C_2 = Y_0$$

A utility-maximising consumer will choose C_1 and C_2 so as to maximise $U = U(C_1, C_2)$ subject to this budget constraint. The solution is two consumption quantities, C'_1 and C'_2, and a maximised level of utility U_0, and is illustrated in Figure 10.2a. We may interpret the vertical axis as being in units of money income. To

see this, note from the budget constraint that if no expenditure took place on good 1 (so $C_1 = 0$), then C_2 is equal to the money income level Y_0.

Now consider the consequence of the price fall of good C_1 from P'_1 to P''_1. The budget constraint rotates anti-clockwise about the point Y_0 on the vertical axis to the new constraint

$$P''_1 C_1 + C_2 = Y_0$$

as shown in Figure 10.2b. Utility maximisation now implies consumption levels of C''_1 and C''_2, and a higher utility level, U_1.

Let us next introduce two of Hicks's measures of individual welfare change:

- The compensating variation (CV) of a change in price is the change in income that would 'compensate' for the price change. More precisely, CV measures the change in income at the new level of prices that would return the individual to his or her old level of utility.
- The equivalent variation (EV) of a price change is the change in income that, with prices remaining at their old levels, would be equivalent to the proposed price change.

These general definitions of CV and EV apply to price falls and price rises, and so the two measures can be positive or negative depending upon which measure

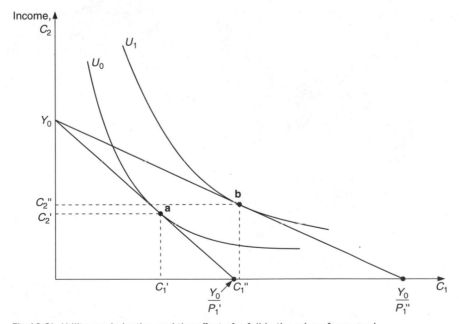

Fig 10.2b Utility maximisation and the effect of a fall in the price of one good.

we are using and in which direction prices change. To assist in your understanding of these rather tricky concepts, we will examine CV and EV for the price fall of good C_1 that we began to examine a few paragraphs earlier.

The compensating variation of the price fall is the quantity of money income which, when taken from the individual after the price fall, leaves him or her at the same level of utility as if the price fall had not occurred, U_0. In other words, it is the amount of money, at the new price level, that we could take from the individual to leave him or her just as happy as at the original price.

We can visualise this quantity with the help of Figure 10.3(a). The points labelled **a** and **b** denote the utility maximising consumption choices before and after the price fall, and correspond to the points **a** and **b** in Figure 10.3(b). Begin at point **b**, at which the slope

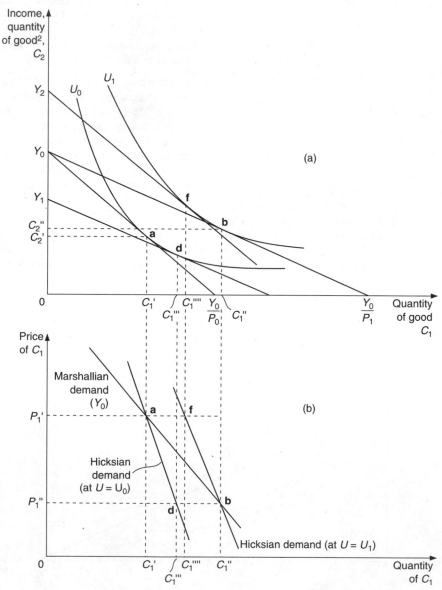

Fig 10.3 (a) The compensating variation of a price fall; (b) Hicksian and Marshallian demands.

of the budget constraint is given by the final price, after the price fall. Keeping relative prices constant, reduce money income until the individual is constrained to have only the original level of utility, U_0, at the point marked **d**. The required income reduction is the amount $Y_0 - Y_1$, which is the compensating variation of the price fall. The CV measures, in units of money income, the utility change from U_0 to U_1, given that prices are fixed at their final level.

The equivalent variation (EV) of the price fall is the quantity of money income which, if given to the individual before the price fall, would leave him or her at the same level of utility as if the price fall had occurred. In other words, it is the amount of money, at the original price level, that we need to give to the individual so that he or she would be just as happy as at the final price. The EV is given by amount $Y_2 - Y_0$ in Figure 10.3(a), leaving the individual at point **f**, and it measures, in units of money income, the utility change from U_0 to U_1, given that prices are fixed at their initial level. The two variations each measure the utility change from U_0 to U_1 in money-income units. They differ from one another because these changes are valued at different sets of prices.

A result that we simply note at this point (but demonstrate later) is that for a normal good (i.e. a good with a positive income elasticity of demand), in the case of a price fall CV is less than EV, and in the case of a price rise, CV is greater than EV. It should also be clear that the CV of a price rise is equivalent to the EV of a price fall, and the EV of a price rise is equivalent to the CV of a price fall. Your comprehension of this conclusion is examined in Problem 1.

Compensated and uncompensated demand functions

An alternative geometrical interpretation is given to CV and EV in Figure 10.3(b). This interpretation has the added advantage that it allows us to distinguish between two types of demand function: uncompensated (Marshallian) demands and compensated (Hicksian) demands. We know that a price change will, in general, have both substitution and income effects. Marshallian and Hicksian demand functions differ in the way in which they deal with these two effects.

Marshallian demand functions are those familiar from standard microeconomic theory. They are the demands which result from maximising utility subject to a budget constraint. So for N goods, $C_1, C_2, \ldots, C_N$, with associated prices P_i $(i = 1, \ldots, N)$ and income Y they are the solutions to the problem of choosing $C_1, C_2, \ldots, C_N$ so as to find

$$\max U = U(C_1, C_2, \ldots, C_N)$$

subject to

$$\sum_{i=1}^{i=N} P_i C_i = Y$$

Marshallian demands are of the form

$$C[M]_i = C_i(P_1, P_2, \ldots, P_N, Y), \quad i = 1, \ldots, N$$

so that the demand for each good is a function of the prices of all goods and of money income. When the demand curve for a particular good is shown diagrammatically, it is usual to give the relationship between the quantity demanded of a particular good and the price of that good, holding all other prices and money income fixed. These demands are uncompensated because no compensation is made to offset the income effect of the price change in question. Movements along a Marshallian demand curve thus represent the combination of the substitution and income effects of a price change.

We can obtain two points that lie on the Marshallian demand curve for our example by transcribing the price and quantity coordinates corresponding to the points **a** and **b** onto the price/quantity space in Figure 10.3(b).

Hicksian demand functions are solutions to the different problem

$$\min E = E(P_1, P_2, \ldots, P_N, U)$$

subject to

$$U = \bar{U}$$

where $\bar{U}$ is a fixed 'target' level of utility, and E denotes money expenditure on consumption. The Hicksian demands will be of the form

$$C[H]_i = H_i(P_1, P_2, \ldots, P_N, \bar{U})$$

so that the demand for the ith good is a function of the prices of all goods, and of the required level of utility.

Diagrammatically, we can portray a Hicksian demand function for one good by showing the relationship between the quantity demanded of a particular good and the price of that good, holding all other prices and utility fixed. These demands are constructed in such a way that compensation is made which eliminates the income effect of a price change. Movements along a Hicksian demand curve thus represent the pure substitution effect of a price change. When we draw a two-dimensional compensated demand curve in price–quantity space, all points on the demand function represent points of constant utility.

To derive the compensated demand function for our example, look again at the exercise we undertook in identifying the CV of a price fall, which we showed to be $Y_0 - Y_1$. Now compare the two points **a** and **d** in Figure 10.3(a). The move from **a** to **d** is the consequence of a fall in the price of the good, holding all other prices constant (in this case just the price of C_2) and holding utility constant (at U_0), and therefore represents the substitution effect of the fall in price of C_2. Points **a** and **d** constitute two points on the Hicksian demand curve for $U = U_0$, as shown in Figure 10.3(b). Note that a second Hicksian demand can be obtained for the utility level $U = U_1$. The two combinations **b** and **f** constitute points on this Hicksian demand.

We are now in a position to provide the alternative geometrical interpretation of CV and EV. To do this, the Marshallian uncompensated demand curve and the two Hicksian compensated demands have been redrawn in Figure 10.4. CV is the area to the left of $H(U_0)$ and between the prices P_0 and P_1. EV is the area to the left of $H(U_1)$ and between the prices P_0 and P_1. Note that the area to the left of the Marshallian demand – the Marshallian consumer surplus of the price change – is not exactly equal to either of the two Hicksian measures of utility change.

Which measure – CV or EV – should we use?

CV and EV are each an exact measure of welfare change. They differ in the manner in which we define the welfare change. A natural question one might ask is which measure is the preferred one. Unfortunately, it is not possible to give an unconditional answer to this question. Once the possibility of multiple price changes and simultaneous changes in income are introduced into the analysis, a number of considerations become relevant to the choice. A discussion of these matters would take us a long way beyond the chosen scope of this text, and we refer the reader to some specialised references in the list of suggested readings at the end of the chapter.

Although the absence of a clear preference for one measure is a somewhat unsatisfactory state of affairs, two factors may reduce any concern that this induces. First, for many problems of interest, the two measures of welfare change yield values that are very similar in magnitude. Any penalty from making the 'wrong' choice may often be quite small. Secondly, as we show in the next section, CV and EV are likely to be of

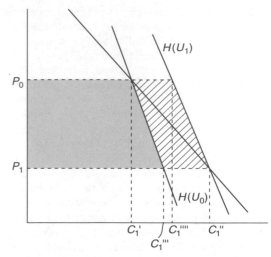

For a fall in the price of C_2:

$$CV = (Y_0 - Y_1) = \int_{P_1}^{P_0} H(U_0)\, dP = \text{shaded area}$$

$$EV = (Y_2 - Y_1) = \int_{P_1}^{P} H(U_1)\, dP = CV + \text{hatched area}$$

Fig 10.4 Compensating variation and equivalent variation.

little practical relevance as they are unobservable magnitudes. We will often have to approximate welfare changes using observable Marshallian demand functions.

Estimating CV and EV in practice

As it stands, CV and EV may not appear to be useful measures of utility changes, as they are based on unobservable demand functions. In practice, we will often be forced to use Marshallian uncompensated demand functions as the basis for obtaining approximations to either CV or EV. The Marshallian consumer surplus of a price change is the area to the left of the Marshallian demand function and between the initial and final price levels. In general, consumer surplus will not be equal to either CV or EV, and so does not provide an exact measure of welfare change. Looking at Figure 10.4, it is clear that, for a price fall, EV is greater than consumer surplus and CV is less than consumer surplus. You can also deduce that consumer surplus measures can provide either upper or lower bounds on the magnitudes of CV or EV.

In many circumstances, however, consumer surplus does not differ greatly from CV and EV, and so can serve as a good approximation to those two welfare measures. The approximation is likely to be good when the relevant price and quantity changes are small, and when the income elasticity of demand for the good in question is low.

One special case illustrates this point, and is worth noting. When the income elasticity of demand for the good in question is zero, then the Hicksian demands become identical to the Marshallian demand function, and so $EV = CV =$ consumer surplus. The reason for this is as follows. Although the price fall will increase real income, that higher real income has no effect on demand. The income effect of the price change is zero. In this case, movements along a Marshallian demand curve will consist only of the substitution effect of a price change. This is exactly what Hicksian demands describe, too. The two Hicksian demands will, in this special case, coincide exactly with the Marshallian demand curve. This conclusion is examined in Problem 2.

Willingness to pay and willingness to accept

In the literature on valuation, the concepts of willingness to pay (WTP) and willingness to accept compensation (WTA) are frequently used as criteria for measuring the benefit to the consumer of a change in the price or quantity of a good. WTP refers to the amount of money income an individual would be willing to pay to secure a welfare improvement, or equivalently to prevent a welfare deterioration. WTA refers to the monetary compensation an individual would require to accept a welfare deterioration, or equivalently, to forego a welfare improvement. The relationship between the concepts of WTP and WTA is shown in Table 10.2.

As we have been considering an example where the price of a good falls and so individual welfare increases, we will continue to couch our discussion in these terms. In this case, we can see that the willingness to pay (WTP) for the price fall is the sum of money a person would be prepared to pay to secure a decreased price of some good, such that his or her utility level would be equal before the price change and after the price change together with money payment. That is

$$U(P_1', Y_0) = U(P_1'', Y_0 - \text{WTP}) = U_0$$

where $U(P_1', Y_0))$, for example, denotes the utility obtained at price P_1' and income Y_0.

The willingness to accept compensation for foregoing a price fall is the quantity of money income which, if given to the individual before the price fall, would leave him or her at the same level of utility as if

Table 10.2 Relationship between willingness to pay (WTP) and willingness to accept (WTA) compensation

WTA compensation for accepting a price rise	$\Leftrightarrow$	WTA compensation for foregoing a price fall
$\Updownarrow$		$\Updownarrow$
CV of price rise (welfare fall)	$\Leftrightarrow$	EV of price fall (welfare rise)
EV of price rise (welfare fall)	$\Leftrightarrow$	CV of price fall (welfare rise)
$\Updownarrow$		$\Updownarrow$
WTP to prevent deterioration	$\Leftrightarrow$	WTP for price fall (welfare improvement)

the price fall had occurred. In other words, it is the amount of money a person would need to receive in compensation for a price reduction that does not occur, so as leave the individual just as happy as he or she would have been at the reduced price.

That is

$$U(P_1'', Y_0) = U(P_1', Y_0 + \text{WTA}) = U_1$$

Once again, WTP and WTA are money measures of the difference between initial and final positions of utility, U_0 and U_1. The difference arises for precisely the same reason that the 'variation' measures differed; that is, because the change is being evaluated at a different set of relative prices in the two cases. Two consequences follow, just as they did for the concepts of CV and EV. Firstly, we would not expect WTP and WTA to be numerically equal. Secondly, as WTP and WTA are, in principle, measured from areas under unobservable compensated demand functions, good estimation of these magnitudes is likely to be very difficult, even for goods for which markets exist. Market data (prices and quantities) relate to uncompensated demand functions, which are not the ones upon which true measures of WTP and WTA should be based.

Compensating surplus and equivalent surplus

We now consider a change in the quantity provided of a *pure public good*. The key difference here arises from the fact that a public good is non-excludable (non-divisible). Therefore, no individual can choose to adjust the level of this good that he or she consumes. Consider a change which increases the quantity of the public good, and therefore makes its price cheaper. Suppose, for the sake of argument, that the consumer is at a utility maximizing position prior to

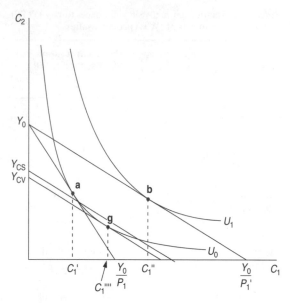

Fig 10.5 The compensating surplus of an increase in quantity.

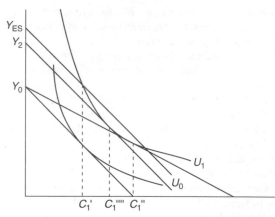

Fig 10.6 The equivalent surplus of an increase in quantity.

the price/quality change. Figure 10.5 represents the utility-maximising consumption levels before and after the change, shown as the coordinates of points **a** and **b** respectively.

In obtaining the CV measure of the utility change from U_0 to U_1, we asked how much income could be taken away from the individual, at the new relative prices, so as to leave him or her at the initial utility level. The answer to this is shown as $Y_0 - Y_{CV}$ in the figure. But this implies that consumption of C_1 is reduced from C_1'' to C_1'''; this is not feasible in this case, as an individual cannot reduce his or her consumption of the public good. *Compensating surplus* is defined as the quantity $Y_0 - Y_{CS}$, the income reduction that would leave the individual at the initial utility level, U_0, and also still consuming the higher quantity of the public good, C_1''. Note that, at point **g**, the consumer is not at a point of tangency of the indifference curve for which $U = U_0$ and the post-income change budget constraint. This arises because there is an additional constraint here. In addition to the usual budget constraint on utility maximisation, an additional constraint arises from the nature of the public good. Once its provision is increased from C_1' to C_1'', the consumer cannot alter his or her consumption of the public good from the level C_1''. It is for this reason that CS is not equal to CV.

The *equivalent surplus* (ES) of a quantity increase corresponds to the benefits an individual loses if a proposed increase in the provision of a public good does not take place. This is illustrated in Figure 10.6. If the consumer were able to adjust consumption, the price fall would lead to consumption changing from C_1' to C_1'', resulting in an equivalent variation of magnitude $Y_2 - Y_0$. However, the good is a public good, and if the project takes place, the individual's consumption is constrained to be C_1'. The ES is the larger quantity $Y_{ES} - Y_0$.

Changes in producer surplus

To this point, we have only considered the welfare changes derived by consumers. But a complete account of all welfare changes may require that other effects are taken into consideration as well. Where a public good is being made available in greater supply, the provider (often government) might incur additional costs in making this provision. Clearly, such additional costs should be subtracted from consumer welfare changes in arriving at a measure of the net welfare gains of the project.

More generally, price or quantity changes may also result in welfare changes to producers, or to the owners of productive resources. We should also take account of any such welfare changes. Fortunately, matters are relatively straightforward here. The concept we need here is that of Marshallian *producer surplus*. Producer surplus can be thought of as the excess of a firm's revenue over the marginal costs of production. In Figure 10.7, which represents a single firm selling in a competitive market at the fixed price P^*, the firm's producer surplus is shown by the shaded area above the marginal cost (supply) curve and below the demand curve for the firm's output. This surplus represents a form of rent to the owners of the

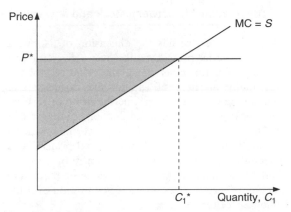

Fig 10.7 Producer surplus.

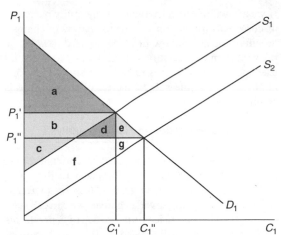

At $\{P_1', C_1'\}$:

$$\left.\begin{array}{l} CS = a \\ PS = b + c \end{array}\right\} \text{Total surpluses} = a + b + c$$

At $\{P_1'', C_1''\}$:

$$\left.\begin{array}{l} CS = a + b + d + c \\ PS = c + f + g \end{array}\right\} \begin{array}{l} \text{Total surpluses} \\ = a + b + c + d + e + f + g \end{array}$$

Therefore *gain in total surpluses* = d + e + f + g

PS is producer surplus; note that here CS is 'consumer surplus', *not* compensating surplus

Fig 10.8 Consumer and producer surpluses.

productive inputs. Clearly, changes in the levels of these rents should be considered whenever all the welfare effects of price or quantity changes are being estimated. It will be convenient to approach our analysis of producer surplus using conventional supply and demand curve analysis. Consider Figure 10.8. As a result of some environmental improvement, the marginal cost schedule of producing good C_1 falls, and so the supply curve shifts from S_1 to S_2. Let us determine the amounts of Marshallian consumer surplus and Marshallian producer surplus at the original market price (P_1'), and then at the final market price (P_1''). Note that we *begin* by calculating the amounts of these surpluses in total for a given price. Having done this, we shall then derive the *changes* in these quantities as the price changes, which will be an appropriate measure of the welfare implications for the firm of a price change.

- Surpluses at the original price and quantity $\{P_1', C_1'\}$:

  Consumer surplus a
  Producer surplus $b + c$
  Total surplus $a + b + c$
- Surpluses at the final price and quantity $\{P_1'', C_1''\}$:

  Consumer surplus $a + b + d + e$
  Producer surplus $c + f + g$
  Total surplus $a + b + c + d + e + f + g$
- Changes in surpluses in move from $\{P_1', C_1'\}$ to $\{P_1'', C_1''\}$:

  Increase in consumer surplus $b + d + e$
  Increase in producer surplus $f + g - b$
  Increase in total surplus $(b + d + e) + (f + g - b)$
  $\qquad\qquad\qquad\qquad = d + e + f + g$

Our concern in this section is primarily with the change in producer surpluses as a result of price and/ or quantity changes. These are given in the 'Increase in producer surplus' line above. Note that we argued earlier that the changes in consumer surplus as shown in Figure 10.8 are only approximations to the true measures of consumer welfare change, based on either EV or CV.

Existent and non-existent markets

If a market exists for the good or service in question, the difficulties that exist in obtaining any of these value measures are, at least in principle, relatively minor. Prices and quantities are observable, and can be used to infer the nature of demand functions, at least for the market as a whole although not necessarily for individuals. However, many environmental resources are not traded in markets, and so preferences are not revealed through market prices and quantities traded. Not surprisingly, valuation is more difficult in these circumstances. The above analysis suggests how one should proceed in principle.

If we are willing to regard any of the utility measures discussed above as appropriate indicators of changes in value, then somehow or other we need to *infer* the relevant demand functions for all users and potential users of the good or resource in question. How one might do this is the subject matter of the rest of this chapter.

General and partial equilibrium analysis

Our objective in valuation can be thought of as finding either the marginal willingness to pay for a good or service, or the marginal willingness to accept compensation for an adverse change. We can call such a value the shadow price of the good. In general, this willingness to pay will depend on the distribution of income and wealth and the allocation of resources throughout the whole economy. The WTP that we want (in most cases) is the WTP for a particular good in the situation where all other goods and services are being traded at Pareto-efficient prices.

One approach to finding such prices is through the use of General Equilibrium Theory (GET). In this approach, an objective is specified, markets are assumed to exist for all goods and services, and market clearing or equilibrium prices and quantities for all goods and services are solved simultaneously. The solution prices from such an approach are the shadow prices we are looking for, as the solution will lead to a Pareto-efficient allocation in every market.

In practice, GET is often too costly to use (or we do not have sufficient information to use it). Our approach in this chapter has been based upon a partial equilibrium framework, rather than that of general equilibrium. In this mode of analysis, we look for a market price/quantity which is Pareto-efficient, making an implicit or explicit assumption that all other markets are allocating resources efficiently. This is the approach we follow in this chapter.

Note, however, that even where the resource or service in question is the subject of market transactions in competitive markets, market failures may exist in this or other markets. In that case, the observed market price will be a poor indicator of the *social* marginal WTP for the resource or service. In such circumstances, some adjustment to observed market prices will usually be required in order to arrive at the appropriate 'shadow price'. It also follows from this that any use we make of the WTP estimates derived from partial analysis may well be invalid if the assumption of Pareto efficiency in all markets is not satisfied.

The relationship between stock and flow values

A resource service has the dimension of a flow; a resource service provides utility over a given interval of time. On the other hand, the resource stock is essentially an item of capital, the existence and magnitude of which determine the flows of services that it can deliver. Sometimes we shall be interested in valuing the flows; at other times we may wish to evaluate the stock itself. Using general principles of (capital) asset pricing, the value of a resource stock can be obtained as the present value of the future stream of service flows it is expected to yield over the 'lifetime' of the resource.

Note that this raises two difficult questions. Firstly, what lifetime should we ascribe to the asset? Secondly, what discount rate should be used when calculating the present value of a stream of income flows? Some suggestions as to how these difficult questions may be answered have already been given in Chapter 2.

Techniques for evaluating environmental resources

The valuations with which we are concerned in this book are of two (related) kinds. We may seek a value for the services provided by an environmental resource, such as a wilderness area, or a natural resource-based recreational facility. Alternatively, the objective could be to value the damages arising from pollution flows, or from reductions in the quality of some environmental resource.

In principle, there are two ways in which we might approach the problem. One method would involve some attempt to evaluate directly the pollution damages or the amenity reductions implied by the worsened quality of the resource. Three approaches we discuss below – hedonic pricing, travel cost techniques and contingent valuation – use this approach in some form. A second, indirect method of valuation consists of two stages. In the first stage, the researcher identifies the physical or biological effects of the pollution on things deemed to be of value to humans, such as crop output, health effects, buildings damage and so on. The second stage involves valuing these physical and biological effects. It may well be the case that these second-step values are relatively easy to do if they relate to goods and services which are marketed. This explains why a two-step approach may be pursued. Dose–response techniques are an example of this indirect two-step method.

It is sometimes suggested that the value of environmental damage can be measured by the cost of cleaning up pollution damage. Whilst this is not true in general, there are some circumstances where it may be valid. However, it is very difficult to know whether the conditions which would make this a valid measure are satisfied in practice. If they are not, the technique will give very misleading valuations. We do not discuss this proposed method of valuation in this book.

Hedonic pricing

The technique of hedonic pricing was developed by Griliches (1971) and Rosen (1974). It consists of a method of estimating the implicit prices of characteristics which differentiate closely related products. Hedonic pricing of unmarketed environmental services is based on the following principle. Suppose that an environmental resource that you wish to value (obtain a shadow price for) is not itself traded in any market, possibly because the resource is a public good. As a result, no market price exists which can reveal preferences or willingness to pay for the resource. Suppose, also, that the resource can be defined in terms of a service it yields or an 'attribute' it embodies. This attribute may, however, be embodied in other goods or assets which are marketed, and which do have observable prices. In such circumstances, statistical techniques (in particular, multiple regression analysis) may enable the investigator to identify the contribution which the attribute in question makes to the price of the traded good. We could then identify an implicit or shadow price for the attribute of interest, and regard this as an estimate of the value of the environmental resource.

In what circumstances might such a valuation route be possible and appropriate? One example might be the value of clean air (or conversely, the cost of atmospheric pollution). Whilst clean air is not a traded good, it is an attribute which seems to influence residential property prices. Evidence from revealed preferences suggests (as we show below) that, other things being equal, a positive relationship exists between the prices that people are willing to pay for housing and the quality of ambient air standards. Examination of property prices might, therefore, enable one to impute the value of clean air.

A second example concerns the risk of serious injury. Decision makers may be required to consider the desirability of a project, one cost of which is an increased risk of serious injury. Different forms of employment may carry different risks of injury, and, at least on *a priori* grounds, one would expect higher risk jobs to be associated with higher wage rates, other things being equal. Hedonic pricing techniques might then be used to estimate the price of increased risk of injury, as reflected through differential wage rates.

Let us now look at this technique in the case of estimating the willingness to pay for clean air.[2] Define X to be an index of the level of air pollution, and assume that the rent[3] that an individual is willing to pay for housing services, R, is a decreasing function of the level of air pollution. That is

$$R = R(X), \qquad R'(X) < 0$$

One possible form for this rent–pollution function is illustrated in Figure 10.9. How could one obtain an estimate of such a rent–pollution function? Assume that data can be collected on housing rents (or house prices, from which rents can be imputed), air quality and a set of attributes which influence housing rents, such as house size, amenities, proximity to employment, and neighbourhood characteristics. A representative sample of properties should be drawn, in such a way that properties in the sample are chosen from a variety of localities with differing levels of ambient air quality. Multiple regression analysis can then be used to estimate the relationship between rents and air pollution, holding all other determinants of house rents at constant values. Box 10.2 presents one application of this technique by Brookshire *et al.*, to estimate the value of air quality improvements in Los Angeles. You are recommended to read this example now.

The outcome of such an empirical exercise will be a rent–pollution function. The hedonic price technique uses information derived from this function to estimate the value of environmental improvements. Thus, in Figure 10.9, if air quality were to improve so that pollution were reduced from X^* to X_1 then the rent an individual would pay would rise from $R(X^*)$ to $R(X_1)$. The difference between these two rent levels (subject to a qualification we shall discuss in a

[2] The presentation in this section follows very closely that given in Brookshire *et al.* (1982).

[3] Note that we are using housing rents as price here, as opposed to the capital or purchase price of the property. Given that the capital value of an asset is the discounted value of its lifetime rents, we could conduct the analysis using either rent or capital price.

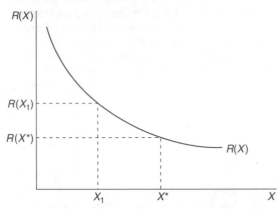

Fig 10.9 The willingness to pay for an improvement in air quality.

moment) represents the individual's WTP for the air quality improvement. Note that this WTP is a flow, a monetary value that an individual would pay in each period for a sustained increase in air quality, rather than a single once-and-for-all payment. The implicit or shadow price of a unit of pollution is then the rate of change of $R(X)$ with respect to X, which we shall denote as $r(X)$. Note that if the rent–pollution function is non-linear (as in Figure 10.9) then the shadow price of pollution $r(X)$ will vary with the level of pollution.

Let us now consider the nature of the qualification mentioned in the last paragraph. Given the arguments in the previous section, you may have noticed that information derived from the estimated rent function will *not* provide the researcher with an exact measure of the true welfare changes arising from air quality improvements. To understand this intuitively, note that the estimated rent function provides information which is related to Marshallian or uncompensated demand functions. But consumer surplus measures derived from Marshallian demands do not provide us with measures of WTP based on CV or EV principles.

Hedonic price technique valuations from the rent function itself do *not* measure the WTP itself. We can, nevertheless, show that for an improvement in environmental quality, the hedonic price estimate will in general overestimate the WTP for that improvement. However, the measure will provide an upper bound for the WTP. For a deterioration in quality, the measure underestimates the WTA, but will give a lower bound for the WTA. This information is likely to be of great value in practice. We have relegated a substantiation of these results to

Appendix 1, to which the reader who is prepared to go through a little additional maths should now turn.

One final point should be mentioned. The hedonic pricing technique will often require that a second step be carried out. We will usually be interested in obtaining an aggregate WTP for some population of individuals. This population is likely to comprise distinct subsets of individuals, living in different localities, and varying in terms of factors such as income and age. The WTP for an environmental improvement will vary with these characteristics. Ideally, the researcher should estimate separate demand curves for the environmental improvement for each of these population subsets.

This can be done by a second-stage regression technique. An inverse demand curve is estimated, in which the implicit price, r, that people in a particular area are willing to pay for environmental improvements (obtained from the first stage, described above) is related to average characteristics such as age and income for that area. So suppose that we have N different areas, each one of which is indexed by the subscript i. We might estimate a model of the form

$$r_i = r_i(X_i, Y_i, \mathrm{AGE}_i, Z_i) + u_i, \qquad i = 1, \ldots, N$$

in which Z denotes a vector of other variables that are thought to be relevant in explaining differences in WTP from one area to another. If estimates of such an equation can be obtained, then it will be possible to obtain estimates of the total WTP for an environmental improvement by a representative citizen of each area, and then to aggregate over all areas and persons to infer the required total WTP.

Problems with and limitations of the hedonic pricing technique

The main limitation of this technique is that it is only capable of measuring that subset of use values for which people are willing to pay, and actually do so (albeit indirectly) through the related market. It has to be recognised from the outset, therefore, that hedonic pricing can only provide us with estimates of some subset of the values in which we might be interested. Furthermore, if we have reason to believe that consumers are not fully informed about the qualities of the attributes being valued, hedonic price estimates are of little relevance.

Secondly, the hedonic price equation (and the second-step demand equation, if this is estimated) will, in most cases, impose rather strong assumptions about *separability* of consumers' utility functions. In

Box 10.2 Valuing improvements in air quality in Los Angeles

Brookshire and his colleagues took a sample of 634 sales of single family homes which occurred between January 1977 and March 1978 in the Los Angeles metropolitan area. Data on two air pollution variables – nitrogen dioxide (NO_2) and total suspended particulates (TSP) – that are collected regularly at air monitoring stations in the area were used in the study. The objective of the study was to estimate the gradient of the hedonic rent function for housing with respect to each of these alternative measures of air pollution, and to calculate rent differentials associated with air quality improvements for various localities within Los Angeles.

Housing sale prices were assumed to be a function of four sets of variables, H, N, A, and Q. These are vectors of explanatory variables, defined as

H = housing structure variables (living area, number of bathrooms, etc.)

N = neighbourhood variables (crime rate, school quality, population density etc.)

A = accessibility variables (distances to centres of employment, beaches, etc.)

Q = air quality variables (total suspended particulate matter and NO_2.)

The estimation procedure was not able to separate out the independent effect of the two air pollution variables, so two hedonic price functions were estimated, one for each measure of pollution. Note that we should interpret the rent–pollution gradient in each equation as a proxy for the effect of changes in a composite NO_2–TSP index.

Estimates of two non-linear hedonic equations are presented in Table 10.3. Brookshire *et al.* searched through a variety of alternative functional forms for the hedonic equation, and the equations reported here are those which had the best statistical fit. In these two equations, note that the dependent variable is the *natural logarithm* of the home sale price (in 1978 US$1000). Thus a change of one *unit in any one of the explanatory variables results in a proportionate change* of the dollar house sale price, where the magnitude of that proportionate change is given by the coefficient estimate attached to the variable in question. However, in the cases where an explanatory variable also enters in logarithmic form, the associated parameter estimate provides information

Table 10.3 Estimated hedonic rent gradient equations[a]

Independent variable	NO_2 equation	TSP equation
Housing structure variables:		
Sale date	0.018 591 (9.757 7)	0.018 654 (9.772 7)
Age	−0.018 171 (−2.338 5)	−0.021 411 (−2.814 7)
Living area	0.000 175 68 (12.126)	0.000 175 07 (12.069)
Bathrooms	0.156 02 (9.609)	0.157 03 (9.663 6)
Pool	0.058 063 (4.630 1)	0.058 397 (4.651 8)
Fireplaces	0.099 577 (7.170 5)	0.099 927 (7.186 6)
Neighbourhood variables:		
Log (crime)	−0.083 81 (−1.576 6)	−0.104 01 (−1.997 4)
School quality	0.001 982 6 (3.945 0)	0.001 771 (3.576 9)
Ethnic composition (% white)	0.027 031 (4.391 5)	0.043 472 (6.258 3)
Housing density	−0.000 066 926 (−9.127 7)	−0.000 067 613 (−9.235 9)
Public safety expenditure	0.000 261 92 (4.760 2)	0.000 261 43 (4.741 8)
Accessibility variables:		
Distance to beach	−0.011 586 (−7.832 1)	−0.011 612 (−7.782 2)
Distance to employment	−0.285 14 (−14.786)	−0.262 32 (−14.158)
Air pollution variables:		
log (TSP)		−0.221 83 (−3.832 4)
log (NO_2)	−0.224 07 (−4.032 4)	
Constant	2.232 5 (2.929 6)	1.052 7 (1.453 7)
R^2	0.89	0.89
Degrees of freedom	619	619

[a] The dependent variable is the natural logarithm of the home sale price in thousands of US$ (1978). Figures in parentheses are the *t*-statistics for the null hypothesis that the coefficient is zero. *Source*: Brookshire *et al.* (1982).

Box 10.2 Continued

about the proportionate change in house sale price that results from a unit proportionate change in the explanatory variable.

So for example, if distance to the beach is increased by one unit (one unit is probably one mile, although Brookshire's paper does not define units), then the home sale price will fall by 0.011 586 in proportionate terms (or by 1.1586%), if all other variables are held constant. A unit proportionate increase in NO_2 concentration (a 100% increase, or a doubling) results, ceteris paribus, in a proportionate decrease in house prices of 0.22407 (that is 22.407%).

Brookshire notes *inter alia* that

1 Approximately 90% of the variation in the home sale price is accounted for by variation in the explanatory variables of the models (see the R^2 statistics).
2 All coefficients indicate the expected relationship between the home sale price and the relevant explanatory variable. All coefficients are

statistically significant at the 1% level except for the coefficients of the crime rate.
3 In their respective equations, the pollution variables have their expected negative influence on sale price and are highly significant. The gradient of the rent gradient with respect to pollution is also consistent with the form suggested in Figure 10.9 above.

Brookshire *et al.* use this information to calculate the rent premium that would be implied if air quality were to improve, for identical homes in given localities. These rent premiums differ from one locality to another, but the results indicate rent differentials from \$15.44 to \$45.92 per month (in 1978 prices) for an improvement from 'poor' to 'fair' air quality, and from \$33.17 to \$128.46 (in 1978 prices) for an improvement from 'fair' to 'good' air quality. In each case, the higher figures are associated with higher income communities.

Source: Brookshire *et al.* (1982).

---

particular, the functional forms of regression model that are usually chosen impose weak separability, permitting rent–pollution and demand functions to be estimated independently of demand equations for other goods that consumers purchase. Standard consumer demand theory and the research evidence from applied studies of consumer demand cast doubt upon the validity of weak separability, particularly when 'large' changes occur, as is often the case when we are dealing with environmental projects.

There are also a large number of econometric pitfalls that beset applied research using hedonic pricing techniques, including problems associated with small sample sizes, uncertainty about choice of relevant variables, sample selection bias and the choice of functional form. We do not intend to discuss these potential problems, but will refer you to specialised references at the end of this chapter. It is worth noting, nevertheless, that if great care is not given to ensuring that the selected regression model is statistically well-specified, the estimates obtained should not be regarded as valid ones.

Valuation techniques based on travel costs

A common method of imputing the values associated with non-marketed recreational or cultural facilities has been through the use of observed travel costs. These techniques have been widely used in Europe,

North America and Australia, and are finding application in developing countries in the estimation of the values of game reserves and tourism developments.

The technique seems to have been first proposed by Hotelling (1931), and subsequently developed by Clawson (1959) and Clawson and Knetsch (1966). Visitors to outdoor recreational facilities, nature reserves and so on usually incur costs, in terms of time and money, in travelling to such sites. Knowledge of these expenditures can be used to infer the values placed by visitors on environmental resources. As in the case of hedonic pricing, the principle being used is that of inferring the value of a set of attributes from expenditure in another market.

The basic principles underpinning this method are very simple. Suppose we consider a particular geographical area, which contains just one wildlife reserve. Our objective is to estimate the (use) value of this reserve. The location of the site in the area we study is represented in Figure 10.10.

Let z_A and z_B denote the number of visits per period to the site from zones A and B respectively, each expressed as a proportion of the population of the zone in question. Let the average travel costs per trip for each visitor from zone A be P_A, and from zone B be P_B. These travel costs should include all relevant costs, including the costs of time spent and the marginal disutility of travel itself (if any). This

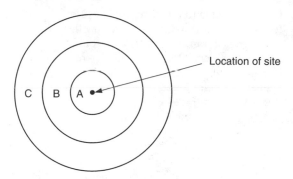

Fig 10.10 The location of a visitor attraction.

information is portrayed in Figure 10.11; our objective is to show that this relationship between travel costs and frequency of visit can be interpreted as a demand curve for the wildlife reserve, and that it can be used to estimate the WTP for this reserve.

We shall use the phrase WTP to denote the total or gross value a consumer derives from a resource to which he or she travels. The term consumer surplus will be used to refer to the excess of this WTP over the total travel costs of reaching the site. So consumer surplus is the net value of the resource, and will be lower than WTP by the amount of travel costs.

For the average visitor from zone A, his or her WTP for z_A trips per period is shown by the area under the cost-trip function between $z = 0$ and $z = z_A$. Given the fact that the typical visitor to the site from zone A will incur travel costs of P_A, his or her consumer surplus is the smaller amount A + B, the shaded area, in Figure 10.11. The gross value of the site to this visitor is equal to this WTP, the net value is this WTP less travel costs, that is his or her consumer surplus.

How do we find the total WTP (or total consumer surplus) for all visitors to the site? This involves two steps. Firstly, multiplying the WTP for each visitor from zone A by the total visitors from zone A gives the total WTP for visitors from zone A. Then repeating this process for each zone, and then summing over all zones, we obtain an aggregate WTP for the site. More formally, the aggregate consumers' surplus is given by

$$\sum_{i=1}^{i=N} n_i \int_{P_i}^{P_0} Z(P) \, dp$$

where $Z = Z(P)$ is the function relating visitor frequency (Z) – total number of visitors divided by population – to average travel cost (P), N is the total number of distinct zones of origin of visitors, n_i is the population of zone i, P_i is the average travel cost for a visitor from zone i, and P_0 is the travel cost for the average visitor from the zone at which the visit rate falls to zero.

This technique can also be used to estimate the increment in value that would result from improvements in the environmental quality of the site. Freeman (1979), for example, analyses the effects on the demand for recreation of a change in water quality. The technique involves augmenting the travel cost visit function with a variable that represents water quality. This allows the researcher to identify the effect on the demand for some given resource site of an improvement in water quality. This is illustrated in Figure 10.12. As a result of an environmental improvement, the attractiveness of the site to visitors is enhanced. For any given population zone, we would expect visitors to be willing to incur greater costs in travelling to the site or a greater number of visits to be generated for a given travel cost. As a result, the (implicit) demand

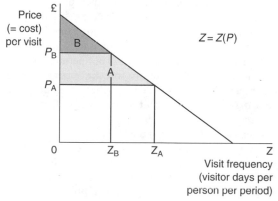

Fig 10.11 Travel costs and visit frequency.

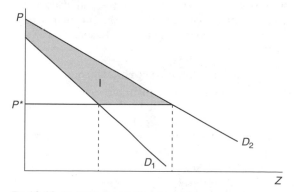

Fig 10.12 An improvement in site quality.

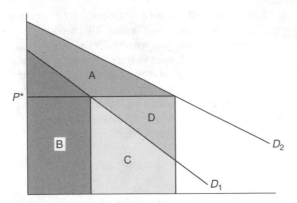

Fig 10.13 The increase in WTP for a site improvement.

curve for the site (the trip generating function) shifts to the right from D_1 to D_2.

If the *actual* cost for the visitor from zone A were P^*, and that remained the average cost after the site improvement, then the increase in *consumer surplus* arising from the improvement is indicated by the (shaded) area denoted I in Figure 10.12. This establishes the increase in consumer surplus for the average visitor from zone A; to obtain the aggregate change, one needs to find the total for each zone, and then sum over all visitor zones. You should now check for yourself by how much the gross WTP for the improvement is increased. The answer is given in Problem 4 at the end of the chapter.

One final point needs to be made here. In this section, we have been equating changes in consumer surplus with welfare changes. Earlier parts of the chapter will have alerted you to the fact that this is not strictly correct, as true measures of welfare change are given by areas under Hicksian or compensated demands, not the uncompensated demands such as that drawn in Figure 10.11. As a result, either we can regard these measures as approximations to the true welfare changes, or we might try and deduce the compensated demands from the uncompensated demands that emerge from the procedures we have just described.

Limitations of the travel cost technique

The major limitation of the travel cost technique is one that we also attributed to hedonic pricing. It is only capable of measuring that subset of values for which people are willing to pay (through the medium of incurring travel costs to visit sites with attributes for which we seek valuations). Travel cost techniques can only provide us with estimates of some of the values in which we might be interested. Another point

is closely related to this: one would expect travel cost techniques to be suitable for measuring the values of a quite limited range of attributes of interest. The approach is very useful for valuing resource-based recreational amenities, where it has been very widely applied, but it has found very few applications outside this particular area.

A number of methodological issues warrant attention. Our presentation of the travel cost technique has modelled the visit frequency to a single site as a function only of the travel costs to that site alone. That is, we have been using the relationship to represent what is often called the trip generating function (TGF). However, in practice, the potential visitor can make his or her travel choice from a number of sites offering similar but not identical experiences and differing in terms of their access to visitors. We would also expect that many factors influence the frequency of visits to any given site. So more generally, if there are n distinct sites available to visit, the frequency of visits to site j might be modelled as

$$Z_j = Z_j(P_1, \ldots, P_n, \Omega), \qquad j = 1, \ldots, n$$

where P_1 to P_n are a set of travel costs to the jth and all other (substitute) sites, and Ω denotes a vector of other explanatory variables, such as income levels, social class, tastes and so on. Nevertheless, it should be clear that the partial relationship between Z_j and P_j, obtained from an estimate of this function, will contain the information we require to impute WTP. Ideally, one should regard the research exercise as that of jointly explaining the visit frequency to each of these n sites. If data were available (which it frequently is not), the best approach would be to estimate all n equations together, using a system estimation technique. An alternative exercise which can also provide very useful information involves estimating the demand for every site separately, and then investigating how parameter estimates vary with differences in environmental attributes across sites. This permits one to obtain a demand function for the environmental attributes themselves. Each of these techniques is very data-demanding, and statistically difficult, and is rarely undertaken.

An awkward empirical question concerns the value which should be assigned to the *time* costs of travel. It is common in empirical work to use some proportion of average wage rates (typically in the range one-quarter to one-half) as a proxy for travel time costs. This procedure is open to much criticism, however. Furthermore, the usual practice of assuming that travel time incurs negative utility is questionable, particularly in circumstances where the travel to the site involves travelling through landscape which has similar qualities to that being visited, or where the travel time is itself pleasurable. As you might expect, serious conceptual problems also arise in dealing with multiple visits to particular sites, trips to poorly defined sites, visits of different lengths of time, and visits which are combined with travelling for other reasons. Whilst it is easy to devise some 'rules of thumb' for valuing such visits relative to the 'pure' case, it is less easy to avoid believing that most such rules are likely to be rather arbitrary ones.

Travel cost studies have to confront the issue of differing welfare measures derived from compensated and uncompensated demand function issues that we have discussed previously. As we have examined this matter at some length already, and because nothing new of substance is introduced by the travel cost approach *per se*, we shall do no more than simply repeat the point that exact measures of WTP should in principle be obtained from compensated demand functions.

Potential issues related to double-counting occur in travel cost studies (and in the other techniques we investigate in this chapter). When a new site is developed, the net addition to welfare will only be equal to the welfare gained from the new site if existing sites have zero substitutability for the new one. In general, as new sites are provided, individuals will change their patterns of travel, and so consumer surplus derived from some existing sites may fall (or may rise if overcrowding pressures are reduced). The point here is that to obtain the net effect on welfare, one must take care to take account of the whole set of effects.

Finally, as with any survey-based statistical analysis, statistically credible results require that valid statistical methods are used. A host of 'problems' arise in travel cost studies, many of which are very difficult to handle given the limited data that are likely to be available to the researcher. There are likely to be problems associated with sample-selection bias, in particular, arising from the fact that the technique draws data only from those who do actually visit, and ignores non-visitors. This can lead to biased coefficient estimates. References to examinations of these difficulties and appropriate responses to them are to be found in the list of suggested reading.

Contingent valuation

The contingent valuation (CV) technique consists of two forms, one employing an experimental approach, based upon simulations or game analysis, the other using data derived from questionnaire or survey techniques. In this survey, we consider only CV using survey methods. The technique is used to estimate either the WTP for an improvement in the quality or quantity of some environmental good, or the WTA for a deterioration in environmental provision. The valuation is termed contingent because the information sought from the game-players or survey respondents is conditional upon some particular hypothetical market context. This context will specify the nature of the change, how it is to be implemented, what it will cost, how payments would be made, and so on. The objective of the simulation or survey is to elicit (hypothetical) monetary bids from a representative sample of the 'population of interest'. These bids are then used as the data from which inference on the shadow price of some environmental gain or loss is conducted.

This technique has found extensive application in recent years. In developed countries, it has been employed to value water quality improvements, the benefits of reduced air pollution, and the option or existence values of wilderness areas or ecologically important species. Applications have been less common in developing countries, but development aid through the IDA at the World Bank has sometimes required CV studies of the benefits of water, sewerage and tourism projects.

Survey design issues

There are several ways in which CV survey data can be collected. The survey data may be collected through personal interview, by returned mailed questionnaires, or by telephone interview procedures. Only the personal interview is likely to yield reliable data, but it is an expensive and time-consuming technique, and may well induce research teams to use small sample sizes, with obviously undesirable consequences. To obtain reliable responses, a very carefully designed questionnaire is required, using structured rather than open-ended questions, and providing the respondent with as much information as possible about the project in question.

There is considerable evidence that the responses received are very sensitive to the manner in which information is provided, and to the content of that information. This raises the question of the means by which the contingent information is best provided. Some of the answers to this question are now widely agreed. Firstly, scenarios presented should be as realistic as possible. The respondent should be presented with a specific problem, requiring specific solutions, told exactly which environmental impacts would occur, and asked how much he or she would be willing to pay in the form of a particular payment method, such as higher prices, higher taxes or a trust fund.

The method by which bids are elicited appears to be have a significant effect upon the WTP values obtained from CV studies. Open bids, in which the respondent is simply asked how much he or she would be willing to pay, are unreliable ways of eliciting information. Superior results seem to emerge from structured bidding processes, involving initial suggestions, and requiring yes or no answers to bids which are incrementally raised from some given starting point.

Sources of bias in estimates

The CV technique relies upon sample evidence to make inferences about a relevant population. A sample estimate is said to be unbiased if the expected value of the sample estimator of the population value is equal to the true (but unknown) population value. There is, of course, no guarantee in general that sample estimators will be unbiased. Sources of bias can arise from unrepresentative sample selection, low response rates in the presence of differential response rates from different subsections of the sample and so on. The CV method is no exception to this, and so careful statistical design of the survey procedure is necessary to minimise the chance of obtaining biased estimators. In addition to bias in the sample estimator, the results of the population estimates can be misleading if errors are made in the choice of the relevant population. Studies of the value of wildlife reserves, for example, often select rather arbitrary delineations of the boundary of the population of interest. These considerations, and several others we have not mentioned, warrant caution in interpreting the results of CV studies.[4]

However, discussion of the CV technique has pointed to a number of additional potential sources of bias, some of which are unique to this approach.

[4] These comments do not apply only to the CV method, of course. Any technique using sample survey methods will face similar problems. Travel cost valuation is another obvious case.

We briefly list these, noting that these are potential biases, most of which should be avoided by careful design of the experiment.

- *Hypothetical bias* may arise because respondents are asked to state WTP for changes which are hypothetical rather than actual. Responses may be unreliable in this case, although whether the unreliability would take the form of a systematic bias (as opposed to being characterised by large estimator variance) is somewhat unclear. We have already suggested that the best CV studies are ones that are as close to real cases as possible. It is also thought that questioning which focuses attention on willingness to pay for future changes rather than willingness to accept compensation for damages already done is most likely to be consistent with scenarios credible to respondents.
- *Information bias* is used to refer to bias that arises from the structure of information presented to the respondent, and upon which bids are conditioned. In particular, the starting points for bids (when these are proposed by the interviewer) have the clear potential to shape the WTP outcomes.
- *Payment vehicle bias*: evidence suggests that the magnitude of bids can be sensitive to the form of payment that would be utilised if the project were to be realised. Some authors have interpreted this as irrational, and so indicative of bias; others argue that rational behaviour can explain why WTP would be related to the means (as opposed to level) of payment, and so would question any imputation of bias.
- *Strategic bias* arises from a respondent's self-interested desire to influence the outcome of the study. If I were strongly in favour of conservation of a natural environment, I might be inclined to propose a very large WTP, in the hope that this enhanced the prospects of the site remaining undeveloped. This is particularly likely if the respondent knows that he or she would not actually be called upon to pay the sum he or she indicated. Clearly, this is an example of the 'free rider' problem in another guise.

Accuracy of results

We have seen that results of CV studies can be misleading or inaccurate. To what extent are they inaccurate? Not surprisingly, it is not possible to answer this question in general. If we regard consistency of findings from different studies over time as indicative of accuracy, practitioners generally argue that we can place considerable confidence in the results of a set of studies taken as a whole. On the other hand, it is often noted that for any individual study, results may be accurate to only one order of magnitude. That is, if the estimated value were 10^2, the true value is very likely to lie in the interval 10^1 to 10^3. Diamond *et al.* (1992) cite evidence that the charitable donations that people purport (in CV studies) to be willing to pay are up to ten times larger than the amounts that are actually provided. Brookshire *et al.* (see Box 10.2), taking hedonic pricing methods as a reference case, find that CV studies are accurate to within ±100% of the values obtained from hedonic price studies.

One particular difficulty of CV appears to be the choice of starting point from which bids are elicited. A number of recent technically sophisticated studies avoid this problem by seeking only accept/reject choices, rather than quantified bids as such. Discrete choice statistical modelling techniques can estimate WTP data from such discrete choices in a sample of respondents, and we have reason to believe that this method offers greater reliability than conventional techniques.

There is some agreement that WTP measures of environmental improvements are more reliable than WTA measures of deteriorations, perhaps because there is little evidence of strategic bias in the former instance. Economic theory suggests that WTA will exceed WTP, but also that the difference should be relatively small in most cases where 'small' changes in quantities or qualities are being proposed. However, many studies have found the difference to be much greater than theory implies. Much effort has been devoted in attempts to explain why this should occur. No consensus has developed regarding the explanation of the discrepancy, but two suggestions figure prominently in the literature.

Firstly, the difference may be entirely rational, in that from a given starting point, consumers may actually value losses more highly than gains. In this case there is no 'problem' to explain: the differences reflect real underlying preferences. A second strand of explanation is based on the premise that respondents often have a very poor understanding of the concept of WTA, or at least understand the term in a way that is very different from its meaning to economists.

Whatever the explanation might be, a consensus has emerged that a WTP measure is more likely to be closely related to its true but unknown counterpart than is the case for WTA.

Assessment of the CV technique

The CV technique is now a widely used tool in economic analysis, and has become a powerful tool of valuation. Its chief merits lie in the very wide applicability of CV, its versatility, and in the fact that it is the only method available which is capable of obtaining estimates of both non-use and use values.

Dose–response valuation methods

Unlike the three valuation techniques we have explored so far, the dose–response procedure does not attempt to measure preferences. Let us consider how this method tries to value an increase in the pollution level. In the first step, estimates are obtained of the consequences (the response) of the pollution 'dose'. These estimates are not in monetary units, but will be in the natural physical units for the medium being affected (such as mass of timber damage, loss of agricultural output, physical damage to buildings, wildlife losses from acidification). Thus, if L denotes units of damage, X units of pollution, and Ω a vector of variables we believe conditions the effect of X on L, we have the relationship

$$L = L(X, \Omega)$$

Our task is to select an appropriate functional form for this relationship, and estimate its parameters using scientific data. Having done this, we can then use this estimated function to estimate the increment in damages that will result from some particular change in environmental pollution. Denote this as ΔL. This completes the first stage.

The second stage involves calculating a monetary value for each unit of damage, which we denote as V. Then the monetary value of the damages associated with the pollution increase is given by $D = V\Delta L$. How this second stage is actually done will vary from one type of damage to another. Where the impacts are primarily felt upon marketed goods or services, then observed prices are often used as indicators of value. For example, agricultural losses are often measured at the market price of the output loss expected from the pollution.

This technique has a number of drawbacks. Firstly, errors can be made in the first step of estimating losses arising from doses of pollution. In particular, where losses are predominantly qualitative rather than quantitative, they tend to be ignored. Secondly, a number of errors can be made in the second step. If impacts are sufficiently large to alter relative prices, then valuation procedures tend to break down. If adjustments to actual or potential damage take place, reducing the observed impacts of pollution changes, a failure to incorporate these costs of adjustment can lead estimated losses to be downward biased. Furthermore, by failing to take account of substitution effects that arise, estimates may also be upward biased. For example, suppose that there is an increase in lower-atmosphere ozone concentrations. If farmers behaved passively, some output would be lost, and it is this loss which the method calculates. But farmers will not usually respond passively. They are likely to substitute ozone-resilient crops for those sensitive to ozone, take measures which counteract ozone damage (perhaps through the use of special fertilisers) or even relocate their production. In each case, these responses will ensure that final net losses are less than the original estimate implied, sometimes greatly less. To obtain post-substitution effect measures of damage will, therefore, require that one augments the basic procedures outlined above with a secondary model of production and consumption responses. Few dose–response studies do this, given the difficult modelling techniques which are likely to be involved.

In conclusion, the monetary estimates of damages obtained from dose–response valuation techniques will not, in general, be equal to the true underlying WTP. However, the technique may be applicable when other methods cannot be used. For example, in cases where the person affected is unaware of the effect, or very badly informed, techniques based upon expressed preferences cannot be used. Furthermore, dose–response valuation is likely to be the cheapest method, and may be enforced by budgetary restrictions.

Obtaining an aggregate social valuation from individual valuations

Our discussion so far has been concerned largely with the individual's valuation of a good or service. In most cases, however, the quantity which is of interest to the environmental economist is the aggregate community (social) value. How do we obtain this? Let us assume that the society of interest is a well-defined set of persons. This community will often coincide with some political community, such as the population of California, or the citizens of Poland, but it need not necessarily do so. The researcher must have in mind such a clearly defined community,

otherwise it is not meaningful to attempt to calculate a social value of the resource services in question.

Within this community, the individuals whose preferences matter when calculating the social value will be all those whose utility is affected by the service in question. It is then usual to assume that the social value in question (i.e. the value for some group as a whole) is obtainable as some aggregate of individual values (based on individual WTPs). A major question now arises of how this aggregate is to be formed. We saw earlier, in Chapter 2, that a social welfare function would be sufficient for this purpose. If we knew the form of that function, this would imply the appropriate method of aggregation. However, in general we will not know this (and perhaps we could not know it); some simplifying assumption is then necessary for us to proceed.

It is common to assume (though such an assumption may be quite wrong!) that income and wealth are distributed in such a way that the marginal utility of income is equal over all individuals. This assumption permits a simple equal-weighted aggregate of individual WTPs to be interpretable as a measure of social welfare.

In those cases where we are dealing with private goods or services, then the social valuation of such a good or service can be derived as the horizontal summation of individual valuations, as shown in Figure 10.14, in just the same way as aggregate demand curves are obtained by horizontal summation of individual demands. Measures of social WTP can be estimated as areas underneath such a social valuation curve. It is different, though, when we are considering public goods or services. In this case, social valuations are obtained by vertical summations of individual valuations, as shown in Figure 10.15.

Irreversibility, option value and quasi-option value

Conventional economic analysis usually assumes that resource-use decisions are reversible. Suppose that, on the basis of information currently available, an agent makes a plan for the use of his or her resources in this period and for all future periods in the relevant planning horizon. Now assume that at some point in the future new information becomes available, and that the optimal programme for resource use changes. If resource use decisions were reversible, the agent

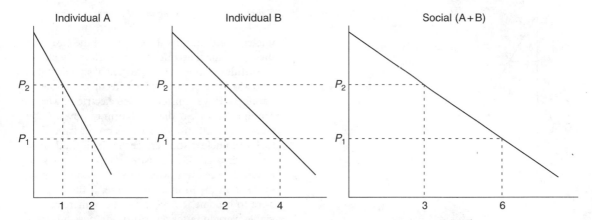

Fig 10.14 Obtaining social valuations for a private good.

could change the pattern of resource use whenever that became optimal to do.

But this kind of reversibility clearly does not apply in all circumstances where decisions are made about the use of environmental resources. The most obvious example concerns exhaustible resources. The use of these is irreversible in the sense that once extracted, that quantity is lost for ever. Suppose that it turns out to have been suboptimal to have undertaken a particular extraction programme, and that an optimal choice would imply (now that more information is available) greater quantities being extracted later and lower quantities earlier. But once the initial plan was implemented, those units already extracted are lost forever. We might regret the initial choice, but some parts of that choice are irreversible.

A second case in which irreversibility is important relates to renewable resources. If a current harvesting rate that was initially thought to be optimal turns out to be excessive, it will often be possible to redeem the situation by temporarily reducing the harvest rate to allow stocks to accumulate to a higher level. But this will not always be possible. If stocks fall below critical levels that are minimum thresholds for species to continue to reproduce over time, then the species will become extinct. Extinction may subsequently turn out to have been a wrong 'choice', but the choice has irreversible consequences.

Finally, another class of irreversibilities concerns decisions to develop wilderness areas or to change the use of some environmental resource system in some significant way. Once 'developed' a wilderness area cannot be returned to its original state, or at least it cannot return to that state in a time scale relevant to human existence. There is a fundamental asymmetry

here: a decision not to develop can be reversed, but a decision to develop cannot be reversed. In the latter case, taking the 'develop' option closes off the 'not develop' option for all future periods. It is this third kind of irreversibility that we focus upon in this section, although you should note that all three forms are closely related to each other.

The Krutilla–Fisher model of wilderness development

Krutilla and Fisher (1975) investigated the conditions under which it would be economically efficient to develop a natural recourse asset such as a wilderness area for commercial uses. They begin by assuming that the asset can be used in only two ways. The first use is extractive, to develop the resource for such things as its logging, mining and hydro power potential. We shall refer to this set of uses as the development use of the resource. Alternatively, the asset can be preserved in its present form, to provide amenity services such as recreational facilities, aesthetic experiences and the existence values arising from ecologically rich habitats. We shall refer to this option as the preservation use of the resource. Two issues are central to the choice about whether the site should be developed.

1 *Irreversibility*. Extractive uses of resources tend to lead to irreversible changes to natural environments, permanently reducing the flow of amenities available from alternative uses of the site. The irreversibility is a consequence of the fact that natural assets are non-producible, at least in time scales that are relevant for human

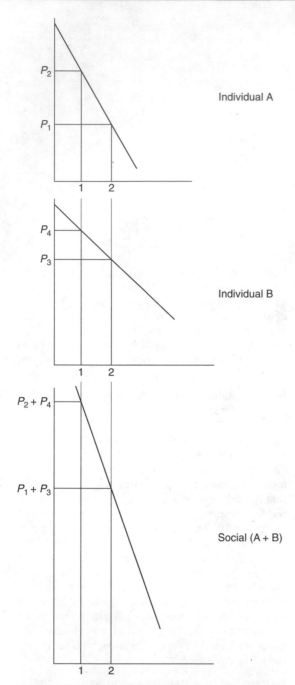

Fig 10.15 Obtaining social valuations for a public good.

planning horizons. An asymmetry that we noted earlier arises here: whilst extractive uses tend to foreclose options in perpetuity, no such implications follow from the preservation use of the resource.

2 *Substitutability and technical progress.* The development option produces extracted intermediate outputs. It is typically the case that these intermediate outputs have relatively close substitutes. Moreover, the degree of substitutability tends to increase over time as technical knowledge develops. If we consider hydro electric power, for example, it is clear that this form of power has many close substitutes, such as power from fossil fuel and nuclear sources. Technological advances have increased these substitution possibilities in recent decades, and will almost certainly continue to do so in the foreseeable future. If fusion power were to become technically and commercially viable, very long-term substitution possibilities will have been opened up. Finally, one would expect that rising demand for the extractive outputs of the development use can be met at decreasing real costs over time, as energy production and conversion benefits from technological innovation.

This contrasts strongly with the preservation benefits of the resource, for a number of reasons.

1 Substitution possibilities for the amenity services of environmental resources are often close to zero, and will not tend to become higher as technical progress progresses.
2 There are strong grounds for believing that future demand for environmental amenities will grow rapidly over time, as economies become increasingly materially affluent. However, technological progress itself cannot augment supplies of these environmental amenities; technology does not enter the production function for natural capital in the way that it does for produced goods.
3 As real income and demand for the amenities provided by environmental assets grow over time, the relative value of these amenities will rise. This contrasts with a falling relative value of material outputs.

Technological change thus has asymmetrical implications: it tends to lower the relative value of extractive outputs, but increase the relative value of amenity services from undeveloped environmental assets.

Let us now look at this problem in a more formal way. In discussing cost–benefit analysis (CBA) in Chapter 2, we noted that the net present value (NPV) of a project is conventionally defined as

$$NPV = \sum_{t=0}^{t=T} \frac{NB_t}{(1+r)^t} \qquad (10.1)$$

in which NB_t denotes the net benefit of the project to the economy in time period t, measured in consumption (or income) equivalent units. In aggregating net benefits over time to arrive at the NPV of the project, r is a consumption discount rate. Our discussion of discounting in Chapter 2 demonstrated that r may be negative, zero or positive. The decision criterion implied by CBA is:

> Do the project if NPV is greater than zero, do not do it otherwise.

Expression 10.1 is appropriate for obtaining the NPV of a project in which net benefits are taken to arise in a finite number of discrete periods. It will be convenient for our purposes if we work with the continuous time analogue of Equation 10.1 which is

$$NPV = \int_{t=0}^{t=T} e^{-rt} NB_t \, dt \qquad (10.2)$$

Now let us decompose net benefit into its constituent parts by writing

$$NB_t = B_t - C_t \qquad (10.3)$$

in which B and C denote total gross benefits and total costs respectively. Let us next adapt the NPV expression for the project that is investigated by Krutilla and Fisher. As the project is development of the natural resources, the project benefits comprise development benefits that we notate as $B(D)$. There are two kinds of project cost. Firstly, establishing and operating the development incurs costs $C(D)$. Secondly, development entails an opportunity cost; once developed, the resources lose some or all their value as preserved assets, yielding amenity services. We denote these foregone preservation benefits $B(P)$. Finally, note that if development does occur, any costs required for preserving the resource (e.g. maintenance, policing, visitor control) will be avoided. These 'costs', denoted $C(P)$, are in effect benefits as regards the NPV of development.

Given these definitions, we may write $B_t - C_t$ in Equation 10.2 as

$$NB_t = B_t - C_t = B(D)_t - C(D)_t + C(P)_t - B(P)_t$$

Therefore, Equation 10.2 may be written as

$$NPV = \int_{t=0}^{t=T} e^{-rt} (B(D)_t - C(D)_t + C(P)_t - B(P)_t) \, dt \qquad (10.4)$$

Equation 10.4 constitutes the conventional expression for calculating the NPV of a development project. But

Krutilla and Fisher suggest it is inappropriate, because preservation benefits tend to increase over time and development benefits tend to fall over time. The expression in Equation 10.4 is not valid because it fails to incorporate these factors. Suppose that the rate of increase of preservation benefits is α and the rate of decrease of development benefits is γ ($\alpha, \gamma > 0$). It is common in empirical studies to proxy α by the trend rate of growth in real *per capita* income and γ by the trend rate of technical progress. We should then apply these to the terms $B(P)$ and $B(D)$ in Equation 10.4. This results in a modified NPV measure, NPV^*:

$$NPV^* = \int_{t=0}^{t=T} e^{-rt} (B(D)_t e^{-\gamma t} - C(D)_t + C(P)_t - B(P)_t e^{\alpha t}) \, dt \qquad (10.5)$$

or

$$NPV^* = \int_{t=0}^{t=T} e^{-(r+\gamma)t} B(D)_t \, dt$$
$$- \int_{t=0}^{t=T} e^{-(r-\alpha)t} B(P)_t \, dt$$
$$- \int_{t=0}^{t=T} e^{-rt} (C(D)_t - C(P)_t) \, dt \qquad (10.6)$$

How will decisions from the Krutilla–Fisher NPV^* differ from those using the conventional NPV measure? The answer is quite simple. If $\alpha, \gamma > 0$, as Krutilla and Fisher suggest, $NPV^* < NPV$. This result follows from the fact that $B(D)_t e^{-\gamma t}$ is always less than $B(D)_t$, and that $B(P)_t e^{\alpha t}$ is always more than $B(P)_t$ under the assumptions that $\alpha, \gamma > 0$. Thus fewer projects will satisfy the criterion that the net present value of a project should exceed zero if it is to be undertaken. The Krutilla–Fisher model leads to a more preservation-oriented rule, but one which is arrived at entirely on the grounds of economic efficiency.

How much difference will this modification make in practice? It is not possible to give a general answer to this question, as the difference will depend not only on the magnitudes of α and γ, but also on the manner in which the benefits and costs are spread out through time. However, given that it is not unreasonable to assume a 2% rate of real income growth and a 3% rate of growth of technical progress, then $\alpha + \gamma = 0.05$, which is of the same order of magnitude as r in many CBA studies. It clearly can, therefore, make a very considerable difference indeed.

Finally, let us note another interpretation that may be put on the Krutilla–Fisher model. The adjustments are equivalent to using different discount rates for benefits and opportunity costs – higher for benefits, lower for costs.

The consequences of irreversibility for resource use

Anderson (1985) provides a very clear intuitive account of some of the implications that irreversibility carries for resource use. We summarise his arguments here. Suppose we have an environmental resource, yielding flows of services (Z) in each of two periods. At this point we assume economic agents are risk-neutral. Imagine we know with certainty the marginal costs (MC) and marginal benefits (MB) derived from the resource services in each of the two time periods. These are the ones illustrated in Figure 10.16. Notice three points about the way this diagram is constructed. Firstly, the two sets of schedules are represented in present value terms, and so the MB and MC curves for period 2 have been discounted at a consumption rate of interest, denoted as r. In view of our discussions in Chapter 2, r may be positive, negative or zero. Secondly, the horizontal axis measures the remaining resource services in each period, and so moving to the right corresponds to more of the resource being conserved. Thirdly, we have assumed that the (discounted) MB is higher in period 2 than in period 1, perhaps because of increasing preferences for environmental services over time. Also, we have assumed that the MC of the services are lower in the second period, perhaps because of technical progress. It would, of course, have been quite reasonable to make the opposite assumption, particularly given the comments we made earlier in summarising the Krutilla–Fisher model.

In the absence of irreversibility, an efficient outcome would involve choosing a consumption level of environmental services in each period which equates marginal costs and benefits. This would lead to Z_1 and Z_2 consumption flows in the two periods. How are matters changed when the use of a resource entails irreversible consequences? To make matters concrete, suppose that the environmental resource were 'developed' for some reason, and were run down to the point where it could yield a maximum of only Z_1 of service flows in period 1. If development were irreversible, this would imply that the maximum feasible flow would be Z_1 in period 2 as well. Therefore, irreversibility implies that the efficient choice of Z_1 and Z_2 in the two periods is not feasible.

In this case, an efficient plan will choose two levels of environmental service consumption, Z_1^* and Z_2^*,

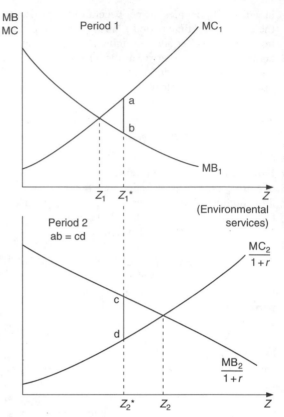

Fig 10.16 Irreversibility and the efficient provision of an environmental service.

such that $Z_1^* = Z_2^*$, and that the marginal loss from holding extra stocks of undeveloped resources in period 1 (that is, ab) is equal to the discounted marginal benefit of having greater stocks in period 2 than would have been the case if more development had taken place (that is, cd). We can now see that irreversibility implies a more 'conservative' plan. Less development of the resource takes place in the first period than would have been the case if wilderness development could be reversed.

Uncertainty

Now let us bring uncertainty into the analysis as well as irreversibility. In particular, suppose that future costs and benefits are uncertain in the following way. There is a probability of p ($0 \leq p \leq 1$) that period 2 MB and MC functions will be those labelled MB_1 and MC_1, and a probability q ($q + p = 1$) that period 2 MB and MC functions will be those labelled MB_2 and MC_2. The efficient plan in this case is the one that

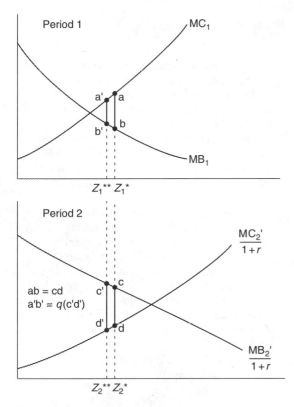

Fig 10.17 Uncertainty and irreversibility.

maximises *expected* net benefits over the two periods. This will require equating the marginal loss from holding extra stocks of undeveloped resources in period 1 to the *expected* discounted marginal benefit of having greater stocks in period 2. This requires equating the distance $a'b'$ to q times the distance $c'd'$ in Figure 10.17.

When uncertainty combines with irreversibility, Anderson's analysis shows that a more conservationist stance should be taken towards resource use than irreversibility alone implies.

Risk aversion: option value

Option value refers to the value that arises from retaining an option to a good or service for which future demand or supply is uncertain. The option value is an additional value to any utility that may arise if and when the good is actually consumed. If we are certain as to our future preferences and the future availability of the resource, option value will be zero. But if we are not certain about either our future preferences or future availability, we may be willing to pay a premium (the option value) to keep the option of future use open. This result was first suggested by Weisbrod (1964), but was the subject of some theoretical controversy at the time. However, Cicchetti and Freeman (1971) demonstrated the existence of option value for risk-averse individuals.

More precisely, suppose that an individual knows what his or her consumer surplus would be in each possible future state of the world, and has a (subjective) probability distribution which gives the probability of each of these possible future states. In this situation, an individual can calculate his or her expected consumer surplus. Define the option price of a resource to be the sum of money that a person would be willing to pay today for the right to consume some quantity of a resource (at a fixed price) in the future. Cicchetti and Freeman showed that a risk-averse individual would have an option price which is greater than his or her expected consumer surplus. The difference between option price and expected consumer surplus is option value. Option value is thus a risk premium, and it will be positive for risk-averse individuals.

Quasi-option value: no risk aversion but uncertainty

Arrow and Fisher (1974) developed the concept of quasi-option value. Quasi-option value refers to another set of utility gains that can be attained by not undertaking irreversible decisions, and so by maintaining options for future use of some resource.

The essence of quasi-option value lies in expectations about future technological advance and the growth of knowledge. Suppose that the passage of time leads to new information becoming available about the benefits of different uses of an environmental resource. If decisions about development are taken later rather than sooner, a greater quantity of this new information can be taken into account when development projects are being appraised. In circumstances where decisions are reversible, there is nogain to be derived from awaiting the growth of new knowledge: choices can be amended accordingly as information evolves. Clearly, this adaptation is precluded when choices have irreversible consequences.

The value of the gains expected from deferring development in these circumstances is known as quasi-option value. An important part of the Arrow and Fisher result is a demonstration that quasi-option value exists whether or not individuals are risk-averse. So the 'precautionary principle' can be lent support by the concept of quasi-option value, and this shows that its validity does not require any assumption of risk-aversion on the part of typical individuals.

The concepts of option value and quasi-option value, together with our earlier summaries of the Krutilla and Fisher model and of the Anderson model, strongly suggest the following conclusion concerning resource development policy. It will be economically efficient to proceed very cautiously whenever any resource use is being proposed that is likely to have irreversible consequences. This conclusion is independent of any particular ecological or ethical arguments that might also justify conservation.

Potential difficulties in environmental resource evaluation

Let us conclude our discussion of environmental resource valuation by noting three potential difficulties. Firstly, it is common for environmental resources to exist in the form of 'multi-dimensional packages'. An example of such a set of resources is a wilderness area, such as the Cairngorms mountain region. This region constitutes an interrelated set of resources/services. Some of these will be marketed or be inputs to products which are marketed (such as sheep products from hill farming), and so the resource in question will command a price reflecting this. On the other hand, many of the items of this resource set (such as unique flora, visual beauty, species diversity) will not be marketed. The market price of the resource set will, in this example, be poorly approximated (and probably be seriously underestimated) by the market value of the land area in question.

Secondly, in matters involving the use (or abuse) of environmental resources, the analyst is often forced to deal with risk or uncertainty. This may arise either because the investigator has poor or incomplete information (particularly, but not exclusively, regarding the future), or because other persons in the community of interest are operating in conditions of risk and uncertainty.

Thirdly, environmental resource stocks exist over time. This raises questions of aggregation of values over time, possible implications of sustainability for valuation, and the span of time horizons over which it is deemed appropriate to make decisions.

Discussion questions

1 Suppose some economic activity were to affect the life expectancy of the average individual. How might one attempt to evaluate
   (a) changes in human life expectancy, and
   (b) changes in the risk of death?
2 Discuss the contention that contingent valuation is, in general, superior to all other techniques for valuing non-marketed goods or services as it is the only technique capable of incorporating non-use values as well as use values.
3 Is the loss of a single species inevitably damaging? Is this true for each species that currently exists?
4 Krutilla has suggested that technological progress has asymmetrical impacts upon the relative value of environmental resources and produced goods and services. In particular, he suggests that technology reduces the relative value of produced goods and increases the relative value of environmental assets. Appraise Krutilla's argument and the suggested amendments he proposes to the cost–benefit analysis of projects with environmental impacts.

Problems

1 Consider a fixed level of income (Y_0) and two prices, P_0 and P_1. Construct a diagram comparable in form to Figure 10.3(a) to demonstrate that the CV of a price rise from P_0 to P_1 is identical to the EV of a price fall from P_1 to P_0.
2 Assume that the income elasticity of demand for good 1, C_1, is zero. Let C_2 denote the composite good 'all other goods than C_1'. Construct a diagram comparable in form to Figure 10.3 to demonstrate that the two Hicksian (compensated) demands (at $U = U_0$ and $U = U_1$) are identical to the Marshallian uncompensated demand for a fall in the price of C_1 from P_0 to P_1. *Hint*: It will be useful to work backwards, remembering that the requirement is that the income effect of the price fall on the quantity demanded of C_1 has to be zero. Indifference curves should be drawn to reflect this requirement.
3 Suppose an individual has the following utility function, where U denotes total utility and Q the quantity of a good or service consumed in a given

period of time:

$$U(Q) = \alpha Q + \frac{\beta}{2} Q^2$$

(a) Obtain the individual's marginal utility function. Assume $\alpha = 10$ and $\beta = -\frac{1}{2}$, and that the individual's consumption rises from Q_1 to Q_2, where $Q_1 = 2$ and $Q_2 = 4$.

(b) What is the individual's marginal utility at Q_1 and Q_2?

(c) Show that total utility can be interpreted as an area under an appropriate marginal utility function, and use this result to obtain the increase in total utility when consumption rises from Q_1 to Q_2.

4 This question makes use of Figures 10.12 and 10.13. Consider the individual whose demand for an environmental resource has increased from D_1 to D_2 as a result of a site improvement, but whose cost of visiting the site remains at P^*. Demonstrate that his or her gross WTP has risen by an amount equal to the sum of the areas A, C, and D in Figure 10.13.

5 Are (a) option values and (b) quasi-option values always positive, or do circumstances exist in which they could be negative? If such circumstances do exist, what are they?

Further reading

Good, practically oriented surveys of valuation are to be found in Winpenny (1991), Turner and Bateman (1990), Pearce and Markandya (1989), Johansson (1987), Kneese (1984) and Pearce and Turner (1990). Discussions of the application of hedonic pricing are Cummings *et al.* (1986), Freeman (1979), Hufschmidt *et al.* (1983), Brookshire *et al.* (1982), Kneese (1984) and Pearce and Markandya (1989). The technique is surveyed in Nelson (1982). Interesting applications may also be found in Marin and Psacharopoulos (1982) and Willis and Garrod (1991).

Travel cost valuation is examined and applied in Freeman (1979), Hanley (1989), Bockstael *et al.* (1987a), Smith and Desvousges (1976), and Smith *et al.* (1983). The principle of contingent valuation is carefully examined or applied in Randal *et al.* (1974), Hanley (1988), Hanley and Spash (1993), Bishop and Heberlein (1979), Schulze *et al.* (1981), Bishop and Welsh (1992), Cummings *et al.* (1986), Mitchell and Carson (1984) and Mitchell and Carson (1989), the

last of which provides an extensive review of case studies.

Option value and option price are analysed in Bishop (1982), Freeman (1985), Desvousges *et al.* (1987) and Boyle and Bishop (1987). Fisher and Hanemann (1987) discuss quasi-option value. Existence value is analysed by Brookshire *et al.* (1983). Wilderness values are discussed in Krutilla's classic paper (1967) and Brookshire *et al.* (1985).

Differences between WTP and WTP valuations in practice are examined in Hanemann (1991) and Knetsch (1990).

Appendix 1

We wish to estimate the willingness to pay for clean air. Let C denote the consumption level of some aggregate commodity, P be the unit price of this consumption commodity, and Y be household income. Define X to be an index of the level of air pollution, and assume that the rent that an individual is willing to pay for housing services, R, is a decreasing function of the level of air pollution. That is

$$R = R(X), \qquad R'(X) < 0$$

Hedonic pricing uses knowledge of this function to estimate the value of environmental improvements. Consider a project that would increase air quality and reduce the pollution concentration from X^* to X^1 (as illustrated in Figure 10.9 above). How much would the consumer be willing to pay for such an improvement? This is the question we now seek to answer.

Assume that each individual has a utility function of the form

$$U = U(C, X), \qquad U_c > 0, \quad U_X < 0$$

so that utility is an increasing function of the consumption good, C, but a decreasing function of the pollution level, X. The individual maximises utility subject to a budget constraint

$$Y = PC + R(X)$$

That is, income is divided between housing rental expenditure, $R(X)$, and expenditure on the composite good, X. Solving this constrained optimisation problem, we find that utility maximisation requires that

$$P\left(\frac{U_X}{U_C}\right) = R'(X)$$

Proof:

Our objective is to maximise

$$U = U(C, X)$$

subject to the constraint

$$Y = PC + R(X)$$

We proceed by forming the Lagrangian function

$$\Upsilon = U(C, X) + \lambda(Y - PC - R(X))$$

where λ is a Lagrange multiplier. The first-order conditions for a maximum require

$$\partial\Upsilon/\partial C = U_C - \lambda P = 0 \qquad (10.7)$$

$$\partial\Upsilon/\partial X = U_X - \lambda R'(X) = 0 \qquad (10.8)$$

$$\partial\Upsilon/\partial\lambda = Y - PC - R(X) = 0 \qquad (10.9)$$

From Equation 10.7 we have

$$U_C = \lambda P \Leftrightarrow \lambda = U_C/P$$

Substituting for λ in Equation 10.8 we obtain

$$U_X - (U_c/P)R'(X) = 0$$

$$U_X = (U_C/P)R'(X)$$

$$R'(X) = P\left(\frac{U_X}{U_C}\right)$$

as required. This completes the proof.

The left-hand side of this expression is the marginal rate of substitution of the consumption good for units of pollution, measured in terms of the price of the consumption good. The right-hand side is the slope of the rent–pollution function. To obtain an intuitive understanding of this condition, let us represent this result diagrammatically, in terms of consumption–air pollution space. Consider an individual with a fixed level of individual income, Y^0, shown in Figure 10.18

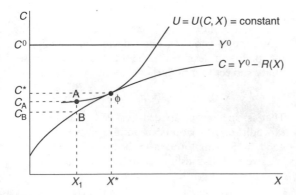

Fig 10.18 The willingness to pay for clean air.

as the horizontal line Y^0. If all income were spent on the aggregate consumption good and none were spent on housing, the quantity C^0 of the composite consumption good could be purchased. For simplicity, choose units of consumption so that $P = 1$. Given this, we can rewrite the budget constraint to obtain

$$C = Y^0 - R(X)$$

which is shown in Figure 10.18. Note that as X rises, so $R(X)$ falls, and so for a given level of Y, C rises, as shown by the function

$$C = Y^0 - R(X)$$

At a point of utility maximisation, the consumer's indifference curve will be tangential to his or her budget constraint. Such an optimum is illustrated by point ϕ in the diagram, corresponding to consumption–air quality pair $\{C^*, X^*\}$.

If air quality were improved in this way, the consumer could reduce consumption from C^* to C_A and still enjoy the same level of total utility as initially, as is clear from the fact that both points lie on the same indifference curve. In other words, he or she would be willing to give up $(C^* - C_A)$ goods for a reduction in air pollution from X^* to X_1. As we have normalised prices so that $P = 1$, this quantity also represents the monetary value of his or her WTP for the environmental improvement.

Therefore, his or her willingness to pay is given by the amount $C^* - C_A$. But how much would knowledge of the rent gradient suggest? The rent gradient would suggest a WTP of $C^* - C_B$, necessarily a larger amount than the correct measure of the WTP.[5]

Given that the hedonic price technique attempts to obtain a valuation from the rent function, we can see that the method does *not* measure the WTP itself. For an improvement in environmental quality, it will in general overestimate the WTP for that improvement. However, the measure will provide an upper bound for the WTP. For a deterioration in quality, the measure underestimates the WTA, but will give a lower bound for the WTA.

As hedonic pricing methods do not, even in principle, measure WTP (or WTA), two questions seem to follow. Firstly, how close an approximation is

[5] Some authors would use the slope of the tangent at the point ϕ, that is the angle Φ (as shown in Figure 10.19) as a basis for estimating WTP. Although this changes matters somewhat, it remains true that this measure is not one of the true WTP.

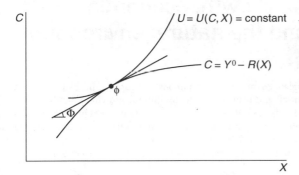

Fig 10.19 Estimating willingness to pay.

the hedonic pricing measure to the true WTP in practice? Secondly, if the approximation cannot be relied upon to be sufficiently accurate, can a method be found which uses the data collected but can (at least in principle) obtain an unbiased measure of WTP?

Perhaps not surprisingly, it is not possible to give an answer to the first of these questions in general. A glance at Figure 10.19 suggests that the error will depend upon the relative curvatures of the indifference curves and the rent–pollution function in the neighbourhood of the initial optimum. Also, the error will vary with the size of the change being considered. Even with complete knowledge of the rent–pollution function, one would need to know consumer preferences to identify the magnitude of the error.

This leads us to the second question. If we were either to know the structure of preferences or to make assumptions that would determine these preferences, then an 'error correction' would be possible. Some studies attempt to do this, by assumptions as to the form of the utility function. However this is beyond the scope of this text; the interested reader can pursue this point by referring to Brookshire et al. directly.

CHAPTER 11

Population growth, economic growth, and the natural environment

Certainly it is a problem to sustain many billions of people, a problem for each human to sustain himself and his/her own family. But the growth in numbers over the millennia from a few thousands or millions of humans living at low subsistence, to billions living well above subsistence, is a most positive assurance that the problem of sustenance has eased rather than grown more difficult with the years. The trend in population size by itself should suggest cheer rather than gloom.

Mark Perlman, page 63, in Simon and Kahn (1984), *The Resourceful Earth*

Introduction

Our objectives in this chapter are to analyse the relationships between population growth, economic growth, and the environment. More specifically, we seek to identify the effects of population growth and economic growth on the natural environment. Although it is likely that economic growth and population growth are interconnected, we shall not explore this link. The organisation of ideas in this chapter is structured around a hypothesis that the level of environmental impacts depends upon the level of *per capita* income, and upon the level of population. Algebraically, we may write this hypothesis as

$$\text{EI} = F\left(\frac{Y}{P}, P\right)$$

where EI denotes the level of environmental impacts, Y/P demotes *per capita* income, and P denotes the level of population. Our task is to examine whether such a relationship exists, and if it does, to identify the nature of that relationship.

We begin by examining population growth. It is estimated that 5.66 billion human beings were living in 1994. Current United Nations forecasts suggest that the world population will continue to grow to about twice this size over the next century, peaking at a level of about 11 billion people by the year 2100. Currently, the world population is rising at about 94 million persons per year. In terms of absolute numbers, this is a higher amount of growth than ever before. However, the percentage rate of population growth is well below its historical peak, and appears to be falling continuously.

In ecological terms, humans dominate the earth; Vitousek and Ehrlich (1986) estimate that nearly 40% of potential net primary productivity (the products of

photosynthesis) of the earth's land surface is appropriated by humans. This proportion appears to be rising rapidly. Whilst there is obviously an absolute constraint on the level to which the proportion can rise, Vitousek argues that catastrophic environmental breakdown would occur well before the figure reached 100%.

Despite widespread views to the contrary, it appears that positive population growth is not inevitable. Most population analysts are agreed that the world's population will peak at some level in the neighbourhood of twice its present size, then remain approximately constant for some time, and will fall thereafter. A number of countries currently have falling populations (for example Germany, Austria, Denmark and Sweden), and many others are expected to move into this category in the near future. In many countries, fertility rates have now fallen below the 'replacement rates' that are required for a population size to be stationary in the long run.

It is often taken to be self-evidently true that the present level of world population is too large, and that catastrophic outcomes will follow if the future level of population is allowed to grow unchecked. But neither of these positions is necessarily correct, as we shall demonstrate in this chapter.

Given the potential importance of population levels upon the natural environment, this chapter examines world and regional population data and projections. We then examine the dynamics of the process of population change, and present the conventional microeconomic theory of fertility. This theory is then used to deduce how measures to control population growth could be constructed.

Later sections investigate the relationship between population size and the availability of food, and the effects on the natural environment of population change. In the final section we switch attention from population effects on the environment to economic growth effects, and examine a claim that economic growth may improve rather than worsen environmental quality.

Perspectives on population growth

In Chapter 1, we discussed the writings of the classical economists, and noted their expectations about the future path of human population. In the writing of Thomas Malthus (1798), one finds something very close to a biologically determined explanation of human population growth. Malthus regards human populations, in common with other biological populations, as having a tendency to grow in a geometrical manner when unchecked by 'environmental' constraints. Whilst it is rare to find a pure Malthusian view of population expressed in contemporary writings, it is not uncommon to find writers presenting pessimistic views regarding the magnitude and consequences of population growth that are not very different from those of Malthus.

We saw in Chapter 1 that the systems analysis simulations of the 1970s and 1980s resulted in a series of very pessimistic forecasts about the consequences of rapid population growth operating in conjunction with limited natural resources. However, within the mainstream of the economics profession, no consensus has emerged about the economic and environmental consequences of continued population increases. The majority of economists reach more optimistic conclusions about the consequences of population growth than those obtained by systems analysts and most environmentalists. Indeed, a number of eminent population economists, including Simon, Kahn and Perlman, find nothing intrinsically bad in population growth, and would certainly deny the validity of any claim that measures to limit population growth are *necessarily* desirable. Before we turn our attention to the causes and consequences of population growth, let us look at the historical path of human population size.

World population: an historical survey

The estimated levels of human population over historical time are shown in Figure 11.1. The broken line describes forecasted future population levels, derived from the 1994 United Nations demographic analyses.

Restricting attention to the last two centuries, an outstanding feature in demographic data is the continuous expansion in human life expectancy. In the last few decades, two other population characteristics are evident: a trend for fertility rates to fall in almost every country, and a slowing down in the rate of population growth in most regions of the world. A fourth important facet of the population growth process is the substantial changes that have taken

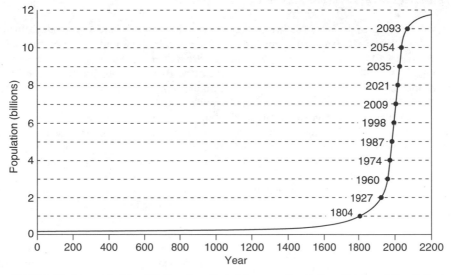

Fig 11.1 World population: actual and projected (*source:* Population Division of the United Nations Secretariat; graph adapted from one published in *The Independent* newspaper).

Table 11.1 Female expectation of life at birth, France (*source*: Perlman, 1984)

(1) INED series		(2) van de Walle		(3) Official statistics	
Dates	$\ddot{e}_0$	Dates	$\ddot{e}_0$	Dates	$\ddot{e}_0$
1740–1749	25.7				
1750–1759	28.7				
1760–1769	29.0				
1770–1779	29.6				
1780–1789	28.1				
1790–1799	32.1				
1800–1809	34.9	1801–1810	36.4		
1810–1819	37.5	1811–1820	38.3		
1820–1829	39.3	1821–1830	38.6		
		1831–1840	38.8		
		1841–1850	40.9		
		1851–1860	40.4	1861–1865	40.6
		1861–1870	41.8	1877–1881	43.6
		1871–1880	43.0		
		1881–1890	45.1	1899–1903	48.7
		1891–1900	46.0	1908–1913	52.4
				1920–1923	55.9
				1928–1933	59.0
				1933–1938	61.6
				1946–1949	67.4
				1952–1956	71.2
1960–				1960–1964	74.4
				1966–1970	75.4

Note: $\ddot{e}_0$ = life expectancy.
Sources: (1) Yves Blavo, La mortalité en France de 1740 à 1829, in *Démographie Historique*, special issue of *Population*, November 1975, page 141; (2) Etienne van de Walle, La mortalité des departments francais ruraux au XIXe siècle, in Hommage à Marcei Reinhard, *Sur la population française au XVIIIe et en XIXe siècles* Société de démographie historique, Paris, 1973, page 584; (3) Alain Monnier, La mortalité, in *La population de la France*, special issue of *Population*, June 1974, page 107. Reproduced with permission from W. R. Lee, *European Demography and Economic Growth*, New York: St. Martins, Press 1979, page 142.

place and are still to occur in the age structure of the world's population. We next examine these four demographic features.

Expansion in life expectancy

Life expectancy has increased for virtually all age groups in the human population. The number of years for which a person can expect to live has increased for members of all age groups in all countries. In historical terms, this has been a relatively recent phenomenon. The developed countries[1] experienced

[1] In this chapter, we use the terms developed and developing to refer to the following partition of the world's countries. The *developed countries* include North America, Europe, Australia, New Zealand and Japan. The *developing countries* include Africa, Latin America (including South America), East and South Asia (excluding Australia, Japan and New Zealand).

major increases in life expectancy throughout the nineteenth century, and life expectancy has continued to rise, albeit more slowly, throughout the twentieth century. By way of illustration, Table 11.1 shows the life expectancy at birth of females in France. In the mid-eighteenth century, a female in France could expect to live for nearly 26 years; by the late twentieth century this expectation had risen to over 75 years.

For the majority of developing countries, the major increases in life expectancy have been compressed into a considerably briefer interval of time, with major improvements taking place after 1945 and continuing to the present day. The main cause of longer life expectancy seems to have been a substantial decline in mortality rates throughout the age structure. A fall in the mortality rate results in increased longevity and, at least initially, a larger average family size. It is widely agreed that this has been the major cause of population growth, particularly in the period after 1945, and continues to account for most of the forecasted increases in population. Mortality rate reductions are largely attributable to public health interventions, and to the control of diseases. Important examples include the vaccination of children, and simple treatments for diarrhoea, the largest cause of death among children in countries of the developing world. The World Health Organisation attributes 400 million deaths in 1985 and 180 million deaths in 1990 to diarrhoea, measles or a combination of the two. While the latter figure is appallingly high, the change does demonstrate the dramatic improvements in mortality that can be obtained relatively quickly by public health measures (*World Resources 1992–93*). Some idea about the magnitude of these changes can be obtained by noting that in developing countries, the annual death rates per thousand people fell from 24 to 11 over a 30-year period from 1955 to 1985. Over the same interval, the death rate in the developed countries fell from 10.2 to 9.5. In large parts of the developing world, therefore, mortality levels are approaching the current levels achieved in the developed world. As a consequence of falling death rates, life expectancy at birth in low and middle income countries has risen from 41 years in the early 1950s to 62 years in 1993. Partly because reductions in the death rate have been more rapid in recent years in the developing countries, it is in these that the largest increments in population are to be expected in the medium-term future.

Population growth rates

A second demographic feature to note is that the proportionate growth rate of population has decreased in recent years in all regions of the world except Africa, as shown in Figure 11.2.

In the developed economies, the average annual rate of population growth has slowed considerably, from 1.19% in 1960–65 to 0.48% in 1990–95. The pattern has been somewhat different in the developing economies. Average growth rates increased marginally from 2.35% to 2.38% between the periods 1960–65 and 1970–75. Subsequently, the rate has fallen continuously, to 2.1% in 1980–85 and to an expected level of 2.06% in 1990–95.

Fertility rates

A third feature that emerges from a study of population statistics, evident in Figure 11.3, is a

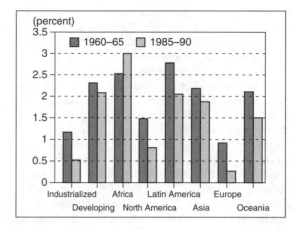

Note: Excludes former USSR.

Fig 11.2 Average annual population growth rates, 1960–65 and 1985–90 (source: *World Resources 1992–93*, Figure 6.1).

trend for fertility rates to fall in most parts of the world. A statistic often used to measure human fertility is the *total fertility rate* (TFR), the expected number of live births during the lifetime of an average female. The fertility rate exhibits large variability, differing considerably between countries and over long periods of time. In 1994, the estimated total number of live births per woman (between the ages of 15 and 49) was 3.6 in the developing countries and 1.9 in developed countries. These broad groupings contain substantial within-group variations, with average fertility rates of 3.0 in North America, 1.7 in Europe, 4.0 in India and 5.8 in Africa.

The global average TFR decreased from 5 in the early 1950s to 3.3 in 1990, a very substantial (34%)

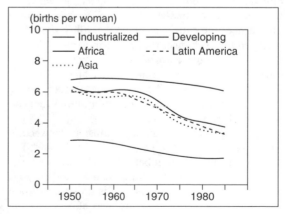

Fig 11.3 Total fertility rates, 1950–85 (source: *World Resources 1992–93*).

reduction. For most countries in the developed world, major falls in the TFR occurred in the nineteenth and early twentieth centuries, and the TFR is expected to remain approximately constant at its present level of 1.9 for the next few decades in those countries. Fertility rates have fallen substantially in developing countries, to an average of 3.7 in 1990, and are still continuing to decrease. Nevertheless, declining fertility rates are certainly not universal; in India, for example, the fertility rate increased by about 50% in the 20 years until 1985, although the rate has now levelled off at about 4 children per female. Whilst the TFR has declined in Africa during the last three decades, it has done so by a relatively small amount, from 6.6 in the 1960s to 6.0 in 1990.

An important, but still unresolved, question concerns the causes of the fertility rate fall that has been observed in most developing countries. Some writers attribute the change to the increased adoption of contraception techniques, claiming that variation between countries in the proportion of women using contraception can explain approximately 90% of the observed variability in fertility rates. It is relatively easy to point to anecdotal evidence that supports the plausibility of this view. For example, over the period 1970 to 1991, the fertility rate in Bangladesh fell from 7 to 5.5 children per woman, whilst the use of contraception increased from 3 to 40%. Correlations between variables cannot, however, inform us about the direction (or even the existence) of causal relationships, and there are many reasons why one might observe positive correlations between variables even when they are not causally related. An alternative view is that the availability of contraception is only likely to be effective in reducing fertility when the demand for a smaller family size has become established; the causes of reduced fertility should be searched for in changes in the determinants of desired family size. Some discussion of the role of contraceptive measures is presented in Box 11.1. We return to this matter later in discussing the microeconomic theory of fertility, and the policy implications that can be derived from that model.

It is important to avoid confusion between a country's total fertility rate and its birth rate. The latter measures the number of live births per year, usually expressed relative to each thousand persons in the population. Birth rate statistics depend upon the total fertility rate, but are also affected by the proportion of women of childbearing age in the population. Global average birth rates have fallen from 37 per 1000 persons in 1950–55 to 27 per 1000 persons in 1980–85.

Fertility rate and birth rate statistics have different uses in making projections of future population levels. Statistics on birth rates, particularly when used in conjunction with death rates measured on a similar basis, are the more useful when projecting short- and medium-term population changes. However, when considering the underlying long-term population trends, the TFR is the more useful measure. Note also that birth rates and death rates are very dependent upon the demographic structure of a country at a particular point in time, whereas the fertility rate is largely independent of that structure. Thus, with large numbers of women having recently entered or just entering reproductive age, the recent downward trend in birth rates will be particularly difficult to sustain.

Population age structures

One consequence of a continuing fall in mortality rates unaccompanied by a contemporaneous and offsetting fall in birth rates is that the age structure of a population alters. For some time, at least, the demographic structure moves in the direction of having a proportionately younger population, and the median age of the population tends to become lower. This can be illustrated by comparing the age structures of Central Africa and Western Europe. In the former group of countries, 48% of the population are less than 15 years old, compared with 18% in Western Europe. Conversely, the proportions aged over 45 years are 9% and 39% in Central Africa and Western Europe respectively.

These age structure differences have important implications for future population levels. Where a country has a relatively young population, a degree of momentum is imparted to the process of population change. As the large cohorts of young persons reach childbearing ages, the numbers of new births will tend to rise, even if fertility rates per person are falling. In other words, even if each woman chooses to bear fewer children, the fact that there will be, in the near future, far more women in childbearing age groups means that the population is committed to substantial rise for some time.

On the other hand, when one projects the age structure forward in time, it becomes clear that a predominantly young population today becomes a predominantly old population some time in the future. United Nations projections of the changing

Box 11.1 Contraception

The importance of contraception and other family planning measures in limiting the rate of population growth is now widely accepted, although considerable disagreement remains about the extent to which the use of contraceptive measures influences the rate of population growth. One of the first systematic investigations into the relationship between contraception and population followed evidence gathered in the World Fertility Survey, a multinational survey of about 400 000 women in 61 countries conducted during the 1970s. The study found significant downward trends in fertility and birth rates during the 1970s in both developing and developed nations, with the only exception being Africa. The reductions in birth and fertility rates are partly attributable to the increased use of contraception, but this was largely the result in turn of increasing preferences for fewer children. Another important causal factor appears to have been a trend towards later marriage.

UN statistics, reported in UNEP (1989), show that the number of governments officially promoting contraception programmes has risen continually since the mid-1970s, whereas those actively limiting contraception has shrunk to just seven in 1988. A United Nations Study (UN, 1989b) of contraceptive practice, conducted in 1988, indicated that 70% of couples in developed economies used some form of contraception, as compared with 45% in developing countries.

Despite the widespread take-up of contraceptive measures in recent years, the rate of use varies considerably between regions of the world. The lowest use is in Africa (14% of couples), Middle Eastern countries and parts of the Indian subcontinent, and appears to be related to religious attitudes towards contraception and the low social status of women in these regions. Outside developed countries, the highest use of contraception is in the newly industrialising countries of Asia (including Thailand and Korea) and South America.

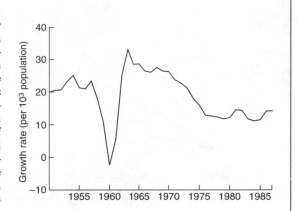

Fig 11.4 Trends in population growth rates in China, 1955–87 (source: State Statistical Bureau of the People's Republic of China, 1988, reported in UNEP, 1991).

China has the highest use rate of contraception in developing countries, so much so, indeed, that when China is excluded from the list of developing countries, the average use rate for that region falls from 45 to 30%. During the two decades from 1950 to 1970, the total fertility rate (TFR) in China was around six children per woman. During the 1970s, family planning services were widely promoted by government, and in 1979 financial incentives were introduced to couples limiting the number of children to one per family (Stein, 1990). By 1990, with approximately 70% of couples using some form of birth control, the TFR had fallen to 2.2 (Sadik, 1990). The effect on population growth rates in China is illustrated in Figure 11.4; note that 1960 was a year in which a series of natural disasters of unusual magnitude struck the country.

Sources: Maudlin (1981), Caldwell (1981), Sadik (1990), Stein (1990), UNEP (1989), UN (1989b, 1990), *World Resources 1990–91* (see Table 4.2) and *World Resources 1992–93*.

age structure of world population to the year 2150, illustrated in Figure 11.5, show this effect clearly.

Population dynamics

An oft-remarked statistical relationship is the high negative correlation between income level and population growth rate. Several attempts have been made to explain this observed relationship, the most well known of which is the theory of demographic transition (Todaro, 1989). This postulates a particular form of relationship between fertility, mortality and economic development. Put into a very simple form, the theory postulates four stages through which population dynamics progress. In the first stage, populations are characterised by high birth rates and high death rates. In some cases, the death rates reflect intentions to keep populations stable, and so include infanticide, infant neglect and senilicide (see Harris and Ross, 1987). In the second stage, rising real

(a)

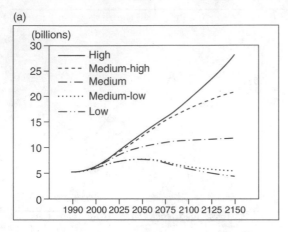

(b)

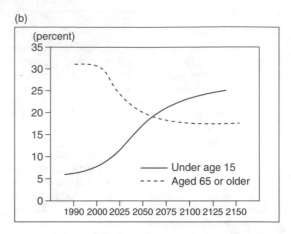

Fig 11.5 (a) Projected population of the world 1990–2150. (b) Changing age structure of world population, 1990–2150. *Source: World Resources 1992–93*, page 80.

incomes result in improved nutrition and developments in public health, which lead to declines in unintended death rates, and lower pressures on families and communities to regulate population. The second stage, therefore, is characterised by rapidly rising population levels. In the third stage of the demographic transition, economic forces lead to reduced fertility rates. These forces are described in the next section of this chapter, and include increasing costs of childbearing and family care, reduced benefits of large family size, higher opportunity costs of employment in the home, and changes in the economic roles and status of women. In the final stage, economies with relatively high income per person will be characterised by low, and approximately equal, birth and death rates, and so stable population sizes.

Schematically, we can represent these transitional stages in an idealised form in the way indicated in Figure 11.6. It is important to realise that this theory is an attempt to explain, in a relatively simple manner, observed population changes over time. The theory appears to describe the observed population dynamics of many of the developed countries quite well. What is much less clear is whether it is of general applicability, or just describes the historical trends of a particular set of countries.

For many of the currently developing countries, the second stage was reached not as a consequence of rising real income, but rather as a consequence of knowledge and technological transfer. In particular, public health measures and disease control techniques were introduced at a very rapid rate. The adoption of such measures was compressed into a far shorter

period of time than had occurred in the early industrialising countries, and mortality rates fell at unprecedented speed. During the nineteenth century, the higher income group of countries typically experienced falls in birth rates relatively soon after falls in mortality rates. However, whilst birth rates are falling in most developing countries, these falls are lagging behind drops in the mortality levels, challenging the relevance of the theory of demographic transition to developing countries. Dasgupta (1992) argues that the accompanying population explosions created the potential for a vicious cycle of poverty, in which the resources required for economic development (and so for a movement to the third stage of the demographic transition) were crowded out by rapid population expansion.

Let us now look in a little more detail at the dynamics of population change. These depend, as we saw in the theory of demographic transition, upon the

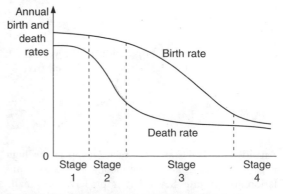

Fig 11.6 The theory of demographic transition.

interplay of changes in death rates and birth rates, but also depend in an important way upon the population age structure. In a country at some point in time, the number of births depends upon

(a) the number of people in their childbearing years, and
(b) the number of children each potential mother bears; this is measured by the *total fertility rate* (TFR), the expected number of live births during the lifetime of an average female.

The TFR can be used to determine the level of fertility that would yield a stationary population, that is a population for which the birth rate and mortality rate are equal and constant over time. This particular level of fertility is known as the replacement rate. To illustrate this point, Tietenberg (1992, page 104) argues that the current United States replacement rate is 2.11. The fertility rate in the US dropped below the replacement rate in 1972, and has remained below it since then. He argues that if the US fertility rate were to remain at its 1984 rate of 1.84 for 25 years, a not unreasonable assumption, the US population would eventually be expected to decline at a rate of 5.25% per year. China reported a

fall in her birth rate below the replacement rate in 1992. Even so, if the current Chinese fertility rate remains constant, her population is expected to rise from 1.13 billion in 1990 to 2 billion by 2050, and subsequently increase further. However, if the fertility rate were to fall slightly, the population could peak at 1.5 billion in 2050, and then decline to 1.4 billion by 2100.

As the information in Figure 11.7 shows, the fertility rate has fallen below the replacement rate in many countries, suggesting that many populations will be falling rather than rising in the not too distant future. United Nations calculations show that fertility will be below replacement rates in most countries before 2050, and below it in virtually all soon after that date.

The economic theory of fertility and the economics of population control

Two important determinants of the rate at which a population changes over time are the number of children born to each female of reproductive age, and

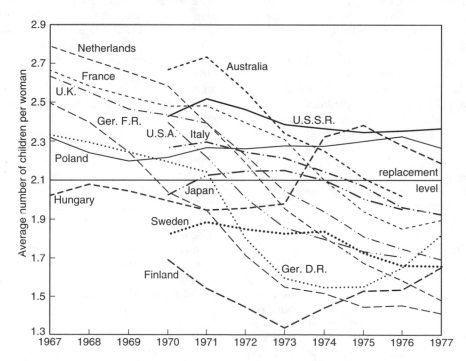

Fig 11.7 Fertility and the replacement level in developed countries (*source:* Perlman, 1984, page 65).

the life expectancy of each child. We have already seen the dramatic increases in life expectancy that have occurred through medical and public health improvements throughout the world. What determines the number of children born to each female of reproductive age? Many people are inclined to answer that it is the availability and take-up rate of contraception. Not only is it somewhat insulting to imply that some people simply 'breed like rabbits' but for the presence of contraception, but such a view seems neither to be plausible nor to fit the evidence obtained from survey work.

Most importantly, the number of children born into each household is primarily the outcome of a choice made by (potential) parents. Family size is, or at least can be, a ·choice variable; contraceptive practices and other family planning devices are the means by which these choices are effected. In this section we describe the conventional microeconomic theory of family size, which sees family size as being determined by the marginal cost of bearing and raising children, and by the marginal benefits derived from children within the family. An important advantage of pursuing this line of analysis is that it offers the prospect of valuable guidelines for policy: attempts to alter desired family size should operate by shifting the marginal cost of bearing and raising children, or the marginal benefits derived from children within the family.

The economic theory of fertility, illustrated in Figure 11.8, begins from the premise that the chosen or desired family size is determined by the marginal costs and benefits of children to the family unit. The marginal costs of children will depend upon the costs of childbearing, child rearing and education, including the opportunity costs of parental time in these activities. We have drawn Figure 11.8 on the assumption that these costs increase mildly with increased family size, but this is merely one of several possibilities. Marginal benefits to the family will be influenced by the psychic benefits of children, the contribution of children to family income, and the extent to which old age security is enhanced by larger family size.

Increasing affluence has been associated with a reduction in the fertility rate; it is interesting to see whether the microeconomic theory of fertility can explain this relationship. We believe it can do so and suggest some reasons why in the answer to Problem 1. Of more direct interest to us here is the possible application of this theory to population control. What measures might government take or

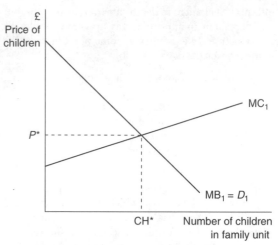

MC = The marginal cost to the family of a child
MB = The marginal benefit to the family of a child
     (= the demand curve for children)

Fig 11.8 The microeconomics of fertility.

encourage that could reduce desired or chosen family size?

1 Increased levels of education, particularly education of women. This might affect fertility through three related routes. First, education may enhance the effectiveness of contraceptive and other family planning programmes; families become more proficient at having the number of children that they choose. Secondly, greater participation in education may contribute towards an increasing status of women; it is now widely agreed that where females have only low status roles in the culture of a society, fertility rates are likely to be high. Thirdly, the microeconomic theory of fertility suggest that increased education will tend to reduce desired family size. It does this by increasing the opportunity cost of child raising (decreasing labour market gender discrimination, allowing females to earn market incomes, and obtain expected real wage rises) and probably by decreasing the marginal benefits of children (for example, salaried workers may be able to provide for old age through pension schemes).

Whatever theoretical arguments suggest, greater education of women appears to be associated with significantly reduced fertility rate. It is easy to find *prima facie* support for the belief that educational improvement results in lower family size. In Zimbabwe, for example, a recent study found that mothers with no formal education had seven children on average, those with primary education six children, and mothers with secondary or higher had four children. As we remarked earlier in this chapter, however, one should be wary of taking correlations between variables of interest as evidence in favour of the existence of real behavioural relationships. In this case, it may well be that cultural differences between different groups of females explain both educational attainment and family size choice, and that education has no independent effect on fertility.

2 Financial incentives can be used to influence desired family size. Financial penalties may be imposed upon families with large numbers of children, or alternatively, where the existing fiscal and welfare state provisions create financial compensation for families with children, those compensations could be reduced or restructured. There are many avenues through which such incentives can operate, including systems of tax allowances and child benefits, subsidised food, and the costs of access to health and educational facilities. There may well be serious conflicts with equity if financial incentives to small family size are pushed very far, but the experiences of China suggest that if government is determined, and can obtain sufficient support, financial arrangements that either increase the marginal cost of children or reduce the marginal benefits of children can be very powerful instruments.

3 Reducing the marginal benefits of children, and providing adequate care for and financial support of the elderly. In many cultures, the marginal benefits of additional children to the family are regarded as being high. As can be seen from Figure 11.8, if the perceived marginal benefits of children were to be reduced, the desired number of children per family would fall. It would be desirable – assuming that one's goal was to reduce the rate of population growth – if these perceived marginal benefits were reduced, without any economic loss to the society as a whole.

First of all, why is it that the marginal benefits of children are high to a family? In some African countries, to give one example, children do constitute wealth to a household. Daughters are, by custom, paid a *bride-price* when they are removed from a household to live with the husband; so a newborn girl represents a real asset from the viewpoint of the family to which the child is born (although the asset value of this bride price is not a real asset to the economy as a whole, of course – why is this?). Sons, on the other hand, represent a valuable source of labour for agricultural production by the household, and become relatively more valuable to the parents as they become older and less able to undertake difficult manual work.

The value of children in the parents' old age may sometimes explain why family sizes are large. This suggests that one approach to reducing desired family size is to introduce an adequate system of support for the elderly, financed by taxation on younger groups in the population. As the tax instrument merely redistributes income, its effect on welfare can be neutral. But by reducing the private marginal benefits of children it can succeed (at little or no real cost) is reducing desired family size.

4 The most powerful means of reducing desired family size is almost certainly economic development, including the replacement of subsistence peasant agriculture by modern farming practices giving farm workers the chance of earning labour market incomes. There may, of course, be significant cultural losses involved in such transition processes, and these should be weighed against any benefits that agricultural and economic development brings. Nevertheless, to the extent that subsistence and largely non-market peasant farming dominates an economy's agricultural sector, there will be powerful incentives for large family size. Additional children are valuable assets to the family, ensuring that the perceived marginal benefits function in Figure 11.8 is relatively high. Furthermore, if no available market incomes are being lost, the marginal cost of the labour involved in raising children is low. Important steps in the direction of creating markets for labour (and reducing desired family size) can be taken by defining property rights more clearly, giving communities greater control over the use of local resources, and creating financial incentives to manage and market resources in a sustainable way.

In this section, we have been discussing the concept and determination of the desired family size. However, reducing the desired family size may not be *sufficient* to lower the rate of growth of population. Another necessary condition is that families have the means to realise these choices. Access to contraception and knowledge about other family planning techniques are also important elements in any population control programme, and should operate in conjunction with the steps we have discussed in this section. What seems clear is that access to contraception is, by itself, unlikely to play a significant part in the control of population size.

1994 UN Conference: Cairo

The resolutions of the 1994 United Nations conference on world population set out a very ambitious target. Whilst its baseline 'no-change-in-policy' scenario projects global population to reach a peak of 12 billion persons in 2100, the UN aim is to initiate policy interventions and cultural changes that will restrict the population to be no greater than 7.27 billion by 2015, peaking at 7.8 billion by 2050.

The proposed control programme contains three key elements: increased education, improved health care and more widespread and effective family planning. The principal emphasis lies in the education and emancipation of women, raising the literacy rate to ensure the conditions for successful birth control programmes, and empowering women to control the number of children they have.

Population, agriculture and the availability of food

A common view is that large-scale and continuing population increases will place increasing pressure on world agriculture, and threaten the availability of adequate supplies of food to future generations. How much justification, if any, is there for such a view?

Johnson (1984), writing over ten years ago, summarised the principal features of the world food system. He noted that a major change which had taken place over the four or five decades to 1980 was that *access* to food by a family had become primarily dependent upon the family's income, and not upon the availability of food to be purchased. By 1980, a food system had become established that was capable of making food available to almost every person in the world, a situation that had been impossible just a few years prior to 1980. This change had taken place in spite of the fact that global population had doubled in the previous 30 years.

Whether the members of a family were able to obtain an adequate amount of nutrition was, therefore, a function of the distribution of income (not the level of income as such) and not of the availability of food. This suggests that programmes to deal with hunger and malnutrition should be tackled by policy directed at reducing inequalities of income within and between countries, rather than by supply-side targeted measures.

In discussing the prognosis for food consumption patterns over the following few decades, Johnson's survey of historical price trends and future supply-side potential led him to the following conclusions:

1 The real price of grains (the major source of calories for poor people) had declined in recent decades. As the graphs in Figure 11.9 indicate, over a long period of time, the trend price of wheat, rice, barley, sugar cane, corn and cotton have been falling. Livestock prices (beef cattle, hogs) have followed a slowly rising price trend, but poultry and eggs showed remarkable and sustained price falls, post-1945. There is very little evidence of rising food scarcity in these real price data.
2 Price volatility varies considerably between different categories of food. However, volatility of price has been greatest for those foodstuffs with the largest degree of government intervention. Paradoxically, perhaps, domestic price stabilisation programmes by large producers have tended to promote international price instability.
3 Resources are available that would permit an increasing rate of growth of *per capita* food production in the developing countries.
4 The food system which had become established by 1980 had substantially reduced the risks of food shortages, hunger and famines resulting from natural disasters.
5 The long-run prospects are in the direction of a gradually declining real price of primary foodstuffs.

Johnson attributes most of the blame for food shortages that have occurred to government intervention in the markets for and movement of food. Serious difficulties arise from trade restrictions and government constraints, which tend to reduce food prices in 'uncontrolled' areas, reducing incentives to supply commercial food crops and to modernise and improve agricultural inputs.

Africa was an exception to the generally optimistic assessment given by Johnson. Whereas *per capita* food production had been rising elsewhere in the world, it fell in Africa, principally as a consequence of political factors (including wars and civil strife) rather than economic conditions. Some regions in

South Asia also exhibited falling *per capita* food production.

Johnson notes several factors which could worsen the long-term prospects for food prices and food availability:

1 Increasing affluence tends to change demand in the direction of meat and away from direct consumption of vegetables and grain. This imparts considerable physical 'inefficiency' in food production, and causes prices to rise, reducing food access to lower-income families.
2 Limited availability of land to bring under cultivations. The scope for expanding the 'extensive margin' of agriculture is now quite restricted. However, the most cost-effective method of obtaining output increases has been through expanding the 'intensive margin' of agriculture. Furthermore, large productivity increases remain to be exploited through land irrigation.
3 Increasing the intensive margin may become more difficult in the future as a consequence of higher energy prices, leading to higher relative prices for inorganic fertilisers. It is also worth noting that since Johnson's article, increasing attention has been paid to the possible unsustainability of highly intensive agriculture, and the potentially very large amounts of environmental damage associated with fertiliser and pesticide use.

To what extent do Johnson's conclusions remain valid ten years later? In general, the conclusions seem to be remarkably robust, as can be seen from the 1994 survey of food and agriculture by the World Resources Institute (*World Resources 1994–95*):

Agricultural production in much of the developing world has been an extraordinary success over the past several decades, but the pressure to grow food will continue as populations rise. With land growing scarcer, most future production gains will have to come from greater average yields per hectare. Yet in Asia, yield gains are generally slowing, while in sub-Saharan Africa the gap between supply and demand is expected to widen.

Two of the many important issues facing agriculture over the next few decades are discussed here. First the use of pesticides in developing countries. Pesticides, one foundation of the remarkable production hikes over the past few decades, continue to underpin many national development strategies in developing countries. Yet considerable research suggests that the benefits of pesticides have been exaggerated and that, as currently used, they pose substantial dangers both to the environment and to human health.

The second issue, agricultural bio-technology, is an important source of hope for the future. Bio-technology offers numerous possibilities for agriculture. But these potential advances are decades away from realisation, carry some risk, and will not displace current agricultural practice altogether. Moreover, while the developing world is most in need of biotechnology's innovations, current research is concentrated on high-value crops grown in the industrialised world.'

Some particularly serious critical issues emerged during the 1980s and early 1990s. The first concerns trends in crop yields (see Figure 11.10). While crop yields have typically continued to increase, they have generally increased at much slower rates in the 1980s than previously. Sub-Saharan Africa poses the second issue we shall mention. *Per capita* food production in Africa has fallen by 20% since 1970, and incomes remain very low. Sub-Saharan African countries will have to import roughly one-third of total food consumption, and may be unable to purchase the necessary quantities. Africa could regularly face serious food shortages during the next few decades unless her income grows or her food output rises. A third worry arises from possible long-term climate changes and the increasing rate of desertification and soil fertility loss, all of which are poorly understood phenomena. These are examined briefly in Box 11.2.

Some commentators take a far more pessimistic view of the future potential for adequate food supply than those expressed by Johnson and by the World Resources Institute. We conclude this section by noting one such view, expressed in a report entitled *Full House* by the Worldwatch Institute in 1985. The report forecasts severe global food shortages in the next 40 years, leading to famine on an unprecedented scale. Lying behind this alarming prediction are the following processes, all operating in conjunction with a rapidly rising global population:

1 Agricultural land is losing fertility and is being lost by increasing urbanisation.
2 New technology has approached the limits of possible increases in grown yields.
3 Reductions in the maximum global marine fishing catch potential.
4 Inequality in the world distribution of income and wealth, which 'fosters overconsumption at the top of the income ladder and persistent poverty at the bottom'. The report argues that 'People at either end of the income spectrums are far more likely than those in the middle to damage the world's ecological health – the rich because of their high consumption of energy, raw materials and

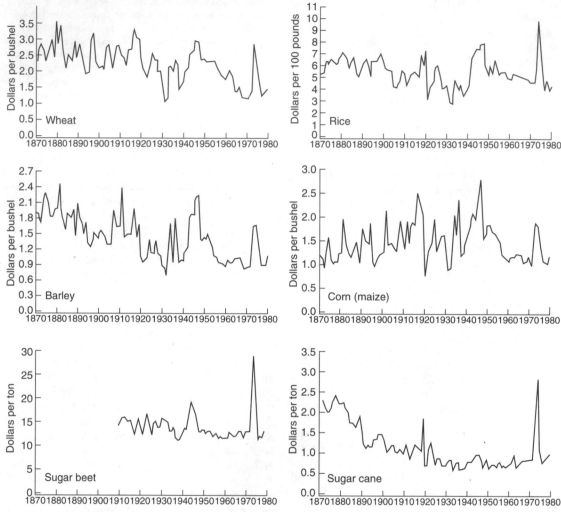

Fig 11.9 Commodity prices received by farmers (deflated by 1967 = 100 W.P.I.).

manufactured goods, and the poor because they must often cut trees, grow crops, or graze cattle in ways harmful to the earth simply in order to survive.'

Population growth and the natural environment

Human population growth, in conjunction with pressures for higher standards of living, has a major impact on the natural environment. As the human population expands, so too do the demands for agricultural land, energy and water resources, and the management and disposal of waste products. Economic activity has led to a range of serious environmental and economic damages, including forest depletion, declining soil fertility, loss of topsoils, desertification, unsustainable rates of water usage, and groundwater and air pollution. Whilst it would be wrong to attribute each of these processes exclusively or primarily to population growth, it is evident that the increasing pressure placed on environmental resources by a growing population will exacerbate these problems.

The worst manifestations of these environmental processes are often to be found in economies with rapidly growing populations and low levels of income *per capita*, particularly where natural endowments of

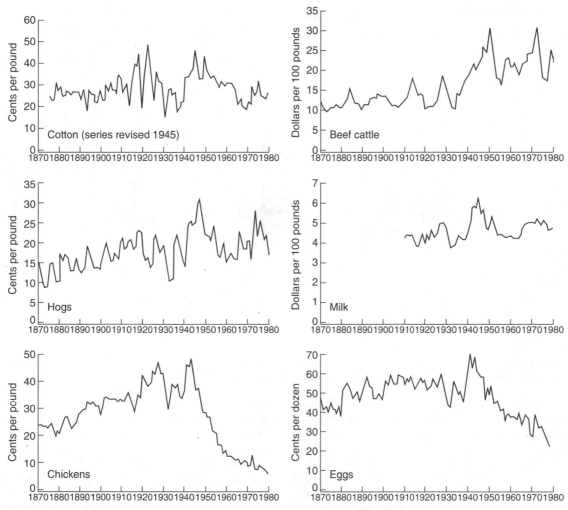

Fig 11.9 Continued.

the resource are already niggardly or have low robustness. However, whilst the most poor developing economies do have a number of serious environmental problems, it is important to realise that these environmental impacts usually take very specific forms, mainly in unsustainable exploitation of soils, forests and freshwater supplies. Collectively the poor developing economies have relatively little impact on air pollution, use few non-renewable resources, and typically have high rates of material recycling. It would be quite wrong, therefore, to regard environmental degradation as being principally a characteristic of developing countries.

Attempts to apportion responsibility for environmental damage between different categories of economy are largely futile and not particularly useful exercises. The way in which such an exercise apportions blame will depend upon how the index of damage is constructed, and there is no single index that can satisfactorily capture the diversity of environmental impacts. But it is worth noting that, on many reasonable measures of environmental impact, damage is predominantly associated not with the levels or rates of growth of the population, but with the level of income per person. If, for example, one focuses on so-called global environmental problems (to be discussed in the next chapter), the problems can be largely attributed to the developed countries, especially those with the greatest concentration of manufacturing industry

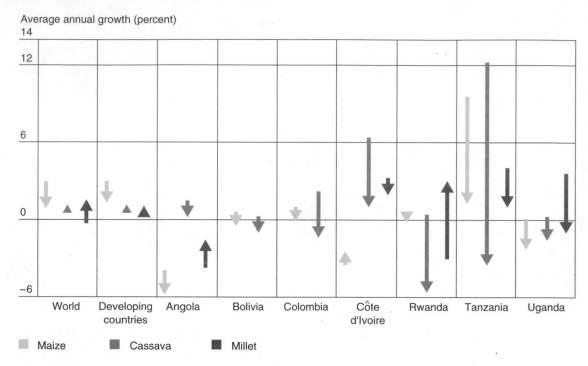

Fig 11.10 Change in crop yields in selected countries, 1970–90. Arrows show change between 1970–80 and 1980–90 (note that millet is not a significant crop in Bolivia or Colombia). *Source:* World Bank data.

and highest rates of *per capita* consumer spending. This is illustrated by some *per capita* resource use ratios recently calculated by the World Resources Institute (WRI). The United States has a *per capita* consumption of petroleum 43 times higher than India, of pulpwood higher by a factor of 386, of beef 11 times greater, and of CO_2 emissions 19 times larger. In its review of the evidence, the WRI claims that the average US citizen has an environmental impact 30 times as great as that of an average citizen in a developing country, and points out that the impacts per person of Japanese and Western European citizens are close to those of their US counterparts.

Economic growth and the natural environment

How does economic growth affect the natural environment? Despite the importance of this question, it is surprisingly difficult to find any clear answer to it. We can get some way towards an answer by some simple reasoning. To the extent that

economic growth involves an increase in material and energy inputs, the potential for adverse environmental impacts is greater. In a world in which no substitution is possible, the materials balance principle demonstrates that material and energy throughputs are proportionate to the level of economic activity, and so growth will inevitably result in deteriorating environmental conditions. However, the growth process is characterised by qualitative changes and substitution effects as well as by quantitative changes. Growth is measured by increases in the value of output, and higher value may not necessarily require higher quantities of inputs. Moreover, as relative resource scarcities change, to the extent that these changing scarcities are reflected in changing prices, substitution effects will take place on both the demand and supply side of economic activity. This implies that it is not appropriate to presume that there are fixed coefficient relationships between the level of economic activity and the level of materials use or discharges of potentially damaging pollutants.

Opinions about the environmental consequences of economic growth tend to reflect the extent to which these substitution possibilities are judged to be

Box 11.2 Declining soil fertility and desertification

In June 1994, a conference of the United Nations Environment Programme (UNEP) took place, at which the specific focus of attention was declining soil fertility and desertification. Delegates to the conference were told that 900 million people were at risk from dependence on agriculture in dryland in the Americas, Africa and Asia, in which soil fertility was being lost at an alarming rate. The UN believes that loss of soil fertility is a greater threat to poor people than global warming or upper atmosphere ozone depletion. UNEP estimates that just under one-tenth of the earth's land surface is significantly degraded, and that an area equal to the size of Italy has been more or less permanently lost to agricultural use.

It is now widely accepted that the predictions, made in the 1970s and 1980s, about the rapidly growing spread of desert areas were severely overestimated and alarmist. Satellite survey makes it clear that deserts expand and contract in natural cycles, and that most of the changes noted in those earlier decades can be attributed to such cyclical behaviour.

However, large areas of land are subject to potential desertification as a result of economic activity. It is also now agreed that desertification is associated with losses of soil fertility and with the agricultural practices that are introduced in attempts to mitigate these losses in soil fertility. In Africa, for example, peasant farms in arid areas lack resources to maintain output as fertility falls, and tend to shift production to more marginal land. Soil fertility soon diminishes in these areas, and so agriculture follows a path of continuously shifting cultivation, but environmental conditions are not conducive to restoring fertility in the vacated land areas. Wood clearing and burning for fuel, and overgrazing of savannah land by cattle, thins roots and leaves soils immune to wind and water erosion. Irrigation has also had unintended effects; whilst often being seen as a way of raising yields, it has often been counterproductive, damaging soil through raising salt to upper soil surfaces.

Institutional factors play an important part in soil fertility losses. Land tenure is often very insecure, and environmental resources in arid regions are often effectively open access resources, destroying any incentives that farmers may have to conserve woodlands and soils. Finally, mention must be made of the effect that crippling poverty has on land degradation. Poverty denies peasant farmers access to credit and the resources necessary for sustainable and conservationist agricultural practices.

What policy initiatives offer hope for controlling or reducing the extent of these environmental and economic problems? Clearly, any changes that can offer the prospect of increasing the levels of real income of farmers in arid regions would be of substantial benefit, making possible the investments that are required for conservationist agricultural policy.

Institutional reforms offer the prospect of significant environmental and economic improvements. It would be desirable to move towards more clearly defined property rights to land and other environmental resources, and to ensure more security in the tenure of land. Property rights need not necessarily be individual-based; relatively small-scale common-property ownership rights can be effective in regulating the demands made on land, provided institutional mechanisms are established that prevent common-property resources degenerating into open-access resources. This implies establishing local incentives to manage resources, enabling communities to regulate access, and reducing restrictions on how resources can be used. For example, simple restrictions prohibiting tree felling are almost certainly counter-productive; they will be largely unenforceable, but will act as severe disincentives for future replanting by local communities.

Source: Press reports during June 1994 on the UNEP Conference on Soil Erosion and Desertification.

possible in the medium and long-terms. At one extreme can be found those who assert that in the long-term, substitution possibilities are very limited, and can be regarded as being approximately zero. Residual and waste flows, and the quantities of harmful pollutants emerging from economic activity, are directly proportional to the level of economic activity as conventionally measured. Some writers appear to hold a diametrically opposed view; properly functioning price mechanisms destroy any fixed relationship between economic activity and the

extent of residual flows. With appropriate relative prices, it would be possible to achieve any pollution-to-economic activity ratio we desire.

These considerations are relevant to the question of whether there are any limits to the economic growth process. Base-run simulations of conventional limits to growth models, such as those reported in Meadows *et al.* (1972) and Barney (1980), tend to accord a very limited scope to substitution effects; in conjunction with assumptions about finiteness of the natural resource stocks and continuing population growth, the conclusion is reached that the currently expected timepath of economic activity is unrealisable. Sustainable economic activity will only become possible if growth is abandoned as a primary objective and substantial changes are implemented that would alter the environmental impact of activity. We have already seen that conclusions from these *Limits to Growth* models were rejected by most economists, mainly on the grounds that the models did not contain a price system, and so did not allow for the kinds of substitution effects that do occur in practice, nor those that could take place with suitable governmental manipulation of the price mechanism to encourage greater pollution control.

There may well be other limits to growth besides those due to physical resource constraints. Fred Hirsch (1976) and Herman Daly (1987) have both analysed other possible forms of limits to growth. We shall now review these contributions. In his book *Social Limits to Growth* (1977), Fred Hirsch argues that the process of economic growth becomes increasingly unable to yield the satisfaction which individuals expect from it, once a society's level of material affluence has satisfied its main biological needs for life-sustaining food, shelter and clothing. There are limits to growth, Hirsch argues, but they are not the material limits of the kind we have just indicated:

> In this sense, the concern with the limits to growth that has been voiced by and through the Club of Rome [as contained in Meadows *et al.*, 1972] is strikingly misplaced. It focuses on distant and uncertain physical limits and overlooks the immediate if less apocalyptic presence of social limits to growth.
>
> Hirsch (1977), page 4

What is the nature of these social limits to growth? Hirsch argues that as the average level of consumption rises, an increasing portion of consumption takes on a social as well as an individual aspect. That is:

> ... the satisfaction that individuals derive from goods and services depends in increasing measure not only on their own consumption but on consumption by others as well.
>
> Hirsch (1977), page 2

This statement clearly applies to the consumption of goods which are associated with the creation of pure public goods externalities. The net satisfaction you and I get from the purchase and use of a car, for example, depends on how many other people do the same; the greater the number of others who use cars, the greater is the amount of air pollution and the

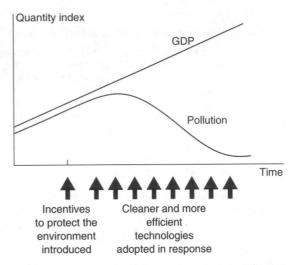

Fig 11.11 Breaking the link between growth in GDP and pollution.

extent of congestion, and so the lower is the net satisfaction our car purchases will yield.

However, Hirsch's main focus is not upon pollution and other environmentally relevant externalities, but on what he calls *position* goods. Position goods are those such that the satisfaction derived from their consumption depends upon one's position in the social structure. Increasing affluence is associated with an increasing proportion of income being spent on such position goods. Consider expenditure on education, in an attempt to raise one's chances of securing sought-after jobs. The utility to a person of a given level of educational expenditure will decline as others attain that level of education too. A breaking-down results in the relationship between individual and aggregate or social gains. Each person

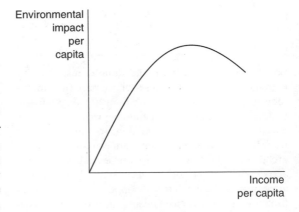

Fig 11.12 The environmental Kuznets curve.

Box 11.3 The links between income and pollution levels

Figure 11.13 (taken from IBRD, 1992, page 11) shows the relationship between four environmental indicators and income levels, using cross-sectional data from a sample of countries at one point in time in the 1980s. For two of these indicators – particulate matter concentrations and urban concentrations of sulphur dioxide – there is an apparent inverted U-shaped relationship between the indicator level and income level. However, the other pair – municipal wastes *per capita* and carbon dioxide emissions *per capita* exhibit continuously positive relationships, with pollution levels *per capita* – showing no tendency whatsoever to fall as income levels rise.

It is unclear whether cross-sectional data of this kind can be used to make valid inferences about changes that are likely to happen over time. Some evidence on such changes is given in Figures 11.14 and 11.15, which show the directions of change in urban concentrations of particulate matter and sulphur dioxide between the 1970s and 1980s in low, middle and high-income countries. The World Bank report summarises Figures 11.14 and 11.15 with

the captions:

> In poor countries even the best city air is bad, but the problem abates as income grows.
> Sulphur dioxide pollution is increasing in poor countries, falling in higher income countries.

although one might argue that it is not valid to draw such strong conclusions from this information.

Finally, Figure 11.16 shows the levels of dissolved oxygen in rivers over the same time interval in countries of different income levels. This does not give support for a claim that growth can improve the environment.

The EKC hypothesis is, of course, referring to some aggregate index of pollution. Whether such an index exhibits an inverted U-shaped relationship with respect to income will depend upon what the index contains, and how its different elements are weighted. If high weighting is given to wastes and greenhouse gases, for example, one can find little evidence for the existence of an EKC. If one regards urban air pollution as having a dominant weight in such an index, it is more likely that the EKC hypothesis will find support.

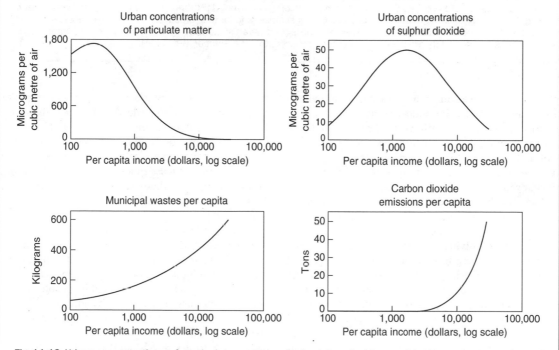

Fig 11.13 Urban concentrations of particulate matter and of sulphur dioxide; municipal wastes *per capita* and carbon dioxide emissions *per capita* from fossil fuels. Estimates are based on cross-country regression analysis of data from the 1980s. *Sources*: Shafik and Bandyopadhyay; World Bank; IBRD (1992), page 11.

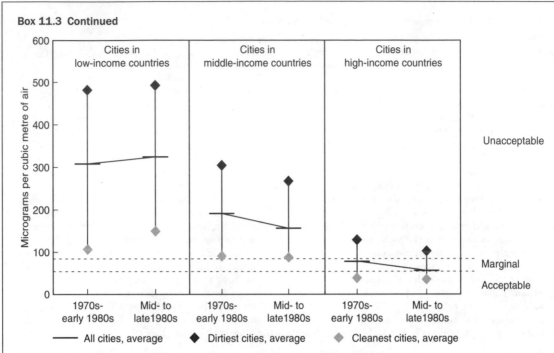

Box 11.3 Continued

Fig 11.14 Urban air pollution levels and trends: concentrations of suspended particulate matter across country income groups. Data are for 20 urban sites in low-income countries, 15 urban sites in middle-income countries, and 30 urban sites in high-income countries. 'Cleanest cities' and 'dirtiest cities' are the first and last quartiles of sites when ranked by air quality. Periods of time series differ somewhat by site. World Health Organization guidelines for air quality are used as the criteria for acceptability. *Source:* IBRD (1992), page 51.

purchasing education seeks to gain individual advantage, but the simultaneous actions of others frustrate these expectations for each individual. As the average level of education rises, individuals will not receive the expected satisfaction gains if the *relative* structure of qualifications remains unchanged.

This breakdown between individual and social gains occurs for many reasons, including the consumption of pure public goods and consumption or production involving externalities that we have examined elsewhere in this book. Hirsch's argument points to a much more widespread divergence between the two, as much consumption behaviour is positional in the sense used by Hirsch. It is important to realise that this is not a psychological argument, and has nothing to do with claims of the form that we get less psychic satisfaction from goods as income levels reach high levels, or as they are easily gained. Hirsch's argument is a material one – given that satisfaction derives from position or place, individual expenditure *cannot* translate into aggregate improvements. One might concede that Hirsch's thesis has some force, but is seriously overstated. If position goods are much less dominant in people's consumption baskets than he asserts, the social limits to growth argument loses much of its force. But if one were to accept the thesis for the sake of argument, does it contain any implications for environmental economics?

Firstly, it suggests that traditional utilitarian conceptions of social welfare may be misleading, or at least in want of very careful interpretation. Simple summation of individual consumption levels to yield a measure of social welfare is highly problematic if Hirsch's argument contains any validity.

Secondly, the social limits to growth argument displaces attention from material (or resource) limits to growth to its social limits. Perhaps the most important implication is that growth, at least in its conventional meaning, is a much less socially desirable objective than economists have usually thought.

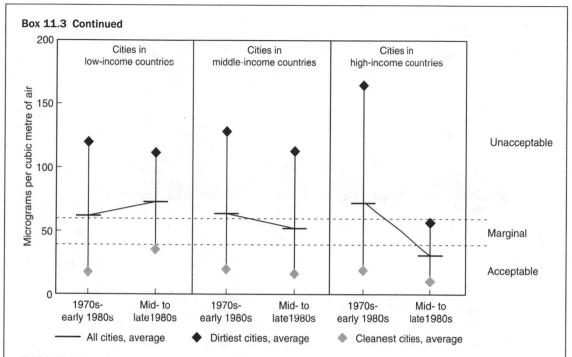

Box 11.3 Continued

Fig 11.15 Urban air pollution levels and trends: concentrations of sulphur dioxide across country income groups. Data are for 17 urban sites in low-income countries, 19 urban sites in middle-income countries, and 42 urban sites in high-income countries. 'Cleanest cities' and 'dirtiest cities' are the first and last quartiles of sites when ranked by air quality. Periods of time series differ somewhat by site. World Health Organization guidelines for air quality are used as the criteria for acceptability. *Source*: IBRD (1992), page 54.

However, nothing in Hirsch's argument suggests any necessary actual limit on the growth process. If individuals choose to alter behaviour to deal with the limits that Hirsch discusses, then environmental consequences may result. If they do not alter behaviour, the argument does not itself suggest any limitations to material growth itself.

Ethicosocial limits to growth

In an important paper, Herman Daly (1987) offers four propositions which he asserts limit the desirability of growth. Daly's thesis is that these propositions are becoming more widely accepted, and as they do, political pressure will ensure that they will become actual limits to growth. The four propositions are

1 The desirability of growth financed by drawdown is limited by the cost imposed on future generations.
2 The desirability of growth financed by takeover is limited by the extinction or reduction in the number of sentient non-human species whose habitat disappears.
3 The desirability of aggregate growth is limited by the self-cancelling effects on welfare.
4 The desirability of growth is limited by the corrosive effects on moral standards of the very attitudes that foster growth, such as glorification of self-interest and a scientific–technocratic world-view.

Biophysical limits to growth

Daly argues that the economic growth process is subject to three fundamental principles. Firstly, *finitude of the overall system* imposes absolute limits because the sources of low entropy materials for conversion into output and the sinks for high entropy wastes from the conversion and consumption processes are finite. Secondly, the *law of entropy* prevents the complete recycling of any used material. These first two principles imply that industrial activity leads to a progressive disordering of the overall ecosystem.

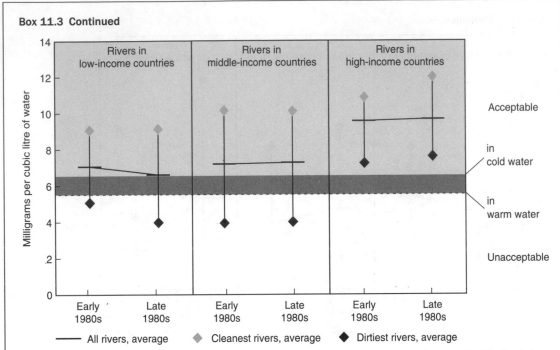

Box 11.3 Continued

Fig 11.16 Dissolved oxygen in rivers: levels and trends across country income groups. Data are for 20 sites in low-income countries, 31 sites in middle-income countries, and 17 sites in high-income countries. 'Cleanest rivers' and 'dirtiest rivers' are the first and last quartiles of sites when ranked by water quality. Periods of time series differ somewhat by site. US Environmental Protection Agency water standards for supporting aquatic life are used as the criteria for acceptability. *Source*: IBRD (1992), page 46.

The third principle is *complex ecological interdependence*; the ecosystem is a set of interrelated, complex systems, necessary for the life support of all natural forms including humans, but the existence of which is at least potentially fragile. The disordering and perturbances associated with economic activity can and increasingly do interfere with the stable operation of this ecosystem.

Can economic growth improve the environment? The environmental Kuznets curve

An idea that has gained considerable support in recent years, not least from the World Bank, is the notion that economic growth can be of assistance to the environment rather than being a threat to it. There are three planks to this belief. Firstly, it may be possible to break the links between economic growth and pollution. This idea is illustrated in Figure 11.11, taken from IBRD (1992). As growth leads to increasing affluence so the incentives to protect the environment become of greater priority and importance in the political agenda. The means of responding to this changed priority include resource substitution, technological innovation and changing patterns of demand in response to relative price shifts.

A second plank of the argument uses empirical data relating to the cross-sectional relationships between income levels and pollution indices for different countries at given points in time, and time-series evidence about the movement of income and pollution indices. These data suggest that, for some classes of pollution at least, the flow levels of the pollutants fall as income rises. Finally, simulation studies show that it may be possible to obtain large reductions in the flows of some damaging residuals through alterations to the structures of relative prices and other incentives. These pollution control programmes do involve real resource costs, and the initial costs may be relatively high. However,

Box 11.4 The environmental Kuznets curve and environmental impacts in the very long run

As we saw in the text, the environmental Kuznets curve (EKC) implies that the magnitude of environmental impacts of economic activity will fall as income rises above some threshold level, when both these variables are measured in *per capita* terms. In this section, we shall assume for the sake of argument that the EKC hypothesis is correct. Michael Common (1995) examines the implications of the EKC hypothesis for the long-run relationship between environmental impact and income. To do this, he examines two special cases of the EKC, shown in Figure 11.17. In one case – what we shall call case **a** – environmental impacts per unit of income eventually fall to zero as the level of income rises. Case **b** is characterised by environmental impacts per unit income falling to some minimum level, *k*, at a high level of income, and thereafter remaining constant at that level as income continues to increase. Note that both of these cases represent very optimistic assumptions; they both embody the basic principle of the EKC, the only difference being whether environmental impacts per unit income fall to zero or just to some (low) minimum level.

Suppose that the world consists of two 'countries' that we denote by the descriptions *developed* and *developing*, which are growing at the same constant rate of growth, g. However, suppose that the growth process began at an earlier date in the developed country and so, at any point in time, its *per capita* income level is higher than in the developing country.

Common investigates what would happen in the long run if case **a**, the highly optimistic version EKC, is true. He demonstrates that the time path of environmental impacts one would observe would be similar to that shown in the upper part of Figure 11.18. Why should there be a dip in the central part of

the curve? For some period of time, income levels in the two countries will be such that the developed country is on the downward-sloping portion of its EKC whilst the developing country is still on the upward-sloping part of its EKC. However, as time passes and growth continues, both countries will be at income levels where the EKC curves have a negative slope; together with the assumption in case **a** that impacts per unit income fall to zero, this implies that the total level of impacts will itself converge to zero as time becomes increasingly large.

But now consider case **b**. Here, no matter how large income becomes, the ratio of environmental impacts to income can never fall below some fixed level, *k*. Of course *k* may be large or small, but this is not critical to the argument at this point; what matters is that *k* is some constant positive number. As time passes, and both countries reach high income levels, the average of the impacts to income ratio for the two countries must converge on that constant value, *k*. However, since we are assuming that each country is growing at a fixed rate, g, the total level of impacts (as opposed to impacts per unit income) must itself be increasing over time at the rate g, going eventually to infinity. This is shown in the lower part of Figure 11.18.

What is interesting about this story is that we obtain two paths over time of environmental impacts

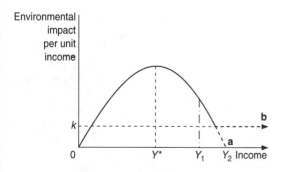

Fig 11.17 Two possible shapes of the environmental Kuznets curve in the very long run (*source*: Common, 1995).

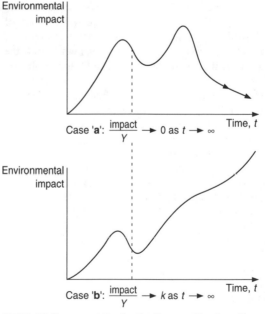

Fig 11.18 Two scenarios for the time profile of environmental impacts.

Box 11.4 Continued

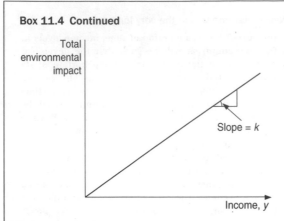

Fig 11.19 A linear relationship between the levels of environmental impacts and income.

which are entirely different from one another in qualitative terms for very small differences in initial

assumptions. In case **a**, k is in effect zero, whereas in case **b**, k is any number greater than zero. Even if environmental impacts per unit of income eventually fell to a tiny level, the total level of impacts would rise to infinity with the passage of time.

Which of these two possibilities – case **a** or case **b** – is the more plausible? Common argues that the laws of thermodynamics imply that k must be greater than zero. If so, the long-run relationship between total environmental impacts and the level of world income would be of the linear form shown in Figure 11.19. Any attempt to infer from the inverted U shape of the EKC that growth will reduce environmental damage in the long run would be incorrect.

Sources: Common (1995), Stern *et al.* (1994)

cost–benefit calculations suggest that pollution control programmes can often yield positive net present values when the averted external costs are included in the calculations. As with any investment programmes, the fact that a pollution control project may be economically advantageous does not ensure that it will be implemented. Developed countries are likely, though, to undertake a larger proportion of such projects given the greater relative strength of demand for environmental improvements and the more plentiful availability of funds for pollution control.

These themes became embodied in a series of articles and reports published in the 1990s (see for example Selden and Song, 1992; Panayotou, 1993; *World Development Report*, IBRD, 1992). Each stressed the *possibility* that economic growth may be a necessary component of a process of environmental improvement. The basic theme of these contributions is the hypothesis that as an economy's *per capita* income increases, the total amount of environmental impact of economic activity initially grows, reaches a maximum, and then falls. This hypothesis is illustrated in Figure 11.12, and the function drawn there has become known as the Environmental Kuznets Curve (EKC).

What is the status of the EKC? As we have already suggested, it is a hypothesis for which its proponents claim empirical and theoretical support. Box 11.3 presents a sample of the sort of evidence that is used

by proponents of the EKC hypothesis, taken from the 1992 World Bank report *Development and the Environment*. This can hardly be regarded as conclusive evidence for the thesis, but one might argue that it is at least consistent with the basic principle underlying the EKC. It is in fact quite difficult to know what kind of empirical evidence would be required to validate the hypothesis, for two reasons. Firstly, the EKC refers to 'environmental impacts', but it is not obvious how such measure should be constructed. More importantly, the EKC might find support for some kinds of impact but not for others. Secondly, the EKC purports to represent a long-term relationship between impact *per capita* and income *per capita* for an individual economy, but data used in empirical testing are often drawn from cross-sections of countries at particular points of time. Whether these data are meaningful in a testing exercise is a moot point. However, we shall remain agnostic in this chapter about the existence of the EKC.

The importance of the Environmental Kuznets Curve lies in its implication that economic growth is a means by which environmental protection can be pursued, rather than a cause of environmental degradation. Official support for the notion that there need be no long-run trade-off between environmental quality and the level of economic activity has recently been given by the incorporation of this principle into World Bank policy statements. The

CASE STUDY   Pesticide and herbicide use in developing countries

The use of pesticides and herbicides has been one of the major elements in the so-called Green Revolution of the developing world, the other components being chemical fertilisers, the development and use of high crop yield varieties, and intensive agriculture. Pesticide use has grown rapidly, largely as a response to these other elements of modern agricultural practice. The use of inorganic fertilisers, irrigation, and high yield crop varieties has led to massive increases in food output, but has had the effect of making crops more vulnerable to pest attack and the spread of viruses. Modern agricultural practice, involving crops grown all year round on monocultural plots, not only provides ideal breeding grounds for crop pests, but renders farmers open to immense risks if the crop fails. Farmers have tended to use pesticides as a preventative measure against possible crop failure, and have often been ignorant or badly informed about the short- and long-term costs of pesticide use. Pressures to use pesticides have also arisen from the 'modern' image that they possess, from the heavy promotion to which they have been subject by agrochemical companies and international agencies, and from the economic pressures to maximise short-term revenue from export sales of cash crops.

The use of pesticides is, of course, not confined to developing countries. North America consumed 26% of the total amount used in 1991, and Western Europe 31%, with most of the remaining 43% consumed in developing nations. However, pesticide use is not growing in North America, and is growing very slowly in Western Europe. The developing countries, on the other hand, are increasing their rates of pesticide use rapidly. In the 1980s, for example, Indonesia, the Philippines, Pakistan and Sri Lanka all increased pesticide consumption at more than 10% annually.

The limited success of pesticides

The era of modern synthetic pesticides began in 1941 with the introduction of DDT. Despite high hopes, pesticide use has not solved the problems for which they were designed. Fifty years later, the percentage of crop loss attributable to insects, weeds and disease has remained more or less constant in the range 30–35% of total crop production. This does represent some success for pesticides of course, as the more intensive agricultural practices tend to increase the proportion of crops lost to these three processes; so pesticide use has at least prevented this proportion from rising.

Pesticide use leads to a number of negative feedback effects. First, the use of pesticides increases the immunity or resistance of pests through the process of genetic adaptation and selection. This is also true of herbicides (used to control weed growth) and fungicides (designed to control fungi and bacteria). Thus, the effectiveness of any given pesticide tends to decline over time, sometimes quite dramatically. This effect also follows from a second consequence of pesticide use – the chemicals used destroy natural predators of crop pests, often far more efficiently than in destroying or controlling the target pest population.

A common response to these problems has been to increase the frequency or magnitude of the pesticide dose, but this has tended to create a vicious cycle, in which pest resistance and pest population explosions due to elimination of natural predators become progressively worse. Increasing pest resistance and secondary pest outbreaks are particularly prevalent in a number of southern countries because of particular climatic conditions.

One illustration of this vicious cycle is provided by cotton, for which developing countries account for two-thirds of global production. Cotton is a highly chemical-intensive crop, consuming more than ten% of total pesticides. Between the 1950s and the 1970s, Central American cotton growers increased the frequency of application of pesticides per season fourfold, from 10 to 40. However, crop yields fell through this period, despite that increased rate of use. In Mexico, efforts to eradicate a particular pest – the boll weevil – led to the population growth of a secondary pest – the tobacco budworm – that proved resistant to pesticides. Crop acreage fell from 300 000 hectares in the early 1960s to less than 500 hectares in 1970.

The environmental costs of pesticide use

Pesticides are designed to kill particular species. Unfortunately, it is not possible to isolate the damaging effects to the largest species, particularly because a very small proportion of the total dose applied – typically less than 1% – actually reaches the target organisms. The rest becomes an environmental contaminant, dissipating as vapour in the air, in watercourses through run-off, or into soils. Through a variety of mechanisms, these contaminants can then do widespread damage to wildlife, plant life, and organisms of soil and water. Many pesticides are highly persistent, with active lives of several years. These accumulate and concentrate at different stages of the food chain, causing direct damage to life. Even more serious may be the effects that intake of pesticides may have on the endocrine

continued

CASE STUDY Continued

and immune systems of animals. The endocrine system of an animal controls its hormone production processes; quite small doses can perturb the operation of the endocrine system, and it is thought that this can pose serious dangers to the reproduction and stability of some populations. The earlier varieties of pesticides, such as DDT, tended to be very persistent (active lives of several decades). These have tended to be replaced by newer chemicals that break down in days or weeks, but which are more acutely toxic to non-target organisms.

Human health

Damage arising to human health from pesticide and herbicide use is particularly serious in developing countries where the number of people subjected to large amounts of pesticide absorption, either indirectly (through food or water consumption, or through airborne pollution) or directly as pesticides are being applied by farm workers, is increasing. Evidence implicates pesticides as causal factors in a number of varieties of cancer, impairment of brain functions, damage to the human endocrine system, impairment of immune system (rendering the affected individuals vulnerable to infectious agents), and many other systemic dysfunctions.

Alternatives to pesticides and herbicides

The most common alternative to systematic use of pesticides and herbicides is integrated pest management (IPM). At the core of IPM is an attempt to reduce crop damages to 'reasonable' levels, using measures which have economic and ecological costs that are not excessive. The central practices of IPM include crop rotation, multiple crop planting, early or delayed planting, 'field sanitation' (such as ploughing in of stubble to remove pest habitats) and the use of 'trap crops' to attract pests away from the economically valuable crop. Biological control – another element of

IPM – operates by the use of natural pest predators, parasites or diseases to keep the target pest population under control. In India, China and elsewhere, for example, a parasitic wasp is used to control corn, cotton, rice and sugar cane pests. IPM does not eliminate the use of pesticides, rather it relegates their use to last-resort measures when economic damage threatens to pass critical threshold levels. Then, at least in principle, the use of pesticides can be controlled in a way that has relatively low ecological impacts. An important new direction of pesticide development is the use of bacteria, viruses or fungi in suspension, replacing previous synthetic chemical pesticides. These have more efficient targeting qualities, and offer the prospect of much-reduced long-term damage.

IPM programmes have had noticeable successes in a number of developing countries, including Cuba and Indonesia. IPM techniques are now being sponsored by the UNFAO in a number of countries, but as yet their use is the exception rather than the rule. Limits to the speed of conversion to IPM are the large training needs that such a programme requires, the creation of an extensive and expensive infrastructural support structure, and the 'public goods' nature of the problem. The success of IPM is related to the proportion of farmers using the system. IPM is a public good, benefiting all farmers in a particular area. But the returns to an individual farmer initiating IPM can be very low, unless he can be confident that others will match his efforts.

This suggests that the introduction and extension of IPM requires public provision, or at the very least, public support, as is the case in the provision of any public good.

Source: World Resources 1994–95, pages 111–18.

following extracts from the preface to IBRD (1992) illustrate the nature of the reasoning that is used to support the idea of the EKC:

> This fifteenth annual *World Development Report* ... also presents an alternative path – one that, if taken, would allow the coming generation to witness improved environmental conditions accompanied by rapid economic development... A twofold strategy is required:
>
> First, take advantage of the positive links between economic efficiency, income growth, and protection of the environment. This calls for accelerating programs for reducing poverty, removing distortions that encourage the

wasteful use of energy and natural resources, clarifying property rights to encourage people and communities to manage resources better, and expanding programs for education (especially for girls), family planning services, sanitation and clean water, and agricultural extension, credit and research.

> Second, break the negative links between economic activity and the environment. The Report describes targeted measures that can bring dramatic improvements in environmental quality at modest cost in investment and economic efficiency.

However, there are several problems associated with the EKC. Firstly, it may provide a reasonable description of the effect of income growth on some classes of pollutants, but it seems to be wholly inadequate for others. In particular, there is little, if any, evidence to believe it applies to impacts associated with energy use. The magnitude of impacts associated with energy use does not bear the inverted U shaped relationship suggested by the EKC, but rather seems to be linearly related to income per person. Furthermore, environmental damage arising from the residuals from energy consumption almost certainly rises rather than falls at high levels of income per person.

A second difficulty relates to the behaviour of the EKC for very high levels of income per person. You will notice that Figure 11.12 remains silent on this. We discuss some alternatives in Box 11.3. The third problem relates to the validity of inferences that some commentators try to draw from the EKC itself. The EKC may be a temporary phenomenon, reflecting substitution and technical possibilities that have been available in the recent past. However, it is by no means clear that these substitution possibilities will be so easily obtained in the future. More importantly, even if one were to concede the validity of the basic EKC, it is by no means the case that this offers comforting results for the sustainability of economic growth.

A critical examination of the nature and implications of the EKC has been undertaken by Michael Common (1995). We summarise his review in Box 11.4. Suffice it to say that Common arrives at the conclusion that in the long run, the best we can hope for is a linear, proportionate relationship between total environmental impacts and the level of income; it might easily be the case that impacts rise more than proportionately to income.

Discussion questions

1 Examine the effects of alternative patterns of land tenure and property rights on the likelihood of soil fertility losses and desertification.
2 How effective are measures designed to increase the use of contraception in reducing the rate of population growth?
3 How may the role and status of women affect the rate of population growth? What measures might be taken to change that role and status in directions that reduce the rate of population growth?

4 Does economic growth inevitably lead to environmental degradation?

Problems

1 Use the microeconomic theory of fertility to explain how increasing affluence may be associated with a reduction in the fertility rate.
2 Suppose that families paid a substantial dowry at marriage. What effect would this have on desired family size?
3 What effect would one predict for desired family size if family members were to cease undertaking unpaid household labour and undertake instead marketed labour?

Further reading

Data and survey material

Good sources of data on the issues discussed in this chapter are found in IBRD (1992) and various editions of the UNEP *Environmental Data Reports* and *World Resources*. See, in particular, UNEP (1991), Part 4, 'Population/settlements', and *World Resources 1992–93*, Chapter 6 'Population and human development' (which includes an analysis of the major causes of death in industrialised and developing countries).

Economic theory

Becker (1960) is the classic original source of the literature on the economics of population. Easterlin (1978) provides a comprehensive and non-mathematical survey of the economic theory of fertility, and his 1980 volume provides an excellent collection of readings.

Food and agriculture

Official data are found in United Nations FAO, *The State of Food and Agriculture* (1979, 1981, 1985, 1989, and subsequent issues). Useful discussions are to be found in Alexandros (1988), Browder (1988), Crosson and Brubaker (1982), Hall *et al.* (1989) and Johnson (1989). An excellent collection of articles on agriculture and development is found in Streeten (1987).

Economic growth and the environment

Durning (1989) discusses the relationships between poverty, development and the environment. The growth–environmental linkages are examined in Pearce *et al.* (1989), IBRD (1992), Common (1995), Dasgupta (1988), Perrings (1987) and Weintraub (1973). Costanza (1991) provides a collection of readings in ecological economics, many of which are relevant to this area.

CHAPTER 12

International and global environmental pollution problems

Isengard began to fill up with black creeping streams and pools. Great white streams hissed up. Smoke rose in billows. There were explosions and gusts of fire. And still more water poured in, until at last Isengard looked like a huge flat saucepan, all steaming and bubbling.

J. R. R. Tolkien, page 595, *Lord of the Rings* (1969)

Introduction

In this chapter we shall investigate problems arising from pollutants for which the zone of influence is geographically very extensive, and whose impacts therefore are not restricted to lie within local or national boundaries. Throughout our analysis of pollution policy in Chapter 9, we were making an implicit assumption that the impacts of pollution emissions were felt only within the territorial domain of a single policy making unit (a nation state or some sub-national governmental unit). In that case, all adverse impacts of the pollution, and the costs of any control measures undertaken, are borne entirely by residents of the political unit in question. Where the impacts of pollution and the costs of control are restricted to regions that are contiguous with political boundaries, the principles we used in Chapter 9 to identify an efficient quantity of pollution and to design and apply 'good' policy instruments are applicable in a relatively straightforward manner.

But this framework may not be appropriate for some types of pollution emissions. *Regional* or *international* pollutants refer to discharges which are transported over large distances by physical processes, including those of atmospheric and water systems. Examples include oxides of nitrogen and sulphur (which are known to be moved over distances of up to 600 miles), and which contribute to the phenomenon known as acid rain. Another example is tropospheric (lower atmosphere) ozone, produced from nitrogen oxides and hydrocarbons in the presence of sunlight. From this point onwards, the term 'regional' pollutant shall be used to encompass both regional and international forms. Another class of pollutants have *global* impacts, arising because they enter the stratosphere (higher-level atmosphere)

and are eventually uniformly mixed. The impacts may differ from place to place, but they are not restricted to zones 'close' to points of emission of the pollutants. In this class are found the various greenhouse gases, and those emissions which act to deplete stratospheric ozone.

Common to all these types of pollution is the fact that the adverse impacts of the pollution, and the costs of any control measures undertaken, are no longer borne entirely by citizens of any single political unit. This adds major complications to the design and implementation of efficient and equitable control programmes.

Not only does the economic theory of externalities and public goods provide a powerful tool for the analysis of pollution problems in general, but it also turns out to be very useful in understanding the particular characteristics of global and regional pollutants. One may think of these as constituting adverse external effects of consumption and production behaviour, which cut across political boundaries. It is important to realise that the use of the word 'externality' here does not refer to the within/outside country distinction; we continue to use the term 'externality' to refer to an action of one party that has unintended and uncompensated effects upon others, irrespective of where those others happen to be located. Of course, for the pollution problems we are discussing in this chapter, these external effects are felt both within the country in which the pollution source happens to be located and in other countries.

Our previous analyses of pollution, externalities and public goods have demonstrated that, in the absence of suitable regulatory mechanisms or incentives to alter behaviour, polluters are likely to regard environmental resources as free goods and so to pollute to levels which are economically inefficient.

This remains true for global and regional pollutants. However, we shall show below that where significant proportions of the adverse impacts are felt in different political units from those where the emission occurs, or where significant proportions of the benefits of pollution control programmes accrue to those living in territories outside those in which the control is effected, the problems are greatly intensified. The likelihood that polluters will regard environmental media as free common property resources is increased, and the private incentives to control emissions will be weak or non-existent.

Of particular importance here is the structure of incentives facing individual governments. We assumed in Chapter 9 that government could, and often would, act in such a way as to maximise the net social benefit of the community. But the community of relevant people is here no longer identical with an individual country's electorate or citizenry. In this case, an individual country has weak incentives to implement pollution control schemes on a unilateral basis. On the contrary, incentives may act in a perverse direction; a country may find it individually rational to not participate in control programmes being undertaken by others, but rather to 'free ride' on those schemes. In some instances, individual rationality may lead a country to generate more pollution if others do less. Exploring these and related issues is the central task of this chapter.

The chapter concludes with three case studies concerning what are often regarded as the most important forms of international or global pollution problems: acid rain, ozone depletion and the Greenhouse Effect.

Regional and global environmental pollution problems: climate change, ozone depletion and acid rain

In a recent survey of environmental issues (Kemp, 1990), the author examined the following environmental problems, all of which he labelled as global environmental problems:

Drought, famine and desertification
Acid rain
Atmospheric turbidity
Depletion of the ozone layer
The Greenhouse Effect
'Nuclear winter'

These problems, actual or potential, could be described as being global in one or more of the following senses. Firstly, even though the impacts might vary between regions, the potential *direct* impacts are global in terms of incidence. This seems to be the case for the Greenhouse Effect, and possibly for ozone layer depletion. However, it does not seem to be a sensible description of acid rain effects; whilst these affect many countries, the impacts of acid rain are not truly global. A second sense of the phrase 'global environmental problem' might be as a name for pollutants or environmental effects that can, *directly or indirectly*, affect individuals throughout the world. This is not, however, a useful meaning for the descriptor 'global', as virtually any pollutant may have indirect effects globally, and so will not be pursued any further here. Finally, global may refer to the nature of the physical processes which operate on the pollutant or which shape the environmental problem prior to the full environmental and economic impacts being felt. In this last sense, only the Greenhouse Effect is truly a global environmental problem, as the greenhouse gases are, to all intents and purposes, characterised by uniform global mixing. High, but imperfect, physical mixing applies in the cases of ozone layer depletion and acid rain, and it seems sensible to refer to these as regional, rather than global, environmental problems.

In this chapter, we consider three of Kemp's six classes of environmental problem: acid rain, ozone depletion and the Greenhouse Effect. Drought, famine and desertification are discussed in Chapter 11. Space constraints and our perception of its relative importance lead us to ignore atmospheric turbidity, and our optimism about the future evolution of international relations accounts for our disregard of the possible, presumably catastrophic, consequences of a nuclear war.

The three pollution forms we shall examine possess the characteristic of being reciprocal externalities. To understand the concept of reciprocal externalities and its consequences, let us look at a simple, hypothetical example. Suppose there are two countries, X and Y, each of which gains utility from consuming a particular good, fossil fuel say. Let F denote the quantity of this good consumed. If the utility enjoyed by X, U_X, depends only on the amount of F that X consumes, F_X, and a similar qualification applies to Y, the two utility functions may be written as

$$U_X = U_X(F_X)$$
$$U_Y = U_Y(F_Y)$$

But suppose that the consumption of fossil fuels results in the emission of a pollutant that affects citizens of both countries. In this case, the utility of country X is affected not only by the consumption of F in country X but also by the consumption of F in country Y. Similarly, the utility of country Y depends upon the consumption of F in both X and Y. The utility functions now become

$$U_X = U_X(F_X, F_Y)$$
$$U_Y = U_Y(F_X, F_Y)$$

An externality occurs when decision makers in country X choose their consumption of F so as to maximise their utility without any regard for the effects of this choice on country Y. If each country maximizes its own utility, ignoring the effect this has on others, the first of these pairs of utility functions is the relevant pair in explaining behaviour. The externality would in this case be reciprocal because each country's behaviour has a spillover effect on the other's utility. The outcome of such 'non-cooperative' behaviour can be shown in Figure 12.1, where country X's choice is represented in terms of pollution levels. Acting non-cooperatively, country X takes account of the pollution which affects it from fossil fuel consumption, but does not take into account the external effects on Y. Utility maximization in this case requires that X consumes fossil fuels to the point where the marginal benefit of additional fossil fuel consumption, NMB, equals the *national* marginal damage of the pollution, represented by the curve labelled NMD. The outcome is that X emits Ψ^* pollution or, equivalently, undertakes $\hat{\Psi} - \Psi^*$ abatement.

Cooperative behaviour implies that the countries act to jointly maximise the second pair of utility functions. This requires that each country consumes fossil fuels to the point where the marginal benefit of additional fossil fuel consumption equals the *total* marginal damage of the pollution, represented by the curve labelled TMD. The cooperative level of pollution, Ψ^{**}, is lower than that which would result if the two countries behave independently. Additional pollution abatement of the amount $\Psi^{**} - \Psi^*$ takes place as a result of cooperation internalizing that part of the externality that spills over national boundaries. The cooperative solution is fully efficient for the two countries when thought of as a single entity. Indeed, if some supranational governmental body existed, acting to maximise total net benefits, and had sufficient authority to impose its decision, then the outcome would be the cooperative one we have just described. If such a single supranational government chose to use a pollution tax as an instrument to bring about fully efficient abatement, the rate of tax would be λ^{**}. This comprises two components: the amount bc, which is the part of the pollution damage affecting the country of origin of the pollutant, and the amount ab which is the damage affecting other countries. But the nub of the problem we discuss in this chapter is that such supranational authorities do not exist, or at least cannot be relied upon to prevail over individual countries acting in ways which they perceive to be in their own interests. The inefficient, non-cooperative outcome is very likely to happen, even though it might be in the interest of all to behave cooperatively. We examine this paradox more closely in the section after next.

Finally, note that each of the classes of pollution investigated in this chapter is characterised by the existence of acute uncertainty. Ignorance extends to the causes, the effects, the value of damages that might occur and the costs of feasible control measures. We do know, however, that the *possible* consequences are very severe, and may even be catastrophic for human populations. There are immense difficulties in making decisions about controlling pollutants in situations where ignorance is endemic, particularly when the costs of control are large. In spite of these uncertainties, some action is likely to be an efficient and optimal strategy, for three reasons. Firstly, the set of possible outcomes if no control is undertaken includes catastrophic consequences; secondly, the costs of enforced, rapid responses taken in the event of damages turning out to be serious are probably very much larger than

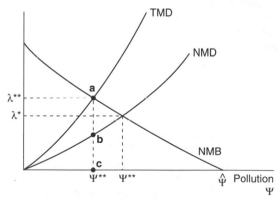

Fig 12.1 National and global efficient pollution levels for a reciprocal externality.

those involved in a planned, preventative programme; and thirdly, because even if the expected value of control measures cannot be shown to be beneficial, the advantages that control now might give in terms of the preservation of future options could still justify that action.

Geographical distribution of costs and benefits of pollution control

The previous section suggested that the actual and potential damages arising from regional and global pollution problems are very large. It is important to make a distinction between the total or aggregate level of these damages (to the world economy, say) and the pollution costs as they apply to particular countries or areas. How are these damages distributed, and in which ways does that distribution matter? We shall try to answer these questions for the case of acid rain pollution and ozone depletion. Distributions of damage arising from greenhouse gas (GHG) emissions will be dealt with in Case Study 3. You will see that the potential costs of pollution damage are very unevenly distributed between nations. This also seems to be the case as regards the costs of abating the pollutants in question, with the costs of pollution control being very unevenly distributed between nations. Furthermore, the degree of correlation between control costs and damage costs appears to be very low; there is little, if any, tendency for countries with high damages to have high control costs, for example. This is likely to create difficulties when attempts are made to secure international agreements over pollution control.

Let us begin by considering the geographical distributions of acid rain damages. The most important point to note is that the pollutant damages are not restricted to lie within the national boundaries of the emission sources. This is evident from the material presented in Case Study 1. Large-scale and systematic reciprocal cross-border acid rain pollution takes place between the countries of Central and Western Europe, and between the individual countries within those areas. These transfers are possible because residual materials in the upper atmosphere can be transported by prevailing winds over very large distances. The United Kingdom appears to have been a major contributor to acid rain pollution. It is estimated that about one-third of the total of relevant UK emissions are deposited in British soils, with most of the rest being carried to, and deposited in, a number of northern European countries, including Germany, the Netherlands, Norway and Sweden.

For geographically large countries, such as the USA, Russia and China, international transfers of pollution are of lower relative importance; however, pollution may carry over sub-national boundaries and where political and administrative control is highly decentralised (as in the United States), cross-state pollution poses similar control problems to cross-national pollution. But even for large countries, transfers of pollutants across boundaries can be very extensive, as in the case of flows between the USA, Mexico and Canada.

The effects of acid rain deposition are also dependent on the ecological characteristics of the receptor areas, with mountain and lake ecologies most at risk. In the USA, studies suggest that the worst-affected regions are the Adirondacks (New York State) and Florida. However, the problems appear to be more acute in Europe than in the USA, suggesting that impacts may differ very substantially depending upon particular characteristics of the ecosystems in impacted regions. Whilst there is little evidence of widespread serious damage to the health of United States forests, some studies report massive forest death in parts of Europe, including France, Germany, Czechoslovakia and Sweden. Figure 12.2, taken from Kemp (1990), illustrates the major acid rain precursor emission centres in North America and Europe, and the areas whose ecology is most sensitive to acid rain damage.

The North is currently far more important than the South in terms of the quantities of emissions of ozone depleting substances (*World Resources 1994–95*). However, this seems set to change in the future as economies of the South undergo rapid economic growth, whilst those in the North attempt to adhere to political commitments. Agreements reached at the *Vienna Convention* and the subsequent *Montreal Protocol on Substances that Deplete the Ozone Layer* require the industrialised countries to phase out the production of chlorofluorocarbons (CFCs) by 1996, and have already led to a decline in global CFC emissions. However, continuing decline will depend upon developing countries substituting away from CFCs as industrial output rises. In China, for example, government forecasts expect CFC emissions to increase from 48 000 metric tonnes in 1991 to 177 000 in 1999 in the absence of control, and to rise rapidly thereafter. China has indicated a willingness to gradually phase out the use of CFCs, but this is

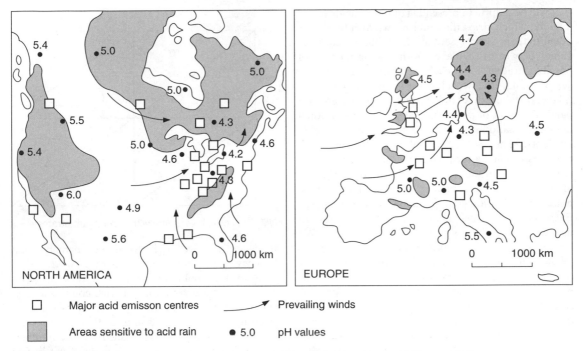

Fig 12.2 The geography of acid rain in North America and Europe (*source*: Kemp, 1990, page 74).

conditional upon similar action being taken elsewhere, technological transfers and financial assistance. China is currently seeking $2.1 billion from the Montreal Protocol fund to cover costs of substitutes in aerosols and refrigerants.

The damage done by ozone depletion does not, of course, match the geographical pattern of production and use. Ozone depletion appears to be greatest at the poles and at high latitudes, decreasing towards the equator. CFC emissions and ozone depletion have two, partially offsetting, effects upon global climate: in their roles as greenhouse gases, CFCs contribute towards a rise in global mean temperatures, but by causing depletion of stratospheric ozone, a cooling effects takes place in the stratosphere, contributing to more localised cooling. On average, these two effects appear to roughly cancel. However, due to the regionally unequal warming effects of CFC emissions, the *patterns* of global climate may be upset, with possibly very serious effects.

Game theory analysis

We have shown that some classes of pollution have effects that operate across national boundaries. The existence of reciprocal externalities implies that expenditures by one country on pollution abatement will give benefits not only to the country doing that abatement but to others as well. Similarly, if a country chooses to spend nothing on pollution control, it can obtain benefits if others do so. Moreover, there may be distinct advantages in not undertaking abatement spending when others do; the most obvious of these potential advantages is the enhanced competitiveness in international trade that a country may gain by avoiding higher costs associated with pollution abatement.

In these circumstances, the pollution control behaviour of each country in a world of many independent countries is likely to be affected by issues of strategic choice. Strategic interaction among a relatively small numbers of actors is often analysed using the techniques of game theory. Game theory permits analysis of choices in situations where the outcome of a decision by one player depends on the decisions of the other players, and where these decisions of others are not known in advance. We shall present a simple introduction to some of the issues of game theory, and explain its relevance to the analysis of environmental issues; at the end of the chapter, you will find suggestions for further reading in game theory.

It will be helpful in presenting our arguments to use a model which strips the problems we wish to discuss down to their barest essentials. To do this we consider games between two players with a finite number of possible strategies that each player may make. Let us suppose that the world consists of two countries (players), labelled X and Y, each of which emits a particular kind of pollutant that crosses the national boundary, and so affects domestic and foreign residents. This is an example of what we have previously called a reciprocal externality. For simplicity, assume that the two countries are equal in terms of population size, income and pollution levels, pollution damages, and pollution abatement costs. Each country must choose whether or not to introduce a pollution abatement programme. We label a decision to introduce the programme as A (abatement) and to not undertake abatement as NA (no abatement). As there are two countries, each of which has two possible courses of action (or strategies), four joint outcomes are possible, as indicated in Figure 12.3.

The numbers in the cells of the matrix of outcomes represent the net benefits (or pay-offs) that each country receives for each pair of strategies chosen by X and Y. Figures have been standardised in the following way: we set net benefits to zero for each country in the case where both countries choose not to abate pollution. Net benefits for each country for all other possible choice combinations are expressed relative to this 'base' case. So we may regard the *not abate* strategy by both countries as a baseline case, against which others can be compared. A number in an upper triangle describes a pay-off to X and a number in a lower triangle describes a pay-off to Y. For example, if X chooses to *abate* and Y *not to abate*, the pay-offs are −3 to X and 5 to Y. Note that numbers in the matrix exhibit a symmetry property – we could reverse the notation of countries without altering any of the values in the matrix cells. This results from our simplifying assumption that the two countries are equivalent in relevant respects.

Before attempting to identify the best strategy for each player, let us look at the *total* pay-offs for the two countries in the four possible outcomes. For the base case where both countries choose the *not abate* strategy, summing individual country net benefits or pay-offs shows that total (world) pay-offs are zero. If both countries select the *abate* strategy, world net benefits are higher, at 6 units. The relative magnitude of these two pay-offs has been chosen to reflect

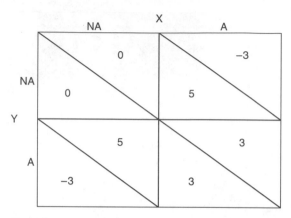

Fig 12.3 A two-player game with a dominant strategy.

an *assumption* we wish to make; namely, that efficiency gains are possible to the world as a whole through pollution abatement. It seems plausible to also assume that if only one country abates, total net benefits to the world will be larger than under no abatement but smaller than where both abate; this assumption is satisfied by the numbers used in this pay-off matrix, as 2 units of net benefit are obtained in the world whenever one (but not both) abates.

How are the world outcomes distributed? If both countries abate, or if both do not abate, then the world net benefits are shared equally between the two countries. This seems reasonable given our assumption of similarity of X and Y. However, assume that Y chooses to abate, whilst X does not abate. As you can see from the entries in the lower left cell, X gains but Y loses relative to the baseline case of no abatement. Why should this be so? It is easy to see why X gains; X incurs no additional abatement costs, but benefits from some of the pollution reduction arising from Y's abatement. Moreover, because Y will now have higher production costs (including abatement expenditure) but X will not, country X will gain a competitive advantage over Y, adding to X's net benefits even further. Country Y suffers for similar reasons: Y has incurred abatement costs, gains some but not all of the total world benefits of her abatement, and suffers a loss of competitive advantage relative to X. By symmetry, identical results follow if the roles of X and Y are reversed in this argument. It is important to stress that these numbers are hypothetical, and have been chosen by the authors to illustrate an argument. Moreover, they are by no means the *only* numbers that are plausible.

Non-cooperative solutions

Let us next examine the best strategy for each country on the two assumptions that, firstly, each behaves to maximise its own benefit, and secondly, no cooperation takes place between the two countries. This behaviour is known as a non-cooperative game. First of all, we can examine the pay-off matrix to see whether each player has a dominant strategy. In game theory, a dominant strategy exists for one player whenever one choice is best for 'him' irrespective of the choice made by the other player. Let us look at the game from Y's point of view. If X chooses to not abate, Y's preferred choice is to not abate, as the pay-off of 0 from strategy NA is greater than the pay-off of −3 from A. If, conversely, X chooses strategy A, Y's preferred strategy is NA. Whatever X chooses to do, it is best for Y to *not abate*, and so *not abating* is Y's dominant strategy. You should confirm, by equivalent reasoning, that the dominant strategy for X is also to not abate pollution. Game theory suggests that when cooperation does not take place, the behaviour that one expects to occur is that given by the dominant strategy of each player, assuming that one exists. So, in our model, we predict that no abatement will take place.

What does this imply for the well-being of the two countries, and the state of the environment? First, the two countries act in a way that is less good for each of them than is feasible. With cooperation, the two countries could get pay-offs of 3 each rather than zero. The non-cooperative solution to the game is inefficient relative to a possible cooperative outcome. In terms of the state of the environment, the non-cooperative solution is less good for the environment than the (cooperatively) efficient outcome – less pollution abatement is taking place than is efficient to do so. Why has this state of affairs come about? One answer is that it reflects the numbers we have chosen for the pay-offs; this is true, but does not really give us any insight into the nature of the 'problem'. To obtain an intuition for what is going on, look at the incentives facing player Y. If X does abate, there is a large benefit to Y from 'free-riding', letting X abate but not abating itself. In this way, country Y could obtain a net benefit of 5 units. Exactly the same argument applies, of course to X. So there is a strong incentive operating on each player to attempt to obtain the benefits of free-riding on the other's pollution abatement. The incentives to free-ride reflect the fact that this is, in essence, a public goods situation. For global

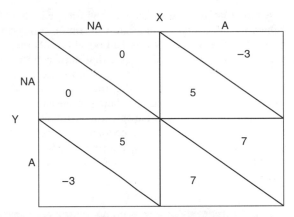

Fig 12.4 A two-player game without a dominant strategy.

pollutants, pollution abatement is a public good; once made available, no one can be excluded from consuming its benefits. Knowing what we do already about public goods, one may have predicted that pollution abatement will tend to be under-provided.

The example we have just looked at was one in which both players had a dominant strategy. But these do not always exist. Let us now look at the pay-offs in a second game in Figure 12.4. It is worth noting that the only difference in the pay-off matrices in Figures 12.3 and 12.4 is that in the latter, the pay-offs from both countries abating together are higher; indeed, the pay-offs to each exceed those obtained by one country free-riding. One might expect this would lead to the choice of both to abate, even in the absence of cooperation. This turns out to be possible but not certain, as you will now see.

The first thing to note is that in this new pay-off matrix, neither country has a dominant strategy. You should now convince yourself of the validity of this assertion. In the absence of dominant strategies for each player, behaviour will depend upon the 'rules' which govern individual behaviour. One possibility is that each player may decide to pursue maximax behaviour. A *maximax strategy* is one that gives rise to the possibility of obtaining the best feasible outcome. The maximax strategies for X and Y are both to abate pollution; to see this, note that if Y chooses to abate, the best she could obtain is 7 units, whereas the best she could obtain by not abating is 5 units. Maximax yields an efficient outcome in this instance, but it is not the only plausible behavioural rule one might imagine is followed, particularly given that maximax strategies are in general ones that imply quite adventurous behaviour.

An alternative assumption one might make is that behaviour takes a *maximin* form. A maximin strategy is one that gives rise to the least bad possible outcome, which in this case would suggest that each country chooses to not abate pollution. This can be seen by noting that if Y chooses to abate, the worst outcome she could obtain would be -3, whereas if she chose to not abate, her worst possible outcome is 0. Since 0 is the least bad of these two outcomes, her maximin choice is to not abate. So maximin behaviour, often considered plausible for risk-averse actors, yields an inefficient outcome.

Cooperative solutions and the difficulties in arriving at them

Our arguments have shown that non-cooperative solutions to games can deliver inefficient outcomes, and can never be better than the best joint outcome possible through cooperation. There are sometimes, in other words, gains to be achieved through cooperative behaviour. In both of the examples we have investigated, the jointly efficient cooperative solution is achieved when the countries agree to abate pollution. Analysis of the Greenhouse Effect, acid

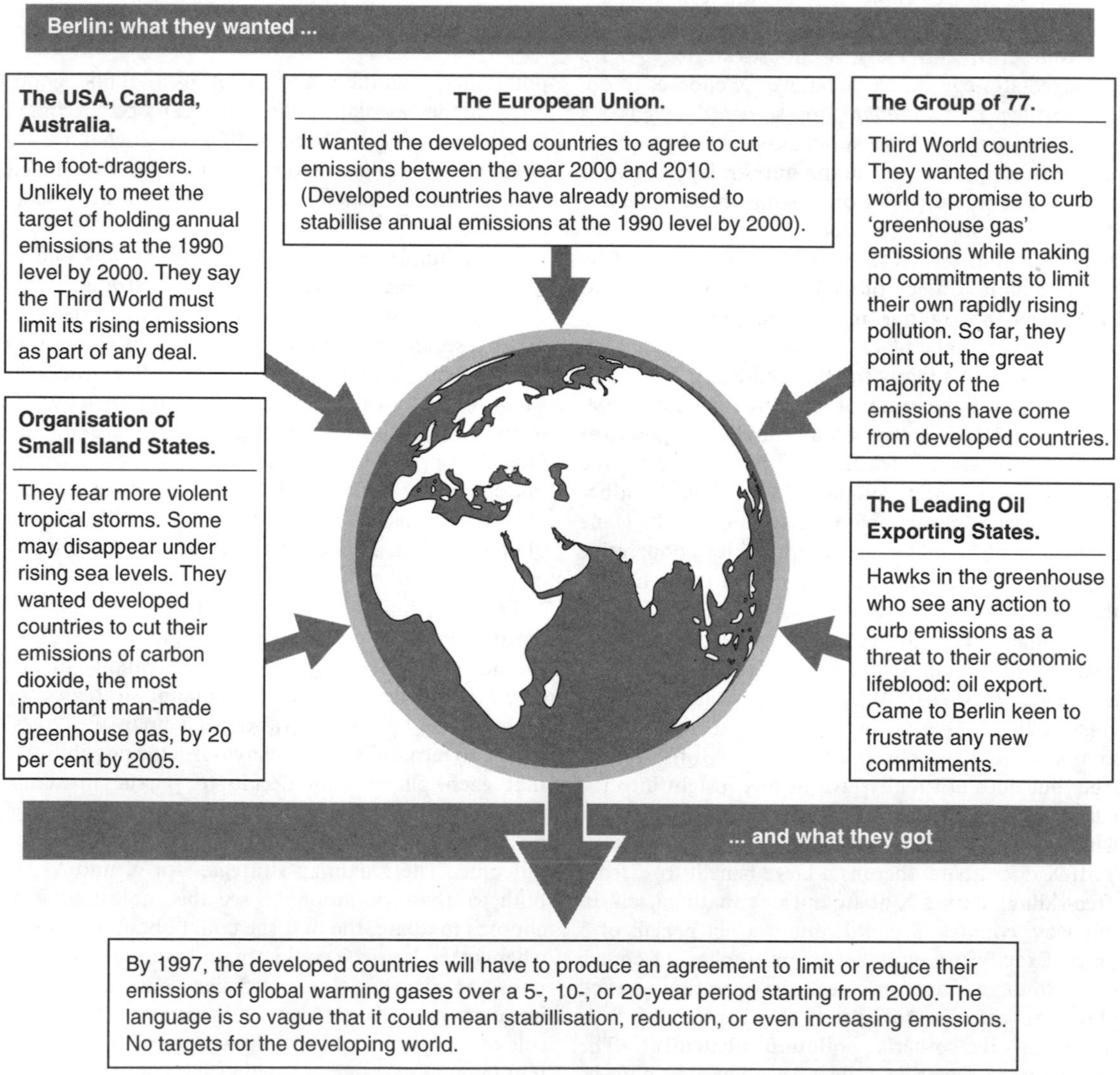

Berlin: what they wanted ...

The USA, Canada, Australia.

The foot-draggers. Unlikely to meet the target of holding annual emissions at the 1990 level by 2000. They say the Third World must limit its rising emissions as part of any deal.

Organisation of Small Island States.

They fear more violent tropical storms. Some may disappear under rising sea levels. They wanted developed countries to cut their emissions of carbon dioxide, the most important man-made greenhouse gas, by 20 per cent by 2005.

The European Union.

It wanted the developed countries to agree to cut emissions between the year 2000 and 2010. (Developed countries have already promised to stabilise annual emissions at the 1990 level by 2000).

The Group of 77.

Third World countries. They wanted the rich world to promise to curb 'greenhouse gas' emissions while making no commitments to limit their own rapidly rising pollution. So far, they point out, the great majority of the emissions have come from developed countries.

The Leading Oil Exporting States.

Hawks in the greenhouse who see any action to curb emissions as a threat to their economic lifeblood: oil export. Came to Berlin keen to frustrate any new commitments.

... and what they got

By 1997, the developed countries will have to produce an agreement to limit or reduce their emissions of global warming gases over a 5-, 10-, or 20-year period starting from 2000. The language is so vague that it could mean stabilisation, reduction, or even increasing emissions. No targets for the developing world.

Fig 12.5 Differing viewpoints at the 1995 Berlin Summit (*source: The Independent*, 8 April 1995).

Box 12.1 The global environmental facility

The Global Environmental Facility (GEF) is a programme, managed jointly by the World Bank, United Nations Development Programme (UNDP) and United Nations Environment Programme (UNEP), to assist developing countries in tackling globally relevant environmental problems. GEF was introduced on a pilot basis, for the three-year period 1991–94.

Financial support from the GEF is intended to provide resources necessary for that portion of an environmental improvement project that would benefit *other* countries, and so would not be undertaken if decisions were taken by comparing costs and benefits to individual nations. In other words, it is targeted at funding the reciprocal externality components of environmental projects. Resources are provided for four particular areas:

- climate change
- biological diversity
- international waters
- ozone depletion

The allocation of GEF expenditure by region in each of these four areas is shown in Table 12.1.

GEF funds are intended to be new, additional contributions. However, controversy has plagued the GEF from the outset in terms of the extent to which GEF funding has in fact been additional, rather than a redirection of existing commitments. It appears to be the case, for example, that funds for defraying the costs of phasing out ozone depleting substances – the Montreal Protocol Multilateral Fund – were assigned to the GEF for distribution, with the result that GEF ozone protection funding has not been additional to previous commitments. A second source

of controversy has centred on the extent and nature of participation in GEF decision making. It has become increasingly understood that effective environmental management requires participation of all relevant donors and recipients, together with non-governmental organisations (NGOs) in an open process. GEF decision-making structures have not been as open as many sponsors hoped, nor have they led to the extent of participation that NGOs have pressed for.

A final source of criticisms of the GEF, made particularly by NGOs and some developing country governments, concerns the fundamentals of environmental assistance itself. In essence, the criticism asserts that the four areas of GEF funding represent issues of interest to, and benefit to, the North, and are not of primary concern to citizens of the South. GEF, it is claimed, is not designed to help the South deal with its own, most pressing, environmental and developmental problems. An ideal world environmental fund, some say, would be focused upon the alleviation of poverty and the transition to sustainable development in Asia and Africa. Looked at in another way, this criticism amounts to an assertion that the GEF suffers from similar weaknesses that development assistance in general has had – it benefits donor countries rather than the recipients, and ties in development with the conservative logic of official agencies such as the World Bank.

Whether or not these criticisms are justified, the *principle* of providing funding to support environmental improvement beyond levels which are justified on a purely national basis is attractive to economists. Consider deforestation in Amazonia, for example. The costs of preventing deforestation are

Table 12.1 Approved expenditures for the Global Environment Facility's Pilot Phase, 1991–94 (million US$) (*source: World Resources 1994–95*, page 230)

Expense category	Africa	Asia	Arab States and Europe	Latin America and Caribbean	Global	Total	Percentage of total
Biodiversity	76.2	75.1	31.6	107.8	12.8	305.5	42
Global warming	55.0	128.5	55.2	29.9	27.4	296.0	40
International waters	16.0	38.0	45.9	19.5	2.6	121.9	17
Ozone	0.0	0.0	3.8	1.9	0.0	5.7	1
Total[a]	147.2	241.6	136.4	159.1	42.8	727.1[b]	100
Percentage of total	20.0	33.0	19.0	22.0	6.0	100.0	

[a] Totals may not add because of rounding.
[b] Total core fund available is $862 million.

Source: Global Environment Facility, Report by the Chairman to the May 1993 Participants' Meeting, Part 1: Main Report, The World Bank, Washington, D.C., 1993, Table 4, page 11.

Box 12.1 Continued

very large to countries in the Amazon basin, whilst only a small proportion of the benefits of reduced deforestation will accrue to Amazonia. An efficient programme requires that *all* the benefits of projects be included when making decisions about the scale of the project to be undertaken. This will only be done if the international or global environmental benefits of lower afforestation can be appropriated by the country undertaking the control. The GEF can thus be viewed as a substitute for a system of emissions charges (or subsidies for emissions abatement) designed to internalize those externalities whose impacts cut across national boundaries.

Source: World Resources 1994–95, Chapter 13.

rain pollution and ozone layer depletion all seem to suggest the possibility of substantial gains from cooperation. We shall see elsewhere in this chapter that cooperation does sometimes occur; however, it appears to take place to a lower extent than one might expect. Why do we not observe cooperative behaviour at *all* times when such gains are theoretically possible?

Several reasons were given in Chapter 9 in our discussion of bargaining solutions to externalities. Cooperation involves bargaining, and bargaining may not occur when numbers of affected parties are high, when bargaining power is unevenly divided between actors, when the expected gains and losses from cooperation differ widely, when property rights are non-existent or not well defined, when bargaining is about public goods, or when, for any reason, the costs of bargaining are large relative to the gains expected from cooperation. Our game theory model was chosen to be very simple; once models are generalised to allow for the factors in this list, the probability of cooperative outcomes being realised is in general reduced.

Finally, cheating or reneging on agreements can sometimes confer large gains on individual cheaters, particularly if the cheating is not detectable, or if compliance to agreements is difficult to enforce. Free-riding can be advantageous both in the context of pure non-cooperation, and where cheating takes place subsequent to the creation of bargained solutions.

International coordination of policy

Our discussion of game theory suggests that uncoordinated or non-cooperative behaviour can lead to highly inefficient patterns of resource allocation where external effects operate across national boundaries. International control regimes pose very difficult political tasks. When private agents fail to achieve efficient outcomes through cooperation *within* one country, a sovereign authority exists which can use its regulatory or incentive powers to steer outcomes in the direction of economic efficiency. However, when sovereign nations acting in isolation fail to act cooperatively, there is no equivalent supranational authority to act in this coordinating role.

Countries may and sometimes do reach negotiated, cooperative outcomes in many circumstances, of course, and it is quite easy to cite examples. The Helsinki Protocol, signed in 1985, bound 21 European states to an agreed 30% reduction of sulphur dioxide emissions (in terms of 1980 base levels) by 1993. But it is instructive to note that 13 countries in the geographically relevant area were not signatories to the Protocol. One of these, the United Kingdom, had very weak incentives to enter into voluntary regulation, with approximately 70% of its sulphur emissions being transported outside UK boundaries by the prevailing westerly winds, and receiving little acid rain deposition from other countries.

The growth and increasing authority of international political structures such as the European Union and the United Nations Organisation offers the prospect of creating vehicles for international coordination of behaviour. Until the collapse of communism in Eastern Europe, a particularly intractable problem had been reciprocal transfers of acid rain pollutants between the countries of Eastern and Western Europe. The scope for internationally negotiated reductions in sulphur and nitrogen emissions has increased with the demise of COMECON, and the prospects for membership of the European Union by a number of Central European states will further enhance the likelihood that mutually beneficial reductions in those pollutants occur. Continuing the example we discussed in the previous paragraph, it is interesting to note that membership of the European Union has required the UK to reduce sulphur and nitrogen oxide emissions, even though she earlier had refused to accede to the

Helsinki Protocol (IBRD, 1992, page 155; French, 1990).

The main vehicle that has been used in attempts to reach cooperative solutions to regional and global environmental problems is that of the intergovernmental conference. At the so-called Earth Summit in Rio de Janeiro, Brazil in 1992, the industrialised nations agreed to stabilise carbon emissions from power stations, industry and traffic at 1990 levels by the year 2000. Such an agreement, whilst relatively modest in terms of the extent of pollution control, represents a major breakthrough in terms of achieving internationally coordinated pollution policy.

The first meeting of the 118 nations that had ratified in Rio the United Nations Climate Protection Treaty, took place in Berlin in 1995. The agenda included proposed reductions in carbon emissions. Progress in securing agreement was hampered by the existence of marked differences of interest between various subgroups within the 118 nations, as explained in Figure 12.5. As a result, no actual reductions were agreed, but the summit accepted in principle the need to reduce emissions below 1990 levels, and to construct a timetable for securing that target. The Berlin summit meeting mandated governments to consider the size of future reductions in emissions and a timetable for implementation, and accepted that a final agreement on these matters would have to be obtained by 1997. It remains to be seen whether this objective is realised.

Decision making and uncertainty

An important characteristic of each of the examples of regional and global pollution problems we are examining in this chapter is that the nature and magnitudes of the damages caused are subject to major uncertainties. In the case of acid rain, uncertainties relate primarily to the magnitudes of the physical and biological effects, rather than to the nature of the effects themselves. There is, of course, an additional uncertainty involved in the subsequent mapping of physical and biological impacts into economic damages.

For ozone depletion, uncertainties are far more pervasive. As Case Study 2 demonstrates, the phenomenon of ozone depletion itself is incompletely understood, and research into the consequences of ozone depletion is in its infancy. Uncertainty is at its most profound as regards the processes and consequences of global climate change, particularly in terms of the regional impacts of the various manifestations of climate change, and the timing of those changes and their consequences.

It is not surprising, therefore, that many countries have been reluctant to undertake substantial amounts of preventative action, particularly where the costs to individual countries are high. Progress on replacing CFC emissions by less harmful substitutes has been relatively successful largely because control costs have been relatively low to date. By contrast, most commentators would probably assess the progress on abating greenhouse gas emissions as being disappointing and inadequately stringent when measured in terms of efficiency levels. Costs of abatement for Greenhouse Effects are far from being negligible, and the rewards of control are highly uncertain to those who choose to implement abatement.

CASE STUDY 1   Acid rain pollution

Causes of acid rain pollution

The phenomenon of acid rain appears to have first been noticed in Scandinavia in the 1950s, when research related acidification of rivers and lakes to the previously unexplained death of freshwater fish. The physical processes underlying acid rain are now generally well understood. Atmospheric stocks of sulphur dioxide and nitrous oxide accumulate primarily from coal and heavy oil-fired power generation. Of secondary importance are emissions of unburnt hydrocarbons and NO_x from vehicle exhausts. Stocks of potential acidic material are transported in the middle and upper levels of the atmosphere by systems of prevailing winds, to distances of up to 600 miles.

Acid rain occurs through two principal processes. In dry deposition, particulate matter is physically deposited, subsequently taking acidic form in conjunction with surface water. The term *acid rain* is, therefore, something of a misnomer as it is not necessarily associated with the process of rain at all. Dry deposition is the most important mechanism of acidification in the south-western United States. By contrast, wet deposition is characterised by acidic substances, particularly sulphuric and nitric acids, being formed in the atmosphere, and subsequently being deposited through rain precipitation or just movements of moist air. A summary of the processes

continued

CASE STUDY 1 Continued

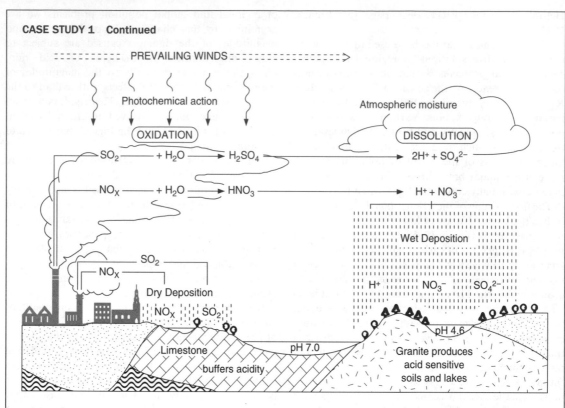

Fig 12.6 Schematic representation of the formation, distribution, and impact of acid rain (*source*: Kemp, 1990).

underlying acid rain deposition is shown in Figure 12.6, taken from Kemp (1990).

Unpolluted rain precipitation is in itself mildly acidic, with global background pH of 5.0. *Acid rain* itself refers to precipitations where the acidity level is unusually severe. The pH measurement index is explained in Box 12.2.

Consequences of acid rain pollution

Major studies of the consequences of acid rain pollution in Europe have been conducted by the Commission of the European Communities (CEC, 1983) and the World Conservation Union (WCU, 1990). An important early 10-year study in the USA was begun by the National Acid Rain Precipitation Program (NARPP) in 1980. Acid rain damage in Europe is amongst the highest recorded anywhere, and appears to be substantially worse than in the USA. The consequences include the following:

1 Increased acidity of lakes where concentrations may kill animal and plant life. Water acidification results in aluminium being leached out of soils, with consequent water poisoning, and fish being starved of salt and oxygen. Damage of this form in

the USA has been rated as modest by NAPAP (1990); recreational fishing is threatened as few species can survive in water with pH levels below 5. Nine percent of lakes studied in the NARPP sample had pH < 5. Worst affected regions in the United States are the Adirondack Mountains in New York State, and Florida, in which 14% and 23% respectively of all lakes have been acidified. By way of contrast, very severe damage has been recorded in Scandinavia. For example, Sweden has 4000 highly acidified lakes, and in southern Norway, lakes with a total area of 13 000 km^2 support no fish, and in another 20 000 km^2 fish stocks have been reduced by 50% (French, 1990). Trout and salmon are particularly badly affected. Similar evidence has been found in studies conducted in Germany, Scotland and Canada.

2 Increased acidity of soils which reduces the number of plants that may be grown. However, current damage to crops is thought to be negligible in the USA (NARPP, 1989) where no significant effects have been observed on crop growth, even at

continued

CASE STUDY 1   Continued

acidity levels ten times that currently prevailing in the eastern United States.

3 Forest destruction due to calcium and potassium nutrient losses by leaching, and replacement by manganese and aluminium, both of which are harmful to root growth. Tree growth may also be affected by direct poisoning of leaves. Acid rain, together with ozone, appears to intensify the effects of natural stresses on some species in mountain locations. Some reports have suggested massive amounts of forest death in Europe, particularly in France (10 000 hectares of serious damage, 30 000 hectares suffering some deterioration), West Germany (in which 2 million hectares, 10% of the total forest area, has experienced serious damage, and over half of all forests some damage), the former East Germany, Czech Republic, Slovakia, and Sweden. Coniferous trees are the most heavily damaged in Europe. Although the majority of American forests appear healthy at present, some concern has been raised about effects on sugar maples and high elevation red spruce in Canada and north-east USA, and on pines in southeast USA and California (French, 1990). Table 12.2 provides data on estimated forest product losses in Europe attributable to *all* sources of air pollution.

4 Acidification of domestic water supplies and sulphate pollution in general probably affects human health, but in ways that are not yet fully identified. One study attributes up to 50 000 deaths per year in the United States to sulphate pollution (Office of Technology Assessment, 1984).

5 Building and infrastructure erosion. Acid rain damages galvanized steel, bronze, limestone and other carbonate stone (including marble and chalk which are converted to soft gypsum) and carbonate-based paints, thus causing culturally important damage, such as that to the Acropolis and the Taj Mahal. Stained glass is so badly eroded that some studies predict a total loss of medieval glass within a few decades.

6 Visibility interference, caused by fine sulphate particles produced by airborne sulphuric acid. In the National Parks of the eastern USA this has caused an estimated 50–60% reduction in visibility.

Which countries are the principal polluters?

The precursors of acid rain are generated from stationary sources, such as coal-burning power plant, ore smelters and industrial boilers, and from mobile-source vehicle emissions. Any country which has high volumes of activity in any of these

dimensions is therefore likely to be a significant contributor to acid rain pollution. However, acid rain deposition is principally associated with the heavily industrialised regions of Europe, the ex-Soviet Union, and North America, where the most heavily polluted areas have levels of sulphur deposition ten times greater than the natural background rate (*World Resources, 1992–93*). China is now the third largest emitter of sulphur (after the ex-Soviet Union and the USA), and has substantial acid deposition in its southern provinces. Meteorological patterns mean that some countries cause particularly severe depositions on their neighbours; for example, 70% of UK emissions are carried by prevailing winds to Germany, the Netherlands, Norway and Sweden, and the heavily industrialised region of Silesia in southern Poland has significant adverse affects on neighbouring regions.

Pollution control programmes

The principal control instruments available to an environmental protection agency are quantity-of-emissions regulation, requirements to install clean-up technology at the points of emission (such as sulphur scrubbing equipment), emissions charges and tradable permit schemes. By raising costs of electricity production using conventional fuels or by imposing quantity constraints on emissions, these instruments should induce substitution in the direction of using (more expensive) low sulphur coal or from coal to other primary fuels.

In the United States, the first substantial control programmes were launched after the passage of the 1970 Clean Air Act. This established a system of local ambient air quality standards, and conferred powers of enforcement on local governments through emission quantity regulations. The Clean Air Act thus constituted a decentralised command-and-control regime, based around targets defined in terms of ambient air quality standards. The system of decentralised control, based on local ambient standards, proved to be rather disappointing in its overall effects. For example, the legislation led to taller emission stacks, which succeeded in attaining local ambient standards, but at the cost of largely passing on the problem to neighbouring areas. Any programme which sets targets in terms of diluting local pollutant concentrations at certain designated measuring sites suffers from this weakness when the pollutant is highly mobile.

Subsequent amendments to the legislation, resulting most recently in the 1990 Clean Air Act, look

continued

CASE STUDY 1   Continued

Table 12.2 Estimated losses of forest products attributable to air pollution, by volume and value (*source: World Resources 1992–93*)

Region/country	Loss of potential harvest attributable to air pollution (million cubic metres per year)	Value of harvest production[a] (million 1987 US dollars per year)
Europe	**82.3**	**$23,022.9**
Nordic countries	11.1	2,925.1
Finland	4.5	1,187.6
Norway	0.8	210.4
Sweden	5.8	1,527.1
European Community	**28.6**	**9,389.1**
Belgium and Luxembourg	0.7	252.6
Denmark	0.4	117.1
France	3.5	1,173.6
Germany (West)	11.9	3,614.0
Germany (East)	4.9	1,160.8
Italy	3.1	1,830.5
Netherlands	0.2	67.4
UK and Ireland	3.7	1,173.1
Alpine countries	**5.8**	**1,573.6**
Austria	3.4	913.4
Switzerland	2.4	660.2
Southern Europe	**7.2**	**1,797.5**
Greece	0.1	23.4
Portugal	1.5	334.1
Spain[b]	X	X
Turkey	2.8	671.4
Yugoslavia	2.8	768.6
Central Europe	**29.6**	**7,337.6**
Bulgaria	2.2	520.9
Czechoslovakia	9.5	2,371.2
Hungary	3.0	789.9
Poland	11.1	2,658.5
Romania	3.8	997.1

[a] Preliminary data; includes roundwood, industrial products, and 'nonwood' benefits.
[b] Data insufficient to allow calculation of pollution effects.
X = not available.

Source: The Price of Pollution: Acid and the Forests of Europe, *Options* (International Institute for Applied Systems Analysis, Laxenburg, Austria, September 1990), page 6.

certain to have far stronger pollution abatement effects. The Act requires sulphur dioxide to be reduced by 10 million tonnes from 1980 emission levels by year 2000, thereby bringing SO_2 emissions down to 8.95 million tonnes, an improvement of over 50%. This is expected to be sufficiently tight control to protect most aquatic systems, although it is not clear how much forest damage this will avoid. The legislation also requires a reduction of nitrogen oxide emissions by 2.5 million tonnes.

Attainment of the targets of the 1990 Clean Air Act will be effected through a system of marketable permits in emissions of the precursors of acid rain. The programme's introduction will be in two phases; in the first stage, permits will be issued for 110 large coal-burning utilities, followed later by permit issues for 2400 smaller generators. The scheme is to be launched in 1995, with permits issued at no charge to generators, allowing emissions of between 30 and 50% of 1985 pollution levels. Whilst the degree of abatement was not determined by any explicit economic efficiency rules, but rather seems to reflect

continued

CASE STUDY 1   Continued

opinions as to what is a necessary 'safety standard', cost–benefit considerations suggest that it is likely that efficiency gains will be secured by the programme. Portney (1989) estimates the annual benefits to the USA to lie in the interval $2–$9 billion whilst control costs are predicted to be $4 billion. The existence of a federal government in the USA facilitates the introduction of pollution control programmes; how easy has it been to abate the precursors of acid rain in Europe where no such unified sovereign governmental structure exists for all relevant areas? We showed earlier, in Section 5, that some voluntary control was agreed in the 1980s by a number of European states, and that the European Community has subsequently extended the coverage and severity of these controls in its member countries. In June 1988, EC Environment Ministers agreed to national reductions in emissions from large combustion plants. These and other agreements have met with some success, with SO_2 emissions falling by more than 20% between 1980 and 1989. At national levels, emission reductions have largely been implemented through command-and-control regulations, although some countries (including France and Sweden) have introduced emission taxes. The UK approach to sulphur emissions control has centred on mandatory abatement investments, including flue-gas desulphurization technology. In the long-term, larger-scale reductions in acid rain precursors in Europe will necessitate the use of either uniform emission taxes, or tradable permit schemes. As yet, no European-wide example of either exists.

Box 12.2 The pH scale of acidity

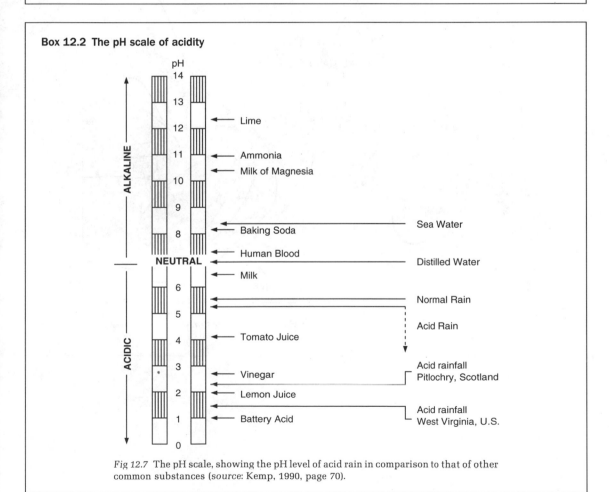

Fig 12.7 The pH scale, showing the pH level of acid rain in comparison to that of other common substances (*source:* Kemp, 1990, page 70).

Box 12.2 Continued

The pH scale is a measure of the extent of acidity of some material. It is constructed so that a falling pH value is indicative of increasing acidity. More precisely, the index is common logarithmic, with a change of one unit in the pH index corresponding to a tenfold change in the concentration of the acid in water. A pH measurement of 7 indicates neutrality; the substance in question lies on the border between being described as acidic and alkaline. Figure 12.7 illustrates the pH scale in comparison with the acidity levels of a set of common substances.

Clean, unpolluted rainwater has a pH value of between 5 and 6 (that is, it is mildly acidic). Over much of north-west Europe, the current pH level of rainwater lies between 4 and 4.5. The lowest rainwater pH level recorded in Europe appears to have been a reading of 2.4, obtained in Scotland. Rainfall in the north-eastern United States currently has a typical pH of 4.4. In Wheeling, West Virginia, one rainstorm gave a pH value of 1.5; to obtain some idea of this level of acidity, note that car battery acid has a pH value of approximately 1.0.

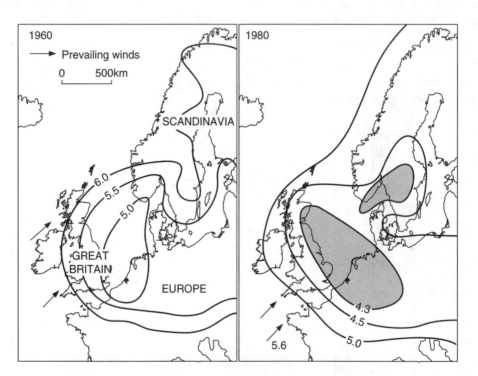

Fig 12.8 The increase in levels of acid rain in north-west Europe, 1960—80 (*source*: adapted from Waugh, 1987).

Box 12.3 Cheap fuel may win over acid rain

Cheap fuel may win over acid rain

ACID rain from the smoke plumes of Pembroke power station in South Wales has long caused acrimony between National Power and government regulators.

So far, Her Majesty's Inspectorate of Pollution (HMIP), cheered on by the environmental lobby, has prevented plans to burn orimulsion — a bitumen based fuel rich in sulphur and heavy metals.

Now that the Government proposes to change the rules by which the new environment agency regulates pollution, the balance of power could shift in favour of the power companies, and the whole issue be reopened.

National Power wants to satisfy peak demand for electricity by switching from occasional burning of expensive heavy fuel oil to almost constant burning of cheaper orimulsion. The bitumin-based fuel from Venezuela has been dubbed "the world's dirtiest fuel".

Using the Environmental Protection Act of 1990, HMIP inspectors have so far insisted that burning orimulsion at Pembroke would be a "new process" which could not be permitted without expensive equipment to take out sulphur and other contaminants.

At the time of the original application to burn orimulsion at Pembroke, David Shaw, executive officer of the River Wye Preservation Trust, estimated that the move would lead to a 13-fold increase in acid rain in the surrounding countryside. "That would affect the watershed of the River Wye, headwaters of the River Severn and other important rivers including the Usk, Dee and the Conway," he said.

After a protracted wrangle over running the station without pollution equipment, National Power put its plans on ice. In August, however, the company revived them, deciding that even with some form of sulphur abatement equipment, burning orimulsion at Pembroke would be viable.

Under existing legislation, National Power would be forced to provide equipment which is the "best practical environmental option".

Yesterday's bill contains a clause stating that the new agency should "have regard to costs and benefits" in exercising its powers. National Power could argue for a cheaper and less environmentally-sound option.

Source: The Guardian, Friday 14 October 1994.

This newspaper article reveals an interesting difference of opinion about how environmental targets should be set. Economists typically espouse an efficiency criterion, arguing that pollution abatement should be taken to the point where marginal control benefits and costs are equalised. The new United Kingdom Environmental Agency is required 'to have regard to costs and benefits' in its adjudications, thereby satisfying, to some extent at least, an efficiency criterion.

But pollution standards in the United Kingdom (and elsewhere) have not usually been established with such a criterion in mind. Instead, targets have tended to be based on perceived minimum safety standards, or upon scientific assessments of 'significant' amounts of pollution. Many environmentalists believe that safety standards are likely to be tighter and more demanding than those set in terms of an efficiency criterion. This is the basis – as the article shows – for the mistrust that many environmentalists have for the guidelines of the Environmental Agency.

Box 12.4 Acid rain games in Europe

In a paper entitled 'Acid Rain Games in Europe' by George Halkos and John Hutton (1993), the authors demonstrate that acid rain causes greater environmental damage than would occur if countries act cooperatively. Using estimates of sulphur dioxide damage and abatement costs, Halkos and Hutton calculate the potential gains to some West European countries from cooperative sulphur dioxide emissions control. The authors use the techniques of game theory to calculate the magnitudes of these potential efficiency gains.

Halkos and Hutton commence by determining cost-efficient abatement cost functions for each country, which measure the cost of eliminating SO_2 emissions from the process of power generation. Abatement costs differ between countries as a result of country-specific factors such as the fuel mix used, the sulphur content of fuels, capacity utilization and the scale for installations. Figure 12.9, taken from Halkos and Hutton, illustrates total abatement costs for one country, the United Kingdom.

The 'staircase' shape of the total abatement cost curve results from marginal cost increases as the scale of abatement rises; as more abatement is applied, polluters switch to different, more expensive control technologies. One useful piece of information that can be derived directly from a total abatement cost function such as this is knowledge of the maximum level of pollution abatement that can be obtained for any given size of control budget.

The second step in the exercise involves the construction of a matrix of transfer coefficients, indicating what proportion of the total emissions from any particular country is eventually deposited in each of the 27 countries being studied. This information is obtained from studies conducted by the Norwegian Meteorological Institute.

Halkos and Hutton then proceed to estimate total SO_2 damage functions. The method of obtaining these estimates is interesting and innovative. First the authors assume, on the basis of recent evidence, that the damage function is convex, rather than linear (see Chapter 8 for an explanation of convexity). There is no way of obtaining direct statistical estimates for the parameters of the damage function, given the almost complete absence of relevant data. However, Halkos and Hutton employ a neat trick to obtain approximate damage estimates. They assume that, for each country, current *national* marginal abatement costs are equated with current *national* marginal damage costs. To understand this, look at Figure 12.10. Halkos and Hutton assume that, when acting uncooperatively, each country considers the costs of pollution control (represented by NMAC) and the damages which it will avoid *in its own country* by doing that abatement (represented by the function labelled NMDC). A country will reduce pollution from the uncontrolled level, $\hat{\Psi}^*$, to the *privately* efficient level, Ψ^*, or equivalently do Z^* abatement.

Note that the fully efficient solution (which we call the cooperative solution) is obtained when each country equates its national marginal abatement costs with the *European* (and not national) marginal damage function. By doing so, the outcome is identical to that which would be economically efficient if all Europe were a single country, and the

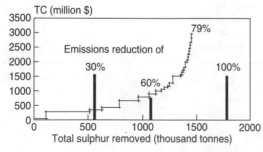

Fig 12.9 United Kingdom year 2000 total abatement cost curve (*source*: Halkos and Hutton, 1993, page 5).

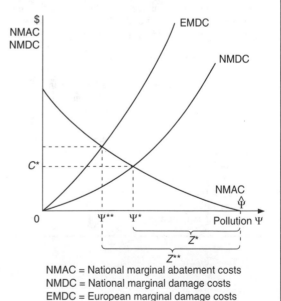

NMAC = National marginal abatement costs
NMDC = National marginal damage costs
EMDC = European marginal damage costs

Fig 12.10 Cooperative and non-cooperative pollution outcomes in the presence of externalities crossing national boundaries.

Box 12.4 Continued

Table 12.3 Acid rain: gains from cooperative behaviour (see text of Box 12.4 for explanation)

	Austria	Italy	FRG	UK	FRG	GDR
Percentages:						
1992 Abatement	18.35	8.40	45.1	11.2	45.1	0.72
Privately efficient abatement (Z^*)	29.49	29.2	62.77	16.7	66.17	1.90
Socially efficient (Europe-wide) abatement (Z^{**})	35.4	35.5	62.41	24.81	63.46	25.24
Total costs of abatement and damage ($m 1985):						
Privately efficient abatement (Z^*)	233.9	720.68	1813.46	479.63	1991.00	84.15
		(954.58)		(2293.09)		(2075.15)
Socially efficient (Europe-wide) abatement (Z^{**})	215.51	729.27	1780.15	496.21	1843.50	156.20
		(944.78)		(2276.36)		(1999.70)
Total efficiency gain		[9.80]		[16.73]		[75.45]

Source: Halkos and Hutton (1993).

European environmental protection agency equates European marginal costs and damages. This would yield Ψ^{**} as the fully efficient pollution level or Z^{**} as the abatement. Notice that the cooperation result is a higher abatement level, Z^{**}, than the non-cooperative solution, Z^*.

Returning to the main thread of our argument, it can be seen from Figure 12.10 that Halkos and Hutton are assuming each country undertakes Z^* pollution abatement. The unobserved marginal damage can be calculated by noting that it is equal to the observable level of marginal abatement costs, C^*. Using this information for each of the 27 countries studied, the parameters of a damage function can then be calibrated. Once this is done, the matrix of transfer coefficients can be used to calculate the total damage each country will experience for any level of SO_2 emissions by each of the 27 countries.

The final step in the analysis involves estimating the magnitudes of the gains that would be obtained from cooperative behaviour as compared with non-cooperative behaviour. Halkos and Hutton's results are presented in Table 12.3, for three pairs of countries. To understand the information given, let us read down the rows.

The first three rows of numbers refer to levels of abatement in percentages. In the '1992 Abatement' row we find (approximate) percentage levels of abatements that the countries actually undertook in 1992; these show very marked variations. For example, in the GDR (the previous East Germany), less than 1% of potential SO_2 emissions were actually abated in 1992; in the FRG (old West Germany) the much greater priority given to environmental

conservation led to over 45% abatement relative to the theoretical unconstrained level. Figures in the second row give the privately efficient abatement percentages (corresponding to Z^* in Figure 12.10). In all cases, these exceed the 1992 abatement levels, implying that none of the five countries abated sulphur dioxide even to the level that would pay positive returns in terms of the own-country pollution reductions that would arise from abatement. The third row presents the socially efficient abatement levels, assuming that each of the pairs of countries shown in the table act in a cooperative manner. Socially efficient pollution abatement occurs when, for the two countries indicated, the sum of total abatement costs and total pollution costs for that pair of countries is minimised. In the case of the two Germanies, cooperative efficiency actually required the FRG to do a little *less* abatement than would be privately optimal, whilst the GDR would have to do much more.

The lower part of the table shows the sum of total abatement and total damage costs for each country and for each pair of countries (in parentheses). Continuing to look at the case of the two Germanies, note that the sum of costs is lower by 75.45 in the socially efficient case (Z^{**}) (costs = 1999.7) as compared with the privately efficient case (Z^*) (costs = 2075.15).

A scrutiny of the costs for individual countries brings out another aspect of this example. For West Germany (FRG), total abatement and damage costs fall by $147 million in moving to the cooperative solution, whereas for East Germany total costs rise by $72 million. For a cooperative solution to be

Box 12.4 Continued

possible, it would be necessary for FRG to give a side-payment to GDR of at least $72 million (but less than $147 million), otherwise both parties would not benefit from the cooperation. Of course, given that the two Germanies are now unified, the new German government might just impose the cooperative solution; whether it chooses to give compensating transfer from West to East becomes a distributional matter.

By way of contrast, the figures demonstrate that for the FRG/UK pair of countries, total costs would rise for the UK in the cooperation case. To induce the UK to undertake cooperation, side payments of at least £16.58 million annually by FRG to the UK would be required. Finally, it must be stressed that the 'total efficiency gains' referred to in the table are obtained by comparison of costs at Z^* and Z^{**}. However, the *actual* levels of current abatement are less in all cases than Z^*, and so the total net benefits in moving from 1992 abatement levels to the socially efficient levels would be greater (and probably substantially greater) than those indicated here.

Source: Halkos and Hutton (1993).

CASE STUDY 2   Stratospheric ozone depletion

Ozone is produced in the upper layers of the atmosphere (the stratosphere and the ionosphere) by the action of ultraviolet light on oxygen molecules. The processes determining the concentrations of upper atmospheric ozone are complex and incompletely understood. What is known is that the ozone concentration is in a constant state of flux, resulting from the interaction of decay and creation processes. Several naturally occurring catalysts act to speed up natural rates of decay; these catalysts include oxides of chlorine, nitrogen and hydrogen. There are large, naturally caused variations in these concentrations by time, spatial location, and altitude. For example, normal dynamic fluctuations in ozone concentrations are as large as 30% from day to night, and 10% from day to day (Kemp, 1990).

During the early 1970s, scientific claims that ozone was being depleted in the stratosphere were first made. These original claims were not satisfactorily verified, but in the mid-1980s the discovery of the so-called hole in the ozone layer over Antarctica led the scientific community to conclude that serious reductions in ozone concentrations were taking place in certain parts of the atmosphere. The downward trend in ozone concentrations was attributed to inadvertent human interference with the chemistry of the atmosphere, related to the prevailing pattern of air pollution. Over the continent of Antarctica, the fall in concentration (relative to its 1975 level) was estimated to be in the interval 60–95%, depending upon the place of measurement (Everest, 1988); see Figure 12.11.

Although much progress has been made towards understanding the chemistry of ozone depletion in the 10 years to 1994, we are still profoundly uncertain even as to the recent historical rates of depletion. Estimates of the actual rates of depletion experienced have been considerably lowered since the initial studies were published, and forecast depletion rates are now much less than early predictions. Current models forecast depletion to be no more than 5% on average over the next 50 years, as compared with initial predictions of depletions of up to 20%. There is also some evidence pointing to very large dispersion in regional depletion rates around these global averages (see Everest, 1988).

There are several ways in which human impacts on the ozone layer take place, as illustrated in Figure 12.12. Two of these – nuclear radiation and aircraft emissions – appear to have relatively little effect at present, but are potentially important. Evidence also implicates a number of other chemicals as ozone depleters, in particular nitrous oxide (associated with traffic and agricultural activity), carbon tetrachloride and chloroform. The dominant anthropomorphic cause of ozone depletion appears to be the emission of CFC gases into the atmosphere. These substances act as catalysts to the decay of ozone, adding to the effects of the natural catalysts we mentioned earlier. Many forms of CFC exist and are being produced currently, two of them – CFC-11 and CFC-12 – being the dominant forms. The most important sources of CFC emissions by quantity are the production, use and disposal of aerosol propellants, cushioning foams, cleaning materials and refrigerative materials. In some cases, such as in aerosol uses, the release of the gas occurs at the time of manufacture or within a relatively short lapse of time after manufacture. In other cases, the release can occur at much later dates as items of hardware such as refrigerators and air conditioning units are scrapped. Table 12.4 (adapted from Quinn, 1986) illustrates the development of the

continued

CASE STUDY 2   Continued

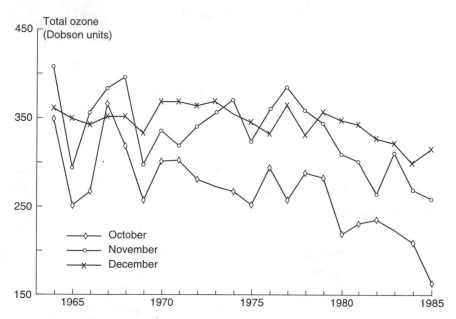

Fig 12.11 Changing ozone levels at the South pole (1964–85) for the months of October, November and December. Dobson units (DU) are used to represent the thickness of the ozone layer at standard (sea-level) temperature and pressure (1 DU is equivalent to 0.01 mm) (*source*: Kemp, 1990).

CFC market and presents estimates of the income elasticity of demand for some CFCs in one important case, the USA. The very high estimated income elasticities of demand show that, if CFC gases are not subject to control, their use would be likely to rise very rapidly as world incomes rise. For example, the estimated elasticity of 4.39 for foam products (in the period 1960–82) implies that for every 1% increase in real income, the demand for CFC-11 for foam products rose by 4.39%.

Long-term forecasts of CFC production, consumption and atmospheric concentration depend critically upon the strength of control measures (if any) which will be undertaken. Tables 12.5 and 12.6 summarise forecasts (from Kula, 1994, based on data in Mintzer, 1987) for these variables over a 90-year period under four different assumptions that could be made about the extent of control. It is also important to recognise that CFC gases are highly stable; the active residence life (i.e. before degradation into harmless elements) of CFCs in the stratosphere is very long (being measured in decades rather than years). Even if controls were to drastically limit current production or use, the damage being caused by the existing stock will continue for several decades subsequently.

What, then, are likely to be the effects of a continuing depletion of the atmospheric ozone layer? The consequences follow from the fact that ozone plays a natural, equilibrium-maintaining role in the stratosphere through

(a) absorption of ultraviolet (UV) radiation, and
(b) absorption of infrared radiation.

The absorption of infrared radiation implies that CFC substances are greenhouse gases, contributing to global climate change. This aspect of ozone depletion is discussed in the following section. Here we focus on the role payed by halons and chlorofluorocarbons (CFCs) in depleting the concentration of ozone in the upper atmosphere and leading to increased UV radiative flows. The ozone layer, therefore, protects living organisms from receiving harmful UV radiation. It is now virtually certain that ozone depletion has increased the incidence of skin cancer among humans. Connor (1993) estimates that a 1% depletion in ozone concentration would increase non-malignant skin cancers by more than 3%, but by rather less for malignant melanomas.

continued

CASE STUDY 2   Continued

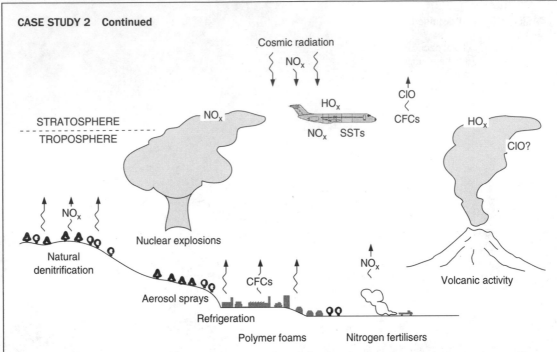

Fig 12.12 Diagrammatic representation of the sources of natural and anthropogenic ozone-destroyers (*source*: Kemp, 1990).

The US EPA has estimated that human-induced changes in the ozone layer will cause an additional 39 million contractions of skin cancer during the next century, leading to 800 000 additional deaths (Kemp, 1990).

Effects which seem likely to occur, but about which much doubt remains, include effects on human immune systems (including activation of the AIDS virus), radiation blindness and cataract formation, genetic damage to plants and animals, and losses to crops and other plant or animal damage. Of particular concern is the apparent damage to marine plankton growth; the importance of plankton in many food chains suggest that this may become a critical issue during the next century. Increased UV radiative flows are also likely to

continued

Table 12.4 Time periods for econometric analysis of historical production of CFCs in the United States

Model	Time period	Comment	Income elasticity of demand
CFC-11, aerosol	1946–1952	Early development period	2.33
	1953–1975	Personal care products market develops	2.96
CFC-11, non-aerosol	1935–1950	Early development period	1.83
	1951–1959	New refrigeration markets develop	3.30
	1960–1982	Urethane foam markets develop	4.39
CFC-12, aerosol	1946–1952	Early development period	2.51
	1953–1975	Personal care products market develops	2.84
CFC-12, non-aerosol	1935–1950	Early development period	2.62
	1951–1957	New refrigeration markets develop	3.02
	1958–1982	Mobile AC market develops	3.17

Source: adapted from Quinn (1986).

CASE STUDY 2   Continued

Table 12.5 Projected total production of CFC-11 and CFC-12 under four different scenarios

| Year | Thousands of tonnes per year | | | |
	Business as usual	High emission	Modest policy	Slow build-up
1990	1100	1100	1100	750
2000	1200	1600	1200	750
2010	1300	2100	1200	750
2020	1400	2600	1200	750
2030	1500	3200	1200	750
2040	1600	4000	1200	750
2050	1800	5400	1200	750
2075	2100	9100	1200	750
Annual growth rate, 1985–2075	0.95%	2.6%	0.35%	0.0%

Source: Mintzer (1987).

accelerate the degradation of polymer plastic materials.

Some indication of the likely magnitudes of the costs and benefits of control is given in a United States EPA 1987 study (reprinted in Kula 1987, page 220), the results of which are reported in Table 12.7. The estimates suggest that huge economic benefits would accrue from even very dramatic CFC control in the USA.

Action to date

International action regarding ozone depletion has been coordinated by the United Nations Environment Programme (UNEP). The first steps towards internationally agreed control measures were taken at the Vienna Convention, Austria, in 1985, at which agreements were made for international cooperation in research, monitoring and the exchange of information. In September 1988, the Montreal Protocol was signed by 24 nations. The signatories to the agreement agreed, as an interim measure, to restrict the domestic consumption of ozone-depleting substances to 1986 levels by 1990, and to limit production to 110% of 1986 levels. The production targets are to be progressively tightened, with limits of 80% and 50% of the 1986 levels by the years 1994 and 1999 respectively.

A second major conference opened in London in March 1989, attended by delegates from more than 120 countries. The London Protocol, signed in July

continued

Table 12.6 Projected atmospheric concentrations of CFCs under four different scenarios

| Year | Business as usual | | High emission | | Modest policy | | Slow build-up | |
	CFC-11 (ppbv)[a]	CFC-12	CFC-11 (ppbv)[a]	CFC-12	CFC-11 (ppbv)[a]	CFC-12	CFC-11 (ppbv)[a]	CFC-12
1980	0.170	0.285	0.170	0.285	0.170	0.285	0.170	0.285
1990	0.303	0.521	0.303	0.521	0.302	0.517	0.282	0.500
2000	0.471	0.793	0.512	0.827	0.464	0.748	0.381	0.693
2010	0.618	1.080	0.815	1.225	0.635	0.987	0.470	0.875
2020	0.826	1.377	1.196	1.714	0.796	1.232	0.547	1.046
2030	1.005	1.687	1.651	2.295	0.959	1.488	0.615	1.206
2040	1.190	2.014	2.198	2.983	1.127	1.756	0.674	1.355
2050	1.379	2.359	2.897	3.828	1.299	2.039	0.726	1.494
2060	1.573	2.720	3.859	4.904	1.474	2.333	0.771	1.625
2075	1.873	3.291	5.749	6.906	—	—	0.829	1.805

[a] ppbv = parts per billion by volume.

Source: Mintzer (1987).

CASE STUDY 2   Continued

Table 12.7 Costs and benefits of CFC control in the United States

Level of control	Discounted benefits ($ billion)	Discounted costs ($ billion)
80% cut	3533	22
50% cut	3488	13
20% cut	3396	12
Freeze	3314	7

Source: EPA (1987).

1990 by 59 nations, agreed to a complete phasing out of halons and CFCs by the year 2000. In addition, controls were agreed on two other substances implicated in the depletion of ozone, carbon tetra-chloride (to be eliminated by 2000) and methyl chloroform (by 2005). A sum of $240 million over the three years 1988–91 was allocated to assist in the funding of projects to substitute from ozone-depleting substances in poorer counties.

As we saw in Chapter 9, the USA introduced in 1978 a ban on the use of halons in aerosol propellants. Unfortunately, the effectiveness of that programme was largely mitigated by the substitution of CFC-11 and CFC-12 for halons. In August 1988, the United States introduced a tradable permits scheme for CFC usage, administered by the US EPA, to meet its responsibilities under the London Protocol. The effectiveness of this scheme was assessed in Chapter 9, Box 9.4.

CASE STUDY 3   The economics of the Greenhouse Effect

The global warming process: causes and consequences

This section contains a discussion of some of the central issues concerning possible global climate change. We begin with an overview of the causes and consequences of global warming.

The economic activity–energy–emissions relationship

Figure 12.13 provides us with a simple schema, in terms of which we can analyse the processes which are collectively known as the Greenhouse Effect. The first step in understanding the global warming process involves relating economic activity at any point in time to an associated level and pattern of energy and material flows, corresponding to which are flows of GHG emissions. For any given level and composition of energy use, the amounts of carbon emissions can be ascertained from coefficients which are known with some accuracy (see Perman, 1994). Carbon emissions are not caused only by fossil fuel use, of course. Another important source is defor-estation, which represents a substantial net con-tributor, but one about whose magnitude we remain very uncertain. Agricultural activity and the decom-position and disposal of waste are important emitters of methane. Chlorofluorocarbon (CFC) emissions are related to the level of activity and choice of techniques in the industrial and personal sectors, and are essentially independent of the level of energy demand. Table 12.8 summarises estimates of current carbon dioxide (CO_2) and other trace gas emissions and atmospheric concentrations, while Table 12.9 describes the economic activities which appear to influence the main forms of GHG emissions.

It is possible to account for GHG emissions by economic sector using energy augmented input–output modelling, as we show in Chapter 14, and much empirical work has been done using this technique. The task is relatively straightforward for carbon emissions, but is more difficult for the non carbon-based GHG emissions.

Perhaps because our knowledge of the causes and magnitudes of carbon pollution is relatively strong, there has been a tendency for policy targets to be couched only in terms of carbon emissions. But this warrants caution, as climate change is dependent upon the changing levels and mix of the whole set of greenhouse gases. Ideally, therefore, we should consider the relative 'warming' contribu-tions of the individual gases, and set appropriate targets for the whole range of relevant gases. Matters are further complicated as there is an important distinction to be drawn between the *instantaneous* impacts and the *long run* (or equilibrium) impacts of each GHG (see Appendix 1). Rather than modelling each gas separately, typical approaches (e.g. Nordhaus, 1991a) use an aggregate index of GHG, expressed in terms of carbon dioxide (or carbon) equivalent mass. Recent estimates of CO_2 equivalence for individual GHGs, and their relative contributions to impact and equilibrium warming, are provided in Appendix 1.

continued

CASE STUDY 3   Continued

The dominance of CO_2 as a GHG clearly emerges from those data.

Emissions forecasting

Whereas *current* additions to the stocks of GHG are well understood in the case of CO_2 and CFCs, and accurately measured *ex post* for other trace gases, forecasting *future* emissions is, of course, less accurate. This requires forecasts of changes in the level of energy demand (which in turn depend on population, price levels, GNP, etc.), its composition by fuel type, and the level of technology applied to the energy production and consumption processes (to determine energy efficiency levels). Of particular importance is the uncertainty surrounding energy demand growth in developing economies. Chandler

(1988), Keepin (1988) and Edmonds (1988) explore this issue with reference to the future energy demand of China, an economy whose emissions will have a very important impact on future atmospheric GHG concentrations.

Among many good examples of energy forecasting that one could cite, is the excellent global energy and emissions modelling using the IEA/ORAU CO_2 emissions model (see Reilly *et al.*, 1987). Reilly *et al* subject that model to a rigorous sensitivity analysis, comparing the properties of the IEA/ORAU model with those of other energy demand models under a variety of assumptions. Reilly finds the median annual rate of CO_2 emission growth to be in the interval 0.5–1.0%. This is substantially lower than post-World War Two experience and lower than that found by most earlier studies. It should be compared with the 3.0% rate assumed in the IPCC (Intergovernmental Panel on Climate Change, United Nations) 1990 Reports. However, uncertainty about the future emission rate was considerable. Of particular importance in shaping model predictions are the assumptions made about labour productivity, end-use efficiency improvements and the income elasticity of demand in developing countries.

Stocks and flows: the relationship between emissions and concentrations

The second step in GHG modelling attempts to relate emissions of GHG to their changing atmospheric concentrations, as the consequent climate responses over time depend primarily upon these concentrations. This relationship between emissions and concentrations depends upon two main factors. The first is the residence time of GHG molecules in the atmosphere in an 'active' form. Secondly, some emissions are absorbed by environmental sinks, and so the capacity and functioning of these sinks will shape the emissions–concentration relationship.

The active lifetime of greenhouse gases is incompletely understood. Estimates have been made of the expected life of different GHG molecules, ranging from a few weeks for tropospheric ozone to 100 years or more for others, such as CFCs. If these lives were stable, we could predict rates of decay. Unfortunately, they are probably not stable, and may depend upon the stock levels and mixes of the various GHGs.

Although many GHG pollutants are long lived, they are not perfectly persistent pollutants. New emissions are adding to stocks whilst decay and transformation processes will be reducing stock

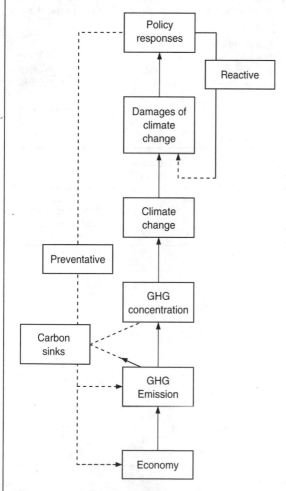

Fig 12.13 Modelling the Greenhouse Effect.

continued

CASE STUDY 3   Continued

levels. It follows that global warming is not an irreversible process (although some of the *consequences* of warming undoubtedly would be).

Our knowledge of the emissions–concentrations relationship is also incomplete because of feedback effects. As atmospheric concentrations change, the capacity of environmental sinks to take up carbon and other pollutants changes. But these dynamics are very poorly understood. Schneider (1989) provides an excellent summary of the current state of knowledge in this area.

Climate change models

In response to altered GHG concentrations, climatic changes occur, through lagged adjustment processes. These processes are usually analysed using large-scale global circulation (GCM) models, which try to represent atmospheric and oceanic dynamic processes. Arising from simulations using GCM models, a reasonably clear picture is now emerging of the probable impacts on global climate, summarised in Table 12.10. Not surprisingly, substantial uncertainties remain, including poorly understood feedback effects. For example, warming will be associated with changes in the nature of cloud cover, altering the net balance of radiative flows. Some scientists maintain that uncertainty is so large that we cannot even be certain of the *direction* of climate change.

Two other well-known limitations of our present understanding warrant emphasis. Firstly, the current state of climate modelling does not permit consideration of transition paths between equilibrium climates. Secondly, regional modelling of climate changes is still in its infancy, providing little guidance on impacts at geographically disaggregated levels. The Intergovernmental Panel on Climate Change (IPCC) Climate Panel 1990 Report states that existing models cannot yet predict likely changes in even the direction, let alone magnitude, of events such as tropical typhoons, hurricanes and winter storms for mid-latitude regions. The uncertainties associated with cloud cover are particularly severe.

The costs of climate change

The next step is to relate climate changes to their associated 'damages', which may be both positive and negative. Climate changes will impact directly

continued

Table 12.8 Sources and growths of greenhouse gas (GHG) emissions

GHG	1990 gross annual emissions (GT)[a]	Net increment to atmosphere per annum (GT)	1990 concentration in atmosphere (ppm)	Annual growth rate (%) of concentration	Annual growth rate (%) of emissions	Emission reductions (%) required to 'stabilise' concentration at current levels
CO$_2$ in carbon equivalent:						
Fossil fuel	5.3–5.6		353			0.5–1.0 (Reilly) 3.0 (IPCC)
Limestone	0.1	} 2.9	(1986–IPCC)	} 0.5		
Deforestation/land	1.0–2.0					
Total CO$_2$	6.3–7.7	2.9	353	0.5		60–80 (50% on EPA data)
Methane			1.67 (EPA–1986)	0.9 0.54 (EPA)		10 (EPA) 15–20 (other studies)
CFC, HFC			0.0006 (EPA–1986)	4.0 1.37 (CFC 11/12)		70–85
N$_2$O			0.34 (EPA–1986)	0.25 0.10 (EPA)		70–80

[a] 1 GT $= 10^{15}$ g = 1 billion (10^9) tonnes, where 1 tonne = 1000 kg.

Sources: Various, including IPCC (1990) and EPA (1989).

CASE STUDY 3   Continued

Table 12.9 GHG emissions by human activity (% of CO_2 equivalents, 1985)

Activity	USA	Rest of OECD	Eastern Europe	CP Asia India	Others
Fossil fuel energy production and use	70	56	79	41	23
CFC applications	25	35	13	4	8
Agriculture	4	7	6	49	36
Other industrial uses	1	2	2	5	3
Forest/wood burning	0	0	0	1	30
Total (%)	100	100	100	100	100
Total gigatonnes of carbon	2.4	2.5	2.2	1.6	3.5

Source: McKinsey (1989).

Table 12.10 Summary of major equilibrium climate responses to a doubling of atmospheric CO_2 concentration

Global–mean surface warming (very probable). For an equivalent doubling of atmospheric CO_2, the long-term global mean surface warming is expected to be in the range of 1.5°C to 4.5°C.

Global–mean precipitation increase (very probable). Increased surface heating will lead to increased evaporation and, therefore, to greater global mean precipitation. Some individual regions might well experience decreases in rainfall.

Reduction of sea ice (very probable). As the climate warms, total sea ice is expected to be reduced.

Polar winter surface warming (very probable). As the sea ice boundary is shifted poleward enhanced surface warming in winter polar regions is likely. Warming of the polar surface air may be as much as three times the global mean warming.

Summer continental dryness/warming (likely in the long term). Marked long-term drying of the soil moisture over some mid-latitude interior continental regions during summer. This dryness mainly caused by an earlier termination of snowmelt and rainy periods, and an earlier onset of the spring-to-summer reduction of soil wetness.

High-latitude precipitation increase (probable). As the climate warms, the increased poleward penetration of warm, moist air should increase the average annual precipitation in high latitudes.

Rise in global mean sea level (probable). A rise in mean sea level is generally expected due to thermal expansion of sea water in the warmer future climate. Far less certain is the contribution due to melting or calving of land ice.

Source: EPA (1988).

upon the physical and ecological environments, again with lagged effects, and these may well induce additional indirect impacts. The magnitudes of damage are uncertain, reflecting the fact that such outcomes are the result of a sequence of processes, each of which introduces additional uncertainties. For any given level of warming, however, current knowledge permits estimates of damage which are sufficiently accurate to make some headway in thinking about desirable policy. The 1990 IPCC Report predicts that by 2020, the sea level will be 4 to 13 inches (10 to 33 cm) higher (best estimate 8 inches or 20 cm), based upon a 'no change of behaviour' scenario. Several inner continental areas will experience much increased probabilities of severe drought and soil degradation. Serious damage to hundreds of millions of people within developing countries by 2020 is expected to operate through effects on farming. Those regions experiencing high population growth and/or decreasing soil fertility are likely to suffer the most.

Nordhaus (1990a, 1990b) discusses preliminary estimates of the likely order of magnitude of damages when measured in monetary terms, based largely upon a wide variety of research evidence collated by the United States Environmental Protection Agency (EPA, 1988, 1989). He suggests that advanced industrial economies will suffer relatively little damage (less than 1% of national income annually over the next half century) because most measured economic activity is insensitive to climatic variation. Only agriculture, forestry and coastal activities are sensitive to any substantial amount, and in the US for example, these sectors generate just 3% of gross national product (GNP).

continued

However, Nordhaus recognises that the impact on some unmarketed activities or resources (such as biological diversity, amenity values and environmental quality) might be severe. For developing countries, prospects are worse. In these economies one-third of GNP arises in agriculture, and productivity is highly sensitive to climate factors, making these regions highly vulnerable to climatic change. Whilst Nordhaus tends to be fairly optimistic in his assessment of the costs of climate change, possibly reflecting the North American orientation of his numerical work, Hansen (1988, 1990) is markedly more pessimistic. His GCM simulations suggest major increases in the frequency of severe drought in many developing countries, and markedly higher likelihoods of desertification, conclusions which are found with greater conviction in simulations from GCM models which are augmented to deal with soil hydrology and vegetative cover.

Whereas some forecasts of the mean value of damage arising from modest increases in world temperature have suggested relatively low levels of damage, a number of authors argue that restricting attention to the mean value of possible outcomes is inappropriate. Barbier and Pearce (1990) and Hansen (1990), for example, point to the inherent uncertainty in our knowledge of climate change outcomes. The risks of global climate change cannot be spread easily, if at all; some consequences of climate change would be irreversible, and the range of possible outcomes includes those for which damage values would be incalculably high. Risk aversion would then imply a different optimal policy rule than the one that would derive from consideration of mean outcomes alone.

Policy responses

We can distinguish between anticipatory and reactive policy. An optimal anticipatory policy would estimate expected costs and benefits of pollution emissions abatement, identify a socially optimal abatement target, and select policy instruments which minimise the expected costs of attaining that target. It is likely (but not certain) that anticipatory policy will be *preventative*, mainly taking the form of attempts to reduce the flows of emissions. Reactive policy would be mainly *adaptive*, attempting to minimise the adverse impacts of climate change *ex post*. More generally, any policy which seeks to reduce expected losses by *ex ante* intervention can be called anticipatory policy. Reactive policy is developed as outcomes unfold,

and is usually designed to minimise adjustment burdens to processes that are regarded as uncontrollable or unforecastable.

Some writers argue that our current state of knowledge is too poor for anticipatory policy to be a rational choice, and that until this knowledge base improves, policy should be reactive or adaptive. On the other hand, if expectations of gains and losses were reasonably accurate, then anticipatory policy is likely to be more beneficial than the alternative option of responding to events *ex post*, as fewer policy options will have been foreclosed and so least-cost programmes can be selected.

If anticipatory or preventative policy is adopted, interventions will probably include measures enhancing fuel efficiency and energy conservation, although these will show rapidly diminishing returns as the scale of abatement rises, or tax/subsidy schemes which encourage substitution between types of fuel. Each of these would change the relationship between economic activity and pollutant emission. Simulation analyses which attempt to project GHG emissions over time typically assume that the combined effects of technical progress and price-driven substitution effects will lead the emissions-to-output coefficient to fall by 1% per annum *even in the absence of policy controls* (Boero et al., 1991). If incentive schemes or regulations were introduced, the coefficient could fall more rapidly. There is also scope for afforestation programmes and other schemes to increase biomass, which can act as carbon sinks, although it is difficult to know how costly these schemes would be to implement on a large scale. Nordhaus (1991a) estimates cost-minimising GHG emissions abatement, and we illustrate his results in Figure 12.14. A GHG emissions reduction of between 10% and 20% (relative to 1990 levels) is achievable at modest cost, with diminishing returns setting in rapidly after that. The 60% cut in emissions recently called for by the IPCC (1990) would, even if efficiently chosen and slowly introduced, cost $300 billion annually in 1992 prices. A more complete survey of recent evidence on abatement costs is given later in this case study.

Adaptive policy measures to minimise the damage associated with (uncontrolled) climate change might include construction of sea walls and other coastal defence schemes, and the development of crop species with high tolerance to climatic fluctuations. Sea defence construction to protect all river deltas of

continued

CASE STUDY 3   Continued

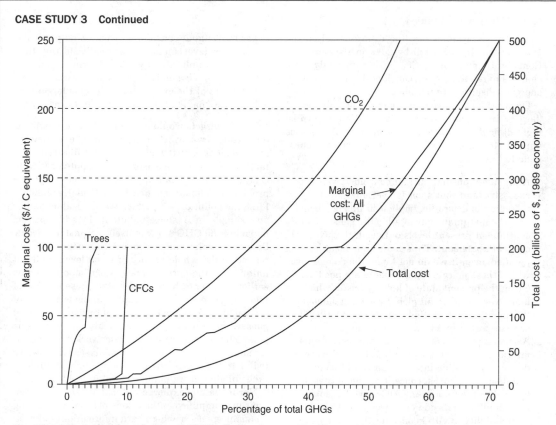

Fig 12.14 Marginal and total costs of GHG reduction (source: Nordhaus, 1991a).

the world against a one-metre sea level rise has been estimated to cost 0.04% of world output over the next century (Nordhaus, 1990b).

Economically optimal targets and least cost control measures

In so far as policy has addressed global warming, two complementary approaches may be discerned. First, attempts have been made to secure internationally agreed targets for emissions of pollutants. In this, there has been some limited success (although it is too early to know whether commitments will be realised). The 1988 Toronto Conference recommended that, as an initial step, global CO_2 emissions be reduced by 20% from their 1988 level by the year 2005, with the brunt of this to be borne by the developed countries. In November 1988, the Hamburg Conference recommended the more stringent target of 30% reduction by developed countries by the year 2000.

Such targets have typically been international, and most countries have made commitments conditional upon all nations acting together. The UK's policy is to stabilise CO_2 emissions at the 1990 level (160 million tonnes per annum) by the year 2005, provided other European Union (EU) countries at least match that objective. A number of countries have made unconditional commitments to national targets and some independent initiatives have been made by groups of countries, such as the EU. Secondly, within some countries, national (and local) emission standards have been established, implemented either by emission quantity/technology regulations, or by the use of tradable emission permit or pollution tax systems.

Within the general objective of reducing GHG emissions, energy efficiency schemes have figured prominently in industrialised economies, largely as a result of the beliefs that such schemes are cost-effective, have desirable additional effects, and low indirect costs. The scope for energy conservation is apparently large; in the period 1973–1982, for

continued

CASE STUDY 3   Continued

example, energy intensity (the ratio of final energy consumption to GDP) fell by 20% in the European Community, suggesting that with sufficiently large changes in relative prices, considerable reductions in energy utilisation are possible.

On what basis have existing emissions abatement 'targets' been established? This question is surprisingly difficult to answer, but a number of premises appear to underpin recent discussions. These include:

1 A presumption that current emission levels are excessive, and that some (as yet unknown) reduction is desirable. Implicit in this is a belief that the marginal costs of allowing emissions to continue at present levels outweigh the marginal costs of abatement. Thus some abatement is justified, even if we do not know the domain over which these marginal net benefits are positive. Given the present state of knowledge (in which we know very little about global warming damage), this position is essentially an article of faith, albeit one supported by informed judgement.

2 A second premise is that in the absence of reliable information on the magnitudes of global warming damage, a sensible interim step would be to stabilise atmospheric concentrations at present levels. For the four main GHGs, the percentage reductions in emissions required to achieve long-term stability in GHG concentrations at current levels were given in Table 12.8. An economist, however, would find it difficult to support the objective that GHG concentrations should be stabilised at present levels. Not only is this target arbitrary, but it would require not just preventing emissions from rising above present levels but also dramatic reductions below those levels. Allowing no concentration rise is likely to be immensely costly, particularly if the adjustment to that goal is rapid (Ingham and Ulph, 1990). A long-term target will almost certainly require stabilisation at some level, but the level and the speed with which we should converge to it should be assessed through dynamic optimization.

3 A third assertion is that targets should be set with reference to long-term environmental goals. For example, Swart et al. (1989) suggest that appropriate indicator variables would be global mean temperature rise, supported by allowable rates of sea level rise. They propose GHG concentrations as monitoring instruments, with emission quotas as short-term national operational objectives. Economists see little validity in setting long-term goals directly in 'environmental' terms

per se. Without considering welfare, no particular rise in sea level can be ranked relative to any other. The same applies to any other environmental variable; an economist regards such variables as indicators of the extent to which some target is being satisfied, but not as targets in themselves.

Ideally, targets would be designed using a dynamic optimizing framework rather than the somewhat arbitrary bases that have dominated discussion so far. We have seen the use of dynamic optimization in Chapters 5 and 6, but applying such models to the problem of climate change is particularly difficult. First, the pollution with which we are dealing here is an example of a stock pollutant. In addition, the impact of the GHG stock is itself non-instantaneous. Damages which arise from GHG emissions are related to the whole history of stock levels, and not uniquely to the current stock. Most importantly, as earlier comments have shown, the present state of knowledge does not permit parametrization of several of the key functions except by using informed guesswork. However, even in the absence of reliable parameter estimates, such a framework can be used for simulations and sensitivity analyses which serve to illustrate the properties of optimal policies under a range of alternative parameter values.

Nordhaus has explored optimal steady-state solutions in a simplified optimal control framework, using 'plausible guesses' where hard information is absent. In an early paper he concluded that

> The current [optimal] control rates are in the 20% [of CO_2 emissions] range for any but the most robust growth trajectories.
>
> Nordhaus (1982), page 241

Nordhaus (1989) estimated the socially optimal level of taxes on carbon-based fuels to be $3 per ton of carbon, which would result in 9% abatement. However, uncertainty is such that the tax may need to be as high as $37 per ton of carbon, resulting in 28% abatement. In a subsequent paper Nordhaus (1990a), using data on costs and benefits from US EPA studies, found the optimal control to be around 17% of total global current emissions.

Emission abatement costs

Given the uncertainties surrounding costs of climate change, some analysts (for example Manne and Richels, 1989) conclude that economic analysis should restrict itself to a more limited objective, concentrating on emission abatement costs and

continued

CASE STUDY 3   Continued

abatement strategies in isolation from their expected benefits. Whilst there are very few convincing economic evaluations of the damages arising from climate change, there are now many empirical studies of abatement costs.

Boero *et al.* (1991), in an excellent survey of the macroeconomic consequences of controlling greenhouse gases, define the different types of abatement costs, and examine the relative merits of a number of alternative modelling methodologies. They classify abatement costs into three types:

(a) possible GDP gains (negative costs) from correction of market failures: so-called 'no regret' policies;

(b) continuing costs in the form of losses from curtailed energy use, consisting of foregone output or resource costs from energy-saving measures;

(c) transitional costs, due to disruption and premature scrapping of capital, and short run labour immobility.

Whilst transitional costs can be very important, few studies consider them explicitly. Most studies concentrate on category (b) costs. Several approaches can be identified in the attempts to measure these costs:

1 *Ad hoc* estimates of marginal costs per unit CO_2 saved for each abatement strategy considered in isolation.

2 Input–output models.

3 The incorporation of a technical abatement module into a macroeconomic model, which measures abatement costs of alternative carbon emission scenarios in terms of foregone consumption possibilities.

4 General equilibrium models, attempting to form a money measure of welfare costs such as the Hicksian equivalent or compensating variation (see Chapter 10 for an explanation of these concepts).

The *ad hoc* approach is exemplified by many of the pairwise comparisons of abatement strategies (e.g. Keepin and Kats (1988) for nuclear power *vis-à-vis* energy efficiency, and Hohmeyer (1988) for fossil versus renewable fuels), by the papers submitted by national governments to the IPCC Policy Panel (e.g. Department of Energy, 1989, for the UK) and by the McKinsey Report to the Ministerial Conference on Atmospheric Pollution and Climatic Change (McKinsey, 1989). This is cost-effectiveness analysis (CEA), discussed at length in Chapter 9, the essence of which is to identify cost-minimising techniques for

achieving certain predetermined goals, subject to the qualifications that only direct costs are measured and substitution possibilities and relative price effects are ignored. CEA ranks available options in terms of cost per unit objective, and so permits a narrowing of the range of options that are deemed worthy of further analysis. In a situation of uncertainty, CEA can be used to suggest where initial efforts may be most effectively deployed.

However, these studies do have serious limitations. The indirect effects that would arise if such schemes were implemented are not explored, and it is not possible to infer a 'best' mix and scale of programmes from the results because the approach has nothing to say about the benefits of various levels of abatement.

Claims are sometimes made that some limitation of global warming is available at negative cost, the so-called 'no regret' possibilities mentioned earlier. Often cited are industrial and domestic energy conservation programmes (Keepin and Katz; 1988, ACE, 1989). These arguments claim the existence of projects which would generate positive net present values but are not currently undertaken. These claims beg an important question: if outputs could be generated at lower cost by alternative techniques or if profitable projects exist, why are these alternatives not already selected? Explanations typically invoke information asymmetries, quantity constraints in capital markets or other causes of market failure. A good review of these explanations can be found in Fisher and Rothkopf (1989). However, one should be wary of viewing evidence of market failure as leading to the existence of a 'free lunch'; the costs of eliminating apparent inefficiencies are often far from negligible, and may outweigh the original efficiency losses associated with the market failure.

Input–output models are discussed at length in Chapter 13, and we restrict our discussion of this technique here to one application. Symons *et al.* (1991) use an input–output approach to examine the sectoral impacts and consumer price effects of a carbon tax on fossil fuels. These results are then used in a micro simulation programme, based upon a system of demand equations (the Institute of Fiscal Studies Simulation Programme for Indirect Taxation, SPIT, described in detail in Barker, 1990) to estimate the effects on consumer demand. Symons *et al.* conclude that a tax rate of 6.5 pence per kilogram of emitted CO_2 would reduce UK CO_2 emissions by 20%.

continued

CASE STUDY 3   Continued

The third approach is exemplified by the work of Manne and Richels (1989, 1990), using a model (Global 2100) which simulates CO_2–energy–economy interactions, which can be used to estimate the costs of carbon emissions limits. The model is highly aggregated to focus upon long-run energy–economy interactions, and permits a variety of assumptions to be made concerning elasticities of substitution (both between energy sources and between energy and other productive inputs) and rates of technological improvement. Costs of emission limits are measured in terms of present values of foregone consumption possibilities. Manne and Richels examine these costs under a set of scenarios reflecting varying degrees of constraint on the availability of emission abatement technologies. It is demonstrated that the costs can be significantly reduced by adoption of the best potential technologies (the least-cost case incurs costs equal to 22% of the baseline, most constrained, case).

Macroeconomic simulation models may be disaggregated to allow for the different energy intensities of different activities and to permit examination of alternative patterns of output and demand associated with alternative price vectors and/or stages of development. Examples of such models include Barker (1990) and Jorgensen and Wilcoxen (1990a,b,c). Other important globally aggregated macroeconomic models developed to date are Anderson and Bird (1990a,b), Cline (1991), Edmonds and Barns (1990a,b), Edmonds and Reilly (1985), and Mintzer (1987).

As Manne and Richels accept, the use of a computable general equilibrium (CGE) framework would permit a richer examination of policy options. Whalley and Wigle (1990) and Burniaux et al. (1991a,b), using the OECD/GREEN model, present CGE models of the consequences of emission abatement policy. Such models focus on static optimality in the allocation of resources, with endogenous prices serving as the means by which shocks (such as the introduction of carbon taxes) bring about new patterns of equilibrium in the allocation of resources. Unlike macroeconomic models, which are most suited to short and medium term analysis and the analysis of adjustment processes, CGE models are inherently long-run in nature, attempting to capture the final general equilibrium in all markets. We discuss CGE models a little further in Chapter 13.

From the various studies cited, it is difficult to ascertain a central tendency of the simulation results, as there is no consensus over choice of scenario investigated, projection time used, nor the proportionate reduction modelled. Results are also conditional upon assumptions made regarding rates of productivity growth in general and for energy, and the availability and cost of backstop fuels. The most complete comparison to date of simulation findings is given in Boero et al. (1991); Table 12.11, based on that comparison, provides a summary of the major simulation results to date. The table is constructed so that increasingly stringent control is applied as one goes down the rows. The first column states the change expected to be achieved in the final year of the projection (given in parentheses), expressed as a percentage of the base case projection for that final year. The second column states the final emission change relative to the 'reference' year (i.e. the year from which the model is parametrized). This latter figure is dependent upon the assumption made regarding actual world growth rates over the simulation period, and will therefore be very unreliable. However, it is included because international GHG diplomacy is usually based upon changes relative to a base reference year.

After standardising the results as far as possible, Boero et al. conclude that 'abatement of 40 to 50% relative to base might tentatively be expected to reduce long-run GDP by no more than 3% (a reduction in the growth rate of no more than one-tenth of 1% over thirty years followed by a resumption of normal growth).' (page S16). However, these cost estimates assume relatively slow adjustment in which no adjustment costs are incurred. Ingham and Ulph (1990) show that these costs are far from negligible, and would rise dramatically under rapid change.

The choice of policy instruments

Chapter 9 of this text was devoted to a general analysis of instruments for pollution control, and so we restrict attention here to a number of points that relate specifically to climate change.

Marketable permits, where control agencies have the flexibility to vary the stock of licences (as in the manner of open-market operations for short-term debt), offer an attractive and potentially efficient instrument for achieving targets in GHG emission abatement. Given that GHGs are uniformly mixing pollutants, an internationally coordinated permit regime would be required. Assuming that an overall global total of permits can be agreed, the method of allocating the quotas between and within nations remains to be decided, which raises major questions

continued

KING ALFRED'S COLLEGE
LIBRARY

CASE STUDY 3   Continued

Table 12.11 Estimates of GDP losses – main global models

Emission change		Study	Loss of GDP per annum at end of projection period (relative to baseline) (%)
Relative to baseline (%)	Relative to reference year (%)		
−37 (2020)	+17 (1985)	Burniaux *et al.* (1991b)	1.8
−39 (2025)	0 (1988)	Edmonds and Barns (1990a)	1.8 – world cooperation
−39 (2025)	0 (1988)	Edmonds and Barns (1990a)	4.0 – OECD action only
−40 (2050)	+162 (1990)	Edmonds and Reilly (1985)	1.0
−50 (2100)	n/a	Nordhaus (1990b)	1.0
−50 (2030)	n/a	Whalley and Wigle (1990)	4.2 – global tax case
−51 (2025)	−20 (1988)	Edmonds and Barns (1990a)	2.3
−68 (2050)	+17 (1990)	Anderson and Bird (1990a)	2.8
−69 (2025)	−50 (1988)	Edmonds and Barns (1990a)	5.7
−75 (2100)	+16 (1990)	Manne and Richels (1990)	5.0
−88 (2075)	−67 (1990)	Mintzer (1987)	3.0 – slow build-up case

of distributional equity and political acceptability. A marketable permit system avoids the need to set explicit national targets for emissions; the pattern of emissions that emerges after emissions trades have taken place will automatically ensure that the abatement burden is distributed between countries in a cost-efficient manner. Whilst tradability is sufficient to attain efficiency, the permit scheme offers a wide choice of different methods of initially allocating the permits, and so allows for whatever distributional targets are deemed to be appropriate. Grubb (1989a) provides an excellent critical survey of the various initial allocation options, and more detailed analyses are found in Hahn and Hester (1989b) and Bertram *et al.* (1989).

Clunies Ross (1990) demonstrates that until a tradable permits market is established, the actual cost that would be imposed on the emission of an extra tonne of CO_2 would be unknown; moreover, once established, the cost may vary considerably from year to year. This price uncertainty may interfere with the efficiency property of the instrument. Of more importance, Clunies Ross shows that high polluter governments (net purchasers of permits) will have little idea of the scale of transfers required in the initial phase, which may produce a reluctance to accept the scheme at all.

Carbon taxes are also appropriate policy instruments for initial action. They generate appropriate signals and incentives, concentrate on that emission which is of greatest importance, can be cheaply administered and generate revenue for other interventions, and can be set at varying levels so as to impose a gradual tightening of control over time. As a longer-term objective, they might be set so that prices of resources (and the goods derived from them) reflect full social costs, as and when more information becomes available. How large would carbon taxes have to be in order to attain reasonable abatement targets? Recent calculations by Barrett (1990) shed some light on this issue. Barrett's estimates of the tax rates required on fossil fuels to reduce CO_2 emissions by 20% in the short term (within three years) and the long-term (within ten years) are reproduced in Table 12.12.

Institute of Fiscal Studies estimates (see *The Economist*, 27 January 1990) suggest the annual revenue raised by these taxes would be $8 billion and $2.9 billion from the high (short run) and low (long run) rates given in Table 12.12. The latter figure is equal to the UK government's tax revenue in 1989/90 from oil and gas production.

Boero *et al.*, in their 1991 survey, quote central tendency estimates of tax rates from existing simulation work. In order to achieve reductions (in long-run equilibrium) of CO_2 emissions by around 40% relative to their uncontrolled levels, a tax rate of between $100 and $300 per tonne of carbon would be required. However, carbon taxes to achieve such magnitudes of global CO_2 reduction, but imposed in OECD countries alone, either would be prohibitively expensive (Burniaux *et al.*, 1991b) or could not achieve the target (Edmonds and Barns, 1990a).

Taxes, either on carbon content or on pollutant emissions more generally, have important implications for the tax structure within economies and the

continued

CASE STUDY 3   Continued

Table 12.12 Tax rates required to reduce carbon dioxide emissions by 20%

	Short run		Long run	
	Tax rate (%)	Change in demand (%)	Tax rate (%)	Change in demand (%)
Gas	40	−4	14	+3
Oil	54	−9	19	+4
Coal	67	−11	24	−25

competitiveness of economies in relative terms. Some analysts have advocated a switch from taxes on labour and capital to taxes on pollution to avoid excessive tax burdens, and schemes have been proposed to penalise nations who attempt to gain competitive advantage by not introducing emissions taxes. Good discussions of these issues are to be found in Grubb (1989a), Bertram et al., (1989), Weizsacker (1989), Hansen (1990), Brown (1989), and Kosmo (1989).

International, intranational and intergenerational compensations

Both climate changes and actions to deal with those changes will alter distributions of income and wealth over generations, across countries and between groups within countries. In this section, we consider briefly some of these distributional issues, commencing with those between nations.

International distribution issues

The direct impacts of global warming will bear down very unequally between different regions of the world. Whilst the strong consensus is that there will be few, if any, 'big winners' there will almost certainly be some very large losers (see Nordhaus, 1990a, and Hansen, 1990). Nordhaus claims that developed countries experiencing a doubling of CO_2 (within 100 years) are unlikely to experience annual losses in excess of 1% of GNP. Whilst he is unable to estimate a comparable figure for developing economies, Nordhaus suggests costs may be considerably higher there, and this is supported by the results of Hansen described previously. On average, therefore, the damage is expected to be inversely related to per capita income. Those economies with the greatest incentive to cut emissions (or otherwise limit climate change) tend to have the poorest resource base to implement preventive and adaptive policies.

If action is taken internationally to prevent global climate change, the potential also exists for substantial reallocations of income and wealth between economies. This is evident in the case of a CO_2 pollution tax, as any such tax, if levied uniformly in terms of carbon emissions, will have substantial effects upon the international terms of trade. The magnitude of these changes (and the associated pattern of receipts from the tax) will depend upon the level of the tax, and upon whether it is levied upon producers (thus acting like an export duty) or consumers (and so acting as an import tariff). The effects of abatement policy instruments upon the international terms of trade have received very little attention in economic analysis so far.

A second aspect of abatement policy instruments is of importance in considering distributional issues. It is commonly assumed that any international programme will involve official resource transfers from more to less affluent nations, partly because this would be a precondition of acceptability, and partly because affluent countries have been predominant contributors to existing stocks of GHG in attaining their current levels of income and wealth, as can be seen in Table 12.13. The literature on marketable permits has paid much attention to the distributional implications of alternative initial allocations of permits. One of the attractions of systems of marketable emission permits is that through the initial allocation of permits, they can attain desired distributions whilst simultaneously sustaining efficiency goals. For example, the widely advocated proposal to allocate permits initially on a per capita basis implies considerable resource shifts from developed to developing countries, whereas allocation on the basis of existing emissions would be distributionally neutral. Having said this, a permit system so designed would require developed nations to have the political will to make substantial transfers. Furthermore, not all 'big emitters' on a per capita basis are affluent, and it will be particularly hard to design schemes acceptable to

continued

CASE STUDY 3   Continued

Table 12.13 Greenhouse index ranking and percent share of global emissions, 1989 (source: World Resources 1992–93, page 13)

Intergovernmental Panel on Climate Change (IPCC)		Rank	World Resources	
Percent	Country		Country	Percent
17.8	United States	1	United States	18.4
13.6	U.S.S.R.	2	U.S.S.R.	13.5
9.1	China	3	China	8.4
4.7	Japan	4	Japan	5.6
4.1	India	5	Brazil	3.8
3.9	Brazil	6	India	3.5
3.4	Germany(a)	7	Germany(a)	3.6
2.2	United Kingdom	8	United Kingdom	2.4
2.0	Mexico	9	Mexico	2.0
1.7	Indonesia	10	Italy	1.8
1.7	Canada	11	France	1.7
1.6	Italy	12	Canada	1.7
1.5	France	13	Indonesia	1.6
1.5	Thailand	14	Poland	1.4
1.5	Poland	15	Thailand	1.4
1.4	Colombia	16	Colombia	1.4
1.1	Myanmar	17	Australia	1.1
1.1	Nigeria	18	South Africa	1.1
1.1	Australia	19	Myanmar	1.1
1.1	South Africa	20	Spain	1.1
0.9	Cote d'Ivoire	21	Nigeria	1.1
0.9	Spain	22	Cote d'Ivoire	0.9
0.8	Korea, Rep	23	Korea, Rep	0.8
0.8	Philippines	24	Czechoslovakia	0.7
0.7	Czechoslovakia	25	Malaysia	0.7
0.7	Malaysia	26	Philippines	0.7
0.7	Romania	27	Romania	0.7
0.7	Viet Nam	28	Lao People's Dem Rep	0.7
0.7	Lao People's Dem Rep	29	Viet Nam	0.6
0.6	Saudi Arabia	30	Saudi Arabia	0.6
0.6	Iran, Islamic Rep	31	Iran, Islamic Rep	0.6
0.6	Argentina	32	Netherlands	0.6
0.5	Venezuela	33	Argentina	0.5
0.5	Netherlands	34	Venezuela	0.5
0.5	Ecuador	35	Yugoslavia	0.5
0.5	Korea, Dem People's Rep	36	Ecuador	0.5
0.5	Yugoslavia	37	Pakistan	0.5
0.5	Peru	38	Peru	0.5
0.5	Pakistan	39	Korea, Dem People's Rep	0.5
0.4	Bangladesh	40	Turkey	0.4
0.4	Turkey	41	Belgium	0.4
0.4	Madagascar	42	Madagascar	0.4
0.4	Zaire	43	Zaire	0.4
0.4	Belgium	44	Bulgaria	0.3
0.3	Sudan	45	Greece	0.3
0.3	Bulgaria	46	Sudan	0.3
0.3	Cameroon	47	Egypt	0.3
0.3	Egypt	48	Bangladesh	0.3
0.3	Greece	49	Cameroon	0.3
0.8	Iraq	50	Hungary	0.3

Sources: 1. Intergovernmental Panel on Climate Change (IPCC), Climate Change: The IPCC Scientific Assessment, J. Houghton, G.J. Jenkins, and J.J. Ephraums, eds. (Cambridge University Press, Cambridge, U.K., 1990). 2. Chapter 24, 'Atmosphere and Climate,' Tables 24.1 and 24.2. Note: a. Data for Germany include both the former Federal Republic of Germany and the German Democratic Republic.

CASE STUDY 3   Continued

several of the Eastern and Central European economies, for example.

Equity within economies

Almost all forms of preventative measure to limit
climate change can have substantial redistributive
effects *within* economies. The case of taxes on carbon
emissions illustrates this. Carbon taxes would be
regressive in impact whether they are additional to or
substitutes for existing taxes. Some evidence on this
is reported in Pearson and Smith (1990), in which it is
shown that a 15% VAT rate on domestic heating fuel
(which was zero-rated in the UK in 1990) would cut
demand by 5.5% overall. However, the demand from
the lowest decile would fall by 10% while that of the
highest by less than 2%, because of the relative
impact of the charge. A dilemma is thus posed for tax
schemes which aim to switch the base of tax from
income to pollution-related expenditures. Although
revenue neutrality may be achieved (which can
prevent loss of national competitiveness), other
transfers would be required if distributional neutrality were sought. Symons *et al.* (1991) use an
augmented input–output framework (described earlier) to demonstrate that a 6.5p/kg carbon tax would
be sufficient to meet a 20% CO_2 emissions reduction.
However, this would have 'dramatic adverse distributional effects for low income households' (page 20).
The authors argue that it is possible to design a larger

CO_2 tax (11–12 p/kg, equivalent to a rate of \$61.5 per
tonne carbon) in conjunction with tax/benefit changes
that maintains fiscal neutrality and largely avoids
those adverse effects upon distribution.

In addition to redistribution between household
groups, there are likely to be substantial sectoral
income shifts as a result of some forms of policy
measure. Jorgensen and Wilcoxen (1990a,b,c) have
employed macroeconomic modelling techniques to
estimate the effects of environmental legislation on
the US economy. The magnitude of potential impacts
can be gauged from Jorgensen's estimate that a 20%
drop in US carbon emissions would be associated
with a 79% fall in US coal output. To the extent that
sectoral production is geographically specialised (as
it certainly is for primary fuel sources), sectoral
impacts will have regionally specific distribution
effects too.

Equity between generations

The issue of intergenerational equity and compensation is more complex. Failure to restrict the growth of
emissions today incurs costs on future generations, in
just the same way as this generation is affected by
warming damages resulting from emissions in earlier
periods. The issues of intergenerational equity and
sustainability were discussed extensively in Chapters 2 and 3, and there is no need to repeat those
earlier discussions here.

Discussion questions

1 Discuss the proposition that marketable emissions
permits are more appropriate than emissions taxes
for controlling regional and global pollutants
because of the much lower transfer costs associated
with the former instrument.

2 Consider the following extracts from an article in
The Independent newspaper (28 March 1995) by the
economist Frances Cairncross:

Work by William Cline, a scrupulous and scientifically
literate American economist, suggests that the benefits
of taking action do not overtake the costs until about
2150. And Mr Cline sees global warming largely in terms
of costs. Yet it is inconceivable that a change of such
complexity will not bring gains ... as well as losses.

Given the difficulties of doing something about climate
change, should we try? Some measures are certainly worth
taking because they make sense in their own right. ...
Removing such [energy] subsidies would make the
economy work more efficiently and benefit the

environment, too.

Indeed, wise governments should go further, and
deliberately shift the tax burden away from earning and
saving ... towards energy consumption.

Beyond that, governments should do little. The most
rational course is to adapt to climate change, when it
happens .... Adaption is especially appropriate for poor
countries once they have taken all the low-cost and
no-cost measures they can find. Given the scarcity of
capital, it makes good sense for them to delay investing in
expensive ways to curb carbon dioxide output. Future
economic growth is likely to make them rich enough to
offset those effects of climate change that cannot be
prevented.

Provide a critical assessment of these arguments.

Problems

Compare and contrast the cost-effectiveness of

(a) a sulphur dioxide emission tax

(b) a sulphur dioxide emission tax levied at the same rate as in (a), together with an arrangement by which emissions tax revenues are used to subsidise capital equipment designed to 'scrub' sulphur from industrial and power generation emissions.

Further reading

Game theory

A good discussion of game theory, at an elementary level, is to be found in Varian (1987), Chapters 27, 31 and 32. See also Maler (1990). Barrett (1990) explores cooperative and non-cooperative outcomes for a range of types of externality. Hoel (1989) demonstrates the worrying result that 'unselfish' unilateral action can result in outcomes which lead to greater levels of emission than in its absence. Dasgupta (1990) shows that cooperation need not require an outside agency to enforce agreements and that such cooperation could be sustained over time by means of norms of conduct.

International coordination of policy

Interesting and informative accounts are given in Grubb (1989a), Hahn and Hester (1989b) and Tietenberg, (1984, 1990).

Acid rain

The scientific basis is well described in Kemp (1990) and a definitive study is to be found in NAPAP (1990), the National Acid Precipitation Assessment Program, 1989 Annual Report. A good analysis of the acid rain issue is to be found in Adams and Page (1985). Biannual editions of *World Resources* provide regular updates of the scientific evidence and economic assessments. Good economic analyses may be found in Feldman and Raufer (1982) and Tietenberg (1989).

Ozone depletion

Kemp (1990), WMO (1991) and French (1990) describe the scientific basis of ozone depletion. Biannual editions of *World Resources* provide regular updates of the evidence, with a good summary given on page 200 of *World Resources 1992–93*. An excellent economic analysis is in Bailey (1982).

The Greenhouse Effect

A more complete presentation of the 'scientific basis' for the Greenhouse Effect, written from the perspective of an economist, is given in Cline (1991). Schneider (1989) and Cline (1989, 1991) provide excellent accounts of the potential climate changes due to global warming, and Common (1989), Hansen (1990) and Nordhaus (1991a) discuss the uncertainties involved in damage estimation. Assessments of the economic costs of measures to reduce GHG emissions are provided in Department of Energy (1989) for the UK, and in Nordhaus (1990a, 1990b) at the global level. Other studies include Barbier *et al.* (1990) and Williams (1989, 1990).

Tietenberg (1984, 1990) discusses the possible use of tradable emissions permits, and a persuasive argument that internationally tradable permits represents the best approach for international action towards the Greenhouse Effect is given in Grubb (1989a). See also Bertram *et al.* (1989) and Hahn and Hester (1989b). For other analyses of policy instruments for controlling global pollutants, see Barbier and Pearce (1990), Baumol and Oates (1988), Opschoor and Vos (1989), Pearce (1991b) and Bertram *et al.* (1989).

Appendix 1

Instantaneous and equilibrium warming contributions of greenhouse gases

Knowledge of the relative importance of different greenhouse gases to global warming is important for a number of reasons. In particular, the information can be used, in conjunction with relative abatement costs, to identify the cost-effectiveness of strategies dealing with the various GHGs (or to design an optimal 'mix' for abatement targets).

Two aspects need to be considered. First, what are the instantaneous impacts of each GHG on climate forcing, and secondly, what is the long-term warming potential of each gas? Warming potential differs from instantaneous impact because of differing residence periods. The instantaneous impact is defined as the product of the increase in atmospheric concentration of a gas and its current per unit radiative impact. Warming potential (or long-term equilibrium effect) is the integral of instantaneous impacts over a suitably chosen time horizon, taking

Table 12.14a Warming potential of GHGs

GHG	Warming potential (relative to CO_2)
CO_2	1.0
CO	2.2
CH_4	10
N_2O	180
HCFC-22	410
CFC-11	1300
CFC-12	3700

Table 12.14b Relative contribution to warming of individual GHGs

GHG	Relative contribution (%)	
	Instantaneous	Total (equilibrium)
CO_2	76.1	94.7
Methane	9.6	0.8
CFCs	11.6	3.3
Nitrous oxides	2.7	1.2

into account decay and transformation processes operating on the stock of the gas.

Lashof and Ahuja (1990) have recently developed an index of these two quantities for the main trace gases. They demonstrate that while the contribution of CO_2 was 57% of the total due to all GHG emissions (in 1985), the overall (long-term integral) warming potential of these emissions was 71.5%. On the latter basis, carbon emissions have a relative importance considerably greater than is conventionally thought to be the case.

On a weight basis, the total global warming potential of different GHGs is calculated as shown in Table 12.14a.

Nordhaus (1990b) reports the estimated contribution of different GHGs to global warming, from 1986 to 2100, using data and projections from the US Environmental Protection Agency. The contributions predicted from the four main GHGs are shown in Table 12.14b.

For further information on the warming contribution of different GHGs, the reader should study Grubb (1989a,b), Nordhaus (1991a) and Lashof and Ahuja (1990). The most complete account is provided in the text by Houghton *et al.* (1990), referenced as IPCC (1990) in the bibliography.

CHAPTER 13

Environmental input–output modelling

Introduction

Sensible and effective environmental policies require an understanding of the relationships between basic economic activities – production, consumption, trade – and the physical environment in which those activities take place. Continued growth in world output and population, allied to greater knowledge of the nature and extent of the impact of economic activity on the environment, has raised fears that current levels of production cannot be sustained without irreparable damage to the environment. Measures are therefore demanded to prevent, limit or repair environmental damage by, for example, reducing carbon dioxide emissions, slowing down or reversing deforestation, encouraging the introduction of 'clean' technologies, and so on.

Although much of the scientific evidence on the nature and effects of economic activities on the environment is still uncertain and controversial, there is enough to establish that measures of environmental protection are essential or prudent over a wide range of economy–environment inter-actions, and that the implementation of many of these measures cannot be left to market forces, for reasons discussed earlier (see Chapter 4). Appropriate policy measures, however, demand a detailed understanding of the environmental impact of particular economic activities and hence the need to *model* the relationship(s) – whether formally or implicitly – between the economy and the environment. For instance, which economic activities result in the emission of carbon dioxide gases, and by how much would particular economic activity levels have to be reduced to bring about a reduction of, say, 20% in CO_2 emissions? What level of 'carbon tax' might be necessary to bring about such a reduction?

What would be the effects of such a tax on the incomes of different types of household? For many policy purposes it is not enough to know simply the nature and direction of the changes brought about by a particular measure (or by the failure to implement a measure): a *quantitative* estimate of the effects of the policy (or of its absence) is needed. It is for this purpose that models of interaction between the economy and the environment are constructed.

As well as predicting the physical and/or economic impact of actual policy measures (including policies of no change), models can be particularly useful in *simulating* the effects of proposed or potential policies, along the lines of '...*if* a carbon tax is introduced, *then* the effect on emissions will be a reduction of x%, *but* GDP growth will also be reduced by y% on average over the next five years...'.

By assessing and comparing the simulated quantitative effects of a range of feasible policy options, governments can hope to identify the 'best' (or least bad) policy or policy mix, avoid policy combinations which are inconsistent or which work in opposite directions, and achieve some kind of optimal trade-off between different, and potentially conflicting economic and environmental objectives.[1] Moreover, such simulation exercises underpin the formulation and implementation of proactive environmental policies, which attempt to anticipate or avoid undesirable outcomes by appropriate preventive

[1] Of course, what is optimal to a government may not seem optimal to other interest groups, such as environmentalists, or the unemployed, or the political opposition, each of whom may, and most probably will, have different social welfare functions (or different perceptions of *the* Social Welfare function), and will attach different weights to particular economic and environmental outcomes.

measures. Although formal simulation modelling is not a precondition for proactive environmental policies, it can powerfully influence public attitudes and policy-making, a recent example being predictions and simulations of the effects of greenhouse gases on global warming. In the absence of quantitative models of economy–environment interaction, policy is more likely to be reactive rather than proactive, which may be too late if environmental damage is irreversible (e.g. species extinction).

As in mainstream economics, a wide variety of model types have been used to examine economy–environment interactions, though given the often pervasive nature of environmental issues and outcomes, system-wide or macro-type models are more common than partial equilibrium models. Included in the former category are materials-balance, input–output and computable general equilibrium (CGE) models, and linear and non-linear programming (optimisation) models. This chapter is largely devoted to a discussion of environmental input–output (I/O) models and their application. I/O models have been used quite extensively in environmental economics, particularly in studies related to energy and pollution, and are the basis of more complex (and data-hungry) variants such as CGE and linear programming models. Although I/O models incorporate a number of simplifying assumptions which require a degree of caution in interpreting the precision of their results, they are mathematically highly tractable, less demanding of data than many other multisectoral models, and offer a flexible and readily understood framework for analysing economy–environment links. It must be stressed, however, that availability and quality of data are still serious impediments to realistic environmental modelling work, including I/O modelling.

The following section presents and explains the basic input–output model and its solution, while the next section shows how the basic model can be extended to incorporate economy–environment interactions, and includes examples of environmental input–output models and their application. These applications are concerned with the 'real' side of the economy, that is, with physical or constant value flows. We then show how the equations of the model can be reformulated to analyse cost and price implications of environmental policies, such as the effects of pollution taxes on industrial costs and retail prices.

Recently, there has been growing interest in the use of computable general equilibrium (CGE) models in simulating and predicting the impact of environmental policies, particularly in cases where

distributional issues (between households, or regions, or countries) are prominent. The last main section briefly reviews the nature of environmental CGE models and their application.

The basic input–output model

The basis of the input–output system is the *transactions table*, which is essentially an extended version of the national accounts (or, in the case of regional input–output, of regional accounts) in which inter-industry transactions – that is, flows of goods and services between industries – are explicitly included and indeed form the centrepiece of the system of accounts.[2] This contrasts with the conventional national accounts in which inter-industry transactions are 'netted out', and the accounts record only the value added by each industry, and the value of sales to final buyers.

Table 13.1 is a hypothetical example of a transactions table, in which all production activities in the economy have been allocated to one of three sectors. Looking along any row of the table shows what the sector on the *left* sold to each sector at the *top*, e.g.

$$
\begin{aligned}
\text{Primary Sector Sales} &= \underset{\text{(Primary)}}{0} + \underset{\text{(Manuf.)}}{400} + \underset{\text{(Services)}}{0} \\
&\quad + \underset{\text{(Households)}}{500} + \underset{\text{(Exports)}}{100} \\
&= \underset{\text{(Total output)}}{1000}
\end{aligned}
$$

Notice that sales are divided between those to intermediate sectors (primary, manufacturing, and services) and to Final Demand (households and exports).[3]

The sum of intermediate and final sales for each sector is gross output. Again for simplicity we assume no government or investment expenditure, which

[2] The reader is warned that this is a highly simplified (though essentially valid) introduction to input–output analysis, designed to facilitate understanding of the environmental input–output models of the following two sections. For a comprehensive guide to input–output analysis, including environmental and energy input–output models, see Miller and Blair (1985).

[3] As a further simplification, transactions between undertakings within the same sector (intra-industry transactions) have been netted out, so that the main diagonal of Table 13.1 is empty.

Table 13.1 Input–output transactions table ($ million)

Purchases from	Sales to					
	Intermediate sector			Final demand		
	Primary	Manufacturing	Services	Households	Exports	**Total output**
Intermediate sectors:						
Primary	0	400	0	500	100	1000
Manufacturing	350	0	150	800	700	2000
Services	100	200	0	300	0	600
Primary inputs:						
Imports	250	600	50			
Wages	200	500	300			
Other value added	100	300	100			
Total input	1000	2000	600			

normally would be included as additional components of Final Demand.

Looking down any column of the table shows what the sector listed at the *top* purchased from each sector on the *left*, e.g.

Primary Sector Purchases =   400   +   0
    (from)   (Primary) (Manuf.)

          +   200   +   600
         (Services)   (Imports)

          +   500   +   300
         (Wages)   (OVA)

        =   2000
       (Total input)

Notice that purchases are divided between those from intermediate sectors (primary, manufacturing, and services), and so-called Primary Input purchases (imports, wages and other value added).[4]

Like the national accounts, transactions tables are normally compiled on an annual basis. They are also typically expressed in value terms, in order to provide a standard unit of account across sectors, though in principle it would be possible to use sector-specific units of account (tonnes, metres, numbers, therms), or a combination of physical and monetary units.

A real transactions table will normally be larger than Table 13.1 because more sectors will be separately identified but the interpretation of it will be the same. A recently compiled input–output table for the UK, for

[4] It is a source of potential confusion, but there is no connection between the Primary *Sector*, which covers production activities such as agriculture, forestry, fishing and extractive industries, and Primary *Inputs*, which conventionally covers the contribution to production of primary factors of production (land, labour and capital), and imports.

example, contains 123 intermediate sectors, and the most recent table for the United States has 480 intermediate sectors. Tables of this size provide a highly detailed snapshot of the structure of an economy and of the interdependence of sectors and agents.

Because of the accounting conventions adopted in the construction of an I/O table, the following will always be true:

1 For each industry: Total output ≡ Total input, that is, the sum of the elements in any row is equal to the sum of the elements in the corresponding column.
2 For the table as a whole:

> Total intermediate sales
> = Total intermediate purchases
>
> Total final demand = Total primary input

The standard national income accounts can be readily derived from the input–output accounts. For example GDP can be estimated from Table 13.1 either:

1 on the income side as:

Wages	$1000m
+ OVA	$500m
=GDP	$1500m

2 on the expenditure side as:

Household expenditure	$1600m
+ Exports	$800m
− Imports	$900m
=GDP	$1500m

The transactions table provides the following balance equation for each industry or sector:

$$X_i = \sum_j X_{ij} + Y_i \qquad i = 1, \ldots, n \qquad (13.1)$$

where X_i = total output of industry i

X_{ij} = sales of industry i to intermediate industry j

Y_i = sales of i to Final Demand.

The basic input–output assumption is now made that

$$X_{ij} = a_{ij}X_j \qquad (13.2)$$

where a_{ij} is a constant. That is, it is assumed that intermediate inputs are a constant proportion of the output of the purchasing industry. So for example if X_j represents the output of the steel industry (tonnes valued at constant prices) and X_{ij} records purchases of iron ore (tonnes valued at constant prices) by the steel industry, we are assuming that iron ore purchases are a constant fraction of the value of steel output (expressed in constant prices); if the output of steel doubles, inputs (purchases) of iron ore will double.

Substituting Equation 13.2 into 13.1,

$$X_i = \sum_j a_{ij}X_j + Y_i \qquad (i = 1,\dots,n) \qquad (13.3)$$

In matrix form, and rearranging,

$$\mathbf{X} - \mathbf{AX} = \mathbf{Y} \qquad (13.4)$$

where $\mathbf{X}$ is an n-element vector of outputs

$\mathbf{A}$ is an $n \times n$ matrix of intermediate input coefficients

$\mathbf{Y}$ is an n-element vector of final demands.

There are n equations in $2n$ variables and n^2 coefficients. If the elements of $\mathbf{Y}$ are specified (or forecast), we can solve the system of equations (subject to necessary and sufficient conditions) for $\mathbf{X}$. From Equation 13.4,

$$(\mathbf{I} - \mathbf{A})\mathbf{X} = \mathbf{Y} \qquad (13.5)$$

i.e.

$$\mathbf{X} = (\mathbf{I} - \mathbf{A})^{-1}\mathbf{Y} \qquad (13.6)$$

where $\mathbf{I}$ is an identity matrix of order n. The solution to the model determines the level and composition of industry outputs necessary to supply a predetermined or forecast level and composition of final demands.

This is the basic input–output model. This type of model has many applications including planning, forecasting, impact studies, studies of structural change, identification of technological linkages, etc. Its validity rests upon a number of assumptions which are clearly – at best – approximations to reality, but used judiciously an input–output model

can be a powerful and insightful tool of analysis. We return to discuss some of these assumptions in the final section of this chapter. In the next section it is shown how the basic model can be extended to incorporate economy–environment interactions. Before reading this section the reader may find it useful to work through Problem 1 at the end of this chapter, which shows the derivation and solution of an input–output model based on the data of Table 13.1.

An environmental input–output framework

Proposals to extend input–output tables and models to include aspects of economy–environment links were first mooted in the late 1960s. The next 10–15 years saw a rapid development of environmental input–output models, including significant contributions (theoretical and applied) by the progenitor of input–output analysis, Wassily Leontief. Although there are some important differences between the models developed by different authors – so that for particular applications the choice of model is important – they all share a common basis of input–output methodology, including constant returns to scale production functions which permit no substitution between inputs (Leontief production functions). We outline below a schematic framework for an extended input–output system which is consistent with a range of model variants, depending on the purpose of the model and data availability.

The basis of Figure 13.1 is recognition that there are three types of linkage between the economy and the environment. First, economic agents extract or exploit natural resources, including obvious forms of exploitation such as extraction of ores and minerals, fish harvesting and so on, but also in less obvious ways such as the 'consumption' of fresh air and landscape.

Secondly, the processing and consumption of these environmental resources yields residuals which are returned to the environment, and which may have undesirable economic, social or health effects, such as air pollution, soil degradation, or loss of habitat. Attempts to eliminate, mitigate or compensate for these effects lead to the third type of economy–environment link, namely activities devoted to abatement or environmental renewal.

In Figure 13.1, the submatrices I and VII correspond to the conventional input–output table, I

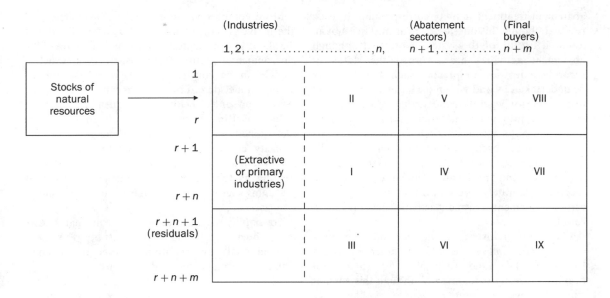

Fig 13.1 An extended input–output system.

recording flows of goods and services between the n intermediate sectors of the economy, and VII recording deliveries to final buyers or users (private and government consumption, investment, exports). For simplicity, we assume here that each 'industry' produces a unique homogeneous 'commodity', thus avoiding the need for a more complex system of accounts which links industries and commodities.

Submatrix II records the extraction or direct use of natural resources by industries, involving a reduction in the vector of stocks of natural resources. Each cell R_{ij} of submatrix II records the amount or volume of resource i, measured in physical units, used or consumed by industry j during a particular time period, say one year. Thus if resource i is water and industry j is water supply, R_{ij} records the volume of water collected and processed by the water supply sector: subsequent sales or deliveries of water to industry and households would appear in row $r + j$ of submatrices I and VII.

Following conventional input–output modelling practice, if we assume a constant proportional relation between inputs of resources and outputs of industries, we can derive a submatrix of resource input coefficients in which the typical coefficient r_{ij} indicates the amount of resource i (in physical units) required per unit of output (typically measured in value units) of industry j. Pursuing the example above, r_{ij} would record the number of gallons of water

required per million dollars output of the water supply industry.

Many of the cells in submatrix II will be zero, since only a limited number of industries are engaged in the direct extraction or harvesting of natural resources. Processed natural resources will be classified as industrial products and distributed along the rows of submatrices I, IV and VII.

Submatrix III records residual wastes generated by each industry, there being a separate row for each type of residual: thus W_{gk} records the amount of residual g generated by industry k in the accounting period concerned. Again following standard input–output practice, if we assume a constant proportional relationship between industry output and residuals generation, we can derive a submatrix of waste coefficients in which the typical element W_{gk} indicates the amount of waste element g produced per million dollars output of industry k. Note that although the elements of submatrix **W** are outputs rather than inputs, they are treated here in an identical way to the input flows in submatrices II and I. Obvious examples of this type of waste production are pollutants generated by industrial production and distribution, an example of which will be considered later in this section.

Columns $n + 1$ to $n + m$ (submatrices IV, V and VI) represent residuals abatement or treatment activities; following Leontief's formulation, there is a unique abatement/treatment activity corresponding to each residual, though this one-to-one relationship is not an essential feature of the system. Note that although abatement activities are accorded the status of separate industries, in practice such activities may be undertaken by and within the industries which are responsible for generating the residual concerned. For instance a firm which generates waste water may undertake water purification 'on site' before discharging the water back into the environment. In the accounting system of Figure 13.1, the mainstream production and purification activities would be recorded separately. Note also that in this schema, certain abatement/treatment activities may operate at zero levels.

Like other industries, abatement industries purchase goods and services from other industries (submatrix IV), and may also absorb natural resources directly (submatrix V, though this submatrix could well be empty). Moreover, like other industries the abatement sectors may themselves generate residual wastes (submatrix VI).

The output of the abatement industries may be expressed in value terms, as are typically the other industries in the table, or in physical units, as the amount of residual treated or eliminated. In the latter case the input coefficients (submatrix IV) would measure (constant) dollar inputs per tonne of residual treated or eliminated. Again, for these industries we assume the Leontief technology of fixed proportional input coefficients.

The final columns of the table record sales or deliveries to final buyers, typically household (private) consumption, government consumption, investment, changes in stocks, exports and (a negative column of) imports, but each of these categories may be further disaggregated. One possibility is to disaggregate the investment column to separately identify capital expenditures directed towards the renewal of natural resources, such as reafforestation, soil regeneration, fish stocks renewal, and so on. These activities then provide a link to the vector of stocks of natural resources at the beginning of the environment–economy–environment sequence in Figure 13.1, and is a step towards closure of the model system.

Submatrix VIII allows for the possibility of direct extraction or use of natural resources by final buyers (e.g. fresh air, untreated water, fish caught for personal consumption, etc.), while submatrix IX includes residual wastes generated by households and other final buyers (CO_2, solid wastes, scrap, etc.).

More complex versions can be constructed, and alternative systems of accounting can be utilised, but the above schema captures the essential features of the environmental input–output system, from which a model can be constructed. Like the basic input–output model described in the previous section, the version presented below is an open, comparative static model in which final demands are exogenous (determined outside the model). There are no explicit capacity constraints on outputs, or limits to the supply of factors of production, which is equivalent to treating factor supplies as completely elastic at prevailing factor prices. We return to these assumptions later.[5]

To simplify the algebra, we assume in what follows that submatrices V and VIII are empty. For the n 'conventional' input–output sectors the balance equations (equilibrium conditions) are

$$X_i - \sum_{j=1}^{n} a_{ij}X_j - \sum_{q=n+1}^{n+m} a_{iq}Z_q = F_i \qquad (13.7)$$

or

$$\mathbf{X} - \mathbf{A_1}\mathbf{X} - \mathbf{A_2}\mathbf{Z} = \mathbf{F} \qquad (13.8)$$

where $\mathbf{X}$ is the output vector for the conventional industries, $\mathbf{Z}$ is the output vector for the abatement industries (to be discussed below), and $\mathbf{F}$ is a vector of deliveries to final buyers. (For convenience we assume here that $\mathbf{F}$ is a vector.) The coefficients $a_{ij} \in \mathbf{A_1}$ and $a_{iq} \in \mathbf{A_2}$ are derived from the system of accounts in Figure 13.1 as

$$a_{ij} = X_{ij}/X_j \qquad (13.9)$$

where X_{ij} is purchases of commodity i by industry j, used to produce output X_j, and

$$a_{iq} = X_{iq}/Z_q \qquad (13.10)$$

where Z_q is the output of abatement sector q (or volume of residual q eliminated).

These assumptions of constant proportional input coefficients mirror those of the basic input–output model of the previous section, and reflect the properties of the Leontief production function, notably constant returns to scale and zero substitution between inputs, in contrast to the more usual neoclassical function used elsewhere in this book.

---

[5] Other than natural resources, inputs of factors of production (labour and capital) are not shown in Figure 13.1, but the system could be readily extended to include them, in a manner similar to that used for natural resource flows.

For the residuals submatrices (III, VI and IX), the production or generation of residuals can be written as

$$P_g = \sum_{j=1}^{n} w_{gj}X_j + \sum_{q=n+1}^{n+m} w_{gq}Z_q + w_{gF} \qquad (13.11)$$

where P_g is the amount of residual g generated by production, by abatement activities, and by final demand. In matrix form

$$\mathbf{P} = \mathbf{W}_1\mathbf{X} + \mathbf{W}_2\mathbf{Z} + \mathbf{W_F} \qquad (13.12)$$

Equation 13.12 measures gross production of residuals. The net production is gross production less the volume treated or eliminated, which is the measured output of the abatement sector. How is this determined? For residual g, the net production (the volume of the residual returned to the environment) can be written

$$\begin{aligned} D_g &= Z_g - P_g \\ &= Z_g - \sum w_{gj}X_j - \sum w_{gq}Z_q - w_{gF} \end{aligned} \qquad (13.13)$$

where Z_g is the volume of residual g eliminated (the output of abatement sector g) and D_g is the net production of g (the volume not eliminated). Unless there is complete elimination, D_g will be typically negative, but its level may be amenable to control, and in ideal circumstances may be taken as a measure of the permitted level of net emission, waste or damage, where marginal damage and abatement costs are equal. By specifying this level as a negative final demand for the residual concerned, we have an equilibrium condition which enables us to determine the output of the abatement activity for that residual. In matrix form,

$$\mathbf{Z} - \mathbf{W}_1\mathbf{X} - \mathbf{W}_2\mathbf{Z} = \mathbf{D} + \mathbf{W_F} \qquad (13.14)$$

We now write the complete model in the following partitioned form:

$$\begin{bmatrix} \mathbf{X} \\ \mathbf{Z} \end{bmatrix} - \begin{bmatrix} \mathbf{A}_1 & \mathbf{A}_2 \\ \mathbf{W}_1 & \mathbf{W}_2 \end{bmatrix} \begin{bmatrix} \mathbf{X} \\ \mathbf{Z} \end{bmatrix} = \begin{bmatrix} \mathbf{F} \\ \mathbf{D} + \mathbf{W_F} \end{bmatrix} \qquad (13.15)$$

$\mathbf{F}$ and $\mathbf{D}$ are the vectors of independent variables $\mathbf{F}$ is final demand for the standard input–output model, and $\mathbf{D}$ is tolerated or permitted emission, waste or damage levels. Once $\mathbf{F}$ and $\mathbf{D}$ are specified, we can solve for $\mathbf{X}$ (industry output levels) and $\mathbf{Z}$ (abatement levels):

$$\begin{bmatrix} \mathbf{X} \\ \mathbf{Z} \end{bmatrix} = \begin{bmatrix} \mathbf{I} - \mathbf{A}_1 & -\mathbf{A}_2 \\ -\mathbf{W}_1 & \mathbf{I} - \mathbf{W}_2 \end{bmatrix}^{-1} \begin{bmatrix} \mathbf{F} \\ \mathbf{D} + \mathbf{W_F} \end{bmatrix} \qquad (13.16)$$

Given the solution vector [$\mathbf{X}$ $\mathbf{Z}$], the level of natural resource consumption can be calculated as

$$\mathbf{N} = \mathbf{R}[\mathbf{X}\ \mathbf{Z}] \qquad (13.17)$$

where $\mathbf{R}$ is a matrix of natural resource input coefficients.

Although there have been numerous applications of environmental input–output models, none have attained the degree of detail and comprehensiveness of the model structure outlined above. Data problems have been severe, particularly in relation to the cost and production structures of abatement activities, but also in the definition and measurement of certain types of environmental degradation. The most common area of application has been in studies of air pollution, using truncated versions of the environmental model which usually exclude abatement activities as distinct sectors. In possibly the best-known such study, Leontief and Ford (1972) computed output coefficients for five air pollutants (particulates, sulphur oxide, hydrocarbons, carbon monoxide and nitrous oxide) across a 90-sector input–output table for the United States. Coefficients were expressed as thousands of tons emitted into the atmosphere per million dollars of output in each industry. Amongst the various applications reported in their study was a projection of air pollution levels in 1980, based on a forecast of final demands in 1980. Results for the 23 principal air-polluting industries are shown in Table 13.2. Note that although the authors adjusted the input–output coefficients (the a_{ij}'s) of the model to account for predicted technological changes between 1963 (the base year of the model) and 1980, they had insufficient information to adjust the pollution output coefficients. To the extent that new technologies incorporate lower emission levels (though this is by no means automatic), the figures in Table 13.2 may have been overestimated.

In a more recent study McNicoll and Blackmore (1993) calculated output coefficients for 12 pollutants[6] for a (preliminary) 29-sector version of the 1989 input–output tables for Scotland. Coefficients were expressed in thousands of tonnes per £ million output, except radioactivity which is measured in thousand becquerels. Applications of the model included a number of simulation studies, two of which involved assessing the impact on pollution emissions of (i)

[6] Carbon dioxide (two measures), sulphur dioxide, black smoke, nitrous oxides, volatile organic compounds, carbon monoxide, methane, waste, lead, radioactivity (air, water, solid).

Table 13.2 Projection of industrial air pollution to 1980 (in thousands of tons, assuming no change in the 1967 pollution characteristics of each industry's technology)

83-order OBE industry	(1) Part.	(2) SO_x	(3) HC	(4) CO	(5) NO_x
7 Coal mining	246.0	0.0	0.0	0.0	0.0
14 Food	2 086.0	463.0	0.0	0.0	0.0
24 Paper	1 314.0	483.0	0.0	0.0	0.0
27 Chemicals	151.0	1 692.0	0.0	0.0	0.0
30 Paint	0.0	0.0	8.0	0.0	0.0
31 Petroleum refinery	1 045.0	3 555.0	1502.0	3225.0	0.0
36 Stone and clay	2 599.0	201.0	0.0	0.0	0.0
37 Iron and steel	2 336.0	0.0	0.0	4375.0	0.0
38 Nonferrous metals	257.0	6 901.0	0.0	0.0	0.0
65 Transportation	774.0	646.0	1420.0	3886.0	1 548.0
68 Utilities	12 335.0	29 163.0	1943.0	3792.0	7 780.0
69 Wholesale and retail trade	0.0	1 147.0	1929.0	0.0	0.0
71 Real estate	315.0	1 555.0	0.0	0.0	925.0
72 Hotels	53.0	262.0	0.0	0.0	156.0
73 Business services	149.0	735.0	0.0	0.0	438.0
75 Auto repair	35.0	172.0	0.0	0.0	102.0
76 Amusements	22.0	108.0	0.0	0.0	64.0
77 Institutions	120.0	592.0	0.0	0.0	352.0
78 Federal enterprises	20.0	99.0	0.0	0.0	59.0
79 State enterprises	26.0	131.0	0.0	0.0	78.0
81 Business travel	24.0	118.0	0.0	0.0	70.0
82 Office supplies	9.0	45.0	0.0	0.0	27.0
83 Scrap	2.0	12.0	0.0	0.0	7.0
Total	23 919.0	47 898.0	6803.0	0.0	11 607.0

Grand total: 105 506.0

Source: Leontief and Ford (1972).

partial substitution by consumers of coal for gas, and (ii) partial substitution of road and air transport for rail transport. For SIM1 (coal for gas), final demand for coal was reduced by £30m, while that for gas was increased by £30m. For SIM2 (greater use of rail), final demand for road transport was reduced by £50m, and air transport by £20m, while final demand for rail transport was raised by £70m. In both cases aggregate final demand was kept unchanged in order to show the effects of different *patterns* of expenditure. Although the figures used are purely illustrative, the approach and discussion are suggestive of how environmental input–output models can be used to quantify and evaluate the effects of policies which influence the pattern, as well as the level, of economic activity. Especially in SIM2, for example, it is interesting that although rail travel is usually considered more environmentally-friendly than road or air transport, the substitution suggests an *increase* in the output of certain pollutants.

Results of the simulations are summarised in Table 13.3. The left-hand columns record the estimated effects of the substitutions on sector outputs, compared with actual 1989 outputs. The right-hand columns show the estimated changes in emissions which would result from the substitutions. For SIM1, the switch from coal to gas results in a fall in the output of all pollutants except solid radioactive waste. For SIM2, the switch from road/air to rail, the results are less clear-cut; emissions of seven pollutants decline, but those of five increase.

Costs and prices

The preceding section described the 'real' side of the model system; inputs and outputs are expressed in physical units, or in constant value terms. However, many of the most interesting and controversial issues in environmental economics involve questions of value, costs and prices. For instance, how would a 'carbon tax' affect the cost of living? What is the 'value' of an unpolluted beach? If electric power

Table 13.3 SIM1 and SIM2 impacts on outputs and pollutants

Sector	Δ gross output (£m)		Pollutant	Δ Output (000 tonnes exep.RA)	
	SIM1	SIM2		SIM1	SIM2
1	−0.04	+0.64	CO_2	−404.7	−287.7
2	−0.001	−0.04	CO_2 (c weight)	−110.4	−78.5
3	−0.02	+0.22	SO_2	−3.0	+0.11
4	−30.21	+0.08	Black smoke	−0.35	−0.06
5	−0.02	−0.02	NO_x	−0.88	−3.84
6	−0.73	−1.06	VOC	−0.14	−3.25
7	−0.27	+2.25	CO	−0.35	−21.16
8	+30.98	+0.60	Methane	−11.46	+0.09
9	−0.01	+0.17	Waste	−655.2	+24.26
10	−0.11	+0.07	Lead	−0.000005	−0.01
11	+0.03	+1.02	RA air	−0.001	+0.009
12	+0.004	+0.27	RA water	−0.00006	+0.0005
13	−0.09	+0.21	RA solid	0.0143	+0.121
14	−0.15	+0.14			
15	−0.009	+1.20			
16	−0.19	+2.13			
17	+0.02	+0.83			
18	+0.05	+0.97			
19	−0.08	+0.48			
20	+0.01	+1.65			
21	−0.42	+15.25			
22	+0.02	+70.29			
23	−0.04	−49.2			
24	+0.01	+0.21			
25	+0.09	−20.49			
26	+0.61	+2.80			
27	+2.64	+5.47			
28	−0.24	+2.89			
House	−5.84	+71.47			

Source: McNicoll and Blackmore (1993).

companies are obliged to halve their emissions of carbon dioxide, by how much will electricity bills rise? Who should pay for pollution, and how?

Some of these questions can be explored using the dual of the input–output model system outlined above. By way of introduction, we return to the basic input–output model described in the second section of this chapter. Equations 13.1 to 13.6 derived the equilibrium conditions for industry outputs, based on the rows of the input–output table. We can also derive equilibrium conditions for prices, based on the *columns* of the table. To do this, we note that

$$X_j = \sum_{i=1}^{n} x_{ij} + m_j + w_j + OVA_j \qquad (13.18)$$

that is, the value of output of sector j covers the cost of purchases from other sectors ($\sum x_{ij}$), plus the cost of imports used in production of product j, plus labour costs, plus other value added, which includes

profit and is essentially the balancing item in the equation. To simplify the exposition, we aggregate imports, labour costs and other value added and state the equation as

$$X_j = \sum_{j} X_{ij} + V_j \qquad (13.19)$$

and refer to V_j as primary input costs. We now assume as before that intermediate inputs are a fixed proportion of industry output, as in Equation 13.2. By substitution in Equation 13.19,

$$X_j = \sum_{i=1}^{n} a_{ij} X_j + V_j \qquad (13.20)$$

Normalising each equation so that the unit of output is unity, and each input coefficient a_{ij} measures the quantity of product i required per unit of j, yields

$$P_j = \sum a_{ij} P_i + v_j \qquad (13.21)$$

i.e. the price of one unit of j equals the sum of quantities of intermediate inputs times their prices plus primary input costs, per unit of output. Rearranging, and in matrix form,

$$(\mathbf{I} - \mathbf{A'})\mathbf{P} = \mathbf{v}$$

i.e.

$$\mathbf{P} = (\mathbf{I} - \mathbf{A'})^{-1}\mathbf{v} \tag{13.22}$$

where $\mathbf{P}$ is a vector of relative prices and $\mathbf{v}$ is a vector of primary input coefficients. Prices are determined by costs of production and, ultimately, by the costs of primary inputs. Given $\mathbf{v}$, the model can be solved to determine equilibrium prices.

The price model can be elaborated to distinguish different types of primary input. For example, if we had not aggregated the three primary inputs in Equation 13.18, the price model could be expressed as

$$\mathbf{P} = (\mathbf{I} - \mathbf{A'})^{-1}(\mathbf{m} + \mathbf{w} + \mathbf{r}) \tag{13.23}$$

where $\mathbf{m}$ is a vector of import cost coefficients, $\mathbf{w}$ a vector of labour cost coefficients and $\mathbf{r}$ a vector of 'other value added' coefficients. Expressed in this form, the model could be used to simulate the effects of a change in import prices, or an increase in wage costs, or any other change or combination of changes in primary input costs. The price effects of changes in technology can also be estimated by making appropriate changes in the $\mathbf{A}$ matrix, and recalculating the price vector $\mathbf{P}$.

As formulated and expressed above, the price model assumes that the effects of any changes will be fully passed on to final buyers, though the actual calculations could be modified to allow, for example, part of the effects of a change in primary input costs to be absorbed by producers. However, as remarked in the previous section input–output models do not permit substitution between inputs (or, to put it in a different way, assume zero elasticities of substitution). In this respect there is a tendency for input–output models to overstate the effects of cost changes.

For the extended environmental input–output system of the previous section, cost-price calculations can be introduced in a manner similar to that outlined above, though in practice a range of approaches have been adopted, governed partly by data availability and partly by the particular form of model. For instance, cost-price equations for the abatement sectors (submatrices IV, V and VI of Figure 13.1) can be formulated as in Equation 13.21, i.e. the price of a unit of abatement is determined by its cost of production. In practice, abatement or elimination activity may be undertaken by and within the industry(ies) which generates the pollution, and it may be difficult to specify a separate and identifiable cost function for the abatement activity. In a study already cited above, Leontief and Ford (1972) estimated the price effects of reducing five types of air pollution by adjusting the value added coefficients of the standard price model. Thus without pollution abatement the standard price model was as in Equation 13.22, i.e.

$$\mathbf{P} = (\mathbf{I} - \mathbf{A'})^{-1}\mathbf{v} \tag{13.24}$$

Undertaking pollution abatement is assumed to raise value added coefficients, a consequence of adding labour and/or capital inputs to the production process. Assuming these costs are passed on to customers, the price effects can be calculated as

$$\mathbf{P^*} = (\mathbf{I} - \mathbf{A'})^{-1}\mathbf{v^*} \tag{13.25}$$

where $\mathbf{v^*}$ is the value added vector incorporating pollution abatement activity, and $\mathbf{P^*}$ is the new vector of equilibrium prices. Note that in this example the pollution abatement effects were subsumed entirely in the value added coefficients, though in reality one would expect abatement activities to also affect the inter-industry coefficients of the $\mathbf{A}$ matrix. In this case the price effects would be measured as

$$\mathbf{P^*} = (\mathbf{I} - \mathbf{A^*})^{-1}\mathbf{v^*} \tag{13.26}$$

where $\mathbf{A^*}$ is the technology matrix amended to incorporate abatement activities. As in the Leontief and Ford application, however, the (engineering) data required to amend the $\mathbf{A}$ matrix may not be available.

Table 13.4 reproduces some of the results of the Leontief and Ford study. Each column shows the estimated effect of a particular air pollution strategy on the relative price of each sector's output. Thus the effect of Strategy (1) is to raise the price of water and sanitary services by an estimated 2.65%, the price of electric utilities by 7.318%, and so on. In contrast Strategy (2) has a negligible effect on water and sanitary services, and raises electric utility prices by an estimated 2.704%. For each sector the original equilibrium price was unity, so the data in the table are price relatives which indicate percentage or proportional changes. For each pollution control strategy, the authors calculated the changes in the vector v required to accommodate the extra labour and capital inputs required, and then solved for the new vector of equilibrium prices using equation (13.25).

Table 13.4 Price effects of four hypothetical air pollution control strategies (1963 price = $1.000 00)

90-order industry	Strategy			
	(1)	(2)	(3)	(4)
1 Water and sanitary services	1.026 50	1.000 56	1.000 79	1.023 22
2 Electric utilities	1.073 18	1.027 04	1.038 10	1.028 94
3 Pulp mills	1.007 02	1.000 59	1.000 83	1.032 22
4 Iron and steel foundries	1.035 07	1.000 72	1.001 01	1.029 18
5 Primary steel	1.021 86	1.000 63	1.000 89	1.014 73
6 Primary nonferrous metals	1.168 24	1.001 51	1.002 13	1.034 05
7 Industrial chemicals	1.006 51	1.000 80	1.001 12	1.102 86
8 Fertilisers	1.008 25	1.000 77	1.001 08	1.046 66
9 Petroleum refining	1.002 22	1.004 43	1.000 61	1.082 60
10 Paving mixtures	1.093 98	1.000 62	1.000 87	1.268 81
11 Cement, hydraulic	1.012 79	1.001 56	1.002 20	1.035 71
12 Lime	1.008 01	1.001 02	1.001 44	1.037 60
13 Coal mining	1.005 04	1.000 88	1.001 24	1.061 03
14 Wholesale trade	1.001 31	1.000 28	1.000 39	1.020 87
15 Grain milling	1.003 87	1.000 40	1.000 57	1.029 41
16 Paints and allied products	1.005 30	1.000 44	1.000 62	1.074 22
17 Secondary nonferrous metals	1.030 43	1.000 51	1.000 72	1.019 20
18 Livestock and livestock products	1.001 81	1.000 32	1.000 45	1.034 00
19 Other agricultural products	1.001 62	1.000 27	1.000 38	1.048 84
20 Forestry and fishery products	1.001 34	1.000 14	1.000 19	1.030 93
21 Agricultural, forestry, and fishery services	1.002 52	1.000 27	1.000 38	1.029 36
22 Iron and ferroalloy ores mining	1.004 03	1.000 84	1.001 18	1.023 61
23 Nonferrous metal ores mining	1.004 77	1.001 01	1.001 42	1.018 41
24 Crude petroleum and natural gas	1.001 58	1.000 35	1.000 49	1.012 01
25 Stone and clay mining and quarrying	1.004 66	1.000 84	1.001 18	1.030 62
26 Chemical and fertiliser mineral mining	1.004 40	1.000 91	1.001 28	1.019 35
27 New construction	1.006 01	1.000 35	1.000 50	1.024 78
28 Maintenance and repair construction	1.004 29	1.000 29	1.000 41	1.021 48
29 Ordnance and accessories	1.006 22	1.000 33	1.000 46	1.010 53
30 Food and kindred products	1.002 11	1.000 34	1.000 49	1.023 64
31 Tobacco manufactures	1.000 86	1.000 15	1.000 21	1.013 59
32 Fabrics, yarn, and thread mills	1.002 48	1.000 58	1.000 82	1.028 91
33 Textile goods and floor coverings	1.002 48	1.000 52	1.000 74	1.029 97
34 Apparel	1.001 61	1.000 37	1.000 52	1.015 89
35 Miscellaneous fabricated textile products	1.002 14	1.000 47	1.000 66	1.020 90
36 Lumber and wood products	1.002 26	1.000 39	1.000 55	1.019 35
37 Wooden containers	1.005 47	1.000 54	1.000 76	1.018 00
38 Household furniture	1.003 93	1.000 40	1.000 56	1.015 77
39 Other furniture and fixtures	1.006 45	1.000 41	1.000 58	1.015 17
40 Paper and allied products	1.004 12	1.000 63	1.000 89	1.028 31
41 Paperboard containers and boxes	1.002 93	1.000 47	1.000 66	1.024 60
43 Printing and publishing	1.001 78	1.000 35	1.000 49	1.014 49
43 Agricultural and miscellaneous chemicals	1.003 47	1.004 49	1.000 70	1.064 16
44 Plastics and synthetic materials	1.003 59	1.000 56	1.000 79	1.062 20
45 Drugs, cleaning and toilet preparations	1.002 35	1.000 34	1.000 48	1.026 19
46 Asphalt felts and coatings	1.003 80	1.000 53	1.000 74	1.189 10
47 Rubber and plastic products	1.002 74	1.000 49	1.000 70	1.024 19
48 Leather tanning products	1.002 10	1.000 45	1.000 64	1.023 79
49 Footwear and other leather products	1.001 75	1.000 33	1.000 47	1.013 46

Source: Leontief and Ford (1972) (table abbreviated).

A similar type of calculation has been used in estimating the probable effects of various forms of 'environmental' taxes on costs and prices. For example suppose the Government decides to impose a tax on energy production, the level of the tax being proportional to the carbon content of the energy units produced. Provided the tax can be expressed as a proportion of output, the value added coefficients of the energy sectors can be adjusted (upwards) to incorporate the new 'tax coefficient' and the overall effects on prices calculated as in Equation 13.25. If sufficient data are available, it may then be possible to estimate the effects of price changes on the cost of living for different types of household, and how household consumption might change in response to these relative price changes.[7] These latter calculations lie outside the scope of the input–output model, though they can be subsumed within the more comprehensive computable general equilibrium framework (see below). Note again that the model assumes that the tax will be fully passed on right through the production network, ultimately falling on final buyers. Value added coefficients could be adjusted by less than the full amount of the tax to allow for the possibility that producers may absorb part of the tax increase, but this would be an independent *ad hoc* adjustment, not an endogenous response triggered through the solution to the model.

If adequate data on abatement costs are available or can be collected, price equations similar to Equation 13.21 can be formulated for the abatement sectors, i.e.

$$P_g = \sum a_{ij}P_i + v_g \qquad (13.27)$$

where P_g is the price or cost of eliminating one unit of pollutant g.

How these equations are used in the extended model depends on the mechanism adopted for paying for abatement or elimination. If legislation obliges the polluter to pay, then polluting industries will buy abatement services from the abatement sectors, and the cost of these services will be included in the polluting industries' prices. The output (equilibrium) price for industry j is now

$$P_j = \sum a_{ij}P_i + \sum a_{gj}P_g + v_j \qquad (13.28)$$

where a_{gj} is the quantity of abatement service g per unit of output which industry j is required to purchase, and P_g is the unit cost of abatement service

g. The general solution to the extended price model is now

$$\bar{\mathbf{P}} = (\mathbf{I} - \bar{\mathbf{A}}')^{-1}\bar{\mathbf{v}} \qquad (13.29)$$

where, $\bar{\mathbf{P}}$, $\bar{\mathbf{v}}$ and $\bar{\mathbf{A}}$ now include the abatement sectors.

Alternatively, abatement/treatment may be financed through general taxation. In this case, polluting industry prices are unaffected (at least directly). Abatement services are provided or purchased by government (central or local) and delivered to consumers as a public service (for example river purification, household waste collection, nuclear waste disposal).

Computable general equilibrium models

Environmental input–output models offer a number of advantages for applied work in policy simulation, forecasting and structural analysis. They are designed to provide a considerable amount of industry/commodity detail, they enable the user to identify and trace the indirect effects of particular exogenous shocks or changes, they are mathematically simple and, subject to fairly minimal conditions, they will always provide an equilibrium solution.

These advantages are obtained at a certain cost which undoubtedly affects the reliability of model results. There are no factor supply equations and no capacity constraints, and as already noted the input–output (Leontief) production functions do not allow for input substitution in response to relative price changes. Agents (producers, owners of factors of production) respond mechanistically to external changes; utility and profit maximising behaviour play no role in these models. Equilibrium conditions are limited to ensuring that, for each sector of production, supply and demand are in balance.

It is possible to address some of these weaknesses by extending or modifying the basic model. Non-linear production functions can be employed, and by treating households as a sector which produces labour services, some account is taken of labour supply. There is also a dynamic version of the input–output model (Leontief, 1970b) in which investment is endogenous. And without too much modification, it is possible to formulate a linear programming version of the basic model which incorporates optimising behaviour in the form of an aggregate social welfare function.

---

[7] For a good recent example of such a study, see Symons *et al.* (1993).

Nevertheless, most environmental input–output models are of the type discussed in this chapter, that is open, comparative static models which are essentially demand-driven. Although from a theoretical standpoint such models have serious shortcomings, from a practical point of view these deficiencies can often be assumed to have a minimal effect, at least in applications where the exogenous changes considered are relatively small. However, concern with the rather limited behavioural basis of input–output models, notably the absence of optimising behaviour central to neoclassical theory, has led to a growing interest in applied general equilibrium models, and in particular to computable general equilibrium or CGE models.

While CGE models bear a superficial resemblance to input–output models, notably in their degree of disaggregation and often incorporating inter-industry flows, their genesis is quite different. They are essentially empirical versions of the Walrasian general equilibrium system and carry over the theoretical (neoclassical) assumptions of that system, which as remarked above are absent from the input–output system and to some extent are antithetical to it. In general, CGE models cannot be solved algebraically, but thanks to the explosion in computing power and the development of solution algorithms they can be solved computationally. These developments have stimulated a rapid growth in applied CGE modelling, particularly on issues related to taxation, trade, structural adjustment and environment.[8]

Even more than input–output models, CGE models are data-hungry and parametrisation is a constant problem. It is rare for parameters to be estimated econometrically; they are usually calibrated from a single data set or are 'imported' from elsewhere. However, CGE models are comprehensive and flexible, have a very large range of potential applications, and are based on explicit micro-economic behavioural assumptions. They are particularly valuable in environmental applications in assessing the distributional and welfare effects of alternative environmental policies, and in identifying the trade-offs between different policy regimes. A major focus of attention in environmental CGE modelling has been the implications of global warming and of alternative abatement policies. A number of models have been designed to simulate the effects of various policy instruments (carbon taxes, energy taxes, emission permits) on demand, output and

incomes, and on the distributional effects of these changes across sectors, regions and household groups. Because of the detail which they provide on potential distributional consequences, CGE models have been valuable in comparing the effects of different policy instruments; for example a CGE modelling exercise by Whalley and Wigle (1989) suggests that with a national production-based tax (to reduce CO_2 emissions) the GDP of developing countries will fall by 4%, whereas with a so-called global tax developing countries will gain 3%. Simulation results of this kind can clearly make an important contribution to the choice of policy instruments and possible compensation arrangements between countries or affected groups. A weakness, common to all CGE models, is the sensitivity of model outputs to initial conditions or assumptions, particularly with respect to substitution possibilities, technological progress, and the treatment of economic agents' expectations. Consequently, different models differ significantly in, for example, the tax level estimated to be necessary to secure a given level of abatement of greenhouse gases.

The OECD Secretariat has developed a multi-sector, multi-region CGE, named GREEN, to examine and compare the effects of alternative policies to achieve global reductions in carbon dioxide emissions. Simulations include one in which industrialised countries – OECD and the former Soviet Union – cut emissions by 20% below their 1990 levels by 2010 and stabilise them thereafter, while emissions in the other three regions in the model – China, India and energy-exporting LDCs – are limited to 50% above 1990 levels. A carbon tax is the chosen policy instrument. Results suggest that average real income across all regions would be about 2.6% lower by the year 2020 compared with the baseline (no change) case, the biggest fall being experienced in

Table 13.5 Percentage changes in household real income relative to the no-trade scenario

USA	+0.3
Japan	+0.8
EU	+0.4
Other OECD	+0.2
Total OECD	+0.4
Energy-exporting LDCs	+4.4
China	+3.5
India	+1.1
USSR	+1.8
Total of all countries/regions	+1.3

Source: Burniaux, J-M. *et al.* (1992).

---

[8] For a good summary of recent work on CGE modelling and applications, see Greenaway *et al.* (1993).

the energy-exporting LDCs (about 10%). In an interesting variant, however, the model is used to re-estimate the consequences of achieving the same emission targets, while allowing countries to trade emission rights. As theory would predict, the possibility of trade in emission rights permits efficiency gains; China, for example, sells some of its emission rights, reduces domestic output of coal, and uses receipts from emission rights sales to import oil, which has a lower carbon content than the equivalent volume of coal, from the energy-exporting LDCs. The figures in the table below imply that all regions gain (in terms of household real income) from trade in emission rights, notably the energy-exporting LDCs, and also China, India and the former Soviet Union.

It is prudent to bear in mind that the ability of complex and necessarily highly stylised models to accurately predict the consequences of specific shocks, particularly large shocks and over long time horizons, is not well proven and results must be treated with caution. However, CGE modelling is an important addition to the menu of modelling techniques in applied economic research. It has a more extensive range of applications than environmental input–output, though it is more difficult to implement empirically, and the latter is likely to remain a standard technique in environmental analysis and simulation for some time to come.

A simple worked example of an input–output model

From Table 13.1, we can define the vector Y as the sum of Household and Export Demand, i.e. $Y = (600, 1500, 300)$. By calculation (not shown here),

$$(I - A)^{-1} = \begin{bmatrix} 1.0833 & 0.2222 & 0.0556 \\ 0.4167 & 1.1111 & 0.2778 \\ 0.1500 & 0.1333 & 1.0333 \end{bmatrix}$$

which is known as the Leontief Inverse. Substituting Y and $(I - A)^{-1}$ into Equation 13.6,

$$X = \begin{bmatrix} 1.0833 & 0.2222 & 0.0556 \\ 0.4167 & 1.1111 & 0.2778 \\ 0.1500 & 0.1333 & 1.0333 \end{bmatrix} \begin{bmatrix} 600 \\ 1500 \\ 300 \end{bmatrix} = \begin{bmatrix} 1000 \\ 2000 \\ 600 \end{bmatrix}$$

as expected since the system is originally in equilibrium.

Now suppose there is an increase in export demand to $(200, 1000, 100)$ so that $Y^* = (700, 1800, 400)$. What is the impact on output? We have

$$X^* = \begin{bmatrix} 1.0833 & 0.2222 & 0.0556 \\ 0.4167 & 1.1111 & 0.2778 \\ 0.1500 & 0.1333 & 1.0333 \end{bmatrix} \begin{bmatrix} 700 \\ 1800 \\ 400 \end{bmatrix} = \begin{bmatrix} 1181 \\ 2403 \\ 758 \end{bmatrix}$$

Note that the increases in output exceed the increases in final demand.

The Discussion Questions and Problems suggest ways in which this simple model can be further developed.

Discussion questions

1 Examine critically the basic assumptions of input–output models, in particular those related to the input–output (Leontief) production function and to factor supplies, and discuss the importance of these assumptions in affecting the validity and accuracy of environmental input–output applications.
2 Discuss how an environmental input–output *or* CGE model could be used to assess the price and output effects of replacing corporate profits tax by a tax on the use of natural resources in production.

Problems

1 In the preceding worked example, the elements of the matrix A were calculated as in Equation (13.2) of the text, that is

$a_{ij} = X_{ij}/X_j$. From the data in Table 13.1

$a_{11} = 0 \quad a_{21} = 350/1000 = 0.3500$

$a_{31} = 100/1000 = 0.1000$

$a_{12} = 400/2000 = 0.2000 \quad a_{22} = 0$

$a_{32} = 200/2000 = 0.1000 \quad a_{13} = 0$

$a_{23} = 150/600 = 0.2500 \quad a_{33} = 0$

hence

$$A = \begin{bmatrix} 0 & 0.2000 & 0 \\ 0.3500 & 0 & 0.2500 \\ 0.1000 & 0.1000 & 0 \end{bmatrix}$$

and

$$(\mathbf{I} - \mathbf{A}) = \begin{bmatrix} 1 & -0.2000 & 0 \\ -0.3500 & 1 & -0.2500 \\ -0.1000 & -0.1000 & 1 \end{bmatrix}$$

(a) Calculate import, wage and other value added coefficients from Table 13.1 analogous to the intermediate input coefficients above. Check that for each column, the sum of intermediate and primary input coefficients is unity.

(b) Use the new output vector $\mathbf{X}^*$ from the worked example to estimate the transactions table consistent with these higher output levels, assuming constant input coefficients for both intermediate and primary inputs. Calculate the new level of GDP.

2 Suppose now we can add the following information about pollution emission and waste to the dataset of Table 13.1:

Pollutant	Industry of Origin			
	Primary	Manufacturing	Services	Total
CO_2	300	3000	400	3700
Waste	4000	2500	150	6650

Where the amounts are in tonnes

(a) Stating carefully your assumptions, calculate the change in emission levels associated with an across-the-board increase of 20% in household expenditure.

(b) Suppose CO_2 emissions can be eliminated by a process which requires $250 of manufacturing inputs, $50 of service inputs, $150 in labour costs, and $50 other value added per tonne of CO_2 eliminated. Show how the input–output model could be extended to incorporate this abatement activity. Assuming the tolerated level of CO_2 emissions is limited to the 'base-year' level of 3700 tonnes, solve the model for levels of output and abatement given a 20% across-the-board increase in household final demand.

3 Following the equation sequence of Section 4, derive and write out the price equations for the basic input–output model based on Table 13.1. Noting that $(\mathbf{I} - \mathbf{A}')^{-1} = [(\mathbf{I} - \mathbf{A})^{-1}]'$, calculate the effect on prices of a 50% increase in import costs in the primary sector, due to the introduction of a tax on basic fuel imports. Why is your calculation likely to overestimate the effects of the cost increase?

Further reading

In addition to the references cited in the text of this chapter, other valuable references on environmental input–output are Ayres (1978), Leontief (1970a), and Pearson (1989).

CHAPTER 14

Accounting for the environment

Introduction

There is now a wide measure of agreement that the conventional system of national accounts, in most countries based upon the System of National Accounts (SNA) designed by the United Nations Statistical Office, is not adequate as a means of measuring or monitoring the impact of environmental changes on income or welfare. This is not surprising, as the development of national accounting (mainly in the 1940s and 1950s) took place in a period in which there was less awareness of, and less concern about, the impact of human economic and social development on the environment. The conceptual basis and scope of the national accounts were governed by definitions of income and wealth which did not make any allowance for the depletion of 'natural' capital or the costs of environmental damage such as pollution. Implicitly, these environmental effects were treated as externalities which, if considered at all, would be assigned zero or negligible values.

This view is no longer tenable, as it is apparent that production and consumption activities have environmental side-effects which impose considerable costs, some of which will be borne by future generations. Although, as will be discussed below, this does not necessarily imply a change in the established SNA, it certainly tempers our interpretation of conventional national accounts aggregates such as gross domestic product (GDP), particularly where these measures are used as proxies for a society's 'welfare' or standard of living.

Criticisms of the conventional system of national accounts centre on three main issues. First, to the extent that the national accounts purport to measure a nation's wealth, they record only man-made capital and ignore natural capital, including economic assets such as exploitable forests, fishing stocks, ores and minerals, and other assets such as fresh air and water, natural parks and wildernesses, and the like, which though typically not subject to market exchange, are valued by society.

Secondly, although the national accounts make allowance for the depletion of man-made capital in arriving at an estimate of net national product or national income, they make no allowance for the depletion of natural resources. Indeed, the value of marketed natural resource asset sales is included in national income, contrary to the accounting treatment of sales of man-made assets. Thus the national accounts overstate 'true' national income, particularly in the case of developing countries which rely heavily on the exploitation of natural resources.

Thirdly, the costs of environmental protection or renovation (so-called defensive expenditures) are included in national income (for example waste disposal, river purification, anti-pollution measures), but no allowance is made for the corresponding environmental damage in calculating net income. The latter can be regarded as environmental degradation, to be treated in a manner similar to depletion of natural resource stocks, and deducted from gross domestic product.

These issues are examined in some detail in the third section of this chapter where we consider ways in which the national accounts may be modified to meet the criticisms noted above. An alternative approach to 'greening' the national accounts is to formulate and develop a quite separate system of environmental accounts, which could complement the conventional SNA but which would not be limited by the SNA framework. In particular, stocks and flows in the environmental accounts could be expressed in physical units, thus side-stepping the formidable problems of valuation involved in incorporating environmental costs and benefits in the SNA. Like the national accounts, environmental accounts would be compiled and published annually, and would provide a means of measuring and monitoring changes in environmental conditions through the compilation of indicators analogous to gross domestic product and related macro-economic indicators in the SNA. This approach is in use in various parts of the world including Canada, the United States, the Netherlands, Norway and France, and is examined in the following section.

Revising the SNA to incorporate, or at least better reflect, environmental costs (and benefits), and developing an alternative system of environmental accounts, are not necessarily mutually exclusive. To some extent the modest proposals for 'satellite' environmental accounts contained in the latest revision of the SNA (United Nations, 1993) represent something of a compromise between the two approaches. Environmental accounting is at an early stage of development and there is considerable debate and contoversy over its direction. The main features of the proposed SNA system are reviewed in the fourth section.

At the present stage of development, the debate on environmental accounting is largely centred on the incorporation of environmental costs and benefits in the national accounts. Debate on the implications of environmental accounting on the form and content of corporate accounts and reports is at a much earlier stage. The final section very briefly reviews environmental accounting at the firm level.

Environmental accounts and environmental indicators

Changes in the physical or natural environment can affect the quality of life of individuals or groups within a society, sometimes positively (for example the purification of a river from chemical pollution) but frequently in a negative way (greater incidence of asthma caused by air pollution). In a wider societal perspective, the scope of relevant environmental impacts includes effects on future generations, such as the depletion of non-renewable natural resources or the extinction of species or unique ecosystems.

The quality of life or welfare of an individual or of a society cannot be precisely defined, but it is common (at least for economists!) to associate welfare with levels of income. One does not have to be an environmentalist to appreciate that this is an imperfect association; however, higher income levels permit higher levels of consumption, and consumption is a major – though by no means the sole – determinant of welfare. It follows that when we assert that a particular environmental change has reduced welfare, this is similar to saying that the incomes of those affected by the change have fallen; or if the effects cannot be allocated to individuals, that there has been a reduction in the aggregate income of the society.

The next two sections discuss how the effects of environmental changes can be expressed in monetary terms, and stress the considerable difficulties involved. In certain cases the value of an environmental change is captured through the market mechanism; examples are differences in house prices which reflect differences in the perceived quality of the local environment, or, more complex, the auctioning of pollution permits, where affected groups may bid for permits to prevent the pollution activity. However, the range of environmental changes which affect the quality of life is considerable, and in the majority of cases there are formidable problems in monetising these changes. These problems are discussed at some length in Chapter 10; in this chapter, they are referred to in the context of incorporating monetary values (however determined) of environmental stocks and flows in a system of national accounts.

Rather than seek to place monetary values on environmental changes, an alternative approach is to develop a system of accounts in physical units, the actual choice of unit being dependent on the conventional or most usual form of measurement of the environmental good concerned. Thus nitrogen oxide emissions might be measured in thousands of tons, loss/gain of natural forest in hectares, decline in species in numbers, and so on. This approach avoids the problem of assigning monetary values to physical or qualitative flows which are not exchanged through a market, but makes it difficult, and some would argue impossible to aggregate the effects of a number of environmental changes since there is no standard unit of measurement or agreed system of weights.

Like other accounting systems, environmental accounts should link opening stocks, flows to and from that stock, and closing stocks. Opening and closing stocks represent the state of the environment at the beginning and end of the accounting period, while flows record the impact (for good or ill) of the actions of economic agents on the environment. This is straightforward enough in the case of (scarce) natural resources, for which estimates are available of the level of economically recoverable reserves (the stock), and the volume of extraction in the accounting period.[1] Similarly, stock and flow measures are available or could be compiled for other environmental variables such as area of protected habitat, area of contaminated land, number of species of flora and fauna, concentrations of particulates in water and air, and so on. In other cases measures of stock cannot be adequately defined or measured (for example fresh air, marine and coastal waters) and we are limited to flow variables which are assumed to affect the *state* of the environment – emissions of carbon dioxide and other greenhouse gases, eutrophication of coastal waters, energy consumption, noise levels in urban areas, etc.

Physical accounts for natural resources and the environment have been compiled for Norway since the mid-1970s, followed soon after by France, Canada and the Netherlands, though each country has developed a distinct system. Other countries such as the USA and the UK are at an earlier experimental stage. A difficulty is in trying to decide what should and should not be included in the environmental accounts, since there are potentially a very large range of variables or indicators. To include too many risks duplication, and confusing the overall picture, while too few may miss an important area of environmental impact. OECD, whose statistical office has played a major role in the development of systems of environmental accounting, has identified a list of nearly 150 environmental indicators, including a 'core' list of 40–50 indicators appropriate for short-term monitoring (OECD, 1994). A similar number of key indicators has been proposed and applied by the Canadian environment ministry, and these are listed in Table 14.1. It will be noted that this list is directed towards environmental quality, and does not embrace the depletion of non-renewable natural resources.

By way of contrast, Table 14.2 lists 46 indicators proposed for the UK in a recent report. The selection of indicators was governed by the following criteria (MacGillivray, 1994, *Environmental Measures*, page 10):

- A time series of the indicator should be available, including recent observations.
- The indicators should be sensitive to action by the UK authorities, and should allow the setting of meaningful targets for the monitoring of actions.

- The data should be uncontentious (as far as this is ever possible) and be from official or otherwise accessible sources.
- They should require little or no additional collection or processing.
- The indicator should have resonance with the intended audience, i.e. be readily understood and be considered appropriate by that audience.

Bearing in mind the distinctive physical, economic and demographic characteristics of the UK and Canada, the coverage of the two lists is similar, but there is greater divergence in the choice of indicators. Note that the UK listing characterises an indicator as describing the *state* of the environment, as identifying a *pressure* on the environment, or as *responding to* an environmental situation or need.

Although the selection of 40–50 indicators, tailored to the conditions of individual countries, may be fully justified, this presents a large and variegated canvas. It would be helpful to try to summarise the overall trend in environmental conditions by means of a single measure or index. There is currently a considerable volume of research and research publications devoted to this issue, an example of which is the Index of Sustainable Economic Welfare (ISEW) (Jackson and Marks, 1994). This is calculated by adjusting the conventional national accounts measure of personal consumption expenditure to take account of environmental costs, though the adjustment also reflects a number of social welfare criteria, such as changes in income distribution. Figure 14.1 compares the movement of GNP and the ISEW for the UK in the period 1950–90; in comparison with GNP, the ISEW suggests virtually no change in the overall level of welfare (as defined by the index) over the 40-year period. Like any other index which combines possibly quite disparate movements in individual components, and is sensitive to the choice of weights, the ISEW must be interpreted with caution. It does, however, illustrate the limitations of GNP or GDP as an index of welfare, especially since the adjustments involved in the calculation of the ISEW are restricted to those environmental costs which can be ascribed a monetary value. For a more extensive discussion of this issue, the reader is referred to Chapter 10. The approach underlying the ISEW, in particular the attempt to value environmental variables, leads to consideration of the potential for integrating economic and environmental accounts, which is the subject of the two following sections.

---

[1] Note, however, that as prices change the levels of economically recoverable reserves may change.

Table 14.1 Canada's preliminary environmental indicators, 1991

Category	Issue	Indicator
Atmosphere	Climate change	Canadian energy-related emissions of carbon dioxide (CO_2) Atmospheric concentrations of CO_2 Global air temperature
	Stratospheric ozone depletion	Canadian production and importation of ozone-depleting chemicals Stratospheric ozone levels
	Radiation exposure	Levels of radioactivity in the air
	Acid rain	Sulphur dioxide (SO_2) and nitrogen oxides (NO_x) emissions
	Outdoor urban air quality	Common air pollutants: nitrogen dioxide (NO_2) and carbon monoxide (CO) levels in urban air and emissions Common air pollutants: SO_2 and total suspended particulates (TSP) levels in urban air and emissions Ground level ozone concentrations Air toxics: lead concentrations in urban air
Water	Freshwater quality	Population served by treated water supply Municipal discharges to fresh water: BOD (biochemical oxygen demand), TSS (total suspended) solids) and phosphorus Pulp and paper mill discharges to fresh water: TSS and BOD Discharges of regulated substances by petroleum refineries to water Concentration of phosphorus and nitrogen in water Maximum observed concentrations of pesticides in water: 2,4-D, atrazine and lindane
	Toxic contaminants in the freshwater system	Contaminant levels in herring gull eggs in the Great Lakes Basin: PCBs (polychlorinated biphenyls) and system DDE (dichlorodiphenyldichloroethylene) Contaminant levels in Lake Trout, a sport fish from the Great Lakes Basin: PBBs and DDT (dichlorodiphenyltrichloroethane)
	Marine environmental quality	Municipal discharges to coastal waters: TSS and BOD Pulp and paper mill discharges to coastal waters: TSS and BOD Volume of significant marine spills Area closed to shellfish harvesting Contaminant levels in seabird eggs: PCBs Contaminant levels in seabird eggs: dioxins and furans
Biota (living organisms)	Biological diversity at risk State of wildlife	Wildlife species at risk Levels of migratory game bird populations
Land	Protected areas Urbanisation Solid waste management	Land under protected status Rural to urban land conversion Municipal solid waste disposal trends
Natural economic resources	Forestry Agriculture	Regeneration success versus total forest area harvested Changes in agricultural land use Amount of chemical fertiliser used and its associated nutrient content Agricultural pesticide application on cultivated land
	Fisheries	Total commercial fish catches in Canadian waters off the Atlantic coast Commercial fish harvest in the Great Lakes
	Water use	Total water withdrawal compared with growth in Gross Domestic Product (GDP) Rates of water withdrawal and consumption by key economic sectors Rates of water recirculation by key industrial sectors Daily household water use per capita
	Energy	Total per capita primary energy use Emissions of CO_2 per unit of energy consumed Fossil fuel intensity of primary energy demand

Source: Environment Canada (1991), published in MacGillivray (1994).

Table 14.2 Suggested environmental indicators for the UK

Theme	Potential indicator idea	PSR[a]	Data? (available and reliable: a = annual p = periodic)	Meaningful? (represents an important phenomenon)	Resonant? (likely to strike a chord with a public audience)
Biodiversity	1 Extinct species	S	x	✓	?
	2 SSSI damage	S/P	x	✓	?
	3 Farmland species index	S	✓a	✓	✓
	4 Declining species	S	x	✓	✓
	5 Habitat status	S	x	✓	✓
	6 Land under active conservation management	R	?	✓	✓
	7 Species Action Plans	R	x	?	x
Quality of life	8 Sustainable Economic Welfare	S	✓p	✓	✓
	9 Asthma cases reported by GPs	S	✓a	?✓	✓
Footprints abroad	10 Timber imports from sustainable sources	P	✓a	✓	✓
	11 Cotton imports from sustainable sources	P	?a	✓	✓
Atmosphere	12 CO_2 emissions	P	✓a	✓	✓
	13 NO_x emissions (from transport)	P	✓a	✓	✓
	14 SO_2 emissions	P	✓a	✓	✓
	15 Areas of SSSI at risk from acid rain	S	x	?	?
	16 HCFC production	P	x	x	?
	17 Critical load exceedance	P/S	x	✓	?
	18 Population exposed to poor air quality	S	?a	x	✓
	19 Other air quality measures	S	?	?	?
Land	20 Hedgerow loss	S/P	✓p	✓	✓
	21 Land use	S	?	?	?
	22 Tree health survey	S	✓a	?	✓
	23 Rates and types of new tree planting	S/R	?a	x	✓
	24 Soil condition	S	x	x	?
Water	25 Nitrate in groundwater	S	✓a	✓	?
	26 Water consumption	P	✓a	✓	?
	27 Water pollution incidents	P	✓a	x	✓
	28 Water quality measures	S	✓a	✓?	✓
Marine	29 Bathing beach standards	S	✓a	?	✓
	30 Coast watch litter	S/P	✓?a	?	✓
	31 Oiled seabirds	S	✓p	?	✓
	32 Fish stocks and catches	S/P	✓a	✓	✓
	33 Oil spill incidents	P	✓a	?	✓
	34 Eutrophication	P	✓a	✓	x
Agriculture	35 Decline in farmland bird species	S	✓a	✓	✓
	36 Expenditure on agri-environment	P/R	✓a	?	✓
	37 Applications of fertiliser/pesticide per farmed hectare	P	✓a	x	?
Energy	38 Energy consumption by fuel type	P	✓a	✓	x
	39 Energy intensity of the economy	S?	✓a	x?	x
Industry	40 Special waste intensity	P	✓a	x	x
	41 Toxic releases	P	x	x	✓
	42 Contaminated land	S	x	x	✓?
Transport	43 Transport km by mode	P	✓a	✓	?
	44 Length of motorways/trunk road lanes	P	✓a	✓	?
	45 Journey length/time	P	✓p	✓	?
Waste	46 Toxic waste trade	P	✓a	✓?	✓

[a] The indicators are either P = environmental pressures, S = state of the environment, or R = societal response to the situation.

Source: MacGillivray (1994).

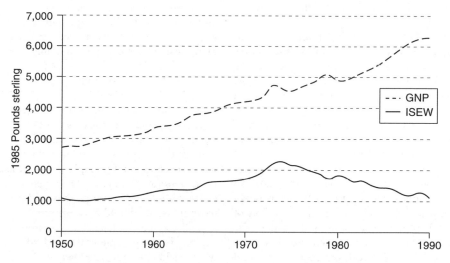

Fig 14.1 Illustrative indicator for the UK: Index of Sustainable Economic Welfare (*source*: Jackson and Marks, 1994).

Integrating economic and environmental accounts

The national accounts contain estimates of the value of goods and services produced in an economy over a particular time period or, what is shown to be the same thing, the value of incomes generated in producing those goods and services or, thirdly and equivalently, the value of expenditure on consuming or investing those goods and services. Economic activities covered by the national accounts are mainly confined to those involving monetary transactions, though there are some exceptions to this – for instance the imputed rent of owner-occupied dwellings, and the value of farm produce consumed by farm households, where in both cases it is fairly easy to place a value on the goods or services produced and consumed, even though market transactions do not take place.

The aggregate sum of the values of all final goods and services produced in an economy over a time period is *Gross Domestic Product (GDP)* which is probably the single most important macroeconomic indicator of a country's (or region's) level of economic development and changes in that level over time. Also important is the closely related *Gross National Product (GNP)*, which is GDP plus or minus the net flow of factor incomes to and from the rest of the world.

However, the production of goods and services entails the use of items of capital – notably buildings, machinery and other man-made equipment – and to offset this capital consumption a certain proportion of current production should be set aside to maintain capital intact. This is depreciation or capital consumption which, deducted from gross national product, yields *net national product (NNP)* or *national income*.

In principle, national income is a better measure than GDP or GNP since it is at least partly based on a concept of sustainability (see below), but GDP/GNP is more widely used, mainly because accurate estimates of capital consumption are difficult and methods of estimation vary considerably between countries. Hence for comparative purposes GDP or GNP is usually preferred.

It is now increasingly argued that allowances for capital consumption or depletion should not be confined to man-made capital, but should also apply to 'natural' capital, including economically exploited (marketed) assets such as farmland, forests, fishing stocks and commercial minerals, and perhaps also (though this is more controversial) non-marketed natural assets such as wildlife areas, rainforest, unique ecosystems and other facets of our natural heritage. In the same way that a certain proportion of income is allocated to maintaining a building or piece of equipment (or is kept in reserve to eventually replace it), so income should be set aside to replace or compensate for the depletion of the national forest, oil and gas reserves, fishing stocks, and so on.

This argument (apart from being intuitively appealing) is firmly grounded in the concept of 'sustainable income' or 'true' income, the origin of which can be attributed to J. R. Hicks's definition of income as the maximum value which a person can consume during a period and still be as well off at the end of the period as at the beginning (Hicks, 1939). It is this concept of income which underlies the allowance for depreciation of man-made capital in the present system of national accounts, and which constitutes the difference between gross national product and national income. On the same principle, gross national product should be adjusted to account for the depletion of natural capital, otherwise income as defined in the Hicksian sense will be overestimated. For countries which are heavily dependent on sales of natural resource products, such as Saudi Arabia or Kuwait, the effect on recorded national income could be dramatic.

This wider definition of capital consumption and its application would bring the level and growth of income closer to the concept of sustainable development, defined by the Brundtland Commission (WCED, 1987) as that rate of development which meets present needs without compromising the ability of future generations to meet their own needs. There is clearly an affinity between Hicksian income and that level and rate of growth of income which permits sustainability, since both imply the maintenance of the initial stock of capital. However, sustainable development is a broader and less precise concept than Hicksian income, and there is as yet no standard definition. We shall not consider this further here (but see Chapter 3), but turn instead to consider how the national accounts measures of capital consumption and national income might be adjusted to reflect the depletion of natural capital.

There are three categories of adjustments to the national accounts which have been proposed to reflect the costs and benefits (in practice, mainly costs[2]) of human activity on the environment. These are the depletion of natural capital, environmental degradation, and defensive expenditures, and we consider each

[2] Understandably, attention tends to be concentrated on (the costs of) damage to the environment, particularly irreversible damage. However, certain activities – works of art and architecture, landscaped gardens and parks, creation and management of special habitats to protect species – enhance the stock of environmental capital and result in a flow of benefits, though again these are seldom monetised.

in turn. A basic requirement is that the relevant stocks and flows of environmental resources can be monetised in a consistent and widely accepted manner, and in many cases this is a major stumbling block.

Depletion of natural capital

The principle here is that stocks of natural resources such as oil and gas reserves, stocks of fish and so on should be treated in the same way as stocks of man-made capital and that a deduction should be made to allow for the depletion or consumption of these natural resources. It is convenient here to distinguish between renewable and non-renewable natural resources, and between resources which yield monetised flows (such as commercial forests, exploited oils and minerals, and so on) and those which yield non-monetised benefits (such as fresh air, lakes and oceans and similar natural resources to which there are no assigned and exclusive property rights).

By way of illustration, let us assume that a country exploits a non-renewable mineral resource, such as oil or coal. Under the present system of national accounting, the net receipts from sales of this resource,[3] let us say R, will be included in Gross National Product (GNP), but no allowance will be made for the depletion of the stock of this natural resource in calculating Net National Product (NNP). Hence

$$NNP = GNP - D$$

where D = depreciation of man-made capital. If, for reasons suggested above, it is considered logical to allow for the depletion of natural as well as of man-made capital, one of two main approaches may be adopted. The first, known as the depreciation method, attempts to value depletion as that part of the receipts from sales of the resource which can be attributed uniquely to that resource. Thus in the above case if extraction costs were zero, the whole of the receipts R would be attributable to the depletion of the resource and net domestic product would be

$$NNP = GNP - D - R$$

If, as would be normally the case, extraction costs are positive and the value R includes an element of labour costs and returns to man-made capital (for example, mining equipment), depletion would then be

[3] For national accounts purposes, R is gross revenue from the sale of the resource *less* purchases of current goods and services required to extract the resource.

less than R. There are a number of ways of calculating the depletion value, for example as gross trading profits from the sale of the resource, *less* an estimated 'normal' return on man-made capital employed in extracting the resource. Thus suppose trading profits from sales of crude oil are $100m, the value of capital equipment used in oil extraction is $500m, and the average return on capital employed in the whole economy is 5%. Then we could calculate the depletion element as $100m − (0.05 × $500m) = $75m. More sophisticated methods, which take into account the relative scarcity of the resource and which therefore require estimates of total (exploitable) reserves of the resource, have also been proposed and tested.[4]

There are two objections to this general approach. The first is that under the depreciation method the measurement of GNP/GDP continues to include receipts from the sale of natural assets, and hence overestimates income from production, or value added. It perpetuates (it is argued) the conceptual error that receipts from sales of natural resources can be treated as rental income rather than as capital consumption.

It is true that the depletion adjustment calculated under the depreciation method corrects for this in moving from GNP to NNP, but this encounters another difficulty, part conceptual, part practical. Suppose the economies of two countries are very similar except that one possesses an abundant supply of a valuable natural resource which it exploits at negligible cost. Although the GNP's of the two countries would differ significantly, applying the depreciation method would result in virtually identical NNP's. This is unsatisfactory on conceptual grounds, since it fails to acknowledge the very real advantage which the citizens of the resource-rich country enjoy, and it is unsatisfactory in a practical way, since the citizens of the resource-rich country would in fact enjoy a higher standard of living.

The User Cost method (El Serafy, 1989) addresses both objections, by adjusting GNP/GDP to exclude asset sales, and by recognising, in its method of calculation of depletion, that ownership of a natural resource confers an income advantage to its owner. Receipts from the sale of a natural resource comprise two elements: capital consumption, or user cost, and income, the relative shares of which depend upon the (physical) level of reserves, the current rate of (physical) extraction, and the choice of discount rate to apply to future flows of income from sales.

[4] See, for example, Repetto *et al.* (1987).

Application of the User Cost method yields the following expression for the share of 'true' income in receipts from natural resource sales:

$$\frac{X}{R} = 1 - \frac{1}{(1+r)^n}$$

where X = true income
R = net receipts from sales (as defined in footnote 3)
r = a discount rate
n = number of years for which current extraction rates could be sustained, i.e. known exploitable reserves divided by the current rate of extraction.

The complementary expression

$$\frac{(R-X)}{R} = \frac{1}{(1+r)^n}$$

gives us the user cost or depletion share. This is inversely related to n (the 'lifetime' of the resource given the current rate of extraction) and r (the rate at which resource owners discount future revenues). If the resource is abundant relative to current use, then n will be large, $1/(1+r)^n$ will be very small, and X (true income) will be close to R (receipts from sales). In the limit, as $n \to \infty$, $X = R$ and all receipts will count as income, which corresponds to current national accounts practice. In effect, then, the current SNA implicitly treats natural resources as inexhaustible.

In contrast, if society decides to lend considerable weight to the consumption possibilities of succeeding generations, the discount rate r will be set at a low level, $1/(1+r)^n$ will be relatively large, and the share of income in receipts from sales will be relatively small. As $r \to 0$, $1/(1+r)^n \to$ unity for any value of n and X, and so $X/R \to 0$.

Table 14.3 shows the share of user cost in receipts from resource sales for various choices of discount

Table 14.3 User cost share of receipts from sales of non-renewable natural resources

Lifetime of resource at current extraction rates (years)	Discount rate (%)				
	1	3	5	7	10
1	98	94	91	87	83
5	94	84	75	67	56
10	90	72	58	48	35
25	78	46	28	17	8
50	60	28	8	3	1
100	37	14	2	0	0

Source: adapted from El Serafy (1989).

Table 14.4 Alternative estimates of depletion of the UK oil and natural gas reserves (£m)

Year	User cost method	Depreciation method[a]	Oil and gas GDP[b]	Total GDP at factor cost
1980	2 600	6 600	8 700	201 017
1981	4 200	9 400	4 800	218 755
1982	5 300	10 700	13 800	138 231
1983	5 200	12 400	16 200	261 038
1984	7 700	15 400	19 600	280 052
1985	2 900	14 200	19 100	306 276
1986	2 800	4 500	9 000	326 182
1987	3 400	5 100	10 100	358 297
1988	2 000	2 000	2 500	397 292
1989	1 700	1 800	2 300	436 180
1990	1 600	2 200	7 700	477 742

[a]Based on the method proposed by Repetto *et al.* (see footnote 4).
[b]Oil and gas GDP means the value-added in the oil and gas extraction sector, i.e. that sector's contribution to GDP.
Source: CSO estimates from Bryant and Cook (1992).

rate and resource lifetimes. With low discount rates and short lifetimes, user cost is nearly 100% of receipts (the income share is close to zero). With long lifetimes and high rates of discount, nearly all receipts count as income. For any given asset lifetime, notice the importance of the choice of discount rate.

The principle underlying the user cost calculation is as follows: From the receipts from sales (R) of an exhaustible natural resource, a certain proportion is set aside and invested at rate of return r in order to yield the same level of true income X indefinitely.[5] (We assume a constant rate of extraction and constant relative prices.) This is consistent with the idea of sustainable development, allowing for substitution of man-made capital for non-renewable natural capital. Combined (produced and natural) capital is sufficient to at least maintain the same rate of income in successive periods.

Table 14.4 shows some alternative estimates of depletion of UK oil and natural gas reserves, applying the user cost method and a variant of the depreciation method. Note that the depreciation method estimates are significantly greater than the user cost estimates,

[5] The present value of the finite series R ($i = 1, \ldots, n$) is

$$R\left[1 - \frac{1}{(1+r)^n}\right] \bigg/ \left(1 - \frac{1}{1+r}\right)$$

while that of the infinite series X is

$$X \bigg/ \left(1 - \frac{1}{1+r}\right)$$

Equating these two sums yields the expressions for X/R and $(R - X)/R$ in the text above.

since the former counts all oil and gas GDP as depletion except that portion attributable to labour or man-made capital used in extraction. The latter, however, attributes an additional income element to the natural resource sale, so that the residual estimate of depletion is typically less. Especially in the early years when prices were high, above-normal profits were substantial and the depreciation estimate of oil and gas depletion accounted for a significant proportion of oil and gas GDP and, in 1982–85, for around 6–7% of total GDP.

Using the depreciation method, the standard or conventional measure of GDP/GNP would be unaffected but *net* domestic/national product would be reduced by the value of oil and gas depletion (in addition to the depreciation of man-made capital). The relative contribution of oil and gas to net domestic product would fall sharply.

With the user cost method, GDP/GNP would be redefined to exclude the user cost depletion estimates, and hence would be less than the conventional measures currently in use. Although the user cost approach is to be preferred on theoretical and practical grounds, it is unlikely to dislodge the conventional measures of GDP/GNP at least until there is comprehensive coverage of the depletion of natural resources and agreement on methods of valuation and calculation.

With respect to renewable natural resources, the principle of maintaining a stock of capital which will sustain a constant rate of income remains the guideline, but the level of expenditure required to maintain capital can be calculated more directly as the volume of replacement investment – for example, timber felled this year should be replaced by an equal area of new planting. Alternatively, the level of expenditure required could be calculated in a comparable manner to that used to calculate consumption of man-made capital (a particular depreciation rate).

In the case of natural resources or environmental assets which are perceived to yield benefits but which are not monetised, estimates of depletion can be based on a variety of methods including replacement or restoration costs, or willingness to pay, though the inclusion of such costs in the national accounts implies a corresponding income flow which the depletion is set against. The conceptual and practical problems here are similar to those which arise in trying to account for environmental degradation, to which we now turn.

Environmental degradation

Degradation occurs when there is a decline in the quality of the natural environment, in particular of air, water and land quality, defining the last-named in a rather broad sense to include areas of natural heritage as well as simply soil quality.

Land, air and water can also be viewed as natural capital and degradation as consumption of natural capital which should be accounted for in the same way as depletion of man-made capital. There is no difference in principle between this case and that of the depletion of mineral resources discussed above, but the practical problems are more severe. It is not always obvious how degradation should be defined and, even if satisfactorily defined, how it should be valued. A common approach has been to establish certain desirable quality standards, and then to measure degradation as the deviation from these quality levels. The value of the degradation can then be calculated as the cost of making good the degradation which has occurred or the cost of achieving the targeted quality standards. For instance, the UK faces a bill of about £15 billion to achieve required European Union water quality standards by the year 2000. This £15 billion could be interpreted as the cumulated value of the water quality degradation which has occurred, though there is clearly an arbitrary element in this since the water quality standards established may be (and indeed have been) changed; moreover, standards may be set which are higher than might occur in the 'natural' environment. Nor is it clear that the quality standards established are those which correspond to the efficient level of abatement, i.e. where the marginal social

cost of the pollution equals the marginal abatement cost.

Where the use of standards and the costs of achieving these standards are inappropriate, alternative methods of valuing degradation must be sought. 'Willingness to pay' (WTP), either to avoid the degradation, or to make it good, has been proposed in many instances. Assuming it is possible to ascertain individuals' WTP in relation to a particular issue, the value of the degradation or its avoidance could be calculated as the sum of the individual WTP 'bids'. A crude version of this approach is often used by conservation bodies such as the Royal Society for the Protection of Birds (RSPB), where an appeal is launched to meet the cost of purchasing, restoring or maintaining a particular area of natural habitat. However, WTP can be invoked in a purely hypothetical way (by asking people what they would be willing to pay), though there is an obvious risk of over-valuation.

The merits and weaknesses of WTP as a method of valuation, and other indirect methods such as Contingent Valuation, are discussed in Chapter 10. From a national accounting standpoint, a disadvantage of WTP is that it includes consumers' surplus, unlike other components of the national accounts which are valued at market prices, and hence gives too much relative weight to the good or service valued by this method.[6]

Abstracting from the considerable problems of valuation, several commentators have urged that in addition to the depreciation of man-made capital and the depletion of natural resources the costs of environmental degradation should be deducted from GDP/GNP to arrive at 'sustainable' national product. Whatever its merits, there are formidable problems in implementing this proposal. Costs of making good or preventing degradation, even when actually undertaken, may be difficult to identify since they may be embodied in, but form only a part of, a larger item of expenditure – for example the purchase of a new machine with a lower emission of particulates, or investment in a new, more up-to-date water filtration plant, where improved environmental performance is an element in but not the main reason

---

[6] Consumers' surplus is the difference between what a consumer is willing to pay for an item, and what he or she actually pays (the market price). Assuming a normal downward-sloping demand curve, there are bound to be some consumers willing to pay more than the prevailing market price.

for the capital expenditure decision. How much of the expenditure should be attributable to making good or preventing degradation? The purchaser may even be unaware of the beneficial impact of the new investment. In addition the incidence of degradation, particularly air and water degradation caused by emissions, is international in its impact, and this raises the question of how the costs of multinational degradation should be allocated. Acid rain in Norway may be caused by factory emissions in the UK, but which country's GDP should be adjusted to reflect its effects? Without actual compensation, Norway bears the cost, even if the responsibility lies with the UK. Other cases are even more complex (see Discussion Questions).

Defensive expenditure

Within the present SNA, expenditures which are expressly designed to protect the environment and to prevent degradation – so-called defensive expenditure – will be included directly or indirectly in GDP. To the extent that expenditure is incurred by producers – for example waste treatment by enterprises – the cost will be incorporated in product prices but not separately identifiable in the national accounts. Expenditure by households, government or non-profit-making institutions, or capital expenditure by enterprises, will be included on the expenditure side of GDP and should in principle be separately identifiable. Some environmentalists argue that such defensive expenditures should be excluded from or at least deducted from GDP, again based on the concept of 'sustainable' income. Apart from the difficulty of measuring indirect defensive expenditure, and some other practical problems, it is not at all clear why defensive *environmental* expenditure should be treated differently from other forms of defensive expenditure, including expenditure on armed forces, preventive medicine and other outlays which do not in themselves yield direct utility. It is true that an increase in GDP which is caused by increased military expenditure, or by an increase in expenditure on environmental protection (assuming some spare capacity in the economy), might not be thought to add to welfare, but this reflects the limitations of GDP as a measure of economic welfare. It may be better to seek an alternative, complementary measure of economic welfare rather than to redefine GDP/GNP in a way which obfuscates its meaning and which introduces substantive elements of value judgement into the compilation of the national accounts.

If defensive expenditure is not undertaken, there is degradation and hence depletion of natural capital. As we have argued, there is a strong case here for including the cost of consumption of natural capital in GDP/GNP, valued at the cost of prevention or restoration,[7] and for deducting an equivalent amount from GDP/GNP to arrive at NDP/NNP, analogous to the treatment of consumption of man-made capital. Previous caveats over the problems of valuation of degradation apply.

The foregoing discussion reveals that while there is a wide measure of agreement that the conventional system of national accounts is inadequate in its treatment of natural capital, there is considerable uncertainty and controversy over the way in which the SNA should be reformed to better reflect environmental costs and benefits, or whether it might be better to construct an alternative but parallel set of environmental accounts. The issues are compounded by major problems of valuation. The authors of the revised (1993) SNA have essentially adopted a compromise position on the integration of the conventional system of national accounts and environmental accounts, which we now consider briefly in the following section.

A satellite system for integrated environmental and economic accounting

The most recent version of the international System of National Accounts (SNA), published in 1993 (United Nations, 1993), addresses for the first time the possible incorporation of environmental costs and assets in the SNA. However, the report does not recommend the integration of environmental accounts into the central or core SNA. Instead it proposes, for those countries interested in and capable of compiling environmental accounts, a system of so-called satellite accounts; these take the standard SNA as a starting point, and then show how the standard SNA stocks and flows might be complemented or modified by the inclusion of stocks and flows arising from the interaction between the economy and the environment. In fact, the section of the report dealing with this is more of a review of

---

[7] We note here, but do not comment further on the fact that the costs of prevention and restoration may be different, and that both may differ from the (social marginal) costs of the degradation. See Chapter 8.

the current state of the art, and a guide to national accounts practitioners who may wish to experiment with environmental accounting, than a firm proposal for a particular design and methodology.

The discussion and presentation are closely modelled on the System of Environmental Economic Accounts (SEEA) proposed in the UN handbook *Integrated Environmental and Economic Accounting* (United Nations, 1992). The SEEA focuses on (i) accounting adequately for the depletion of scarce natural resources, and (ii) measuring the costs of environmental degradation and its prevention. The basic structure of the SEEA and its links with the SNA are illustrated in Table 14.5, which can also be used to explain the derivation of the main aggregates of the satellite environmental accounts.

The shaded part of Table 14.5 covers the conventional SNA aggregates. Row i records opening assets, $K0_{p.ec}$ being the value of stocks of man-made (produced) capital, and $K0_{np.ec}$ the value of stocks of natural resources (oil and gas, cultivated forests, etc.) regarded as economic assets by the SNA.[8] Row ii records total supply, comprising domestic production (**P**) and imports (**M**).

Row iii shows how total supply is used. A proportion of supply is used in further production (**Ci**); the balance is either exported (**X**), consumed by households or government (**C**), or invested (**Ig**).

Column 1 shows the cost structure of domestic production P, comprising the cost of goods and services used in production (**Ci**), the cost of consumption of fixed (man-made) capital (**CFC**), and the balancing value-added, or net domestic product (**NDP**). Note that **NDP** + **CFC** = Gross Domestic Product. Consumption of fixed capital also appears as a negative item in Column 4; gross investment **Ig** *less* capital consumption **CFC** = net investment **I**.

Row v yields the familiar national accounts identity

$$\mathbf{NDP} = (\mathbf{X} - \mathbf{M}) + \mathbf{C} + \mathbf{I}$$

Rows ix and x include various adjustments to the stock of produced and non-produced assets, including adjustments to account for changes in prices of assets, destruction of assets due to natural disaster, and certain other changes which affect the level of stocks of assets. For produced economic assets, opening stocks $K0_{p.ec}$ plus net investment **I**, plus or minus adjustments $Rev_{p.ec}$ and $Vol_{p.ec}$, gives closing stocks $K1_{p.ec}$ (or opening stocks in the next accounting period). For non-produced economic assets, the entries $Rev_{np.ec}$ and $Vol_{np.ec}$ denote corresponding adjustments to opening stocks $K0_{np.ec}$, resulting in closing stocks $K1_{np.ec}$. The 'Other changes in volume of assets' $Vol_{np.ec}$ include changes in known economic reserves of natural assets.

The non-shaded part of the table shows how the system can be extended to incorporate other environmental accounts, which may be expressed in physical or monetary units, or both. Expressed in physical units, these additional flows can be viewed as supplementary to the SNA; expressed in monetary units, they can be used to obtain environmentally-adjusted measures of domestic product.

The additional column 6 covers natural capital not classified as economic (because their usage does not involve market or quasi-market transactions), such as air, uncultivated land, particular ecosystems, virgin forest, and most forms of surface water. The additional row vi records the use or consumption of non-produced natural assets, Use_{np} – i.e. the depletion/degradation of natural capital, analogous to **CFC** for man-made capital. Use_{np} itself comprises $Use_{np.ec}$ – the depletion of economic natural assets such as sub-soil minerals, commercially exploited forests, and so on – and $Use_{np.env}$ – the degradation of other natural assets caused by human activities, such as air, water and soil pollution, extinction of species, and so on. These are entered as negative elements in columns 5 and 6, hence reducing the stocks of natural assets.

Row vii – 'Other accumulation of non-produced natural assets' – records the transfer of assets from the non-economic to the economic category. For example, improved techniques of extraction have enhanced reserves of economically recoverable oil; the quantity or value of the increase in reserves would appear as a positive entry in column 5, and as an equal but negative entry in column 6. By construction, the entries in this row will sum to zero.

The addition of rows vi and vii to the table will affect one of the entries in the SNA part of the table, namely 'Other changes in volume of (non-produced) assets', $Vol_{np.ec}$. In the SNA, this item includes changes in stocks of economic natural assets, whether through depletion/degradation, or the transfer of assets from the non-economic to the economic category. In the SEEA, these components of $Vol_{np.ec}$ will be recorded in rows vi and vii of column 5.

If the entries in the additional column and rows are expressed in physical units, this completes the table. The SNA monetary aggregates remain unchanged.

---

[8] We retain the somewhat cumbersome notation used in the UN text, for ease of cross-reference.

Table 14.5 Basic structure of the SEEA

		Economic activities					Environment
					Economic assets		Other non-produced natural assets 6
		Production 1	Rest of world 2	Final con-sumption 3	Produced assets 4	Non-produced natural assets 5	
Opening stock of assets	i				$K0_{p.ec}$	$K0_{np.ec}$	
Supply	ii	P	M				
Economic uses	iii	Ci	X	C	Ig		
Consumption of fixed capital	iv	CFC			−CFC		
Net domestic product	v	NDP	X − M	C	I		
Use of non-produced natural assets	vi	Use_{np}				$-Use_{np.ec}$	$-Use_{np.env}$
Other accumulation of non-produced natural assets	vii					$I_{np.ec}$	$-I_{np.env}$
Environmentally adjusted aggregates in monetary environmental accounting	viii	EDP	X−M	C	$A_{p.ec}$	$A_{np.ec}$	$-A_{np.env}$
Holding gains/losses	ix				$Rev_{p.ec}$	$Rev_{np.ec}$	
Other changes in volume of assets	x				$Vol_{p.ec}$	$Vol_{np.ec}$	
Closing stock of assets	xi				$K1_{p.ec}$	$K1_{np.ec}$	

Source: United Nations (1993).

The environmental data supplement the monetary accounts by linking levels of economic activity with changes in the environment. However, if these environmental changes can be monetised, the conventional SNA aggregates can be modified to reflect the use of environmental assets.

Row viii records the modified data. In column 1, the consumption of natural capital (Use_{np}) is deducted from **NDP** (net domestic product) to give **EDP** – environmentally adjusted domestic product, which approaches the concept of sustainable income. Columns 2 and 3 remain unchanged. Columns 4–6 introduce the concept of net accumulation in place of net capital formation in the SNA. In fact, for produced assets, net accumulation is the same as net capital formation, so that $A_{p.ec} = I$. For non-produced economic assets, net accumulation is the sum of depletion/degradation $Use_{np.ec}$ (negative) and additions to economic reserves $I_{np.ec}$ (positive), hence

$A_{np.ec}$ can be positive or negative. Net accumulation of other non-produced natural assets ($A_{np.env}$) is always negative.

The accounting identity between net production and expenditure noted in the equation above now becomes

$$EDP = (X - M) + C + A_{p.ec} + (A_{np.ec} - A_{np.env})$$

Since $A_{p.ec} = I$, and $I_{np.ec}$ and $-I_{np.env}$ cancel out, the term inside the brackets is equal to $-Use_{np}$, which is also the difference between NDP and EDP, hence the identity is maintained.

Presented as a satellite account, the SEEA has a number of obvious merits. It integrates environmental and economic accounts while maintaining continuity and consistency in time series of national accounts by retaining the conventional SNA definitions and aggregates. As satellite accounts, it is less important to attempt to achieve comprehensive coverage of environmental assets before compiling integrated accounts. For certain environmental assets, for example oil and gas, scarce sub-soil minerals and commercial forestry, there are sufficient data on stocks, flows and market values to include them in a set of integrated accounts. In other cases, for example emissions of industrial pollutants, data on physical quantities may be adequate, but valuation may be difficult. As additional data become available, or acceptable methods of valuation are developed, the coverage of the satellite accounts can be extended.

The SEEA also proposes a more transparent treatment of expenditures on environmental protection (referred to in the preceding section as defensive expenditures), by proposing a finer breakdown of the ISIC codes which relate to environmental protection, and by transferring protective expenditures which are undertaken as ancillary activities from their industries of origin to the relevant sub-sector of environmental protection services. A possible sub-sectoral breakdown suggested in the SEEA is shown in Table 14.6. Thus for example if a paper plant collects and treats waste water from its manufacturing process, the expenditures associated with that activity should be transferred from paper manufacturing to subsector 90.2 – collection and treatment of waste water. This would make it possible to identify more exactly the levels of expenditure on environmental protection (and, as some environmentalists have proposed, to adjust the measure of domestic product to exclude such defensive expenditures). However, as remarked in the previous section of this chapter, it is often difficult to separately identify these ancillary expenditures. For example, the cost of catalytic converters

in vehicles is included in the vehicle price and it may not be feasible to separately identify the cost of the exhaust system, and more particularly the part of the vehicle running expenses attributable to exhaust gas cleaning. Nevertheless, environmental protection services, like other services, are growing in importance in relation to overall economic activity, and this in itself supports the case for a greater degree of detail in classification.

Considerable progress has been made in recent

Table 14.6 Two-digit ISIC categories that identify environmental protection services

Code	Category
37	Recycling
90	Sewage and refuse disposal, sanitation and similar activities
90.1[a]	Collection, transport, treatment and disposal of waste
90.2[a]	Collection and treatment of waste water
90.3[a]	Cleaning of exhaust gases
90.4[a]	Noise abatement
90.5[a]	Other environmental protection services n.e.c.
90.6[a]	Sanitation and similar services

[a] Proposed SEEA breakdown.
Source: United Nations (1993).

Box 14.1 Directions for the European Union on environmental indicators and green national accounting

As a follow-up to the Fifth Environmental Action Programme (CEC, 1992), the European Commission has proposed a harmonised system of integrated economic and environmental indicators and accounts for the member states of the European Union. The main features of the Commission's proposal (CEC, 1994) are

- establishment of a European System for Integrated Environmental and Economic Accounting (ESEA) (which would be closely modelled on the SNA satellite accounts framework);
- establishment of a European System of Environmental Pressure Indices (ESEPI). This will comprise a set of physical indicators and a system of weighting coefficients which may be used to combine indicators into so-called environmental pressure indices – for example, physical measures of emissions of particulates combined to provide a pressure index for air quality;
- combining the more conventional indices of economic performance (growth rates, GDP *per capita*, and so on) with the new indices of environmental pressure, to form a European System of Integrated Economic and Environmental Indices (ESI);
- the development and extension of work on 'greening' the National Accounts, at this stage primarily through the satellite accounts approach, and by improving the methodology and enlarging the scope of monetary valuation of environmental assets and environmental damage.

A useful by-product of this proposal may be greater focus on environmental problems and policies of an international or regional dimension, which as noted in Chapter 12 may not be regarded as priorities at a national level.

years in understanding of the conceptual issues involved in 'green accounting', in methods of valuation (the trickiest problem being that of valuing degradation), and in the compilation of the necessary data. However, the achievement of fully integrated economic and environmental accounts remains a long-term goal, and not necessarily the optimal objective from an environmentalist perspective. In the short to medium term, we will almost certainly see the parallel development of more sophisticated systems of environmental indicators, along with the development and regular publication of satellite monetary accounts of environmental stocks and flows linked to the national accounts. This twin-track approach to environmental accounting may eventually prove a preferred alternative to a unified, fully integrated system of environmental and economic accounts.

Environmental accounting at the firm level

Throughout this chapter the discussion of environmental accounting has been at the national accounting – or 'macro' – level. Ultimately, however, the successful implementation of a system of environmental accounts will require the collection, monitoring and reporting of information by individual organisations, including corporations. Although an increasing number of companies include references to environmental matters in their annual reports, and growing public concern has led manufacturers of consumer products to seek green labelling for their products, environmental accounting at the firm level is in its infancy – indeed at the pre-natal stage.

Despite, or perhaps because of lack of much progress in implementation, there is a growing volume of

---

Box 14.2 Guidelines for environmental accounting at the firm level

Policy
- Statement of environmental policy (or steps being taken).
- Steps taken to monitor compliance with policy statement.
- Statement of compliance with policy statement.

Plans and structure
- Structural and responsibility changes undertaken in the organisation to develop environmental sensitivity (e.g. VP of environment; committees; performance appraisal of line managers).
- Plans for environmental activities – introduction of Environmental Impact Assessment; Environmental Audit; Investment Appraisal criteria; etc.
- Talks with local green groups; plans to work with community, etc.

Financial
- Amount spent on environmental protection – capital/revenue; reaction to/anticipation of legislation; voluntary/mandated; damage limitation/pro-active (enhancement) initiatives.
- Anticipated pattern of future environmental spend – to meet legislation, as voluntary; capital/revenue.
- Assessment of actual and contingent liabilities (e.g. 'Superfund' type problems); impact on financial audit; impact on financial results.

Activity
- Compliance with standards audits; procedures for, results of and issuance of compliance with standards report.

- Environmental audit and issuance of summary/ results.
- Physical units analysis on (e.g.) materials, waste and energy.
- Analysis of dealings with regulatory bodies/fines/ complaints.
- Awards/commendations received.
- Analysis of investment/operating activity influenced by environmental considerations.
- Analysis/description of voluntary projects undertaken (e.g. tree planting; schools liaison).

Sustainable management
- Identification of Critical, Natural Sustainable/ Substitutable, and Man-Made Capital under the influence of (not necessarily 'owned' by) the organisation.
- Statement of transfers between categories.
- Estimates of sustainable activities.
- Estimates of 'sustainable costs' which would have to be incurred to 'return the organisation (and thus future generations) to same position as they were in before the activity'.
- Assessment and statement of input/output resource flows and changes therein.

An alternative or complementary reporting form might recognise the different dimensions of environmental impact – such as resources used; emissions; waste energy; products; transport; packaging; health and safety; toxic hazards; biosphere; built environment; visual environment;community interaction.

Source: adapted from Gray (1994).

current research and debate on the scope and method of environmental accounting and reporting at the firm level. A good critical review is contained in Gray (1994). The United Nations Centre for Transnational Corporations has proposed a system which includes both financial information (actual and anticipated environmental expenditures, potential environmental liabilities including possible remedial costs) and non-financial information (statements of the firm's environmental policy and activities in implementing that policy). This latter part of the proposal can be described as 'Compliance-with-Standard' reporting, in which the firm accounts to society for its success or failure in meeting environmental standards established either by law or by professional or trade associations.

The UN proposals have not yet been adopted at member country level, and it is virtually certain that legislation, rather than voluntary agreement, will be needed to ensure implementation, since except in rare instances of concerted consumer pressure there are no financial incentives or penalties to impel firms to introduce environmental accounts and reports. It is also worth noting, as Gray (1994) emphasises, that there is a profound difference between the relatively modest proposals for environmental accounting, and corporate reporting for sustainable development, which would necessitate a much more extensive volume of information on the firm's use of and impact on the natural environment. Accounting and reporting for sustainable development is still at the exploratory and experimental stage. Box 14.2 reproduces a checklist of quantitative and qualitative information requirements including basic environmental accounts and compliance-with-standard reporting, but extending to the kind of information needed for sustainable development reporting. As a general standard for company accounts and reports, this is some way into the future.

Discussion questions

1 Five European countries have access to the water resources of the River Rhine, which are intensively used for commercial and industrial purposes. Discuss (a) methods of valuation of Rhine water quality degradation caused by human use, and (b) the allocation of these costs between the countries affected.

2 Discuss the arguments for and against the exclusion or deduction of defensive or preventive environmental expenditure from GDP. Identify other components of GDP which, it could be argued, should be excluded for identical or similar reasons.

3 Discuss the distinction between 'economic' and 'non-economic' environmental assets. Compile a short list of three or four specific non-economic environmental assets, and identify the costs and benefits associated with those assets and how these might be valued for national accounts purposes.

4 Devise a checklist for the qualitative and quantitative information which a university should be asked to furnish as a basis for an environmental audit of its functional activities.

Problems

1 A mineral resource is extracted and sold, yielding £20m annual gross revenue to the owners Purchases of goods and services used for extraction are £4m, labour costs are £2m and capital equipment is valued at £30m. The average rate of return on capital in the mineral extraction sector is 4.5%. At current extraction rates, reserves will be economically exhausted in five years. Assume a constant rate of extraction, a fixed extraction technology, and constant relative prices. Calculate a depletion rate for this mineral resource and hence the contribution of this extraction activity to gross and net national product, stating any necessary additional assumptions.

2 Given the valuation problems inherent in assessing many forms of environmental damage or degradation, is it better to concentrate efforts on developing a comprehensive system of physical environmental accounts, rather than attempt to incorporate environmental costs and benefits into the conventional system of national accounts?

Further reading

A good discussion of environmental accounts is to be found in Hamilton *et al.* (1994). An excellent and comprehensive analysis is provided in Ahmad *et al.* (1989). See also Jackson and Marks (1994) and OECD (1994a).

References

ACE (1989) *Solving the Greenhouse Dilemma: A Strategy for the UK*. Association for the Conservation of Energy, 9, Sherlock Mews, London W1M 3RH, UK, June 1989.

Adams, D.D. and Page, W.P. (1985) *Acid Deposition: Environmental, Economic and Policy Issues*. Plenum, New York.

Ahmad, Y.J., El Serafy, S. and Lutz, P. (eds) (1989) *Environmental Accounting for Sustainable Development*. World Bank, Washington.

Alexandros, N. (ed.) (1988) *World Agriculture: Towards 2000*. New York University Press, New York.

Anderson, D. and Bird, C.D. (1990a) *The Carbon Accumulation Problem and Technical Progress*. University College, London, UK and Balliol College, Oxford, UK, September.

Anderson, D. and Bird, C.D. (1990b) *The Carbon Accumulation Problem and Technical Progress: a Simulation Study of the Costs*. University College, London, UK and Balliol College, Oxford, UK, December.

Anderson, F.J. (1985) *Natural Resources in Canada: Economic Theory and Policy*, Second Edition. Nelson, Canada, 1991.

Anderson, L.G. (1981) *Economic Analysis for Fisheries Management Plans*. Ann Arbor Science Publishers, Ann Arbor, MI.

Andreasson, I.-M. (1990) Costs for reducing farmer's use of nitrogen in Gotland, Sweden. *Ecological Economics* 2(4), 287–300.

Arrow, K. (1963) *Social Choice and Individual Values*. Wiley, New York.

Arrow, K. and Fisher, A.C. (1974) Environmental preservation, uncertainty and irreversibility. *Quarterly Journal of Economics* 88, 313–319.

Atkinson, G. and Pearce D.W. (1993) Measuring sustainable development. *The Globe*, Issue No 13, June 1993, UK GER Office, Swindon.

Atkinson, S.E. and Lewis, D.H. (1974) A cost-effectiveness analysis of alternative air quality control strategies. *Journal of Environmental Economics and Management* 1, 237–250.

Ayres, R. U. (1978) *Resources, Environment and Economics*, John Wiley, New York.

Ayres, R.U. and Kneese, A.V. (1969) Production, consumption and externalities. *American Economic Review* 69(3) (June), 282–297.

Bailey, M.J. (1982) Risks, costs and benefits of fluorocarbon regulations. *The American Economic Review*, 72, 247–250.

Baker, P., McKay, S. and Symons, E.J. (1990) *The Simulation of Indirect Tax Reforms: SPIT*. Institute of Fiscal Studies Working Paper, 90/11, UK.

Barbier, E.B. (1989a) *Economics, Natural Resources Scarcity and Development: Conventional and Alternative Views*. Earthscan, London.

Barbier, E.B. (1989b) The global greenhouse effect: economic impacts and policy considerations. *Natural Resources Forum* 13(1).

Barbier, E.B., Burgess, J.C. and Pearce, D.W. (1990) *Slowing Global Warming: Options for Greenhouse Gas Substitution*. London Environmental Economics Centre, London.

Barbier, E.B. and Markandya, A. (1990) The conditions for achieving environmentally sustainable development. *European Economic Review* 34, 659–669.

Barbier, E.B. and Pearce, D.W. (1990) Thinking economically about climate change. *Energy Policy* 18(1), 11–18.

Barker, T. (1990) *Review of Existing Models and Data in the United Kingdom for Environment-Economy Linkage*. Cambridge Econometrics. Department of Applied Economics, University of Cambridge, UK.

Barnett, H.J. (1979) *Scarcity and Growth Revisited*. In V. Kerry Smith (ed.), Scarcity and Growth Reconsidered. Johns Hopkins Press, Baltimore, MD.

Barnett, H.J. and Morse, C. (1963) *Scarcity and Growth: The Economics of Natural Resource Availability*. Johns Hopkins University Press/Resources for the Future, Baltimore, MD.

Barney, G.O. [Study Director] (1980) *The Global 2000 Report to the President of the United States*. In 3 volumes, Pergamon Press, New York.

Barrett, S. (1990) *Pricing the Environment: The Economic and Environmental Consequences of a Carbon Tax*. Briefing Paper, London Business School, London, UK.

Bator, F.M. (1957) The simple analytics of welfare maximisation. *American Economic Review* 47, 22–59.

Baumol, W.J. and Oates, W.E. (1988) *The Theory of Environmental Policy*. Second Edition, Cambridge University Press, Cambridge. [First Edition, 1975].

Beauchamp, T.L. and Bowie, N.E. (1988) *Ethical Theory and Business*. Third Edition, Prentice Hall, Englewood Cliffs, New Jersey.

Becker, G. (1960) *An Economic Analysis of Fertility*. In *Demographic and Economic Changes in Developed Countries*. Princeton University Press, Princeton, New Jersey, pp. 209–231.

Beckerman, W. (1972) Economists, scientists and environmental catastrophe. *Oxford Economic Papers*.

Beckerman, W. (1974) *In Defence of Economic Growth*. Jonathan Cape, London.

Bell, F. and Leeworthy, V. (1990) Recreational demand by tourists for saltwater beach days. *Journal of Environmental Economics and Management*, 18-3, 189–205.

Benson, J. and Willis, K. (1991) *The Demand for Forests for Recreation*. University of Newcastle, Newcastle.

Bentham, J. (1789) *An Introduction to the Principles of Morals and Legislation*. London.

Berndt, E. and Field, B. (eds) (1981) *Measuring and Modelling Natural Substitution*. MIT Press, Cambridge, Massachusetts.

Bertram, I.G., Stephens, R.J., and Wallace, C.C. (1989) *The Relevance of Economic Instruments for Tackling the Greenhouse Effect*. Economics Department, Victoria University, New Zealand, Report to the New Zealand Ministry of the Environment, August.

Bishop, R.C. (1978) Endangered species and uncertainty: the economics of a safe minimum standard. *American Journal of Agricultural Economics* **60**, 10–18.

Bishop, R.C. (1982) Option value: an exposition and extension. *Land Economics* **58**, 1–15.

Bishop, R. and Heberlein, T. (1979) Measuring values of extra-market goods: are indirect measures biased? *American Journal of Agricultural Economics* **61**(5), 926–930.

Bishop, R.C. and Welsh, M.P. (1992) *Existence Value and Resource Evaluation*, Unpublished paper.

Blaug, M. (1985) *Economic Theory in Retrospect*. (4th edition), Cambridge University Press, Cambridge.

Bockstael, N.E, Hanemann, W.M. and Strand, I.E. (1987a) *Measuring the Benefits of Water Quality Improvements using Recreational Demand Models*. Environmental Protection Agency Co-operative Agreement CR-811043-01-0.

Bockstael, N.E, Strand, I.E. and Hanemann, W.M. (1987b) Time and the recreational demand model. *American Journal of Agricultural Economics* **69**, 293–302.

Boero, G., Clarke, R. and Winters, L.A. (1991) *The Macroeconomic Consequences of Controlling Greenhouse Gases: A Survey*. UK Department of the Environment, Room A11, Romney House, 43 Marsham Street, London SW1P 3PY, UK. [Summary and full text available].

Boulding, K.E. (1966) *The Economics of the Coming Spaceship Earth*. In H. Jarrett (ed.), *Environmental Quality in a Growing Economy*, Resources for the Future/Johns Hopkins Press, Baltimore, pp. 3–14.

Boulding, K.E. (1981) *Evolutionary Economics*. Sage, Beverley Hills, California.

Boyle, K.J. and Bishop, R.C. (1987) Valuing wildlife in benefit–cost analysis: a case study involving endangered species. *Water Resources Research* **23**, 942–950.

Bromley, D. W. (ed.) (1995) *The Handbook of Environmental Economics*. Blackwell, Oxford.

Brookshire, D.S, Thayer, M.A., Schulze, W.D. and D'Arge, R.C (1982) Valuing public goods: a comparison of survey and hedonic approaches. *American Economic Review*, March, 165–177.

Brookshire, D., Eubanks, L. and Randall, A. (1983) Estimating option price and existence values for wildlife resources. *Land Economics* **59**(1), 1–15.

Brookshire, D., Thayer, M., Tschirhart, J. and Schulze, W. (1985) A test of the expected utility model: evidence from earthquake risks. *Journal of Political Economy* **93**(2), 369–389.

Broome, J. (1992) *Counting the Cost of Global Warming*. White Horse Press, Cambridge.

Browder, J.O. (ed.) (1988) *Fragile Lands of Latin America: Strategies for Sustainable Development*. Westfield Press, Boulder, Colorado.

Brown, G. and Field, B. (1978) Implications of alternative measures of natural resource scarcity. *Journal of Political Economy* **86**, 229–244.

Brown, G.M. and Field, B. (1979) The adequacy of measures for signalling natural resource scarcity. In V.K. Smith (ed.), *Scarcity and Growth Reconsidered*. Johns Hopkins University Press/Resources for the Future, Inc., Baltimore, MD.

Brown G. and McGuire C.B. (1967) A socially optimal pricing policy for a public water agency. *Water Resources Research* **3**, 33–44.

Brown I. (1989) Energy Subsidies in the United States. In *Energy Pricing: Regulation Subsidies and Distortion*. Surrey Energy Economics Centre Discussion Paper No. 38, University of Surrey, UK, March 1989.

Brown, K. and Pearce, D.W. (1994) *The Causes of Tropical Deforestation*. UCL Press, London.

Brown, L.R. (1981) *Building a Sustainable Society*. Norton, New York.

Bryant, C. and Cook P. (1992) *Environmental Issues and the National Accounts*. Economic Trends No. 469, HMSO, London.

Burniaux, J-M., Martin, J.P., Nicoletti, G. and Martins, J.Q. (1991a) *GREEN – A Multi-Region Dynamic General Equilibrium Model for Quantifying the Costs of Curbing CO_2 Emissions: A technical Manual*. OECD, Department of Economics and Statistics Working Paper No 104, OECD/GD(91)119, Resource Allocation Division, OECD, June.

Burniaux, J-M., Martin, J.P., Nicoletti, G. and Martins, J.Q. (1991b) *The Costs of Policies to Reduce Global Emissions of CO_2: Initial Simulation Results with GREEN*. OECD, Department of Economics and Statistics Working Paper No 103, OCDE/GD(91)115, Resource Allocation Division, OECD, June.

Burniaux, J-M., Martin, J.P., Nicoletti, G. and Martins, J.O. (1992) The costs of international agreements to reduce CO_2 emissions, in *European Economy, The economics of limiting CO_2 emissions*, Special Edition No. 1, Commission of the European Communities, Brussels.

Burrows, P. (1995) *Nonconvexities and the Theory of External Costs*. In Bromley D.W. (ed.), *The Handbook of Environmental Economics*. Blackwell, Oxford.

Business Week (1991) Saving the planet: environmentally advantaged technologies for economic growth. Special supplement, December 30.

Caldwell, J.C. (1981) *Fertility in Africa*. In N. Eberstadt (ed.), *Fertility Decline in the Less Developed Countries*, Praeger, New York. pp. 97–118.

CEC (Commission of the European Communities) (1983) *Acid Rain: A Review of the Phenomenon in the EEC and Europe*. Graham and Trotman, London.

CEC (Commission of the European Communities) (1992) Fifth Environmental Action Programme. Office for Official Publications of the European Communities, Luxembourg.

CEC (Commission of the European Communities) (1994) Directions for the EU on Environmental Indicators and Green National Accounting. Office for Official Publications of the European Communities, Luxembourg.

Chandler, W.U. (1986) *The Changing Role of the Market in National Economies*. Worldwatch Paper 72, Worldwatch Institute, Washington, DC.

Chandler, W.U. (1988) *Climatic Change* **241**, 13.

Chiang, A.C. (1984) *Fundamental Methods of Mathematical Economics*. Third edition, McGraw-Hill, New York.

Chiang, A.C. (1992) *Elements of Dynamic Optimisation*. McGraw-Hill, New York.

Cicchetti, C.V. and Freeman, A.M. (1971) Option Demand and Consumer Surplus, Further Comment. *Quarterly Journal of Economics* **85**, 528–539.

Cipolla, C.M. (1962) *The Economic History of World Population*. Penguin, Harmondsworth.

Ciriacy-Wantrup, S. von (1952) *Resource Conservation, Economics and Policies*. University of California Press, Berkeley and Los Angeles, CA.

Clark, C. (1990) *Mathematical Bioeconomics:The Optimal Management of Renewable Resources*. Second Edition. [1976: First Edition], Wiley, New York.

Clawson, M. (1959) *Methods of Measuring the Demand for and Value of Outdoor Recreation*, Resources for the Future, Reprint Number 10, Washington, DC.

Clawson, M. (1977) *Decision Making in Timber Production, Harvest, and Marketing*. Research Paper R-4, Resources for the Future, Washington, DC.

Clawson, M. and Knetsch, J. (1966) *Economics of Outdoor Recreation*. Johns Hopkins University Press, Baltimore, MD.

Cline, W.R. (1989) *Political Economy of the Greenhouse Effect*. Mimeo, Institute for International Economics, Washington, USA, August.

Cline, W.R. (1991) Scientific basis for the greenhouse effect. *The Economic Journal* **101**, 904–919.

Clunies Ross, A. (1990) Transfers versus licenses as incentives to governments for environmental correctives. Paper submitted to the Development studies Association Annual Conference, University of Strathclyde, Dept. of Economics, 100 Cathedral Street, Glasgow, UK, 1990.

Coase, R. (1960) The problem of social cost. *Journal of Law and Economics*, **3**, 1–44.

Cobbing, P. and Slee, W. (1993) A contingent valuation of the Mar Lodge Estate. *Journal of Environmental Planning and Management* **36**, 1.

Cole, H.S.D., Freeman, C., Jahoda, M. and Pavitt, K.L.R. (eds) (1973) *Thinking about the Future: A Critique of the Limits to Growth*. Chatto and Windus, London, for Sussex University Press.

Common, M. (1988) *Environmental and Resource Economics: An Introduction*. Longman, London.

Common, M. (1989) *The Greenhouse Effect: An Economic Perspective on Origins and Responses*. Unpublished paper, Centre for Resources and Environmental Studies, Australian National University, P.O. Box 4, Canberra, Australia.

Common, M. (1995) *Sustainability and Policy: Limits to Economics*. Cambridge University Press, Sydney.

Common, M. and Perrings, S.C. (1992) Towards an ecological economics of sustainability, *Ecological Economics* **6**(1), 7–34.

Commoner, B. (1963) *Science and Survival*. Ballantine, New York.

Commoner, B. (1972) *The Closing Circle*. Jonathan Cape, London.

Connor, S. (1993) Ozone depletion linked in rise to harmful radiation. *The Independent*, 23 April.

Conrad, J.M. (1995) *Bioeconomic Models of the Fishery*. In Bromley, D.W. (ed.), *The Handbook of Environmental Economics*, Blackwell, Oxford.

Conrad, J.M. and Clark, C.W. (1987) *Natural Resource Economics: Notes and Problems*. Cambridge University Press, New York.

Conway, G.R. (1985) Agroecosystem analysis. *Agricultural Administration* **20**, 31–55.

Conway, G. (1992) Sustainability in agricultural development: trade-offs with productivity, stability and equitability. *Journal for Farming Systems Research and Extension*.

Costanza, R. (ed.) (1991) *Ecological Economics: The Science and Management of Sustainability*. Columbia University Press, New York.

Cropper, M.L. and Oates, W.E. (1992) Environmental economics: a survey. *Journal of Economic Literature*, **XXX**, 675–740.

Crosson, P.R. and Brubaker, S. (1982) *Resource and Environmental Effects of US Agriculture*. Johns Hopkins University Press for Resources for the Future, Baltimore, MD.

Cummings, R., Brookshire, D. and Schulze, W. (eds) (1986) *Valuing Environmental Goods: An Assessment of the Contingent Valuation Method*. Rowman and Allenheld, Lanham, Maryland.

Daly, H.E. (1973) *The Steady State Economy: Toward a Political Economy of Biophysical Equilibrium and Moral Growth*. In Daly, H.E. (ed.), *Toward a Steady State Economy*. W.H. Freeman, San Francisco, CA.

Daly, H.E. (1974) *The Economics of the Steady State*.

Daly, H.E. (1977) *Steady State Economics*. Freeman, San Francisco, CA.

Daly, H.E. (1987) The economic growth debate: what some economists have learned but many have not. *Journal of Environmental Economics and Management*, December, Vol. 14, 4.

D'Arge, R.C. and Kogiku, K.C. (1972) *Economic Growth and The Environment*. Review of Economic Studies, 40, 61–78.

Darnell, R.M. (1973) *Ecology and Man*. W.C. Brown, New York.

Dasgupta, P. (1982) *The Control of Resource*. Basil Blackwell, Oxford.

Dasgupta, P. (1990) The environment as a commodity. *Oxford Review of Economic Policy* **6**(1), 51–67.

Dasgupta, P. (1992) *The Population Problem. Faculty of Economics and Politics*, University of Cambridge. (Manuscript).

Dagupta, P. (1993) *Natural Resources in an Age of Substitutability*. Chapter 23 in Kneese, A.V. and Sweeney, J.L. (eds) (1993) *Handbook of Natural Resource and Energy Economics*, Volume 3.

Dasgupta, P, and Heal, G.M. (1974) The optimal depletion of exhaustible resources. *Review of Economic Studies, Symposium*, May, pp. 3–28.

Dasgupta, P. and Heal, G. (1979) *Economic Theory and Exhaustible Resources*. Cambridge University Press, Cambridge.

Debreu, G. (1959) *Theory of Value*. Wiley, New York.

Department of Energy (1989) *An Evaluation of Energy Related Greenhouse Gas Emissions and Measures to Ameliorate Them*. Energy Paper No 58, January, HMSO, London, UK.

Desvousges, W., Smith, V. and Fisher, A. (1987) Option price estimates for water quality improvements. *Journal of Environmental Economics and Management* **14**, 248–267.

Deverajan, S. and Fisher, A.C. (1980) Exploration and Scarcity. *Journal of Political Economy* **90**, 1279–1290.

Deverajan, S. and Fisher, A.C. (1982) *Measures of Resource Scarcity under Uncertainty*. In V. Kerry Smith and Krutilla, J.V. (eds), *Explorations in Natural Resource Economics*, Johns Hopkins University Press/Resources for the Future, Baltimore, MD.

Diamond, P., Hausman, J., Leonard, G. and Denning, M. (1992) *Does Contingent Valuation Measure Preferences? Experimental Evidence*. In *Contingent Valuation: A Critical Assessment*. Cambridge Economics, Cambridge, Massachusetts.

Domar, E.D. (1957) *Essays in the Theory of Economic Growth*. Oxford University Press, New York.

Dornbusch, R. and Poterba, J. (eds) (1991) *Economic Policy Responses to Global Warming*.

Durning, A.B. (1989) *Poverty and the Environment: Reversing the Downward Spiral*. Paper No. 92, Worldwatch Institute, Washington, DC.

Easterlin, R.A (1978) *The Economics and Sociology of Fertility: A Synthesis*. In C. Tilley (ed.), *Historical Studies of Changing Fertility*. Princeton University Press, Princeton, New Jersey,

Easterlin, R.A (1980) (ed.) *Population and Economic Change in Developing Countries*. University of Chicago Press, Chicago, IL.

Eberstadt, N. (1981) (ed.) *Fertility Decline in the Less Developed Countries*. Praeger, New York.

EC (1988) Main Findings of the Commission's Review of Member States' Energy Policies. Commission of the European Communities COM(88), Final Vol 11.

EC (1992) *Towards Sustainability*. Commission of the European Communities, background report ISEC/B19/92, 21 July.

Ecstein, O. (1958) *Water Resources Development: The Economics of Project Evaluation*. Harvard University Press, Cambridge, MA.

Edmonds, J.A. (1988) *Climatic Change* **13**, 237.

Edmonds, J. and Barns, D.W. (1990a) *Estimating the Marginal Cost of Reducing Global Fossil Fuel CO_2 Emissions*. PNL-SA-18361, Pacific Northwest Laboratory, Washington, DC, USA.

Edmonds, J. and Barns, D.W. (1990b) *Factors Affecting the Long Term Cost of Global Fossil Fuel CO_2 Emissions Reductions*. Global Environmental Change Programme, Pacific Northwest Laboratory, Washington, DC, USA.

Edmonds, J. and Reilly, J.M. (1985) *Global Energy: Assessing the Future*. Oxford University Press, New York.

Ehrenfeld, D. (1988) *Why Put a Value on Biodiversity?* In E.O. Wilson, (ed.), *Biodiversity*. National Academy of Science Press, Washington, DC, pp. 212–216.

Ehrlich, P. (1970) *The Population Bomb*. Ballantine.

Ehrlich, P. and Ehrlich, A. (1981) *Extinction: The Causes and Consequences of the Disappearance of Species*. Random House, New York.

El Serafy, S. (1989) *The Proper Calculation of Income from Depletable Natural Resources*. In Ahmad, Y.J., El Serafy, S. & Lutz, P. (eds), *Environmental Accounting for Sustainable Development*, World Bank, Washington, DC.

Environmental Ethics: See in particular Summer 1982 Symposium Issue.

EPA (1988) *The potential effects of Global Climate Change on the United States*. J.B. Smith and D.A. Tirpak (eds), US Environmental Protection Agency, 1988. (In 3 volumes.)

EPA (1989) *Policy Options for Stabilising Global Climate*. Draft Report to US Congress, Lashof, J.A. and Tirpak, D.A. (eds), US Environmental Protection Agency, February 1989. (In two volumes).

EPA (1991) *Final Regulating Impact Analysis of National Primary Drinking Water Regulations for Lead and Copper*. US Office of Drinking Water, US Environmental Protection Agency, Washington, DC.

EPA (1993) United States Environmental Protection Agency 33/50 Programme: Third Progress Update, EPA Report No 745-R-93-001, Washington, DC.

Everest, D. (1988) The Greenhouse Effect, Issues for Policy Makers. Joint Energy Programme, Royal Institute of International Affairs, London.

FAO: See United Nations FAO.

Feldman, S.L. and Raufer, R.K. (1982) *Emissions Trading and Acid Rain: Implementing a Market approach to Pollution Control*. Rowman and Littlefield, New Jersey.

Fisher, A.C. (1979) *Measurements of Natural Resource Scarcity*. In V. Kerry Smith (ed.), *Scarcity and Growth Reconsidered*. Johns Hopkins Press, Baltimore, MD.

Fisher, A.C. (1981) *Resource and Environmental Economics*. Cambridge University Press, Cambridge, UK.

Fisher, A.C. and Hanemann, M. (1987)

Fisher, A.C. and Peterson, F. (1976) The environment in economics: A survey. *Journal of Economic Literature*, March.

Fisher, A.C., and Rothkopf, M.H. (1989) Market failure and energy policy. *Energy Policy* **17**(4), 397–406.

Forrester, J.W. (1971) *World Dynamics*. Wright-Allen Press, Inc., Cambridge, Massachusetts.

Freeman, A.M. (1979) *The Benefits of Environmental Improvement: Theory and Practice*. Johns Hopkins University Press, Baltimore, MD.

Freeman, A.M. (1985) Supply uncertainty, option price and option value. *Land Economics* **61**(2), 176–181.

French, H. (1990) *Clearing the Air*, In *State of The World, 1990*. L.R. Brown (ed.), Norton, New York.

Georgescu-Roegen, N. (1971) *The Entropy Law and The Economic Process*. Harvard University Press, Cambridge, Massachusets.

Goodpaster, K.E. (1978) On being morally considerable. *The Journal of Philosophy*, 75.

Goodstein, E.S. (1995) *Economics and the Environment*. Prentice-Hall, Englewood Cliffs, New Jersey.

Gordon, H.S. (1954) The economic theory of a common-property resource: the fishery. *Journal of Political Economy*, April.

Gray, L.C. (1914) Rent under the assumption of exhaustibility. *Quarterly Journal of Economics* **28**, 466–489.

Gray, R.H. (1994) Corporate reporting for sustainable development: accounting for sustainability in 2000 AD. *Environmental Values*, 3, 17–45.

Greenaway, D., Leybourne, S.J., Reed, G.V. and Whalley, J. (1993) *Applied General Equilibrium Modelling: Applications, Limitations and Future Development*, HMSO, London.

Griliches, Z. (1971) *Price Indexes and Quality Change*. Harvard University Press, Cambridge, Massachusetts.

Grubb, M. (1989a) *The Greenhouse Effect: Negotiating Targets*. Royal Institute of International Affairs, London.

Grubb, M. (1989b) *On Coefficients for Determining Greenhouse Gas Emissions from Fossil Fuels*. IEA Expert Seminar on technologies to reduce greenhouse gas emissions, Paris, March (IEA/OECD).

Hahn, R.W. (1984) Market power and transferable property rights. *Quarterly Journal of Economics* **99**, 763–765.

Hahn, R.W. (1989) Economic prescriptions for environmental problems: how the patient followed the doctor's orders. *The Journal of Economic Perspectives* 3, 95–114.

Hahn, R.W. and Hester, G.L. (1989a) Where did all the markets go? An analysis of the EPA's emission trading program. *Yale Journal of Regulation* 6, 109–53.

Hahn, R.W. and Hester, G.L. (1989b) Marketable permits: lessons for theory and practice. *Ecology Law Quarterly* 16, 361–406.

Hahn, R.W. and Noll, R.G. (1982) *Designing a Market for Tradeable Emissions Permits*. In W.A. Magat (ed.), *Reform of Environmental Regulation*. Ballinger, Cambridge, Massachusetts.

Halkos, G. and Hutton, J. (1993) *Acid Rain Games in Europe*. Discussion Papers in Economics No. 93/12, University of York , UK.

Hall, D.C. *et al.* (1989) Organic food and sustainable agriculture. *Contemporary Policy Issues*, 7, October.

Halliday, D. and Resnick, R. (1988) *Fundamentals of Physics*. Third Edition, Wiley, New York.

Hamilton, K., Pearce, D.W., Atkinson, G., Gomez-Lobo, A. and Young, C. (1994) *The Policy Implications of Natural Resource and Environmental Accounting*. CSERGE Working Paper GEC 94–18. University College, London.

Hanemann, M. (1991) Willingness to pay and willingness to accept: how much can they differ? *American Economic Review* **81**(3), 635–647.

Hanley, N. (1988) Using contingent valuation to value environmental improvements. *Applied Economics* **20**, 541–549.

Hanley, N. (1989) *Problems in Valuing Environmental Improvements from Agricultural Policy Changes: The Case of Nitrate Pollution*. Discussion Paper No. 89/1, Economics Department, University of Stirling.

Hanley, N. and Spash, C. (1993) *Cost–Benefit Analysis and the Environment*. Edward Elgar, Aldershot, England.

Hansen, J. (1990) *Greenhouse and Developing Countries*. Paper presented at the symposium 'Environment and Economics in the Developing Countries', Association of the Bar of the City of New York, 23 May.

Hansen, J. *et al.* (1988) Global climate changes as forecast by Goddard Institute for Space Studies three dimensional model. *Journal of Geophysical Research* **93**(D8), 9341–9364.

Harberger, A.C. (1971) Three basic postulates for applied welfare economics: an interpretative essay. *Journal of Economic Literature* **9**, 785–797.

Hardin, G. (1968) The tragedy of the commons. *Science*, **168**, 13 December.

Harris, D.P. (1993) *Mineral Resource Stocks and Information*, Chapter 21 in Kneese, A.V. and Sweeney, J.L. (eds), *Handbook of Natural Resource and Energy Economics*. Volume 3, Elsevier Science Publishers, Amsterdam.

Harris, M. and Ross, E.B. (1987) *Death, Sex and Fertility: Population Regulation in Preindustrial and Developing Societies*. Columbia University Press, New York.

Harrison, D. Jr. (1983) *Case Study 1: The Regulation of Aircraft Noise*. In T.C. Schelling (ed.), *Incentives for Environmental Protection*, MIT Press, Cambridge, Massachusetts.

Harrod, R.F. (1936) *The Trade Cycle*. Oxford University Press, Oxford.

Harrod, R. (1948) *Towards a Dynamic Economy*. St Martins Press, London.

Hartwick, J.M. (1977) Intergenerational Equity and the Investing of Rents from Exhaustible Resources. *American Economic Review* **67**, 972–974.

Hartwick, J.M. (1978) Substitution Among Exhaustible Resources and Intergenerational Equity. *Review of Economic Studies* **45**, 347–354.

Hartwick, J.M. and Olewiler, N.D. (1986) *The Economics of Natural Resource Use*. Harper and Row, New York.

Heal, G.M. (1981) *Economics and Resources*. In R. Butlin (ed.), Economics of the Environment and Natural Resource Policy. Westview Press, Boulder, Colorado.

Heal, G. (1990) *The Optimal Use of Exhaustible Resources*. Chapter 18 in Kneese, A.V. and Sweeney, J.L. (1985) *Handbook of Natural Resource and Energy Economics*, Volume 3, Elsevier Science Publishers, Amsterdam.

Heijman, W. (1990) *Natural Resource Depletion and Market Forms*. Wageningen Economic Papers, Wageningen Agricultural University, The Netherlands.

Herfindahl, O.C. and Kneese, A.V. (1974) *Economic Theory of Natural Resources*. Charles E. Merrill Publishing, Ohio.

Hicks, J.R. (1939) *Value and Capital*. Oxford University Press, Oxford.

Hicks, J.R. (1941) The rehabilitation of consumers' surplus. *Review of Economic Studies* **8**, February, 108–116.

Hirsch, F. (1976) *The Social Limits to Growth*. Harvard University Press, Cambridge, Massachusetts.

Hirsch, F. (1977) *Social Limits to Growth*. Routledge & Kegan Paul, London.

Hirschborn, J. (1991) Technological potential in pollution prevention, *Pollution Prevention* **1**(2), 21–24.

Hoel, M. (1989) *Global Environmental Problems: The Effects of Unilateral Action Taken by One Country*, Working Paper No 11, Department of Economics, University of Oslo.

Hogan, W.H. and Manne, A.S. (1979) *Energy–Economy Interactions: The Fable of the Elephant and the Rabbit?* In Pindyck, R.S. (ed.), *Advances in the Economics of Energy and Resources*. Volume 1, JAI Press, Greenwich, Connecticut.

Hohmeyer, O. (1988) *Social Costs of Energy Consumption.* Springer, Heidelberg, Germany.

Holdgate, M.W. (1989) *Climatic Change: Meeting the Challenge.* Commonwealth Secretariat, London.

Holling, C.S. (1973) Resilience and stability of ecological systems. *Annual Review of Ecological Systems* **4**, 1–24.

Holling, C.S. (1986) *The Resilience of Terrestrial Ecosystems: Local Surprise and Global Change.* In W.C. Clark and R.E. Munn (ed.), *Sustainable Development of the Biosphere*, Cambridge University Press, Cambridge.

Hotelling, H. (1931) The economics of exhaustible resources. *Journal of Political Economy* **39**, 137–175.

Hufschmidt, M.M. *et al.* (1983) *Environment, Natural Systems and Development: an Economic Valuation Guide.* Johns Hopkins University Press, Baltimore, Maryland.

Hume, D. (1739) *A Treatise on Human Nature.* In *Hume's Moral and Political Philosophy.* 1968, Hafner, New York.

Hume, D. (1751) *An Enquiry Concerning the Principle of Morals*, in *Hume's Moral and Political Philosophy*, 1968, Hafner Publishing Co., New York.

Hunt, W.M. (1980) Are 'Mere Things' Morally Considerable? *Environmental Ethics* **2**(1).

Huppert, D.H. (1990) *Managing Alaska's Groundfish Fisheries: History and Prospects.* University of Washington Institute for Marine Resources Working Paper, May.

IBRD (1992) *World Development Report 1992.* The World Bank, Oxford University Press, Oxford.

IEA (1990) *Energy and The Environment: Policy Overview.* Organisation for Economic Co-operation and Development, Paris.

Ingham, A. and Ulph, A. (1990) *Market-based Instruments for Reducing CO_2 Emissions – The Case of UK Manufacturing.* Discussion Paper in Economics and Econometrics, No 9004, University of Southampton, UK, November.

IPCC (1990) *Second Draft Reports of the Intergovernmental Panel On Climate Change (Climate, Impact and Policy Groups)*, April 1990. The report of the first group (Climate) has been published as: Houghton, R., Jenkins, G.J., and Ephraums, E (1990) *Climate Change: the IPCC Scientific Assessment.* Cambridge University Press, Cambridge, UK.

Jackson, T. and Marks, N. (1994) *Measuring Sustainable Development – a Pilot Index: 19550–1990.* Stockholm Environment Institute and New Economic Foundation, London & Stockholm.

Jevons, W.S. (1865) *The Coal Question: An Inquiry Concerning the Progress of the Nation and the Probable Exhaustion of our Coal Mines.* Second edition, Macmillan, London.

Jevons, W.S. (1871) *The Theory of Political Economy.* First edition, Macmillan, London.

Johansson, P-O. (1987) *The Economic Theory and Measurement of Environmental Benefits.* Cambridge University Press, Cambridge.

Johansson, P-O. (1990) Valuing environmental damage. *Oxford Review of Economic Policy* **6**(1), 34–51.

Johnson, D.G. (1984) In Simon, J.L. and Kahn, H., *The Resourceful Earth*, Basil Blackwell, Oxford.

Johnson, M.G.M. (1989) *Leading Issues in Economic Development.* Fifth Edition, Oxford University Press, New York.

Jorgensen, D. and Griliches, Z. (1967) The explanation of productivity change. *Review of Economics and Statistics* **34**, 250–282.

Jorgensen, D.W and Wilcoxen, P.J. (1990a) *The Costs of Controlling US Carbon Dioxide Emissions.* Paper presented at Workshop on Economic/Energy/Environmental Modelling for Climate Policy Analysis, Washington, DC, USA, 22–23 October.

Jorgensen, D.W and Wilcoxen, P.J. (1990b) *Global Change, Energy Prices, and US Economic Growth.* Paper presented for the Energy Pricing Hearing, US Department of Energy, Washington, DC, USA, 20 July.

Jorgensen, D.W and Wilcoxen, P.J. (1990c) Environmental legislation and US economic growth. *RAND Journal of Economics*, **21**(2), 314–340.

Just, R.E., Hueth, D.L. and Schnitz, A. (1982) *Applied Welfare Economics and Public Policy.* Prentice-Hall, Englewood Cliffs, New Jersey.

Kahn, R.F. (1931) The relation of home investment to unemployment. *Economic Journal*, 173–198.

Kaldor, N. (1957) A model of economic growth. *Economic Journal*, 591–624.

Kant, I. *Groundwork of the Metaphysic of Morals.* Section II, Various translations and editions.

Keepin, B. (1988) *Climatic Change* **13**, 233.

Keepin, B and Kats, G. (1988) Greenhouse Warming: Comparative Analysis of Nuclear and Efficiency Abatement Strategies. *Energy Policy* **16**(6), 538–561.

Kemp, D.D. (1990) *Global Environmental Issues: A Climatological Approach.* Routledge, London.

Keynes, J.M. (1936) *The General Theory of Employment, Interest and Money.* Macmillan, London.

Klassen, G.A.J. and Opschoor, J.B. (1991) Economics of sustainability or the sustainability of economics: different paradigms. *Ecological Economics* **4**, 93–115.

Kneese, A.V., Ayres, R.V. and D'Arge, R.C. (1970) *Economics and the Environment: A Materials Balance Approach.* The Johns Hopkins University Press, Baltimore, MD.

Kneese, A.V. (1984) *Measuring the Benefits of Clean Air and Water.* Resources for the Future, Washington, DC.

Kneese, A.V. and Schulze, W.D. (1985) Ethics and Environmental Economics. Chapter 5 in Kneese, A.V. and Sweeney, J.L. (eds), *Handbook of Natural Resource and Energy Economics*, Volume 1.

Kneese, A.V. and Sweeney, J.L. (1985a) *Handbook of Natural Resource and Energy Economics.* Volume 1, Elsevier Science Publishers, Amsterdam.

Kneese, A.V. and Sweeney, J.L. (1985b) *Handbook of Natural Resource and Energy Economics.* Volume 2, Elsevier Science Publishers, Amsterdam.

Kneese, A.V. and Sweeney, J.L. (1993) *Handbook of Natural Resource and Energy Economics.* Volume 3, Elsevier Science Publishers, Amsterdam.

Knetsch, J. (1990) Environmental policy implications of disparities between willingness to pay and compensation demanded. *Journal of Environmental Economics and Management* **18**, 227–237.

Koopmans, T.C. (1973) *Some Observations on 'Optimal' Economic Growth and Exhaustible Resources.* Cowles Foundation Discussion Paper, No 356.

Kornai, J. (1986) *Contradictions and Dilemmas: Studies on the Socialist Economy and Society.* MIT Press, Cambridge, Massachusetts.

Kosmo, M. (1989) *Money to Burn? The high price of Energy Subsidies.* World Resources Institute, Washington, DC.

Krebs, C.J. (1985) *Ecology.* Harper and Row, New York.

Krupnick, A.J. (1986) Costs of alternative policies for the control of nitrogen dioxide in Baltimore, MD. *Journal of Environmental Economics and Management* **13**, 189–197.

Krutilla, J.V. (1967) Conservation reconsidered, *American Economic Review* **54**(4), 777–786.

Krutilla, J.V and Fisher, A.C. (1975) *The Economics of Natural Environments.* Johns Hopkins University Press, Baltimore, MD.

Kula, E. (1994) *Economics of Natural Resources, the Environment and Policies.* Second Edition, Chapman and Hall, London.

Lashof, D. and Ahuja, D.R. (1990) Relative contributions of greenhouse gas emissions to global warming. *Nature* **334**, 529–531, 5 April.

Layard, P.R.G. and Walters, A.A. (1978) *Microeconomic Theory.* First Edition, McGraw-Hill, Maidenhead.

Layard, R. and Glaister, S. (eds) (1994) *Cost–Benefit Analysis.* Second Edition, Cambridge University Press, Cambridge.

Leach, G. (1975) *Energy and Food Production.* International Institute for Environment and Development.

Lecomber, R. (1975) *Economic Growth versus the Environment.* Macmillan, London.

Lele, S.M. (1991) Sustainable Development: A Critical Review. *World Development* **19** 607–621.

Leontief, W. (1970a) Environmental repercussions and the economic structure: an input–output approach, *Review of Economics and Statistics* **52**, 262–277.

Leontief, W. (1970b) The dynamic inverse. In A.P. Carter and A. Brody (eds), *Contributions to Input–Output Analysis,* North-Holland, Amsterdam.

Leontief, W. and Ford, D. (1972) Air pollution and the economic structure: Empirical results of input–output computations. In A. Brody and A.P. Carter (eds), *Input–Output Techniques,* North-Holland, Amsterdam.

Leontief, W. *et al.* (1977) *The Future of the World Economy.* Oxford University Press, New York.

Leopold, A. (1949) *A Sand County Almanac, with Essays on Conservation from Round River.* New York 1970, first published 1949.

Lind, R. (ed.) (1982) *Discounting for Time and Risk in Energy Policy.* Johns Hopkins University Press, Baltimore, MD.

Locke, J. (1960)   *Second Treatise on Civil Government.* Cambridge University Press, New York [Laslett Edition].

Lovelock, J. (1989) *The Ages of Gaia: A Biography of Our Living Earth.* Oxford University Press, Oxford.

Ludwig, D., Hilborn, R. and Walters, C. (1993) Uncertainty, Resource Exploitation and Conservation: Lessons from History. *Science* **260**, 17–18.

Maass, A., Hufschmidt, M., Dorfman, R., Thomas, H.A., Marglin, S. and Fair, G. (1962) *Design of Water Resource Systems.* Harvard University Press, Cambridge.

MacGillivray, A. (1994) *Environmental Measures.* Environmental Challenge Group, London.

Maddox, J. (1971) *The Doomsday Syndrome.* Macmillan, London.

Maler, K.G. (1985) Welfare Economics and the Environment. Chapter 1 in Volume 1, Kneese, A.V. and Sweeney, J.L. (eds), *Handbook of Natural Resource and Energy Economics,* Elsevier Science Publishers, Amsterdam.

Maler, K.G. (1990) International Environmental Problems. *Oxford Review of Economic Policy* **6**(1), 80–107.

Maloney, M.T. and Yandle, B. (1984) Estimation of the cost of air pollution control regulation. *Journal of Environmental Economics and Management* **11**, 244–63.

Malthus, T.R. (1798) *An Essay on the Principle of Population as it Affects the Future Improvement of Society.* Ward-Lock, London.

Manne, A.S. (1979) ETA Macro. In R.S. Pindyck (ed.), *Advances in the Economics of Energy and Resources,* Vol. 2, JAI Press, Greenwich, CT.

Manne, A.S. and Richels, R.G. (1989) CO_2 *Emission Limits: An Economic Analysis for the USA.* Mimeo, Stanford University and Electric Power Research Institute, Paolo Alto, CA, USA, November 1989. (Published in *The Energy Journal* (April 1990), 11(2), 51–74).

Manne, A.S. and Richels, R.G. (1990) CO_2 *Emission Limits: A Global Economic Cost Analysis.* Paper presented at the workshop on Energy/CO_2 Data, International Institute for Applied System Analysis, Laxenburg, Austria, January 22–23. Published in *The Energy Journal* (1991), 12(1).

Marglin, S. (1963) The social rate of discount and the optimal rate of investment. *Quarterly Journal of Economics* **77**, 95–111.

Marin, A. and Psacharopoulos, G. (1982) The reward for risk in the labour market: evidence from the United Kingdom and a reconciliation with other studies. *Journal of Political Economy* **90**.

Markandya, A (1992) The Value of the Environment: a State of the Art Survey. In Markandya, A. and Richardson, J. (eds), *The Earthscan Reader in Environmental Economics.* Earthscan, London.

Markandya, A. and Richardson, J. (eds) (1992) *The Earthscan Reader in Environmental Economics.* Earthscan, London.

Marshall, A. (1890) *Principles of Economics.* Macmillan, London.

Marx, K. (1960 edition) *Capital* (in 3 volumes). Foreign Languages Publishing House, Moscow.

Maudlin, W.P. (1981) *Patterns of Fertility Decline in Developing Countries, 1970–75.* In Eberstadt, N. (ed.), *Fertility Decline in the Less Developed Countries,* Praeger, New York, 72–96.

McGartland, A.M. (1984) *Marketable Permit Systems for Air Pollution Control.* PhD Dissertation, University of Maryland.

McKinsey (1989) *Protecting the Global Environment.* McKinsey and Company, Report to Ministerial Conference on Atmospheric Pollution and Climatic Change, Noordwijk, The Netherlands, November.

McNicoll, I.H. and Blackmore, D. (1993) *A Pilot Study on the Construction of a Scottish Environmental Input–Output System,* Report to Scottish Enterprise, Department of Economics, University of Strathclyde, Glasgow.

Meadows, D.H., Meadows, D.L., Randers, J. and Behrens, W.W. (1972) *The Limits to Growth: A Report for The Club of Rome's project on the Predicament of Mankind.* Earth Island, Universe Books, New York. [Also known as Club of Rome Report].

Menger, K. (1950) *Principles of Economics.* Free Press, New York.

Mikesell, R (1977) *The Rate of Discount for Evaluating Public Projects*. American Enterprise for Public Policy Research, Washington, DC.

Mill, J.S. (1857) *Principles of Political Economy*. J.W. Parker and Son. [6th ed. 1865, Augustus M Kelly, New York.]

Mill, J.S. (1863) *Utilitarianism*.

Miller, R.E. and Blair P.D. (1985) *Input–Output Analysis; Foundations and Extensions*, Prentice-Hall, Englewood Cliffs, New Jersey.

Mintzer, I.M. (1987) *A matter of degrees: The Potential for Controlling the Greenhouse Effect*. Research Report 5, World Resources Institute, Washington, DC, USA.

Mishan, E.J. (1967) *The Costs of Economic Growth*. Staples Press, London.

Mitchell, R. and Carson, R. (1984) *A Contingent Valuation Estimate of National Freshwater Benefits*. Technical Report to the United States Environmental Protection Agency. Resources for the Future, Washington, DC.

Mitchell, R. and Carson, R. (1989) *Using Surveys to Value Public Goods: The Contingent Valuation Method*. Resources for the Future, Washington, DC.

Munro, G. (1981) The Economics of Fishing: An Introduction. In J.A. Butlin (ed.) *The Economics of Environmental and Natural Resources Policy*. Westfield Press, Boulder, CO.

Munro, G. (1982) Fisheries, extended jurisdiction and the economics of common property resources. *The Canadian Journal of Economics* **15**, August.

NAPAP (1990) *National Acid Precipitaion Assessment Program*. 1989 Annual Report to the President and Congress, Washington, DC, 1990.

Nelson, J.P. (1982) Highway noise and property values: a survey of recent evidence. *Journal of Transport Economics and Policy* **XIC**, 37–52.

Nordhaus, W.D. (1972) *World Dynamics: Measurement without Data*. Cowles Foundation Discussion Paper. Reprinted in *The Economic Journal*, December 1973, 1156–1183.

Nordhaus, W.D. (1973) The allocation of energy resources. *Brookings Papers on Economic Activity* **3**, 529–570.

Nordhaus, W. (1982) How fast should we graze the global commons? *American Economic Review, Papers and Proceedings* **72**, 242–46.

Nordhaus, W. (1989) *The Economics of the Greenhouse Effect*. Mimeo, Department of Economics, Yale University.

Nordhaus, W. (1990a) Greenhouse economics. *The Economist*, 7 July.

Nordhaus, W. (1990b) *An Intertemporal General Equilibrium Model of Economic Growth and Climate Change*. Yale University. Paper presented at Workshop on Economic/Energy/Environmental Modelling for Climate Policy Analysis, Washington, DC, USA, 22–23 October.

Nordhaus, W. (1991a) To slow or not to slow: the economics of the greenhouse effect. *The Economic Journal* **101**(407), 920–937.

Nordhaus, W. (1991b) The cost of slowing climate: a survey. *The Energy Journal* **12**, 37–65.

Nordhaus, W. and Yohe, G.W. (1983) *Future Paths of Energy and Carbon Dioxide Emissions*. In *Changing Climate, op cit*, under NAS (1983).

Norgaard, R.B. (1975) Resource scarcity and new technology in U.S. petroleum development. *Natural Resources Journal* **15**, 265–295.

Norgaard, R.B. (1984) Coevolutionary development potential. *Land Economics* **60**, 160–173.

Norgaard, R.B. (1988) *The Rise of the Global Economy and the Loss of Biological Diversity*. In E.O. Wilson (ed.), *Biodiversity*. National Academy of Science Press, Washington, DC.

Nozick, R. (1974) *Anarchy, State and Utopia*. Johns Hopkins Press, Baltimore, MD.

OECD (1985).

OECD (1994a) *Environmental Indicators*. OECD, Paris.

OECD (1994b) *Project and Policy Appraisal: Integrating Economics and Environment*. OECD, Paris.

Office of Technology Assessment (1984) *Acid Rain and Transported Air Pollutants: Implications for Public Policy*. US GPO, Washington, DC.

Opschoor, J.B. and Vos, H.B. (1989) *The Application of Economic Instruments for Environmental Protection in OECD Member Countries*. OECD, Paris.

Page, T. (1973) *The Non-Renewable Resources Subsystem*. In H.S.D. Cole, C. Freeman, M. Jahoda and K.L.R. Pavitt (eds), *Thinking About the Future: A Critique of the Limits to Growth*. Sussex University Press, London.

Page, T. (1977) *Conservation and Economic Efficiency*. Johns Hopkins Press for Resources for the Future Inc., Baltimore, MD.

Page, T. (1982) Intergenerational Justice as Opportunity. In MacLean, D. and Brown, P. (eds) *Energy and the Future*, Rowman and Littlefield, Ottowa.

Palmer, A.R., Mooz, W.E., Quinn, T.H. and Wolf, K.A. (1980) *Economic Implications of Regulating Chlorofluorocarbons from Nonaerosol Applications*, Report No. R-2524-EPA prepared for the United States Environmental Protection Agency by the Rand Corporation, June.

Panayotou, T. (1993) *Empirical Tests and Policy analysis of Environmental Degradation at Different Stages of Economic Development*. Working Paper WP238, Technology and Employment Programme, International Labour Office, Geneva.

Pareto, V. (1897) *Cours d'Economie Politique*. Lausanne.

Pearce, D.W. (ed.) (1991a) *Blueprint 2: Greening the World Economy*. Earthscan, London.

Pearce, D.W. (1991b) The role of carbon taxes in adjusting to global warming. *The Economic Journal* **101**(407), 938–948.

Pearce, D.W. (1994) Assessing the social rate of return from investment in temperate zone forestry. In R. Laynard and S. Glaister (eds), *Cost–Benefit Analysis* (2nd edition), Cambridge University Press, Chapter 17.

Pearce, D.W. and Turner, R.K. (1990) *Economics of Natural Resources and the Environment*. Harvester Wheatsheaf, Hemel Hempstead.

Pearce, D.W. and Markandya, A. (1989) *Environmental Policy Benefits: Monetary Valuation*. OECD, Paris.

Pearce, D.W., Markandya, A. and Barbier, E.B. (1989) *Blueprint for a Green Economy*. Earthscan, London.

Pearce, D.W., Barbier, E. and Markandya, A. (1990) *Sustainable Development: Economics and Environment in the Third World*. Edward Elgar, Aldershot, UK.

Pearson, P.J.G. (1989) Proactive energy–environment policy strategies: a role for input–output? *Environment and Planning* **A21**, 1329–1348.

Pearson, M. and Smith, S. (1990) Taxation and environmental policy: some initial evidence. *Institute of Fiscal Studies Commentary*, **19**.

Perlman, M. (1984) *The Role of Population Projections for the Year 2000*. In Simon and Kahn (1984), *op cit.*

Perman, R. (1994) The economics of the greenhouse effect. *Journal of Economic Surveys* **8**(2), June.

Perrings, C. (1987) *Economy and the Environment*. Cambridge University Press, Cambridge.

Peterson, F.M. and Fisher, A.C. (1977) The exploitation of extractive resources: a survey. *Economic Journal* **87**, December, 681–721.

Pezzey J. (1992) Sustainability: an interdisciplinary guide. *Environmental Values* **1**, 321–362.

Pigou, A.C. (1920) *The Economics of Welfare*. Macmillan, London. [Fourth edition 1932.]

Pollock Shea, C. (1988) *Shifting to Renewable Energy*. In L. Starke (ed.), *State of the World 1988*. Worldwatch Institute, Washington, DC., 62–82.

Portes, R.D. (1970) *The Search for Efficiency in the Presence of Externalities*. In P. Streeten (ed.), *Unfashionable Economics: Essays in Honour of Lord Balogh*. Weidenfeld and Nicholson, London, 348–361.

Portney, P.R. (1989) Policy watch: economics and the Clean Air Act. *Journal of Economic Perspectives* **4**(4), 173–182.

Portney, P.R. (1990) *Air Pollution Policy*. In P. Portney (ed.) *Public Policies for Environmental Protection*. Resources for the Future, Washington, DC.

Quinn, E.A. (1986) *Projected Use, Emission and Banks of Potential Ozone Depleting Substances*. Rand Corporation Report, No 2282, EPA, Washington, DC.

Ramsey, F. (1928) A mathematical theory of savings. *Economic Journal*, **38**.

Randall, A. and Farmer, M.C. (1995) Benefits, Costs and the Safe Minimum Standard of Conservation. In D.W. Bromley (ed.), *The Handbook of Environmental Economics*, Blackwell, Oxford.

Randall, A., Ives, B. and Eastman, C. (1974) Bidding games for valuation or aesthetic environmental improvements. *Journal of Environmental Economics and Management* **1**, 132–149.

Rawls, J. (1971) *A Theory of Justice*. Oxford University Press, Cambridge, Massachusetts.

Redclift, M. (1992) The meaning of sustainable development. Geoforum **23**(3), 395–403.

Reilly, J.M., Edmonds, J.A., Gardner, R.H. and Brenkert, A.L. (1987) Uncertainty analysis of the IEA/ORAU CO_2 emissions model. *Energy Journal* **8**(3), 1–30.

Repetto, R. (ed.) (1985) *The Global Possible*. Yale University Press, New Haven, CT.

Repetto, R., Wells, M., Beer, C. and Rossini, F. (1987) *Natural Resource Accounting for Indonesia*. World Resources Institute, Washington, DC.

Ricardo, D. (1817) *Principles of Political Economy and Taxation*. Reprint, 1926, Everyman, London.

Roach, F., Kolstad, C., Kneese, A.V., Tobin, R. and Williams, M. (1981) Alternative air quality policy options in the four corners region. *Southwestern Review* **1**, 29–58.

Robbins, L. (1935) *An Essay on the Nature and Significance of Economic Science*.

Rosen, S. (1974) Hedonic prices and implicit markets: product differentiation in pure competition. *Journal of Political Economy* **82**, 34–55.

Rosenberg (1973) Innovative responses to materials shortages. *American Economic Review*, Vol. 63(2).

Royal Commission on Environmental Pollution (1994) *Eighteenth Report: Transport and the Environment*. HMSO, London.

RSPB (1994) *Environmental Measures: Indicators for the UK Environment*. Royal Society for the Protection of Birds, Sandy, Bedfordshire.

Sadik, N. (1990) *The State of The World Population*. United Nations Population Fund, New York.

Samuelson, P.A. (1956) Social indifference curves. *Quarterly Journal of Economics* **70**.

Sarokin, D. (1992) *Toxic Releases from Multinational Corporations*. The Public Data Project, Washington, DC.

Schaeffer, D.J., Herricks, E. and Kerster, H. (1988) Ecosystem health. I. Measuring ecosystem health. *Environmental Management* **12**(4), 445–455.

Schaeffer, M.D. (1954) Some aspects of the dynamics of populations important to the management of the commercial marine fisheries. *Bulletin of the Inter-American Tropical Tuna Commission* **1**, 25–26.

Schaeffer, M.D. (1957) Some consideration of population dynamics and economics in relation to the management of marine fisheries. *Journal of the Fisheries Research Board of Canada* **14**, 669–681.

Schmidheiny, S. (1992) *Changing Course: A Global Perspective on Development and the Environment*. MIT Press, Cambridge, Massachusetts.

Schneider, S.H., (1989) The greenhouse effect: science and policy. *Science* **243**, February, 771–781.

Schulze, W.D., Brookshire, D. and Saddler, T. (1981) The social rate of discount for nuclear waste storage. *Natural Resources Journal* **21**(4), 811–832.

Schumacher, E.F. (1973) *Small is Beautiful: Economics as if People Mattered*. Harper Torch Books, London.

Selden, T.M. and Song, D. (1992) *Environmental Quality and Development: Is There a Kuznets Curve for Air Pollution?* Department of Economics, Syracuse University, Syracuse, New York.

Sen, A. (1987) *On Ethics and Economics*. Blackwell, Oxford.

Seskin, E.P., Anderson, R. Jr. and Reid, R.O. (1983) An empirical analysis of economic strategies for controlling air pollution. *Journal of Environmental Economics and Management* **10**, 112–124.

Simon, J.L. and Kahn, H. (1984) *The Resourceful Earth*. Basil Blackwell, Oxford.

Sinclair, P. (1991) *High Does Nothing and Rising is Worse: Carbon Taxes Should Keep Declining to Cut Harmful Emissions*. The Manchester School.

Singer, P. (1993) *Practical Ethics*. Second edition. Cambridge University Press.

Slade, M.E. (1982) Trends in natural-resource commodity prices: an analysis of the time domain. *Journal of Environmental Economics and Management* **9**, 122–137.

Smart, B. (1992) *Beyond Compliance: A New Industry View of the Environment*. World Resources Institute, Washington, DC.

Smith, A. (1776) *The Wealth of Nations* (Cannan, E. ed, 1961). Methuen, London.

Smith, V.K. (ed.) (1979) *Scarcity and Growth Reconsidered*. Johns Hopkins University Press, for Resources for the Future, Baltimore, MD.

Smith, V.K. and Desvousges, W.H. (1976).

Smith, V.K., Desvousges, W.H. and McGivney, M.P. (1983) The opportunity cost of travel time in recreational demand models. *Land Economics* **59**, 259–278.

Smith, V.K. and Krutilla, J.V. (1979) The Economics of Natural Resource Scarcity: An Interpretive Introduction. In V. Kerry Smith (ed.), *Scarcity and Growth Reconsidered*. Johns Hopkins University Press, Baltimore, MD.

Smith, V.L. (1972) Dynamics of waste accumulation versus recycling. *Quarterly Journal of Economics* **86**, 600–616.

Solow, R.M. (1956) A contribution to the theory of economic growth. *Quarterly Journal of Economics*, 65–94.

Solow, R.M. (1974a) Intergenerational equity and exhaustible resources. *Review of Economic Studies, Symposium*, May, 29–46.

Solow, R.M. (1974b) The economics of resources and the resources of economics. *American Economic Review*, May. Reprinted in R. Dorfman and N. Dorfman (eds) *Economics of the Environment: Selected Readings*, New York, Norton. 1977.

Solow, R.M. (1986) On the intergenerational allocation of natural resources. *Scandanavian Journal of Economics* **88**(1), 141–149.

Solow, R.M. (1991) *Sustainability: An Economist's Perspective*. Paper presented at Woods Hole Oceanic Institution, Massachusetts, June 14, and reprinted in Dorfman, R. and Dorfman, N. (1993) *Economics of the Environment: Selected Readings*, Third edition, W.W. Norton, New York.

Spash, C.L. and d'Arge, R.C. (1989) The greenhouse effect and intergenerational transfers. *Energy Policy*, April 88–96.

Spofford, W.O. Jr. (1984) *Efficiency Properties of Alternative Source Control Policies for Meeting Ambient Air Quality Standards: An Empirical Application to the Lower Delaware Valley*. Discussion Paper D-118, November, Resources for the Future. Washington, DC.

Stein, D. (1990) Family planning with chinese characteristics. *China Now* **133**, 15.

Stern, D.I., Common, M.S. and Barbier, E.B. (1994) *Economic Growth and Environmental Degradation: A Critique of the Environmental Kuznets Curve*. Discussion Papers in Environmental Economics and Environmental Management, No. 9409, The University of York, August.

Streeten, P. (1987) *What Price Food? Agricultural Policies in Developing Countries*. St Martin's Press, New York.

Swart, R.J., de Boois, H. and Rotmans, J. (1989) Targeting climate change. *International Environmental Affairs* **1**, Part 3.

Symons, E.J., Proops, J.L. and Gay, P.W. (1991) *Carbon Taxes and Carbon Dioxide Emission*. Unpublished Discussion Paper, Department of Economics and Management Science, University of Keele, Staffs., ST5 5BG, UK.

Symons, E.J., Proops, J.L.R. and Gay, P.W. (1993) *Carbon Taxes, Consumer Demand and Carbon Dioxide Emission: A Simulation Analysis for the UK*, mimeo, Department of Economics, University of Manchester, Manchester, UK.

Tietenberg, T.H. (1984) *Marketable Emission Permits in Theory and Practice*. Paper presented at the Conference, Economics of energy and Environmental Problems, Yxtaholm, Sweden, 6–10 August.

Tietenberg, T.H. (1989) Acid rain reduction credits. *Challenge* **32**, March/April.

Tietenberg, T.H. (1990) Economic instruments for environmental regulation. *Oxford Review of Economic Policy*, **6**(1), 17–34.

Tietenberg, T. (1992) *Environmental and Natural Resource Economics*. Third Edition, Harper Collins, New York.

Todaro, M.P. (1989) *Economic Development in the Third World*. Fourth edition. Longman, New York.

Tolkien, J.R.R. (1969) *The Lord of the Rings* (in one volume). George Allen and Unwin, London.

Toman, M., Pezzey, J. and Krautkraemer, J. (1993) *Economic Theory and 'Sustainability'*. Department of Economics, University College London, Discussion Paper in Economics No 93–15, August 1993.

Turner, R.K. and Bateman, I. (1990) *A Critical Review of Monetary Assessment Methods and Techniques*. Environmental Appraisal Group, University of East Anglia.

Ulph, A. Ulph, D. and Pezzey, J. (1991) *Should a Carbon Tax Rise or Fall Over Time?* Discussion Paper Number 91/309, Department of Economics, University of Bristol, 8 Woodland Road, Bristol, BS8 1TN, UK.

UN (1989a) *World Population Prospects 1988*. Population Studies No. 106, United Nations Department of International Economic and Social Affairs, New York.

UN (1989b) *Levels and Trends of Contraceptive Use as Assessed in 1988*. Population Studies No. 110, United Nations Department of International Economic and Social Affairs, New York.

UN (1990) *Demographic Yearbook 1988*. United Nations Department of International Economic and Social Affairs, New York.

UN (1994).

UNEP (1987) *United Nations Environment Programme: Environmental Data Report*. First edition 1987/88, Basil Blackwell, Oxford. [Published periodically in updated versions.]

UNEP (1989) *United Nations Environment Programme: Environmental Data Report*. 2nd edition 1989/90, Basil Blackwell, Oxford. [Published periodically in updated versions.]

UNEP (1991) *United Nations Environment Programme: Environmental Data Report*. 3rd edition, Basil Blackwell, Oxford. [Published periodically in updated versions.]

United Nations (1992) *Integrated Environmental and Economic Accounting*. United Nations, New York.

United Nations (1993) *Systems of National Accounts 1993*. United Nations, New York.

United Nations Centre for Transnational Corporations (1992), *International Accounting*. UNCTC, New York.

United Nations FAO (Food and Agriculture Organisation) *The State of Food and Agriculture* (1979, 1981, 1985, 1989, and subsequent issues), Rome, Italy.

Varian, H.R. (1987) *Intermediate Microeconomics*. Second edition, W.W. Norton, New York. [First edition, 1980.]

Vitousek, P.M., Ehrlich, P.R. (1986) Human Appropriation of the Products of Photosynthesis. *BioScience* **36**, 368–373.

Walras, L (1954) *Elements of Pure Economics*. Richard D. Irwin, Homewood, Illinois.

Warnock, G.J. (1971) *The Object of Morality*. Methuen, New York.

Watson, R.A. (1979) Self-consciousness and the rights of non-human animals. *Environmental Ethics* **1**(2), 99.

Waugh, D. (1987) *The World*. Thomas Nelson and Sons, Surrey, UK.

WCED (World Commission on Environment and Development) (1987) *Our Common Future*. Oxford University Press, and United Nations, New York.

WCU [World Conservation Union] (1990) *Environmental Issues in Eastern Europe: Setting an Agenda*. The Royal Institute of Environmental Affairs, Energy and Environment Programme, London.

Weintraub, E.R. (1973) *General Equilibrium Theory*. Macmillan Press, London.

Weisbrod (1964) Collective consumption services of individual consumption goods. *Quarterly Journal of Economics* **78**(3), 471–477.

Weizsacker, E.U. von. (1989) *Global Warming and Environmental Taxes*. International Conference on Atmosphere, Climate and Man, Torino, Italy, January 1989.

Whalley, J. and Wigle, R.M. (1989) *Cutting CO_2 Emissions: the Effect of Alternative Policy Approaches*. Paper presented at the NBER conference on AGE modelling, San Diego, CA.

Whalley, J. and Wigle, R.M. (1990) The International Incidence of Carbon Taxes. Paper presented at conference on 'Economic Policy Responses to Global Warming', Rome, 4–6 October, October 1990 revision. National Bureau of Economic Research, Cambridge, MA; and Wilfrid Laurier University, Waterloo, Canada. Published in *Energy Journal* (1991) **11**(4).

Wilen, J.E. (1985) Bioeconomics of Renewable Resource Use. Chapter 2 in Kneese, A.V. and Sweeney, J.L. (eds) *Handbook of Natural Resource and Energy Economics*. Volume 1, Elsevier Science Publishers, Amsterdam.

Williams, R.H. (1990) *Low-Cost Strategy for Coping with CO_2 Emission Limits (A Critique of 'CO_2 Emission Limits: an Economic Cost Analysis for the USA' by Alan Manne and Richard Richels)*, Centre for Energy and Environmental Studies, Princeton University, Princeton, USA. Published in *Energy Journal*, 1990, **11**(4).

Williams, R.H. (1990) *Will Constraining Fossil Fuel Carbon Dioxide Emissions Cost so Much?* Centre for Energy and Environmental Studies, Princeton University, Princeton, USA.

Willis, K.G. and Garrod, G.D. (1991) *The Hedonic Price Method and the Valuation of Countryside Characteristics*. ESRC Countryside Change Initiative Working Paper 14, University of Newcastle.

Wilson, E.O. (1980) Extract from article published in *Harvard Magazine*, January–February.

Wilson, E.O. (ed.) (1988) *Biodiversity*. National Academy of Science Press, Washington, DC.

Winpenny (1991) *Policy appraisal and the Environment. A Guide for Government Departments*. HMSO, London.

WMO [World Meteorological Organisation and United Nations Environment Programme] (1991) *Scientific Assessment of Stratospheric Ozone, 1991*. Executive Summary, 22 October.

World Meterological Organisation (UNO) (1988) *The Changing Atmosphere: Implications for Global Security*. Conference Proceedings, 27–30 June. WMO-710, Toronto, Canada.

Worldwatch Institute (1985) *Full House*.

WR (1990/91) *World Resources 1990–91*. World Resources Institute, Oxford University Press, Oxford.

WR (1992/93) *World Resources 1992–93*. World Resources Institute, Oxford University Press, Oxford.

WR (1994/95) *World Resources 1994–95*. World Resources Institute, Oxford University Press, Oxford.

WWF (1993) [The World Wildlife Fund]: *The Right to Know: The Promise of Low-Cost Public Inventories of Toxic Chemicals*. WWF, Washington, DC.

Young, J.T. (1991) Is the entropy law relevant to the economics of natural resource scarcity? *Journal of Environmental Economics and Management* **21**(2), 169–179.

Name Index

Subject Index

KING ALFRED'S COLLEGE
LIBRARY